AFFECTIVE DISORDERS IN CHILDHOOD AND ADOLESCENCE —An Update

Child Behavior and Development

Series Editor Dennis P. Cantwell, MD

Suicide in Children and Adolescents. Syed Arshad Husain and Trish Vandiver, editors.

Attention Deficit Disorders. Lewis M. Bloomingdale, editor.

Affective Disorders in Childhood and Adolescence–An Update. Dennis P. Cantwell and Gabrielle A. Carlson, editors.

Emotional Disorders in Children and Adolescents: Medical and Psychological Approaches to Treatment. G. Pirooz Sholevar, Ronald M. Benson, and Barton J. Blinder, editors.

Clinical Treatment and Research in Child Psychopathology. A. J. Finch, Jr., and Philip C. Kendall, editors.

Autism: Diagnosis, Current Research, and Management. Edward R. Ritvo, Betty Jo Freeman, Edward M. Ornitz, and Peter Tanguay, editors.

The Hyperactive Child: Diagnosis, Management, Current Research. Dennis P. Cantwell, editor.

AFFECTIVE DISORDERS IN CHILDHOOD AND ADOLESCENCE

An Update

Edited by

Dennis P. Cantwell, M.D.
Joseph-Campbell Professor of Child Psychiatry
University of California, Los Angeles

Gabrielle A. Carlson, M.D.
Associate Professor of Child Psychiatry
University of Missouri, Columbia

SP

SP MEDICAL & SCIENTIFIC BOOKS
a division of Spectrum Publications, Inc.
New York

To Susan

Suzi, Denny, Coleen, Erin, and Marianne

To Harold

Gregory and Jonathan

and

To Mr. and Mrs. Frederick W. Davis

SPECTRUM PUBLICATIONS, INC.
175-20 Wexford Terrace
Jamaica, NY 11432

Library of Congress Cataloging in Publication Data
Main entry under title:

Affective disorders in childhood and adolescence.
(Child Behavior and Development)
Bibliography: p.
Includes index.
1. Depression in children. 2. Affective disorders in children. 3. Adolescent psychopathology. I. Cantwell, Dennis P. II. Carlson, Gabrielle A. III. Series. [DNLM: 1. Affective disorders–In adolescence. 2. Affective disorders–In infancy and childhood.
W1 CH644M / WM 171 A25595]
RJ506.D4A38 1983 618.92'89 83-13672
ISBN 0-89335-189-X

Second Printing

Printed in the United States of America

Preface

The first two books in this series on Child Behavior and Development dealt with the Hyperactive Child Syndrome (Attention Deficit Disorder) and with Infantile Autism. These are two of the most investigated and best established syndromes in child psychiatry.

Affective disorders, that is depressions and manias, are probably the most investigated and best established syndromes in adult psychiatry. However, it is only recently that investigators have turned their attention to depressions and manias in children and adolescents. Focusing on clinical, research, and management aspects, this present monograph is an attempt to collect in one place much of what we know about depression and mania in children and adolescents.

The first section deals with the phenomenology of affective disorders in children and adolescents. Issues regarding classification and diagnostic criteria are reviewed and case studies are presented. The second section deals with the issues of alternative forms of depression and relates common school-related problems to affective disorders. The third section on assessment discusses various assessment instruments in some detail. The fourth section on possible etiologic factors concentrates on those biologic areas that are the subject of most of the etiologic research at the present time. Likewise, the last section on management deals with those therapeutic interventions which have been the subject of the most intense research in this area.

Acknowledgements and thanks are due to all of the contributors for taking time from their busy schedule to prepare their chapters; to Lori Faigin, Susan Cantwell, and Adeline Butkus for their work in typing, indexing, and proofing the manuscript; and to Maurice Ancharoff of Spectrum Publications for his encouragement and assistance.

In addition, the preparation of this monograph was supported in part by Grants MH35116 and MH08467 from the National Institute of Mental Health.

July 1983

Dennis P. Cantwell, M.D.
Gabrielle A. Carlson, M.D.
Los Angeles, California

Contributors

Richard Bedrosian, PhD
Director
Massachusetts Center for Cognitive Therapy
West Borough, Massachusetts

Dennis P. Cantwell, MD
Joseph-Campbell Professor of Child Psychiatry
Director, Residency Training in Child Psychiatry
University of California at Los Angeles
Neuropsychiatric Institute
Los Angeles, California

Gabrielle A. Carlson, MD
Associate Professor of Psychiatry (Child)
Division of Child Psychiatry
University of Missouri
School of Medicine
Columbia, Missouri

William J. Chambers, MD
Assistant Clinical Professor of Psychiatry
New York State Psychiatric Institute
New York, New York

Donald J. Cohen, MD
Professor of Pediatrics, Psychiatry, and Psychology
Yale University
Child Study Center
New Haven, Connecticut

Maurice Eisenbruch, MD
Visiting Fellow
Department of Social Medicine and Health Policy
Harvard Medical School
Boston, Massachusetts

Robert Elkins, MD
Vice President of Operations
Medical Director
Continental Care Corporation
Columbia, Maryland

Gary Emery, MD
Director
Los Angeles Center for Cognitive Therapy
Los Angeles, California

Judy Garber
Department of Psychology
University of Minnesota
Minneapolis, Minnesota

Moshe Lang, Dip Psych, MA, MAPS
Director
Williams Road Family Therapy Centre
President
Victorian Association of Family Therapists
Windsor, Victoria, Australia

Thomas L. Lowe, MD
Assistant Professor of Psychiatry
Department of Psychiatry
Division of Child Psychiatry
University of South Florida
College of Medicine
Tampa, Florida

Theodore A. Petti, MD
Associate Professor of Child Psychiatry
Director, Youth and Child Section
Office of Education and Regional Programming
University of Pittsburgh
Western Psychiatric Institute and Clinic
Pittsburgh, Pennsylvania

Joaquim Puig-Antich, MD
Director of Child Psychiatry
Clinical Research Service
Associate Professor of Clinical Psychiatry
Columbia University
College of Physicians and Surgeons
New York, New York

Judith L. Rapoport, MD
Chief, Section of Child Psychiatry
Department of Health, Education, and Welfare
Public Health Service
Alcohol, Drug Abuse, and Mental Health Administration
National Institute of Mental Health
Bethesda, Maryland

Anne Rehmet, MA
Director of Admissions
The Winston School
Dallas, Texas

Michael Strober, PhD
Associate Professor of Psychiatry
Mental Retardation and Child Psychiatry Program
University of California at Los Angeles
Neuropsychiatric Institute
Los Angeles, California

Mary Ann Tabrizi, MA, RN
Research Coordinator
New York State Psychiatric Institute
New York, New York

Miriam Tisher, MA, MAPS
Clinical Psychologist
Counseling Services
Caulfield Institute of Technology
Caulfield East, Victoria, Australia

Warren A. Weinberg, MD
Associate Professor
Pediatrics and Neurology
University of Texas Health Science Center at Dallas
Medical Director
The Winston School
Dallas, Texas

Table of Contents

SECTION I

Phenomenology

Introduction

On more than one occasion, the forward movement of science has been impeded when prevailing theoretical beliefs have biased observers against believing their own eyes and ears. This has been the case to some extent in depressive disorders in children: for a long time, dogma declared that adult-type depression could not exist in children. However, the rapidly accumulating phenomenological, psychological, and biological data on adult affective disorders have provided both impetus and guidance to those of us interested in childhood affective disorders. As Dr. Cantwell discusses in Chapter 1, there has been an evolution in thinking, supported by a growing body of research, that depressive disorders in children not only exist but are not strikingly dissimilar from adult depressive disorders. Yet, it would be a perpetuation of the same "theoretical" beliefs to limit our observations and data gathering solely to what has been applicable to mature adults because the immature organism is, in many ways, different. Clearly we are still in the process of formulating what childhood depression is, and what it is not.

The first section of this volume reviews important conceptual issues on the subject of classification and diagnosis. The diagnostic dilemmas of childhood and adolescent affective disorders are addressed by literature review in Chapters 1 and 2; case history material in Chapters 3 to 5; and data from ongoing studies of childhood and adolescent depression in Chapters 2 and 6.

Affective Disorders in Childhood and Adolescence--
An Update. Edited by D.P. Cantwell and G.A. Carlson.

1

Depression in Childhood: Clinical Picture and Diagnostic Criteria

Dennis P. Cantwell, MD

The study of depression in both adults and children has been somewhat hampered by a lack of precision in terminology. The term "depression" has both psychiatric and nonpsychiatric usage. Even when used in a purely psychiatric sense, the term depression can have several different meanings. It may refer simply to dysphoric mood, which is a universal part of human experience. Dysphoric mood as a *symptom* can occur as a response to loss or disappointment and/or can exist for no particular reason. When dysphoric mood is seen as a symptom in psychiatrically ill patients, it may or may not be part of a depressive *syndrome* or a depressive *disorder*, and it may or may not be a part of another psychiatric disorder.

The concept of depression as a syndrome as opposed to a symptom implies more than simply dysphoric mood. When the word depression is used to mean a syndrome, the implication is that dysphoric mood occurs in combination with a number of other symptoms and that these symptoms regularly occur together. These symptoms are not limited to affective changes, but they also include vegetative and psychomotor disturbances, cognitive changes, and motivational changes. The clinical syndrome of depression may occur as a primary problem. It may also occur with a wide variety of physical and mental disorders, including such diverse conditions as rheumatoid arthritis, Cushing's disease, alcoholism, antisocial personality, anxiety disorders, and schizophrenia.

The concept of a depressive disorder connotes even more than the concept of a depressive syndrome. When the word depression is used to refer to a disorder, the implication is that not only is there a depressive syndrome causing some degree of incapacity, but that there is also a characteristic clinical picture, a characteristic natural history, a characteristic response to treatment, and also possible family, environmental, and biological correlates.

In adult psychiatry, the concept of depression both as a syndrome and as a disorder is well-accepted. In adults, several different depression disorders have been delineated on the basis of differing clinical pictures. These disorders seem to differ not only in clinical picture, but also in natural history, response to pharmacological treatment, family history of mental illness, and biochemical and neurophysiological characteristics.

Andreasen (1982) has reviewed the major controversies surrounding the depressive syndrome in adults. She points out that these controversies revolve around the limits of the concept of affective disorder and the methods of subclassifying affective disorder. Andreasen has reviewed the delimitation of the boundary between depression and normality. Here an attempt is made to exclude relatively mild or brief situational disorders, for example, in response to death of a spouse, from the concept of major affective disorder. On the other side there is the problem of a delimitation between affective disorders and schizophrenia and between affective disorders and anxiety disorders.

In adult life patients may present with affective disorders colored by psychotic symptomatology. In some cases the picture may be confusing enough to demand a diagnosis such as schizo-affective disorder for which there are no absolute diagnostic criteria. It is also true that patients with anxiety disorders may develop secondary depressive episodes, and patients with primary affective disorders may present with associated symptoms of anxiety. While these delimitations do present clinical difficulty at times, their discrimination in adults is considerably clearer than in children.

As with the study of any psychiatric syndrome in children or adults, the starting point must be the delineation of the core clinical picture. This has proved difficult and somewhat controversial in children. Four major schools of thought can be identified in the literature, each with a somewhat different view on the question of the clinical picture of a depressive syndrome in childhood.

Proponents of the first school of thought feel that depression as a clinical syndrome, analogous to that which occurs in adults, simply does not occur in prepubertal children. There are a variety of reasons offered by proponents of this school for their view. The more psychoanalytically oriented feel that the classical clinical depressive syndrome, analogous to that which occurs in adults, cannot occur in children because of the lack of a well-developed and well-internalized superego during the preadolescent age period. Rie (1966), in a classic review article, stated "familiar manifestations of adult nonpsychotic depression are virtually nonexistent in childhood." More recently, Lefkowitz and Burton (1978) proposed a different reason for their belief that the clinical syndrome of depression should not be considered as a definite entity in childhood. They pointed out that the symptoms touted as being indicative of a depressive syndrome are transitory developmental phenomena in children that disappear over time. Their interpretation of the available literature was that there are marked variations of the prevalence of "depressive" symptoms with children's age and also that many symptoms supposedly characteristic of depression occur very commonly in normal children. Therefore, they concluded that these clinical manifestations were neither deviant statistically nor indicative of psychopathology.

In contrast to the first school of thought, which suggests that depression as an independent clinical syndrome really does not exist in children, proponents of the second and third school of thought do suggest that depression does exist in childhood. However, they feel it is characterized by a rather "unique" set of symptoms that are not necessarily the symptoms indicative of depression in adult life. Proponents of the second school of thought feel that the clinical picture of depression in childhood consists of certain unique characteristics and symptoms which occur in addition to those that indicate depression. This literature was reviewed by Kovacs and Beck (1977). They listed a number of authors as representing this school of thought, all of whom had enumerated certain "characteristic" depressive symptoms and features. However these unique symptoms tend to differ from author to author in the mood area, in the cognitive area, in the psychomotor area, and in the neurovegetative area.

These authors do not state that the clinical syndrome of depression in childhood does not consist of symptoms analogous to what is seen in adults, such as dysphoric mood, anhedonia, and vegetative symptoms. What they do say is that in addition to those core symptoms, this unique set of symptoms distinguishes depression occurring in children from depression occurring in adults. However, it is not clear in most cases whether these authors consider these unique symptoms to be essential features that must be present for the depressive syndrome to be diagnosed or whether they consider them to be associated features that may be present in children who have definite depressive disorders similar in clinical picture to that seen in adults. This is an important distinction, and actually, this school of thought makes theoretical sense. For example, in the Diagnostic and Statistical Manual (DSM-III), after much debate, it was decided that there would be no separate category of childhood depression with different clinical criteria. Rather, it was felt that the essential features of a major depressive episode were identical for children, adolescents, and adults. However, it was also felt that there are age-specific associated features described for different age and developmental levels. These do not occur as part of the diagnostic criteria. Instead, it is stated that separation anxiety is a characteristic associated feature in prepubertal children. In adolescent males it is stated that negative and antisocial behavior, grouchiness, sulkiness, withdrawal from social activities, and school difficulties are common associated features occurring with the core essential features of the depressive syndrome.

Since infants, children, and adolescents are at different developmental stages dynamically, morally, cognitively, and physically, it is not surprising that there might be different associated features in children and adolescents of different ages who have the same essential features of a major depressive disorder.

However, it must be stated that this issue is far from resolved. The DSM-III associated features, which are detailed in the text, were derived purely from clinical experiences. To date there are no clinical studies of large numbers of children of different ages and different sexes who have essential features of an adult similar to a depressive syndrome to determine if they have characteristic associated features which differ from those children of the same age with other psychiatric disorders and from normal children of the same age.

Puig-Antich and his associates (1978) have indeed shown that there is a strong relationship between separation anxiety and major depressive disorder in prepubertal children. In their preliminary report of a study of 13 prepubertal children who met Research and Diagnostic Criteria (RDC) requirements for major depressive disorder, the investigators found that all had developmentally excessive separation anxiety. However, Puig-Antich has also found that many children with major depressive disorder do not have separation anxiety at all and others only have mild symptoms of separation anxiety. Finally, there are children who present with the full clinical picture of both a major depressive disorder and a separation anxiety disorder, and children who present with a purely separation anxiety disorder.

Moreover, Gittelman-Klein and her associates (1971) have shown that children with separation anxiety disorder and school refusal have a high likelihood of positive response to tricyclic antidepressants. However, this response cannot be considered an antidepressant response because it was independent of the presence of depressed mood.

Further research with larger groups of patients diagnosed by operational criteria will be necessary to clarify the relationships in children between the essential and associated features of major depressive disorder, separation anxiety disorder, anorexia nervosa, conduct disorders, and attention deficit disorder with hyperactivity—all of which may occur alone or in combination with a depressive disorder.

The third school of thought regarding the clinical picture of depressive disorder in childhood can be called the "masked depression" or "depressive equivalent" school. Those who espouse this view differ from those described above in that they feel that the essential clinical features of a major depressive disorder are not present in children in the form that they are present in adults. Rather, they postulate that an underlying depression is responsible for the manifest behavior which may include such diverse behaviors as conduct disorder, hyperactivity, enuresis, learning disabilities, and somatic complaints. This underlying, unexpressed depressed affect is postulated to account for the manifest behavior even in the face of the absence of dysphoric mood, anhedonia, and other characteristic symptoms of depression as we know it in adults. Thus, the second and third schools of thought are somewhat similar.

However, those who espouse the second view feel that the unique characteristic symptoms of childhood depression do not completely mask the more typical depressive syndrome. The masked depression school states that these unique symptoms do in fact completely mask the core essential features of the depressive syndrome.

There are a number of problems with this latter concept. Probably the most important one is that the behaviors cited as masking depression by various authors cover the entire range of psychopathology in childhood. It is not made clear how these various behaviors are linked to the underlying unexpressed depressive affect. It is also not made clear how one decides when dealing with a child with a conduct disorder whether the disorder is or is not masking a depression. The term "masked depression" has been used so vaguely and so loosely that with time the concept has lost credibility in the United States.

In 1977, Kovacs, and Beck reviewed the literature on masked depression. They pointed out that the term was probably misleading and unnecessary. They noted that many of the behaviors listed as masking depression in children were often presenting complaints of depression in adults, and that in adults they are not considered to be masking depression but rather are part-and-parcel of the depressive syndrome. Carlson and Cantwell (1979b) amplified this view in a study of children referred to a psychiatric clinic. Of 102 children referred to the UCLA Neuropsychiatric Institute for evaluation, 28 met a diagnosis for some DSM-III affective disorder. Fourteen of the children had a primary affective disorder in which the child had no preexisting psychiatric disorder of any type. However, in the other 14 cases, there was a preexisting psychiatric disorder. Most commonly this was an overt behavior disorder such as attention deficit disorder with hyperactivity or conduct disorder. In these cases the overt behavior disorder predated the onset of the depressive episode by many years and was often considered to be the presenting problem for psychiatric evaluation. In some cases the significance of the overt behavior problems overshadowed the depressive symptomatology in the parents' eyes. However, careful clinical evaluation revealed the true depressive syndrome. Thus, the overt behavior disorder did not completely mask the depressive symptomatology. There were other children with anxiety disorders and anorexia nervosa which also predated the onset of the depressive episode. However, these children were again rather easily distinguished from those children with anxiety disorders and anorexia nervosa who did not have a complicating secondary depression. Thus, in 14 cases with secondary affective disorder, the other psychiatric symptomatology did not mask the depressive symptoms, but rather was present as an additional diagnosis that usually predated the onset of the depressive disorder. Carlson and Cantwell concluded that to an alert clinician conducting a thorough diagnostic evaluation, the depression would not be masked. More often the mask rests on the face of the clinician than on the face of the child.

Petti (this volume) likewise has reviewed the variety of forms of presentation of depression in children. He correctly points out that children with somatic complaints, hyperactivity, attention deficit disorder, learning problems, academic achievement problems, and a wide range of other problems have often presented with secondary episodes of depression. The significant depression is often overshadowed by the morass of other symptomatology with which the child may present. Again, with careful clinical evaluation it can be seen that the depressive syndrome does indeed exist and is not completely masked by the other symptomatology.

The fourth school of thought regarding the clinical picture of depression in childhood has most recently emerged. The proponents of this school state that if one looks for the clinical picture of depression in children in a way analogous to the way it has been looked for in adults, it can indeed be found. Moreover, they feel that it may be an underdiagnosed condition in childhood. This view was expressed at the Fourth Congress of the European Pedopsychiatrists in Stockholm in August of 1971. (The proceedings of this manual were published as a book, *Depressive States in Childhood and Adolescence* (Annell, 1972).)

With the recognition that there are children who present with the clinical picture of depression similar to the way adults present with a depressive syndrome, two related questions arise for both research and clinical purposes: How common is this adult-like depression syndrome in children? What should the diagnostic criteria be for the diagnosis of depression in childhood? The answer to the first question depends to a large extent upon the criteria used for the diagnosis of depression.

There are a variety of studies by Albert and Beck (1975), Carlson and Cantwell (1979a), Kupferman and Stewart (1979), and others reviewed by Kashani and associates (1981) which give widely varying rates for major depressive disorder in children. Albert and Beck found significant depression in approximately 60 percent of girls and 50 percent of boys enrolled in a parochial school. These children were aged 11 through 13. Kashani and Simonds (1979) studied randomly selected children in the general population and found DSM-III major depressive disorder in 1.9 percent of the children studied. However, more than 17 percent demonstrated clinically significant sadness or depression. Comparing symptomatology in these children with significant sadness to the children without significant sadness, it was found that the sad children demonstrated more somatic complaints, more hyperactivity, more low self-esteem, more aggressive behavior, and more school refusal. Thus, although only 1.9 percent met strict DSM-III criteria for affective disorder, a significantly larger number had persistent sadness; this sadness was associated with other symptomatology that could suggest a subclinical form or an early manifestation of depression.

In a general population study on the Isle of Wight conducted by Rutter and his colleagues, only 1.4 per 1,000 children aged 10 to 12 years of age in the general population met the criteria for a major depressive disorder. These criteria were rather idiosyncratic. However, many more children demonstrated sad mood as part of symptomatology of other psychiatric disorders.

Petti (1978) found that 59 percent of psychiatric inpatients met modified Weinberg criteria for depression. McConville found a prevalence rate for depression of 53 percent, and Pearce (1977) found a prevalence rate of 23 percent, all among psychiatric inpatients. Carlson and Cantwell found a prevalence rate of 27 percent of psychiatric inpatients and outpatients using strict DSM-III criteria. Weinberg, using his own criteria (Weinberg et al, 1972), found a prevalence rate of 58 percent of children presenting to an outpatient educational diagnostic center. Thus, these studies and others give widely varying rates for major depressive disorder in children. Although there are a variety of reasons for these discrepancies in prevalence rates, including the wide age range, different sex ratios, different patient samples (ie, inpatient versus outpatient, general population versus psychiatric population), the most important reason is probably the use of different diagnostic criteria or no criteria at all and the use of nonstandardized methods of evaluation to make a diagnosis.

What should the operational criteria be for the diagnosis of depression in childhood? Should they be modified adult criteria? Or should the criteria be modified for use with children? As mentioned previously, the approach taken in DSM-III is that the criteria for a major depressive episode with regard to essential features are exactly the same in infants, children, and adolescents as they are for adults. It is stated in the text, however, that there may be age-specific associated features that differ in infants, children, and adolescents. However, these are not part of the diagnostic criteria.

The concept of operational diagnostic criteria for depression and indeed for other psychiatric disorders owes its roots to the Washington University Psychiatric Group in St. Louis (Feighner et al, 1972). This group published a set of operational criteria for psychiatric research in adults which have been termed the Feighner criteria (after the senior author of the article in which these criteria were set forth). The Feighner criteria were the starting point for operational criteria for a larger group of psychiatric disorders developed by Spitzer, Endicott, and Robins (1978), which carry the name of Research Diagnostic Criteria (RDC). The RDC were the starting point for the development of DSM-III diagnostic criteria for an even larger group of psychiatric disorders.

The Feighner criteria and the RDC criteria were developed for research purposes. For these purposes it is important to have a group of patients which is as homogeneous as possible. Thus, the criteria tend to be stricter. The DSM-III criteria were developed by a committee primarily for use by clinicians. For clinical purposes it is important to have a minimum of false negatives so that people who require services can obtain them. Thus, the criteria tend to be broader. Table 1 lists the Feighner criteria, the RDC criteria, and DSM-III

Table 1 Feighner–RD, Spitzer–RDC, and DSM-III Criteria for Depression

Feighner–RD	Spitzer–RDC	DSM-III
A. Dysphoric Mood–Depressed, sad, discouraged, despondent, irritable, etc.	A. One or more distinct periods of dysphoric mood, pervasive loss of interest or pleasure	A. Dysphoric mood or anhedonia
B. Other features at least five of the following	B. At least five of the following	B. Other symptoms: at least four of the following:
1. Poor appetite and weight loss	1. Appetite increase/decrease, weight gain/loss	1. Appetite/weight gain/loss
2. Sleep difficulty (insomnia or hypersomnia)	2. Sleep disturbance: insomnia, hypersomnia	2. Sleep difficulty
3. Loss of energy	3. Loss of energy, fatigability	3. Loss of energy
4. Agitation or retardation	4. Psychomotor agitation or retardation	4. Loss of interest or pleasure in usual activity
5. Loss of interest in usual activities (including sexual drive)	5. Loss of interest/pleasure in social contact or sex	5. Self-reproach, inappropriate guilt
6. Feelings of self-reproach or guilt	6. Self-reproach or guilt	6. Diminished concentration
7. Diminished ability to think or concentrate	7. Diminished ability to think, concentrate	7. Suicidal tendencies
8. Recurrent thoughts of death or suicide	8. Recurrent thoughts of death, suicide	C. Duration: At least two weeks
		D. Exclusions:
		1. Schizophrenic symptoms
		2. Organic mental disorder
		3. Residual-type schizophrenia
		4. Simple bereavement

C. Duration: at least 1 month with no other preexisting psychiatric condition or medical illness that could account for depressive symptomatology	C. Duration: At least one week
D. There are patients who fulfill the above criteria, but who also have a massive or peculiar alteration of perception and thinking as a major manifestation of their illness. These patients are currently classified as having a schizoaffective psychosis.	D. Sought help, medicated: functional impairment
	E. Exclusion criteria suggesting schizophrenia 1. Delusions discordant for depression 2. Non-affective hallucinations for several days or intermittently for a week 3. Auditory hallucinations 4. More than one month of delusions or hallucinations without depressive symptoms 5. Preoccupation with delusion or hallucinations discordant for depression 6. Formal thought disorders

criteria for major depression. It can be seen that they resemble each other to a large degree. They do differ in duration in that the Feighner criteria require at least one month; the RDC criteria a duration of at least one week; and the DSM-III criteria a duration of at least two weeks. The Feighner criteria require the presence of dysphoric mood or a pervasive loss of interest or pleasure in all activities (anhedonia). The Feighner and the RDC require five other symptoms out of a list of seven. The exclusion criteria are essentially the same, with an attempt to rule out schizophrenia in the Feighner and RDC criteria, and to rule out schizophrenia, organic mental disorder, and simple bereavement in DSM-III criteria. The Feighner criteria specifically rule out other preexisting psychiatric conditions or medical illness that could account for depressive symptomatology. RDC and DSM-III criteria require that one make both diagnoses if both are present. For example, if anorexia nervosa and depression are present, then anorexia nervosa and depression are both diagnosed. The Feighner criteria would not make the diagnosis of depression in the face of a preexisting anorexia nervosa.

A different approach has been taken by other investigators in the field of childhood depression. They have modified criteria for childhood depression so that the essential features, rather than the associated features, are different from those required for the diagnosis of adult depression. Operational criteria for the diagnosis of depression in childhood have been presented by Ling et al (1970), Weinberg et al (1973), Petti (1978), Poznanski (1981), and others. The Weinberg criteria probably have had the biggest impact on the field. Petti's criteria, the Bellvue Index of Depression (BID), are actually a modification of the Weinberg criteria which allow for each symptom to be scored from 0 to 3. The Weinberg criteria were originally derived by modifying the adult Feighner criteria. And, since the Feighner criteria bear a strong resemblance to the DSM-III criteria, it is not surprising that the Weinberg criteria and the DSM-III criteria would be similar. However, there are some significant differences. Table 2 presents a detailed comparison of the Weinberg criteria and the DSM-III criteria.

In early work, Weinberg not only listed the various criteria for the diagnosis of depression, but also listed specific symptoms that would qualify for the presence of the criteria. It can be seen that while the DSM-III criteria require either dysphoric mood or anhedonia, the Weinberg criteria require both dysphoric mood and self-depreciatory ideation. The Weinberg criteria then require only two or more of the other eight major symptoms, while the DSM-III criteria require four or more of the eight other symptoms with some specific requirements for children under the age of six. While there is a large degree of overlap between the DSM-III criteria and the Weinberg criteria, there are some criteria in the Weinberg group wich do not have direct counterparts in the DSM-III group and vice versa. The duration for the Weinberg criteria is one

Table 2 DSM-III and Weinberg Criteria for Depression

Weinberg	DSM-III
INCLUSION	
Both	*Either*
I. Dysphoric Mood (Melancholy)	A. (1) Dysphoric Mood
a. Statements or appearance of sadness, loneliness, unhappiness, hopelessness and/or pessimism	(2) Loss of interest or pleasure in all or almost all usual activities and pastimes (anhedonia)
b. Mood swings, moodiness	
c. Irritable, easily annoyed	
d. Hypersensitive cries easily	
e. Negative, difficult to please	
II. Self-depreciatory Ideation	
a. Feeling of being worthless, useless, dumb, stupid, ugly, guilty (negative self-concept)	
b. Belief of persecution	
c. Death wishes	
d. Desire to run away or leave home	
e. Suicidal thoughts	
f. Suicidal attempts	
Two or more of the following eight:	*Four* or more of the following eight:
III. Aggressive Behavior (Agitation)	(Two of nos. 1-4 in children under six)
a. Difficult to get along with	(3) Psychomotor agitation or retardation, not only subjective feelings of restlessness or being slowed down (in children under six, hyopactivity)
b. Quarrelsome	
c. Disrepectful of authority	
d. Belligerent, hostile, agitated	
e. Excessive fighting or sudden anger	
IV. Sleep Disturbance	(2) Insomnia or hypersomnia
a. Initial insomnia	
b. Restless sleep	
c. Terminal insomnia	
d. Difficulty waking in morning	
V. Change in School Performance	(7) Complaints or evidence of diminished ability to think or concentrate, such as slowed thinking or indecisiveness not associated with marked loosening of associations or incoherence
a. Frequent complaints from teachers re: daydreaming, poor concentration, poor memory	
b. Loss of usual work effort in school subjects	
c. Loss of usual interest in nonacademic school activities	
VI. Diminished Socialization	(May correspond to A-2 above)
a. Decreased group participation	
b. Less friendly, less outgoing	
c. Socially withdrawing	
d. Loss of usual social interests	

Table 2 *(continued)*

Weinberg	DSM-III
VII. Change in Attitude Toward School a. Does not enjoy school activities b. Does not want or refuses to attend school	(No direct counterpart)
VIII. Somatic Complaints a. Non-migraine headaches b. Abdominal pain c. Muscle aches or pains d. Other somatic concerns or complaints	(No direct counterpart)
IX. Loss of Usual Energy a. Loss of usual personal interests or pursuits other than school; eg, hobbies b. Decreased energy; mental and/or physical fatigue	(5) Loss of energy; fatigue
X. Unusual Change in Appetite and/or Weight	(1) Poor appetite or significant weight loss (when not dieting) or increased appetite or significant weight gain (in children under six consider failure to make expected weight gains)
(May correspond to VI above)	(4) Loss of interest or pleasure in usual activities, or decrease in sexual drive not limited to a period when delusional or hallucinating (in children under six, signs of apathy)
(May correspond to II above)	(6) Feelings of worthlessness, self-reproach, or excessive or inappropriate guilt (either may be delusional)
(May correspond to II above)	(8) Recurrent thoughts of death, suicidal ideation, death wishes, or suicide attempt
Duration of at least 1 month	*Duration* of at least two weeks
A *change* in the child's usual behavior	(No such requirement)
EXCLUSION	
Not clear	Not due to Organic Mental Disorder or Uncomplicated Bereavement, or superimposed on: Schizophrenia, Schizophreniform Disorder or Paranoid Disorder When affective symptoms are *absent* neither of the following may dominate the clinical picture: (1) preoccupation with a mood–incongruent delusion or hallucination (2) bizarre behavior

month as opposed to two weeks in the DSM-III criteria, and no specific exclusion criteria are given by Weinberg. When one looks at individual symptoms that might qualify for the criteria being scored positive, it can be seen that being described as "negative and difficult to please" is indicative of dysphoric mood in the Weinberg criteria, and "desire to run away or leave home" is indicative of self-depreciatory ideation. Thus, a patient with both of those symptoms, a "change in school performance" such as "poor concentration" and "frequent daydreaming," along with a "change in attitudes towards school" would allow the patient to be given a diagnosis of depressive disorder according to Weinberg criteria. These symptoms are quite common in children with overt behavior disorder, such as conduct disorder and attention deficit disorder with hyperactivity. Thus, on the surface it appears as if the Weinberg criteria are broader than DSM-III criteria, and that using these criteria would result in a much more heterogeneous group of patients than using the DSM-III criteria. In a systematic study by Carlson and Cantwell (in press), that is precisely was was found.

As part of their study of 102 randomly selected children presenting for psychiatric evaluation to the Neuropsychiatric Institute, Carlson and Cantwell compared the utility of Weinberg criteria and DSM-III criteria in the diagnosis of depression. Using both the Weinberg and the DSM-III criteria and the information obtained from the parent, from the child, and from parent and teacher rating scales, the following groups of children could be created:

1. Those who met DSM-III criteria for the diagnosis of one of the affective disorders;

2. Those in whom the parent described enough signs and symptoms to meet the Weinberg criteria for depression. (The Weinberg criteria for depression include a "change from a previous functioning." Thus, these children met the criteria for acute symptomatology and were called the "acute parent Weinberg group" since the symptoms were detailed by their parents.)

3. A group of children who themselves described sufficient signs and symptoms to meet the Weinberg criteria ("child Weinberg").

4. Those in whom both parent and child describe signs and symptoms which meet the Weinberg criteria. (This group was called "both Weinberg.")

5. Those children in whom the parents could describe enough signs and symptoms to meet the criteria described by Weinberg but either could not establish the discrete onset of each symptom or noted that the symptoms had been present for more than three years. (This group was called the "chronic parent Weinberg group.")

As mentioned above, out of the 102 children, 28 met DSM-III criteria for some affective disorder: 14 had a primary depression and 14 had a secondary depression. All but five of these 28 children who met DSM-III criteria for depression fell into one of the above Weinberg groups. Thus, 17.8 percent of the 28 children meeting DSM-III criteria did not meet Weinberg criteria at all.

Nine (or 32 percent) were in both the acute parent and the child Weinberg group. Five (or 17.8%) were in the child Weinberg group alone. Four (or 14.2 percent) were in the acute parent Weinberg group alone. Three (or 10.7 percent) were in the chronic parent Weinberg group alone, and two (or 7.1 percent) were in the chronic parent group and not the acute child Weinberg group criteria. Of the five children who did not meet any of the Weinberg criteria, two had reoccuring depressions, and three denied feeling depressed but admitted to a loss of pleasure in usual activities.

In contrast, a total of 34 of the 102 children met Weinberg criteria as described by Weinberg himself, that is, including the criteria that the symptoms had to be a change from usual functioning. However, an additional 28 parents described chronic depressive symptomatology in their children. Only 3 of 28 children met simultaneous DSM-III criteria for affective disorder as opposed to 20 of the 34 children of the acute Weinberg group described above. However, it is significant that even when the acute symptomatology is met, as described by Weinberg in 34 cases, only 20 children met DSM-III criteria leaving 14 (or 41.1 percent) who did not meet DSM-III criteria. In these 14 children there was a mixture of behavior disorders, anxiety disorders, undiagnosed mental disorders, and one case of childhood psychosis. Thus, it seems quite clear from the results of the Carlson and Cantwell study that the Weinberg criteria and the DSM-III criteria identify largely different groups of children with only some overlap. The great majority of those children who meet DSM-III criteria also meet Weinberg criteria. However, there is a substantially large number of children who meet Weinberg criteria but not DSM-III criteria. Thus, if one were to use the two sets of criteria to identify depressed patients in a study of the dexamethasone suppression test, other biological correlates, family history studies, etc, one would likely obtain different results simply because the patients presented with different disorders.

Similar results have been presented by Poznanski (1981) who compared her own criteria with the Weinberg and DSM-III criteria. Only future studies will determine which criteria are "right" in the sense that they identify a more homogeneous group of patients with regard to natural history, family history treatment, etc. However, it should be kept in mind when reading studies along these parameters that the diagnostic criteria used to identify the children as depressed are likely to lead to different groups of children if different criteria are used.

To summarize what has been said about the clinical picture of depression in childhood, there does seem to be a converging body of evidence from a variety of investigators in different centers suggesting that there is indeed a clinical syndrome of depression in childhood that manifests itself in its essential features similar to the way the depressive syndromes are manifested in adult life. There are children presenting for psychiatric evaluation who, when carefully evaluated, do have a DSM-III-diagnosable affective disorder. It is true that many of these children have other associated symptoms. Indeed, a fair number qualify for other DSM-III diagnoses as well. However, these symptoms and other disorders generally do not mask the depressive syndrome in the sense that they completely obliterate the essential features of the depression. It may be that there are age-specific associated symptoms in children presenting the essential features of a depressive syndrome that are a result of different developmental and age levels. The concept of masked depression has been vaguely and loosely used so that at present it seems to have little clinical or research use.

Given that there is a depressive syndrome in childhood and adult-like features, there are many remaining questions which should be asked. Some of these are: How should this depressive syndrome be subclassified? Does the presence of this depressive syndrome, and even more importantly, any subtypes of the syndrome carry with it the same implications with regard to natural history, treatment, biological correlates, etc, that this diagnosis carries with it in adults? These questions are addressed in later chapters in this book.

REFERENCES

Albert N, Beck AT. Incidence of depression in early adolescence: a preliminary study. *J Youth Adolescence* 1975;4:301-307.

Andreasen NC. Affective disorders: concept, classification, and diagnosis. In Paykel ES, ed. *Handbook of affective disorders*. New York: Guilford Press, 1982:24-42.

Annell AL. *Depressive states in childhood and adolescence*. Stockholm: Almquist and Wiksel, Stockholm, 1972:

Carlson GA, Cantwell DP. A survey of depressive symptoms in a child and adolescent psychiatric population. *J Am Acad Child Psychiatry* 1979a; 18 4:587-599.

Carlson GA, Cantwell DP. Unmasking masked depression in children and adolescents. *Am J Psychiatry* 1979b; 137 4:445-449.

Carlson GA, Cantwell DP. Diagnosis of childhood depression—a comparison of Weinberg and DSM-III criteria. *J Am Acad Child Psychiatry* 1981; 21: 247-250.

Feighner JP, Robins E, Guze SB, et al. Diagnostic criteria for use in psychiatric research. *Arch Gen Psychiatry* 1972; 26:57-63.

Gittelman-Klein R, Klein DF. Controlled imipramine treatment of school phobia. *Arch Gen Psychiatry* 1971; 25:204-207.

Kashani JH, Husain A, Shekim WO, et al. Current perspectives on childhood depression: an overview. *Am J Psychiatry* 1981; 138:143-153.

Kashani J, Simonds JF. The incidence of depression in children. *Am J Psychiatry* 1979; 136:1203-1205.

Kovacs M, Beck AT. An empirical clinical approach toward definition of childhood depression. In *Depression in childhood: diagnosis, treatment and conceptual models*. Schulterbrandt JG, ed. New York: Raven Press, 1977: 1-25.

Kupferman S, Stewart MA. The diagnosis of depression in children. *J Affective Disord* 1979; 1:117-123.

Lefkowitz MM, Burton N. Childhood depression: a critique of the concept. *Psychol Bull* 1978;85:716–726.

Ling W, Oftedal G, Weinberg W. Depressive illness in childhood presenting as severe headache. *Am J Dis Child* 1970;120:122–124.

McConville BJ, Boag LC, Purohit AP. Three types of childhood depression. *Can J Psychiatry* 1973;18:133-178.

Pearce J. Depressive disorder in childhood. *J Child Psychol Psychiatry* 1977; 18:79–82.

Petti, TA. Depression in hospitalized child psychiatry patients: approaches to measuring depression. *J Am Acad Child Psychiatry* 1978;17:49–59.

Petti TA. Imipramine in the treatment of depressed children, in *Affective disorders in childhood and adolescence*. New York: Spectrum Publications, 1983.

Poznanski E. Diagnostic criteria for depression in childhood. Presented at the Annual Meeting of the American Academy of Child Psychiatry in Dallas, Texas, October 1981.

Puig-Antich J, Blau S, Marx N, et al. Prepubertal major depressive disorders: pilot study. *J Am Acad Child Psychiatry* 1978;17:695–707.

Rie HE. Depression in childhood: a survey of some pertinent contributors. *J Am Acad Child Psychiatry* 1966;5:653–685.

Rutter M, Tizard J, Whitmore K. *Education and health behavior*. New York: Wiley, 1970.

Spitzer RL, Endicott J, Robins E. *Research diagnostic criteria for a selected group of functional disorders*. 3rd ed. New York: New York State Psychiatric Institute, 1978:

Weinberg, WA, Rutman J, Sullivan L, et al. Depression in children referred to an education diagnostic center. *J Pediatr* 1973;83:1065–1072.

Affective Disorders in Childhood and Adolescence--
An Update. Edited by D.P. Cantwell and G.A. Carlson.

2

Issues in Classification

Dennis P. Cantwell and Garbielle A. Carlson

PRINCIPLES OF PSYCHIATRIC CLASSIFICATION

The basic principles of classification in child psychiatry have been discussed fully by Rutter (1978) and Spitzer and Cantwell (1980). The most important are:

1. There is no right or natural way to classify the psychiatric disorders of childhood. Traditional classification systems, including the Diagnostic and Statistical Manual (DSM)-I, DSM-II, GAP, and the newer DSM-III, have categorical classification systems. However, Achenbach (1980) has reviewed the evidence for the validity and stability of empirically defined syndromes of behavior produced by factor, pattern, and cluster analysis. Only some of these empirically derived syndromes have counterparts in DSM-III, although there does tend to be a large degree of overlap. There are empirically derived syndromes that have no apparent counterpart in DSM-III, and likewise there are DSM-III diagnostic categories that apparently have no counterpart among the empirically derived syndromes of behavior. There are many reasons why this may be so. Spitzer (1980) has started that "no diagnostic category has ever been added to a classification of mental disorders for clinical use that was a syndrome first identified by a mathematical procedure designed to generate diagnostic categories."

Etiology is not necessarily the best basis for classification. Etiology is a good basis for classification in disorders due to specific bacterial agents which can be isolated and tested for sensitivity and treated with specific antibiotics. However, this is not necessarily so in the rest of general medicine. For example, a descriptive-phenomenological approach to fractures (simple versus compound) offers much more information than an etiological one which would state whether the fracture was due to having been hit with a hammer or by a car.

2. For any classification system to be successful, it must be based on facts and not on theoretical concepts. This is particularly difficult in child psychiatry. There is a relative lack of hard, concrete facts in child psychiatry regarding natural history, familial pattern of illness, developmental changes in symptom pattern, etc, for various disorders. In child psychiatry, one man's fact is often considered another man's fantasy.

3. The diagnostic categories in the classification system must be reliable. A system cannot be valid if it is not reliable. Even if a classification system has reliability—that is, clinicians can agree with a high degree of reliability on diagnoses applied to a series of cases—it still may not have validity.

Spitzer (1980) has pinpointed the major sources of unreliability in psychiatric diagnosis. These include information variance, observation and interpretation variance, and criterion variance. Information variance arises from the fact that different clinicians evaluating the same case obtain different types of information on which to base their diagnosis. Observation and interpretation variance occurs when clinicians, even though they elicit the same information and make the same observations, differ in what they remember and in how they interpret what they see and hear. Criterion variance occurs when there are differences in the criteria that clinicians use to make a certain diagnosis. For example, if a child has hyperactivity, inattentiveness, and impulsive behavior, and also may have some conduct disorder symptoms, some clinicians will diagnose both attention deficit disorder with hyperactivity and conduct disorder. Others will only make a diagnosis of conduct disorder and ignore the symptomatology of attention deficit disorder with hyperactivity.

There is also subject variance and occasion variance because a patient may actually have a different condition at different times, and may present differently on different occasions. Technically these are also sources of unreliability in diagnosis; since these reflect true facts, however, they do not represent actual disagreement in diagnosis but, instead, a true change on the part of the patient (Spitzer, 1980).

There are very few studies that have examined the relative contributions of information variance, criterion variance, and observation and interpretation variance to diagnostic unreliability. There is a study by Ward et al (1962) of agreement between psychiatrists, using DSM-I as the diagnostic system, on the diagnosis of psychiatric disorders in adults. This study indicated that nearly two thirds of the diagnostic disagreements were due to criterion variance. Apparently, there are no comparable studies with children. Criterion variance can be minimized by the use of operational diagnostic criteria for each psychiatric disorder. Such criteria have been specified by Feighner et al (1972) and by Spitzer et al (1978) for psychiatric disorders in adults. The DSM-III classification of psychiatric disorders of both adults and children also specifies operational diagnostic criteria for each diagnosis.

4. The diagnostic categories must have validity. Spitzer (1980) has denoted the types of validity that should be distinguished when the validity of a classification system is being considered. These include face validity, descriptive validity, predictive validity, and construct validity. Face validity is the first step in the identification of a diagnostic category. One obtains descriptions from experienced clinicians on what they think the essential features of a particular

disorder should be. Many of the categories in the childhood section have only face validity. Some have descriptive validity. As Spitzer and Cantwell (1980) point out, it is necessary initially to include categories which have only face validity; but if more powerful types of validity, such as descriptive validity and predictive validity, cannot be demonstrated after a thorough investigation, then the categories probably should not be continued in further editions of the classification system.

When the category has descriptive validity, it justifies the assumption that this category represents a distinct behavioral syndrome rather than a random collection of clinical features. A category that has little descriptive validity is characterized by symptoms which are commonly seen in persons with other types of mental disorders or in persons with no mental disorder.

From the clinical standpoint, probably the most important type of validity is predictive validity—that is, how the various types of mental disorders described in the system differ in ways *other* than in their clinical picture. Such knowledge can be helpful in predicting natural history, biological correlates, differential responses to treatment, etc. In child psychiatry, to a much greater degree than in adult psychiatry, there are many categories that have little predictive validity. In child psychiatry, there is a relative lack of knowledge about the natural history of various psychiatric disorders both with and without treatment, and an even greater lack of knowledge regarding the response of different syndromes to different types of psychiatric intervention.

5. Any classification system classifies psychiatric *disorders* of childhood; it does not classify *children*. Thus, it is correct to say, "Tommy Jones has infantile autism." It is incorrect to say, "Tommy Jones, the autistic," just as it would be incorrect to say, "Tommy Jones, the diabetic." Clearly, in most psychiatric disorders of childhood, there is no homogeneity within a diagnostic category. The diagnostic classification system classifies disorders, and it is not equivalent to a diagnostic formulation. A diagnostic classification system tells us what patients have in common with other patients who have similar clinical syndromes. A diagnostic formulation tells us what makes Patient A different from Patient B, even though they have the same clinical syndrome.

6. To be clinically useful, a classification system must provide adequate differentiation and adequate coverage. The "ultimate system" would be both jointly exhaustive and mutually exclusive. A patient would present with only one disorder, and all patients who walk through our doors would have disorders that are described somewhere within the system. We know from studies of adult psychiatric patients that as many as 25 percent receive a diagnosis of "undiagnosed mental disorder" (Goodwin and Guze, 1979). Studies that have used similar criteria for adolescents (Welner et al, 1979) suggest that the figure is even higher.

In addition to providing adequate coverage, the system must provide adequate differentiation between syndromes. An overall rubric such as "adjustment reaction of childhood" may cover nearly every child we see. It is obviously useless for differentiation between syndromes that require differential types of intervention or have different natural histories without treatment.

7. It must be recognized that psychiatric disorders in childhood do not exist as discrete entities with complete discontinuity between one disorder and another, or between the category of psychiatric disorder and normality (Spitzer, 1980). This is very similar to what is found in general medicine with categories such as essential hypertension. That there is not a complete discontinuity between disorders and between a category of psychiatric disorder and normality does not obviate the usefulness and need for a classification system (Spitzer, 1980).

8. In contrast to a classification system of psychiatric disorders of adult life, a child psychiatric classification system must have a developmental framework. Much more is known about the traditional, well-described syndromes seen in adults such as schizophrenia and affective disorder. However, child psychiatrists see a number of conditions which are considered normal at one time of life but may be pathological at another. (For example, bedwetting at age two versus bedwetting at age 12.) While all of psychiatry must contend with the question of distinguishing abnormality from normality, the child psychiatrist has the added problem of defining normality for different ages and developmental levels.

9. Finally, and most importantly, for a diagnostic classification system in child psychiatry to be worthwhile, it must be practical and clinically useful in everyday clinical practice. While it is true that diagnostic classification systems have multiple purposes, the most important one is clinical usefulness. Certainly, a classification system is a vitally necessary basis for communication in child psychiatry, which has many divergent etiologic viewpoints. A classification system is useful for information retrieval, prediction, developing concepts to be used within a scientific discipline, and forensic and legal uses. But the system cannot be so complicated and so difficult to use that mental health practitioners will avoid using it in everyday clinical practice.

This chapter will briefly review the issues in classification of affective disorders in adults. Then, specific issues relating to the classification of affective disorders in children will be reviewed.

CLASSIFICATION OF AFFECTIVE DISORDERS IN ADULTS

Andreasen (1982) has reviewed the controversies regarding the classification of affective disorders in general. These include: Should the classification be categorical or dimensional in nature? Should it be unitary, dichotomous, or multiple? And how do we determine whether the various subgroups created in the classification have any validity?

With regard to the categorical versus dimensional question, all of the "official" psychiatric nomenclatures in the United States (DSM-I, DSM-II, and DSM-III) have been categorical systems. These classification systems emphasize psychiatric disorders as discrete entities. Thus, a patient either has a major affective disorder or he does not. He either has schizophrenia or he does not. On the other hand in a dimensional approach, what one has is not a patient whose disorder belongs to one nosological entity or another, but rather a patient who represents a profile of descriptive dimensions of behavior. For example, there may be a depressive factor, an anxiety factor, a psychotic factor, a conduct factor, and others. Dimensional systems are becoming increasingly common with the use of techniques such as factor and cluster analysis. Achenbach (1980) has recently described the dimensional approach he has developed with his colleagues. Using factor and cluster analysis, he has shown that there are clusters that correspond to DSM-III categories, that there are DSM-III categories with no corresponding clusters, and that there are mathematically derived clusters with no corresponding DSM-III categories.

Generally, the sources of data for these dimensional systems involve rating scales completed by parents and teachers. These raw sources of data are then subjected to factor analytic procedures creating dimensions of behavior. Then, cluster analysis may be used to create groups of children based on their factor scores on these dimensions of behavior. The dimensional and categorical approaches are not entirely oppositional. They can be considered as complimentary approaches to the classification of childhood behavior problems. What is probably most important is which system offers the most with regard to predictive validity. That is, does the patient's disorder, belonging to one categorical class or another, predict more about natural history, response to treatment, biological correlates, etc than do his scores on these various dimensions of behavior? To date, this is an unanswered, unresearched question, although studies in this area are going on at the present time.

Regarding the unitary versus dichotomous versus multiple approach to the classification of depression, British psychiatrists, pioneered by Sir Aubrey Lewis (1934) and in more recent times by Robert Kendell (1976), have suggested that depression should not be further subtyped. That is, depressive disorders are in fact various states of a continuum, and depression should be considered a unitary condition rather than several discrete depressive disorders. On the other hand, most of the popular classifications of depression are dichotomous in nature, such as, "psychotic" versus "neurotic," "endogenous" versus "reactive," "bipolar" versus "unipolar," "primary" versus "secondary," "pure depressive disorder" versus "depression spectrum disorder," and "agitated" versus "retarded." As with the question of whether a categorical or a dimensional approach is better, the ultimate answer to whether or not one way of subclassifying depressive disorders is better than another depends on its predictive validity. There are many classification systems now in use for affective disorders in adult life. Some of these are "official," such as ICD-9 and DSM-III; many are unofficial. In addition, there are several that have been proposed for childhood depression which are different again from those that are currently in use in both clinical and research centers for the classification of depression in adult life. In general, the official classification systems tend to be created by organizations such as the World Health Organization and the American Psychiatric Association. Like any classification system, these official classification systems have multiple uses, but by and large they are designed for use by the practicing clinician. Since those used by the clinician must have adequate differentiation and adequate coverage, they tend to be broader and more inclusive than more specialized unofficial classification systems which are developed by researchers, often for their private use. Research studies involving biological correlates, treatment outcome, etc, if they are to provide useful information, must begin with homogeneous groups of patients. For this reason, research based classification systems tends to be more narrow. ICD-9 is used by psychiatrists all over the world with very different theoretical orientations and very different backgrounds. It was created by a committee with a multinational representation. Thus, it is not surprising that such a classification system tends to be very broad and all-inclusive. The classification of affective disorders in ICD-9 (Table 1) involves 17 different subtypes of affective disorder listed under nine different main headings within the classification system. One of these (Category 313.1, misery and unhappiness disorder), is a disorder listed under the overall rubric of "disturbance of emotions specific to childhood and adolescence." This category is listed as "excluding depressive neurosis," thus indicating that it is meant to be used specifically for children with a clinical picture probably analogous to depression in adults. It should be pointed out, however, that ICD-9, like DSM-II and other previous official systems, does not provide operational diagnostic criteria for the diagnosis of each disorder; thus, it is difficult to know how depressive neurosis is excluded from this particular category in childhood other than by age.

There are a variety of problems with the ICD-9 classification of affective disorders which are beyond the scope of discussion in this chapter. It suffices to say that the classification system seems to have been unaffected by major research findings in the field over the last five years.

The DSM-III classification (Table 2) for affective disorders was created to meet the need of both clinicians and researchers. There are three major areas where affective disorders may be classified: under the broad heading of "affective disorders," under the broad heading of "psychotic disorders not elsewhere classified," and under the broad heading of "adjustment disorder."

Table 1 Classification of Affective Disorders in ICD-9

295	Schizophrenia
	Schizoaffective type
296	Affective psychoses
	Manic-depressive psychosis, manic type
	Manic-depressive psychosis, depressed type
	Manic-depressive psychosis, circular type, currently manic
	Manic-depressive psychosis, circular type, currently depressed
	Manic-depressive psychosis, circular type, currently mixed
	Manic-depressive psychosis, circular type, currently unspecified
	Manic-depressive psychosis, other and unspecified
298	Other non-organic psychoses
	Depressive type
	Excitative type
300	Neurotic disorders
	Neurotic depression
301	Personality disorders
	Affective
308	Acute reaction to stress
	Predominant disturbance of emotions
309	Adjustment reaction
	Brief depressive reaction
	Prolonged depressive reaction
311	Depressive disorder, not elsewhere classified
310	Disturbance of emotions specific to childhood and adolescence
	Misery and unhappiness disorder

The latter two broad categories have only one subclassification: schizoaffective disorder under "psychotic disorders not elsewhere classified" and adjustment disorder with depressed mood under the broad heading of "adjustment disorder." Thus, under the broad rubric of affective disorders, most of the affective disorders may be found in DSM-III. There are two major subdivisions here: "major affective disorders" and "other specific affective disorders." The major affective disorders contain two major subgroupings: bipolar disorder and major depression. Bipolar disorder is subdivided as manic, depressed, or mixed.

Major depression is subclassified at the fourth digit as a single episode or recurrent. The current episode may also be further subclassified at the fifth digit to reflect certain characteristics such as the presence of psychotic features, and in the case of a major depressive episode the presence of melancholia. This latter term is used to describe a severe form of depression, particularly responsive to somatic therapy with clinical features that have previously been

Table 2 Classification of Affective Disorders in DSM-III

Affective Disorders
Major Affective Disorders
Bipolar Disorder
Manic
Depressed
Mixed
Major Depression
Single Episode or Recurrent
With or Without Melancholia
With or Without Psychotic Features
Other Specific Affective Disorders
Cyclothymic Disorder
Dysthymic Disorder
Psychotic Disorders Not Elsewhere Classified
Schizoaffective Disorder
Adjustment Disorders
With Depressed Mood

characterized as "endogenous" in nature. The term endogenous was not used because it implies to many the absence of a possible precipitating stress which is not necessarily true in all cases.

The "other specific affective disorder" category is subclassified into cyclothymic disorder and dysthymic disorder. In both of these conditions a full affective syndrome, that is, a depressive or manic episode, is not present. In cyclothymic disorder there are symptoms characteristic of mania and depression, and in dysthymic disorder there are characteristic symptoms of depression. But the symptoms are not severe enough or of long enough duration to meet the criteria for a full affective syndrome. (These disorders must be present for at least two years.) In the major affective disorders, bipolar disorder and major depression, a full affective syndrome must be present in order for the diagnosis to be made. (There is no category of unipolar mania since it is felt that most people presenting with a manic episode will eventually develop a depression.)

Schizoaffective disorder is not listed either under schizophrenia or under the affective disorders, but instead is listed as residual category for those patients whose clinical picture does not clearly meet criteria for either schizophrenic disorder or affective disorder as described in DSM-III. There are no diagnostic criteria specified for schizoaffective disorder, and it is the only such category in DSM-III.

There are a variety of unofficial classification systems of depression generally developed by researchers who are interested in studying particular aspects of affective disorder. Many of these have been around for a long time and have been shown to have some degree of validity with regard to such aspects as family, natural history, treatment, and laboratory studies. One of the oldest is the endogenous-reactive dichotomous classification scheme of depression. The original concept of the endogenous subtype was that, in contrast to a reactive subtype, it arose from within the individual. Thus, endogenous connotes a biological origin, while a term like "reactive" connotes a response to some environmental stress. At the same time, endogenous has often been used to mean "psychotic" or severe, and reactive has often been used to mean "neurotic." The endogenous depressions in general are characterized by a set of characteristic symptoms which include: a distinct autonomous quality of severely depressed mood, an inability to respond to pleasant changes in the environment, psychomotor retardation, difficulty in concentration, and vegetative symptoms such as weight loss and terminal insomnia. Thus, in DSM-III the term endogenous was dropped in favor of the term "with melancholia" to indicate the phenomenological aspect of the picture without implication of etiology.

Likewise, the term "reactive" has also been used almost synonymously with neurotic when it is used to describe depressive disorder. Unfortunately, the term neurotic also entails multiple meanings—that of a neurotic disorder and that of a neurotic process. Factor analytic studies also suggest that as with the endogenous depressions, there is a characteristic set of symptoms that tend to occur in those individuals with the neurotic-reactive type of depression. These include a precipitating factor, a sudden onset, a clinical picture of irritability, mood that is responsive to the environment, and features such as self-pity, hysterical personality features, and immaturity. Andreasen (1982) has reviewed various studies attempting to validate the endogenous-reactive dichotomy of depressive disorder classification. There does seem to be strong evidence that with regard to natural history, certain laboratory studies, and a response to certain types of treatment, they do in fact differ. For example, endogenous depressions do seem to have a better prognosis, both long- and short-term, and they respond better than reactive depressions to antidepressants and to electroconvulsive therapy. They are also characterized by a differential response to methylamphetamine challenge and break-away from dexamethazone suppression. Thus, there are data to suggest that the endogenous-reactive dichotomy does have some validity. The problems lie with the imprecise terminology and the multiple meanings of the various terms like endogenous, reactive, psychotic, and neurotic.

Winokur (1979) has proposed a system of classification which is based on antecedent factors, current clinical picture, and family history of psychiatric illness. The first division of affective disorder is into primary and secondary types.

The primary affective disorders, those which occur without preexisting psychiatric illness, are further subdivided into a bipolar type and a unipolar type.

The bipolar type is characterized by episodes of depression and mania, and the unipolar type is characterized only by episodes of depression. The unipolar type is further subdivided into a sporadic, familial pure, and depression spectrum disorder. The sporadic depression describes patients who have no family history of any major psychiatric illness. The familial pure depression group describes patients who have a family history of depressive disorder only. Depression spectrum disorder describes those patients with a family history of other psychiatric disorders such as somatization disorder, antisocial personality, and alcoholism, which may occur alone or in combination with depression.

The validity of the primary-secondary, bipolar-unipolar, and the subdivisions of the unipolar types have been reviewed recently by Cantwell and Carlson (1979), Andreasen (1982), Schessler et al (1980), and Andreasen and Winokur (1979). Some of the findings for the validity of these subtypes will be discussed in the context of similar findings in childhood depression.

CLASSIFICATION OF AFFECTIVE DISORDERS IN CHILDREN

In addition to the classification systems outlined above, which were developed to classify affective disorders in adults, there are a number of classification systems that have been developed specifically to classify affective disorders in children.

One approach is based on developmental theory, that is, since children have different capabilities and issues at different ages, the phenomenology of depression must present in an age-appropriate context (Glaser, 1968; Malmquist, 1971; Phillips, 1978; Bemporad and Wilson, 1978). After discussing the divergence between analytic theory and clinical observation regarding childhood depression, Bemporad and Wilson (1978) state "it is no longer a question of whether adult-like depression can occur in childhood but rather how the cognitive and affective limitations at various stages of development modify the experience and expression of emotions in general." While some authors (Philips, 1978; McKnew and Cytryn, 1979) include Spitz' notion of anaclitic depression (1946) as an example of depression in infancy, Bemporad and Wilson reject that notion. Given not only what we know of the infant's capacities to demarcate himself or another, responses of infants to lack of stimulation, and animal models of response to deprivation and loss, these authors, along with Sandler and Joffe (1965) conclude that depression-like states of infancy are more likely a "basic psychobiologic reaction to deprivation."

Depression (as opposed to inhibition or sadness) in preschool children is also difficult to conceptualize. The emotional lability of exuberance to fears at a moment's notice is well-known and, as described in Chapter 4, is felt by some to be nascent manic depression. Certainly children who experience problems with separation/individuation, or who respond to parental limitations of their willful behavior by becoming clinging and inhibited, appear unhappy. The cognitive and affectual limitations of this period prevent the child from understanding future time, anticipating consequences of behavior, or even maintaining mood changes over anything but brief periods of time. Whether the particular temperaments, genetics, on environmental situations which predispose children to future depressions can be discerned at this time remains to be proven.

Middle childhood has been the time when "masked" depression or depressive equivalents are most often evoked. Children from six to nine are in a transition period; their cognitive maturity level determines their ability to understand reality in a way that promotes the signs and symptoms of depression, and their ability to express feelings in a way that others can identify as depression. Bemporad and Wilson (1978) conclude "middle childhood is a time in which prolonged unhappiness is possible in response to different types of environmental stress." The distinction between situational dysphoria (Gittelman-Klein, 1977) and true major depression is currently the subject of much research.

The presence of a depressive syndrome even as late as late childhood and early adolescence was once rejected by classical psychoanalytic theory. Depression was considered impossible because the child does not have a sufficiently formulated super ego to direct aggression towards his own ego (Rochlin, 1959) or because the child does not have a sufficiently stable self-representation to suffer loss of self-esteem in the face of a diminished ego ideal (Rie, 1966). Sandler and Joffe (1965) resolve the issue by considering depression "a basic psychobiologic affective reaction which, like anxiety, becomes abnormal when it occurs in inappropriate circumstances, when it persists for an undue length of time, and when the child is unable to make a developmentally appropriate adaptation of it." As with middle childhood, the interaction between the pathoplastic effects of age and the clinical picture of depression need further investigation. A number of theoretical issues which preclude adult manifestations of depression have not been substantiated by clinical observation. For instance, hopelessness and despair for the future, part of the clinical picture of adult depression, are said to be incompatible with children before formal operational thinking because of their limited temporal orientation. However, in their study of 102 psychiatrically disturbed children and adolescents, Carlson and Cantwell (1982) found that pessimism about the future was endorsed with almost equal frequency among depressed prepubertal children and adolescents.

Another approach to classification attempts to describe different symptom pictures which the proponent feels constitute examples of childhood depression. In a seminal two-part article in the *New England Journal of Medicine*, Malmquist (1971) presented a classification of childhood depression which used both etiology and development level as organizing factors. There were five major subgroups, the first two based on known etiology: depressions associated with known organic diseases and those described as deprivation syndromes or reality-based reactions to impoverished or nonrewarding environments. The other three major types were based on developmental level: syndromes associated with difficulty in individuation, latency types, and adolescent types.

Among the problems with this proposed classification scheme include the fact that there is a mixture of etiologic and theoretical frameworks as a basis for classification, and many of the conditions would not be considered affective disorders in the DSM-III framework (such as "schizophrenia with predominant affective components").

McConville and associates (1973) postulated three types of depression in childhood: the affectual, self-esteem, and guilt types. Affectual type was characterized by expressions of sadness, helplessness, and hopelessness, and was more common in children aged six to eight.

The second type, negative self-esteem, was characterized by "thought feelings" about depression. This became more common after the age of eight. McConville postulated that these "thought feelings" about depression emanated from fixed ideas about negative self-esteem. This type was felt to be partly due to a direct and continually experienced loss, as in children who were shifted from foster home to foster home.

The third type, guilt, occurred in only a small number of children. These children felt that they were wicked, and that they should be dead or be killed, either because they were bad themselves or because they wished to be reunited with a dead person. A punitive superego was felt to be an etiologic factor in this type of depression. This group was found to be more common in older children (after age 11), when the last stage of piagetian thinking was just beginning.

Differences in clinical symptomatology were investigated from a "prime symptom list." Fifteen depressive items were selected on the basis of clinical frequence. The first five related to the affectual depression group, the second five to the negative self-esteem group, and the third five to the guilt depressive group. Other than differences in age, it is unknown whether outcome, association with other symptomatology or other psychiatric disorders, and response to different types of therapeutic intervention distinguished these three types of depression.

In a later study, McConville and Boag (1973) suggested that these different subtypes were not actually independent diagnoses. They hypothesized that the three types represented a series of stages of expression of mourning depressive processes in children. These successive stages were determined largely by the interplay of affectual and cognitive factors in children of different ages. They investigated a number of other factors to see if they distinguished the three groups. These included sex distribution and possible etiologic factors such as loss of parents or siblings, rejection by the family, family history of depression, and different therapeutic responses. In this study, it was found that the three groups described in the previous paper were not found in "pure" fashion. The affectual (D-1 group) consisted of six cases and the negative self-esteem (D-2 group) consisted of 42 cases. There were no children who had a pure D-3 or guilt depression. However, 19 children were found who had a combination of a D-1 and D-2 type, and six children were put in a "D-3 miscellaneous" group because they had either D-3 plus D-1, D-3 plus D-2, or D-3 plus both D-1 and D-2. There were 73 children in the entire depressed group. Thus, for this study there were four main groups: D-1, D-2, D-1 + D-2, and D-3 miscellaneous. D-1 and D-1 + D-2 types were found more commonly in females while the D-3 miscellaneous group was more common in males. However, these differences were not statistically significant due to the small numbers involved. Loss of significant others was highly represented in the depressed group as a whole. It was particularly high in D-1 and D-3 miscellaneous types. However, no significant figures are given.

It was found that rejection of the child by the family averaged approximately 50 percent for all four major groups studied. A family history of depression was lowest in the D-2 type (38 percent), with the highest family history of depression occurring in the D-3 miscellaneous group (100 percent). Sixty-seven percent of the D-1 children had a family history of depression, and 58 percent of the D-1 + D-2 group did. Again, no significance figures are given.

No systematic studies were done with different therapeutic interventions. All of the children were involved in a variety of individual, group, and family therapy modalities, with some children being treated with medication. The course of individual psychotherapy of the four groups was described as being somewhat different, and group therapy was especially felt to be effective with the D-2 (negative self-esteem) type. Medication was not used systematically, so no clear comment could be made about the relative efficacy of antidepressant medication. It was found that 100 percent of the D-3 children and 58 percent of the D-1 + D-2 children were treated with imipramine as opposed to 17 percent of the D-1 group and 14 percent of the D-2 group.

When attempting to assess the mean therapeutic change on a 1 to 4 scale, less change was found in the D-2 group than in the other groups. It was also found that the D-2 group tended to stay in the residential setting longer than the other three groups. But these differences did not reach statistical significance. An attempt was made to evaluate the change in the family during the length of stay in the hospital. Seven children in the D-2 group and five in the D-1 + D-2 group required further placement after discharge from the hospital.

Thus, although there are problems with this study, it does suggest that the course of therapy and changes in therapy may be different for some of the subtypes described by McConville and his group.

In an early article, Frommer (1968) postulated that there were three groups of depressives in her population: enuretic depressives, pure depressives, and phobic depressives. She compared 54 children with enuretic depression, 74 with pure depression, and 62 with phobic depression on a variety of symptomatic, demographic, and treatment factors. All three groups were compared with 74 "neurotic" children who had a variety of emotional disorders without depression. The data are presented in a number of large tables as well as in textual description. Frommer reported that the enuretic depressives consisted of 31 boys and 23 girls. Many had serious difficulties in school and serious learning problems. They were considered to be immature for their age. Antisocial behavior was frequent as was social withdrawal. The disorder tended to be insidious with no identifiable onset. This group had the highest incidence of rejection by parents, family discord, and parental mental illness.

Frommer felt that amitriptyline was the drug of choice in the enuretic depressives, but that MAO inhibitors would be the first choice if there were a clear-cut precipitating factor with an accompanying change or regression in behavior. Therapeutic groups were found to be useful for depressive children, and removal from the home to a specially geared boarding school was considered to be the most effective treatment in some cases.

With regard to prognosis, it was her belief that the depression in this group may clear up months or years before the enuresis and/or encopresis. She hypothesized that these children's difficulties may stem from delayed maturation, of which the enuresis may sometimes be a manifestation.

The pure depressive group (or the children with uncomplicated depression, as Frommer termed them) consisted of 29 boys and 35 girls. Characteristic features were irritability, weepiness, and a tendency to recurrent explosions of temper or misery. Difficulty in sleeping, nightmares, and sleepwalking were also common. This group of depressive subjects was the only one in which a fairly large number complained spontaneously of feeling depressed. Suicidal ideation and attempt was almost exclusively limited to this group. Anxiety and lack of confidence were not prominent features of the pure depressive group. Nearly half were described as warm and outgoing and had many friends, but antisocial behavior was present in somewhat less than quarter.

MAO inhibitors were considered the drug of choice, except for those who showed a marked pattern of early morning awakening, in which tricyclics might be a better treatment. As to prognosis, the duration of illness up to the time of referral did not seem to influence the results of treatment to any great extent, provided that the current conditions were favorable for the child's recovery.

Children in the phobic depressive group included 22 boys and 40 girls, a markedly different sex ratio from the other two groups. While Frommer stated that these children had "typical depressive symptoms in full measure," they were considered to be less moody and more apathetic. Somatic complaints were common, and nearly half of the children had developed their illness by the age of seven. Characteristic symptoms of anxiety were obviously present in addition to the depressive symptomatology. There was a markedly lower incidence of parental mental illness in this group compared to the other two.

Therapy with MAO inhibitors alone or with tranquilizers was considered the best treatment. Regarding prognosis, cases of recent onset were seen as responding well to simple antidepressant drug treatment, providing that a phobic conditioning mechanism had not been well-established before drug treatment. However, in more chronic cases, regular psychotherapy and intensive medication was considered necessary. Chronic symptomatology with improvement and relapses following minor precipitants seemed to indicate a poor prognosis. Frommer asserted that some apparently phobic depressive children in childhood and preadolescence progressed to a psychotic illness in puberty.

The neurotic group of 74 children included 50 boys, a very different sex ratio from the phobic depressive group. These children did not have a depressive affect but had many physical problems and became ill at an early age. Parental deprivation was high. Psychotherapy, group treatment, and placement in special boarding schools were felt to be the best therapy, with drug treatment playing a small role. Prognosis was guarded. Some of the children were thought improved, and subsequently developed a depressive illness which responded to antidepressant treatment.

Special mention was made of 16 boys and 3 girls who made up an atypical group, with depressive features combined with extreme forms of temper outbursts which alternated with brief states of reasonableness. Family history of depressive illness was not common. Frommer stated that this was an illness very much like what others have described as an early form of manic depressive disease and that a small dose of lithium carbonate might be an effective response.

This is one of the few studies that has looked somewhat systematically at different types of depressive children and compared them regarding symptomatology, family history, response to treatment, prognosis, etc. Unfortunately, there are no operational criteria for the diagnosis of depression in general, or for any of the three specific subtypes. Indeed, in studying the pattern of symptomatology in the three groups it is difficult at times to tell what makes the child depressed. Without any statistical handling of the data it is not easy to determine which of the differences in the many tables are statistically significant given the different numbers in the four major groups compared. The family history may not have been inquired into systematically or blindly. At the time the study was done, structured interviews such as the FHRDC (Andreason et al, 1977) were probably not used. The use of tricyclics and MAO inhibitors was not explored systematically; indeed no data are given with regard to criteria for improvement other than anecdotal reports. Nevertheless, this is an early attempt to look at different subtypes of depression in children.

More recently Cytryn et al (1972) proposed a classification scheme of childhood depression which is based on both severity of the depressive phenomena and on putative etiologic factors. They describe a typical depressive syndrome characterized by the symptoms regularly associated with the depressive disorder in adults. These they divided into acute and chronic types. The acute type supposedly occurred in children without preexisting psychiatric pathology who only had mild family psychopathology. The chronic type occurred in children who had poor preexisting premorbid adjustment and came from much more pathological homes. However, the family psychopathology described plus the fact that the children improved shortly after removal from the home suggests that their acute and chronic types, particularly the acute type, would not qualify for a major affective disorder diagnosis by DSM-III criteria. In their view, by far the most common type of depression and the third subtype they describe was that of masked depression. They believed that the masked depression could be diagnosed by an examination of verbal expression, dream content, fantasy content, and certain facets of mood and behavior. They later elaborated on this scheme, suggesting that the three subtypes may in fact reflect the child's developmental stage. Thus, depressive themes would be seen in fantasy and dream before the child verbalized depression. If these defenses failed, verbal expression of depressive feelings would occur, and depression and other behaviors which mask the depression would become obvious.

In a more recent assessment of their classification scheme, Cytryn and his colleagues (1980) used DSM-III criteria to rediagnose the 12 children who originally were judged as having their form of acute depressive reaction. Eleven were rediagnosed by DSM-III criteria as having major depressive disorder, single episode, and one as having separation anxiety disorder. Of the 11 children who had originally received their chronic depressive reaction diagnoses, none were DSM-III–diagnosed as having major depressive disorder recurrent, and two as atypical depressive disorder. Finally, in their masked depression group, which numbered 13 children originally, two received a DSM-III diagnosis of recurrent major depressive disorder, two of atypical depressive disorder, one of avoidant disorder, two of schizoid disorder, and seven of unsocialized conduct disorder. Their conclusion was that the DSM-III classification system was a very valid way of classifying and diagnosing depression in childhood. Of particular note is the fact that their acute and chronic depressive reaction groups corresponded much more closely to DSM-III diagnoses of one of the affective disorders than their masked depression group did, half of whom had conduct disorder by DSM-III criteria.

Carlson and Cantwell applied the nosology of primary and secondary depression to their sample of 28 children and adolescents who met DSM-III criteria for affective disorder (Carlson and Cantwell, 1979, 1980a, 1980b). The differences between the two groups are summarized in Table 3. In general,

Table 3

	Primary affective (n = 14)	Secondary affective (n = 14)
Mean age	13.8 years (range 9–17)	12.9 years (range 7–16)
Prepubertal/adolescent	5/9	6/8
Male/female	7/7	7/7
Mean Childrens Depression Inventory Score	19.9 ± 10.6	23.7 ± 13.5
Depressive Symptoms (percent)		
Dysphoric mood	71	71
Low self-esteem	64	86
Anhedonia	50	79
Fatigue	64	50
Somatic complaints	64	50
Suicidal ideation	85	93
Hopelessness	71	71
Family History		
Pure depression or bipolar manic depressive illness	6	–
Depressive spectrum	4	10*
Undiagnosed	3	2
Unknown or adopted	–	2
No illness	1	0
Precipitants for Referral		
Depressive behavior	–	3
Suicidal behavior	5	3
Deteriorating school perf.	4	–
School refusal	1	1
Family conflict	4	2
Conduct problems	–	3
Anorexia nervosa	–	2
Informal Follow-up		
Functioning well	4	1
Return to premorbid functioning†	2	4
Continued episodes	1	1
Suicide	–	1
Unknown	6	7

*Includes two with just sociopathy and alcoholism.
†Not necessarily good but no further episodes.

youngsters with secondary depression were more chronically disturbed (by definition), although interestingly, their parents first brought them to psychiatric attention for superimposed depressive symptoms or suicidal behavior in 43 percent of cases. Regarding depressive symptoms, there were no significant differences between the two groups. The commonly held "depressive equivalents" such as somatic complaints, hyperactivity, aggressiveness, and rule violation were seen much more frequently in children with secondary depression and reflected their primary psychiatric diagnosis. Also, families of youngsters with secondary depression had considerably more "depressive spectrum" disorders than those with primary affective disorder.

As this investigation was an interview rather than treatment study, no comment can be made about treatment response. What information is known about half of the children five years after their interview reflects the fact that those with secondary depression continue to suffer from their primary problem, though the depressive symptoms have remitted. Four children with primary affective disorder (including one receiving lithium) are functioning well. One girl who committed suicide had depression secondary to anorexia nervosa. She also had juvenile onset diabetes mellitus and severe family conflict.

Data are insufficient to draw conclusions about the validity of the primary/secondary distinction in childhood depression. Except for the fact that primary affective disorder occurs twice as often as secondary affective disorder in adults, our findings concur with those of Andreasen and Winokur (1979).

To summarize what has been said about classification, the two official classifications now in use (ICD-9 and DSM-III) represent different approaches to the classification of affective disorders in adults. The DSM-III classification system seems to correspond much more closely to what is known from current research in the area of affective disorders. Very little work has been done in subclassifying affective disorders in childhood along DSM-III lines in the sense that it is not known whether these various subtypes exist in childhood and if so whether they carry the same implications with regard to natural history, family pattern of illness, response to treatment, etc. Likewise, there are a number of unofficial classification systems such as the endogenous-reactive, neurotic-psychotic, and the primary-secondary–unipolar-bipolar subdivisions. To date very little work has been done in this area with childhood depression. But what has been accomplished suggests that there may be fruitful ways of subtyping the affective disorders in childhood as there are in adults.

REFERENCES

Achenbach TM. DSM-III in light of empirical research on the classification of child psychopathology. *J Am Acad Child Psychiatry* 1980; 19 3:395–412.

Andreasen NC. Affective disorders: concept, classification, and diagnosis. In: Paykel ES, ed. *Handbook of affective disorders*. New York: Guilford Press, 1982:24–42.

Andreasen NC, Winokur G. New experimental methods for classifying depression. *Arch Gen Psychiatry* 1979; 36:447–452.

Andreason et al. The Family History Method using diagnostic criteria, reliability and validity. *Arch Gen Psychiatry* 1977; 34:1229–1235.

Bemporad JR, Wilson A. A developmental approach to depression in childhood and adolescence. *J Am Acad Psychoanal* 1978;6:325–352.
Cantwell DP, Carlson G. Problems and prospects in the study of childhood depression. *J Nerv Ment Dis* 1979; 167 9:522–529.
Carlson GA, Cantwell DP. A survey of depressive symptoms in a child and adolescent psychiatric population: interview data. *J Am Acad Child Psychiatry* 1979; 18:587–599.
Carlson GA, Cantwell DP. A survey of depressive symptoms, syndrome and disorder in a child psychiatric population. *J Child Psychol Psychiatry* 1980a; 21:19–25.
Carlson GA, Cantwell DP. Unmasking masked depression in children and adolescents. *Am J Psychiatry* 1980b; 137:445–449.
Carlson GA, Cantwell DP. Suicidal behavior and depression in children and adolescents. *J Am Acad Child Psychiatry* (in press, to be published in July 1982).
Cytryn L, McKnew DH Jr. Proposed classification of childhood depression. *Am J Psychiatry* 1972; 129:149–155.
Cytryn L, McKnew DH Jr., Bunney WE Jr. Diagnosis of depression in children: a reassessment. *Am J Psychiatry* 1980; 137:22–25.
Feighner JP, Robins E, Guze SB, et al. Diagnostic criteria for use in psychiatric research. *Arch Gen Psyciatry* 1972; 26:57–63.
Frommer EA. Depressive illness in childhood. In: Coppens A, Walk A, eds. *Recent developments in affective disorders.* Ashford, Kent: Headley Brothers, 1968:117–136.
Gittelman-Klein R. Definitional and methodological issues concerning depressive illness in children. In: Schulterbrandt JG, Raskin A, eds. *Depression in childhood.* New York: Raven Press, 1977:69–80.
Glaser K. Masked depression in children and adolescents. *Ann Prog Child Psychiatry Child Dev* 1968; 1:345–355.
Goodwin DW, Guze SB. *Psychiatric diagnosis.* New York: Oxford University Press, 1979:
Kendell RE. The classification of depressions: a review of contemporary confusion. *Br J Psychiatry* 1976; 129:15–28.
Lewis AJ. Melancholia: a historical review. *J Ment Sci* 1934; 80 328:1–42.
Malmquist CP. Depressions in childhood and adolescence. *N Eng J Med* 1971; 284:887–893.
McConville BJ, Boag LC. Therapeutic approaches in childhood depression. Presented at the Annual Meeting of the Canadian Psychiatric Association, Vancouver, Canada, 1973.
McConville BJ, Boag LC, Purohit AP. Three types of childhood depression. *Can J Psychiatr* 1973; 18:133–138.
McKnew DH, Jr., Cytryn L. Urinary metabolites in chronically depressed children. *J Am Acad Child Psychiatry* 1979; 18:608–615.
Phillips I. Childhood depression: the mirror of experience, interpersonal interactions, and depressive phenomena. In: Feuch AP, Berlin IN, eds. *Depression in children and adolescents.* New York: Human Sciences Press, 1978.
Rie HE. Depression in childhood: a survey of some pertinent contributors. *J Am Acad Child Psychiatry* 1966; 5:653–685.
Rochlin G. The loss complex. *J Am Psychoanal Assoc* 1959; 7:299–316.

Rutter M. Classification. In: Rutter M, Hersov, eds. *Child psychiatry*. London: Blackwell Scientific Publications, 1978:359–384.

Sandler J, Joffe WG. Notes on childhood depression. *Int J Psychoanal* 1965; 46:88–96.

Schlesser MA, Winokur G, Sherman BM. Hypothalamic-pituitary-adrenal axis activity in depressive illness. *Arch Gen Psychiatry* 1980;37:737–743.

Spitz RA. Anaclitic depression. *Psychoanal Study Child* 1946; 11:313–342.

Spitzer RL. Classification of mental disorders and DSM-III. In: Kaplan HI, Freedman AM, Sadock BJ, eds. *Comprehensive textbook of psychiatry* III. Williams & Wilkins, 1980:

Spitzer RL, Cantwell DP. The DSM-III classification of the psychiatric disorders of infancy, childhood, and adolescence. *J Am Acad Child Psychiatry* 1980; 19:356–370.

Spitzer RL, Endicott J, Robins E. Research diagnostic criteria: rationale and reliability. *Arch Gen Psychiatry* 1978;35:773.

Ward CH, Beck AT, Mendelson M, Mock JE, Erbaugh JK. Reasons for diagnostic diagreement. *Arch Gen Psychiatry* 1962;7:198–205.

Welner A, Welner Z, Fishman R. Psychiatric adolescent inpatient. *Arch Gen Psychiatry* 1979;36:698–700.

Winokur G. Unipolar depression: is it divisible into autonomous subtypes? *Arch Gen Psychiatry* 1979;36:47–52.

Affective Disorders in Childhood and Adolescence--
An Update. Edited by D.P. Cantwell and G.A. Carlson.

3

Case Studies in Prepubertal Childhood Depression

Gabrielle A. Carlson and Dennis P. Cantwell

General issues of classification and diagnostic criteria for childhood depression have been described in previous chapters. It is obvious to most clinicians that in diagnosing affective disorders in children we have not uncovered a new population of children never before considered disturbed. Rather, by using operational criteria, we are reclassifying disturbances in a way that will be more consistent and ultimately more accurate, allowing for better treatment, prediction, and research.

The degree of continuity between children and adults who meet DSM-III criteria for affective disorders has not been established, nor has a consistent group of age-related "associated features" and circumstances that modify the presentation of the illness.

The following cases of prepubertal children are described phenomenologically in some detail. The discussion concentrates on issues specific to the diagnosis of depression based on operational criteria, as well as addressing age-specific issues and diagnostic ambiguities.

CASE HISTORIES

Case 1: Major Depression, Single Episode, with Melancholia in a 9½-Year-Old Boy

Presenting Problem

R. was brought to the hospital emergency room by his parents because he had been riding his skateboard in a dangerous intersection hoping to be killed. Parents had only mild concerns about this behavior; more bothersome to them was the recent onset of R.'s "poor conduct" at home and school. Strangely, R. pleaded with the doctor to hospitalize him before he actually did kill himself. His extremely serious, sad countenance and his statements of feeling sad, guilty for the grief he caused everyone, self-loathing, and anhedonia, with no evidence of psychosis or longstanding behavior problems, suggested the diagnosis of depression from the start. His suicidal behavior and adamance for admission prompted that decision.

History of Present Illness

While the family initially presented as intact and somewhat concerned, a very bizarre history ultimately emerged from R. (verified subsequently by parents). R., who was unusually coherent and sensitive for his age, said he felt his problems began when he came to live with his parents. Parents had given R. to a relative shortly after birth and pretended they were dead. Just as precipitously, they demanded him back when he was 6½. R. had to adjust not only to having dead parents but also to finding out they were alive and to the sudden loss of the aunt who raised him. As neither R. nor the aunt wanted him to go, there was a fight and parents refused to have further contact with her. Although parents identified R.'s conduct problems as having a gradual but recent onset, R. dates the onset of his problems to a feeling he had on the plane returning to his parents several years earlier that he was "going to do something wrong."

In spite of the foregoing, R. became attached to his mother. However, his parents were rigid disciplinarians and threatened him by saying he would cause a heart attack (mother had coronary artery disease) or spell (described later) in the mother or by using physical punishment that bordered on abusive. Family turmoil was described by R. as "mommy gets mad and takes it out on Daddy; Daddy takes it out on me, and I take it out on myself." In a resigned way he also noted "my parents took me back so they will have someone to put their burdens on."

History from parents and school ultimately revealed a behavior change a few months earlier. R. had begun getting into trouble in school for not completing assignments, bothering other children, and getting into more fights (though the teacher considered R. only a minor problem). He had occasional episodes of fecal incontinence, nightmares (he said he often could not sleep), and had begun to engage in minor antisocial activities (petty theft, running away from home for a few hours, about which he felt very guilty). R. acknowledged that he felt bad inside (not only unhappy but wicked—the only way he could account for behavior which displeased his parents) and felt hopeless that the future would be better; he stated that nothing was any fun anymore, and thought he would be better off dead. Appetite was unimpaired; there was no evidence of delusional thinking, hallucinations, phobia, obsessive thoughts, or compulsions. He admitted to a "short fuse" and described his fights with other boys with some bravado. There was no history of serious conduct disorder or abuse of the rights of others.

The most striking aspects of R.'s mental status were his seriousness and frequent hypoactivity. However, while he often appeared subdued, sometimes he would be unable to articulate his feelings, and become silly, "hyperactive," and distractible. On those occasions, he would also be prankish and irritable. He vacillated from extreme dependence to risk-taking, "superman" behavior. He was, however, a very appealing "spunky" youngster who made warm relationships easily with adults and fairly well with peers.

Developmental History

R. was premature, weighing 3 lb at birth. There were no other problems, however, and development was normal.

Psychologic Testing

Revealed a youngster with a WISC Verbal 105, Performance 90, Full-Scale IQ 97, much lower than one would have guessed on interacting with him. The lower performance tasks were attributed to some psychomotor slowing. Projective testing revealed themes of abandonment or violent endings for people.

School Performance

Academic testing revealed at least fourth grade skills and performance. The teacher noted R.'s main school problems to have been depression and preoccupation with personal problems: "He is sensitive and highly perceptive but his inner turmoil interferes with his work which ranges from creative and high level to disorganized and sloppy. He often refused to do anything . . . Even though he was scoring at near seventh grade levels [he was in the fourth grade] on reading vocabulary subtests [of the California Achievement Test], his self-disappointment when he could not do as well as he thought erupted into anger, tears, and total refusal to finish the test."

Family History

R.'s mother, whom he physically resembled, was in her late 30s. She had been granted a medical disability from the Women's Army Corps and the family lived on her disability and social security checks. Her medical history was fraught with seven pregnancies (of which only two children lived), five back operations, and two coronary artery bypass surgeries. She was subject to intermittent paranoid psychotic episodes (called "spells") which began suddenly, could last for hours to days, and often terminated with heavy alcohol intake. They were extremely frightening to behold and, according to R.'s mother, to experience. There was no evidence of depression or mania before, during, or after these spells. They were not alcohol-induced. Her warmth, thought processes, and relationship with her son (and his therapist) between these "spells" suggested a more episodic but atypical affective disorder rather than a schizophrenic disorder. She had run away from home at age 16 and knew little about her family. Her husband had never been employed, appeared generally inadequate, and had a family history of alcoholism.

Treatment Course

Although R. felt safer (both from abuse, "spells," and the damage he felt he inflicted) in the hospital, he remained moderately depressed. He was given the Short Beck Depression Inventory (BDI) on admission and scored 18 (cutoff for adults with moderate depression is 8) (Albert and Beck, 1975). After two weeks, a trial of imipramine was begun at 100 mg/day. By six weeks his depressive symptoms had improved considerably (Short BDI score was 7). He noted feeling sad only when angry, rather than all of the time. He was sometimes disappointed in himself but the self-loathing and "bad" feelings had diminished. He noted some fatigue, loneliness, and boredom, but school performance, concentration, and sleep had improved.

Additional treatment included intensive psychotherapy and family therapy initially with the goal of brief hospitalization and outpatient follow-up. Family therapy and early discharge proved futile as the degree of family psychopathology became unmasked and R.'s fear for his own safety was understood. Moreover, his mother, hospitalized for her third cornoary bypass operation, died during surgery. Interestingly, R. noted a qualitative difference between the grief felt at the loss of his mother and his depressive symptoms. While he did not feel guilty or responsible for her death, however, he wondered "if she still kept an eye on me from behind some cloud so I'll behave good."

Medication was discontinued at hospital discharge. His Short BDI score was 3. R. was seen in supportive therapy through the following year; however, the father moved precipitously and R.'s treatment was terminated abruptly. When R. was 15, he ran away from home because of continued conflict and abuse from his father. He found his way back to his therapist who initiated social service intervention.

R. recalled his experience and depression vividly and felt the therapist had "saved his life." He denied feeling depressed since but obviously bore the scars of someone chronically undervalued and at least psychologically abused. He remained serious, caring, and resourceful. His future goal was to join the Marines.

Discussion

This example underscores a number of important clinical issues in the diagnosis of childhood depression. First, the child is often more aware of his mood state and other depressive symptoms than the parents. The parents' major concern was R.'s misbehavior. They had great difficulty acknowledging R.'s depression (possibly because they felt responsible for it). This child might previously have been considered as having a "masked" depression and certainly displayed a number of symptoms sometimes called "depressive equivalents" (fighting, delinquency, occasional fecal soiling, deteriorating school performance). He was so articulate at describing the affective, cognitive, and neurovegetative features of his depression, and at providing a remarkably accurate chronology, one needed hardly resort to equivalents to make the diagnosis. (Although his mother's death was unfortunate, it was interesting that R. voluntarily distinguished between his feelings when his mother died and his depressed mood.)

While further study is necessary for substantiation, there may be some diagnostic significance to the fact that R.'s "feeling bad" antidated the onset of the more age-related concomitants or "associated features." We have seen children who develop these "equivalents" secondary to their depression. We have also seen many children whose depressive symptoms postdate their conduct problems and/or encopresis. The temporal relationship of these "equivalents" to the course of the depression may be more important than simply their presence or absence.

In this youngster, as in others we have seen, there is often a relative underactivity. It appears to this author, however, to be listlessness and lack of energy and to be less pervasive than the total system slowing seen in adult psychomotor retardation. Conversely, the hyperactivity and irritability, rather than being chronic as it is in youngsters with attention deficit disorder, occurs when the youngster seems to be trying to avoid feeling sad.

Published case histories of depressed youngsters usually describe clear-cut family histories of affective disorder. While R.'s mother had an episodic disorder, episodes appeared neither manic, depressive, or even schizoaffective in nature. As is often the situation in cases referred to teaching institutions (versus private practice) psychiatric histories of extended families are, like the families themselves, unavailable.

R. was treated before either dexamethadone suppression tests or imipramine blood levels were being done on a regular basis. It was clear, however, that different aspects of R.'s depression responded to different interventions. The imipramine diminished R.'s irritability, suicidal ideation, insomnia, and severe dysphoria. His helplessness/omnipotence was addressed with some success in therapy and by the milieu.

Six years later, R. met no criteria for a psychiatric disorder (though he was not free from emotional problems) and had had no recurrence of depression or suicidal ideation.

Case 2: Major Depression in a 7½-Year Old Girl with Preexisting Attention Deficit Disorder and Developmental Reading and Arithmetic Disorder

Presenting Complaint

T. was referred by her private psychiatrist who felt her "marked depression and low threshold for frustration" required more attention than was obtainable on an outpatient basis. T.'s mother had been unaware of T.'s feelings and had her evaluated because of her longstanding temper tantrums and her inability to function in school.

History of Present Illness

T. was a normal infant described as easy to take care of, but one who had difficulties in any new situation. When she was two years old, her parents divorced. Between that time and her evaluation, she was shuttled back and forth across country at least five times to be cared for by either parent as their individual financial or marital status changed. Her mother stated that T.'s disciplinary problems began at the time of the divorce (age two) and that "no one has ever been able to get her to do anything." This extended to school where she was working below grade level, was found to be inattentive, poorly coordinated, had some "immaturities" (letter and number reversal), and no peer relationships. T. was also described as very impulsive and extremely emotionally labile. She was suspended from school because she was disruptive and needed more supervision than the school could provide.

Since neither parent was aware of how sad T. felt and both denied they had ever heard her make comments like she wished she were dead, she was a bad person, etc, it could not be ascertained when T.'s depressive symptoms began. Besides the problems previously mentioned, however, both parents (separately) commented on T.'s sleep problems (difficulties getting to sleep and staying asleep) and enuresis (one to two times per week). Her mother stated that T.'s three major fears were of abandonment, being alone, and not being loved.

Mental Status

The following descriptions were excerpted from T.'s therapist's mental status exam. The first interview had to be terminated as T. screamed, hit herself (only) with clenched fists, and rolled around the floor for the duration of the meeting. The next meeting was more successful.

"T. related and had mannerisms of a much younger child," she did things in extremes, eg, speech was either shouts or whispers; her affect could change suddenly from calm to screaming and crying.

"She showed great difficulty turning on and off expressed emotion." T. described herself as sad, having no good qualities, and said that no one liked her.

She was quite preoccupied with minor injuries. Her only stated fear was that something might happen to her mother (however, problems with separation were also noted). Thought process, intellect, and sensorium were unremarkable.

In addition to the above, the research interview revealed there were no activities that gave her any pleasure. T. admitted to being aggressive and angry when she felt sad; she had thought about dying and tried to kill herself by jumping off a roof (a fall which was considered accidental by mother), and felt hopeless about the future. She said she felt tired most of the time and did not have much appetite (though there was no evidence of weight loss).

Although T. spoke about her sadness and low self-esteem with her therapist, during the research interview she was clearly able to talk better about her feelings and problems through the use of puppets than she was on direct examination. Thus, the "doctor puppet" went through the systematic interview, and the lamb puppet (T.'s) answered the questions. T. had to use a third puppet to discuss her suicidal feelings (eg, "Has the little lamb ever felt so sad or terrible she wished she were dead?" "No, but the turtle has." Up popped a turtle puppet who then described the roof incident).

School Report

Although IQ testing put her in the normal range (WISC V = 113, P = 105, FSIQ = 109) this third grader was performing at a mid-first grade level in reading and arithmetic. Her teacher described her as "a depressed, confused child with extremely poor self-concept, poor peer relationships, and consequently an underachiever." On the Connors Teacher Rating Scale (Connors, 1977), items endorsed as "most of the time" were "tearful on arrival to school," "cries often and easily," "quick or drastic mood changes," "tantrums and unpredictable behavior," "sullen," "often unhappy," "overly sensitive," and "complains often of aches and pains."

Family History

Although no family history of depression was noted in T.'s workup, specific questioning of her mother revealed she had had a depressive episode several years earlier where she felt low, she was tearful, lost 10 lb because of poor appetite, had insomnia, and was barely able to function because she had no energy and could not concentrate. She contemplated overdosing with pills but did not because "she felt responsible for the kids." This lasted several months and went untreated. She denied any other psychiatric problems except for "stress-related migraine headaches." T.'s mother felt her own mother was depressed, drank secondary to it, and died at age 56 of cirrhosis of the liver. Mother knew little of T.'s father's psychiatric problems ("There was nothing obvious.") but said both his parents were heavy drinkers.

Treatment Course

T. was treated with psychotherapy, consistency and limit-setting by the ward school milieu, and an approach of ignoring her tantrums and providing her with success experiences. After two months, a trial of amitriptyline was begun. With 75 mg dosage, T. noted that she "felt better" and said the medicine helped her control her temper tantrums. She was discharged to residential placement two months later, having made substantial gains in self-control, but still experienced separation problems, "fears of developing close relationships," and problems with peers.

Follow-up One Year Later

T. was considerably more composed and friendly and by report of parent, placement, and self had made considerable gains. She again resorted to puppets to acknowledge she did not have as many friends as she liked. She denied feeling depressed any longer, but said she sometimes wished she were dead when other kids hurt her feelings. Her mother was about to move to a new neighborhood and T. was very worried about starting a new school. She also admitted to worrying about the dark, being left alone, and that her mother might die. Although she had improved academically, she still met criteria for developmental reading and arithmetic delays.

Discussion

Like patient 1, T. presented primarily as a behavioral problem. Since her parents divorced at age two, a time in which temper tantrums and oppositional behavior are not unknown, it is difficult to actually date the onset of her behavior problems. Moreover, at age 7½, she herself was unable to provide a reliable chronology of when she started to feel bad about herself, have sleep problems, low energy, little interest, etc. Her parents, unaware that she had such feelings, had no idea when they began. Delineating an actual episode in these circumstances is close to impossible.

One need not be rigid in obtaining information systematically from children. By using puppets, for instance, the research interviewer, who had no relationship with T., was able to complete a detailed, structured interview. On follow-up interview one year later, the use of puppets again enabled T. to recall her previous problems and discuss their current state.

In addition to meeting criteria for major depression, T. probably meets criteria for attention deficit disorder without hyperactivity (on Axis I) and developmental reading and arithmetic disorders on Axis II. Disentangling how these disorders relate is also difficult. Some would argue that the depression was responsible for both academic and behavioral problems. The authors hypothesized that the impulsivity and developmental delay antedated the depressive symptoms and gave her a diagnosis of secondary affective disorder. Some corroboration for this ordering is found in the persistence of the developmental delays academically noted on one-year follow-up when her depression had improved.

Cases 1 and 2 are similar and highlight a frequent finding in depressed children. Both children suffered from inordinate losses—shifting of parenting figures and preemptory changes in home and school. It is not surprising that fears of abandonment and regression associated with separation should be prominent parts of their clinical picture. How much of these children's abandonment concern is "unrealistic worry" (as required by DSM-III for separation anxiety disorder diagnosis), as opposed to quite realistic given their experience, is a difficult distinction to make. On the other hand, many of the children admitted to the children's psychiatric inpatient unit have suffered similar (and worse) deprivation. Obviously not all of the youngsters respond to these losses with a major depressive episode.

T. had a less ambiguous family history than R. since her mother gave a clear history of depression. In both cases, a number of family members were alcoholic. More family history data comparing children with depression and other psychiatric disorders should be collected before any conclusions can be drawn about the relationship of alcoholism to childhood depression.

Finally, long-term follow-up will be necessary to determine whether these children will function like adults with occasional depressive episodes or will develop other adult psychopathology.

Case 3: Major Depression with Psychotic and Melancoholic Features and Atypical Eating Disorder in an 11½-Year-Old Boy

Presenting Problem

S., an 11½-year-old-boy, seemed to have the acute onset of fear of getting fat after the sudden death of an obese acquaintance of the family. S. was previously considered healthy and, in fact, conscientious about eating the right food and staying in shape. However, fear of getting fat (and thus dying) and associated obsessive behavior (a massive exercise program, frequent weighing, hiding food) was of major concern to the family. S. began complaining of stomach pains and was also noted to be increasingly withdrawn and self-depreciatory. Ultimately, he refused to swallow anything, became increasingly hostile toward family members, and acted slightly bizarrely, contemptuously calling members of his family "pieces of food." While by admission he had lost 10 lb (duration of symptoms had been nine weeks) his height and weight were still just over the third percentile for his age.

At S.'s admission, his doctor described him as looking young for his age, scrawny, hunched, and fidgety. His voice was soft, with a monotonous tone.

He said he felt mad and sad, his mood being a "2 or 3 out of 10." He had a low opinion of his worth: "I'm really spoiled and I have always been spoiled. People shouldn't be giving me so much attention and spending so much money on me."

His worries, besides getting fat, included that his parents and friends might get killed in a car accident. He didn't think he would ever get out of the hospital, didn't really care what happened to himself, and, when asked about what animal he'd like to be, said he would like to be a crocodile because it could "swim away and not be bothered by anyone." He admitted to having insomnia (initial and terminal) and nightmares about being chased by food.

A research interview found all the above as well as psychomotor retardation, anhedonia, suicidal thinking ("I would kill myself if I could"), and numerous somatic complaints. He described his abdominal pain and felt there were monsters in his stomach. Discussion of monsters, in fact, took up 25 percent of his spontaneous conversation. His intelligence seemed somewhat above average and there was a faint glimmer of a sense of humor. He remarked with the only smile in the interview that when his mother would return from the grocery store with food, he would think "here comes Mom with the enemy." Except for the stomach monsters and thoughts about food, there was no evidence of delusional thinking. When asked to draw a picture of what he thought his stomach looked like, S. drew an excellent, anatomically correct picture of the human heart.

Past History

The patient's history was unremarkable except that he seemed somewhat shy, rigid, perfectionistic, and always concerned about his body and getting sick. School performance was good. Peer and family relationships were not considered a problem.

Family History

S. was the middle of three children. The family was cohesive, intelligent, and concerned—what conflicts or problems they had were not commensurate with the magnitude of S.'s psychopathology. S.'s maternal grandmother was treated successfully with electroconvulsive therapy for a midlife depression. S.'s mother became depressed while taking antihypertensive medication but the depression abated with its cessation. Both mother and father have a number of other family members with alcohol problems.

Hospital Course

It was necessary to feed S. through a nasogastric tube as he persistently refused to eat for several months. He was given a trial of doxepin, 5 mg/kg, to which he did not respond. He was treated with play therapy, guided imagery, milieu therapy, and family therapy. Five months after admission S. began to complain again of frequent, cramping abdominal pain. Reevaluation of these complaints revealed that he had acute pancreatitis. For the following month he was treated with hyperalimentation, at the conclusion of which both his stomach pain and preoccupation with food disappeared and he resumed eating.

At follow-up, one year later, S. was no longer depressed and his weight was normal. He recalled his problem earlier as being afraid of getting fat and that he wasn't having fun anymore. He acknowledged that he was "not quite back to normal," however, because he still worried about eating fattening food. He also still sat holding his stomach. His preoccupation with monsters seemed to have changed to a strong interest in robots. He was reserved though not unfriendly and more compliant than the usual 13-year-old. His thinking was also more concrete than had impressed the interviewer earlier. On telephone contact five years later S. was not interested in further contact. His parents stated he had not required further treatment and was doing well in school, with peers, and with family members.

Discussion

Although S. was diagnosed during his hospitalization as having anorexia nervosa, his symptomatology approximated that of a delusional depression. Not only did S. articulate the whole panoply of depressive signs and symptoms, his fear of weight gain was due to his delusional perception that food killed rather than that he was obese and needed to lose weight. Furthermore, his delusion of monsters in his stomach was a mood congruent, somatic delusion. Finally, unlike the previous cases, the onset of S.'s disorder was acute. His past history was not riddled with losses and severe parental psychopathology.

The relationship of S.'s acute pancreatitis to his psychiatric disorder is unclear. Acute pancreatitis is relatively uncommon in otherwise healthy children with no history of cystic fibrosis, mumps, or family history. It is interesting that he resumed eating (after five months of nasogastric tube feeding) when the pancreatitis subsided. On the other hand, at the follow-up interview, he identified his psychiatric symptomatology rather than his abdominal pain as being his primary problem and still had some residual concerns about food. It is also interesting to note that of the nearly 100 youngsters diagnosed as having anorexia nervosa treated at UCLA for the past 15 years, only two have required long-term feeding by nasogastric tube. One was S. who meets criteria for major depression and possible atypical eating disorder. The other is an adolescent with severe depression who will be described in a later chapter.

S. did not respond to doxepin and it was the only drug tried. The pills were pulverized and fed nasogastrically. How well the 5 mg/kg correlated with adequate blood levels is unknown. In addition, Puig-Antich (personal communication) has found that youngsters with psychotic depressions need higher blood levels before they respond to imipramine. Thus, whether S. would have responded to adequate treatment with a different drug is unknown.

S.'s family history of depression and alcoholism does not help us in our distinction between eating and depressive disorders as such histories have been found in both populations of youngsters. The only remarkable finding was the absence of both the degree of interactional psychopathology found in psychosomatic families and the degree of loss and deprivation found in many children with depression. The autonomous aspect of S.'s symptomatology, the pervasive anhedonia, and the significant weight loss meet criteria for major depressive episode with melancholia.

S. is now 16 years old. According to his parents he is eating and functioning normally. In follow-up studies at UCLA, this outcome is more consistent with that of an acute depression than eating disorder (Cantwell et al, 1977; Strober and Carlson, 1982).

Case 4: Recurrent Major Depression in a 12½-Year-Old Boy

Presenting Problem

D. had had a long history of somatic problems (mainly gastrointestinal and ear, nose, and throat). Over the year before the Neurophsychiatric Institute (NPI) referral (beginning at age nine) he missed most of the school year because of ear, chest, stomach, and low back pain. There was no shortage of pediatricians involved and one pediatrician, shortly before a tonsillectomy and myringotomy were to be performed to alleviate the ear, nose, and throat complaints, finally referred D. and his parents for psychiatric evaluation.

Psychiatric history revealed that beginning with a move to another school, D. became markedly withdrawn and listless and began to gain weight. He stayed home most of the time complaining of physical aches and pains which succeeded also in keeping him out of school. He had no appetite or sleep problems, and though he denied being depressed, he stated he was rarely happy and remained bored most of the time at home.

When after surgery, D. refused to eat solid foods (and ultimately lost 25 lb) and began to speak only in whispers, he was referred for inpatient treatment. He was ten years old. Mental status was notable for the following: D. was withdrawn and lethargic, was depressed-looking, and spoke only when asked to speak. He whispered whatever he did say. He was sullen and never showed any affect other than a pained expression as he intermittently held his stomach and moaned. He said he did not eat because he was not hungry. He denied suicidal ideation, fears, phobia, obsessions, or delusions.

Psychologic testing revealed a very bright youngster who answered slowly what he would answer, but responded with an "I don't know" to most items on the Thematic Apperception Test (TAT) or Rorschach.

Family History

Mother gave the history of being abused as a child and having multiple caretakers. Her own mother "had a nervous breakdown" but nothing else is known. Mother was guarded in discussing herself but denied a history of psychiatric disorder. Father described himself as having had periods of being withdrawn (like his son) as a child and adolescent. He now described himself (and is described) as an adult as having a violent temper and a drinking problem. He meets criteria for dysthymic disorder but not major depression. Family problems were severe though both parents were "devoted" to D.

School Comments

In addition to noting D.'s withdrawal and somatic preoccupations, teacher felt D. had a great deal of trouble concentrating and was extremely indecisive.

Hospital Course

D. was given a choice of eating 700 calories in food or meritene for each meal with the option of being tube-fed if he did not eat within the time constraints provided. He never required tube feeding. His whispers and somatic complaints (after thorough evaluation) were ignored. His family was engaged in treatment with the goal of "de-enmeshing" D. and helping him to be more independent. It took about two months before he began to speak audibly, and six months before he began to eat normally. He was discharged after eight months of hospitalization.

Second Admission

D. evidently had no problems with school attendance or eating for the next two years. In the setting of increased family strife, he began to withdraw, languish at home, complain of abdominal pain, and ultimately stopped eating. As these symptoms marked the beginning of his problem the first time, his parents and pediatrician referred him promptly "before things got worse." He was transferred from the medical hospital (to which he had been admitted with possible dehydration) for psychiatric inpatient treatment at age 12½.

Those who had known D. on his prior admission felt his symptoms and behavior were of similar kind but less severe. He spoke, but in a quiet voice, did little unless pushed, was often tearful and whining, was preoccupied with aches and pains, and was somewhat preoccupied with food. While he lost 5 to 6 lb, he continued to eat in the hospital. The inability to make decisions, which had been somewhat problematic before, was incapacitating. Moreover, D. was extremely irritable and sarcastic in a way not noted on previous admission.

When asked about how he felt, D. denied he had any problems but his abdominal pain. He denied self-esteem problems, hopeless feelings, or suicidal ideation. He did admit feeling bored frequently, to feeling like crying for no reason, to having little energy, and to getting angry and annoyed easily. While he acknowledged liking to have fun, he could think of nothing that gave him pleasure. He didn't enjoy eating but had no sleep problems. He was unable to say when he began having the aforementioned feelings or whether they represented a change from his usual self.

Psychologic Testing

On the Wechsler Intelligence Scale for Children–Revised (WISC-R), D. functioned in the superior range in total and all subtests scores, except for coding where his relatively weak performance (scaled score 9) was compatible with his reduced mental efficiency. On this admission D. was more forthcoming on projective tests. The psychologist noted "most of his characters were sad, and if a character was not sad, he was either dead or angry because he had been the victim of a terrible injustice . . . When confronted with stress, D. tends to avoid, deny or flee from the stressor. There was no evidence of thought disorder."

A dexamethasone suppression test was performed shortly after admission. With 1 mg dexamethasone administered at 11 PM, the serum cortisol drawn at 4 PM the following day was 8.4 mg/100 ml. As levels of 5 mg/100 ml or greater are considered evidence of nonsuppression, it was felt that D.'s response was similar to that observed in depressed adults (Carroll et al, 1981). In addition to the inpatient therapy approach, D. was given imipramine, 150 mg daily. With this regimen, his irritability and cognition improved, the somatization diminished, and his activity level increased. He was discharged to outpatient follow-up after a four-month hospitalization. Although D. had clearly improved, he still lacked any insight into his symptoms and behavior, let alone the kinds of factors that produced them.

Discussion

Unlike many of the children we have interviewed, D. denied feeling depressed or having self-esteem or guilt problems. His professed and observed anhedonia, concentration problems, anorexia, and lethargy/psychomotor retardation qualified him for the diagnosis of major depression. Unlike Case 3, his family functioned like a psychosomatic family (Minuchin et al, 1978). Hypochondriacal/somatic features complicated D.'s presentation but seemed to represent an exacerbation of his usual functioning. During his first hospitalization, the major thrust of treatment was family and individual psychotherapy.

When D.'s symptoms recurred, a more aggressive approach was taken to treat the depressive symptomatology. A positive dexamethasone suppression test supported antidepressant treatment which was subsequently undertaken. Symptom resolution was more rapid. Although depressive psychopathology largely resolved, the somatic preoccupations were still present though more muted.

Patients 3 and 4 present with somatic rather than behavioral concomitants to their depression. Again, however, it was not necessary to infer depressive psychopathology. While there appears to be a definite interaction between the youngster's premorbid personality and the psychopathology for which the child ultimately required treatment, the individual factors did not so modify the depressive symptoms as to "mask them."

Case 5: Major Depression in a Ten-Year-Old Boy with Preexisting Attention Deficit Disorder

Presenting Complaint

T. was a ten-year-old male referred for continuing problems at home and in school.

History of Present Illness

T. was referred by his mother for evaluation primarily upon pressure from the school. T.'s fifth grade teacher reported that he "had problems with temper, poor attitude, lack of control, inability to perceive a situation and evaluate it, living in a fantasy world, foul language, hyperactivity, poor concentration, poor school work, disrupting the class, frequent temper tantrums, and unpredictable behavior." Although T. attended a regular public school (as he had been since kindergarten), it was quite clear that his behavioral problems were longstanding. School records revealed oppositional behavior, disobeying rules, impulsivity, and difficulty in interpersonal relationships with both peers and school officials, dating back to kindergarten. Despite this, and despite the fact that T. had a tested IQ of over 130 and was not even functioning at grade level work, T. had never been referred for any kind of special help in the school. The prevailing attitude of T.'s teacher, the school psychologist, and the school principal seemed to be, "T. can control himself if he wants to. He just doesn't seem to want to behave."

T.'s mother also revealed that T. has been inattentive, hyperactive, and fidgety for as long as she could remember. In desperation, T.'s mother had him evaluated by a pediatric neurologist. The neurologist felt that T. had longstanding attentional problems and specific learning delays with a superimposed depression characterized by feelings of self-depreciation, sadness, and death wishes. Depressive symptoms (which included dysphoric mood, rather marked anhedonia, marked appetite change with a 20 lb weight gain over a six-month period, social withdrawal, frequent crying spells, frequent temper tantrums and getting into fights, dependency on and clinging to the mother, initial and terminal insomnia, and feelings of guilt and hopelessness) had begun about two years after the suicide of T.'s father. T.'s father committed suicide during a one-month separation from the mother after a 22-year marriage. T. felt himself somewhat guilty for the separation. "If I wouldn't have been so bad, maybe my mom and dad would have stayed together, and then he wouldn't have killed himself." At the same time, he also tended to blame his mother for the suicide because it occurred while they were separated.

When T. was initially seen, he presented with a sullen, belligerent, hostile attitude. However, after several sessions, his depressed mood, poor self-image, hopelessness, strong feelings of guilt about his father's suicide, pervasive anhedonia, and strong suicidal ideation became evident. He felt numb, lonely because he was unable to make any friends and got into frequent fights, picked on by his teachers who he felt "did not understand that he did not want to do things he did, but simply couldn't control himself." He was very eager to enter into a plan of intervention.

Developmental and Medical History

Developmental history was significant for rapid onset of almost all milestones, a history of activity and impulsivity from a very early age, and a long history of multiple accidents.

Family History

The father, a retired pilot, killed himself at the age of 43 after being depressed for about a year. During the year before the suicide, there were frequent marital conflicts with both parents drinking heavily. The father had previously made an unsuccessful attempt which the mother had not taken seriously. The father also may have had attention deficit disorder as a child. T.'s mother, a college graduate in spite of earlier learning problems, was in therapy for depression for about six months before the husband's suicide and for about six months after the suicide.

Many first and second degree relatives on both sides of T.'s family had histories of alcoholism, antisocial behavior, and multiple depressions.

Treatment Course

With a good deal of pressure from the therapist the school district approved placement in a private school for children with learning disabilities and emotional problems. At the same time, T. was seen on a regular basis both alone and with his mother and started on imipramine therapy which reached a maximum dosage of 150 mg per day (less than 2 mg/kg body weight). Attempts to raise the dose above this level met with complaints of headaches, blurred vision, and other somatic adverse effects. T. was unable to function in the private school, however, and the director of the school felt that they would no longer be able to manage T. on an outpatient basis. T.'s depression seemed to have increased and he talked to the staff intermittently about committing suicide.

T. was hospitalized for four months on an inpatient psychiatric ward and received individual and family therapy as well as milieu treatment and special education. After a period of observation without medication, he was restarted on imipramine to more appropriate dosage levels without complaints of side effects. His peer relationships improved with a social skills training program designed to increase T.'s ability to deal with his peers. School performance improved dramatically. He felt in better control of his attentional problems and impulsivity though he still required more structure and consistency than his mother could provide.

Thus, after four months of inpatient care, he was discharged to a residential treatment center. After seven months in residential placement, T. was able to attend a regular boarding school, and at follow-up 2½ years after he was initiallly seen, T. was doing extremely well personally, academically, and socially. He had not experienced any recurrence of his depression. He had been medication-free for over a year.

Discussion

T. had a longstanding history of inattentiveness, hyperactivity, and impulsivity, in the classroom. Despite the fact that these problems had dated back to and were documented in the class records since kindergarten, by fifth grade T. had been given no special help by the school. Following the death of the father figure, T. developed a superimposed depression. The depression remained untreated for quite a while. However, even with major therapeutic intervention on an outpatient basis including special schooling, individual and family therapy, and the use of medication, hospitalization was required. T. responded rapidly to the therapeutic program in the hospital. He progressed from there to a residential treatment center, and then to a regular boarding school geared for children with high academic abilities and no behavioral or emotional problems. He has functioned for more than a year in that school and has done well in every way. At his 2½ year follow-up he was functioning well in all areas.

Case 6: Major Depression with Psychotic Features in a 10½-Year-Old Girl

Presenting Complaint

Y., a 10½-year-old prepubertal girl, was transferred from a pediatric ward to which she had been admitted for persistent refusal to eat and a 12 lb weight loss. Although the initial diagnosis was presumed to be anorexia nervosa, it became apparent that Y.'s reasons for not eating were considerably more complex.

History of Present Illness

Past history revealed that Y. had always been a shy, anxious child acclimating to any changes and separations with difficulty. Her father, Mexican by birth, was very authoritarian and insisted he be in total control of "his women" (wife and two daughters). He viewed everything outside his immediate family with suspicion and allowed little interchange between his family and others. Thus, Y.'s anxiety associated with separations had multiple origins. Further, the mother had begun to bridle under the repression she felt and family strife had increased. Y.'s symptom seems to have developed in the context of beginning school in the fall and increased marital discord.

Y. had also recently seen *The Exorcist* on cable television and was very upset by the famous vomiting scene. Shortly thereafter she began to experience abdominal pain and nausea when eating, gradually began to eat less (her weight initially dropped from 90 to 82 lb), and then stopped eating altogether. She was hospitalized by her pediatrician for a medical workup. No unusual food habits were noted and the pediatrician also noted that although Y. had previously been a normally active youngster, she would sit alone and do nothing all day if left alone in her hospital room. She was transferred to a psychiatric hospital when no organic reason was found for weight loss and her refusal to eat persisted.

At psychiatric interview on admission Y. said that her weight (78 lb) was just about right. Somewhat more guardedly she said she feared "someone bad will poison my food." Who or why was unclear. She also admitted (though not consistently) to hearing her dolls and toys talking at night. (She couldn't hear what they were saying.) She stated, "I know dolls can't really talk but I hear them and it scares me." Since watching *The Exorcist* she also feared that the "scary things on TV will happen to me." Clear hallucinations with depressive, persecutory, or even discernable content were denied.

Other depressive symptoms to which Y. admitted included feeling bored, lonely, and sad, having trouble concentrating, feeling angry but being unable to express it, and feeling uncertain about the future. There was no diurnal variation. She did have insomnia and nightmares. She specifically denied suicidal ideation. She also worried a great deal about her parents and had more difficulty adjusting to the ward than the usual child.

At interview, she looked very sad, never smiled, barely answered questions, and, in fact, rarely moved and had definite latency of response.

Psychologic Testing

Testing revealed a youngster with Verbal, Performance, and Full Scale IQ (FSIQ) scores of 101. There was no evidence of thought disorder. Her themes reflected anxieties about the dark and monsters. There was some suggestion of hypervigilance from the number of "eye" responses on the Rorschach. Testing was otherwise unremarkable.

Family History

Both parents, currently in their 40s, had past histories of severe financial and affective deprivation. The father became depressed in late adolescence and was treated with an unknown medication. He considers himself to have been chronically anxious and depressed since. His own father was an alcoholic. The patient's mother reportedly became depressed two years before this evaluation and was seen briefly in outpatient treatment. Of her three sisters, she says two are suffering from depression. Her mother had no known psychiatric problems and her father was shot at the age of 40.

Hospital Course

While the food delusion and vague hallucinations disappeared in about ten days, Y. remained sad and anhedonic for the first month of hospitalization. She rarely interacted with peers and seemed preoccupied and uninterested in school. Her father's fear of medication prevented even obtaining a dexamethasone suppression test (DST) until he began to trust Y.'s doctor and staff. A DST ultimately revealed nonsuppression to 0.5 mg of dexamethasone. Cortisone levels were 13.7 mg/100 ml at 4 PM after an 11 PM drug administration the night before. She had been started on a cognitive behavioral therapy approach, charting her moods and learning to define her feelings. Although her mood improved with her therapist, this did not generalize to ward or school. She ultimately began a course of imipramine to which she had at least partially responded by discharge. She admitted that she had been depressed on admission and claimed her mood and outlook had improved. She was more spontaneous and assertive in her interactions. She remained somewhat irritable, oppositional, and shy. It was unclear how much of this represented residual depressive symptoms. There was no evidence of her delusions or hallucinations at discharge. There was never any evidence of formal thought disorder.

Her post-hospital course has been stable. Menarche occurred two months after discharge.

Discussion

The phenomenology of Y.'s psychotic depression represents an interesting mixture of cultural, environmental, and temperamental variables in a genetically vulnerable youngster. Her initial abdominal pain and nausea and ultimate explanatory delusion that her food was poisoned probably represents a combination of the anorexia of depression, her identification with the possessed little girl from *The Exorcist*, and her internalizing repeated admonitions from her father that anything outside the family was to be regarded with suspicion and fear. It is interesting that the other youngster with a psychotic depression (Case 3) complained of abdominal pain, refused to eat, and had food delusions.

Psychotic depressions in our experience are fairly uncommon. The frequency and significance of food-related delusions remains to be investigated.

In our experience, hallucinations in psychotically depressed youngsters are neither as intense nor persistent as they are in adolescence or adulthood. Unlike anhedonia, irritability, and pessimism, hallucinations have disappeared early in hospitalization before pharmacotherapeutic intervention. Although Y.'s initial paranoia and hallucinations prompted inclusion of schizophrenia in the differential diagnosis, the acuteness of onset, transience of psychosis, and prominence of other depressive symptoms and signs and ultimate improvement on antidepressants makes that diagnosis less likely. Although the DST is compatible with a diagnosis of depression, we have also had positive DSTs in a few children with unequivocal chronic schizophrenia.

Finally, in our experience, psychotic symptoms in childhood depression become more common with the approach of puberty. It is probably significant that Y.'s episode occurred just before menarche.

SUMMARY

Until we have unequivocal validation of the depressive disorder diagnostic category, we must look to consistency of clinical picture, family history, treatment response, natural history and laboratory studies for tentative validation. Cases 1 and 6 represent instances of clear signs and symptoms of depression, such that the age of the subjects was virtually irrelevant. In fact, were the subjects middle-aged adults, there would have been little question of diagnosis.

Cases 2 and 5 present more common diagnostic dilemmas. In both cases, it appeared that behavioral problems antedated the onset of more typical depressive psychopathology. Again it is unclear whether these youngsters had major depressions from the start which manifested differently at earlier ages or whether they had two diagnoses—attention deficit disorder followed by a depressive episode. Both youngsters improved with tricyclic antidepressants. These drugs are also useful in attention deficit and separation anxiety disorders. Family history also suggests mixed psychopathology. Attending to the depressive symptoms did result in an overall improvement in both children, however. Since one of the purposes of a diagnosis is to suggest a treatment regimen, we feel that there is at least clinical validation for identifying depressive histories in children with complex symptom pictures.

Cases 3 and 4 are described because of the medical aspects of their differential diagnosis. In both cases, abdominal pain with subsequent cessation of eating and weight loss were presenting complaints. Given the history of somatic preoccupation of both youngsters, it is perhaps not surprising that their depressive symptoms emphasized physical rather than behavioral manifestations.

The fact that all of these children were hospitalized does not imply that major depression in prepubertal children is necessarily an inpatient diagnosis. It probably does reflect the severity of depression, since these children by and large were nonfunctional at home, in school, and at play.

In summary, we feel the phenomenology of depression in a given child seems to reflect his/her dynamic issues, personality attributes, developmental abilities, and environmental circumstances within the confines of recognizable signs and symptoms of depression.

REFERENCES

Albert N, Beck AT. Incidence of depression in early adolescence: a preliminary study. *J Youth Adolescence* 1975;4:301-307.
Cantwell DP, Sturzenberg S, Burroughs J, et al. Anorexia nervosa–an affective disorder? *Arch Gen Psychiatry* 1977;34:1087-1093.
Carroll BJ, Feinberg M, Greden JF, et al. A specific laboratory test for the diagnosis of melancholia. *Arch Gen Psychiatry* 1981;38:15-22.
Connors K. Connors teachers rating scale. In Guy W, ed. *ECDEU manual.* National Institute of Mental Health, 1977:35-38.
Minuchin S, Rosman BL, Baker L. *Psychosomatic families: anorexia nervosa in context.* Cambridge, Mass: Harvard University Press, 1978.
Strober M, Carlson GA. Bipolar illness in adolescents with major depression. *Arch Gen Psychiatry* 1982;39:349-555.

Affective Disorders in Childhood and Adolescence--
An Update. Edited by D.P. Cantwell and G.A. Carlson.

4

Bipolar Affective Disorders in Childhood and Adolescence

Garbielle A. Carlson

There has been intermittent interest in juvenile manic depressive illness (bipolar) (BMDI) since the time of Kraepelin. As the phenomenologic, biologic, and genetic issues have been articulated and tools developed to clarify them, we are, perhaps, in a better position to reexamine the questions both of childhood antecedents of MDI and actual appearance of recognizable MDI in children.

This chapter will address itself mainly to diagnostic issues of prepubertal and adolescent bipolar manic depressive illness, though treatment and natural history will be discussed briefly at the end.

The often quoted review of Anthony and Scott (1960) enunciated the issues of controversy surrounding the existence of childhood BMDI. These are: (1) BMDI originates in the mood variations that are part of normal infant and early childhood development. The "extremes" of cheerfulness and negativism seen in the toddler are thus considered by some to be embryonic manic depression; (2) The opposing viewpoint, however, dismisses these mood changes as little more than personality disturbance or normal variation; interpretation of the more active phases as "mania" and their absence as "depression" is erroneous. Everyone agrees, then, over the existence of "mood swings" in early and mid-childhood; the question is whether or not these ups and downs are prodromata or an early form of BMDI.

In reviewing the question of childhood BMDI, we need to define both what is meant by childhood, and the point at which normal extremes become BMDI. Traditionally, illnesses beginning from age 0 to 19 are said to have a "childhood onset." A review of the literature reveals, however, that a number of such childhood cases in fact begin in adolescence. As will be discussed later, there is little doubt that BMDI occurs with some frequency in early adolescence. Prepubertal BMDI appears to be a more uncommon entity, however, and is decidedly rare to absent in early childhood.

The distinction between normal extremes, cyclothymia, and BMDI is one of severity, duration, and probably relative autonomy. Just as one can formulate a depressive spectrum from sadness, through grief, depression, and melancholia, one can similarly envision a spectrum from normal mood variation through emotional lability, cyclothymia, and full-fledged BMDI. Emotional lability implies extremes in mood of brief duration out of keeping with environmental input. Cyclothymic disorder requires by DSM-III (APA, 1980) criteria "a two-year history of numerous periods during which some symptoms characteristic of both depressive and manic syndromes were present but not of sufficient severity and duration to meet the criteria for a major depressive or manic episode." Manic episodes must last one week or require hospitalization; depressive episodes must last two weeks. Again, episodes are *often* (not always) autonomous in that there are no obvious precipitants. Severity is even more difficult to define than duration and rests on clinical judgment, and the individual's, family's, or community's tolerance for symptoms and behavior.

Let us briefly review the phenomenology of BMDI in adults. Although still considered a mood disorder, perhaps the most striking and consistent feature of BMDI is its changes in activity level (Bunney, 1977). In mania, the activation level is rapid: energy is increased; movement, speech and thought are fast; need for sleep is diminished. Normal premorbid preoccupations are expanded so that features such as religiosity, hypersexuality, and paranoia are often aggrandized features of what existed previously. Interests and involvement in activities are increased; the patient is gregarious and intrusive. A smoker now smokes four packs per day; a student is writing the greatest book in the world, etc. Although mood may be high, euphoria becomes dysphoria with depression, crying, or anger with the slightest provocation. Irritability and lability are as common as euphoria (Winokur et al, 1969). It is now well-recognized that the most frenetic psychosis can be quite consistent with severe mania (Carlson and Goodwin, 1973). The difference between hypomania and mania is one of velocity and lack of control.

Where mania is everything in fast motion, the depression of BMDI is slow motion. Psychomotor retardation presents with slowed action and thought; mutism and seeming catatonia can occur in severe cases. Hypersomnia, apathy, loss of interest in food, sex, and friends occurs. Instead of the expanded view of mania, the person's views are constricted. He is hopeless and worthless, the future is black, there is little point in eating, bathing, or waking. Occasionally, these morbidly depressed persons become delusional and hallucinate. For those who can articulate it, depression is far more complex and dysphoric than sadness (Winokur et al, 1969).

Finally, in the least controversial cases, the hallmark of BMDI is its episodic nature. There is a clear distinction between each state and between that state and "euthymia." While both the intensity and duration of mania and depression may vary from slight to severe, diagnosis is easiest when the cycles and episodes are clearest. The dilemma is greatest in mixed manic/depressive states, in single episodes where a course has not been established, where the cross-sectional phenomenology blends schizophrenic and affective features, and in "emotionally unstable character disorders"—dysthymic or cyclothymic disorders where some features are present, but clear episodes may be lacking and symptoms may be indistinguishable for personality factors.

PREPUBERTAL BIPOLAR MANIC DEPRESSIVE ILLNESS

In applying the description of adult BMDI to prepubertal children, it is obvious that the more stringent the criteria for BMDI, the less common it is. When Anthony and Scott reviewed the literature in 1960 using the following strict criteria, only three cases were found, all of whom were 11 years old (that is, not young children).

Criteria

1. Evidence of an abnormal psychiatric state at some time of the illness approximating Kraepelin's classical clinical description (1921).
2. Evidence of a positive family history suggesting a manic depressive diathesis.
3. Evidence of an early tendency to a manic depressive type of reaction as manifested in:
    a. A cyclothymic tendency with gradually increasing amplitude and length of oscillations.
    b. Delirious manic or depressive outbursts occurring during pyrexial illness.
4. Evidence of a recurrent or periodic illness with at least two observed episodes.
5. Evidence of a diphasic illness showing swings of pathologic dimension.
6. Evidence of an endogenous illness indicating that the phases of the illness show minimal tolerance to environmental events.
7. Evidence of a severity of illness indicated by the need for inpatient treatment, heavy sedation, or electroconvulsive therapy.
8. Evidence of an abnormal underlying personality of an extroverted type.
9. Absence of features of schizophrenia or organic states.
10. The evidence of current, not retrospective assessments.

The DSM-III criteria for mania and depression (Table 1, Chapter 1) essentially require items 1, 4, 5, 7, and 9 of the Anthony-Scott criteria. Positive family history and specific premorbid personality type, while helpful, are not necessary.

With less stringent criteria more children seem to be diagnosable as having BMDI. Weinberg et al (1973) and Weinberg and Brumback (1976) speculated that adult Feighner criteria (Feighner et al, 1972) for both depression and mania would need modification for children (Table 2, Chapter 1). It is unclear how valid their premise and criteria are since neither reliability studies, double-blind observations of medication trials, nor longitudinal studies have been carried out yet on children diagnosed by these criteria. Carlson and Cantwell (in press) found that, in comparison to DSM-III depression criteria, the Weinberg Depression criteria were considerably broader and subsumed children that would meet DSM-III criteria for other diagnoses. The quality of the symptoms enumerated for mania may need greater precision as well. Many youngsters with conduct disorder and/or attention deficit disorder deny problems, are aggressive, grandiose, and distractible, and have sleep problems. They meet criteria for mania, but it is unlikely that all these children are misdiagnosed manics since follow-up studies of such children do not find bipolar outcomes in greater numbers than the general population (Robins, 1966; Dahl, 1971; Glueck, 1940).

Finally, as has been noted in Chapter 1, many of the symptoms noted for mania are not pathological at certain ages. Gesell's description (1940) of the "out of bounds" four-year-old encompasses intermittent periods of silliness, grandiosity, sleep problems, finicky appetite, garrulousness, and what could be called flight of ideas except that the prelogical language of a four-year-old is replete with such associations.

There have been a number of case reports published of children diagnosed as manic with a first episode of BMDI at age 12 or earlier. Although the data usually had not been gathered systematically or the case histories reproduced with specific criteria in mind, Anthony and Scott's methodology specifically comparing phenomenology of mania and depression in eight younger (under age nine) and six older (nine to 12 years) children has been reviewed and updated (Weinberg and Brumback, 1976; Thompson, 1976; Feinstein and Wolpert, 1973; McKnew, 1974; Dyson and Barcai, 1970; Barrett, 1931; Varsamis, 1972; McHarg, 1954; Warneke, 1975; and Anthony and Scott, 1960).

In over 75 percent of all cases, family histories positive for depression, manic depression, cyclothymia, alcoholism, and suicide were noted. In fact, the positive family history was often instrumental in the child's final diagnosis.

"Premorbid history" revealed that six out of eight younger children had other problems: four were hyperactive, one was deaf, one had a severe trauma (electrical burn) preceding onset of illness. In the other two cases with onsets at 15 months and 3½ years, no "premorbid" history is reported. It is also more difficult to delineate discrete episodes in the younger children. Duration of episodes, except in Weinberg and Brumback's (1976) data, is rarely noted. In the six older children, previous psychiatric disorder is not mentioned. However, episodes are quite obvious.

Regarding the basic affective criterion of euphoria or irritability, we find elation noted in only one of eight younger children, an eight-year-old (McKnew, 1974), (though a five-year-old was called "cheerful") (Thompson, 1976), but in four of six older children. The major affective component for younger manics was, in general, irritability, aggressive behavior, and emotional lability.

A similar dichotomy was noted for depressive symptoms. Crying or irritability was described in six of eight of the younger children and three of the six older children. Looking depressed or complaining of depression was noted in only one of the younger and five of the older children.

Aberrations in thought content and self-esteem (gradiosity, paranoia, hallucinations) were uncommon in young children. Grandiosity was described in one four-year-old (Weinberg and Brumback, 1976) who had "fantasies about being able to fly and believed herself to be an airplane." Another eight-year-old "expressed many grandiose ideas about his abilities, strength and wealth, but never had a complete break with reality" (McKnew, 1974). Where to draw the line between gradiosity and the imagination of children, especially in some exuberant preschoolers, needs to be established if the term is to have any meaning. The older children, however, were clearly grandiose and one reported mood-congruent, visual, and auditory hallucinations.

Low self-esteem, guilt, paranoia, and morbid preoccupation were also uncommonly reported in the depressive episodes of younger "bipolar patients" but noted in most of the older children.

Increased psychomotor activity (hyperactivity, distractibility, push of speech) were the most consistently noted symptoms in both younger and older children though in older children rapid thoughts and flight of ideas were additionally reported. The difficulties in diagnosis between manic and hyperactive children who are also described as motor driven, distractible, and ignorant of the negative consequences of much of their behavior will be discussed below.

Psychomotor retardation was described in one younger child whereas lethargy and/or "little speech" were noted in many of the older children. The cases reported by Weinberg and Brumback were only described as having tantrums and aggression (psychomotor agitation).

Among the vegetative symptoms that occur in mania is reduced need for sleep. A precise description of the sleep disturbance is necessary in the developmental context of the child. In a well-known longitudinal study of normal children, 33 percent of boys at 21 months showed restless sleep (MacFarlane et al, 1971). At three years, 26 percent of children were still having sleep problems (Earls, 1980).

Unfortunately, Brumback and Weinberg were the only ones scrupulously noting insomnia in their cases and this occurred both during their manic and depressive phases.

In summary, it appears from case descriptions that manic and depressive episodes as they are described in adults are virtually absent in young children. We would postulate that the advent of puberty would have some impact on the phenomenology of mania or depression. There is evidence that sleep patterns (Anders, 1982), and activity levels (Rutter et al, 1967) change with adolescence. Perhaps these changes are responsible for the kind of psychomotor retardation or acceleration that is characteristic of bipolar depression and mania in older children and adolescents and adults. The speculation that biologic aspects of changes associated with puberty rather than the cognitive changes account for the "adult" phenomenology is supported by observations of both BMDI and mentally retarded persons (Carlson, 1979). As has been reported elsewhere, the typical changes in activity level, mood, and sleep are present in cycles of mania and depression in the most profoundly retarded individuals—changes that would not be present if those symptoms were based on their cognitive or "ego" strengths.

If we broaden the criteria of BMDI even further than Weinberg and Brumback (1976), we find a number of proponents of the "variant" and "prodromata" hypothesis. This hypothesis says that disturbed youngsters with genetic loadings for BMDI have "variants" of the disorder regardless of what the presenting complaints are. Response to lithium is ultimate confirmation.

Annell (1969) has reported 12 cases, only three of whom were prepubertal, whose psychopathology included delinquency, periodic catatonia, suicide attempts, hyperactivity, psychosomatic disorders, "extremely disorderly conduct at school," and two cases of MDI, one having anorexia nervosa and depression. Nine of these youngsters had abnormal electroencephalograms. All but two responded to lithium (one ten-year-old with periodic school disturbance and one 13-year-old with periodic catatonia felt to be postencephalitic). Five of 12 families had histories of major affective disorder, four had a variety of periodic disorders (schizophrenia, alcoholism, tics), two had unknown family histories, and one had a history of epilepsy and mental retardation.

Annell cast a broad net and based her decision of whether to use lithium on the periodicity of symptoms, regardless of what they were. If we use Annell's data to correlate lithium response in children with psychopathology of parents, we find the following: of the five families with known major affective disorder, one of the offspring (one with MDI, one with periodic stupor) responded well, one with hyperactivity had some improvement but was still unstable, and two (one with periodic stupor and one with periodic school disturbance) had slight to absent responses, respectively. Of the four families with periodic psychosis, schizophrenia, or alcoholism, all offspring (two had periodic stupor, one had severe premenstrual distress, one made suicide attempts) had good lithium response as did the youngsters who were adopted or had epilepsy/mental retardation in the family. Thus, from Annell's data, families with periodic psychopathology predicted better lithium response in their offspring than families with major affective disorder.

The three children described by Annell (1969) with psychopathology described in childhood include a nine-year-old adopted girl who was "alternately boisterous and passive," who developed clear symptoms of depression at 13 years, 10 months and who responded to lithium; a seven-year-old boy with attacks of stupor, who, as an adolescent was dysphoric and paranoid between stuporous periods, and who became "pleasant and composed" when he took lithium at age 19; a ten-year-old boy (whose mother had BMDI) who had severe behavior problems in school, but who did not respond to lithium alone.

It is obvious from accumulating research that lithium effects are wide-ranging and, at this time, positive lithium response cannot, in and of itself, be diagnostic of BMDI any more than nonresponse can be conclusive evidence against the diagnosis.

A number of other authors (Dyson and Barcai, 1970; Davis, 1979; White and O'Shanick, 1977; and Weinberg and Brumback, 1976) have reported youngsters with early histories of hyperactivity and family histories of affective disorder. Dyson and Barcai (1970) felt these children could be distinguished from cases of "attention deficit disorder" (hyperactivity), either because they lacked the soft signs and learning disabilities associated with hyperactivity or because they did not respond to stimulant drugs.

There are a number of similarities between the cross-sectional symptoms of mania and hyperactivity. DSM-III criteria for attention deficit disorder with hyperactivity (ADDH) (as the hyperactivity or minimum brain dysfunction syndrome is now called) includes easy distractibility and inattention, impulsivity, and excessive motor behavior as the essential features. The volatility, irritability or low frustration tolerance, and thoughtless impulsive behavior especially in interpersonal relationships seen in this disorder is similar to that in a manic episode, though the author has not found the gregarious, infectiously humorous charm of at least some people with mania in children with ADDH. Other ADDH criteria call for onset before age seven and a duration of at least six months.

The differential diagnosis between ADDH and mania is simplified when there is an acute onset of symptoms, a clear history of discrete episodes, or when symptoms begin de novo in an older child. The waters are considerably muddied in younger children, children whose parents are poor historians, or who come from foster care or placements without past histories. Moreover, if we decide the episodic nature of BMDI is not one of its essential features or, at least, that the "variant syndrome" does not have episodes, differential diagnosis becomes more complicated. The absence of soft neurologic signs or poor response to stimulant drugs does not necessarily a bipolar patient make. Soft signs are not among the essential criteria for ADDH since their presence is variable; finally, at least 15 percent of hyperactive children do not respond to stimulant drugs. If ten percent of school age children have ADDH, and 15 percent of those are really bipolar patients in that they do not respond to stimulants, one percent of the elementary school population already identified as troubled would have BMDI. This is not in keeping with observations to date.

Some studies have either specifically examined the possibility that hyperactivity and BMDI are linked or can be cited that explore this hypothesis. Greenhill et al (1973), in a double-blind study, compared lithium, dextroamphetamine, and placebo in nine hyperactive children aged seven to 14 years and considered to be lithium nonresponders. While lithium improved the behavior in two children with some affect laden symptoms, the improvement was only transient. Whitehead and Clark (1970) used lithium alternating with thioridazine and placebo in seven hyperactive children aged five to nine with unimpressive results for lithium.

Clearly these sample sizes are too small to be conclusive. In contrast to adult psychiatry, however, lithium has not yet taken the field of child psychiatry by storm. The presence of a positive family history of BMDI may improve the chance of lithium response as noted by Dyson and Barcai (1970), White and O'Shanick (1977), and Weinberg and Brumback (1976). Given the wide range of symptoms and disorders on which lithium has some effect, however, the presence of a positive response in these children does not establish that they have BMDI.

Other studies shedding light on the BMDI variant of hyperactivity theory include family studies of hyperactive children (Morrison and Stewart, 1971; Cantwell, 1972). These have not found a higher incidence of affective disorder in family members than in the general population, however. Were families divided by whether children did or did not respond to stimulants, perhaps a higher loading of affective disorder would be found among the families of the stimulant nonresponders.

Finally, follow-up studies of hyperactive children and children conduct disorder (Dahl, 1971; Robins, 1966; Glueck, 1940) have not found bipolar outcomes in numbers higher than general population predictions.

At this time it must be concluded that if a subgroup of ADDH children indeed have BMDI, the group is very small.

Another "variant" described separately by Feinstein et al (1982) and Davis (1979) is that of affective instability which may or may not come to psychiatric attention. This term connotes rapid shifts in mood (over minutes and hours) without environmental input adequate to explain such shifts. Explosive anger, violent outbursts, and aggressiveness are variously described and the child has, according to Feinstein, little ability to dampen his reactions. These outbursts are supposed to be different qualitatively from the temper tantrums present in other childhood disorders and sound similar to what was described in the past (DSM-I) as emotionally unstable character disorder (EUCD).

Rifkin et al (1972a, 1972b) studied a group of adolescents and young adults who fit this description and were diagnosed as being EUCD a number of years ago. Although the affective instability was found to be greatly improved by lithium, the frequent finding of soft neurologic signs (Quitkin et al, 1976) and the fact that on follow-up over one third of the patients had improved spontaneously suggests some degree of developmental delay or cerebral immaturity rather than nascent affective disorder.

Can we learn anything about early forms of BMDI from studies of offspring of bipolar parents? Although there are a number of studies of children of depressed parents (reviewed in Chapter 14), until recently, data from unipolar and bipolar parents were combined. Two recently published studies that do examine offspring of bipolar parents find conflicting results. Mayo et al (1979) examined 25 children, aged five to 17 years, from 12 families and found three had been psychiatrically hospitalized, and five had been in outpatient treatment. The children were diagnosed by DSM-III criteria as having behavior disorders (nine), depression (two), paranoia (one), and learning disability with depression (one). Anxiety, sleep disturbance, depressive symptoms, isolating behavior, and fearful behavior were the symptoms found most often. Using virtually the same methodology, Laroche et al (1981) examined 17 eight to 18-year-old children from ten bipolar families and found that none was considered sufficiently disturbed to warrant psychiatric diagnosis, except one child with a learning disability. Interview items of note on the children's Psychiatric Rating Scale were tension, depression, and preoccupation with topics of anxiety. Kestenbaum (1979) reported three children of bipolar parents who had affective storms, attentional problems in school, and psychological test patterns indicative of high verbal and low performance scores on the WISC. Waters (1980), in a letter to the *American Journal of Psychiatry* reported that in 19 children (aged six to 15 years) of bipolar parents he "found the psychopathology of the 11 [he] judged to be disturbed was not distinctive in any way from the rest of the patients" in his clinical practice. In contrast, in an examination of 48 offspring of 16 bipolar parents with a mean age of 27 years, 18 met criteria for major affective disorder, eight for other psychiatric disorders. Mean age of onset for the major affective disorder was 16 years and none had come to psychiatric attention earlier.

The complexities of deciding how much of the pathology in offspring of bipolar subjects represents incipient BMDI, how much represents a response to an intermittently disruptive illness in the parents, and how much represents nonspecific difficulties will require some of the methodologies that are being used to separate such issues in schizophrenia. Unfortunately, the long age of risk of BMDI adds an additional complication.

The author suggests that those studying offspring of bipolar parents take into account the age of onset of the parents' illness in relationship to the age of the child. Finally, the degree of disruptiveness presented by the parents' illness should also be considered, since the environmental impact of a parent whose illness is well-controlled with lithium is likely to be different from one whose cycles are frequent, stormy, and uncontrolled.

The question of how frequently and with what symptomatology BMDI presents, especially in children under age nine, thus has not been answered. Lowe and Cohen (1980) have used the following genetic model to begin classifying some of the foregoing observations:

1. Children who present with disorders whose symptoms resemble adult BMDI and which respond to the same treatments, and have the recognized biologic concomitants, which continue into adult life, can be said to have syndrome both *phenotypically* and *genotypically* similar to the adult syndrome.

2. Offspring of bipolar patients who present with hyperactivity, periodic stupor, schizophreniform disorders, etc, which either respond to the same treatments and have the same biologic concomitants or, in adulthood come to resemble classical BMDI, would have a disorder of the *same genotype* but *different phenotype.*

3. Symptoms or behaviors, for example, mood swings in preschoolers, and those with affective instability, which seem to even out with maturity will have syndromes with some *phenotypic similarities* to BMDI but *genotype dissimilarity.*

BMDI IN ADOLESCENCE

If the existence and phenomenology of BMDI in early childhood remains unclear, the appearance of this disorder in early adolescence is not. Precise epidemiologic figures on the incidence of BMDI are unavailable since episodes of mania and depression are often overlooked or misinterpreted. For example, first episodes of BMDI may be mild and not come to psychiatric attention. It is only when an episode occurs in later years and requires treatment that past history often reveals mood swings beginning around puberty. Moreover, without a preexistent cyclothymic personality or previous episodes to alert the clinician that he/she is dealing with an episodic disorder, the diagnostic significance of a first episode is often overlooked. In addition, the assumption still exists that aberrant, wild behavior is part of adolescent turmoil or that depression is reactive to one of the many vicissitudes of adolescence. Finally, until recently clinicians felt that any psychosis in adolescence was indicative of a schizophrenic illness (Carlson and Strober, 1978).

BMDI in adolescence is apparently not a major public health problem; the following widely disparate figures reflect on its rate of occurrence. Kasanin and Kaufman (1929) found that one to two percent of admissions who were 14 to 18 years old had BMDI; Olsen (1961) found 6.2 percent of patients with manic depressive psychosis had an onset between 13 and 19 years of age; Wertham (1929) observed that 18 percent of 2,000 manic patients were admitted before age 20. Kraepelin (1921) found that with each year into adolescence the frequency of onset of MDI increased; in fact, Perris (1968) found that 40 percent of his bipolar sample noted the onset of this illness between ages 15 and 25.

The phenomenology of adolescent BMDI presents its own set of complexities. A review of some of the older literature citing follow-up studies specifically of bipolar patients (Olsen, 1961; Landolt, 1957) and a study of the numerous case reports begin to show some consistencies in the diagnostic dilemmas posed by adolescent BMDI.

Olsen (1961) identified 28 patients in the late 1940s whose onset of illness was between 13 and 19 years of age. Interestingly, childhood psychopathology in 15 was negligible; of the other 13, two were cyclothymic, two retarded, two "imaginative"; three had periodic problems. This group was also described as "queer and obstinate" and had poor peer relationships. In describing actual cases, a number of Olsen's samples had manic episodes presenting as behavior problems with specific antagonism toward the family and with hysterical or schizophreniform features. Manic episodes also alternated with depressive episodes noted for their paranoia and psychomotor retardation. Organic brain syndrome was often part of the differential diagnosis.

Landolt (1957) followed 60 BMDI patients whose onset of symptoms was between ages 13 and 22. Premorbid personalities came in three categories: schizoid, dependent, extroverted. Eighteen of the 60 were noted to have clinical pictures with "schizophrenic coloring." Although nine of her sample were found to have catatonic schizophrenia on follow-up, most of those with "schizophrenic coloring" were in the recovered group.

Kasanin (1930) and Campbell (1952) described a number of youngsters whose manic episodes were remarkable for their wildness and whose depressive episodes by their psychomotor retardation. Where previous personalities were described, the picture varied: "extrovert," "nervous," "model boy," "happy-go-lucky but undisciplined," "good in school," "excitable," and "sensitive" were descriptions noted.

A number of case reports (Berg, 1974; White and O'Shanick, 1977; Coll and Bland, 1979; Engstrom et al, 1978; vanKrevelen and vanVoorst, 1969; Preodor and Wolpert, 1979) and several series (Hudgens, 1974; Carlson and Strober, 1978a, 1978b; Hassanyeh and Davison, 1980) enlarge upon these earlier observations.

These reports reveal premorbid personality varies and is not invariably either cyclothymic or extroverted. Intellectual and school performance also varies; several youngsters, in fact, had borderline to mild mental retardation. Family histories were often but not always positive for affective disorders.

The disgnostic errors made in identifying adolescent manic or depressive episodes have been, basically, twofold. Mild episodes have been most often misdiagnosed as adjustment reactions, behavior disorders, or narcissistic personality disorders. Severe episodes have been confused with schizophrenia.

A persistent clinical issue has been whether the pathoplastic effect of adolescence changes the phenomenology of BMDI to appear more psychotic. A recent report by Ballenger et al (1982) strongly suggests this to be the case, as least in mania. These authors compared the frequency of "schizophrenic" symptoms (delusions, auditory and visual hallucinations, catatonia, paranoia, Schneiderian first rank symptoms, confusion, thought disorder, ideas of reference, bizarre behavior, past diagnosis of schizophrenia, past other diagnosis) in nine patients whose episodes were observed before age 21 with 12 whose episodes were observed after age 30. Both groups of patients were equally responsive to lithium and had similar family histories of affective disorder. However, adolescents had every psychotic symptom more frequently than adults. This was statistically significant for delusions, which occurred in 88 percent of adolescent manic episodes and 33 percent of the adult manic episodes, and ideas of reference which occurred in 44 percent and 0 percent of patients respectively. Furthermore, in six of the nine adolescent manics whose episodes were observed into early adulthood, the frequency of psychotic symptoms diminished. The study did not examine psychosis in depression nor did is ascertain how much of the psychotic phenomenon had to do with earlier versus later episodes of illness. This study strongly suggests that manic episodes occurring in adolescence have more psychotic features than episodes occurring later in the person's life.

The interplay of personality, stressors, and age seem to color the presentation of BMDI. Given the importance of correctly treating the condition, we contend these variables should not mask the condition. The following annotated case report, reprinted with permission from the *Journal of Clinical Psychiatry*, elaborates how those variables interact in one case.

CASE REPORT

The patient, pseudonym Janet, is the second of three girls born and raised to age six in China. She was always considered to be a sociable albeit quiet child, generally apprehensive of change and sensitive to criticism. Her childhood was otherwise unremarkable and there was no evidence of premorbid personality characteristics of extroversion or cyclothymia.

In the summer of 1965, she, her sisters, and mother emigrated to the United States, where the girls were raised for a year by their maternal grandmother until the mother found suitable work. Janet suffered most from the impact of this emigration: she cried herself to sleep every night and was extremely anxious in school where she began formal education with the handicap of a strange language, novel and incomprehensive surroundings, and lack of maternal support. The family, including the father, was reunited after a year, however, and Janet settled down both at home and school. [A history of separations or object loss is not an uncommon developmental precursor in manic-depressive illness, although recent evidence questions the diagnostic specificity of this finding. Similarly, despite the purported significance of premorbid cyclothymic personality in the pathogenesis of manic depressive psychosis, this has not been corroborated in detailed study of adolescent manic-depressive patients. Thus, her psychosocial history and personality dynamics, while informative, are not diagnostically revealing.]

Family psychiatric history was not completely available because the mother had no specific knowledge of her father or his family: moreover, both of Janet's parents were reluctant to divulge information pertaining to other family members. However, the mother has had one depressive episode subsequent to the onset of Janet's illness which was responsive to imipramine. [Although the presence of a positive family history of affective disorder is helpful in making a diagnosis of MDI, the relative youth of parents of adolescent patients and the long age risk of MDI should not preclude the diagnosis in its absence. In this case, the daughter's diagnosis alerted psychiatrists to the true nature of the mother's lethargy, withdrawal, and somatic complaints.]

Janet's first episode of illness began in later summer of 1971 (one year postmenarche) at age 12 and coincided with the arrival of her maternal grandmother, whom Janet had come to dislike intensely. Also noteworthy was the fact that Janet was entering junior high school, of which she was extremely apprehensive. The initial request for psychiatric evaluation (September 1971) was precipitated by the mother, who observed Janet becoming increasingly despondent, stating repeatedly "It's too much for me: I want to kill myself." Noted, however, in Janet's initial psychiatric evaluation was a recent past history of extreme nervousness (which, to this family meant hyperactivity), extreme talkativeness, sleep loss, and multiple somatic complaints—all of which were considered to be out of character for her. [This behavior recurred in a subsequent manic episode when it was recognized as such; see later.] At intake Janet described herself as being "nervous, dumb, and needing help." [Although unable to articulate her subjective experience as that of depression, such an impression was clearly conveyed by the mother's characterization of her difficulties and Janet's own appearance and general demeanor.] Her interviewer described her as coherent, tense, depressed, and imminently psychotic. The diagnosis of adjustment reaction of adolescence was made and she was referred for outpatient group therapy without further diagnostic evaluation. In the group, she was noted to be "withdrawn, shy and inhibited." By Spring of 1972, however, she had returned to her more characteristic euthymic state and was, therefore, terminated from outpatient treatment.

In retrospect, it appears that Janet displayed a transient yet diagnosable hypomanic or manic episode though the intake worker was not alert to the significance of the abrupt behavior change. This was followed shortly thereafter by an evident depression of approximately eight months duration in which self-critical ideation, withdrawal, and lethargy were predominant clinical manifestations and were a clear contrast to the preceding hyperactivity and push of speech. The initial diagnosis of adjustment reaction was likely deemed appropriate by the attending psychiatrist in view of the stressful life circumstances (school, grandmother's arrival) concurrent with the onset of symptomatology. This observation bears witness to the excessive usage of this clinical diagnosis in adolescents whose behavior deviations actually reflect crystallization of major psychiatric illness.

In September 1972, prior to her entry into a new parochial school, Janet returned again to the outpatient clinic complaining of vivid and frightening nightmares. The attending psychiatrist described her mental status as overtly psychotic with prominent paranoid ideation and had her admitted for inpatient treatment. Janet, on the other hand, attributed her need for hospitalization to "requiring too much time to dress in the morning, sleeping too much, and having a sore throat." [In this context, she was evidently referring mainly to her incapacitating psychomotor retardation and lethargy, about which her family had complained.] During the early phase of this hospitalization, she was observed to cry a gret deal and repeatedly express the fear that she was "going crazy." Chart notes described her as being confused, having thought blockage, and disconnected speech. [On follow-up interview, Janet recalls this as a period when her thoughts were so slow and concentration so poor that she was neither able to fully comprehend what others were saying nor respond promptly or effectively. She ascribed her "craziness" to these cognitive abnormalities.] Her paranoia was characterized by the belief that other patients on the ward were accusing her of being a drug addict, sexually promiscuous, and of hating her parents. She manifested guilt-laden ruminations related to her self-described "sinful thoughts of pregnancy and for being unworthy of her mother's sacrifices for her." Additionally, on several occasions during the early course of this hospitalization she reported hallucinations of a voice stating "Janet is going to die." [Despite the chart diagnosis of schizophrenia, the guilt-ridden, self-depreciatory content of her delusional ideation and hallucinations were conspicuous and consonant with her affective state; moreover, the thematic contents of her psychotic symptomatology are not only discriminating features of depressive illness, but are also especially pertinent to Janet who, in her euthymic state, is very preoccupied with issues related to moral conduct, drug use, and her intrafamilial relations. Hence, Janet's case reflects the intertwining of pathoplastic aspects of her characterological dynamics with distinguishing clinical properties of her affective illness.]

Initial treatment with a variety of phenothiazines was unsuccessful. However, by February 1973, Janet's more florid psychotic symptoms had remitted and she was now reported to be significantly depressed. Her dysphoria, withdrawal, and lethargy persisted and her poor appetite with resultant weight loss was subsequently noticed and documented in the charts. After a gradual lightening of mood and improvement in interpersonal relations, Janet was discharged in September 1973, to a day school for emotionally disturbed children. [Although some may attribute this constellation of affective symptoms to post-psychotic depression, it is most likely that her primary depression was gradually resolving with the psychotic elements, initially overshadowing the core affective manifestations, remitting first. This speculation is in accord with the observations of Winokur and colleagues (1969) and Carlson and Goodwin (1973), regarding the order of disappearance of pathologic symptoms during the course of a single affective episode.]

Except for a weight gain of 50 lb, Janet functioned reasonably well during Spring 1975, when her therapist noted she was becoming increasingly irritable and hyperactive. Janet described her subjective state in terms of "having to do things fast." Similarly, her parents reported that she was very nervous and insomniac, identifying this behavior as similar to that which preceded her first psychiatric evaluation in 1971 (her first hypomanic episode). She was boisterous, unusually talkative, emotionally labile and irritable. Her school teachers complained she was completely out of character: hysterical, uncontrollable, provocative, paranoid, and unpredictable. After three months, the implications of these symptoms were realized, and her mania and the periodicity of her affective state was recognized; she was diagnosed as manic depressive and admitted for lithium treatment in June 1975. While on the ward, she was described in nursing notes as intrusive, hypersexual, hyperactive, paranoid, labile, and occasionally combative and bizarre (wearing outlandish clothes and changing them often). Although most of the time she appeared euphoric and without insight, she occasionally became extremely frenetic and verbalized that she was frightened because she didn't comprehend what was happening to her.

Janet's symptoms remitted after two weeks of lithium treatment (1,800 mg/day) though she remained hospitalized for several months due to her unstable family environment.

Janet was treated with lithium carbonate and weekly psychotherapy and has not required hospitalization for the last six years. Over the fall and winter of 1975-1976, however, she began to complain increasingly of boredom, hating school, and of sleeping more than usual. In January 1976, her school commented that her grades had dropped precipitously and that her concentration and initiative had diminished. She began gaining weight again (having lost 40 lb during her manic episode). Psychological testing, which had not been administered previously, revealed a verbal score of 91, performance score of 71, and full-scale of 80—considerably lower than had been expected from past school performance. This significant interscale scatter was interpreted as indicating possible deficits in psychomotor processes, short-term memory, or sustained concentration. Although she denied being depressed at the time, her total score on the Beck Depression Inventory put her in the moderately depressed range. [She recognized the multiple concomitants of depression but never identified them phenomenologically as such to herself or others; again, her lethargy, self-depreciation, and withdrawal were the most conspicuous clinical features.] Since her prior history was to remit spontaneously in spring, antidepressants were not added to her lithium regimen and, predictably, a few weeks later she began to look brighter and feel better. By May 1976, her grades had improved significantly and her Beck Depression Inventory score no longer registered significant levels of depressive symptomatology. Repeat psychological testing revealed a verbal IQ of 98, performance IQ of 86, and a full-scale IQ of 94. Improvement registered mostly on timed performance subtests where her previous psychomotor retardation and diminished concentration no longer handicapped her functioning. She remained on lithium, ultimately obtained a degree in vocational nursing, and at current follow-up, 11 years after onset of illness, is contemplating marriage. She remains shy and anxious about change. There has been no suggestion of further episodes on lithium and medication will likely be suspended when she wishes to get pregnant.

After reviewing the literature on early onset BMDI, the following conclusions regarding phenomenology may be drawn.

1. Contrary to the criterion of extroverted personality required by Anthony and Scott (1960) for BMDI, no particular premorbid personality seems to predispose the disorder. Whether particular dynamics or personality type presage specific (for example, psychotic) symptomatology as once suggested by Campbell (1952) remains to be proven.

2. Family histories positive for affective disorder are often noted.

3. Onset of the full-fledged disorder is often acute and dramatic even when there is an earlier history of problems. Psychosis and psychomotor retardation are frequently part of the episodes of illness.

These observations are particularly useful in predicting who, in a cohort of adolescents first presenting with depressive symptomatology, are at possible risk for a bipolar course. Strober and Carlson (in press) have followed sixty 13 to 16-year-olds psychiatrically hospitalized with a major depressive episode and found that 12 (20 percent) subsequently developed mania an average of 28 weeks after initial admission. Comparing the 12 with a known bipolar course to the 48 as yet unipolar revealed that the variables of particular predictive significance included: (1) rapid onset of the depressive episode; (2) psychomotor retardation; (3) concurrent presence of psychotic features; (4) positive family history of bipolar illness or three generations of affective illness in the family; (5) hypomanic response to antidepressant medication.

TREATMENT OF PREPUBERTAL AND ADOLESCENT BMDI

The crux of treatment in BMDI is establishing a diagnosis. As has been noted, this is not easy in prepubertal children and adolescents. Youngerman and Canino (1978) have summarized the literature on lithium treatment in these age groups (including some of the data described earlier in this chapter). They concluded:

1. Where the disorder resembles adult BMDI the age of the patient is not a factor in lithium responsiveness.

2. Where there is a positive family history of BMDI and the child or adolescent has a disorder "broadly characterized as mood disturbance," even if the affective symptom is not the major psychiatric problem, a positive lithium response is likely. In young children the presenting symptomatology may be similar to attention deficit disorder; in older children and adolescents, mixtures of psychotic or organic features may be predominant.

Systematic studies of lithium carbonate in children and adolescents with BMDI have yet to be published. Most clinicians, therefore, treat BMDI in young people combining their knowledge of adult psychopharmacology and child psychiatry. The reader should refer to the now numerous discussions of lithium management (for example, *Primer of Lithium Therapy* by Jefferson and Greist, 1977).

Of specific note in young people is their higher tolerance and need for higher doses of lithium for treatment and higher blood levels (0.8 to 1.4 MEQ/liter) for prophylaxis. This is because of their efficient renal clearance of the drug (Schou, 1972). The presence of organic features (soft neurologic signs, abnormal electroencephalograms) do not appear to be contraindications to the drug (Youngerman and Canino, 1978).

Other age specific treatment issues for young people include: (1) When and under what circumstances to start lithium prophylaxis? (2) How long to continue medications? (3) How to reinforce treatment compliance? (4) What other treatments should be included in the regimen?

Until studies are published which address themselves specifically to the foregoing issues, decisions must be based on individual circumstances and common sense.

1. When to start? The frequency, severity, duration, and support system available to the patient largely determine when to start and how long to

continue medication. A teenager with an obvious devastating manic episode should not have to wait for several more episodes before beginning acute and prophylactic treatment. A youngster who is receiving lithium to see if his nonspecific symptoms respond may need to have the medication stopped (if response has not been clear-cut) to evaluate whether he is better with or without medication. Even in the case of mild episodes of depression and mania, if they occur with frequency (at least two per year), the youngster may have a less stormy adolescence on medication and will be better able to cope with the other age-appropriate demands of making relationships, finishing school, and identifying himself as other than flagrantly psychiatrically ill.

2. How long to continue? In the author's experience, affective episodes, though muted, are still often discernible even with lithium therapy. If this is the case, prophylaxis should be continued. The follow-up data cited earlier suggested that young people may have a flurry of episodes at the onset of their disorder and not have another for many years. It is, therefore, probably wise to hedge on the question, "Will I have to take this for the rest of my life?" Not only is a "yes" frightening, it does not take into account future research or specific needs such as pregnancy that advise a drug holiday. (Since there is evidence that lithium may have teratogenic effects on the fetus [Weinstein and Goldfield, 1975], lithium treatment in women anticipating pregnancy should be used with caution. Situations exist, however, where episodes are so destructive that the uncertainty of a child with a cardiac anomaly is preferable to a mother who makes a serious suicide attempt or contacts syphilis while sexually promiscuous.)

3. Treatment compliance is not just an issue with adolescents though frequently a teenager's need to feel in complete control of his/her life exacerbates the problem. Education of the youngster and family on the nature of the disorder is imperative. Long-term availability of a consistent treatment source is important. A person might need to experience several episodes before being convinced that a medication trial is helpful. Consultation with someone who has weathered several episodes with the teenager and whom the teenager trusts and who can help the teenager analyze the risk/benefit ratio adds immeasurably to treatment success.

The risk of suicide needs to be considered in treating young (and old) bipolar patients. No one can be forced to take a medication prophylactically; however, it is preferable to know and have the family know when a person is refusing medication than have that person lie and give everyone a false sense of comfort until the next lithium blood level is drawn and noncompliance is obvious.

4. Other treatment? This again depends on the individual case. Unless all problems subside with medication administration (which has never been the author's experience), one is left with all of the usual "bread and butter"

issues of what is necessary for the specific child: school consultation, family therapy, individual therapy, hospitalization, residential placement, etc. There is no question that psychotherapy in an adolescent whose mood swings are under some control is considerably more effective than the converse. The old premise that one needs to suffer with mania and depression to benefit from therapy should be relegated to the same category as flogging chairs, wall restraints, and divination.

NATURAL HISTORY OF BMDI IN CHILDREN AND ADOLESCENTS

Natural history studies of BMDI in adults have found that the course is variable. By definition there must be at least two episodes of illness. Usually there are more. Much of the prognosis depends on the disruptiveness of the episodes, the degree of euthymia achieved between episodes, and, in recent years, responsiveness to lithium. BMDI was always considered to have a "good" prognosis relative to schizophrenia. However, while manic depressive patients do not "deteriorate" as schizophrenics do, and their diagnosis does not change, long-term studies reveal that about one third of patients are chronically incapacitated by their disease (Carlson et al, 1974). Moreover, suicide may be a fatal outcome in as many as one out of six cases (Guze and Robins, 1971).

There are several reasons why one might speculate that childhood or adolescent-onset BMDI might have a worse prognosis than adult-onset BMDI. The early onset may reflect a worse disease. Schizophrenia beginning in childhood and adolescence seems to have a worse prognosis than older-onset schizophrenia. Grappling with any serious disorder during one's formative years may be more difficult than doing so when one's education is complete, permanent relationships have been established, and one's sense of identity is relatively stabilized.

Carlson et al (1977) reviewed several studies which, between them, described 99 cases whose BMDI began in adolescence. Atypical, often psychotic features were noted in early episodes of these cases but the periodicity of symptoms and ultimate resemblance to classical mania and depression allowed the BMDI diagnosis to be made. Criteria for good outcome varied but approximately half of the patients were functioning well (including some cases in which there were no further episodes) and a fourth were chronically disabled. Comparing 28 BMDI patients whose mean age of onset was 15.8 years with 20 whose onset was 50.6 years, Carlson et al (1977) found no significant difference in mean episode frequency per year, educational achievement, or functioning at job, within the family or community. The percentage of those functioning reasonably well (about 60 percent) and those chronically ill (about 20 percent) did not confirm the hypothesis that adolescent-onset bipolar patients had a worse prognosis than older-onset patients.

Whether adolescent-onset BMDI patients have a higher suicide rate than their older-onset counterparts remains to be determined. In the mean 19.3 year follow-up of 28 adolescent-onset BMDI subjects, one had committed suicide. However, two of six bipolar patients in a study reported by Welner et al (1980) committed suicide within the ten years the follow-up encompassed. What percentage of the rapidly increasing suicide rate in 15 to 19-year-olds is comprised by young bipolar patients is unknown.

In summary, BMDI is not a benign disorder. Although systematic prospective, long-term studies of early onset BMDI have not been carried out, there is no evidence that the disorder beginning in childhood or adolescence is intrinsically more devastating than it is in adults. Variables such as the time spent psychiatrically ill, the intermorbid functioning of the patient, and the support system available (family, friends, treatment) are probably more important to long-term functioning than age of onset.

REFERENCES

American Psychiatric Association: Diagnostic and Statistical Manual (DSM-III). Washington, DC: ADA, 1980.

Anders TF. Neurophysiological studies of sleep in infants and children. *J Child Psychol Psychiatry* 1982; 23:75–83.

Annell AL. Lithium in the treatment of children and adolescents. *ACTA Psychiatr Scand* 1969; 207(Suppl):19–33.

Annell AL, ed. *Depressive states in childhood and adolescence.* Halstead Press Division of John Wiley & Sons, 1971.

Anthony J, Scott P. Manic depressive psychosis in childhood. *J Child Psychol Psychiatry* 1960; 1:52–72.

Ballenger JC, Reus VJ, Post RM. The "atypical" presentation of adolescent mania. *Am J Psychiatry* 1982; 139:602–606.

Barrett AM. Manic depressive psychosis in childhood. *Int Clin* 1931; 3:205.

Berg I, Hullin R, Allsopp M, et al. Bipolar manic-depresive psychosis in early adolescence—a case report. *Br J Psychiatry* 1974; 125:416–417.

Bunney WF, Jr. The switch process in manic depressive psychosis. *Ann Intern Med* 1977; 87:319–355.

Campbell JD. Manic depressive psychosis in children—report of 18 cases. *J Neu Ment Dis* 1952; 116:424–439.

Cantwell DP. The hyperkinetic syndrome. In Rutter M, Hersov L, eds. *Child psychiatry modern approaches.* Oxford: Blackwell Scientific Publications, 1977:524–555.

Cantwell DP. Psychiatric illness in the families of hyperactive children. *Arch Gen Psychiatry* 1972; 27:414–417.

Carlson GA, Kotin J, Davenport Y, Adland M. A follow-up of 53 bipolar manic-depressive patients. *Br J Psychiatry* 1974; 124:134–139.

Carlson GA. Affective disorder in mental retardates. *Psychiatr Clin North Am* 1979; 2:499–510.

Carlson GA, Cantwell DP. (in press), Diagnosis of childhood depression—a comparison of Weinberg and DSM-III criteria. *J Am Acad Child Psychiatry.*

Carlson GA, Davenport YB, Jamison K. A comparison of outcome in adolescent and late onset bipolar manic depressive illness. *Am J Psychiatry* 1977; 134:919–922.

Carlson GA, Goodwin FK. The stages of mania. *Arch Gen Psychiatry* 1973; 28:221–228.

Carlson GA, Strober M. Affective disorder in adolescence: issues in misdiagnosis. *J Clin Psychiatry* 1978a; 39, 59:63–66.

Carlson GA, Strober M. Manic depressive illness in early adolescence: a study of clinical and diagnostic characteristics in six cases. *J Am Acad Child Psychiatry* 1978b; 17:138–153.

Coll PG, Bland R. Manic depressive illness in adolescence and childhood—review and case report. *Can J Psychiatry* 1979; 24:255–263.

Dahl V. A follow-up study of a child psychiatric clientele with special regard to manic depressive psychosis. In Annell AL, ed, *Depressive states in childhood and adolescence.* Stockholm, Sweden: Almquist & Wiksell, 1971:534–541.

Davis RE. Manic-depressive variant syndrome of childhood: a preliminary report. *Am J Psychiatry* 1979; 136:702–705.

Dyson WL, Barcai A. Treatment of children of lithium responding parents. *Curr Ther Res* 1970; 12:286–290.

Earls F. The prevalence of behavior problems in three-year-old children: a cross national replication. *Arch Gen Psychiatry* 1980; 37:1153–1157.

Engstrom FW, Robbins DW, May JG. Manic depressive disease in adolescence: a case report. *J Am Acad Child Psychiatry* 1978; 17:514–520.

Feighner JP, Robin E, Guze SB, et al. Diagnostic criteria for use in psychiatric research. *Am Gen Psychiatry* 1972; 26:57–63.

Feinstein SC, Wolpert EA. Juvenile manic-depressive illness clinical and therapeutic considerations. *J Am Acad Child Psychiatry* 1973; 12:123–136.

Feinstein SC, Feldman-Rotman S, Woolsey AB. Diagnostic aspects of manic-depressive illness in children and adolescents. In Shafii M, Shaffi S, eds. *Essentials of human development and child and adolescent psychiatry.*

Gessel A. *The first five years of life.* New York: Harper and Row, 1940.

Glueck S, Glueck E. *Juvenile delinquents grown up.* New York: The Commonwealth Fund, 1940.

Greenhill LL, Rieder RO, Wender PH, et al. Lithium carbonate in the treatment of hyperactive children. *Arch Gen Psychiatry* 1973; 28:636–640.

Guze S, Robins E. Suicide and primary affective disorders. *Br J Psychiatry* 1970; 117:437–438.

Hassanyeh F, Davison K. Bipolar affective psychosis with onset before age 16: report of ten cases. *Br J Psychiatry* 1980; 137:530–539.

Hudgens RW. *Psychiatric disorders in adolescents.* Baltimore: Williams and Wilkins, 1974.

Jefferson JW, Greist JH. *Primer of lithium therapy.* Baltimore: Williams and Wilkins, 1977.

Kasanin J. The affective psychoses in children. *J Neu Ment Dis* 1952; 116: 424–429.

Kasanin J, Kaufman MR. A study of the functional psychoses in childhood. *Am J Psychiatry* 1929;9:307.

Kestenbaum CJ. Children at risk for manic-depressive illness: possible predictors. *Am J Psychiatry* 1979; 136:1206–1208.

Kraepelin E. *Manic depressive insanity and paranoia.* Edinburgh: Livingstone, 1921.

Landolt AD. Follow-up studies on circular manic depressive reactions occurring in the young. *Bull NY Acad Med* 1957; 33:65–73.

Laroche C, Cheifetz PN, Lester EP. Antecedents of bipolar affective disorders in children. *Am J Psychiatry* 1981; 138:986–988.

Lowe TL, Cohen DJ. Manic in childhood and adolescence. In Belmaker RH, vanPreag HM, eds. *Mania–an evolving concept.* New York: Spectrum Publications, 1980:111–117.

MacFarlane JW, Allen L, Honzik MP. The developmental study of the behavior problems of normal children between 21 months and 14 years. In Jones HC, Bayley N, MacFarlane JW, Honzik MP, eds. *The course of human development.* Waltham, Mass: Xerox College Publications, 1971:67–82.

Mayo JA, O'Connell RA, O'Brien JD. Families of manic-depressive patients: effect of treatment. *Am J Psychiatry* 1979; 136:1535–1539.

McHarg JF. Mania in childhood. *Arch Neurol Psychiatry* 1954; 72:531–539.

McKnew DH, Jr, Cytryn L, White I. Clinical and biochemical correlates of hypomania in a child. *J Am Acad Child Psychiatry* 1974; 13:576–585.

Morrison JR, Stewart MA. A family study of the hyperactive child syndrome. *Biol Psychiatry* 1971; 3:189–195.

Olsen T. Follow-up study of manic-depressive patients whose first attack occurred before the age of 19. *ACTA Psychiatr Scand [Suppl]* 1961; 162:45–51.

Perris C. The course of depressive psychoses. *ACTA Psychiatr Scand* 1968; 44:238–248.

Preodor D, Wolpert EA. Manic depressive illness in adolescence. *J Youth Adoles* 1979; 8:111–130.

Quitkin F, Rifkin A, Klein DF. Neurologic soft signs in schizophrenia and character disorders. *Arch Gen Psychiatry* 1976; 33:845–853.

Rifkin A, Leviton SJ, Galewski J, et al. Emotionally unstable character disorder. A follow-up study. II. Prediction of outcome. *J Biol Psychiatry* 1972a; 4:81–88.

Rifkin A, Quitkin F, Carillo E, et al. Lithium carbonate in emotionally unstable character disorder. *Arch Gen Psychiatry* 1972b; 27:519–523.

Robins LN. *Deviant children grown up: a sociological and psychiatric study of antisocial personality.* Baltimore: Williams & Wilkins, 1966.

Rutter M, Greenfeld D, Lockyer L. A five to fifteen year follow-up study of infantile psychosis: II. Social and behavioral outcome. *Br J Psychiatry* 1967; 113:1183–1199.

Schou M. Lithium in psychiatric therapy and prophylaxis. A review with special regard to its use in children. In Annell AL, ed. *Depressive states in childhood and adolescence.* Stockholm, Sweden: Almquist and Wiksell, 1971.

Stewart MA, Morrison JR. Affective disorder among the relatives of hyperactive children. *J Child Psychol Psychiatry* 1973; 14:209–212.

Strober M, Carlson G. Clinical, genetic and psychopharmacologic predictors of bipolar illness in adolescents with major depression. a 3 to 4-year prospective follow-up investigation. *Arch Gen Psychiatry* (in press).

Thompson RJ, Jr, Schindler FH. Embryonic mania. *Child Psychiatry Hum Dev* 1976;6:149–154.

vanKrevelen D, vanVoorst J. Lithium in the treatment of a cryptogenic psychosis of a juvenile. *ACTA Paedopsychiatr* 1969;26:148–152.

Varsamis J, MacDonald SM. Manic depressive disease in childhood: case report. *Can J Psychiatry* 1972;17:279–281.

Warneke L. A case of manic-depressive illness in childhood. *Can J Psychiatry* 1975;20:195–200.

Waters B. The outlook for children of manic-depressive patients. (Letter to the editor) *Am J Psychiatry* 1980;137:1126.

Weinberg WA, Brumback RA. Mania in childhood. *Am J Dis Child* 1976;130:380–385.

Weinberg WA, Rutman J, Sullivan L, et al. Depression in children referred to an educational diagnostic center: diagnosis and treatment. *J Pediatr* 1967;83:1065–1072.

Weinstein MR, Goldfield MD. Cardiovascular malformations with lithium use during pregnancy. *Am J Psychiatry* 1975;132:529–531.

Welner A, Welner Z, Fishman R. Psychiatric adolescent inpatients 8 to 10 year follow-up. *Arch Gen Psychiatry* 1980;36:698–700.

Wertham F. A group of benign chronic psychoses: prolonged manic excitements. *Am J Psychiatry* 1929;86:17–78.

White JH, O'Shanick G. Juvenile manic-depressive illness. *Am J Psychiatry* 1977;134:1035–1036.

Whitehead PL, Clark LD. Effect of lithium carbonate, placebo, and thioridazine on hyperactive children. *Am J Psychiatry* 1970;127:824–825.

Winokur G, Clayton PJ, Reich T. *Manic depressive illness.* St. Louis: CV Mosby, 1969.

Youngerman J, Canino I. Lithium carbonate use in children and adolescence: a survey of the literature. *Arch Gen Psychiatry* 1978;35:216–224.

Affective Disorders in Childhood and Adolescence--
An Update. Edited by D.P. Cantwell and G.A. Carlson.

5

Affective Disorders in Adolescence

Gabrielle A. Carlson and Michael Strober

The subject of affective disorders in adolescents has been especially shrouded in controversy because of the supposed difficulties in unravelling the problem of "adolescent turmoil." Thus, while writers have advanced discrepant viewpoints, empirical data to support or refute them is sparse. Whereas some authorities contend that adolescent depression is an identifiable diagnostic entity similar to that seen in adults (Carlson and Strober, 1978a), others argue that extrapolation of adult depressive phenomenology to young persons is highly fallible and recommend we search for nontraditional, adolescent-specific "equivalents" of depressive disorder (Glaser, 1967).

General methodological and theoretical problems in the study of depression in childhood and adolescence have been detailed by Gittelman-Klein (1977). The purpose of this chapter is to critically examine the questions of affective disorders in early adolescence, and to consider the possible impact of this developmental period on the phenomenological expression of affective disorders.

EPIDEMIOLOGIC CONSIDERATIONS

Epidemiologic data serve as one point of reference for questions concerning the recognition and magnitude of adolescent depression. Although estimates of depressive morbidity in young populations are not available, we can, nonetheless, turn to nationwide statistics compiled by the United States Public Health Service on psychiatric diagnosis in adolescents to shed some light on these issues. These data provide useful indices of the frequency of depressive diagnoses in adolescents with treated mental disorder, as well as age-related comparisons of the prevalence of depression in persons receiving psychiatric care.

Table 1 shows the percent distribution of primary diagnoses among nearly all adolescent and adult patients treated in general hospital, state, and county psychiatric inpatient units in the United States for 1975 (United States Department of Health, Education, and Welfare, 1977a, 1977b). Considerable variation by age and type of facility in the prevalence of depressive diagnoses can be seen.

Table 1 Percent Distribution of Primary Psychiatric Diagnoses by Age of Patient and Type of Treatment Facility, 1975

	Under 18	18-24	25-64
	Public general hospitals[a]		
Depressive disorders[d]	13.8	16.5	25.7
Schizophrenia	19.9	44.7	38.0
Neuroses[e]	3.3	1.9	3.0
Personality disorders	11.7	14.5	6.0
Transient situational disorders	19.2	5.9	3.0
	Private general hospitals[b]		
Depressive disorders[d]	19.0	31.5	43.0
Schizophrenia	15.1	29.9	17.2
Neuroses[e]	8.3	6.2	7.0
Personality disorders	6.7	10.5	3.4
Transient situational disorders	29.6	6.0	2.6
	State/county mental hospitals[c]		
Depressive disorders[d]	2.7	8.7	–
Schizophrenia	17.7	40.0	–
Neuroses[e]	3.8	1.9	–
Personality disorders	10.4	13.1	–
Transient situational disorders	54.3	3.2	–

[a]Total n = 139,352; under 18, n = 11,067.
[b]Total n = 376,185; under 18, n = 31,623.
[c]Total n = 385,237; under 18, n not available.
[d]Includes psychoneurotic depression, psychotic depressive reaction, manic-depressive reaction.
[e]Excluding psychoneurotic depression.
Reprinted with permission from *Psychiatric Clinics of North America.*

Note, for example, the rate of depression in juvenile admissions (under 18 category) to state and county facilities (27.7 percent) compared to that in public (13.8 percent) and private general hospitals (19 percent)—a disparity related possibly to the larger number of chronic (presumably schizophrenic) patients generally serviced in state and county facilities. Even so, the data in Table 1 suggest, at the minimum, that the prevalence of treated depression increases steadily with advancing age. Also to be noted in Table 1 is that among patients under 18 years of age, the diagnosis of transient situational disturbance exceeds depression in frequency in each type of treatment facility.

These figures are generally similar to foreign reports, discussed by Henderson et al (1971), of rates of first admission for major mental illnesses among adolescents, including the categories of depressive psychosis and psychoneurotic depression. A comparison of rates per 10,000 population aged 15 to 19 in five countries—Australia, New Zealand, Canada, Enland, and Czechoslovakia—shows that among females, rates for depressive psychosis (subcategorization unspecified) vary from a low of 0.2 in Australia to a high of 3.5 in England, whereas for males these figures range from 0.2 in Australia to 2.0 in England. In general, admission rates for the less restrictive diagnosis of psychoneurotic depression are about three to four times greater, although rates of both affective diagnoses are exceeded by schizophrenia, personality disorder, and transient situational disturbances in four of the five countries. Again, even taking into consideration transnational differences in actual morbidity risk and diagnostic fashion, these figures can be viewed as supporting the contention that depression illness has a disproportionately low rate of occurrence in adolescence compared to other major nosological entities.

Two other studies superfically appear to lend confirmation to this notion. Rutter et al (1976) reported a prevalence of clear-cut depressive disorder of less than 0.2 percent in ten and 11-year-old children surveyed in the Isle of Wight investigations, compared to 0.4 percent at age 14. Similarly, Weiner and Del Gaudio (1976) in a survey of diagnostic stability in adolescent psychopathology also comment on the negligible incidence of depressive illness at this age, noting that only one case of diagnosed "affective psychosis" was recorded among 1,334 adolescent patients listed in the Monroe County Cumulative Psychiatric Case Register in 1961 and 1962.

Although instructive, conclusions drawn from these studies must be tempered because of the methodological flaws. While a detailed analysis of these problems is beyond the scope of this chapter, the more serious ones deserve brief mention.

First, these data obviously do not reflect recent advances in the general nomenclature of depressive illness or other contemporary systems for subtype categorization. We know, for instance, that depression is not a single homogeneous entity, and have come to recognize the value of multiaxial classifications based on symptomatic, social, genetic, biological, and temporal variables. Also bearing on this issue is a recent report by Akiskal and colleagues (1978) that, in many cases, atypical or neurotic depression—by far the most frequent assignment in adolescents with mood disturbance—is a precursor of later, unequivocal episodes of primary affective disorder. Hence, it is impossible to deduce from the data available the proportion of certain subtypes of affective disorder in adolescents diagnosed broadly as depressed.

Another related problem in discussions of depression in both childhood and adolescence is the failure to distinguish between the symptomatic, syndromal, and disease connotations of the term "depression." Without such specificity, and because of this semantic confusion, comparison across studies and synthesis of data is impeded.

On a more practical note, we have found that clinicians often refrain from inquiring into the full range and variety of psychopathology with adolescent patients, citing the young person's propensity to deny such problems, the need to establish immediate trust and rapport, and concern over the damaging influence of psychiatric labeling at such a young age. Because of this tendency to be less explicit in questioning adolescents with emotional problems, diagnoses are apt to reflect variable and hastily contrived judgments about the presence or absence of symptomatology.

Perhaps more problematic, however, is the influence upon diagnostic judgments of traditional notions of adolescence as an unstable phase of life, in which signs of deviance are held to be commonplace and normal. Even though recent evidence basically discredits these assertions (Weiner, 1970), many practitioners remain wary of employing certain diagnostic labels with young persons. Accordingly, it is reasonable to infer that many cases of depressive disorder are actually buried in the more ubiquitous and diagnostically muddled category of adolescent adjustment reaction.

A last remaining problem worth noting briefly concerns the historically broad defintion of schizophrenia in American psychiatry, and emerging evidence that this label is often applied indiscriminately to patients with psychotic phenomenology more properly categorized in the affective spectrum. Elsewhere, we have argued that similar errors in diagnostic assignment occur with psychotically depressed and manic adolescents as well, much more frequently than heretofore realized (Carlson and Strober, 1978a, 1978b).

In sum, we feel we can look upon the above statements as support for the suggestion that depressive illness in adolescence is considerably more prevalent and identifiable than current opinion and available epidemiological data suggest.

Indeed, this suggestion is in line with data reported by Winokur et al (1969) and Perris (1966), which indicate that between 30 and 40 percent of adult manic depressive patients first become manifestly ill during their adolescence. Even a reexamination of Rutter's data (1976) reveals that of the 135 adolescents felt to have a psychiatric disorder, many had predominant symptoms of depression and anxiety, and might have, with an interview designed more specifically to make psychiatric diagnoses, been given diagnoses of affective disorder.

Also worthy of note are two studies of admissions of adolescents to the Washington University Renard Hospital, both involving the use of more explicit and standardized data collection procedures and criteria for diagnostic assignment. In one study, King and Pittman (1969) found that 26 patients (40 percent) in a sample of 65 consecutive admissions fulfilled criteria for either major depressive episode or mania, with a comparably lower proportion receiving a diagnosis of schizophrenia. Similarly, Hudgens (1974) demonstrated a predominance of affective disturbances in a larger cohort of adolescent admissions to the Renard facility. Of 110 psychiatric patients evaluated, 19 received a primary diagnosis of depressive disorder, 11 were manic, 14 were classified "undiagnosed, most like depression," and two presented with a mixture of depressive and nondepressive symptomatology—a yield of affective disorder or affect-laden syndromes in over 40 percent of the sample.

Clearly, these latter two studies yield a prevalence of admission for affective disorder that is far greater than the national estimates derived from Public Health Service statistics highlighted in Table 1. In view of prior discussion, we believe these discrepancies are due far less to different rates of depressive illness among sample populations than to more accurate detection of this entity through refined operational diagnostic methods.

CLINICAL PHENOMENOLOGY

Like prepubertal depression, notions concerning the existence of adolescent affective disorder can be described as: (1) it does not exist or is extremely rare; (2) it exists, but its characteristic features appear as various other forms of behavioral deviance ("depressive equivalents"); and (3) affective disorder, defined by adult criteria, can be detected in adolescents. The concept of "masked depression" or "depressive equivalents," which is discussed briefly later in this chapter, is difficult to validate in the absence of a long-term, prospective study and would seem to reinforce the belief that more precise characterization of juvenile and adolescent affective disorder is not possible. Accordingly, our focus for discussion will be those adolescents who meet criteria for adult affective disorder, including the primary and secondary subtypes, using the definitions developed at Washington University (Woodruff et al, 1967).

Primary Affective Disorder, Bipolar Type

Bipolar affective disorder in adolescents is described in Chapter 4.

Unipolar Depression

Given the long age of risk for bipolar manic depressive illness, a diagnosis of unipolar depression in an adolescent suffering a first episode of depression cannot be made with certainty. Nevertheless, for this discussion we shall define adolescents as having unipolar depression if they have no other preceding or concurrent psychiatric diagnosis, if there is no family history of bipolar manic depressive illness, and if they meet established operational criteria (DSM-III) (American Psychiatric Association, 1980) for major depressive disorder.

In Table 2 we show the comparative prevalences of a broad range of phenomenological and descriptive features in 28 probands with unipolar depression from the authors' study sample of 130 hospitalized adolescent and other major series of adolescent and adult depressive patients. Of 33 symptom

Table 2 Comparative Analysis of Symptomatology and Related Features in Adolescents and Adults with Depressive Disorder

	Percent of sample exhibiting symptom			
	Adolescents		Adults	
Symptom	Current study (n = 28)	Hudgens (n = 19)	Baker et al (n = 100)	Woodruff et al (n = 54)
1. Dysphoria	93	95	100	93
2. Loss of interest	71	79	77	89
3. Loss of pleasure	46	–	36	50
4. Sad appearance	71	–	–	74
5. Crying episodes	43	32	61	50
6. Inability to cry	29	–	44	–
7. Feelings of worthlessness	64	–	38	74
8. Hoplessness	43	89	56	61
9. Self-reproach	54	–	–	59
10. Guilty thoughts	32	63	32	24
11. Impaired concentration	82	–	67	19
12. Agitation	18	84	67	93
13. Irritability	54	42	60	67
14. Excessive worry	39	–	69	30
15. Problems making decisions	57	–	67	59
16. Thought slowed	46	–	67	69
17. Reduced speech	32	–	–	74
18. Loss of energy	61	58	97	57
19. Psychomotor retardation	21	–	60	26
20. Initial insomnia	61	63	77	59
21. Restless sleep	43	63	–	46
22. Early awakening	39	32	65	61
23. Diurnal variation	25	–	46	33
24. Anorexia	68	74	80	87
25. Weight loss or gain	61	53	61	78
26. Lack of reactivity	39	–	–	–
27. Distinct quality to depression	54	–	–	72
28. Thoughts of death or suicide	61	89	63	41
29. Somatic complaints	50	42	25	74
31. Suicidal acts	32	68	15	11
31. Obsessional symptoms	7	–	14	–
32. Depressive delusions	14	–	16	11
33. Auditory hallucinations	4	–	9	2
34. Acute onset	57	–	–	–
35. Prior depressions	18	–	–	–
36. Positive family history	43	–	–	–
37. Paranoid ideation	14	–	6	7
38. Depersonalization or derealization	7	–	13	4
39. Thought disorder	11	–	6	–
40. First rank symptom(s)	11	–	8	–

Reprinted with permission from *Psychiatric Clinics of North America.*

variables recorded (items 1 to 33) in our group, 17 occurred in at least 50 percent of the population; moreover, classic endogenous symptoms (items 3, 9, 10, 12, 19, 21, 22, 24, 25, 26, 27) were common in these teenagers, and four patients (14 percent) displayed delusions of guilt, sin, or nihilism. Nonaffective forms of psychotic behavior were seen in some of our patients–including paranoid ideation, formal thought disorder, and first rank symptoms–although these were relatively infrequent, with occurrence rates comparable to those reported for adults with depressive illness. It is also relevant to note that 12 of our patients (43 percent) came from families with positive histories for affective disorder, and in five multiple generations were affected. Such observations support very convincingly the validity of our descriptive-phenomenoligical evaluation and classification of these young depressive patients.

As we have noted, many authorities maintain that unambiguous expression of depressive phenomenology is rare before late adolescence. Overall, we see little evidence in Table 2 to support this contention. Instead, one is struck by the similar occurrence of these symptoms both in our patients and in adult probands. In addition, in only eight of our 28 patients (29 percent) do nonaffective symptoms–purported to represent equivalent expression of depression–coincide with or immediately precede development of the full depressive syndrome. Finally, the frequency of positive family history of affective disorder lends additional credence to the affective diagnosis of these teenagers. In short, in our sample of rigorously diagnosed adolescent depressive patients, there does not appear to be an especially significant incidence of "atypical" or "masked" depressive symptoms. Of course, one cannot generalize this conclusion to the adolescent population at large at the present time. Only through prospective study of larger cohorts of maladjusted adolescents can be know for certain whether certain nondepressive forms of adolescent deviance prove to be forerunners of adult depression. The following case histories illustrate the clinical features of unipolar depression in adolescence.

CASE REPORTS

Case 1: The older of the two girls, C. had always been a reserved individual. At age 15½ just as she had begun to become somewhat more comfortable socially in high school, her father's job forced the family to relocate across country. C. seemed to adjust to this move but approximately nine months later, at the beginning of 11th grade, noticed she was having a great deal of trouble concentrating on school work. As she was an honors student, this troubled her greatly and her family sought psychiatric treatment for her.

C. presented as a very quiet adolescent with a blank, often downcast facial expression. She denied feeling depressed and stated that she had no feelings except anxiety about her studies and the fact that she could not get excited about doing things with her friends. She slept 12 hours per night, took a three-hour nap after school, and still felt tired. She had lost 10 lb, though was not concerned as she had been a little overweight. She was not suicidal, denied guilt or self-esteem problems, and was uncertain about the future.

Her conversation was laboriously slow and circumstantial. The interviewer felt tired just listening to her speak. It was clear how cognitively impaired this bright (IQ 135) adolescent was.

Further history revealed a youngster who had an obsessive personality (but no specific obsessions or compulsions) and who did not "fit" into her family of aggressive extroverts. There was no family history of affective disorder, however, and parents were concerned and committed to C.'s improvement if not always understanding of her personality.

C. was unable to tolerate amitriptyline but her depressive symptoms responded to 250 mg of imipramine. She remained a shy, socially insecure adolescent, however. She was advised to continue psychotherapy to help her with interpersonal skills and medication when she attended college in another state.

C. was not heard from again until eight months later when a psychiatrist whom she had consulted at college called for information. He had hospitalized C. for paranoid and somatic delusions. He had been aware of her past psychiatric history but did not feel that her cessation of antidepressant medication when she started college had any bearing on her current symptomatology. The psychiatrist reported that C. had lost 35 lb over the preceding three months, slept most of the time, and was frightened that she was going to die. Although less psychotic with thioridazine therapy, her doctor felt she still required hospitalization.

At some urging, her doctor had a dexamethasone suppression test done. When the 4 PM cortisol level after a prior 11 PM administration of 1 mg of dexamethasone revealed a level of 25 μg/100 ml, she was restarted on imipramine and was well enough for discharge on imipramine alone in three weeks. Although C. had to drop that quarter in college, she was able to return to school subsequently where she has continued to function relatively well.

Case 2: S., 16 years old at the time of her first psychiatric hospitalization, was described by her parents as a shy and naive person. While her mother was an introverted woman, with whom S. had little closeness, and her father was an unstable though more demonstrative man who often deserted the family for days at a time, there was no specific family history of psychiatric illness.

S. first became depressed in the summer of 1975, coinciding with growing friction between her parents. This change in mood was not immediately apparent, however, being overshadowed by the parents' marital conflict as well as her lifelong pattern of shyness. It was not until her decreased appetite and resultant weight loss became severe that help was sought. She was brought first to a family physician who recommended psychiatric counseling at a community clinic. She was seen there at frequent intervals for two months, during which time her weight loss and withdrawal became more severe. At home, her parents now recognized she had grown more obviously depressed and tearful and were concerned about her uncharacteristic withdrawal from the other children. Frustrated by her continued silence and weight loss, her therapist referred her for medical hospitalization, and she was subsequently transferred to the adolescent ward at UCLA in Winter 1976.

On admission, her appearance was one of profound depression and emaciation. Initially, she volunteered few spontaneous comments, responding in a terse, barely audible voice when questioned directly. On the ward, she typically sat alone with arms folded tightly around her, resisting attempts to involve her with peers and routine ward activities. Because of her refusal to eat, a diagnosis of anorexia nervosa was considered, but dismissed when no evidence of body image distortion, food preoccupation, or surreptitious vomiting could be found. Gradually, after growing more comfortable with the staff, S. described a history of depression and suicidal thinking dating back to the previous summer. She described growing feelings of worthlessness, pessimism about her future, sleep irregularities, anorexia, somatic concerns, slowed thinking, and loss of pleasure. She depicted herself as ugly and unwanted, and life as confusing, trivial, and meaningless. It became apparent that her continuing refusal to eat represented a willful method of suicide. When this showed no evidence of change, force-feeding of meals was instituted.

Multiple trials of antidepressants brought little symptomatic relief, and S. remained seriously depressed for an additional three months. By late May, she began to eat voluntarily, showed significant improvement in her self-esteem, and made rapid strides socially and academically. Continued hospitalization was deemed necessary, however, to help her cope more effectively with general family problems, her parents' deteriorating marital situation, and post-hospital plans. Feeling more hopeful of her future, she finally decided that a return home would not be in her best interest and was discharged in December 1976 to a residential setting. She remained there for nearly one year while attending a local community college. Although still depicting herself as shy, she began dating periodically. S. remained well until April 1979, at which time she had been living with a grup of girlfriends, and working successfully. Then, following an unpleasant sexual experience, she experienced a second depression, lasting until July, though not accompanied by the same degree of vegetative disturbance as before. Nevertheless, her job and social relating suffered and she again became suicidal. This episode remitted in several months. For the past two years she has been asymptomatic, is working full-time, and has recently been married.

Secondary Depression

The concept of secondary affective disorder was discussed in Chapter 2. The following case history illustrates the development of secondary depression in an adolescent diagnosed as having attention deficit disorder.

H. was a 14 year old boy with a lifelong history of behavior and medical problems. He was considered hyperactive as a toddler and grade school child with fidgety, restless behavior, poor impulse control, a quick temper, and distractibility. He had been in special classes since first grade and was hospitalized for a week at age eight for treatment of his hyperactivity. According to his mother, as he entered adolescence his restless behavior diminished, but six months before evaluation he was caught by the police as he was returning a bicycle he had stolen. He was suspended from school several times for fighting and for smoking marijuana, and also started drinking heavily.

One month before evaluation his mother reports he became withdrawn, would not leave his room or go out with friends, no longer had fun doing anything, slept all day, and was awake all night. He told his mother "I don't want to live," and his probation officer reported this as well. This behavior was clearly different from anything in the past.

He had been asthmatic since birth, and eczema developed at age three. As a consequence of steroid treatment he has remained small in stature. Both his size and his skin problems have caused him obvious distress.

Significant in his family history was his father's death when H. was an infant. His father was an alcoholic and died in a car accident. Many paternal family members are alcoholics or drug abusers. His maternal grandmother was hospitalized several times for unipolar depressions. A maternal aunt has peptic ucler disease and several cousins are narcotic addicts. The patient's mother admitted an alcohol problem in the past, but denied such now and has worked steadily as a draftsperson for several years. No one on either side of the family has graduated from high school. H. has an older sister, of whom he is fond, and who has no psychiatric problems. His brother, two years older, has recently become involved in minor skirmishes with the law.

During the interview, H. presented as a small, wiry adolescent who looked considerably younger than his age. He spoke with much bravado about his illegal escapades and admitted that others were concerned about his depression. However, while he was sad much of the time, used to hate himself and had thought about killing himself, he stated he was not depressed. Another obvious discrepancy between word and action was his denial of a sleep problem; on further questioning, however, he indicated that he often lay in bed awake until 3 AM. He said with gusto he had had great sex with four different girls, yet getting undressed in front of anyone made him panicky—"unsettled his appetite." Crowds, spiders, and school had similar effects. He had numerous somatic complaints of headaches, fatigue, and malaise. His activity level was also remarkable. He was extremely active, and could not sit still or stay in his chair; he was so distractible that he needed to be prompted to attend to the interview and was aware of every extraneous noise in the hall. He was obviously irritated by some of the questions, but related to the interviewer most of the time in an overly friendly manner. His attention deficit disorder and affective disorder were both obvious by history and mental status examination.

H.'s depressive symptoms remitted with hospitalization and psychotherapy which he continued as an outpatient for the next 1½ years.

Follow-up one year later found H. free of major depression, though experiencing some dysphoria and flare-ups of eczema. He was attending school but living away from home. He was no longer engaged in antisocial behavior.

Systematic follow-up examination has not yet been carried out on adolescents with secondary affective disorder. Two facts are obvious to the authors, however. The depressive disorder seems to have its own natural history and may abate either spontaneously or with antidepressant treatment. The primary diagnosis remains relatively unchanged. For example, one of the girls with anorexia nervosa and depression was treated with amitriptyline for her irritable mood, withdrawn behavior, insomnia, and difficulty concentrating. While antidepressant medication noticeably improved her mood, sociability, and motivation, her phobic avoidance of weight gain and obsession with food remained unchanged. The second fact is that the chaotic family situations from which these teenagers come complicate their course and treatment immeasurably.

SUMMARY

Although the clinical boundaries and prodomal features of affective disorder in adolescents remain unclear, for many young persons the phenomenology of their illness is similar to that of adults. The conflicts presented by this particular developmental period coexist with but do not substantially alter the primary features of depression and mania. Looking beyond the issue of depressive phenomenology, the question of whether affective disorder proves more protracted or malignant when beginning in adolescence requires additional research (Carlson et al, 1977), as does the thornier problem of whether certain forms of pathology seen often in adolescence (for example, anorexia nervosa, drug usage) constitute affective spectrum disorders.

Parts of this chapter have been reprinted from *Psychiatric Clinics of North America*, 2:511, 1979, with permission of the publisher.

REFERENCES

Akiskal HS, Bitar AH, Puzantian VR, et al. The nosological status of neurotic depression. *Arch Gen Psychiatry* 1978; 35:756–766.

American Psychiatric Association: Diagnostic and Statistical Manual (DSM-III). Washington, DC: APA, 1980.

Baker M, Dorzab J, Winokur G, et al. Depressive disease: classification and clinical characteristics. *Compr Psychiatry* 1971; 12:354–365.

Carlson GA, Davenport YB, Jamison K. A comparison of outcome in adolescent and late onset bipolar manic-depressive illness. *Am J Psychiatry* 1977; 134:919–922.

Carlson GA, Strober M. Affective disorder in adolescence: issues in misdiagnosis. *J Clin Psychiatry* 1979; 39:63–66.

Carlson GA, Strober M. Manic depressive illness in early adolescence: a study of clinical and diagnostic characteristics in 6 cases. *J Am Acad Child Psychiatry* 1978; 17:138–153.

Gittelman-Klein R. Definitional and methodological issues concerning depressive illness in children. In: Schulterbrandt JG, Raskin A, eds. *Depression in childhood.* New York: Raven Press, 1977:69–85.

Glaser K. Masked depression in children and adolescents. *Am J Psychother* 1967; 21:565–574.

Henderson AS, Krupinski J, Stoller A. Epidemiological aspects of adolescent psychiatry. In: Howells JG, Ed. *Modern perspectives in adolescent psychiatry.* New York: Brunner/Mazel, 1971.

Hudgens RW. *Psychiatric disorders in adolescents.* Baltimore: Williams & Wilkins, 1974:38–89.

King L, Pittman GD. A six year follow-up study of sixty-five adolescent patients: predictive value of presenting clinical picture. *Br J Psychiatry* 1969; 115:1437–1441.

Perris C. A study of bipolar (manic-depressive) and unipolar recurrent depressive psychoses. *ACTA Psychiatr Scand (Suppl)* 1966; 194:9–189.

Rutter M, Tizard J, Yule W, et al. Isle of Wight studies, 1964–1974. *Psychol Med* 1976; 6:313–332.

U.S. Department of Health, Education, and Welfare: Primary diagnosis of discharges from non-federal general hospital psychiatric inpatient units, United States–1975. Mental Health Statistical Note no. 137, 1977a.

U.S. Department of Health, Education, and Welfare: Diagnostic distribution of admissions to inpatient services of state and county mental hospitals, United States–1975. Mental Health Statistical Note no. 138, 1977b.

Weiner IB. *Psychological disturbance in adolescence.* New York: John Wiley and Sons, 1970:

Weiner IB, Del Gaudio A. Psychopathology in adolescence. *Arch Gen Psychiatry* 1976; 33:187–193.

Winokur G, Clayton PJ, Reich T. *Manic depressive illness.* St. Louis: CV Mosby, 1969.

Woodruff RA, Murphy GF, Herjanic M. The natural history of affective disorders: I. symptoms of 73 patients at the time of index hospital admission. *J Psychiatr Res* 1967; 5:265–263.

Affective Disorders in Childhood and Adolescence--
An Update. Edited by D.P. Cantwell and G.A. Carlson.

6

Clinical and Biological Perspectives on Depressive Disorders in Adolescence

Michael Strober

Clinical and theoretical traditions have long maintained that regression and turmoil are universal landmarks of normal adolescent development bearing little relationship to adult patterns of psychiatric illness. However, epidemiologically based studies of adolescent cohorts in North America and Great Britain during the past 15 years have found little direct support for these ideas (Coleman, 1978). As a result, greater emphasis is now being placed on attempting to more reliably define psychopathologic disorders in teenage patients and expanding knowledge of their rate of occurrence, empirical descriptors, and long-term prognosis.

Clearly, this thrust has been most evident in the depressive disorders (Puig-Antich, 1980). Suffice it to say that substantial evidence is accumulating to suggest that explicit and operationally defined diagnostic criteria can be used with adolescents to identify conditions approximating adult-like depressions, and that these conditions are a greater source of psychiatric morbidity in the teenage population than previously supposed (Carlson and Strober, 1979; Strober et al, 1981).

There is an emerging core of agreement that the extension of adult diagnostic criteria to child psychiatric populations is necessary to bring some order to the proliferating theoretical conceptions and clinical analyses of juvenile depression. However, beyond such refinements in diagnosis and phenomenology, there are no systematic data available concerning the nosologic validity of depressive states in adolescence, nor has much consideration been given to how biological processes and other developmental influences that naturally occur with puberty trigger the diathesis to depression in teens. Along similar lines, a further question that may be raised when considering adolescent depression in its developmental context is whether maturational factors operative at this stage of life give rise, at least in certain instances, to clinically atypical expressions of depressive disorder–the speculation (Cantwell et al, 1977; Strober et al, 1982) that variants of anorexia nervosa fall within the affective spectrum being a case in point.

Also worthy of note is the increasing realization that depression is not a unitary disease form but rather a common pathway for multiple etiologies, and divisible into more restrictive clinical-descriptive subtypes. Yet few insights are available at present concerning these matters in adolescents. The point at issue is that progress toward diagnostic syndrome validation must begin by verifying in adolescent populations the existence of genetic, biological, and predictive correlates deemed relevant to the nosologic discrimination of adult depression.

In this chapter, data are summarized from an ongoing project designed to objectively classify and validate patterns of depressive psychopathology in early and middle adolescence. Findings to be presented will illustrate how genetic and biological sources of validating evidence can serve as a guide for empirical inquiry in adolescent psychiatry.

SAMPLE AND METHODS

Since 1976, 88 patients (63 females, 25 males) with a presumptive diagnosis of major depressive disorder have been identified from among 529 consecutive admissions to the Adolescent Service of the UCLA Nueropsychiatric Institute. Patients were evaluated by experienced clinicians, using a detailed and structured psychiatric interview, the Schedule for Affective Disorders and Schizophrenia (SADS) (Spitzer and Endicott, 1978), and unmodified Research Diagnostic Criteria (RDC; Spitzer et al, 1978a, b). The total cohort ranged in age from 13 to 17 years (mean age 15.8) and were predominantly Caucasian from middle class socioeconomic backgrounds.

At the time of the patient's admission, information concerning differential familial patterns of psychiatric illness was ascertained by direct interview of biological parents and second-degree relatives (grandparents, aunts, uncles) using the lifetime version of the SADS and RDC. We have been able to personally interview over 90 percent of parents and 50 percent of second-degree relatives. Psyciatric diagnoses of noninterviewed relatives were obtained using the family history method described by Andreasen et al (1977).

In light of recent investigations concerning neuroendocrine markers of primary depressive illness, assessments of pituitary-adrenal regulation have been conducted on 38 of the 88 depressive probands using the overnight dexamethasone suppression test (DST) (Carroll et al, 1981). Each patient received a 1 mg dose of oral dexamethasone at 11 PM after a baseline blood sample was obtained. Blood samples for serum cortisol determinations were then obtained at 4 PM and 11 PM the following day. An abnormality in pituitary-adrenal suppression was defined as failure to reduce serum cortisol levels to below 5 μg/100 ml at either 4 PM or 11 PM.

RESULTS

Descriptive Validity

The frequencies of RDC subtypes of depression in the 88 probands were as follows: primary, 77 percent; secondary (that is, preceded by major non-affective psychiatric illness), 23 percent; endogenous, 45 percent; psychotic, 14 percent; retarded, 20 percent; agitated, 8 percent; situational, 47 percent; and incapacitating, 20 percent. Because the RDC scheme does not treat diagnostic subtypes as mutually exclusive categories, many of these patients received multiple classifications. As the figures indicate, there appears to be clinically significant diversity in the phenomenologic expression of depression in this cohort.

Independent SADS-RDC assessments were carried out on 40 of the probands to evaluate interrater reliability of the RDC rules for subtype classification. Resulting Kappa Coefficients of agreement for the eight subtypes were as follows: primary, 0.79; secondary, 0.72; endogenous, 0.74; psychotic, 0.82; retarded, 0.70; agitated, 0.63; situational, 0.58; and incapacitating, 0.60. For the most part, the reliabilities are quite satisfactory and compare favorably to coefficients of agreement reported for adult depressives (Spitzer et al, 1978).

Because the SADS is sufficiently inclusive, it allows for the grouping of certain individual symptoms into more global dimensions of depressive psychopathology. Using item assignments described in Endicott and Spitzer (1978), summary scale scores were calculated for 65 of the depressive probands and assessed for internal reliability using Chronbach's alpha. Reliabilities were as follows: depressive mood and ideation = 0.81; endogenous features = 0.71; depression-associated features = 0.69; suicidal ideation and behavior = 0.74; delusions and hallucinations = 0.82. These coefficients appear to suggest that the depressive state in adolescents lends itself to reliable and homogeneous quantitative description at the dimensional level.

Genetic Relation to Adult Depression

There is now an abundance of evidence that psychiatric illnesses concentrate in families such that the lifetime risk in blood relatives of affective individuals exceeds the averaged expected rate of illness in the general population. Accordingly, evidence of increased rates of depressive illness in the parents and second-degree relatives of adolescents exhibiting symptoms of major depression would offer reasonably persuasive evidence of syndrome validity. To explore this issue, morbid risk estimates for different categories of psychiatric illness were determined for more than 600 parents and second-degree relatives of adolescent probands with primary major depression, schizophrenia, or conduct disorder. In each case, psychiatric diagnoses of relatives were made without knowledge of the proband's diagnostic status. Morbid risks for familial schizophrenia and affective illness were determined using the Weinberg abridged method of age-correction, assuming a risk period of 15 to 59 years for affective illness and 15 to 39 years for schizophrenia. Age-correction was not undertaken in computing risks for antisocial personality.

Findings are summarized in Table 1. Clearly, secondary cases of affective illness concentrate in relatives of adolescents with major depression: the 21.7 percent morbid risk in these relatives is significantly greater than the 8.0 percent risk found in relatives of schizophrenic probands ($\chi^2 = 10.22$, $p < 0.005$) and the 6.5 percent risk in relatives of the conduct disorder group ($\chi^2 = 13.21$, $p < 0.001$). Relatives of depressive probands were also found to have a 6.3 percent risk for bipolar illness, which is nine times greater than the expected 0.7 percent lifetime risk for this condition in the general population (Krauthammer and Klerman, 1979). Importantly, the findings also reveal that schizophrenia was rare in the family pedigrees of depressive probands, and that the rate of antisocial personality, while somewhat greater than the expected risk of this condition in the general population, is still far lower than the rate of sociopathy documented in relatives of conduct disorder adolescents.

To illuminate the possible mode of familial transmission within the cohort, a subset of 35 probands with primary subtype of major depression was screened for the presence of two or more ancestral secondary cases of affective disorder in their pedigree. According to Slater (1966), a single major dominant gene transmission of illness should be reflected in a marked tendency for affected

Table 1 Morbid Risks for Psychiatric Illnesses in Blood Relatives of Adolescents with Depression, Schizophrenia, and Conduct Disorder

	Illness in relatives[a]		
Adolescent probands	Affective disorder	Schizophrenia	Antisocial personality
Major depression (n = 20)	21.7 ± 3.4	1.0 ± 0.7	5.6 ± 1.6
Schizophrenia (n = 20)	8.0 ± 2.3	9.9 ± 2.1	2.9 ± 1.2
Conduct disorder (n = 20)	6.5 ± 2.1	2.0 ± 1.0	21.7 ± 2.9

[a]Morbid risks are based on illness in the pooled group of parents and second-degree relatives.

relatives to be distributed unilaterally in a pedigree, that is, situated either on the paternal or maternal side, whereas in polygenetic inheritance the distribution of unilateral to bilateral pairs of affected relatives should approximate a 2:1 ratio. The number of bilateral pairs corrected for family size is obtained by the formula: Bilateral pairs = [2 (number of paternal cases) (number of maternal cases)] /N - 1, where N equals the total number of secondary cases in the pedigree.

A total of 13 probands had at least two ancestral cases of affective disorder. From the distribution of secondary cases of affective disorder on the paternal and maternal side in these 13 probands, a total of 21.0 unilateral pairs and 10.0 bilateral pairs were observed, nearly equivalent to the expected 2:1 ratio and thus consistent with a hypothesis of polygenetic heritability.

Thus, as a whole, the findings presented would seem to justify the treatment of primary major depression in adolescents as a nosologically distinctive form of psychopathology sharing predisposing familial-genetic factors in common with adult affective illness. However, in view of the increasing speculation that patients with the endogenous or melancholic states of depression have greater descriptive and biological specificity, evidence of familial differnces was sought between age and SES-matched subgroups of 25 endogenous and 25 nonendogenous primary depressives, drawn from the original sample of 88. These data are summarized in Table 2. The most noteworthy finding is that the adolescents with endogenous depressions were found to have a more extensive family history than their nonendogenous counterparts: a significantly greater percentage of endogenous patients had affective illness present in two ascendant generations ($\chi^2 = 4.25$, $p < 0.05$), and they were more likely than nonendogenous patients to have family pedigrees containing a member with the more severe bipolar type of affective illness, although this difference did not reach significance. On the other hand, more nonendogenous than endogenous depressive patients reveal family histories of antisocial personality, but a gain, the difference

Table 2 Clinical and Familial Differences between Adolescents with Endogenous and Nonendogenous Primary Depression

Variable	Group (n = 25)	
	Endogenous (%)	Nonendogenous (%)
Family history of affective illness	72	64
Family history of mania	28	8
Family history of suicide	36	24
Family histories of alcoholism	68	76
Affective illness in two ascendant generations	52	20
Family history of antisocial personality	4	20
Divorce or marital separation	40	48

did not attain significance. The groups were found to be comparable in terms of family histories of affective disorder, alcoholism, suicide, and divorce/separation.

Neuroendocrine Dysfunction

The 38 patients on whom DST results are available include nine with secondary depression, 18 with primary endogenous depression, and 11 with nonendogenous depression. A failure to suppress serum cortisol below the normal criterion of 5 μg/100 ml was detected in 12 of the 38 (32 percent). The proportions of nonsuppressors within these three subtypes were as follows: secondary depression, one of nine (11 percent); endogenous depression, 9 of 18 (50 percent); and nonendogenous depression, two of 11 (18 percent). Thus, nine of the 12 (75 percent) nonsuppressors met criteria for endogenous depression whereas only nine of the 26 (35 percent) probands with normal post-dexamethasone suppression were classified as endogenous (Fisher exact $p < 0.05$). Among endogenous probands, suppressors and nonsuppressors were not found to differ in age, sex, or multigeneration history of affective disorder; however, nonsuppressors received somewhat higher mean scores on the SADS item for psychomotor retardation ($p < 0.10$).

CONCLUSION

The data summarized offer impressive support for the applicability of RDC classifications of major depression in adolescent populations. Ratings on major symptom dimensions appear to be internally consistent and the division of patients into more clinically homogeneous subtyes reliable. The observed differences in familial patterns of psychiatric morbidity affirm the nosologic distinctiveness of primary major depression from other forms of psychiatric disturbance extant in the adolescent population; preliminary analyses conducted on a subset of depressed probands indicate that further affective illness has some merit. And, finally, the finding that the pituitary-adrenal disinhibition characteristic of adults with endogenomorphic depression (Brown and Shuey, 1980; Carroll et al, 1981) was also found in association with a primary endogenous subtype of depression in this young cohort indicates the cross-developmental generality of this marker, and the substantial commonality between adolescent and adult depressive patients in certain genetic-pathophysiologic processes. It is evident that the joint application of clinico-genetic and biological paradigms to juvenile populations holds considerable promise for future studies of the depressive disorders.

REFERENCES

Andreasen NC, Endicott J, Spitzer RL, Robins E. The family history method using diagnostic criteria: reliability and validity. *Arch Gen Psychiatry* 1977; 34:1229–1235.

Brown WA, Shuey I. Response to dexamethasone and subtypes of depression. *Arch Gen Psychiatry* 1980; 37:747–751.

Cantwell D, Sturzenberger S, Burroughs J, Salkin B, Green J. Anorexia nervosa: an affective disorder. *Arch Gen Psychiatry* 1977; 34:1087–1091.

Carlson G, Strober M. Affective disorders in adolescence. *Psychiatr Clin North Am* 1979; 2:511–526.

Carroll BJ, Feinberg M, Greden JF, Tarika J, Albala AA, Haskett RF, James N, Kronfol Z, Lohr N, Steiner M, Vigne JP, Young E. A specific laboratory test for the diagnosis of melancholia: standardization, validation, and clinical utility. *Arch Gen Psychiatry* 1981; 38:15–22.

Coleman JC. Current contradiction in adolescent theory. *J Youth Adol* 1978; 7:1–11.

Endicott J, Spitzer RL. A diagnostic interview: the schedule for affective disorders and schizophrenia. *Arch Gen Psychiatry* 1978; 35:837–884..

Krauthammer C, Klerman GL. The epidemiology of mania. In: Shopsin B, ed. *Manic illness.* New York: Raven Press, 1979:11–28.

Puig-Antich J. Affective disorders in childhood: a review and perspective. *Psychiatr Clin North Am* 1980; 3:403–424.

Slater E. Expectation of abnormality on paternal and maternal sides: a computational model. *J Med Genet* 1966; 3:159–161.

Spitzer RL, Endicott J. *The schedule for affective disorders and schizophrenia.* New York: New York State Psychiatric Institute, 1978.

Spitzer RL, Endicott J, Robins E. *Research diagnostic criteria for a selected group of functional disorders.* New York: New York State Psychiatric Institute, 1978a.

Spitzer RL, Endicott J, Robins E. Research diagnostic criteria: rationale and reliability. *Arch Gen Psychiatry* 1978b; 35:837–844.

Strober M, Carlson G, Green J. Reliability of psychiatric diagnosis in adolescents: interrater agreement using DSM-III. *Arch Gen Psychiatry* 1981; 38:141–145.

Strober M, Salkin B, Burroughs J, Morrell W. Validity of the bulimia-restricter distinction in anorexia nervosa: parental personality characteristics and family psychiatric morbidity. *J Nerv Ment Dis* 1982; 170:345–351.

SECTION II

Alternative Forms of Depression

Overview of Masked or Alternate Forms of Depression

Gabrielle A. Carlson

As noted in Chapter 2, one school of thought regarding childhood depression has held that rather than being demonstrated in a clinically obvious way, depression in children and adolescents is "masked." As we have learned to ask children more systematically how they think and feel, it appears that depression is not as hidden as originally believed (Carlson and Cantwell, 1980).

Yet certain clinical pictures seem to coexist frequently with the syndrome of depression—clinical pictures whose onsets are fairly specific to children and adolescents. The question that arises is whether depression in children is protean in its presentation or if it is associated in some specific way to these other disorders.

The interaction between school distress and childhood depression provide one arena for discussion. Weinberg, in Chapter 7, discusses his thinking and research on the impact of depression in children on school performance. Whether we speculate that a child placed in a classroom situation with demands inappropriate to his abilities subsequently developed low self-esteem, depression, helplessness, and hopelessness, or that a depressed child had his performance impeded by poor concentration and feelings of hopelessness, school failure and depression are often associated. Another group of children with school problems, those with "school phobia," separation anxiety," and/or school refusal often are found to be suffering from symptoms of depression. Tisher describes her systematic investigation of the interaction between depressive symptoms and school phobia in Chapter 8 and she and Lang devised a rating scale (The Children's Depression Scale) (Chapter 11) to measure depression.

Another disorder which seems to be associated with childhood depression is conduct disorder. Carlson and Cantwell (1980) found that behavior problems were the calling card for a number of children with depressive disorder. Puig-Antich (1982) reviewed the literature on this association and reported his finding that 16 of 43 prepubertal boys who met Diagnostic and Statistical Manual-III (DSM-III) criteria for major depression also met criteria for conduct disorder. Moreover, the 13 boys who received imipramine treatment responded with an amelioration of depressive symptoms in 11 cases, and the conduct disorder behaviors subsided. The relative onset of these two disorders may be of some importance to whether the antisocial behaviors are simply part of the clinical picture of some kinds of depression, since the depressive symptoms usually were first to appear both in the first episode and, when it occurred, during relapse. We might speculate that when associated with depression, antisocial behaviors (like psychotic symptoms) represent a subtype of depression. Unlike psychotic symptoms, however, antisocial behaviors may be associated with a stormier clinical course and worse outcome. Further study of this subject is clearly needed.

The foregoing discussion has focused on the coexistence of childhood affective disorder and other psychiatric syndromes. If we hypothesize that the child's age may considerably alter the appearance of a particular syndrome, we can turn to Ballenger et al's recent finding (1982) that psychotic symptoms in mania are much more frequent in adolescents than adults. While schizophrenia has not been a "mask" for affective disorder in the traditional sense, like behavior and school related problems, psychotic symptoms may distract the clinician from ascertaining or recognizing affective symptoms.

Another disorder with an onset in childhood and adolescence which may be associated with affective disorder is anorexia nervosa. Family history (Winokur et al, 1980; Strober et al, personal communication) and antidepressant studies (Needleman and Waber, 1977; Barcai, 1977) suggest a relationship. Carlson and Cantwell (1980) found five of 28 subjects meeting criteria for affective disorder had anorexia nervosa as their primary diagnosis.

Somewhat more intriguing to the question of association are those adolescents who on follow-up some years later have had no recurrence of anorexia nervosa, but have had episodes of depression (Cantwell et al, 1977). The following case history illustrates this point.

A 16-year-old girl, M., presented with a fairly classical history for anorexia nervosa. She wa slightly overweight, and followed directions to go on a diet to improve her running speed (she was a competitive runner). Several months later, the dieting got out of control and help was sought. M., who was 5′2″, was convinced she was fat in spite of her 30 lb weight loss to 65 lb; and she was obsessed with the fear of having fat legs. She exercised relentlessly but never vomited. Her thinking was rigid and concrete. Her mother, who never validated M.'s thoughts or feelings also did not want her to grow up. Neither on referral, psychiatric hospitalization, nor discharge eight months later, did M. have any signs or symptoms of depression. These were repeatedly asked given the authors interest in the subject. Although M. had regained her weight and was able to maintain it after discharge, she recognized that her feelings about food were abnormal (that more than a few bites of food could cause her to expand voluminously). One year later, during one of her weekly therapy sessions, M. reported she felt acutely depressed, miserable, weepy, and hopeless; she wasn't sleeping and had lost all interest in school and friends. She said she had never felt so miserable and, in fact had never felt anything like this previously though she reiterated she had been disgusted and tired of being "anorexic." She responded within a week to imipramine and within six weeks "felt normal about food." Three months later she forgot to take her medication over a five-day skiing weekend and her depressive feelings (without food pre-occupation) began to recur. Resumption of medication ended the symptoms. She continued medication for six months, which included beginning college. She has continued to be symptom-free, slightly *over* weight, for the past three years. Interestingly, her father had had one episode of depression at age 30; his mother had had a late life depression.

Whether one invokes "masked" depression or alternate forms of depression related to age, it is clear that certain syndromes are associated with concurrent or future diagnosis of affective disorder and the nature of those relationships will require continued investigation.

REFERENCES

Ballenger JC, Reus VI, Post RM. The "atypical" presentation of adolescent mania. *Am J Psychiatry* 1982; 139:602-606.

Barcai A. Lithium in adult anorexia nervosa–a pilot report on two patients. *ACTA Psychiatr Scand* 1977; 55:97-101.

Cantwell DR, Sturzenberger S, Burroughs J, et al. Anorexia nervosa–an affective disorder? *Arch Gen Psychiatry* 1977; 34:1087-1093.

Carlson GA, Cantwell DP. Unmasking masked depression in children and adolescents. *Am J Psychiatry* 1980; 137:445-449.

Needleman HL, Waber D. The use of amitriptyline in anorexia nervosa. In Vigersky RA, ed. *Anorexia nervosa.* New York: Raven Press, 1977: 357-363.

Puig-Antich J. Major depression and conduct disorder in prepuberty. *J Am Acad Child Psychiatry* 1982; 21:118-123.

Winokur A, March V, Mendels J. Primary affective disorder in relatives of patients with anorexia nervosa. *Am J Psychiatry* 1980; 137:695-698.

Affective Disorders in Childhood and Adolescence--
An Update. Edited by D.P. Cantwell and G.A. Carlson.

7

Childhood Affective Disorder and School Problems

Warren Weinberg and Anne Rehmet

The function of an educational evaluation center is to assess children who are having difficulties in school. Children are referred to these centers for evaluation of learning and behavior related to learning failure and classroom behavior problems. Often it is the classroom behavior of these children that accounts for their being referred by the teacher for evaluation and treatment. Parents frequently report a change in the child's mood, affect (feelings), sleep, interests, and homework effort concomitant with the negative comments being offered by the teacher to the parent. The referred child is described by parents and teachers as hyperactive, irritable, aggressive, agitated, inattentive, moody, lethargic, and generally disruptive. It is possible that a cycle of primary affective illness (depression or mania) accounts for the behavior of these children and their inability to behave and achieve in an acceptable manner similar to non-referred children with or without developmental severe learning disabilities.

RELATIONSHIP OF AFFECTIVE ILLNESS TO LEARNING DISABILITIES AND SCHOOL PERFORMANCE

Although affective illness in childhood has been infrequently discussed in medical literature as a cause of children's social, physical, or academic incapacitation, any of these symptoms can cause conflicts in school classroom situations and other social settings and can result in referral of the child to a physician for evaluation of school problems (Brumback and Weinberg, 1977b; Huessy and Cohen, 1976; Husain, 1979; Kovacs and Beck, 1977; Weinberg et al, 1973). It is apparent from previous investigations (Weinberg et al, 1973; Brumback et al, 1977) that childhood depression independent of learning disabilities might be a common condition in children who are doing poorly in school. In that study, all but one of 72 children manifested a learning disability as determined by the Symbol Language Battery (Weinberg, 1975) and psychometric test scores.

Children diagnosed as depressed did not differ from those diagnosed as non-depressed in respect to type of learning disability, age, sex, or IQ. Other publications discuss the relationship of hyperactivity and school problems to childhood emotional and learning disorders (Eisenberg, 1966; Fish, 1971; Kenney et al, 1971; Werry, 1968). However, these childhood "emotional" disorders have not been clearly defined.

Since poor school performance and school failure are part of the clinical picture of many depressed children, a possible relationship between depression and mental retardation (Rideau, 1971) or other intellectual disturbances has been suggested (Malmquist, 1977). Another study (Brumback et al, unpublished) found no difference in IQ and achievement test scores between the depressed and nondepressed group in learning disabled children. The results suggest that the poor school performance of depressed children neither results from nor produces a reduction in basic school skills. Indeed, poor school performance in learning disabled children might possibly be an expression of disinterest in participation and the defeatist self-depreciatory feelings related to primary depression. However, it is common for others to conclude that depression, frustration, and discouragement are secondary to learning disabilities and do not constitute a primary condition.

The relationship to school problems of affective illness, its cyclical nature of gradual worsening followed by improvement with recovery, was investigated at Winston School in Dallas, Texas. Do learning disabled children manifest depressive illness and is affective illness manifested by their families? Would children diagnosed as having affective illness still have school-related behavior problems while attending a school designed for children and young adolescents with developmental specific learning disabilities? Do children at Winston School manifest a cyclical behavioral disorder; if so, who are these children?

Winston School is a school for children, grades one through nine (chronological age six years, zero months through 14 years, 11 months), with developmental specific learning disabilities. The curriculum is designed to allow children to bypass the use of language and symbol skills which are developmentally delayed (Weinberg, 1975, 1979). Emphasis is on the acquisition and utilization of information through multimedia resources. The faculty is trained to pursue the child's learning and communicative assets. The student is not penalized for his/her limitations. There are no known inappropriate school stresses in this educational environment.

The mean physical growth, height, weight, and head circumference of the Winston School student population is at the 50th percentile for the general population and classic neurologic examination is normal in this group of developmental specific learning disorders. This student population is of normal intelligence, and the students are free of primary conduct problems or thought disturbance. Ninety-six percent manifest severe specific learning discrepancy with 80 percent having multiple severe specific learning discrepancies (Table 1).

Table 1 Percentage of New Winston School Students with Severe Learning Discrepancies as Defined by P.L. 94-142 (1975–1976 to 1978–1979)*

Number of Severe Discrepancy	n	%
No discrepancy	6	4
One discrepancy	27	16
Two discrepancies	46	28
Three discrepancies	36	22
Four discrepancies	25	15
Five discrepancies	16	10
Six discrepancies	6	4
Seven discrepancies	2	1
Total	164	100

Average number of discrepancies per student = 2.8

Symbol Language Skill Categories	n	Severe Discrepancies (%)
Oral Expression	106	65
Basic Reading Skills	98	60
Written Expression	97	60
Mathematical Calculation	53	33
Reading Comprehension	51	31
Listening Comprehension	37	23
Mathematical Reasoning	15	9

*1975-1976, n = 55; 1976-1977, n = 30; 1977-1978, n - 28; 1978-1979, n = 51.

A method of determining whether or not a child has a severe learning discrepancy has been provided through the New York Board of Regents–State Education Department, Office of Education of Children with Handicapping Conditions. The method was developed by the New York Child Service Demonstration Program, Title VI-G as a consideration for Public Law 94-142. The exact formula is: Chronologic age IQ/300 + .7 − 2.5 = Severe discrepancy level (in grade equivalents). This method provides a standard by which two percent of the population qualify as having a severe learning discrepancy between achievement and intellectual ability. A severe discrepancy exists when achievement "falls at or below 50 percent of an individual's expected achievement level when intellectural ability, age and previous educational experiences are considered" (Smith et al, 1977).

Using the seven criteria skills for specific learning disabilities as stated in PL 94-142, the performance of students at Winston School was analyzed for the following symbol language skills: (1) basic reading skills; (2) reading comprehension; (3) listening comprehension; (4) oral expression; (5) written expression; (6) mathematical calculations; and (7) mathematical reasoning. The categories of symbol language skills in which most Winston School students had severe learning discrepancies were in oral expression, basic reading skills, and written expression—60 to 65 percent of Winston School students. The next grouping was mathematical calculations (33 percent) and reading comprehension (31 percent). This was followed by listening comprehension (23 percent) and mathematical reasoning (9 percent) (Table 1).

During and at the end of each school year, the headmaster and medical director of Winston School review each individual student with respect to behavior problems. The students are coded one of three ways for behavior problems observed during the time of the review: (1) clinically significant problem: a problem that persists for more than ten days. It may be persistent or recurrent through the school year. The problem is disruptive to classmates and teachers and limits the student's participation in the Winston School educational process. The problem is reported to the student's parents and clinical management for the student is requested; (2) "mini" problem: this problem is less severe than the clinically significant problem in duration and intensity. Typically, the problem lasts for only a few days, but is of sufficient severity for school faculty to note, report, and record the problem. This problem level may also be recurrent during the school year. Clinical management is discussed with the parents but not directly requested; and (3) no problems.

All 167 students enrolled in Winston School for the first four years of operation are included in this analysis. In addition to the above coding, all students at the initial clinical visit and before entrance into Winston School are clinically diagnosed using the following groupings: (1) no problem; (2) hyperactivity but no depression; (3) hyperactivity and depression; (4) depression; and (5) "mini" depressive syndrome. Children and adolescents with primary conduct disorder, thought disturbance, autism, and subnormal intelligence are not acceptable for admission to Winston School.

Tables 2 and 3 show the frequency and percentage of total Winston School student populations per year and new Winston School students per year in relationship to pre-entrance behavior diagnostic category. As noted in Table 2, the total Winston School student population for the year 1978–1979, 40 percent of the children manifest depression and 21 percent have depression plus hyperactivity. Table 4 shows the percentage per year of new Winston School students with a family history of affective illness. The percentage ranges from 68.6 to 95.8 percent per year of new Winston School students having a strongly positive family history for affective illness.

Data presented in Table 5 indicates that the percentage of students having no problem during the school year increases over a four-year prospection. It shows that the four-year population starts with a high level of problems and decreases over time, but problem periods of a cyclical nature continue.

The next question to answer is whether or not it is the same children who have behavior problems over time. Table 6 displays the frequency of problems

Table 2 Frequency Distribution for Total Winston School Populations by Behavior Diagnosis at Entrance

Diagnosis	1975-1976 n	1975-1976 %	1976-1977 n	1976-1977 %	1977-1978 n	1977-1978 %	1978-1979 n	1978-1979 %
No problem	10	18	16	22	18	21	19	16
Hyperactivity but No Depression	9	16	11	15	12	14	19	16
Hyperactivity and Depression	13	24	15	20	18	21	26	21
Depression	17	31	25	34	31	36	49	40
"Mini" Depressive Syndrome	7	11	6	08	7	08	9	07
Total	55	100	73	100	86	100	122	100

Table 3 Frequency Distributions and Percentages for New Winston School Students per Year by Behavior Diagnosis at Entrance

Diagnosis	1975-1976 n	1975-1976 %	1976-1977 n	1976-1977 %	1977-1978 n	1977-1978 %	1978-1979 n	1978-1979 %
No problem	10	18	8	27	3	11	5	09
Hyperactivity but No Depression	9	16	4	13	3	11	8	15
Hyperactivity and Depression	13	24	7	23	8	28	11	20
Depression	17	31	11	37	12	43	28	52
"Mini" Depressive Syndrome	6	11	0	0	2	07	2	04
Total	55	100	30	100	28	100	54	100

for the four-year population. Only 40 percent have no behavior problems over the four years. No students had only one problem period. The mean number of problem periods for this group is 2.7 over an eight-period time interval. It is evident there are no constant behavior problem students. There are some (seven of 25) with frequent (three to six) problem periods; and eight of 25 have two problem periods over four years. Most of the problems are manifested by the same students but most of the students are manifesting recurrent problems. Table 7 demonstrates two three-year prospections. The results show 1.5 and 1.4 problem periods per three-year follow-up, but with the addition of the fourth year (Table 6), the mean problem period increases to 2.7. Again, a cyclical or recurrent behavior disorder is suggested.

Table 4 Percentage of New Winston Students with a Family History of Depression, Mania, and/or Manic-Depressive Illness (Family History at Entrance)

1975-1976 (n = 55; 4 adopted)		1976-1977 (n = 30; 4 adopted)		1977-1978 (n = 28; 4 adopted)		1978-1979 (n = 54; 4 adopted)	
68.6%	31.4%	88.5%	11.5%	95.8%	4.2%	80%	20%
n = 35	n = 16	n = 23	n = 3	n = 23	n = 1	n = 40	n = 10
		No affective illness				Affective illness	

The depression groups have increased in number and percentage whereas the most difficult problem groups, depression with hyperactivity, have demonstrated a mild decline in numbers by diagnosis before entering Winston School (Tables 2 and 3).

The next area to be addressed is the relationship of clinical diagnosis before entering Winston School to the occurrence of behavior problems during enrollment at Winston School. Table 8 through 12 display the data by each diagnosis. The children with both depression and hyperactivity present the greatest problem at Winston School. The next most problem-prone group is children with depression, followed by children with only hyperactivity. Very few children with a clinical diagnosis of no problem manifest problems while at Winston School.

Does the frequency and recurrence of behavior problems relate to the clinical diagnosis established before entrance to Winston School? Table 13

Table 5 Percentage of Winston School Students Over Time Having Behavior Problems at Winston School (Four-Year Prospection)

	1975-1976				1976-1977			
	During		End		During		End	
	%	n	%	n	%	n	%	n
CS	28.0	7	0.0	0	16.0	4	4.0	1
MP	24.0	6	4.0	1	24.0	6	12.0	3
NP	48.0	12	96.0	24	60.0	15	84.0	21
Total	100.0	25	100.0	25	100.0	25	100.0	25
	1977-1978				1978-1979			
	During		End		During		End	
	%	n	%	n	%	n	%	n
CS	20.0	5	4.0	1	4.0	1	4.0	1
MP	12.0	3	8.0	2	28.0	7	4.0	1
NP	68.0	17	88.0	22	68.0	17	92.0	23
Total	100.0	25	100.0	25	100.0	25	100.0	25

CS = clinically significant problem; MP = "mini" problem; NP = no problem.

Table 6 Frequency of Behavior Problems for Winston School's Four-Year Population (Four-Year Prospective Study: n = 25)

	n	Total Number of Problems
No problem	10	0
One problem period	0	0
Two problem periods	8	8 × 2 = 16
Three problem periods	1	1 × 3 = 16
Four problem periods	2	2 × 4 = 8
Five problem periods	2	2 × 5 = 10
Six problem periods	2	2 × 6 = 12
Seven problem periods	0	0
Eight problem periods	0	0
Total	25	52

Average number of problem periods = 2.7.

Table 7 Frequency of Behavior Problems for Winston School's Two Three-Year Populations (Two Three-Year Prospective Studies

	1976-1977–1978-1979 (Not here in 1975-1976) n	1976-1977–1978-1979 (Here in 1975-1976) n
No problem periods	8	10
On problem period	5	6
Two problem periods	2	3
Three problem periods	4	2
Four problem periods	0	3
Five problem periods	2	1
Six problem periods	0	0
Total	21	25
Average number of problem periods	1.5	1.4

Table 8 Percentage of Students with a Clinical Diagnosis of No Problem Having Behavior Problems at Winston Schools

	During School		End of School	
Category of Problem	%	n	%	n
		1975-1976		
Clinically significant	20.0	2	0.0	0
"Mini" problem	10.0	1	0.0	0
No problem	70.0	7	100.0	10
Total	100.0	10	100.0	10
		1976-1977		
Clinically significant	12.5	2	6.2	1
"Mini" problem	18.7	3	0.0	0
No problem	68.8	11	93.8	15
Total	100.0	16	100.0	16
		1977-1978		
Clinically significant	0.0	0	0.0	0
"Mini" problem	5.6	1	5.6	1
No problem	94.4	17	94.4	17
Total	100.0	18	100.0	18
		1978-1979		
Clinically significant	0.0	0	0.0	0
"Mini" problem	5.3	1	0.0	0
No problem	94.7	18	100.0	19
Total	100.0	19	100.0	19

Table 9 Percentage of Students with a Clinical Diagnosis of Hyperactivity (But No Depression) Having Behavior Problems at Winston Schools

	During School		End of School	
Category of Problem	%	n	%	n
	1975-1976			
Clinically significant	33.3	3	11.1	1
"Mini" problem	22.2	2	11.1	1
No problem	44.5	4	77.8	7
Total	100.0	9	100.0	9
	1976-1977			
Clinically significant	9.1	1	0.0	0
"Mini" problem	9.1	1	0.0	0
No problem	81.8	9	100.0	11
Total	100.0	11	100.0	11
	1977-1978			
Clinically significant	41.7	5	0.0	0
"Mini" problem	8.3	1	8.3	1
No problem	50.0	6	91.7	11
Total	100.0	12	100.0	12
	1978-1979			
Clinically significant	10.5	2	5.3	1
"Mini" problem	21.1	4	10.5	2
No problem	68.4	13	84.2	16
Total	100.0	19	100.0	19

displays the frequency and average number of problem periods by diagnosis during school years 1976-1977, 1977-1978, and 1978-1979 (three-year prospective study, n = 46). Students with the clinical diagnosis of hyperactivity *and* depression manifest the greatest number of problem periods (2.7), followed by children with only depression (1.4) before entrance into Winston School, and then by hyperactive children (1.1). The frequency for Winston School students with the diagnosis of no problem manifesting problem periods was minimal (0.6).

These findings support a relationship between clinical diagnosis before entering Winston School and manifestation of behavior problems during attendance at Winston School. The majority of the students fulfill criteria for a positive clinical behavior diagnosis of affective illness (depression) before entering Winston School. The family history of these children is strongly positive for the same condition. Winston School students manifesting no clinical behavior

Table 10 Percentage of Students with a Clinical Diagnosis of Hyperactivity and Depression) Having Behavior Problems at Winston Schools

	During School		End of School	
Category of Problem	%	n	%	n
		1975-1976		
Clinically significant	76.9	10	23.1	3
"Mini" problem	15.4	2	15.4	2
No problem	7.7	1	61.5	8
Total	100.0	13	100.0	13
		1976-1977		
Clinically significant	40.0	6	6.7	1
"Mini" problem	33.3	5	20.0	3
No problem	26.7	4	73.3	11
Total	100.0	15	100.0	15
		1977-1978		
Clinically significant	55.6	10	16.7	3
"Mini" problem	11.1	2	5.5	1
No problem	33.3	6	77.8	14
Total	100.0	18	100.0	18
		1978-1979		
Clinically significant	30.8	8	7.7	2
"Mini" problem	34.6	9	23.1	6
No problem	34.6	9	69.2	18
Total	100.0	26	100.0	26

problem before entering Winston School continue free of behavior problems during their stay. Students fulfilling the criteria for both depression and hyperactivity have a prominent likelihood of manifesting behavior problems at Winston School; these problems are often recurrent over time. This observation strongly suggests a cyclical nature for the manifest clinical problem. Students with only depression or hyperactivity also seem to manifest cyclical problems but with less likelihood of occurrence. For the child who is hyperactive only, there are seemingly fewer problem periods.

The behavior of the general student population at Winston School seems to improve over time (Tables 8-12). It is difficult to define the variables that account for the improvement in the behavior of the students. It is noteworthy that the number of depressed students who are admitted has increased. There is a slight reduction in the number of students admitted who are both hyperactive

Table 11 Percentage of Students with a Clinical Diagnosis of Depression Having Behavior Problems at Winston Schools

	During School		End of School	
Category of Problem	%	n	%	n
		1975-1976		
Clinically significant	29.4	5	0.0	0
"Mini" problem	23.5	4	0.0	0
No problem	47.1	8	100.0	17
Total	100.0	17	100.0	17
		1976-1977		
Clinically significant	16.0	4	0.0	0
"Mini" problem	20.0	5	8.0	2
No problem	64.0	16	92.0	23
Total	100.0	25	100.0	25
		1977-1978		
Clinically significant	29.0	9	12.9	4
"Mini" problem	9.7	3	16.1	5
No problem	61.3	19	71.0	22
Total	100.0	31	100.0	31
		1978-1979		
Clinically significant	14.3	7	6.1	3
"Mini" problem	18.4	9	4.1	2
No problem	67.3	33	89.8	44
Total	100.0	49	100.0	49

and depressed (Tables 2 and 3). It is possible that depression without hyperactivity is less characterized by agitation, irritability, and "acting out" behaviors when compared to depression plus hyperactivity, a predicted antecedent of manic depressive illness. It is also possible that depression in some children is "reactive" or "masked" and not manifested in this education setting relatively "free" of certain stresses.

TREATMENT

Diagnosis of an affective disorder is requisite to initiating appropriate treatment. Empirically, the natural history by retrospective study is similar to that of adults. The average length of a depressive cycle persists from six to 18 months

Table 12 Percentage of Students with a Clinical Diagnosis of "Mini" Depressive Syndrome Having Behavior Problems at Winston Schools

	During School		End of School	
Category of Problem	%	n	%	n
		1975-1976		
Clinically significant	0.0	0	0.0	0
"Mini" problem	33.3	2	0.0	0
No problem	66.7	4	100.0	6
Total	100.0	6	100.0	6
		1976-1977		
Clinically significant	33.3	2	0.0	0
"Mini" problem	0.0	0	0.0	0
No problem	66.7	4	100.0	6
Total	100.0	6	100.0	6
		1977-1978		
Clinically significant	28.6	2	14.3	1
"Mini" problem	0.0	0	0.0	0
No problem	71.4	5	85.7	6
Total	100.0	7	100.0	7
		1978-1979		
Clinically significant	22.2	2	0.0	0
"Mini" problem	0.0	0	0.0	0
No problem	77.8	7	100.0	9
Total	100.0	9	100.0	9

without drug management. Probably less than half of depressive episodes last longer than one year and, by history, some children have been and remain depressed for several years, if not longer.

Thereapy can involve alteration of the enviornment; offering protection and avoidance of inappropriate stresses (Brumback and Weinberg, 1977a; Krueger, 1979; Pearce, 1977); psychotherapy; and medical (drug) therapy. By educating the family to understand the nature of the child's depression, tension over the child's behavior can be reduced. A depressed child should neither be rejected nor punished but should receive increased affection, understanding, protection, supervision, and reassurance. That an exasperating child should receive extra understanding is probably the hardest concept for a family to accept. Teachers must try to reward the depressed child for his successes and not stress his difficulties. He should be allowed to stay in his regular classroom

Table 13 Frequency of Behavior Problems by Clinical Diagnosis for Winston School Years 1976-1977, 1977-1978, and 1978-1979 (Three-Year Prospective Study: n = 46)

	Clinical Diagnosis				
Problem Periods	Total	Problem	Hyperactivity Only	Depression Only	Hyperactivity and Depression
No problem periods	18	8	3	7	0
One problem period	11	1	2	6	2
Two problem periods	5	1	0	2	2
Three problem periods	6	0	2	1	3
Four problem periods	3	1	0	1	1
Five problem periods	3	0	0	2	1
Six problem periods	0	0	0	0	0
Total	46	11	7	19	9
Average number of problem periods	1.4	.6	1.1	1.4	2.7

pursuing his assets and avoiding social peer group isolation and unproven remedial, tutorial programs. Social workers, counselors, psychiatrists, and other physicians must be supportive of the depressed child. Medical therapy generally should avoid hospitalization, except occasionally for protection and for initiation of drug therapy. Hospitalization can result in isolation, emotional deprivation, and be viewed by the child as further punishment and rejection.

Proper management involves treatment, support, reassurance, protection, avoidance of confrontations, and supervision by parents, teachers, and friends, both at home and at school. Specific school curriculum should emphasize the developmental "bypass" strategies for success in classroom tasks (Weinberg, 1975, 1979). The children are encouraged to pursue their socially acceptable assets, skills, and interests. The children are reassured that they will recover and that parents, friends, teachers and physicians will offer the needed support through the recovery period. Since judgement is poor during a period of depression, supervision and protection while pursuing assets in the usual living environments are important. Punishment, often tried by parents and teachers in the past, is not successful and can be prevented through appropriate attitudes and proper environmental planning by parents and teachers.

Drug management for the treatment of depression in children remains controversial, as does the understanding that depression as a primary illness occurs in children. Medication, appropriately prescribed, can be very useful. Stimulants, frequently tried in "hyperactive" children and occasionally used as part of the treatment of adult depression, such as methylphenidate and dextroamphetamine, have the advantage of an immediate positive effect in reducing the depression. However, the disadvantage of stimulants is that their effect is of relatively short duration and tolerance develops, requiring larger doses with less effectiveness (Beck, 1973; Freedman et al, 1975). In children, one positive effect of stimulants is to reduce hyperactivity; however, stimulants worsen the depressive symptoms of agitation, irritability, crying spells, insomnia, and poor appetite. The major tranquilizers (phenothiazines) reduce agitation and anxiety but have little effect on other aspects of the depression.

The best and most specific medications for depression at the present time are the tricyclic drugs of which imipramine and amitriptyline are the prototypes (Freedman et al, 1975; Rapoport, 1976). These drugs alleviate depressive symptoms in over 90 percent of children (Brumback and Weinberg, 1977a; Frommer, 1968; Ossofsky, 1974; Puig-Antich et al, 1975; Weinberg et al, 1973).

The tricyclic antidepressant medications have not been approved by the United States Food and Drug Administration (FDA) for use in children under 12 years of age, except for imipramine in enuresis. Yet, several empirical studies and observations (Brumback et al, 1977; Brumback and Weinberg, 1977c; DeLong, 1978; Frommer, 1968; Kuhn and Kuhn, 1972; Puig-Antich et al, 1978; Weinberg et al, 1973) have demonstrated significant benefit. Clinically, it has been observed that the tricyclic group of drugs is both safe and beneficial in the lifting of the child's depression and often in preventing further cycles.

This group of drugs is beneficial in alleviating dysphoric mood, self-deprecation, somatic complaints, sleep disturbances, and restoring energy and interest. Decreased aggressiveness follows later. In some children coincident administration of a major tranquilizer may reduce the aggressiveness and agitation more rapidly. Improvement is noted in three to 14 days as therapeutic dosage is achieved. A phenothiazine or haloperidol is sometimes needed for control of the irritability and agitation and for complete stabilization of mood.

The dosage range for the tricyclic antidepressant medications in children remains empirical. Generally, benefit is noted when dosage is 1 to 3 mg/kg per day and not exceeding 150 mg per day in the heavier, older adolescent. The FDA has recommended for experimental and research purposes not to exceed 5 mg/kg of body weight for 24-hour periods (Hayes et al, 1975). The FDA has also advised baseline and serial electrocardiograms when dosage approaches 5 mg/kg per day in order to prevent cardiac arrhythmias and cardiac conductive problems that are known to occur with high doses and overdosage of the tricyclics (Hayes et al, 1975; Martin and Zaug, 1975; Petit and Biggs, 1977; Winsberg et al, 1975).

The most commonly used tricyclics, amitriptyline, followed by imipramine and the desipramine, is offered on a trial-and-error basis as follows: (1) Two to five years of age: 20 to 50 mg per day with two-thirds to three-quarters of the total dose given at bedtime; (2) six to 11 years of age: 50 to 100 mg per day with two-thirds to three-quarters of the total dose given at bedtime; and (3) 12 to 15 years of age (depending upon physical maturity and size: 50 to 150 mg per day with two-thirds to three-quarters of the total dose given at bedtime.

A trial dose of a small amount of tricyclic, for example 20 to 50 mg at bedtime depending upon age and size, is given during the first week with maximum dosage as stated above achieved within two to three weeks after the start of medication.

Dosage schedule for the commonly used phenothiazines, thioridazine or chlorpromazine, is 30 to 60 mg in three to four divided doses per day in the three- to six-year-old child. For older school age children and young adolescents the usual dosage is 50 to 150 mg per day in three to four divided doses. Haloperidol dosage ranges between 1 and 4 mg per day in three to four divided doses. Haloperidol is used if a phenothiazine is not successful in controlling the manic component or agitation.

Maximum dosage for a tricyclic (for example, imipramine) should be achieved within two to three weeks with improvement above the 50 percent level noted shortly thereafter with or without the addition of a phenothiazine. If improvement does not occur, a trial on the second tricyclic (for example, amitriptyline) is then offered using a similar schedule with the same expectations. If this is not successful within another two to four weeks, then desipramine or nortriptyline is offered. It is recommended that amitriptyline should be tried first, followed by imipramine, then desipramine, and finally nortriptyline. Of course, time is passing and depression in most possibly lifts without specific management in six to 18 months. In choosing a tricyclic to offer, it is helpful if another family member has been successfully managed with tricyclic drugs. It is statistically predictable, though not always clinically, that family members respond favorably to the same tricyclic (Baldessarini, 1975; Bielski and Friedel, 1976).

Fifty percent improvmeent is defined as the child is able to participate in his usual environments but still manifests symptoms of depression as observed by either or both parents, teachers, and friends. Sixty to 70 percent improvement is defined as when the child's performance is approaching his usual non-depressed self, functioning satisfactorily in his usual endeavors but still having "too many moments" of the depressive symptomatology. Eighty percent improvement is defined as complete restoration of the child to his usual pre-depressed state. By direct interview, though, the recovered child may continue to have depressed feelings, but they are "not too much" by the child's own estimation. A responder to a given tricyclic antidepressant medication with or without a phenothiazine should achieve an 80 percent level of improvement in one to three months.

Telephone calls from the parent at three to ten-day intervals during the initial treatment period are helpful to allow knowledge of response, change in dosage or medication, and observation for adverse effects. It is the experience of the author that serious side effects are rare for the dosage listed above. A rash in one patient and hypertension in a second have been noted in a large cohort of tricyclic-treated children and young adolescents. Constipation, hesitancy and difficulty in voiding, dizziness suggesting orthostatic hypotension, and uncomfortable dry mouth are likewise rare in children and young adolescents. Acceptable adverse effects are a mild intentional tremor and a mild tachcardia.

Worsening behavior occurs with tricyclics in specific or general drug non-responders. Increased dysphoria, agitation, and/or sedation are evident within several days. Also, tricyclics can worsen or trigger an episode of mania suggesting a bipolar illness, manic depressive disease.

Dyskinesias have not been noted in children and young adolescents with the above schedule of phenothiazines. Undue sedation, worsening of behavior, and even promotion of manic-like behavior have been observed in depressed children on phenothiazines. Rashes are uncommon (rare) as a hepatic toxicity.

Severe dyskinesia, as an idiosyncratic reaction, can occur within one to five days after beginning haloperidol. This reaction is an emergency and is alleviated with intravenous diphenhydramine, 25 to 50 mg.

Until the medication is discontinued, a depressed child is seen at monthly intervals for office examination with emphasis on the affective symptomatology and physical examination. Since depression is a recurrent illness, routine visits at six to 12-month intervals after full recovery are advised.

The beneficial drug regimen is continued until the child has been asymptomatic for a period of three to six months. The child is then weaned from the medication over a period of one to three months. There is a subgroup of depressed children who seemingly remain asymptomatic only if a maintenance dose of tricyclic is continued at bedtime for an indefinite period of time.

Treatment of the rarer manic syndrome often requires hospitalization for protection, supervision, and family relief. Youngerman and Canino (1978) have reviewed the literature on the use of lithium carbonate in treating mania in children and adolescents. Recent reports (Brumback and Weinberg, 1977c; DeLong, 1978; Frommer, 1968; Weinberg and Brumback, 1976; White and O'Shanick, 1977a) have suggested the benefit of lithium carbonate, but it has not been approved by the FDA for use in children under 12 years of age. Control of the mania with lithium is sometimes followed by a depressive cycle and the addition of a tricyclic antidepressant medication is helpful in that group of manic children, again suggesting a bipolar illness.

Phenothiazines and haloperidol, in the dosage schedule described above, are other drugs clinically beneficial in the control of manic behavior in some children. At this point in time, though, there remains an absence of controlled studies in the treatment and course of mania in children.

NEEDS FOR FUTURE STUDY

Further replication and refinement of the research cited in this chapter is essential to validate the diagnostic criteria for primary affective illness(es) in children.

Pursuit of physiological and biochemical correlates of primary affective illness should be encouraged. Epidemiological studies should be conducted in populations of school children to determine the percent variance of school problems that are represented by primary affective illness. Studies relating to the controversy of genetics versus environment need major emphasis in defining both its cause, natural course, and beneficial treatment. It is possible that developmental specific learning disorders are a genetic marker of affective illness and/or an epiphenomenon of "school problems." Longitudinal studies are needed to determine the natural history of the illness, its incidence, and prevalence.

Investigation of the response of this criteria-specific illness to antidepressant medication and other methods of treatment is urgently indicated. More specific differentiation of subgroups of children with primary and/or secondary depression, manic depressive illness, and hyperactivity might be possible thus allowing the most successful method for prevention and treatment to become known and implemented.

SUMMARY

Diagnosis and treatment of affective illness, possibly primary, in children has been reviewed in this chapter. Criteria for the diagnosis of this condition in children has been presented. This criteria, based upon the adult criteria with select modification, has been utilized in diagnosing affective illness in children and young adolescents referred to educational diagnostic centers because of school-related learning or behavior problems.

School skills of children with affective illness do not differ from other children in the referred population. Evaluation of intelligence and learning disabilities indicates no difference between groups with or without depression. It is evident that school behavior problems result, at least in part, from a cyclical behavior disturbance, possibly as a manifestation of primary affective illness.

Proper management of the child's environment and specific drug treatment are recommended. Results from a prospective study of children with developmental specific learning disorders attending school in an ideal environment indicate that, in a large subgroup, affective illness occurs and seems to be recurrent. Most at risk are children who manifest both hyperactivity and depression.

Clinically, hyperactive children whose behaviors, mood, and feelings are worsened by stimulant medication are probably only significantly hyperactive when depressed. This may be an antecedent of "bipolar" manic depressive disease. It may be that some children fulfilling the critiera for depression are depressed secondary to inappropriate schooling, or that appropriate schooling is "masking" their depression.

Affective illness, possibly primary, is a common cause of school-related behavior problems in children. The majority of children manifesting the disturbed behavior characteristic of affective illness are infrequently recognized and offered beneficial treatment. They are shunned by schools, families, and friends, often receiving inadequate education as social outcasts (Poznanski et al, 1976). From this group of chronically rejected, depressed children probably emerge the individuals who, during a further depressive (or manic) episode as young adults, are involved in self-destructive and antisocial acts. Early detection and appropriate treatment of children with affective illness will hopefully prevent their school and personal failure, social withdrawal, antisocial activity, and suicide (Brumback and Weinberg, 1977a, b).

REFERENCES

Baldessarini RJ. Bases for amine hypothesis in affective sideorders: critical evaluation. *Arch Gen Psychiatry* 1975; 32:1087–1093.

Barcai A. Predicting the response of children with learning disabilities and behavior problems to dextroamphetamine sulfate. *Pediatrics* 1971; 47: 73–80.

Beck AT. *The diagnosis and management of depression*. Philadelphia: University of Pennsylvania Press, 1973.

Bielski R, Friedel R. Prediction of tricyclic antidepressant response–a critical review. *Arch Gen Psychiatry* 1976; 33:1479–1489.

Brumback RA, Weinberg WA. Childhood depression: an explanation of a behavior disorder of children. *Percept Mot Skills* 1977a; 44:911–916.

Brumback RA, Weinberg WA. Relationship of hyperactivity and depression in children. *Percept Mot Skills* 1977b; 45:247–251.

Brumback RA, Weinberg WA. Mania in childhood II. Therapeutic trial of lithium carbonate and further description of manic-depressive illness in children. *Am J Dis Child* 1977c; 131:1122–1126.

Carlson GA, Goodwin FR. The stages of mania: a longitudinal analysis of the manic episode. *Arch Gen Psychiatry* 1973; 28:221–228.

Delong GR. Lithium carbonate treatment of select behavior disorders in children suggesting manic-depressive illness. *J Pediatr* 1978; 93:689–694.

Eisenberg L. The management of the hyperactive child. *Dev Med Child Neurol* 1966; 8:593–598.

Feighner JP, Robins E, Guze SB, et al. Diagnostic criteria for use in psychiatric research. *Arch Gen Psychiatry* 1972; 26:57–63.

Fish B. The "one child, one drug" myth of stimulants in hyperkinesis. *Arch Gen Psychiatry* 1971; 25:193–203.

Freedman AM, Kaplan HI, Sadock BJ, eds. *Comprehensive textbook of psychiatry*. 2nd ed. Baltimore: Williams & Wilkins, 1975.

Frommer EA. Depressive illness in childhood. Recent developments in affective disorders. Coppen A, Walk A, eds. *Br J Psychiatry* special publication 1968; 2:117–136.

Hayes T, Panitch M, Barker E. Imipramine dosage in children: a comment on "Imipramine and electrocardiographic abnormalities in hyperactive children." *Am J Psychiatry* 1975; 132:546–547.

Kenny T, Clemmens R, Hudson B, et al. Characteristics of children referred because of hyperactivity. *J Pediatr* 1971; 79:618–622.

Kotin J, Goodwin FK. Depression during mania: Clinical observations and theoretical implications. *Am J Psychiatry* 1972; 129:679–686.

Kovacs M, Beck AT. An emprical-clinical approach toward a definition of childhood depression. In: Schulterbrandt JG, Raskin A, eds. *Depression in childhood: diagnosis, treatment, and conceptual models*. New York: Raven Press, 1977:1–25.

Krueger DW. The depressed patient. *J Fam Pract* 1979; 8:363–370.

Kuhn V, Kuhn R. Drug therapy for depression in children. In: Annell AL, ed. *Depressive states in childhood and adolescence*. New York: Halsted Press, 1972:455–459.

Malmquist CP. Childhood depression: a clinical and behavioral perspective. In: Schulterbrandt JG, Raskin A, eds. *Depression in childhood: diagnosis, treatment, and conceptual models*. New York: Raven Press, 1977:33–59.

Martin G, Zaug P. Electrocardiographic monitoring of enuretic children receiving therapeutic doses of imipramine. *Am J Psychiatry* 1975; 132:540–542.

Ossofsky H. Endogenous depression in infancy and childhood. *Compre Psychiatry* 1974; 15:19–25.

Pearce JB. Annotation: depressive disorder in children. *J Child Psychol Psychiatry* 1977; 18:79–82.

Petit J, Biggs J. Tricyclic antidepressant overdose in adolescent patients. *Pediatrics* 1977; 59:283–287.

Poznanski E, Krahenbuhl V, Zrull J. Childhood depression. *J Am Acad Child Psychiatry* 1976; 15:491–501.

Puig-Antich MD, Blau S, Marx N, et al. Prepubertal major depressive disorder. *J Am Acad Child Psychiatry* 1978; 17:695–707.

Rapoport JL. Psychopharmacology of childhood depression. In: Klein DF, Gittleman-Klein R, eds. *Progress in psychiatric drug treatment*. New York: Brunner/Mazel 2, 1976:493–505.

Rideau A. Les etats depressifs du debile profond jeune. In: Annel A-L, ed. *Depressive states in childhood and adolescence*. Stockholm: Almqvist and Wiksell, 1971:126–132.

Smith RT, Smith WJ, Smith LM. *M-G Percepts no. 6*. Spring Valley, New York, 1977.

Weinberg W. Delayed symbol language skills and their relationship to school performance. In: Swaiman K, Wright F, eds. *The practice of pediatric neurology*. St. Louis: The C. V. Mosby Co, 1975:898–911.

Weinberg WA. Winston School Report No. 1 to the Professional Advisory Board, July 27, 1979.

Weinberg W, Brumback R. Mania in childhood. case studies and literature review. *Am J Dis Child* 1976; 130:380–385.
Weinberg W, Rutman J, Sullivan L, et al. Depression in children referred to an educational diagnostic center: diagnosis and treatment. *J Pediatr* 1973; 83:1065–1073.
Werry JS. Developmental hyperactivity. *Pediatr Clin North Am* 1968; 15: 581–599.
White JH, O'Shanick G. Juvenile manic-depressive illness. *Am J Psychiatry* 1977a; 134:9–12.
Winokur G, Clayton P, Reich T. *Manic depressive illness*. St. Louis: The C. V. Mosby Co, 1969.
Winsberg B, Goldstein S, Yepes L, Perel J. Imipramine and electrocardiographic abnormalities in hyperactive children. *Am J Psychiatry* 1975; 132:542–545.
Youngman J, Canino I. Lithium carbonate use in children and adolescents. *Arch Gen Psychiatry* 35:216–224.

Affective Disorders in Childhood and Adolescence--
An Update. Edited by D.P. Cantwell and G.A. Carlson.

8

School Refusal: A Depressive Equivalent?

Miriam Tisher

Descriptions of school refusal vary from paper to paper, but generally refer to fairly dramatic inability or unwillingness by the child to attend school, clinging to home and/or parent(s), separation anxiety, intense ambivalence, concern over death or loss, etc. Frequently, fear of teacher(s), anxiety over school performance, and rejection by friends at school are cited by children and families as "the cause," but most writers on school refusal explain it as family-related or associated (Cooper, 1966; McDnald and Sheperd, 1976; Waldron et al, 1975).

The literature on childhood depression has increased over the last ten to 15 years and although there is still some debate regarding whether or not it is a "syndrome" or "symptom" and regarding its specific qualities, there is general movement towards agreement that some children are in fact depressed and pragmatic moves to measuring depression are being made (Kovacs, 1980/81).

Looking at the two bodies of literature–that on school refusal and that on childhood depression over the last two decades–interesting similarities are apparent. With respect to both, there has been a debate which centered on whether they refer to syndromes or symptoms; with respect to both there has been challenge as to the reality of the sets of behaviors as separate entities with distinct clinical meaning or relevance. In following both sets of literature, we see increasing consensus as to the syndrome nature of the behaviors in question.

The relationship between school refusal and depression is far from clear. It has been explicitly written about in one study (Agras, 1959), referred to in some detail in some (Baker and Wills, 1978; Davidson, 1961; McDonald and Sheperd, 1976; Waldron et al, 1975) and discussed in terms of antidepressant medication, for example, imipramine, on others (Gittelman-Klein, 1975; Gittelman-Kelin and Kelin, 1973). Some writers (Cytryn and McKnew, 1974; Glaser, 1967; Sperling, 1959; Toolan, 1962) have described school refusal as one of many behaviors which are depressive equivalents–avenues which the child uses to give expression to his/her depression which is otherwise generally masked.

At the same time, reviews of school phobia such as that by Gordon and Young (1976) makes no mention of depression.

This chapter draws on data from a study carried out in 1970 where a severe school refusing group was compared with a group of regular attenders (Lang, 1974; Tisher, 1974; Lang et al, unpublished). Some of the specific links between depression and school refusal are drawn out and discussed.

THE STUDY

The Group

School refusal was defined operationally as referring to children aged nine to 16 years who:

1. were not attending school and had been continually absent for more than one month;
2. during school hours would stay mainly at home or with their parents;
3. had no diagnosed organic or physical illness as the reason for non-attendance (commonly recognized psychosomatic symptoms such as headaches were not regarded as illness);
4. for at least two weeks had had attempts made unsuccessfully by appropriate agencies to help them return to school.

The control group consisted of regular school attenders, namely children who had not missed more than ten school days during the year which was nearing completion.

The groups were matched for age, sex, and particular school, grade, or form. Matching for school and form was intended both to control the variable of school environment and its possible contribution to school refusal (Eysenck and Rachman, 1965) and to provide some degree of matching of socioeconomic status through geographical area (Lancaster-Jones, 1969).

Sampling

School Refusing Group

All known treatment and educational guidance agencies in Melbourne, Australia, a city of 2.5 million with approximately 348,000 children, were approached and requested to supply details of all school refusing children known to them who were aged nine years and over (nine years was used as the lower age limit because children under this age would have difficulty in comprehending the tests used). The investigators examined these details and identified 41 cases who met the above criteria. The family of each child was approached and requested to cooperate. Of the 41 families, 40 cooperated. Of these, 13 (30 percent) were not attending clinics or agencies at the time of the investigation.

Of the 40 families, 39 were of Anglo-Saxon background with all children born in Australia. The remaining family was Yugoslavian and came to Australia in 1957.

Regular Attenders

The schools of all school refusing children were approached and for each school refusing child, headmasters were requested to supply names, addresses, and telephone numbers (if any) of three children who had not missed more than ten school days in 1970, whose birthdays were closest to a specified date of birth (that of the matched school refusing child), who were of the same sex as the school refuser, and who were in the same grade or form as the school refuser was, or would have been, in 1970.

Thirty-seven control group families were approached and 32 agreed to participate immediately. Of the five others, two families were rejected because they had insufficient English and three did not agree to cooperate. In these five cases, the second family on the list supplied by the headmaster cooperated.

The control group consisted exclusively of Australian-born children and in all cases their parents were of Anglo-Saxon origin.

Measures

It was considered important to look at a range of personality variables, as well as anxiety and depression in particular. Anxiety was identified because of the particular centrality ascribed to anxiety and separation anxiety by many writers (Eisenberg, 1958; Johnson et al, 1941; Johnson, 1955; Goldenberg and Goldenberg, 1970; Gordon and Young, 1976; Jackson, 1964; McDonald and Sheperd, 1976; Waldron et al, 1975); depression because it had been noted by several writers (see above) and because of the writer's considerable clinical experience which consistently pointed up the significance of depression in the school refusing children and their families.

Personality Variables

Three scales from the Institute of Personality and Ability Testing (IPAT) were used–the 16 Personality Factors (16 PF) (adult) (Cattell, 1970), the High School Personality Questionnaire (HSPQ) (12 to 18 years) (Cattell, 1969), and the Children's Personality Questionnaire (CPQ) (under 12 years) (Cattell, 1959). The three forms yield scores on a series of first order and second order factors regarding a number of personality variables and are comparable across the age ranges of children and adults.

All first order factors common to both the CPQ and HSPQ, the second order factors of introversion and anxiety, and the criterion measure of neuroticism were used.

Anxiety

Anxiety was further tested by Sarason's General Anxiety (GA) and Test Anxiety (TA) scales. These are self-report questionnaires with items such as "Do you worry whether your mother is going to get sick?," and "Are you frightened by lightning and thunder storms?."

Depression

The Childrens Depression Scale (Lang and Tisher, 1978) and the Childrens Depression Scale–Adult Form were used. These measures are described fully in another chapter of this book and are self-report for the child, using cards and boxes in a game format. The Adult Form require parents and/or others to report their perceptions of the child.

Family Perceptions

The test used was the Family Relations Test of Bene and Anthony (1957). The results were assessed on the basis of the number of positive and negative messages sent to the family members and on a score for paternal overprotection and maternal overindulgence.

FINDINGS

The School Refusing Group

There were 25 boys and 15 girls. The average age of the children was 13 years and one month; the range was 9 to 16 years. The children had been absent from school for an average of 10.3 months: 17 children (42.5 percent) for less than three months and 12 (30 percent) for more than 12 months.

Seventeen children (42.5 percent) showed a sudden onset to the school refusing behavior, while for the remaining 23 children the onset was gradual. A sudden onset was more frequent among girls than boys ($p < 0.01$).

Fourteen children (35 percent) showed severe separation difficulties–the child "hardly ever leaves home or mother." Ten (25 percent) showed moderate difficulties, and six (15 percent) mild difficulties. In ten (25 percent), little or no separation difficulties could be ascertained.

Table 1 Length of Continuous Absence from School

Months	Boys	Girls	Total
1–3	11	6	17
4–6	4	3	7
7–12	2	2	4
13–23	1	3	4
24+	7	1	8
Totals	25	15	40
Average years, months	11.3	8.4	10.3

Table 2 Pattern of Onset of School Refusal

Type of Onset	Boys	Girls	Total
a. The child was always happy at school and there is no history of academic or social problems. The school refusal is *sudden*.	5	9	14
b. Sudden onset to an episode previous to the current one. After an absence from school the child returns and the readjustment appears relatively good until a relapse occurs. Alternatively, there may be spasmodic attendance subsequent to the first episode, leading to complete nonattendance again.	1	2	3
c. Gradual escalation of the problem: the child over a period of at least two years is unhappy about school, reluctant to attend, and suddenly stops attending.	5	1	6
d. Similar to (c), ie, gradual escalation of the problem, but there is spasmodic attendance building up to complete nonattendance.	6	3	9
e. Chronic problem with continued irregular attendance and poor adjustment since the child began school.	8	0	8
Totals	25	15	40
Onset Categories			
Sudden (a & b)	6	11	17
Gradual (c, d, e)	19	4	23
Totals	25	15	40

$\chi^2 = 9.337$, $p < 0.01$.

Table 3 Separation Behavior, School Refusing Children

	Boys	Girls	Total
Child hardly ever leaves home or mother	5	9	14
Child occasionally goes out only when accompanied by a limited number of familiar people	9	1	10
Child goes out by himself to a limited number of familiar places, or child goes accompanied to a wide variety of places	3	3	6
Child goes almost everywhere by himself, but with some difficulties	0	0	0
Child could go almost anywhere without any difficulty	4	2	6
Child leaves home without parents' consent for short periods of time	4	0	4
Child frequently leaves home for long periods of time without parents' consent	0	0	0
	25	15	40

Comparison of School Refusers and Regular Attenders

The families of school refusers were on the average larger, particularly the boys' families.

Fathers and mothers of school refusers were older than fathers and mothers in the control group. Seventeen fathers and ten mothers were over 50 in the school refusing group, compared with two fathers and one mother, respectively, in the regular attenders group. The school refusers had fewer years of completed education than the regular attenders, probably because of their poor attendance. The fathers and mothers of school refusing children had fewer years of education and the fathers were of lower occupational status than their counterparts in the families of regular attenders. Using scores on Factor B of the IPAT scale as an indication of level of intelligence, children, mothers, and fathers in the school refusing group obtained lower scores.

The two groups did not differ with regard to whether mother was working, nor were there any discernible trends regarding ordinal position in the family.

Among the school refusers, one mother and one father had died; among the regular attenders, one father had died. However, in the school refusing group ten fathers were separated from their wives and their children; in the regularly attending group one mother only was similarly separated. This difference is significant ($p < 0.01$).

Table 4 Comparison of the School Refusing and Regularly Attending Groups on Social and Family Variables

Characteristics		School refusing group (n = 40) $\bar{x}$	SD	Regularly attending group (n = 37) $\bar{x}$	SD	
Number of children in the family	Total	4.00	2.42	3.11	1.01	< 0.05
	Boys	4.52	2.51	3.27	1.21	< 0.05
	Girls	3.00	2.32	2.87	1.11	NS
Age of father		48.62	8.66	43.70	8.12	< 0.001
Age of mother		45.46	7.22	38.60	7.29	< 0.001
Level of intelligence[a]	Child	4.46	1.72	6.03	1.39	< 0.01
	Mother	5.33	1.27	6.43	1.31	< 0.05
	Father	4.41	1.75	6.56	2.31	< 0.05
Number of years completed education	Child	6.30	1.36	7.16	1.59	< 0.001
	Mother	7.79	1.66	8.74	2.55	< 0.05
	Father	7.97	2.36	10.80	2.96	< 0.001
Occupational status[b] of father		3.52	1.57	2.19	1.53	< 0.001

[a]On the basis of score obtained by subjects on Factor B of the pertinent IPAT Scales (for father school refusal group, n = 17; regularly attending group n = 25).
[b]According to occupational categories taken from Krupinski and Stoller (1968): 1 = highest, 5 = lowest occupation.

Comparison of School Refusers and Regular Attenders on Measures Used

Personality Factors

Scores on the IPAT Scales show that seven of 13 first order factors and all three second order factors (neuroticism, anxiety, and extraversion) differentiated between the two groups of children and that four of the first order factors and one of the second order factors discriminated between the groups of mothers.

Table 5 Fathers' Absence from Home–Frequency Table

	Father absent from home	Father present at home	Total
School refusing	11	29	40
Regularly attending	1	36	37
	12	65	77

$\chi^2 = 8.984$, $p < 0.01$.

Table 6 Differences between School Refusing and Regular Attending Children on Personality Factors (IPAT Scale) (Cattell, 1959; 1969)

IPAT factor	School refusing group $\bar{x}$ score	School refusing group SD	Regularly attending group $\bar{x}$ score	Regularly attending group SD	p Value (Wilcoxon matched pairs)
First order					
A	4.2	1.9	5.51	1.64	< 0.01
B	4.5	1.72	6.02	1.38	< 0.01
C	4.98	2.07	6.00	2.54	NS
D	5.9	2.01	5.59	2.07	NS
E	4.5	1.96	6.46	1.99	< 0.01
F	4.57	2.13	5.70	1.89	< 0.01
G	5.02	2.09	5.70	2.23	NS
H	3.82	2.20	6.76	1.94	< 0.01
I	5.2	2.22	5.02	2.03	NS
J	6.55	2.04	5.21	1.69	< 0.01
O	6.12	2.12	4.86	2.04	< 0.01
Q_3	4.42	1.78	5.24	1.89	NS
Q_4	6.42	1.92	5.92	1.91	NS
Second order					
Extraversion	4.06	2.02	6.09	2.00	< 0.01
Anxiety	6.02	2.14	5.35	2.09	< 0.05
Neuroticism	6.28	1.66	4.96	1.82	< 0.01

Anxiety

The school refusing children are more anxious than the regular attenders both on the IPAT second order factor of Anxiety (Table 6) and on the results of the General Anxiety and Text Anxiety Scales (Table 8).

Depression

The results of the Childrens Depression Scale and Childrens Depression Scale–Adult Form show that the school refusing children were more depressed than the regular attenders both on their self-report and on the assessment of their mothers.

There is a wide disparity between the mean Childrens Depression Scale and Childrens Depression Scale–Adult Form scores in the regularly attending group but not in the school refusing group. This discrepancy is elaborated upon in the Discussion section later.

Family Perceptions

School refusing children sent a greater number of messages in the Bene and Anthony test to their mothers, both positive and negative, than did the regular

Table 7 Comparison of Mothers of School Refuers and Mothers of Regular Attenders of the 16 Personality Factors (C Form) (Cattell, 1970)

IPAT factor	School refusing group		Regularly attending group		p Value (Wilcoxon matched pairs)
	x̄ score	SD	x̄ score	SD	
First order					
M.D.	4.85	2.09	4.60	2.11	NS
A	5.26	1.92	4.14	1.76	< 0.05
B	5.33	1.27	6.43	1.31	< 0.01
C	5.26	1.55	6.70	1.47	NS
E	6.10	1.96	5.76	2.30	NS
F	4.85	1.70	5.35	1.88	NS
G	4.95	1.92	5.24	2.20	NS
H	5.95	2.15	5.70	2.46	NS
I	5.70	1.88	5.76	1.53	NS
L	5.49	1.81	6.03	1.53	NS
M	4.28	1.95	4.51	1.75	NS
N	5.33	1.82	6.14	1.73	NS
O	5.00	2.04	5.14	1.69	NS
Q_1	5.46	1.81	6.57	1.85	< 0.05
Q_2	5.00	1.93	5.90	1.86	< 0.05
Q_3	5.36	2.13	4.78	1.36	NS
Q_4	5.82	2.11	5.54	1.87	NS
Second order					
Extraversion	5.70	1.68	4.72	1.28	< 0.05
Anxiety	5.58	1.24	5.36	1.43	NS
Cortertia	6.04	1.56	5.87	1.56	NS
Neuroticism	5.83	1.55	5.71	1.21	NS

attenders (significant for the total and a trend for both positive and negative messages separately).

There were no differences in messages sent to fathers, "Mr. Nobody," or self. However, school refusing children showed greater levels of maternal and paternal overprotection and overindulgence.

Table 8 Comparison of Scores in School Refusers and Regularly Attending Group on Sarason's Test Anxiety and General Anxiety Scales (Sarason et al, 1960)

	School refusing group (n = 40)		Regular attending group (n = 37)		p Value (Wilcoxon matched pairs)
	x̄ score	SD	x̄ score	SD	
Specific measures					
Test anxiety	13.02	7.11	8.81	6.40	0.025
General anxiety	14.10	5.86	11.65	7.08	0.05

Table 9 Scores for CDS and CDS–Adult Form for School Refusers and Regularly Attending Groups

Measure	School refusing group		Regularly attending group		
	$\bar{x}$ score	SD	$\bar{x}$ score	SD	p Value
CDS	157.0	28.3	116.9	35.3	< 0.00
CDS– adult form	159.7	24.5	102.8	18.3	< 0.00
	(Ch. N = 40)		(Ch. N = 37)		(37 pairs)
	(Mo. N = 39)		(Mo. N = 36)		(36 pairs)

CDS = Children's Depression Scale.

Table 10 Comparison of School Refusing and Regularly Attending Groups on the Bene and Anthony Family Relations Test

Items		School refusing (n = 31) $\bar{x}$ score	Regularly attending (n = 25) $\bar{x}$ score	p Value (*t* test, one tail)
Sent to mother	Positive	9.81	7.44	< 0.10
	Negative	2.65	2.2	NS
	Total	12.52	9.52	< 0.05
Sent to father	Positive	5.48	6.16	NS
	Negative	3.52	2.6	NS
	Total	9.00	8.68	NS
Sent to "Mr. Nobody"	Positive	13.29	15.8	NS
	Negative	13.90	16.08	NS
	Total	35.90	42.88	< 0.10
Sent to self	Positive	0.58	0.48	NS
	Negative	1.29	1.48	NS
	Total	5.06	3.56	< 0.10
Maternal and paternal overprotection and overindulgence		3.39	1.6	< 0.005

A PROFILE OF SCHOOL REFUSING CHILDREN

School refusing children have been absent from school for nearly 12 months; their school refusal was a little more likely to have had a gradual onset and they probably have difficulties separating from home and parents. They are likely to have come from a large family with older parents, their family tends to be of lower socioeconomic status and they are likely to have completed fewer years of education than their regularly attending counterparts from the same school. Both the school refusing children and their parents may demonstrate a lower level of intelligence. They are much more likely to come from a family where the parents do not live together.

They differ from their regularly attending counterparts by being more anxious, depressed and more involved with their mothers; they see themselves as overprotected and overindulged by their mothers and fathers. They are more introverted, neurotic, reserved, submissive, guilt-prone, shy, sober, and internally restrained. Their mothers are more extroverted or likely to seek social contact than are the mothers of their regularly attending mate, but otherwise there are not many personality differences between the mothers of the two groups.

This finding of relatively little difference between mothers in the two groups is not consistent with most reports in the literature (Agras, 1959; Jackson, 1964; Johnson et al, 1941). Clinical experience of pathology in families of children who refuse school is difficult to measure using personality scales. On the other hand, an explanation consistent with the recent systems theory view of school refusal, is that while children are refusing school as a symptom of family dysfunction, other members of the family (in this case mothers) are able to remain symptom-free. This explanation fits with the author's clinical experience of working with families of school refusing children. As different members of the child's family are able to experience and share their distress, the child's symptoms are reduced and he/she becomes able to return to school. Investigators who have found similar patterns include Firestone et al (1978), Hawkes (1981), and, in a more general sense, Framo (1972).

There are other inconsistencies between the findings of this study and those of other studies. School refusal was operationally defined so as to preclude mild/transient symptomatology, and sampling was not limited to children and families in contact with helping or psychiatric agencies. Thus, there were more children with gradual onset, from larger families, with lower levels of socioeconomic status education and intelligence.

The importance of sampling in studying school phobia has also been noted by Hampe et al (1973). They report that, provided the sample size is large enough and in the absence of economic barriers to treatment, the distribution of intelligence among school phobic children is similar to that in the general population. This finding also contradicts many reports in the literature that school refusing children have a high level of intelligence (Eisenberg, 1958; Talbot, 1957; Coolidge et al, 1964; Adams et al, 1966). Hampe et al describe their sample as representing "the population of school phobic children whose parents are willing to seek help"; thus, the sample being described is still not a direct sampling of the population of persons with the disorder, as is the sample described in this chapter.

In contrast to general claims in the literature (Johnson et al, 1941; Waldron et al, 1975), a substantial minority of children (25 percent) showed little or no separation difficulties.

DISCUSSION

There is no doubt from the profile of the school refusing child that he/she is anxious, overprotected, overindulged, and depressed, among other things. The finding of anxiety is not new; anxiety has been associated with school refusal by many writers, since Johnson (1941) identified school phobia as equivalent to separation anxiety. Depression in children has been variously defined in the literature, but much of the recent literature in particular has focused upon overt expressions of depression (Kovacs, 1980; Poznanski and Zrull, 1970; Sandler and Joffe, 1965). Thus, if a child looks miserable or weepy, if he/she has social problems, describes feelings of guilt, low self-esteem, and concerns about death, and loss of him/herself or others, it is now likely that depression will be suspected. And the strength of such self-report measures as the Childrens Depression Scale and the Childrens Depression Inventory (CDI) (Kovacs and Beck, 1977) is that they permit children who wish to communicate their depression to do so.

It is largely on the basis of the Childrens Depression Scale, a direct self-report measure, as well as the Childrens Depression Scale–Adult Form, that the school refusing children are considered depressed. It seems, given an opportunity to communicate their depression, that these children are able to do so. Furthermore, these self-reports are generally in agreement with the ways in which their parents perceive them.

Mothers of regular attenders, however, report their children as considerably less depressed than the children report themselves. Three explanations may be suggested for this. It may be that the differences between reports of regularly attending children and their mothers reflects healthy individuation while in school refusing families there is considerably more enmeshment (Minuchin, 1974). This explanation is consistent with the suggestion made earlier that the relative lack of personality difference between the two groups of mothers may be due to the success of the symptom-bearing of the child in the families of the school refusing children. Or it may be that where there is severe disturbance, mothers are more attuned to their children's symptomatology and consequently describe it more accurately and in greater agreement with their children. Thirdly, parents of regular attenders may respond to the "trials of childhood" through a perspective of seeing the problems and depressions of their children as fairly mild. In any event, the differences identified here in perceptions should be clarified and followed up in further research.

The thrust of this chapter is the relatively new finding of significant depression associated with school refusal. What meaning can be attached to the finding of depression in school refusing children? The first point which should be made is that, given the general background and familial variables which are part of the school refusing child's familial network or system, it is not surprising that he/she is depressed. In fact, one could readily argue that the depression may be expected in a family situation with generally low socioeconomic, educational, and intellectual levels and parental separation. In addition to these factors, this child has already been absent from school for significant periods of time—a statement of social "failure" by him/her—and it would be appropriate for feelings of depression to be associated.

In the wider context, then, not only is depression present, but it is related to the family and social circumstances as well as to the symptomatology of long-term school refusal.

Why has relatively little recognition been given to the presence of depression in school refusal? Two interrelated factors are involved in this question. The reports in the literature are all about clinical samples only, and it may well be that many of the findings reported relate more to that variable than to the school refusal variable (with some notable exceptions where clinical control groups are used, such as Hersov, 1960). It is likely that families seeking help are still fighting the symptomatology and may well be of higher socioeconomic status. The sampling of the study reported in this chapter specifically did not limit itself to families attending clinics. Lefkowitz and Burton (1978) make the point that referral behavior varies with parents' education and socioeconomic status. They call for identification of base levels of childhood depression in the community against which clinical incidence can be assessed.

Secondly, a measure was used which gave children an opportunity to communicate their depression clearly; again, such an attempt has not been reported before. This may simply have to do with the fact that attempts to measure depression in school refusal using self-report scales have not been reported previously.

It is likely that there are many situations and issues in community groups to which it is appropriate for children to react with depression. Examples which come readily to mind include marital conflict, death, parental separation, academic underachievement, migrant conflict, and adjustment, and poverty. Perhaps the point which needs to be made here is that a diagnosis of depression in a child has considerably more meaning when interpreted in the light of information about the broader systems to which the child belongs (at least the family and school networks). Thus, while this study shows a relationship between school refusal and depression, it also provides contextual data about the broader social systems of the children to which both their school refusal and their depression are related. Bolman (1970) makes a similar point when he argues for the importance of "collecting multilevel data that will gradually permit the clinical behavioral sciences . . . to develop therapeutic approaches that fit the complexity of the problem."

Furthermore, in attempting to explain some of the results of this study, a systemic view has been proposed where the children's school refusal and depression are related to needs by other members of their families for them to continue with their symptomatology so that the system will not be upset or changed. The study described in this chapter was not designed to obtain data of this sort.

To summarize, school refusal represents a fairly dramatic rejection by children of one of the two major networks in their lives (the school) in favor of closer enmeshment in the other (the family). An intensive examination of a range of variables associated with children who show a severe form of this behavior brings to light a large range of significant factors. The family involvement and anxiety factors were expected; the depression was anticipated but not previously empirically demonstrated in the literature; many of the social and family variables were not expected and are contrary to reports in the literature. It is unclear whether the depression and the social/family variables are directly related to the sampling, which was also different from other reports in the literature in that it addressed the population in total rather than the clinical groups of that population. In further work on school refusal and in particular its association with depression, it would be very important to carefully control socioeconomic status and intactness of family as well as age, sex, and school environment.

The importance of the study and of this chapter generally is to alert the clinician, teacher, and parent to the likely prevalence of depression in school refusal. This depression may be readily observable—overt—or it may be masked. Either way, an opportunity for the child to express any depression he/she may experience should be permitted. The group reported in this sample is severe in its school refusal; it is important to use these results to predict earlier signs of both depression and school refusal. There are periods in a child's school life—for example preschool to school transition, move from primary to high school—that are critical changeover times and some mild degree of school reluctance or school refusal may be appropriate. But if this persists, it may be useful to suspect depression. Awareness of some of the early signs of depression may then permit preventive action as well as increased understanding of the behavior involved.

REFERENCES

Adams PL, McDonald NF, Huey WP. School phobia and bisexual conflict: a report of 21 cases. *Am J Psychiatry* 1966; 123:541.

Agras S. The relationship of school phobia to childhood depression. *Am J Psychiatry* 1959; 116; 6:533–536.

Baker H, Wills U. School phobia: classification and treatment. *Br J Psychiatry* 1978; 132:492–499.

Bene E, Anthony J. *Manual for the family relations test.* The National Foundation for Educational Research in England and Wales. London, 1957.

Bolman WM. Systems theory, psychiatry and school phobia. *Am J Psychiatry* 1970; 127; 1:25–32.

Cattell RB. *IPAT children's personality questionnaire: the CPQ.* Institute for Personality and Ability Testing, Illinois, 1959.

Cattell RB. *Junior and senior high school personality questionnaire HSPQ.* Institute for Personality and Ability Testing, Illinois, 1969.

Cattell RB. *Handbook for the sixteen personality factor questionnaire 16 PF.* Institute for Personality and Ability Testing, Illinois, 1970.

Coolidge JC, Brodie RD, Feeney B. A ten-year follow-up study of 66 school-phobic children. *Am J Orthopsychiatry* 1964; 34:675–684.

Cooper M. School refusal: an inquiry into the part played by school and home. *Educat Res* 1966; 8:223–229.

Cytryn L, McKnew DH. Factors influencing the changing clinical expression of the depressive process in children. *Am J Psychiatry* 1974; 131; 8:879–881.

Davidson S. School phobia as a manifestation of family disturbance. *J Child Psychol Psychiatry* 1961; 1:270–287.

Eisenberg L. School phobia: a study in the communication of anxieties. *Am J Psychiatry* 1958; 114; 8:712.

Eysenck HJ, Rachman S. *The causes and cures of neurosis.* London: Routledge and Kegan Paul, 1965:212–222.

Firestone A, Goding GA, Stagoll B. Family therapy—a diagnostic scheme. Melbourne: Bouverie Clinic, 1978.

Framo JL. Symptoms from a family transactional viewpoint. In: *Progress in group and family therapy*, Sager CJ, Kaplan HS, eds. New York: Bruner & Mazel, 1972:271–308.

Gittelman-Klein R. Pharmacotherapy and management of pathological separation anxiety. *Int J Ment Heath* 1975; 4:255–271.

Gittelman-Klein R, Klein DF. School phobia: diagnostic considerations in the light of imipramine effects. *J Nerv Ment Dis* 1973; 156; 3:199–215.

Goldenberg H, Goldenberg I. School phobia: childhood neurosis or learned maladaptive behavior? *Except Child* 1970; 37; 3:220–226.

Glaser K. Masked depression in children and adolescents. *Am J Psychother* 1967; 21:565–574.

Gordon D, Young RD. School phobia: a discussion of aetiology, treatment and evaluation. *Psychol Rep* 1976; 39; 3:783–804.

Hampe E, Miller L, Barrett C, Noble H. Intelligence and school phobia. *J Sch Psychol* 1973; 11; 1:66–70.

Hawkes R. Paradox and a systems theory approach to a case of severe school phobia. *Aus J Fam Ther* 1981; 2; 2:56–62.

Hersov LA. Persistent non-attendance at school. *J Child Psychol Psychiatry* 1960; 1:130–136.

Jackson L. Anxiety in adolescents in relation to school refusal. *J Child Psychol Psychiatry* 1964; 5:59–73.

Johnson AM, Falstein EI, Szurek SA, Svendsen M. School phobia. *Am J Orthopsychiatry* 1941; 11:702–711.

Johnson AM. School phobia workshop, 1955, discussion. *Am J Orthopsychiatry* 1957.

Kovacs M. Rating scales to assess depression in school-aged children. *ACTO Paedopsychiatr* 1981; 46:305–315.

Kovacs M, Beck AT. An empirical-clinical approach toward a definition of childhood depression. In: *Depression in childhood: diagnosis, treatment and conceptual models*, Schulterbrandt JG, Raskin A, eds. New York: Raven Press, 1977.

Krupinski J, Stoller A. Occupational hierarchy of first admission to the Victorian mental health department, 1962–1965. *Aust NZ J Sociol* 1968; 4:55–63.

Lancaster-Jones F. *Dimensins of urban socal structure: the social areas of Melbourne, Australia.* Canberra: Australian National University Press, 1969:Chap 6.

Lang M. *Depression in school refusal* (unpublished thesis). Australia: Melbourne University, 1974.

Lang M, Tisher M, Goding GA. An empirical study of school refusal. (unpublished dissertation), 1975.

Lang M, Tisher M. *Childrens depression scale.* Melbourne: Australian Council for Educational Research, 1978.

Lefkowitz MM, Burton N. Childhood depression: a critique of the concept. *Psychol Bull* 1978; 85; 4:714–726.

McDonald JE, Sheperd G. School phobia: an overview. *J Sch Psychol* 1976; 14; 4:291–304.

Minuchin S. *Families and family therapy.* Massachusetts: Harvard University Press, 1974:Chap 3.

Poznanski E, Zrull JP. Childhood depression: clinical characteristics of overtly depressed children. *Arch Gen Psychiatry* 1970; 23:8–15.

Sandler J, Joffe WG. Notes on childhood depression. *Int J Psychoanal* 1965; 46:88–96.

Sarason SB, Davidson KS, Lighthall FF, et al. *Anxiety in elementary school children.* New York: John Wiley and Sons, 1960:Chap 4.

Sperling M. Equivalents of depression in children. *J Hillside Hosp* 1959; 8:138–148.

Talbot M. Panic in school phobia, school phobia workshop, 1955. *Am J Orthopsychiatry* 1957:286–295.

Tisher M. *Anxiety in school refusal* (unpublished thesis). Australia: Melbourne University, 1974.

Toolan JM. Depression in children and adolescents. *Am J Orthopsychiatry* 1962; 32:404–415.

Waldron S, Jr, Shrier DK, Stone B, Tobin F. School phobia and other childhood neuroses: a systematic study of the children and their families. *Am J Psychiatry* 1975: 132; 8:802–808.

Section III

Assessment

Assessment of Childhood Depression: An Overview

Dennis P. Cantwell

The diagnostic process in child psychiatry can be conceptualized as geared toward answering a number of questions (Cohen, 1976). These questions include:

1. Does the child who is being presented for evaluation have any type of psychiatric disorder? This question can be taken further: does the child have a significant problem in development—a problem that is manifested as an abnormality in behavior, emotions, relationships, or cognition; and one that is of sufficient severity and/or duration to cause distress, disability, or disadvantage?
2. Does the clinical picture of the child's disorder fit a known and recognized clinical syndrome?
3. Since all psychiatric disorders in childhood are probably of multifactorial etiology, what are the intrapsychic, familial, social, and biological roots of the disorders in the *individual child*, and what are the relative strengths of each of these roots?
4. What forces maintain the problem?
5. What forces facilitate the child's normal development?
6. What are the individual child's strengths and competencies?
7. Untreated, what will be the likely outcome of this child's disorder? The answer to this question depends partly on the natural history of the clinical syndrome described in the answer to question 2. It also depends on the answers to questions 3 to 6. The natural history of the child's disorder determines the urgency and level of intervention. Obviously, a disorder which will pass with time, leaving no residual effects, requires much less urgent and much less severe intervention than a disorder which is likely to be significantly disabling without treatment. The natural history of a child's disorder also offers a test of the efficacy of treatment. For a treatment to be considered efficacious, the outcome must be better than that which could be predicted on the basis of no treatment.
8. Is intervention necessary in this case?
9. What types of intervention are most likely to be effective?

Treatment planning in child psychiatry depends not only on the answer to question 2—what diagnostic syndrome is the child suffering from—but also on the answers to questions 3 to 7.

The tools available to the practitioner in the diagnostic process include an interview with the parents about the child; family interviews; an interview with the child; behavior rating scales completed by parents, teachers, and significant others in the child's life; a physical exam; a neurological exam; and laboratory studies including psychological testing.

Only in rare cases do the physical and neurological exam and laboratory studies, including psychological testing, contribute to making a *specific diagnosis* in child psychiatry (Gittelman, 1980). This does not mean that they do not play an important part in many cases in providing other information regarding the *diagnostic formulation*. Laboratory studies do not exist for the diagnosis of specific psychiatric disorders in childhood, with the exception of such things as chromosomal studies in certain cases of mental retardation, and specific psychometric testing for confirmation of the diagnosis of some specific developmental disorders.

In general, the defining of any clinical syndrome in childhood is done on the basis of the interview with the parents, the interview with the child, and the behavior rating scales. In one of the few studies of the reliability and validity of the diagnostic procedures in child psychiatry, Rutter et al (1970) found that the interview with the parents was the single best instrument for detecting children with psychiatric disorders. It was only rarely that children who were considered to be normal by their parents, and normal on the basis of parent-teacher rating scales, were considered to be psychiatrically disturbed by psychiatrists based *solely* on the interview with the child.

The use of behavior rating scales has been fostered primarily in research settings, particularly in psychopharmacological research settings. However, clinicians who have used behavior rating scales in these settings have found them to be helpful in the diagnostic process, even in nonresearch settings. It is the data from behavior rating scales generally completed by parents and teachers, and in other instances completed by mental health workers, that have led to the empirically derived syndromes of behavior described by Achenbach (1980). It is surprising how little work has been done on the reliability and validity of the diagnostic process in child psychiatry.

This chapter will discuss some specific aspects of the assessment of depression in childhood. In the assessment of childhood depression, the major question to be answered is question number 2: What type of psychiatric disorder does the child have? In essence, what one is asking here is: Does the child meet the diagnostic criteria for depression as outlined in the Diagnostic and Statistical Manual-III (DSM-III) (or more idiosyncratic criteria for depression in childhood like the Weinberg criteria)? An elaboration of question 2 is: What subtype of depression does the child present with (such as the endogenous subtype in Research Diagnostic Criteria (RDC) criteria or melancholoic subtype in DSM-III criteria)?

What specific tools are available to the clinician and to the researcher in assessing children for depression? They can be classified into four general types: interviews with the parent about the children, interviews and observations of the child himself or herself, rating scales, and laboratory studies. Rating scales include those completed by the child himself (self-rating scales), those completed by parents, those completed by teachers, those completed by peers, and those completed by clinicians.

The term "laboratory study" here is used in its broadest sense to include not only traditional laboratory studies such as biological measures, but also psychological testing. As has been pointed out above, psychological tests that have been shown to be reliable and valid can be considered to have the same utility as a biological laboratory measure.

As part of a report on the proceedings of the Conference on Depression in Childhood Depression sponsored by the National Institutes of Mental Health (NIMH) in 1977, the subcommittee on assessment looked at the issue of measurement instruments and data collection. Seven areas were felt to be important in the content of the measurement instruments: (1) facial expression and motoric behavior; (2) social responsivity/social adjustment (particularly the way the child relates to parents, peers, and teachers); (3) task performance; (4) problem-solving strategies (including affective, behavioral, and cognitive); (5) concepts of the self, world, and motivation; (6) mood and affective expression; and (7) biochemical and biophysiological variables. The possible data-gathering approaches could include: observational methods, self-ratings and description, and ratings and description of the subject by others.

Since the time of that report there has been an increasing body of research in the area of childhood depression. As part of this increased research has come the development of instruments specifically to be used with children. These have been reviewed in detail by others (Kazdin, 1981; Kovacs, 1981; Orvaschel et al, 1980). Some highlights will be reviewed in this chapter as an attempt to aid the clinician and the researcher as to the availability of measurement instruments and their current state of development.

INTERVIEWS

The assessment of children presenting for psychiatric evaluation traditionally begins with an interview with the parent or parents about the child's problem. This has been discussed in detail in another chapter by Puig-Antich. What will be briefly mentioned here are the various semi-structured interviews that have been developed over the past few years. These began as research instruments, but have begun to find utility in clinical settings as well. Interviews for use by clinicians with parents to detail child symptomatology include: the Kiddie-SADS, the Diagnostic Interview for Children and Adolescents (DICA), the Diagnostic Interview Schedule for Children–Parent Form (DISC-P), the Interview Schedule for Children (ISC)–parent form, and the Columbia Psychiatric Interview (COLPA). Some of these interviews are geared toward assessing general psychopathology, while others are more specific for depression such as the Kiddie-SADS (although the Kiddie-SADS does assess psychopathology in other areas as well).

Generally the approach underlying all of the interviews is the same, that is, the use of the semi-structured interview guarantees that certain questions about certain symptomatic areas are asked of all parents. The interviews differ in a variety of parameters: the age range of the children for which they are to be used, the comprehensiveness of the psychopathology that is covered, the extent and structure of different probes that are used in specific symptomatic areas, and certain aspects of coding. Probably the most comprehensive, from the standpoint of psychopathology covered, is DISC-P. This is an NIMH-generated interview analogous to the adult DIS. It is keyed to DSM-III diagnostic categories to that all DSM-III diagnoses can be made. In addition, the interview is ultimately envisioned to be used by nonclinicians. Thus, it is very highly structured with a standard amount and type of probes to be used after each positive and negative response.

The interviews mentioned above also have versions which can be used directly with the child subject himself or herself. In addition, Hodges et al (1981) have developed the Child Assessment Schedule (CAS) as a diagnostic interview for children. The Child Assessment Schedule consists of two parts. In the first part, the interviewer asks the child a series of about 75 questions which address multiple topics. The topics covered include: school, friends, activities and hobbies, family, fears, worries, self-image, mood, somatic concerns, expression of anger, and thought disorder. In addition, there is a second part, which is observational, upon which the interviewer can record observations and judgments made after completing the interview with the child. There are more than 50 items in the observational section. Hodges and her colleagues estimate that the interview takes only about 45 minutes to one hour to complete with the average child.

As pointed out by Puig-Antich in another chapter in this volume, it does seem that there are certain symptoms that are probably more validly obtained from children than from parents and vice versa. Herjanic in her studies of the DICA has demonstrated that there is a large degree of overlap between symptoms reported by parents and teachers. However, she has also demonstrated that there are certain symptoms that tend to be reported more by parents and likewise certain symptoms that tend to be reported more by children. Thus, when using the semi-structured interviews with parents and children, it is not surprising that different results will be obtained, and some clinical judgment must be used in assessing where the weight should be put with each individual child-parent combination.

Many of the interviews mentioned above, both for parents and children, still are in the development state and are being refined. Ultimately the DISC and DISC-P will be used in epidemiologic studies to determine prevalence rates of DSM-III diagnosable psychiatric disorder in the general population. More details about each of these interviews can be found in review publications by Kazdin (1981) and by Orvaschel et al (1980).

RATING SCALES

Rating scales have been devised for use by the patient (self-rating scales) and also by the use of significant others in the child's environment, including parents, teachers, and peers. Finally, clinician-completed rating scales, analogous to the Hamilton Rating Scale, have also been developed. Like the interviews, some of these rating scales are designed to assess general psychopathology as well as depression. Others are designed to specifically look at the extent and severity of depressive symptomatology.

Self-Rating Scales

The Children's Depression Scale (CDS) developed by Lang and Tisher is described in detail in Chapter 8. The Children's Depression Inventory (CDI) is another self-rating scale, designed by Kovacs and Beck (1977) to measure severity of depression. The CDI, in its original form, was created by Kovacs and Beck by modifying certain items on the adult Beck Depression Inventory. The CDI has been used in studies by Albert and Beck (1975), by Kovacs and her colleagues (1977), and by Cantwell and Carlson (1981). The origianl CDI has been modified several times by Kovacs, both with regard to its scoring format and to the content of the items.

Cantwell and Carlson (1981) factor-analyzed the original version of the Children's Depression Inventory and came up with four factors. The first factor was a "dysphoria self-image factor," consisting of eight items, which explained 26 percent of the variance. This factor could also be considered to be a severity of depression factor. The second factor consisted of five items explaining seven percent of the variance. The five items were fatigability, indecisiveness, crying spells, self-accusation, and sense of failure. The third factor consisted of only two items, somatic preoccupation and sleep disturbance, and explained six percent of the variance. The fourth factor consisted of two items, anorexia and weight loss, and explained four percent of the variance. In the t test analysis of children diagnosed as depressed by DSM-III criteria, factor one discriminated between those diagnosed as depressed and those diagnosed as nondepressed, psychiatrically ill at the < 0.0001 level; factor two at the < 0.04 level. Factors three and four did not distinguish the two groups significantly.

In a discriminant function analysis, factors one and two correctly classified 82.8 percent of those without affective disorder and 76.2 percent of those with an affective disorder. The overall classification rate was 81 percent. A jackknife classificiation procedure produced the same results. Using factors three and four, the discriminant function analysis did not improve the classification rate.

Considering that the affective disorder diagnosis was made on the basis of a traditional clinical evaluation, which included information from the parent and teachers as well as from the child, the results obtained from the independent self-rating done by the child alone on the CDI should be considered promising.

More recently, Birleson (1981) has developed a self-rating scale for childhood depression. Birleson derived the self-rating scale by comparing prepubertal depressed children to three control groups, a psychiatrically disordered clinic group who did not have depression, a normal group from a normal school, and a group from a residential school for maladjusted students. The final version of the self-rating scale was determined by looking at which items from a larger initial inventory discriminated depressed groups from the other three groups. Birleson's initial study demonstrated that the self-rating scale had high internal consistency, factorial validity, and satisfactory stability, although it still needed work on further validation with an independent depressed group. The final version consisted of 18 questions to which the subject responds as to how he has felt over the past week to each particular statement. For example, the statement "I look forward to things as much as I used to" is either checked off as "most times," "sometimes," or "never." Scoring is on a zero, one, two basis.

Some authors question whether self-report inventories with children will be as useful as they have been with adults. Self-report inventories with adults and children of course are subject to certain sources of bias and distortion. But with children it should be recognized that language and cognitive skills at different age levels will probably influence the child's interpretation of the items that are asked by the rating scale and may play a greater role in variance than they do with adults.

Parent Rating Scales

Behavior rating scales completed by parents have a long history in child psychiatry, particularly in the research area. Rutter developed a parent rating scale which was very useful for screening for psychiatric disorders in the Isle of Wight epidemiological study (Rutter et al, 1970). The Conners Parent Rating Scale was developed primarily for use in psychopharmacologic research (Guy, 1976). The Child Behavior Checklist developed by Achenbach has been used to collect large amounts of epidemiological data.

Most of these scales, particularly the Rutter and the Conners, do not have many items pertaining to the child's mood state. However, the Achenbach has more such items. However, as has been noted elsewhere, the diagnosis of a depressive disorder in childhood is heavily dependent on subjective phenomenon rather than on observable behavior. Thus, it is not clear whether the presence or absence of depressed mood and accompanying psychiatric symptoms to make a diagnosis of major depressive disorder can be picked up by rating scales developed for use by parents and teachers. Puig-Antich has recently experimented by adding 49 items pertaining to specific symptoms in major depressive disorder to the Conners questionnaire. The CDS developed by Tisher and Lang does have a version to be completed by the child's parents. The CDI likewise could be reworked so that a version could be completed by parents as well, and Carlson is currently experimenting with just such a modification. However, much more work needs to be done with these instruments to see how effective they will be in discriminating depressed children from children with other types of psychiatric disorders.

Teacher Rating Scales

The same criticisms of parent rating scales that were made above can be made of teacher rating scales. Rutter, Achenbach, and Conners do have rating scales to be completed by teachers as well as by parents. Again, these are both general psychopathology rating scales, and only the Achenbach has a significant number of mood items on it. There is one specific teacher rating scale developed for the assessment of depressive symptomatology in children by Petti called the Teacher Affect Rating Scale (TARS). This teacher rating scale is composed of 26 items, rated on a scale from zero to three, which correspond to "not at all" to "very much." The teacher is instructed to complete the rating scale on the basis of the child's behavior during the past week. Petti has found three factors in a factor analysis: factor one (a behavior factor), factor two (a learning factor), and factor three (a depression factor) (Petti, unpublished data).

On the basis of preliminary testing, the TARS seems to be a worthwhile instrument, but it is still in its developmental stage. Again, a major and unanswered question is how well teachers will do in picking up depressive behaviors, which are more subjective, compared with how they do in picking up more overt behaviors, such as in children with attention deficit disorder with hyperactivity.

Clinician Rating Scales

Clinician rating scales, such as the Hamilton, have been used in the study of affective disorder with adults for quite a long period of time. More recently, three specific clinician rating scales have been developed for use with children. One, the Children's Depression Rating Scale (CDRS), was developed by

Poznanski et al (1979) by modifying the original Hamilton Scale. The data base is information obtained from the child, from parents, and from medical personnel (including nursing staff). The 16 items cover a wide variety of behaviors, all of which are scored from zero to two or from zero to five, with higher scores indicating greater pathology. Interrater agreement in the preliminary studies has been high, and total scores seem to correlate highly with clinical assessment of depression. It is unclear, however, exactly what weight is given to the varying reports from parents, medical personnel, the child himself, etc., and also what questions are asked of the various individuals to make the ratings. More work needs to be done on validation and on correlation with the clinical diagnosis of depression. But the CDRS is an obvious step in the right direction, modeled after a rating scale which has been used very successfully with adults.

The Children's Affect Rating Scale (CARS) developed by Cytryn and McKnew (1972) is also completed by clinicians who have either conducted or observed a structured psychiatric interview with the child. Three subscales describe mood and behavior, verbal expression, and fantasy. A child is rated from zero to nine on each of the three subscales. The CARS is in its initial stages of development and needs much more work on its psychometric properties and on its ability to distinguish depressed children from children with other psychiatric disorders.

Petti developed the Bellvue Index of Depression (BID) as a clinician rating scale, which is slightly different from the two above. The BID is actually a semi-structured interview for children ages six to 12 consisting of 40 items. The items are rated on a four-point scale, from zero to three (from "not at all" to "very much"). The duration of the problem is rated as "less than one month" to "always." The items covered by the BID are those specified by Weinberg as his operational diagnostic criteria for depression. Petti added a quantitative rating to the items and also an interview format. The BID is similar to the CDRS in that it is completed after collecting information from the child, the parents, and from significant others. Again, as with the CDRS, it is not quite clear how the different sources of information are weighted should there be a discrepancy on certain items. More work is needed on reliability and validity of the instrument. But its major value would seem to lie in providing a quantifiable severity rating of multiple symptoms along with ratings of duration. Both the CDRS and the BID would seem to be useful for following patients in therapeutic studies and/or natural history studies.

Rating Scales Completed by Significant Others

In addition to parents and teachers, there are significant others who could be called upon to complete rating scales. For inpatients this could be nursing staff or other ward staff closely connected with the child's day-to-day workings on the ward. For children in residential treatment centers, it might be house parents or cottage parents. For schools it could be peers. Peer ratings have been used to measure a variety of aspects of childhood behavior. Pelham (in press), for example, has recently found success in peer ratings of hyperactive children which has led to significant therapeutic interventions. Lefkowitz and Tesiny (1981) have developed a Peer Nomination Inventory for Depression (PNID) which consists of 20 items. This requires that an individual child be evaluated by many peers in his classroom setting. The 20 items on the PNID include two that describe popularity, four that describe happiness, and 14 that describe what are considered to be observable aspects of depression. All of the peers are required to nominate one or more of the other children in the group in response to several specific questions. A given child's score for depression is the sum of the number of nominations he or she has received across all of the questions on the PNID. Reliability studies have been impressive, but validity studies have been somewhat lacking. Validity studies have correlated PNID scores with other reports of depression: self-reports, teacher reports, etc. Correlations between scores on the PNID and self-ratings of depression, such as the CDI and teacher ratings of depression, have only been moderately positive. PNID scores, however, were shown to correlate with school performance, self-concept, teacher ratings of work skills and social behavior, peer ratings of happiness and popularity, and other measures. However, apparently the PNID has not been validated against clinical diagnosis of depression. Thus we do not know how well the PNID will discriminate children with a depressive *disorder* from children with depressive *symptoms* as part of other psychiatric disorders. Factor analysis of the 14 depression and four happiness items yielded four factors. The first three, loneliness, inadequacy, and dejection, do seem to consist of meaningful aspects of depression. From the standpoint of psychometric work, the PNID is one of the better scales to be developed. However, how practical this will be as a useful tool in everyday clinical practice and/or psychiatric research is an open question.

LABORATORY STUDIES

Other chapters in this volume have addressed the issue of biological validation of the depressive syndrome in childhood using measures analogous to those which have been used in adults, such as the dexamethasone suppression test and cortisol secretion. Electromyogram recordings have also been proposed as biological indicators of depression. At the moment it is safe to say that most of these biological validation measures are still in their development stage in the study of children with depression.

As mentioned above, psychological tests which have been shown to be reliable and valid can also be considered to be laboratory tests in the same way that biological measures can be. It has long been assumed in some circles that projective psychological testing carries this same type of diagnostic specificity that biological validation laboratory measures have had. Cytryn and McKnew (1972) have used projection techniques to measure fantasy in children with depression, and there are other projective tests, such as the Rorschach, the TAT, the CAT, figure drawings, and others, which can be scored for depressive themes. However, they have not been applied to a large degree in a systematic way in the study of childhood depression. Whether they would add anything over and above what can be gleaned from other areas of the evaluation that have been discussed above, such as interviewing parents, interviewing the children, etc., is very much an open question. Gittelman's (1980) comprehensive review of the use of projective psychological testing in diffierential diagnosis in child psychiatry gives less than enthusiastic support for their reliability and validity in differential diagnostic procedures.

SUMMARY AND CONCLUSIONS

The area of assessment of childhood depression is in a very active research stage at the moment. Interviews with parents, interviews with children, rating scales to be completed by the patient, by the parent, by teachers, by peers, and by clinicians all are in the developmental stage. The development of such instruments in crucial for other areas in the field to flower. Natural history research and treatment research depend on instruments which are sensitive to changes in clinical status and which can reliabily and validly measure depression.

Many of the instruments are still in early developmental stages. Others have a fair amount of research behind them. All of the instruments, especially the various rating scales, need work on internal consistency, reliability (both test-retest and interrater), and on validity. Intercorrelation between measures of different types, such as clinician rating scales, independent interviews with parents, and teacher rating scales, are very important. Self-rating scales may have special limitations with younger children because of cognitive and linguistic variables. Kazdin (1981) has pointed out that there are validational methods, such as convergent and discriminant validation, that can be used to determine whether depression or some other disorder explains the performance on a particular scale and also whether the measure of depression assesses a distinct clinical syndrome. Very few such attempts have been made with measures to study childhood depression. However, preliminary work on the instruments that have been developed does look promising.

REFERENCES

Achenbach, TM. DSM-III in light of empirical research on the classification of child psychopathology. *J Am Acad Child Psychiatry* 1980; 19; 3:395–412.

Albert N, Beck AT. Incidence of depression in early adolescence: a preliminary study. *J Youth Adol* 1975; 4:301–307.

Birleson P. The validity of depressive disorder in childhood and the development of a self-rating scale: a research report. *J Child Psychol Psychiatry* 1981; 22:73–88.

Cantwell DP, Carlson GA. Factor analysis of a self-rating depressive inventory for children: factor, structure and nosological utility. Presented at the American Academy of Child Psychiatry Annual Meeting in Dallas, Texas, October 1981.

Cohen DJ. The diagnostic process in child psychiatry. *Psychiat Ann* 1976; 6; 9:29–56.

Cytryn L, McKnew DH, Jr. Proposed classification of childhood depression. *Am J Psychiatry* 1972; 129:149–155.

Gittelman R. The role of psychological tests for differential diagnosis in child psychiatry. *J Am Acad Child Psychiatry* 1980; 19; 3:413–438.

Guy W. *ECDEU Assessment Manual for Psychopharmacology*. National Institute of Mental Health, Psychopharmacology Research Branch. Rockville, Maryland: U.S. Department of Health, Education, and Welfare. ECDEU: Early Clinical Drug Evaluation Unit of Psychopharmacology Research Branch, 1976.

Hodges K, McKnew D, Cytryn L, et al. The Child Assessment Schedule (CAS) Diagnostic Interview: a report on reliability and validity. *J Am Acad Child Psychiatry* 1982; 21:468–473.

Kazdin AE. Assessment techniques for childhood depression—a critical appraisal. *J Am Acad Child Psychiatry* 1981; 20:358–375.

Kovacs M. Rating scales to assess depression in school age children. *ACTA Paedopsychiatr* 1981; 46:305–315.

Kovacs M, Beck AT. An empirical clinical approach toward a definition of childhood depression. In: *Depression in childhood: diagnosis, treatment, and conceptual models.* Schulterbrandt JG, ed. New York: Raven Press, 1977:1–25.

Kovacs M, Betof NG, Celebre JE, et al. Childhood depression—myth or clinical syndrome. University of Pennsylvania, (unpublished manuscript) 1977.

Lefkowitz M, Tesini EP. Assessment of childhood depression. *J Consult Clin Psychol* 1981; 48:43–51.

Orveschel H, Sholomskas D, Weissman M. The assessment of psychopathology and behavior problems in children: a review of scales suitable for epidemiological and clinical research, 1967–1969. DHHS Publication No. ADM80-1037, 1980.

Pelham WE, Bender ME. *Peer relationships in hyperactive children: description and treatment*. Greenwich, CT: JAI Press.

Poznanski EO, Cook SC, Carroll BJ. A depression rating scale for children. *Pediatrics* 1979; 64; 4:442–450.

Rutter M, Tizard J, Whitmore K. *Education, health, and behavior*. London: Longman Group, 1970.

Affective Disorders in Childhood and Adolescence-- An Update. Edited by D.P. Cantwell and G.A. Carlson.

9

The Clinical Assessment of Current Depressive Episodes in Children and Adolescents: Interviews with Parents and Children

Joaquim Puig-Antich, William J. Chambers and Mary Ann Tabrizi

HISTORY

Methods of clinical assessment in child and adolescent psychiatry have undergone considerable evolution during the last 20 years, in a close, two-way relationship with progress in diagnostic classification systems. Such advances have been largely fueled by similar advances in adult psychiatry and by the increasing number of treatment techniques.

Initially, a substantial proportion of child psychiatrists totally disregarded classification systems in consonance with the psychodynamic-psychoanalytic unitary view of mental illness in childhood and they focused on degree of severity of the clinical picture (Szurek, 1956). Unconscious mental conflict was seen as the root of mental disorder and the task of the child psychiatrist was to find out what conflicts were underlying every abnormal behavior, in order to make the child aware of them through interpretive work. It was thought that making the unconscious conscious would produce therapeutic benefit in all mental disorders, regardless of diagnosis or severity. Although lip service was paid to "constitutional factors" by several prominent members of this unitary etiological model of childhood mental disorder more interested in diagnostic approaches (Beres, 1956; Mahler, 1968; Freud, 1970), the only treatment method remained psychotherapy. Consistent with this model, the clinician was interested in assessing worries, preoccupations, and symbolic meanings in order to infer unconscious psychic conflict. Symptoms were viewed as ephemeral surface manifestations, and treatment was directed toward fostering the healthy development of the child's personality. Symptoms were seen as a manifestation of conflict-dependent, arrested, or abnormal development and, therefore, they would disappear once the conflict was worked through and psychological development was "moving again" in the proper direction. In the interview with the parents, the clinician was especially interested in a chronicle of the child's social relationships in early childhood with the parents, and with parental reaction to and expectations from the child, as these were thought to be extremely important determinants (and later, reflections) of pathogenic psychic conflict.

This unitary model came to be seriously challenged during the 1960s and 1970s by other models of child psychiatric disorder. The evidence supporting such models came from findings in three main research areas: epidemiology, behavior therapy, and pediatric psychopharmacology. As will be seen, findings in these three areas have resulted in major shifts in both assessment methods and classification systems.

Behavior Therapy

The basic tenet of the theoretical underpinning of this therapeutic modality is that behavior is dependent on immediate antecedents and immediate contingencies, and that by changing these, the therapist can reliably alter behavior away from maladaptation (Yule, 1976).

Needless to say, such focus in the present ("here and now") was very contrary to the psychodynamic approach, and substantial theoretical arguments ensued without a great deal of cross-fertilization (Mischel, 1968). To be administered properly, behavior therapy necessitates a careful behavioral description including antecedents and consequences of each behavior. This functional analysis therefore shifted the focus to behavioral phenomenology, to observation, to "microanalysis" of behavior, and to careful description and identification of strictly defined single behaviors, which could be reliably assessed.

In addition, the hypotheses advanced by behaviorists were by and large testable, and its practitioners, mostly psychologists, were trained in research methodology and design. Research designs to test effectiveness of behavioral interventions were developed following the scientific method. These represented clear advances in the field. On the other hand, some behaviorists (Skinner, 1953) and psychodynamicists (Szurek, 1956) shared a disregard for phenomenological child psychiatric diagnosis, although due to different theoretical reasons.

Epidemiology

Epidemiology is a powerful tool for generating and testing hypotheses regarding etiology of behavioral disorders, besides its better known goal to arrive at prevalence rates for different disorders, traits, or characteristics in the general population. The early epidemiological studies of childhood behavioral disorders chose to collect data on behavioral "bits," unrelated to diagnostic categories (Lapouse and Monk, 1959; Gersten et al, 1976; Pringle et al, 1966). Many relatively discrete individual behaviors were listed and had to be rated on a dichotomous scale by either the parent, the teacher, or, in adolescents, the child himself. These rating scales were then subjected to factor or cluster analyses in order to identify behavioral patterns or "dimensions." The dimensional approach has since been very useful in child psychiatry, but it should be noted that it has been mostly used for data collected from sources other than the child himself—namely, teachers and parents. Therefore, it is likely to be more apt to identify observable behaviors than "inner" psychic phenomena like mood, obsessions, or hallucinations, unless they are accompanied by persistent overt specific behavioral correlates.

The Isle of Wight study (Rutter et al, 1970) was one of the first child psychiatric studies to use well-defined diagnostic categories and standardized structured interviews with the child himself. As part of that study, Rutter and Graham (1968) demonstrated the fact that ten-year-olds can be reliably interviewed, and that the information obtained is not only reliable, but also valid. This was a major advance which unfortunately did not have much of an early impact in child psychiatric practice in this country except for a few exceptions. The diagnostic categories used were clinically derived, and some of the broader categories (emotional and conduct disorders) were validated by dimensional methods and by other clinical characteristics. Many of the diagnostic categories had been derived in reference to adult psychiatric disorders, which they clinically resembled.

Pediatric Psychopharmacology

During the late 1960s and the 1970s pediatric psychopharmacology developed substantially. Several properly controlled double-blind studies demonstrated the effectiveness of stimulant drugs in the treatment of the hyperkinetic syndrome (attention deficit disorder with hyperactivity) (Gittelman-Klein, 1975). The need for reliable rating scales to properly diagnose and measure stimulant drug effects in this disorder led to the development of the Conners' Parent and Teacher Questionnaires (Conners, 1969), the Behavior Problem Checklist (Quay, 1977), and others.

The symptoms of attention deficit disorder are mainly observable and can be assessed reliably by teachers and by independent observers. Thus, these rating scales focus on strictly defined individual behaviors.

Another major advance in pediatric psychopharmacology was the evidence produced by Gittelman-Klein and Klein (1973) supporting the effectiveness of imipramine in a specific type of school phobia (separation anxiety disorder). In that study, both observational measures and the child's self-report were used to assess drug effects. The report from the child was shown to be the most sensitive method of differentiation between drug and placebo effects. This disorder is characterized by both behavioral and emotional symptoms.

In an effort to develop a drug-sensitive child psychiatric rating scale including both the child's own report and observational measures, the Child Psychiatric Rating Scale (CPRS) was developed (1975) as a collaborative effort of several researchers in the field.

ASSESSMENT OF MAJOR DEPRESSION IN CHILDREN AND ADOLESCENTS: SEVERAL PRINCIPLES

The existence of major depression in prepuberty has been controversial. Nevertheless, during the 1970s child psychiatrists became increasingly interested in this disorder. At present there is a substantial consensus on its existence and exciting research is ongoing as evidenced in this book (Weinberg et al, 1973; Cytryn et al, 1980; Carlson and Cantwell, 1980).

When our group entered this field, our first question was "can major depression in children be diagnosed using the same symptomatic criteria which have been established for adult patients: the Research Diagnostic Criteria (RDC)?" (Spitzer et al, 1972). After reviewing the clinical instruments available for children we found none which assessed all symptoms of RDC major depression. We therefore wrote a depression supplement for the CPRS, and demonstrated that prepubertal depression can be diagnosed using exactly the same criteria as for adult depression (Puig-Antich et al, 1978). Weinberg et al (1973) had already used criteria derived from adult depression to diagnose depressed children. However, these criteria were substantially modified, resulting in conceptually much looser categories. Given that diagnostic validation (after demonstration of reliability of the assessments was to be the next step), it seemed to us prudent not to widen the diagnostic category without sufficient cause, as this may have markedly and unnecessarily hampered any validation strategies.

It should be underlined that this emphasis on *symptoms* led to more emphasis in *talking* with the child as opposed to *playing* with the child as a means of psychiatric assessment.

Although the assessment of psychodynamic constellations and symbolic meanings through play is an important part of the general psychiatric assessment of children, it has only a minor, if any, role to play in the clinical process of arriving at a diagnosis of major depression. Play interviews by and large do not assess symptoms. Furthermore, we have found it distracting for both the child and the interviewer. In assessing symptoms like depressive mood or anhedonia, the child must pay attention to relatively new concepts and questions, think, and answer, and he is more likely to do that in an interview situation without the distraction of toys.

Most clinical researchers interested in prepubertal and/or adolescent depression strongly emphasize the diagnostic importance of the interview with the child (Cytryn et al, 1980; Carlson and Cantwell, 1980; Puig-Antich et al, 1978). This represents a major shift from the past, when most child psychiatrists used information from parent and teacher to reach a diagnosis (or a treatment recommendation) without paying much attention to what the child said in a usually nonstructured interview. This is historically surprising because Rutter and Graham (1968) and also Herjanic et al (1975) had already demonstrated that children *are* reliable reporters. This emphasis on the child interview is probably due to the fact that the most crucial symptoms of depression are "inner" symptoms which may completely escape observation by others, and therefore, can only be accurately reported by the child.

Once it was clear that we could use unmodified RDC criteria for major depressive disorder in order to identify depressed children the next questions were "what is the nature of prepubertal major depression?" and "what is the relationship between child and adult major depressive disorders?" To attempt to answer this question meant to undertake a series of validation studies as described in Chapter 11. But before such studies could be undertaken, it was necessary to decide what interview schedule could be developed to reliably measure all symptoms in the depressive syndrome in children and adolescents.

At the present time there are three diagnostic instruments available to measure the depressive syndrome under the age of 18 years. All three instruments are in advanced stage of development. These instruments are:

1. *Diagnostic Interview for Children and Adolescents (DICA)*, developed by Herjanic. This schedule records information obtained in the interview with the child. It does not record the interview with the parent. It covers the child's lifetime, not the present episode.

2. *Interview Schedule for Children (SCI)*, developed by Kovacs. It also records the interview with the child. A separate form differently structured covers the interview with the parent. It also covers the child's lifetime, and includes all symptoms which have been reported in the literature as part of depression in childhood.

3. *Schedule for Affective Disorders and Schizophrenia for School-Age Children (Present Episode) (Kiddie-SADS-P, K-SADS-P)*, developed by Puig-Antich and Chambers. This schedule records information from the interview with the child and with the parent. Both interviews follow exactly the same structure and summary ratings are achieved item by item. The K-SADS-P measures psychopathology during the current episode of disorders only.

Although there are important differences in scope and method among these schedules, a final critique and comparison of these instruments should await their finished form and is beyond the scope of this chapter.

Instead, in what follows, we will discuss the rationale for the development of the K-SADS-P and the main technical difficulties encountered in assessing the different symptoms in the depressive syndrome from both parent and child.

Once it was clear that we were going to assess in children the same symptoms routinely assessed in adult depression, it made sense to adapt for children the instrument which had proven to be reliable in adults in assessing the symptoms included in RDC criteria for major depression (Endicott and Spitzer, 1978).

In adult populations, symptomatic assessments are mainly based on patient interviews. Other sources of information are used only when the patient has severe cognitive impairment or when the clinician suspects distortions in self-report. In contrast, with children, two sources of information besides the patient have been used routinely in clinical practice and research: the parent and the school. These are necessary because of the cognitive limitations inherent to the developmental stage of the prepubertal child, which make it usually impossible for him to provide an accurate chronological structure for the present episode of illness. During most of prepuberty, time concepts like three weeks and three months are not distinguished. At the same time, it is difficult for others, such as parents and teachers, to be aware of the child's mood and feeling states. Therefore, although the child's ability to report past status is limited, most clinicians working with depressed children think the child is the best reporter for present state and place great emphasis on the interview with the child to evaluate current emotional status (Cytryn et al, 1980; Carlson and Cantwell, 1980; Puig-Antich et al, 1978). The emerging consensus seems to be that, in the assessment of psychiatric symptoms which are manifested mostly intrapsychically and which reflect subjective phenomena (emotions, feelings, ideas), information obtained from the child is essential. Thus, inappropriate guilt, obsessions, depressive mood, self-esteem, delusional beliefs, suicidal preoccupations, anxious worries, hallucinations, and other symptoms may remain totally unknown to parents, especially when they are not clearly associated with specific changes in behavior. This situation is more likely the older the child, as with increasing age children tend to become more private about their inner life. The ability of prepubertal children to give accurate information has been studied by several investigators during the last decade, and there is little question now that well-trained, skilled interviewers are able to elicit reliable information from children regarding their own mental state (Rutter and Graham, 1968; Herjanic et al, 1975; Herjanic and Campbell, 1977). The validity of the child interview data is further suggested by the Isle of Wight follow-up, where previous data obtained from the children's interviews and interviews with parents were more predictive of later psychopathology than ratings by teachers and parents (Rutter M, personal communication, 1979).

Sensitive parents are usually the best informants for observable behavior, including past verbal statements by the child, and for providing the interviewer with a chronological framework for the unfolding of the present episode of disorder. Regarding the child's intrapsychic affective and cognitive content, the extent and quality of parental information improves when their children are younger and more communicative, when the child's intrapsychic symptoms clearly alter behavior, and when they are empathic, relatively free of psychopathology, and know their child well, and their relationship to the child has a positive emotional tone.

In the case of prepubertal children, we find it advisable to interview the parent first about the child's symptoms and history. Initially, this interview should be unstructured, allowing the parent to give a spontaneous report of all presenting problems, and how they developed. Thus, a chronology for onset and course for each one of the problems and/or symptoms can be established. Once the mode of onset of the child's present episode, duration, and all presenting problems are clear, the interviewer proceeds to a comprehensive semi-structured assessment of salient symptoms of most child psychiatric disorders for the current episode. For purposes of evaluation of treatment effectiveness, it is imperative to obtain a measure of severity for each symptom during a fixed period of time (for example, a week) preceding the assessment.

Following the parent interview, the clinician interviews the child about his own symptoms. It is useful to start the interview with a brief assessment of language abilities, time concepts, and general intelligence, so that the wording of questions can be adapted to the child's level of understanding. This also helps the rater in determining the relative weight to place on the child's report when arriving at summary ratings. Needless to say, children with low IQs (below 60) or with severe language problems cannot be interviewed. Some children will remain verbally silent throughout the interview, but will nod yes or no to questions. If the child's intelligence and comprehension are within normal limits and if he nods yes or no to all questions, a complete symptomatic assessment is possible.

The clinician follows the same format (unstructured/semi-structured) with the child as with the parent, and asks the same questions in simple language so that the child can understand. Repeating the same inquiry with different wording, and directly asking the child if he understood the question and if he can repeat it in different words, are the best way to monitor comprehension.

While interviewing the child, the clinician should monitor agreement between parent and child. If the reasons for the disagreement are not obvious, it is useful to confront the child with the parental report and to ask him why he thinks his/her parent answered differently. Frequently the disagreement can be clarified in this manner. Persistent disagreement can be clarified by talking with the parent and the child together at the end of the interviews. Nevertheless, the clinician should be careful because in this situation the child may agree out of fear of the parent and not out of conviction. Ultimately the clinician must exercise judgment in determining summary ratings where disagreements persist. Studies of the relative merits of structured and unstructured interviews in child psychiatry have shown that rigidly structured interviews in which all questions are predetermined might miss important information. Unstructured assessments tend to be incomplete because of the failure to inquire about possibly present symptoms, leading to false negatives. A semi-structured interview as described above, has been found to be preferable in the evaluation of children, as it combines the advantages and avoids the disadvantages of both extremes (Cox and Rutter, 1977).

ASSESSMENT OF THE INDIVIDUAL SYMPTOMS IN THE DEPRESSIVE SYNDROME

Depressive Mood

A child's negative answer to an inquiry about sadness is not equivalent to absence of depressive mood. We routinely ask for eight different labels for depressive mood: "sad feeling inside which is with you most of the time." Depressed prepubertal children can usually identify one (or sometimes several) as the persistent dysphoric feeling they have had no name for. Adolescents can usually be more articulate but it is also advisable to inquire about all eight labels. It is interesting how many children report no sadness, but identify one of the other seven labels as present.

The duration and periodicity of depressive mood during the day and during the week should be assessed very carefully in order to differentiate relatively universal short-lived periods of sadness from true depressive mood. In children who report the coexistence of two or more of the seven labels, it is important to ask if the two (for example, sadness and emptiness) occur together or separately. If separate, total duration should be the addition of the durations of each dysphoric mood.

Time estimates are more likely to be inexact the younger the child is. The use of standard time units (hours, etc) in our experience does not improve matters because frequently they are not clearly understood by the child. We have found it much more useful to refer to other types of time units which mean something to the child: "the whole morning," "the whole afternoon until you go home," "from the time you get up until you get to school," "from breakfast to lunch," "from dinner to the time you go to sleep," etc. It can be easily seen that when such time estimates from the child are placed in the context of the chronological structure of the child's average day as obtained from the parent, it becomes much easier to have approximate estimates of duration of dysphoric mood. A good general way to approach duration is to ask about diurnal variation of mood: "Do you feel worse (more sad, empty, etc) in the morning or in the afternoon?" "At what time do you begin to feel better?" "Does this happen every day?" "Also on weekends?." The clinician must be careful to assess for how long the child felt worse. Some children will report that they feel worse in the morning, by which they mean the short period between getting up and eating breakfast. This is not diurnal variation of mood (or of fatigue).

Lack of reactivity of dysphoric mood is a very important characteristic which helps to identify severity of the disorder (endogenous versus nonendogenous subtype). In children and adolescents with marked separation anxiety, separation situations may be a very specific trigger of sad mood. Thus, children with pathological separation anxiety may have feelings of sadness (and anxiety) which are entirely dependent on the presence or absence of the mother. When a child presents sadness which only occurs when separated from major attachment figures, but never in the presence, we do not count this as a symptom of the depressive syndrome. If the child feels also dysphoric in the presence of the attachment figure for a substantial period of time and feels worse during separation, then we count this as a symptom of the depression syndrome. The limits between the diagnoses of major depressive disorder and separation anxiety disorder are difficult to determine because a significant proportion of children fit criteria for both diagnoses. A full discussion of this diagnostic problem is published elsewhere (Puig-Antich and Gittelman, 1980).

Most parents are able to report depressed mood in their depressed children. Frequently their report is based more in their empathic perception of the child's mood than on actual statements of the child, but we have found that parental reports tend to agree with the child. Some parents, though, are remarkably insensitive, and our data tends to show that when disagreement occurs in prepuberty, the child is usually a better reporter. Some adolescents can be very threatened by admitting to persistent sadness or other feelings and will deny, with tears in their eyes, that they feel sad. In such cases the parental report, confirmed by the adolescent's behavior, is the best guide for clinical purposes.

Quality of mood different from reaction to a loss which occurred when the patient was not depressed is a very important sign of major depression, endogenous subtype in adult patients. Parents are frequently ignorant about this symptom which requires access to relatively fine distinctions of inner experience. Adolescents by and large have no difficulty in reporting on this aspect of dysphoric mood when properly asked. It is helpful to ask first about losses they have sustained *when they were not depressed* and how they felt at the time. Then a comparison with current feelings can be easily made. We have found it essential to inquire about losses when not depressed. If the patient was depressed at the time, his reaction to the loss is likely to be similar in quality to depressed mood and a false negative rating will ensue.

Young children have much difficulty understanding this relatively abstract concept. By age ten, most children are able to understand it and to answer appropriately when the questions are carefully explained in simple concrete language which is meaningful to them. Therefore, in young children, quality of mood cannot be assessed reliably, because of their developmentally expected cognitive limitations.

Excessive Guilt

The crucial anchor points for the assessment of excessive guilt are feeling guilty for an inordinate length of time (weeks) after doing something wrong, feeling guilty about things that are objectively not the child's fault, feeling that he should be punished much more than he is, and, finally, delusional guilt in which the child is convinced that he is the worst person that ever existed and/or that he is being persecuted, the world will come to an end soon, or he will become terribly sick because of how bad he is. One example of delusional guilt appeared in a 12-year-old boy who was absolutely certain he was the worst person ever born, "worse than the worst criminal," and that death would not be a punishment fit for him because it would end his suffering. Instead, he felt that he should be condemned to live in complete isolation (his worst fear) for the rest of his life. When asked about what was his worst crime, he responded that he was not helpful to his sisters and parents, and that the way he was feeling was causing them pain. Such extreme degree of excessive guilt is the exception in depressed youngsters, but lesser intensities of this symptom are quite common.

Parents tend to be ignorant about the presence or absence of this symptom in their children, except in the more severe cases, for the same reasons explained earlier when discussing quality of mood. Therefore, the bulk of the evidence will come from the child interview.

The first step in this assessment is to make sure that the child understands the concept of guilt. We usually ask the child to explain what feeling guilty means. Quite frequently he will say that it refers to being accused of something which somebody else did and/or being punished for it. Other times they say it has to do with a verdict of guilty. It is therefore essential to clarify the concept before assessing it. We have found it very helpful to explain very concretely along these lines: "How do you feel after you have done something wrong?" "Do you feel that way for a long time afterwards?" "Do you sometimes feel bad for things other people did wrong, but you felt it was your fault?" "Do you ever feel (guilty) and don't know why?".

Some children understand concrete examples better: "I am going to tell you about three children and you tell me which one is most like you. The first is a child who does something wrong, then feels bad about it, goes and apologizes to the person, the apologies are accepted, and he just forgets about it from then on. The second child is like the first but after his apologies are accepted, he just cannot forget about what he had done and continues to feel bad about it for one or two weeks. The third is a child who has not done much wrong, but who feels bad and guilty for all kinds of things which are really not his fault like . . . Which one of these three children is like you?

It is also useful to double-check the child's understanding of the questions by asking him to give an example, such as the last time he felt guilty "like the child in the story."

Anhedonia: Lack of Interest

Although these symptoms are in their essence inner experience, they are quite frequently accompanied by relatively obvious behavioral indices. We have found parental reports as helpful as the child's reports. Younger children, under eight or nine years, tend to have difficulty understanding negative concepts (like lack of interest or pleasure). It is therefore useful to phrase questions in the affirmative mode: "Do you feel you have more fun than your friends or less fun than your friends?" "During your free time, like at home, can you keep yourself occupied?" "What things (hobbies) do you like to do?" "Do you enjoy them as much as before?".

The assessment of these two symptoms in children and adolescents has some potential pitfalls. In adults, the clinician goes back to how things were before the patient got ill. Thus, if the patient used to especially enjoy five activities and now he only enjoys and/or is interested in two of them and no others, the symptom would be rated moderate. But in children and adolescents a new factor should always be considered: children's interests change with development. Therefore, clinical judgment should be exercised in this regard. A decrease in the total number of interesting and/or pleasurable activities is more informative for assessment purposes than a change in interests.

A second caveat is also in order. In certain urban areas parents are understandably quite strict about their children being outside, and keep them at home for a very substantial part of the day. Also, mothers of depressed children are frequently depressed and withdrawn themselves and may totally abdicate their responsibility for providing the child with varied stimulation. A child therefore may say that he feels bored a great deal and has much less fun than his friends because he has no opportunities to enjoy himself, or because he cannot enjoy anything in spite of having the opportunities. The latter is a sign of depression in the child, the former is not. Appropriate questioning of both the parent and the child can usually differentiate these two situations which have quite different diagnostic meaning.

A third caveat has to do with situation specificity. Children with separation anxiety disorder are in distress when they cannot enjoy anything at school. Nevertheless, they are totally free of symptoms when at home and/or in the presence of the major attachment figure. It should be clear from this that to be counted positive, anhedonia and lack of interest should be cross-situational.

Boredom, lack of enthusiasm, and lack of initiative (compared to the time before onset of present episode) are, in our experience, good indicators of anhedonia and of lack of interest. We have found these concepts easier for children, and some parents, to understand. Given that boredom is frequently reported by many children, it is probably wise to require boredom to occur cross-situationally for at least 50 percent of awake time in order to count it positive. It is also important to make sure that boredom persists in spite of availability of stimulation.

Suicidal Ideation and Behavior

Quite frequently we have found parents to be totally unaware of suicidal thoughts, plans, and even behavior in their child. Except for very few angry adolescents who deny any difficulties while their parents report convincing descriptions of suicidal behavior or statements, the child is by and large the best source of information for this symptom.

Suicidal ideation is quite frequent in depressed children, but the clinician is unlikely to obtain this information unless he directly asks the child. We are aware of no deleterious effects on the child when the question is put to non-suicidal children. On the other hand, suicidal depressed children felt quite relieved at being able to talk openly about their thoughts and plans or even acts which they usually kept to themselves.

Although successful suicide is rare in prepuberty (Shaffer, 1974), suicidal ideation and even attempts are not. Children who report suicidal attempts usually say that they were feeling so bad that they contemplated death as a remedy, an end to their pain. Surprisingly, in our experience, they by and large understand the finality and irreversibility of death. On the other hand, careful inquiry into the method of their unsuccessful attempts reveals insufficient cognitive competence to carry out their wish. Thus a nine-year-old attempted to hang himself twice by using a towel tied to the shower rod. As in adults, attempts carried out in private underscore the seriousness of the child's suicidal wish.

A crucial distinction regarding dangerous behavior to the self in children is between impulsive and suicidal acts. Impulsive behavior arises before thinking, in the absence of a wish to harm or kill oneself, and is characteristic of children with conduct disorder and/or attention deficit disorder, sometimes combined with low IQ. Suicidal behavior is always preceded by thoughts and ruminations about suicide and a clear suicidal wish. Suicidal gestures, which also occur in children, are always accompanied by suicidal wishes although the determination to kill onself is definitely much weaker and there is a strong manipulative, dramatic tint to the child's or adolescent's actions. The distinction between gestural and truly suicidal behaviors cannot always be made. These behaviors in children are likely to represent different points in a continuum; therefore, conservative clinical management, when in doubt, is always called for. Only direct questioning of the child can clarify the differential diagnosis between impulsive and suicidal behavior. Such questioning should be gradual: "Have you ever thought about killing yourself?" "Have you thought about how you would do it?" "Have you ever tried it?" "What is the closest you have come to doing it?" "What did you do?" "Did you really want to die?" "What happens after death?" "Why did you want to die?" "How many times have you tried it?"

Assessment of suicidal risk should be especially careful in youngsters fitting both criteria for major depression and conduct disorder. Shaffer (1974) has shown that successful suicide tends to occur in adolescents presenting conduct disturbances, and the final act usually follows a disciplinary crisis.

Changes in Sleep Patterns

Children and adolescents with major depressive disorder as a group report considerable sleep difficulties which can fall under various subcategories: difficulty falling asleep, circadian shift of sleep period, intermittent awakenings, early morning awakening, increase in sleep period requirement, and a feeling of not sleeping well (nonrestorative sleep). It is important to assess all six patterns of sleep difficulties in order to properly determine the presence or absence of sleep pattern changes.

Difficulty falling asleep (DFA) is probably the most frequently reported symptom, sometimes associated with excessive separation anxiety. We rate this symptom positive when the child spends at least one hour in bed without being able to fall asleep, after he decides to go to sleep. There is a problem in this population, in that bedtimes are dictated by parents, and the child adapts to such training. Nevertheless, it should be realized that social pressures significantly determine bedtime in adults also. Although the social pressures come from different sources, they are still social pressures and, at least in our opinion, the determination of usual bedtime in childhood and adulthood have more similarities than differences.

Other children, especially older ones and adolescents, reset their bedtime to a later time than usual, in the absence of social pressure to do so, and frequently against social and familial influences. The child will report that now he cannot fall asleep before the new late bedtime. We do not know if bedtime shifts and difficulty falling asleep represent the same or different symptoms. Frequently both symptoms coexist, so that the child may go to bed when depressed much later than his regular bedtime and still have substantial difficulty falling asleep.

In some adolescents with major depressive disorder, these bedtime shifts become extreme and constitute an almost complete 180 degree circadian shift: they sleep during the day and are awake all night. The mechanisms underlying such pronounced changes are unknown at present. Nevertheless, it is probably advisable to attempt to assess in such cases the role of oppositional behavior characteristic of some adolescents. Thus, the circadian shifts of an adolescent who can switch bedtimes at will may have a very different diagnostic significance than that of an adolescent who cannot do so, given no other environmental circumstances.

Interrupted sleep is also relatively frequent in the report from depressed youngsters. It is important to exclude middle of the night awakenings to urinate without difficulty falling back to sleep, as well as awakenings from anxiety dreams. Early morning awakenings (EMA) is reported less frequently. To be rated positive it should occur at least 30 minutes before usual time of awakening. It is useful to ask the child if he wakes up spontaneously before he has to, or before his parent calls him, and if he feels that he would like to sleep more but cannot.

Increases in sleep period requirements are reported more frequently by depressed adolescents, in whom substantial hypersomnia is not rare. The actual questioning for these symptoms should include naps and also an estimate of the total number of hours slept per 24-hour cycle. Daytime napping to compensate for sleep difficulty during the night does not constitute hypersomnia. The estimate of the total number of hours slept should be compared to the child's usual sleep time before the depressive episode and to age norms before reaching a decision on the presence or absence of these symptoms. We do not rate this positive if the child's daily sleep time does not increase by at least one hour.

All the symptoms described under this section on sleep constitute changes in sleep patterns associated with major depression. Nevertheless, in order to count any of these symptoms positive we have one more requirement: the patient should report that upon final awakening he does not feel well-rested or that he feels like he did not sleep well, and this feeling of nonrestorative sleep should persist after breakfast. We still do not know if the feeling of nonrestorative sleep per se, even if unaccompanied by any of the sleep pattern changes described above, should or should not be accepted as a symptom of sleep difficulty in major depression in children and adolescents.

Changes in Appetite and/or Weight

Anorexia is a very frequent, and mostly unsubstantiated, parental complaint in any pediatric practice. Given its importance as one of the symptomatic criteria for the depressive syndrome, it behooves the clinician to assess this symptom by as objective measurement as possible. When loss of appetite is accompanied by weight loss, the latter serves as a validating criterion provided that the patient is not refusing to eat on grounds of dieting or excessive fear of obesity, in which case the differential diagnosis with anorexia nervosa has to be made.

Weight loss in children and adolescents cannot be assessed by simply comparing measured weight from the past (preferably before the depressive episode) to the present. Because children's and adolescent's weight normally increases as a function of time, if the youngster's weight remains stationary over several months, this in itself constitutes weight loss (except in older adolescents). The ideal situation occurs in children in whom the pediatrician had past weights. Weight percentile can then be determined according to standard tables for children (or adolescents) before the onset of the episode and at assessment time. A percentile fall over ten points is the minimum cut-off point we accept to rate weight loss positive.

Nevertheless, this ideal situation does not always occur. In such occasion semi-quantitative indices can be used like clothes becoming baggy, belt needing to be tightened, or changes in appearance. In prepuberty it is frequent to find depressive episodes of long duration and insidious onset, which makes it more difficult to properly assess weight loss. In such eventuality any past weight before the time when the patient has been most depressed is probably sufficient if compared to another measurement at or near the peak of depressive syndrome severity. If the patient is getting better at the time of assessment, current weight is probably a poor index of weight loss.

When the available evidence for weight loss is not conclusive, the assessment of anorexia becomes more important. It is advisable to ask about any period of time during the present episode of disorder when the child's appetite has been decreased as compared to before the onset of illness. In the interview with the parent, the clinician should ask appropriate questions to discriminate between changes in pattern of food intake, changes in preferences, or changes in total amount of food consumed, as parents tend to report these three as lack or loss of appetite. When in doubt, and if the child is reportedly "anorexic" at the time of the assessment, a prospective three-day dietary assessment can be very helpful at arriving at a final rating. In the interview with the child it is helpful to focus on the loss of the appetite for food. Some children develop a "sweet tooth" when depressed. At present we do not rate this as anorexia if the total amount of food consumed appears not to be decreased and if the child reports a good appetite for sweets. Nevertheless, this should alert the clinician to the possibility of loss of taste which is probably a reflection of pervasive anhedonia. In cases where the depressive episode is over two years in duration with a relatively chronic course, the clinician finds himself in search for a baseline for food intake. We find it acceptable to ask the child and the parents how the child's food intake compares to that of his peers. Unavoidably, a rating of anorexia cannot be achieved with reasonable certainty in some prepubertal children. In adolescents this situation rarely arises.

The assessment of increased appetite and excessive weight gain in children and adolescents follows the same methodology and is subject to the same "caveats" as the assessment of their opposites. Only two points need to be made:

1. During the pubertal growth spurt, marked increases in appetite and weight are the norm. Ideally, growth tables considering weight/height ratios should be used (Hamill et al, 1977). The clinician should ask about growth spurts when any period of increased appetite is reported, and should be careful to use this as a correction factor in his final rating.

2. During a depressive episode, a youngster can have a period of anorexia and/or weight loss, and another period of increased appetite or weight gain. Thus, a positive rating of one set of symptoms does not preclude the assessment of the other set.

Difficulty Concentrating and/or Slowed-Down Thoughts

The concept of slowed-down thoughts in our experience is not understood by and large by prepubertal children, although it is a useful, descriptive term in the assessment of concentration difficulties in adolescents.

In prepuberty concentration difficulties are hard to assess without direct input from the teacher. The parent can report on gross indices of poor concentration ability, like a drop in school performance as reflected in the child's marks. Nevertheless, the clinician should be aware that low scholastic marks do not necessarily indicate concentration difficulties. A depressed younster may not be doing well in school because he has completely lost his interest in school work and activities (which should be rated as lack of interest), or because of a variety of interpersonal difficulties with peers or teachers, or because of severe separation anxiety with excessive preoccupation with parental well-being during the school period. Neither of the above should be specifically rated as concentration difficulties.

Conversely, lack of impairment of school performance does not necessarily indicate normal concentration ability. When properly asked, a child may report that he now needs more effort to concentrate and complete his school tasks than he needed before he started feeling depressed. Such a statement supports a positive rating for concentration difficulties.

Parental reports about the child not completing his tasks or of "hyperactivity" do not support a positive rating of poor concentration in themselves because of their lack of specificity.

Some of the questions we have found helpful in interviewing prepubertal children about concentration difficulties are: "Do you have trouble keeping track of what the teacher says in class?" "Do you have trouble paying attention to what she says or to your work?" "Do you know what concentration means?" "Can you tell me what it means?" "Do you have trouble concentrating when you read? . . . study? . . . or when dong school or homework?" "Is it harder for you to do your work now?" If the child shows any indication of possible difficulty in this area, the clinician should follow by asking the child for a description of what the problem seems to be: "Do you have trouble reading (or keeping track while doing your work, etc) because you cannot understand it? . . . or because you just don't care? . . . or because you are worried about something? . . . or because you just can't pay attention for long and keep getting distracted?" "Can you pay attention to things you like to do, like TV shows, building blocks, etc?"

The younger the child, the more critical the information from the teacher becomes in the assessment of concentration. Although both parents and child may be able to give secondhand reports of the teacher's comments and opinion, these are not good substitutes for direct teacher information because they are likely to be distorted by the information bearer to fit his/her own needs. A comprehensive discussion of the role of teacher information in the differential diagnosis of prepubertal major depression is beyond the scope of this chapter.

Fatigue, Excessive Tiredness, and Lack of Energy

Complaints of tiredness are not frequent among well children, and their presence therefore is a good indicator of disorder. Both parents and children tend to be highly reliable informers for this symptom, which is relatively easy to assess. Frequently, children and parents confuse tiredness with sleepiness and daytime napping, and the clinician should clarify the two concepts so that the different ratings remain specific and a single behavior does not contribute to two different criteria.

We do not rate fatigue positive unless evidence is forthcoming that the child is regularly and unusually tired at times (lasting for at least one hour) out of proportion to the activities carried out. Diurnal variation of fatigue is frequently present. Depressed children will frequently report that they feel tired most of the morning and become less fatigued as the day goes on. Interestingly, diurnal variation of fatigue does not always parallel diurnal variation of mood. In the assessment of these symptoms, the clinician should guard against false positive responses secondary to concreteness of prepubertal children. Thus, a child may report feeling very fatigued regularly and further inquiry reveals that he is referring to tiredness after playing his regular one-hour soccer game. Intense, pervasive sense of fatigue and lack of energy are not unusual among depressive youngsters, who may feel exhausted almost all of the time.

Psychomotor Agitation and Retardation

Inability to sit still and development of different habits (frequent picking and/or rubbing on skin, clothes, or hair) are the most frequent signs of psychomotor agitation in prepubertal children. In adolescents, pacing, nonstop talking, and hand-wringing, which are rare in prepuberty, become more frequent.

Slackness of body movement, sluggishness, slowness in carrying out simple routine tasks (getting dressed, walking), and difficulty maintaining a conversation can be the result of any combination of the following items: slowed-down speech, monotonous speech, long latency of response, and markedly decreased amount of speech. Sometimes the child is barely understandable because of the weak nature of his voice when depressed.

Psychomotor changes are easily observable and therefore parents and teachers are the best sources of information. It is important to rate actual observations by others (including the clinician's observation during the interview with the child) and not to accept as sufficient evidence the child's report of feeling slowed-down or speeded-up.

Psychotic Symptoms

Although hallucinations and delusions are not as intrinsic a part of the depressive syndrome, the presence of psychotic symptoms (especially hallucinations) is not unusual, and it may have major diagnostic and prognostic importance. We will therefore describe what we consider to be the most relevant aspect of their systematic assessment in depressed youngsters.

Hallucinations

In children under 18 years, as in adults, the presence of hallucinations per se does not militate against the diagnosis of major depressive disorder. These symptoms should be routinely assessed in every child with a presumptive diagnosis of major depression, and if present, a differential diagnosis of the symptom should be undertaken.

Children are the best informers regarding these symptoms, which depressives quite frequently keep to themselves. We have found it most helpful to approach this subject directly: "Do you ever hear voices when you are alone or when no one is talking to you?" "Do you ever see visions? . . . or see things that are not there?" "Do you ever smell things that other people cannot smell?" "Do you ever feel that someone is touching you when no one is there? . . . or things crawling on your skin when nothing is there?" A positive answer to any of these questions is *not* tantamount to a positive rating for hallucinations. Prepubertal children in particular are very concrete, and they refer to instances where their keen senses were more sensitive than those of adults around them, etc. Therefore, it is crucial to ask the child to explain what did he perceive and under what circumstances.

Visual illusions should not be confused with hallucinations. Illusions occur in the periphery of the visual field or under conditions of semi-darkness, and are based on a real stimulus, the perception of which is distorted under conditions of poor visual resolution. Thus, a child may "see a robber" instead of the coat hanging in the darkness of his bedroom. Illusions disappear instantaneously when visual conditions improve: when he focuses his vision on the stimulus or when the light is turned on. Illusions are frequent in childhood, and they are likely to be associated with anxiety. Their diagnostic meaning is therefore quite different from that of hallucinations. Two other phenomena specific to children and adolescents should be differentiated from true hallucinations: the imaginary friend and eidetic imagery. Although some children may insist on clearly and even visibly perceiving their imaginary companions through one or more senses, such "perception" can usually be turned on and off at the child's will, and their presence does not cause distress.

Once the presence of a true hallucination is established, the first step is to inquire about its timing in the 24-hour sleep/wake cycle. First of all, some children report as hallucinations their dream experiences. Questions as simple as: "Do you hear or see these things when you are awake or asleep?" "Only when asleep or sometimes also when you are awake?" are sufficient to establish these points. The presence of hypnagogic and hypnopompic hallucinations should always be assessed. This type of hallucination occurs exclusively in the half-awake or half-asleep state, either at the start or at the end of the sleep period. As in adults, the presence of hypnagogic or hypnopompic hallucinations in children and adolescents does not indicate psychosis, but should not be disregarded by the clinician. The finding of such specific hallucination should lead to questions about excessive daytime sleepiness, sleep paralysis and cataplexy (narcoleptic tetrad), and to an appropriate referral to a sleep/wake disorder center, as narcolepsy can also affect youngsters (Navalet et al, 1976).

The differential diagnosis of drug abuse, drug withdrawal, and "organic" hallucinatory state falls beyond the scope of this chapter, as it rarely poses a problem in the assessment of children with possible major depression. In adolescents this problem may sometimes occur, but differential diagnosis follows the same guidelines as in adults.

Once the presence of *true, functional, nonsleep-related hallucinations* is established, it is advisable to systematically assess all different types of content and form of auditory hallucinations: command, commenting voices, conversing voices, religious, persecutory, and others.

In our experience the depressive hallucination in children can be characterized by three criteria:

1. Temporal consistency with the depressive syndrome: the child never hallucinated outside the depressive episode.
2. Thematic consistency with depressive mood: the content of the hallucinations is congruent with depressive mood. Thus, the voices tell the child to kill himself or that he is no good.
3. The form of hallucinations: in pure major depression conversing and commenting voices do not occur. Instead, the child hears one voice talking directly to him, most frequently with command suicidal content. If the child hears several voices, all voices talk to him and not among themselves.

When auditory hallucinations in children with major depression fit all three criteria, the hallucinations are classified as depressive and the disorder is subtyped as psychotic. When in a child with major depression and auditory hallucinations none of this criteria are met, we provisionally classify them as schizoaffective/depressed, following RDC criteria for adults. We do not as yet know if the larger diagnosis is valid in children or how many of these criteria for hallucination should or should not be met as a cut-off point for their classification.

Finally, where the child locates the "source" of the auditory hallucinations has been considered important by some authors for the diagnosis and prognosis of psychotic disorders of childhood (Bender, 1970). Specifically, the child should be asked if the voices come from inside his head, from inside the rest of his body or from outside his head. If the voices come from only inside his head, it is important to ask: "Are these voices you *hear* or do you mean just your *thoughts*?" The concept of hallucination involves an abnormal perception, in this case auditory. Being aware, even very aware, of his own thoughts should never be classified as a hallucination unless the child actually *hears* his thoughts aloud. We do not know if the outside/inside location of depressive hallucinations in children and adolescents has any prognostic or diagnostic implications. This must await further work.

Delusions

The assessment of delusions in prepubertal children poses problems of similar nature to those found in assessing hallucinations, but they are more difficult to resolve. In contrast to hallucinations, in which a relatively definite cut-off point exists (the existence of clear perception not based on external stimulus), there is no such clear delimitation between elaborated fantasies, cultural beliefs, overvalued ideas, and definite delusions. The more extreme delusions are easy to recognize if the clinician's inquiries are specific. Thus, in the section on excessive guilt we have an example of a definite delusion of guilt. We find it advisable to routinely assess the following types of delusions: referential persecutory, guilt, sin or poverty, nihilistic, thought insertion, thought withdrawal, thought broadcasting, thought reading, delusions of control or influence, somatic, grandiosity, etc.

In contrast to hallucinations, we have found it helpful to approach this subject more generally: "Does your imagination ever play tricks on you?" "Do you know about things other people don't seem to know about?" "Do you believe in things other people or your parents don't seem to believe in?" If there is any possible doubt about the presence of delusions, the clinician should proceed to ask the relevant questions regarding each individual type of delusion. If at the end of this assessment the clinician has rated any of them either definite or suspected, the clinician must inquire further regarding the tenacity with which such beliefs are held and to challenge their logic: "Are you sure that this is so? . . . or do you think that it just may be so?" "Why are you sure? . . . how do you know?" It is characteristic of definite delusions that the child or the adolescent is definitely sure but cannot provide logical evidence for his beliefs.

One of the major difficulties, especially in prepuberty, is that delusions in child psychiatric disorders in general and in major depression specifically are rare, and therefore the clinician rarely becomes very proficient in their assessments. Another problem is that a few prepubertal children will, on interview, describe what appears to be a persecutory delusion on purely phenomenological grounds, but without any other major signs of psychopathology. Sarnoff (1976) has described this as benign paranoia of latency-age children and he reported that on follow-up these children did very well and did not become psychotic. Such youngsters may have had no more than elaborate fantasies and/or overvalued ideas during a developmental period; but, as indicated before, sometimes the differential diagnosis between the later and definite delusions cannot be made with certainty.

As with hallucinations, once the presence of definite delusions has been established, the next task is to determine if these are depressive or nondepressive in nature, by using temporal and thematic consistency criteria with major depression, as was described for hallucinations. In our experience, four types of delusions can occur in major depressive youngsters: guilt, sin or poverty, somatic, persecutory, and nihilistic. The common link is that the child will say that this is happening because he is such a terrible person. When these delusions occur in major depressive disorder, we provisionally classify the disorders as schizoaffective/depressed, following RDC criteria for adults. Not until a sufficient sample of these patients has been collected will we be able to have any evidence for or against the validity of this diagnosis in youngsters.

SUMMARY

Studies on child and adolescent major depression have provided a great deal of stimulation in the last few years for the development of interview techniques for the psychiatric assessment of this population. All investigators, as the work progresses, are moving toward increasing reliance on the interview with the child. This represents in our view a major advance in child psychiatry and is bound to substantially alter child psychiatric practice in years to come. Preliminary ongoing studies tend to indicate that children over six years of age can be assessed as reliably as adults, but that it is also necessary to interview the parents about the child's symptomatology. In Chapter 11, preliminary evidence on the validity of the assessment of major depressive disorder in children will be provided.

REFERENCES

Bender L. The maturation process and hallucinations in children. In: Keup W, ed. *Origins and mechanisms of hallucinations.* New York/London: Plenum Press, 1970:95–102.

Beres D. Ego deviation and the concept of schizophrenia. *Psychoanal Study Child* 1956; 11:164–235.

Carlson G, Cantwell D. Unmasking masked depression. *Am J Psychiatry* 1980; 137;4:445–449.

Children Psychiatric Rating Scale (CPRS) Assessment Battery for Pediatric Psychopharmacology. NIMH Rev, July, 1975.

Conners CK. A teacher rating scale for use in drug studies with children. *Am J Psychiatry* 1969; 126:152–156.

Cox A, Rutter M. Diagnostic appraisal and interviewing. In: Rutter M, Hersov L, eds. *Child psychiatry*. London: Longman V.K., 1977:271–305.

Cytryn L, McKnew D, Bunney W. Diagnosis of depression in children: reassessment. *Am J Psychiatry* 1980; 137:22–25.

Endicott J, Spitzer RL. A diagnostic interview: the schedule for affective disorders and schizophrenia. *Arch Gen Psychiatry* 1978; 35:837–844.

Freud A. The symptomatology of childhood: a preliminary attempt at classification. *Psychoanal Study Child* 1970; 25:19–41.

Gersten JC, Langner TS, Eisenberg JG, et al. Stability and changes in types of behavioral disturbance of children and adolescents. *J Abnorm Child Psychol* 1976; 4:111–127.

Gittelman-Klein R. Review of clinical psychopharmacological treatment of hyperkinesis. In: Klein DF, Gittelman-Klein R, eds. *Progress in psychiatric drug treatment.* New York: Brunner/Mazel, 1975:661–674.

Gittelman-Klein R, Klein DF. School phobia: diagnostic considerations in the light of imipramine effects. *J Nerv Ment Dis* 1973; 156:199–215.

Hamill PVV, Dridz TA, Johnson CL, et al. NCHS growth curves for children–birth-18 years, United States. Hyattsville, Maryland: National Center for Health Statistics, 1977; DHEW publication no. (PHS)78-1650; series 11; no. 165.

Herjanic B, Campbell W. Differentiating psychiatrically disturbed children on the basis of a structured interview. *J Assoc Child Psychol* 1977; 5:127–134.

Herjanic B, Herjanic M, Brown F, Wheatt T. Are children reliable reporters? *J Assoc Child Psychol* 1975; 3:41–48.

Lapouse R, Monk MA. Fears and worries in a representative sample of children. *Am J Orthopsychiatry* 1959; 29:803–818.

Mahler M. *On human symbions and the vicissitudes of individuation: infantile psychosis.* New York: Int. University Press, 1968.

Mischel W. *Personality and assessment.* New York: Wiley, 1968.

Navalet Y, Anders T, Guilleminault C. Narcolepsy in children. In: Guilleminault C, Dement WC, Passouant P, eds. *Narcolepsy.* New York: Spectrum, 1976:171–177.

Pringle MLK, Butler NR, Davie R. *Eleven thousand seven-year-olds.* London: Longmans, 1966.

Puig-Antich J, Blau S, Marx N, et al. Prepubertal major depressive disorder: pilot study. *J Am Acad Child Psychiatry* 1978; 17:695–707.

Puig-Antich J, Gittelman R. Depression in childhood and adolescence. In: Paykel ES, ed. *Handbook of affective disorders.* London: Churchill, 1980.

Quay HC. Measuring dimensions of deviant behavior: the behavior problem checklist. *J Abnorm Child Psychol* 1977; 5:277–289.

Rutter M, Graham P. The reliability and validity of the psychiatric assessment of the child: the interview with the child. *Br J Psychiatry* 1968; 114: 563–579.

Rutter M, Tizard J, Whitmore K. *Education, health and behavior.* London: Longmans, 1970.

Sarnoff C. *Latency.* New York: Jason Aronson, 1976:300–334.

Shaffer D. Suicide in childhood and early adolescence. *J Child Psychol Psychiatry* 1974; 15:275–291.

Skinner BF. *Science and human behavior.* New York: Macmillan, 1953.

Spitzer RL, Endicott J, Robins E. Research diagnostic criteria: rationale and and reliability. *Arch Gen Psychiatry* 1972; 35:773–782.

Szurek S. Psychotic episodes and psychotic maldevelopment. *Am J Orthopsychiatry* 1956; 26:519–543.

Weinberg WA, Rutman J, Sullivan L, et al. Depression in children referred to an education diagnostic center. *J Pediatr* 1973; 83:1065–1072.

Yule W. Behavioral approaches. In: Rutter M, Hersov L, eds. *Child psychiatry.* London: Blackwell, 1973:923–948.

Affective Disorders in Childhood and Adolescence--An Update. Edited by D.P. Cantwell and G.A. Carlson.

10

The Children's Depression Scale: Review and Further Developments

Miriam Tisher and Moshe Lang

Until the early 1960s, depression in children was rarely if ever mentioned in textbooks on child psychiatry and generally not diagnosed clinically. Since that time, however, interest in childhood depression has increased considerably and an ever-increasing number of papers on childhood depression is being published. In reviewing the status of the Children's Depression Scale (CDS), some perspective of the literature concerning definition and measurement of childhood depression is useful.

DEFINITION

Many authors writing in the 1970s agree upon a set of behaviors which are consistent with childhood depression. Kovacs and Beck (1977) (Table 1) provide a good summary of these characteristics, which include weepiness, looking or feeling miserable, weepy, or unhappy, low self-esteem, persistent somatic problems which are not of physical origin, irritability, and social withdrawal (Connell, 1973; Frommer, 1967; Glaser, 1967; Kovacs and Beck, 1977; McConville et al, 1973; Murray, 1970; Pozanski and Zrull, 1970).

While there is general agreement regarding the characteristics above, there are some important disagreements in the literature which should be noted.

The question of "masked" versus "overt" depression continues to be debated. Those who argue for masked depression claim that behavior such as truancy, lying, stealing, school phobia, enuresis, encopresis, hyperactivity, hypochondriasis, and delinquency, are indirect or masked ways in which children express their depression (Connell, 1973; Cytryn and McKnew, 1974; Bakwin, 1972; Fromer, 1967; Glaser, 1967; Ling et al, 1970; Renshaw, 1974). Other writers such as Anthony (1977) question whether by terming so many behaviors depression we are in fact contributing anything to the understanding of childhood depression.

A second question arising from the literature is whether depression is a syndrome or a mood state. Kovacs and Beck (1977) firmly draw the distinction between "... depression as a sad, despondent mood, and depression as a clinical syndrome (a collection of symptoms)." Murray (1970), identifies eight major symptoms which he considers indicate the presence of childhood depression as a syndrome.

A third issue is whether and when depression is normal or appropriate and when it is pathological. Lefkowitz (1977) and Lefkowitz and Burton (1978) review the literature and find that in epidemiological studies of deviant behavior in children, for example, the work of Lapouse and Monk (1958), approximately 20 percent of the general child population has been reliably judged to possess the symptoms of depressive disorder observed in clinical samples.

One of the important findings reported recently is that depression in children is manifested differently depending on the age of the child. McConville et al (1973) suggest that affectual depression would be most common in youngest children (six to eight years), that self-esteem depression would be most common in middle children (eight to ten years), and that guilt depression would be most common in oldest children (ten to 13 years). Cytryn and McKnew (1974) identify some of the factors which influence the changing clinical picture of childhood depression with age.

MEASUREMENT

To date, to our knowledge, two serious attempts have made to measure depression in children, neither of which has been published for general use. The first of these is the Wiggins and Winder Peer Nomination Inventory (Siegelman, 1966), in which 113 boys in grades four, five, and six were asked to rate each other on 58 items which covered five areas, one of which was depression, and the others aggression, dependency, withdrawal and likability. The second measure is the Children's Depression Inventory (Kovacs and Beck, 1977). Kovacs and Beck have adapted the BDI (Beck Depression Inventory), a scale which has been used widely with adults to measure depression, for use with children by changing or omitting items as necessary.

The Children's Depression Scale

Raskin (1977), after reviewing definitions of depression in children and measurement issues associated with depression in children, argues for the importance of what he calls a "laundry list" of symptoms and signs of childhood depression and of several simultaneous rating scales which are completed by the child, teacher, and others. He further argues for the separation of symptoms and behaviors which are associated with mood and those which extend longer, for example, loss of appetite and loss of interest in activities previously enjoyed. We were pleased to note that the CDS in fact meets the criteria set up by Raskin.

In terms of definition, we see depression as a range of behaviors, feelings, and attitudes which varies in intensity and in extent. We expect that childhood depression is present to varying degrees throughout the population as well as having a role in various specific groups such as bereaved children, underachieving children, and psychiatric populations, particularly groups of children diagnosed as suffering from depression.

In terms of measurement, in the CDS we combine two types of measurements; we ask the child himself or herself to report on themselves, that is, self-report, and we ask for reports from others who know the child well, for example, parents, teachers, nurses. We also ask for a systematic clinical judgment by clinicians or testers, that is, a rating on each of ten scales.

Development of the CDS

Toward the end of 1967, we were interested in studying a sample of severe school refusing children and their families and comparing them with a matched control group of children who attend school regularly. On the basis of our clinical experience we had some expectations or hypotheses about the sorts of variables that would be important; these included separation anxiety, dependency, and, very importantly, depression in the children and in the families generally. While there were many scales to measure anxiety, personality disturbance, and so on, there was no scale available to measure depression in children; in fact at that time there was debate and some opposition in the literature to the concept that childhood depression could be an issue (Rie, 1966). As no scale of childhood depression was available, we decided to develop our own. A brief summary of the development of the scale follows.

The first step was to develop an empirical definition of childhood depression. We arrived at such a definition by summarizing the features reported in the literature as part of the symptomatology of childhood depression:

1. Affective response: feelings of sadness and unhappiness, weeping (Despert, 1952; Frommer, 1967; Harrington and Hassan, 1958; Poznanski and Zrull, 1970; Sandler and Joffe, 1965; Ushakov and Girich, 1971; Ling et al, 1970).

2. Negative self-concept: feelings of inadequacy and low self-esteem, feelings of worthlessness, helplessness, hopelessness, unlovability (Poznanski and Zrull, 1970; Sandler and Joffe, 1965).

3. Decrease in mental productivity and drive: boredom, withdrawal, lack of energy, discontent, little capacity for pleasure, inability to accept help or comfort, motor retardation (Sandler and Joffe, 1965; Stack, 1971; Ushakov and Girich, 1971).

4. Psychosomatic problems: headaches, abdominal pains, insomnia or other sleep disturbances (Agras, 1959; Harrington and Hassan, 1958; Poznanski and Zrull, 1970; Sandler and Joffe, 1965; Stack, 1971; Ling et al, 1970; Frommer, 1968; Kuhn and Kuhn, 1972).

5. Preoccupation with death or illness of self or others, suicidal thoughts, feelings of loss (real or imagined) (Agras, 1959; Despert, 1952; Frommer, 1967; Harrington and Hassan, 1958; Poznanski and Zrull, 1970; Ushakov and Girich, 1971).

6. Difficulties with aggression: irritability, temper outbursts (Frommer, 1967; Harrington and Hassan, 1958; Poznanski and Zrull, 1970; Stack, 1971).

For the purpose of constructing the CDS, these features constituted a definition of childhood depression, and in developing the CDS an attempt was made to include items pertinent to all these features.

Items were developed on the basis of close inspection of psychotherapy records and TAT and sentence completion records of clinically depressed children as well as descriptions of depressive phenomena and experiences reported in the literature. In phrasing the items, the aim was to describe the depressed child's experience in such a way that he or she would recognize the feelings or attitudes described by the item if they were in any way part of his or her experience.

These items were administered to a range of children in treatment at the time of scale construction. The children were subsequently requested to comment, modify, and/or suggest new items as they thought appropriate.

Description: Scales and Subscales

CDS

The full CDS contains 66 items, 48 depressive (for example, "Often I feel I'm not worth much," "Often I feel lonely") and 18 positive (for example, "I enjoy myself most of the time"). The two sets of items are retained as independent scales and scored separately, yielding a depressive score and a positive score.

Within the two main scales of the CDS certain items which refer to similar features of childhood depression have been grouped together as subscales. The depressive scale contains five such subscales and the positive scale contains one such subscale. Each is briefly described here.

Affective Response (Aff. Res.): Refers to the feeling state and mood of the respondent. Items are:

7 Often school makes me miserable
10 Sometimes I wish I was dead
27 I feel like crying often when I am at school

32 Often I feel miserable/weepy/unhappy
33 Sometimes I feel that life is not worth living
45 When I am away from home I feel very unhappy
51 Sometimes I don't know why I feel like crying
54 I feel that life is miserable for me

Social Problems (Soc. Prob.): Refers to the difficulties in social interaction, isolation, and loneliness of the child. Items are:

16 Often I feel nobody cares for me
18 Often I feel lonely
20 Often I can't show anybody how unhappy I feel inside
28 When I am at school I often feel lonely and lost
40 Most of the time I feel nobody understands me
49 Nobody knows how unhappy I really am inside
56 Often I feel I am no use to anyone
64 When I am away from home I feel empty inside

Self Esteem (Self Est.): Refers to the child's attitudes, concepts, and feelings in relation to his/her own worth and value. Items are:

9 Often I feel I'm not worth much
19 Often I am annoyed with myself
25 I hate the way I look or the way I act
35 Often I hate myself
38 Often I feel ashamed of myself
52 Sometimes I wonder whether I may be a very bad person inside
53 When I fail at school I feel that I am a nobody
58 Most of the time I feel I am not as good as I wish to be

Preoccupation with Own Sickness and Death (Sick/Death): Refers to the child's dreams and fantasies in relation to his/her sickness and death. Items are:

12 Often I wake up during the night
13 I feel more tired than most children I know
14 Most of the time I am not interested in doing anything
26 Often I don't feel like waking up in the morning
30 Often I feel dead inside
48 I feel tired most of the time when I am at school
60 I often imagine myself hurt or killed

Guilt (Guilt): Refers to the child's self blame. Items are:

21 Often I feel as if I'm letting my mother/father down
23 Sometimes I believe that my mother/father do or say things which make me feel as if I've done something terrible to them
37 Sometimes I am afraid that I do things which might harm or upset my mother/father

39 Often I feel I deserve to be punished
46 I sometimes feel upset becuase I don't love my mother/father as much as I should
47 I feel that people love me even though I don't deserve it
55 Sometimes I believe that I do things which could make my mother/father ill
61 I sometimes feel upset because I can't give my mother/father the attention and love that they need

Pleasure (Plsr.): Refers to the presence of fun, enjoyment, happiness in the child's life, or to his/her capacity to experience these things. Items are:

1 I enjoy myself most of the time
2 I'm always looking forward to the next day
8 I'm always keen to do lots of things when I am at school
22 I get fun out of the things I do
24 Often I enjoy myself at school
41 I'm a very happy person
65 I feel I'm a beautiful person
66 I'm successful in most of the things I try

The items in each of these subscales are mutually exclusive, that is, each item belongs to only one subscale. Thee are nine depressive items which do not cluster together and which do not belong to any of the subscales. These are scored as Miscellaneous D items. Similarly, there are ten positive items which do not belong to a subscale; these are scored as Miscellaneous P items.

Miscellaneous D items are:

3 I feel that there is a lot of suffering in life
4 When somebody gets angry with me I get very upset
6 When I feel very angry I usually end up crying
42 Often my schoolwork makes me miserable
43 Often I am upset about my mother's health
50 Sometimes in my dreams I am hurt or killed
59 Often I'm very upset because I don't get the opportunity to do things I want to do
62 Often I feel I'm not getting anywhere
63 Sometimes I feel there are two persons inside me pulling me in different directions

Miscellaneous P items are:

5 I feel proud of most of the things I do
11 Most of the time my mother/father make me feel the things I do are pretty good
15 In our family we all have lots of fun together
17 When somebody gets angry with me I get angry in return

29 I feel my mother/father are very proud of me
31 It is all right to feel angry
34 I sleep like a log and never wake up during the night
36 I have many friends
44 I spend my time doing many interesting things with my father
57 Many people care about me a lot

Different children manifest their depression in different ways; these subscales allow several aspects of childhood depression to be considered separately.

CDS–Adult Form

The CDS–Adult Form is intended for use with parents, siblings, teachers, and relatives of the child to yield another index of the child's depression. The items of the CDS were rephrased, for example, from "Often I feel I'm not worth much" to "Often he feels he is not worth much" (for boys) and "Often she feels she is not worth much" (for girls).

Rather than relying upon the respondent only, that is, the child, by using the CDS in conjunction with the CDS–Adult Form, the tester has information about the child's depression from at least two, and perhaps more, sources.

A systematic version of what commonly happens in a clinician's office is thus provided, that is, the child's state of feeling and behavior is explored with the child, the parents, the siblings, and perhaps teachers or relatives. All the information obtained is then used to provide an index of depression in the child which is more reliable and comprehensive than would be the case if only one respondent's information were being relied on.

Table 1 shows experimental and control group mean scores, F values, and significance level values, based on analysis of variance for each of the CDS and CDS–Adult Form items.

Of the 48 depressive items, 35 discriminate between the depressed and nondepressed children and 47 discriminate between the two groups of mothers. Of the 18 positive items, 11 discriminate between the two groups of children and 12 discriminate between the two groups of mothers.

Each of the 66 items of the CDS is printed on a separate card. The cards/items are presented one by one to the child or adult in order, that is, 1 through 66.

Five boxes are provided, each with a slit in the top. These boxes are labeled "Very Wrong --," "Wrong –," "Don't know/Not sure?," "Right +," and "Very Right ++." They are set up in a row in front of the child or adult, from left to right as follows:

Very Wrong --	Wrong –	Don't Know Not Sure ?	Right +	Very Right ++

Table 1

	CDS				CDS adult form			
Item no.	Exp $\bar{x}$ n = 40	Cont $\bar{x}$ n = 37	F values	p	Exp $\bar{x}$ n = 39	Cont $\bar{x}$ n = 37	F values	p
3	3.950	3.649	1.125	NS	3.462	3.243	0.832	NS
4	3.725	3.351	1.700	NS	4.538	3.919	14.796	000
6	2.975	2.324	3.987	.049	3.846	2.919	10.081	002
7	4.075	2.595	27.308	.000	4.206	2.027	96.141	000
9	3.125	2.784	1.347	NS	3.615	1.811	68.286	000
10	2.950	2.703	0.491	NS	3.462	1.946	32.408	000
12	3.225	2.784	1.808	NS	3.385	2.081	24.872	000
13	3.150	2.081	18.330	000	3.256	1.892	26.968	000
14	2.950	1.757	19.235	000	3.026	1.486	38.606	000
16	2.925	2.297	5.049	.028	3.256	1.838	36.035	000
18	3.625	2.649	12.988	.001	3.718	2.189	45.879	000
19	3.750	2.919	11.817	.001	3.538	2.703	15.474	000
20	3.725	2.622	15.042	000	3.897	2.514	37.990	000
21	3.450	3.000	2.282	NS	3.103	2.135	19.950	000
23	3.400	2.622	7.260	.009	3.179	1.811	40.233	000
25	2.650	2.432	0.494	NS	3.051	1.757	46.433	000
26	3.875	3.405	2.350	NS	3.872	2.486	27.071	000
27	2.675	1.622	16.080	000	3.513	1.838	47.624	000
28	2.975	1.432	40.809	000	3.692	1.676	86.033	000
30	2.825	1.919	9.504	.003	3.256	1.919	36.858	000
32	3.575	2.189	27.289	000	3.821	2.000	70.830	000
33	3.150	2.432	4.521	.037	3.179	1.811	30.813	000
35	3.325	2.541	7.923	.006	3.333	2.054	27.193	000
37	3.525	3.000	2.922	NS	3.308	2.649	7.750	.007
38	3.425	2.541	10.952	.001	3.256	2.432	14.786	000
39	3.050	2.865	0.425	NS	2.949	2.432	5.276	.024
40	3.650	2.135	32.617	000	3.974	2.081	68.307	000
42	3.675	2.514	19.063	000	3.718	2.000	50.633	000
43	3.275	2.541	6.637	.012	3.077	1.892	22.853	000
45	2.830	2.000	10.726	.002	2.897	2.081	10.364	002
46	2.550	2.081	3.349	NS	2.923	1.892	20.654	000
47	3.325	2.595	9.414	.003	3.231	2.324	15.807	000
48	3.400	1.973	26.007	000	3.308	1.838	45.081	000
49	3.575	2.216	22.547	000	3.872	2.000	116.213	000
50	2.600	2.459	0.175	NS	2.897	2.378	4.962	.029

Table 1 (continued)

	CDS				CDS adult form			
	Exp $\overline{x}$	Cont $\overline{x}$			Exp $\overline{x}$	Cont $\overline{x}$		
Item no.	n = 40	n = 37	F values	p	n = 39	n = 37	F values	p
51	3.325	2.351	11.862	001	3.436	2.216	21.359	000
52	2.975	2.405	4.502	037	2.846	1.838	19.696	000
53	3.525	2.514	11.593	001	3.436	2.000	38.324	000
54	3.100	1.541	49.524	000	3.564	1.757	60.072	000
55	2.800	2.108	5.478	022	2.769	1.622	27.363	000
56	3.150	2.054	14.310	000	3.103	1.676	38.816	000
58	3.775	3.054	6.639	012	3.513	2.403	31.522	000
59	3.825	2.784	15.021	000	3.769	2.649	22.233	000
60	2.400	2.162	0.644	NS	2.641	2.054	8.513	005
61	3.050	2.162	9.397	003	2.692	1.787	24.899	000
62	3.850	2.405	33.419	000	3.641	2.189	38.637	000
63	3.300	2.351	9.212	003	3.231	1.973	35.192	000
64	2.925	1.973	12.841	001	3.026	2.000	23.470	000
1P	2.425	1.730	8.595	004	2.615	1.703	18.017	000
2P	3.025	2.351	6.857	011	3.000	2.081	25.374	000
5P	2.775	2.541	0.920	NS	2.154	1.892	2.372	NS
8P	3.425	2.270	17.000	000	2.718	1.838	17.296	000
11P	2.225	2.324	0.144	NS	2.256	1.865	3.488	NS
15P	3.000	2.273	7.067	010	3.103	2.378	11.461	001
17P	2.350	2.703	1.535	NS	1.897	2.649	9.008	004
22P	3.125	1.703	29.725	000	3.231	1.730	54.374	000
24P	2.925	2.297	7.235	009	2.718	2.054	9.135	003
29P	3.025	2.757	0.912	NS	2.436	2.405	0.021	NS
31P	3.150	2.832	0.836	NS	2.178	2.270	9.606	003
34P	2.875	1.730	17.241	000	3.205	1.973	27.584	000
36P	3.650	2.676	11.676	001	3.436	2.946	3.259	NS
41P	3.000	2.162	10.878	001	2.769	2.162	6.818	011
44P	3.625	3.270	2.001	NS	3.103	3.865	1.019	NS
57P	2.775	2.459	1.462	NS	2.308	2.108	0.801	NS
65P	2.625	1.649	20.266	000	2.282	1.622	10.827	002
66P	3.275	1.838	34.233	000	2.897	1.784	22.380	000

[a] Experimental (Exp) and Control (Cont) group means ($\overline{x}$), F values, and significance level values based on analysis of variance for each of the CDS and CDS adult form items where Very right = 5, Right = 4, Don't know = 3, Wrong = 2, Very wrong = 1.

This format ensures that the respondent focuses attention on one item at a time and that he/she is not unduly influenced by earlier items; it forces the respondent to manipulate each item separately and to take an active role while doing the CDS, possibly reducing the effects of response set. Most of the children who have used the CDS have enjoyed its game-like quality. Administration, scoring, and interpretation details are set out in the manual of the CDS (Lang and Tisher, 1978).

Description of Sample

The CDS was administered to a total sample of 96 children, 76 mothers, and 54 fathers. The breakdown of the sample is shown in Table 2.

The experimental group consisted of relatively severe cases of school refusal. The control group consisted of regular school attenders who had not missed more than ten school days during the year and who were matched with the school refusing children for age, sex, school, and year.

The clinic population includes children aged between nine and 16 years who were attending Bouverie Clinic, a child psychiatric clinic, for a variety of childhood psychiatric problems other than school refusal.

We found that the scale worked very well in discriminating between these three groups of children (Lang and Tisher, 1978). We further found that the children "enjoyed" using the scale, and that the use of the scale opened up considerable communication both between the child and ourselves and between the child and the parents. Although we had not used the scale with a group of depressed children, we considered on the basis of this initial pilot project that it was sufficiently promising to publish the scale as a research edition so that it could be widely used by many investigators and so that hopefully we could use the responses from different people and data collected by different investigators in pruning the scale further and producing a first edition. The Children's Depression Scale was published by the Australian Council for Educational Research, in August, 1978 (Lang and Tisher, 1978).

Table 2 Distribution of Sample

	Children				
Group	Boys	Girls	Total	Mothers	Fathers
Experimental	25	15	40	39	20
Control	22	15	37	37	34
Clinic population	12	7	19	0	0

All children were aged between nine and 16 years ($\bar{x}$ age: 13 years, 1 month).

USES OF THE CDS

1. The CDS enables the clinician to establish the extent of the child's depression both from the child's responses and from the responses of others (parents, teachers, etc) about the child. Preliminary results (Tables 3 and 4) indicate that parents generally tend to obtain lower scores than their children.

While parents in both groups tend to score lower than their children, this pattern is more consistent in the normal group than in the depressed group. In the depressed group, there is a slight tendency for parents (particularly mothers) to score higher than their children on the depressive scales (not on the positive scales).

Table 3 Parents and Children–Control Group

	Parents		Children			
	$\bar{x}$	SD	$\bar{x}$	SD	T value	p
Dep.	102.78	18.59	116.89	35.78	−2.18	< 0.03
Aff. Res.	15.32	3.81	17.43	6.09	−1.78	NS
Soc. Prob.	16.14	3.68	17.38	7.00	−1.10	NS
Self Est.	17.26	3.79	21.19	7.29	−3.02	< 0.00
Sick/Death	13.79	2.74	16.08	5.04	−2.53	< 0.01
Guilt	17.12	3.44	20.43	7.12	−2.58	< 0.01
p Scale	38.59	4.79	41.54	9.07	−2.40	< 0.02
Plsr.	15.32	2.18	16.00	4.90	−0.92	NS

Mean and SD scale and subscale scores of parents (CDS–Adult) and children (CDS) (n = 37 matched pairs).

Table 4 Parents and Children–Experimental

	Parents		Children			
	$\bar{x}$	SD	$\bar{x}$	SD	T value	p
Dep.	159.77	24.82	156.95	28.65	0.56	NS
Aff. Res.	27.74	5.82	25.70	6.44	1.84	NS
Soc. Prob.	28.22	5.51	26.55	6.47	1.47	NS
Self Est.	26.06	5.25	26.55	5.16	−0.51	NS
Sick/Death	21.81	5.53	21.83	5.55	−0.01	NS
Guilt	23.93	4.37	25.15	5.35	−1.36	NS
p Scale	49.15	10.46	53.27	11.45	−2.85	< 0.00
Plsr.	22.23	5.97	23.83	5.94	−2.05	< 0.04

Mean and SD CDS–Adult scores of parents and children's CDS scores (n = 40 matched pairs).

There are several possible interpretations for this finding. It may be that the parents of the depressed child are confronted by their child's depression in a way that makes it impossible for them to deny his or her depression. Hence the greater agreement between the scores. It is possible that the normal parent, while perhaps aware of his or her child's unhappiness, can see it in a broader context or as a transitory phenomenon and sees the child's depression in a more hopeful or positive light. Hence the greater discrepancy between the scores of parents and children in the normal group.

It may be that in the depressed families there is an enmeshed system between the parents and the child in which the boundaries become weak and therefore the child is unable to keep to him or herself the feelings of unhappiness. Consequently, it is shared and mutually amplified (Minuchin, 1974). In normal families, on the other hand, boundaries between parents and child are clearer. The child aged between nine and 16 years is likely to keep some of his feelings to him/herself. This would account for the greater discrepancy between parents' and children's score.

In any event, estimation of depression in the child can be done in the context of differences between scores of parents and child.

2. The CDS gives the clinician a clearer understanding of the nature of the child's depression by providing scores on a range of subscales which represent different areas of depression. For example, a child may score high on all subscales except social problems on which he/she does not receive a high score. This suggests that social functioning is an area of relative strength in a child who is otherwise depressed and points to a direction for therapy. Or a child may receive low scores on all subscales except the pleasure subscale, where he/she scores high. This suggests that the child is having difficulties in enjoying him/herself and that this is a problem area–although his/her general score on depression may be low.

3. The CDS permits the clinician to compare the child's responses with those of parents and others and to compare responses of mothers, fathers, and others with each other; this gives the clinician some understanding of the child's depression as it relates to the context in which he/she lives. For example, if the child receives a low score on depression, that is, he/she reports him/herself as not depressed, but both parents report him/her as depressed, questions may be raised in the clinician's mind–is the child unable/unwilling to communicate his/her depression? Are the parents' perceptions inappropriate? Are they perhaps seeing the child as depressed because they have problems of their own, etc. Or, if the CDS is given to all children in the family, not just the child with the present problem, other children in the family, hitherto perceived by the parents as "fine" or "very happy" may use the CDS to communicate their depression. This occurred with one family who came for treatment because of problems with one child, and the discussion of the CDS results resulted in a marked

change of family dynamics–mother and father became aware of the distress of the other child and realized that the "identified patient" was not the only or main problem.

The CDS has therapeutic uses in that it facilitates communication in the family and also between the family and the therapist. In our clinical use of the CDS with families we have had some dramatic and very rewarding experiences with families, where parents have for the first time often found out from the children that they are depressed and what sort of things are worrying their children. We have found parents grateful for being alerted to the possibility that their children are unhappy. We have found children relieved for the opportunity to tell their parents of feelings and attitudes which they have often been bottling up inside them for fear that their parents might not understand, or be angry with them, or feel that they have failed as parents. Perhaps the most useful aspect of the CDS in this context is that the items are written down on cards for the family members to read. In itself, this shows that the feelings stated are not unique to themselves, that others feel similarly, and that it is perhaps permissible for children to feel the way they do. In reviewing the uses to which the CDS has been put since its publication, we regret that more people have not used the CDS with families and we hope that rewriting the adult form, in paper and pencil form (see later, section on Research) will facilitate this use of the CDS in a family context.

RECENT DEVELOPMENTS AND RESEARCH

Questionnaire

In September 1979, that is, a year after publication, a questionnaire was devised and sent to all known users of the CDS. All in all 97 questionnaires were sent out.

Of the 97 respondents to whom the CDS was sent, 16 were overseas users (Canada, Japan, United Kingdom, United States, Norway, New Zealand, Israel, and Germany). Forty replies were received, and these are summarized briefly. Fifteen of the respondents were guidance officers with the counselling, guidance, and clinical services division of the education department. Most other respondents came from a range of positions, including consulting psychologists, university positions, court counsellors, social workers, and clinical child workers. In descriptions of their jobs, most people worked with children and families either in a clinical or school setting. Four people worked primarily in research.

At the time of reply, most respondents had been using the CDS for between nine and 12 months and the overwhelming majority used it mainly with children (that is, they used the CDS, not the CDS–Adult Form). It is interesting that only one person reported using it with persons outside the nuclear family, namely with nurses in a hospital situation and comments that it was very valuable in this context.

Many respondents (74 percent) describe the subscales of the CDS as important. Two open-ended questions about the CDS were asked:

1. "The most useful things to me about the CDS are as follows." By far the most frequently expressed comment is that the CDS allows and encourages children to talk about things they did not usually express, to talk about things which otherwise are difficult for them to open up about, that it greatly improves and facilitates rapport between the child and the therapist, and that it encourages children to talk to the therapist.

The CDS was seen to provide an objective test and re-assurance for the user about his or her subjective opinions about the child. Many people felt that the boxes were extremely important and that they were much better than the pencil and paper form or other card-sorting tests that were available. Other useful things about the CDS include its usefulness in opening up communications between members of the family, its use in highlighting problem areas in the child's environment, its appeal to the child which frequently led to relief, and its opening up of areas as potential follow-up with the client. Several persons particularly found the subscales helpful in the context of diagnosis. Other useful things noted include research use, use of the CDS–Adult Form, especially where the children were too young or insufficiently verbal to do the CDS themselves, the school related questions for use in schools, the simplicity of administration, the opportunity to compare parent's and children's scores, and the format of the record form, namely, having the deciles on the scoring sheets so that there is no need to look up in the manual.

2. "The things I would like to change about the CDS are as follows." Most comments related to administrative difficulties, for example, scoring, confusing card colors, specific wording. Some requests for larger standardization samples were also made.

Ongoing Research and Preliminary Results

Some of the ongoing research using the CDS is briefly described in this section. There may of course be considerably more work in progress than we report; we only report work of those researchers who have made contact with us. We are interested in hearing from others similarly engaged.

Except where otherwise acknowledged, reported are our statistical analyses of results sent to us by researchers. We express appreciation to workers in the field for their cooperation. Professor Kodaki at Shimane University in Izumo, Japan, has translated the CDS into Japanese and has used a paper and pencil form of the CDS with 389 boys and girls in normal schools from fifth grade to

12th grade, that is, aged nine years through to 18 years. We have carried out some statistical analysis of these results (Tables 5 and 6).

Of the variables age and sex, age contributes to differences in scores more heavily than sex. With respect to sex differences, girls obtain higher scores on social problems ($p < 0.002$) and on full D scale (approaching significance, $p < 0.059$). With respect to age, boys over 14 years obtain higher scores on all depression scales and subscales except sickness/death. The pleasure subscale and p scale scores are opposite in direction to the depression scale and subscale scores; this may reflect some interesting cultural differences or it may be that in the process of translation some of the specific colloquial meanings of the items are different. It may also be that the reverse scoring procedures have been carried out differently.

Erica Frydenberg, in Melbourne, Australia, is looking at childhood depression in a normal school population of 11-year-olds. The CDS and other measures of childhood depression, including the Children's Depression Inventory, are being used. The relationship between general abilities, educational achievement, socioeconomic status, and depression is being investigated. Use of several measures of depression will yield important findings regarding validity of the CDS and some of its correlates. The relationship between cognition and

Table 5 Japanese Sample: Age Differences

Variable	Age	$\bar{x}$	SD	Value	DF	p
Affective response	14 years and older	17.952	4.855	2.94	387	< 0.003
	Under 14 years	16.415	5.367			
Social problems	14 years and older	20.257	4.89	3.62	387	< 0.000
	Under 14 years	18.465	4.67			
Self-esteem	14 years and older	25.687	5.611	7.03	387	< 0.000
	Under 14 years	21.654	5.492			
Sickness/death	14 years and older	16.583	3.782	0.89	300.43	< 0.374
	Under 14 years	16.195	4.502			
Guilt	14 years and older	22.348	4.367	3.21	387	< 0.001
	Under 14 years	20.969	3.852			
Full D scale	14 years and older	129.703	22.163	4.55	383	< 0.000
	Under 14 years	119.000	23.370			
Pleasure	14 years and older	23.604	4.616	3.36	387	< 0.001
	Under 14 years	25.226	4.765			
Full P scale	14 years and older	53.696	7.676	2.88	387	< 0.004
	Under 14 years	55.956	7.502			

n = 230 for 14 years and older; n = 159 for under 14 years.

Table 6 Japanese Sample: Sex Differences

Variable	Sex	$\overline{x}$	SD	Value	DF	p
Affective response	Boys	16.502	4.417	3.21	365.35	< 0.001
	Girls	18.149	5.632			
Social problems	Boys	19.313	4.744	0.86	387	< 0.391
	Girls	19.737	4.999			
Self-esteem	Boys	23.118	5.979	3.12	387	< 0.002
	Girls	24.964	5.685			
Sickness/death	Boys	16.631	3.902	1.00	387	< 0.319
	Girls	16.217	4.272			
Guilt	Boys	21.626	4.132	0.74	387	< 0.458
	Girls	21.943	4.301			
Full D scale	Boys	123.140	21.425	1.89	374.64	< 0.059
	Girls	127.604	24.774			
Pleasure	Boys	24.436	4.905	0.70	387	< 0.483
	Girls	24.098	4.572			
Full P scale	Boys	54.989	7.780	0.95	387	< 0.341
	Girls	54.247	7.574			

Boys n = 195; girls n = 194.

depression is also being looked at; high and low CDS scorers will be given verbal and numerical tasks to perform. Following from Beck's work with adults, the prediction is that high CDS scorers will judge their performance poorly, predict further performances poorly, and will be more reluctant to perform further cognitive tasks.

Tonkin and Hudson, also working in Melbourne, have completed a study titled "The Childrens Depression Scale: Some Additional Psychometric Data" (Tonkin and Hudson, 1980). They report upon a sample of 60 pupils of a Melbourne outer-city primary school–"Almost all of the children lived in high-rise accommodation and were of migrant background." The children were aged nine to 13 years, including 33 boys and 27 girls. Tonkin and Hudson report that girls score higher than boys but that there are no significant differences among the age groups. The mean scores of children in their sample are considerably higher than mean scores of normal children reported in the CDS manual–an interesting finding which is discussed below in relation to results of other studies. Tonkin and Hudson administered the CDS on a test-retest basis, each child being given the scale twice; the interval between test and retest ranged from seven to ten days. Subscale coefficient alphas ranged from 0.54 to 0.77 and the overall scale coefficient alpha was 0.92. The test-retest correlation

Table 7 Gardiner Sample: Age Differences

Variable	Age	x̄	SD	Value	DF	p
Affective response	Up to 11.2 years	21.888	5.904	0.53	188	< 0.596
	11.3 years and over	21.409	6.278			
Social problems	Up to 11.2 years	24.250	6.037	1.04	188	< 0.299
	11.3 years and over	23.236	7.021			
Self-esteem	Up to 11.2 years	24.838	6.357	0.33	188	< 0.744
	11.3 years and over	24.518	6.859			
Sickness/death	Up to 11.2 years	20.488	5.047	0.14	188	< 0.891
	11.3 years and over	20.382	5.352			
Guilt	Up to 11.2 years	25.825	5.681	1.34	188	< 0.182
	11.3 years and over	24.618	6.428			
Full D scale	Up to 11.2 years	146.863	26.938	0.77	188	< 0.443
	11.3 years and over	143.482	31.930			
Pleasure	Up to 11.2 years	22.738	4.767	0.38	188	< 0.705
	11.3 years and over	23.036	5.753			
Full P scale	Up to 11.2 years	39.938	8.678	0.74	188	< 0.458
	11.3 years and over	40.945	9.612			

Up to 11.2 years, n = 80; 11.3 years and over, n = 110.

was 74 for each of the depression and positive scales (Tonkin and Hudson, 1980).

A study was begun at the Austin Hospital in Melbourne under the direction of Bruce Tonge, MD, using the CDS to look at depression in children who are hospitalized. The CDS was administered to children on their first day of hospitalization, on the fifth day of hospitalization, and the follow-up was carried out six months later after their return home. Nurses and parents were also asked to complete the CDS Adult Form. Unfortunately, owing to staff shortages, this study has not yet been completed.

Gardiner has completed a study: "An Investigation of the Relationships between Lateral Preferences and Personality and Emotional Characteristics in Children" (Gardiner, 1980). Gardiner used the Eysenck Personality Questionnaire (Junior) (EPQ) and the CDS with 192 children and reports that "the hypothesis that there are significant relationships between lateral preferences and personal and emotional characteristics in children cannot be accepted."

Analysis of CDS scores indicates no sex or age differences (Tables 7 and 8). The absence of age differences is consistent with results of Tonkin and Hudson and may be expected as his sample also spanned a small age range of nine to 12 years, with most children aged 10 and 11). The absence of sex differences,

Table 8 Gardiner Sample: Sex Differences

Variable	Sex	$\bar{x}$	SD	Value	DF	p
Affective response	Boys	22.102	6.440	1.03	188	< 0.304
	Girls	21.186	5.813			
Social problems	Boys	23.876	6.930	0.41	188	< 0.683
	Girls	23.480	6.383			
Self-esteem	Boys	24.829	7.184	0.34	188	< 0.734
	Girls	24.500	6.158			
Sickness/death	Boys	20.250	5.463	0.43	188	< 0.666
	Girls	20.578	5.008			
Guilt	Boys	24.921	6.198	0.43	188	< 0.669
	Girls	25.304	6.111			
Full D scale	Boys	145.773	32.197	0.37	188	< 0.711
	Girls	144.157	27.910			
Pleasure	Boys	17.284	5.130	0.74	188	< 0.461
	Girls	17.833	5.093			
Full P scale	Boys	40.602	8.946	0.11	188	< 0.911
	Girls	40.451	9.493			

Boys n = 88; girls n = 102.

however, is interesting in the light of results reported in the CDS Manual (Lang and Tisher, 1978) and by Tonkin and Hudson which showed that girls scored higher than boys. These comparative results are further discussed below.

A table of correlations between CDS and EPQ scores was obtained (Table 9). Nearly all the correlation coefficients reported in the table are significant, indicating that scale and subscale scores of the CDS correlate positively with psychoticism and neuroticism and negatively with extraversion as well as with the lie scale. The highest level of correlation is between the full D scale score and neuroticism—a finding which may be expected in view of Eysenck's description of "... the typical high N scorer as being an anxious, worrying individual, moody and frequently depressed. He is likely to sleep badly, and to suffer from various psychosomatic disorders" (Eysenck, 1975). Overall, the scale and subscale scores correlate most highly with neuroticism, although the pleasure scale and subscale scores are also highly correlated negatively with extraversion. Eysenck described "the typical introvert" as "a quiet, retiring sort of person, introspective, fond of books rather than people; he is reserved and distant except to intimate friends" (Eysenck, 1975). It is appropriate that this sort of person will be unable to enjoy life as expressed in the pleasure scale and subscale scores, also in the 0.27 correlation with social problems scores.

Table 9 Correlation Between CDS Scale and Subscale Scores and EPQ Scores

	PSYCH	EXTRA	NEURO	LIE
SUBAFF	0.1665 (190) S = 0.011	−0.2743 (190) S = 0.001	0.6050 (190) S = 0.001	−0.1415 (190) S = 0.026
SUBSOC	0.1644 (190) S = 0.012	−0.274 (190) S = 0.001	0.4925 (190) S = 0.001	−0.0327 (190) S = 0.327
SUBSELF	0.1685 (190) S = 0.010	−0.1610 (190) S = 0.013	0.5385 (190) S = 0.001	−0.1598 (190) S = 0.014
SUBSD	0.2509 (190) S = 0.001	−0.1508 (190) S = 0.019	0.5441 (190) S = 0.001	−0.1583 (190) S = 0.015
SUBGUILT	0.1761 (190) S = 0.008	−0.0432 (190) S = 0.277	0.3617 (190) S = 0.001	−0.1453 (190) S = 0.023
SMISCD	0.1003 (190) S = 0.084	−0.0870 (190) S = 0.116	0.5413 (190) S = 0.001	−0.6133 (190) S = 0.012
FULLD	0.2048 (190) S = 0.002	−0.2083 (190) S = 0.002	0.6356 (190) S = 0.001	−0.1572 (190) S = 0.015
SUBPLEA	0.1618 (190) S = 0.013	−0.4817 (190) S = 0.001	0.3228 (190) S = 0.001	−0.3145 (190) S = 0.001
SMISCP	0.0279 (190) S = 0.351	−0.4370 (190) S = 0.001	0.2645 (190) S = 0.001	−0.1582 (190) S = 0.015
FULLP	0.1064 (190) S = 0.072	−0.5192 (190) S = 0.001	0.3291 (190) S = 0.001	−0.2673 (190) S = 0.001

Correlations with the psychoticism and lie scale scores are more difficult to comment upon—Eysenck says of the p scale: "The nature of the p variable can of course only be guessed at, at the moment" (Eysenck, 1975). Of the lie scale, he states, "The main difficulty seems to be that in addition to measuring dissimulation, the L scale also measures some stable personality factor which may possibly denote some degree of social naiveté," and "hence the scale must measure some stable personality function; unfortunately little is known about the precise nature of this function" (Eysenck, 1975).

Table 10 Showing Comparative Mean and Standard Deviation Scores on Full D Scale for Different Samples Studies

Sample		Total D score $\bar{x}$	SD
Lang and Tisher (1978)			
Control group	Boys (n = 22)	106.3	36.5
	Girls (n = 15)	132.5	30.3
Experimental group	Boys (n = 25)	153.6	25.3
	Girls (n = 15)	162.6	31.9
Clinical group	Total (n = 19)	134.5	23.9
Tonkin and Hudson (1980)	Boys (n = 33)	132.46	24.24
	Girls (n = 27	141.32	25.95
Gardiner (1980)	Boys (n = 88)	145.773	32.197
	Girls (n = 102)	144.157	27.910
Kodaki (1980)	Boys (n = 195)	123.140	21.424
	Girls (n = 194)	127.604	24.774

The results of the six samples reported to date have been put together for preliminary comparative purpose and are set out in Table 10. Total depression scores only are reported and scores for boys and girls are reported separately. Inspection of the table indicates that, with the exception of Gardiner's sample, girls consistently obtain higher scores than boys. It is important to look at the differences in scores between samples. For example, the scores in both Tonkin and Hudson's sample and Gardiner's sample are more similar to the scores of the clinical group reported by Lang and Tisher than to their control group. Unfortunately, no socioeconomic correlational data is available with respect to the three samples other than that of Lang and Tisher. However, both Tonkin and Hudson's sample and Gardiner's sample deal mainly with 11 to 12-year-olds (while Lang and Tisher dealt with nine to 16-year-olds) and both report that their samples are from outer-city schools; indeed Tonkin and Hudson's were almost all migrant and from high-rise accommodation and Gardiner's sample including a heavy percentage of migrant children. Findings of levels of depression comparable to that of a general clinical control group may be entirely appropriate, and certainly foreshadow the importance of a wide-scale assessment of depression in the community. Scores of the Lang and Tisher control group are lower than scores of children from other samples; the control group was obtained on the basis of empirical criteria which probably yielded a supernormal sample-children who had not missed more than ten school days of an entire school year. These children probably also knew they were participating because they were a "normal" group and this may have influenced them to respond in a "normal" way.

The Japanese sample shows scores between those of the Lang and Tisher control group and those of the two outer-city samples. It is also interesting that in the Japanese sample, older children obtain higher scores than younger children. In the Gardiner sample and Tonkin and Hudson sample, no age differences are present; however, this is probably due to the small age range in both these samples. However, the age range in the Japanese sample is similar to that in the Lang and Tisher sample, where age differences were not significant, but tended to be in the direction of younger children obtaining higher scores. Again, the importance of cross-cultural comparison is highlighted.

The data available for proper interpretation of this table is unfortunately sparse. Nonetheless, we report it because it opens up questions about levels and areas of depression in difference groups in the community.

Further Developments

In addition to the work of Professor Kodaki in translating the CDS into Japanese, negotiations are presently in progress for translation of the CDS into several other languages (Italian, Dutch, Spanish, French, and Hindu).

Several changes in the next edition of the CDS may be foreshadowed. The CDS–Adult Form will be produced in paper and pencil form; the reverse scoring of the positive items will be altered so as to be consistent with scoring of depression items; and the colors of the cards will be more distinguishable from each other. The preliminary norms suggested in the research manual will be updated and reported on the basis of larger samples.

We plan to develop the CDS–Adult Form for use with younger children and are devising items that would be appropriate for use with preschool children. We hope to develop a brief form of the CDS–Adult Form so that teachers and others can rate children on the essential features of depression even if they do not have the time to complete the full CDS–Adult Form. Use of the subscales for rating purposes would be a good starting point, that is, rating children on affective response, social problems, self-esteem, preoccupation with own sickness and death, guilt, and pleasure.

It is clear that in measuring depression it is important to obtain a profile of depression in different areas (subscales) as well as global scores of depression. We plan to look at the subscales statistically and try to determine how the different subscales of depression interrelate with each other, and the extent to which their interrelationships or their relative significance is a function of age, family variables, etc. We also intend to use independent diagnostic criteria to identify a group of depressed children (while being aware of the difficulties in discovering such a sample–see Raskin, 1977), a group of children attending clinics or hospitals for reasons other than depression, and a normal group in the community, and compare CDS scores of children in all three groups.

Finally, we are working toward establishing the extent and nature of childhood depression in the general community as well as in specific groups of children, such as those who under-achieve academically, children of parents who are separated, children who are bereaved, children who are hospitalized, and so on.

Two and a half years after publication of the CDS, we are encouraged by the high level of interest shown in the scale and by research, both ongoing and foreshadowed.

We look forward to hearing from clinicians and researchers who use the scale and to working together in further developments in the area of childhood depression.

REFERENCES

Agras S. The relationship of school phobia to childhood depression. *Am J Psychiatry* 1959; 116; 6:533–536.

Annell AL. *Depressive states in childhood and adolescence.* New York: Halsted Press, 1972.

Anthony EJ. Discussion of Dr. Malmquists' chapter: childhood depression: a clinical and behavioural perspective. In: Schulterbrandt JG, Raskin A, eds. *Depression in childhood.* New York: Raven Press, 1977:61–63.

Bakwin H. Depression—a mood disorder in children and adolescents. *Md State Med J* 1972; 21; 6:55–61.

Connell HM. Depression in childhood. *Child Psychiatry Hum Dev* 1973; 4:71–85.

Cytryn L, McKnew DH. Factors influencing the changing clinical expression of the depressive process in children. *Am J Psychiatry* 1974; 131; 8:879–881.

Despert IK. Suicide and depression in children. *Nerv Child* 1952; 9:378–389.

Eysenck HF, Eysenck SBG. *Manual of the Eysenck personality questionnaire, junior and adult.* Great Britain: Hodder and Stoughton, 1975.

Frommer E. Treatment of childhood depression with antidepressant drugs. *Br Med J* 1967; 1:729–732.

Gardiner C. An investigation of the relationships between lateral preferences and personality and emotional characteristics in children (unpublished thesis). University of Adelaide, March, 1980.

Glaser K. Masked depression in children and adolescents. *Am J Psychother* 1967; 21:565–574.

Harrington J, Hassan J. Depression in girls during latency. *Br J Med Psychol* 1958; 31:43–50.

Kuhn V, Kuhn R. Drug therapy for depression in children. In Annell AL, ed. *Depressive states in childhood and adolescence.* Ibid. 1971-1972.

Kovacs M, Beck A. An empirical-clinical approach toward a definition of childhood depression. In: Schulterbrandt JG, Raskin A, eds. *Depression in Childhood.* New York: Raven Press, 1977:1–25.

Lang M, Tisher M. *Childrens Depression Scale.* Melbourne: Australian Council for Educational Research, 1978.

Lapouse R, Monk MA. An epidemiological study of behavior characteristics in children. *Am J Public Health* 1958;48:1134–1144.

Lefkowitz MM. Discussion of Dr. Gittelman-Klein's chapter: definitional and methodological issues concerning depressive illness in children. In: Schulterbrandt JG, Raskin A, eds. *Depression in childhood.* New York: Raven Press, 1977:81–85.

Lefkowitz MM, Burton N. Childhood depression: a critique of the concept. *Psychol Bull* 1978;85;4:714–726.

Ling W, Oftedal G, Weinberg W. Severe childhood headache as sign of depression. *Mod Med Aust* 1971;(May 17):71–72.

Ling W, Oftedal G, Weinberg W. Severe childhood headaches as sign of depresion. *Am J Dis Child* 1970;120:122–124.

McConville BJ, Boag LC, Purohit AP. Mourning responses in children of varying ages. *Can J Psychiatry* 1970;15:253–255.

McConville BJ, Boag LC, Purohit AP. Three types of childhood depression. *Can J Psychiatry* 1973;18:133–138.

Minuchin S. *Families and family therapy.* Massachusetts: Harvard University Press, 1974:Chap. 3.

Murray PA. The clinical picture of depression in school children. *Ir Med J* 1970;63:65–66.

Poznanski E, Zrull JP. Childhood depression: clinical characteristics of overtly depressed children. *Arch Gen Psychiatry* 1970;3 (July):8–15.

Raskin A. Depression in children: fact or fallacy. In: Schulterbrandt JG, Raskin A, eds. *Depression in childhood.* New York: Raven Press, 1977: 141–146.

Rensahw DC. Suicide and depression in children. *J School Health* 1974;44: 487–489.

Rie HE. Depression in childhood: a survey of some pertinent contributions. *J Am Acad Child Psychiatry* 1966;5:653–685.

Sandler J, Joffe WG. Notes on childhood depression. *Int J Pschoanal* 1965; 46:88–96.

Siegelman M. Psychometric properties of the Wiggins and Winder Peer Nomination Inventory. *J Psychol* 1966;64:143–149.

Stack JJ. Chemotherapy in childhood depression. In: Annell AL, ed. *Depressive states in childhood and adolescence.* Ibid. 1972:460–466.

Tonkin G, Hudson A. The Childrens Depression Scale: some additional psychometric data, in press.

Ushakov GH, Girich YP. Special features of psychogenic depressions in children and adolescents. In: Annell AL, ed. *Depressive states in childhood and adolescence.* Ibid. 1972:510–516.

Section IV

Etiologic Factors

Overview of Etiologic Factors

Dennis P. Cantwell

As is emphasized elsewhere in this book, all psychiatric disorders in childhood probably have a multifactorial etiology, and depression is no exception to this rule. In 1975, Akiskal and McKinney attempted to integrate ten conceptual models of depression into a comprehensive clinical framework for the understanding of depression in adults. Their ten models of depression represented five schools of thought. These five schools of thought were: the psychoanalytic school, the behavioral school, the sociological school, the existential school, and the biological school.

There were four models that were considered to belong to the psychoanalytic school: the aggression turned inward model, in which there was a conversion of aggressive instinct into depressive affect. This is the Abraham-Freud model (Abraham, 1960; Freud, 1950). In their review of this literature, Akiskal and McKinney stated that even though this probably was one of the most widely held psychological conceptualizations of depression, they felt there was less systematic evidence to support it than there was for other models.

A second psychoanalytic view is Bibring's model (1965). This model was looked upn by Akiskal and McKinney as a "loss of self-esteem" model in which the patient experienced helplessness in attaining the goals of the ego ideal. In contrast to the first model, hostility in Bibring's model was inconstant, and was a secondary phenomenon brought about by object losses or by factors that prevented the attainment of the ego ideal.

A third psychoanalytic model postulated by authors such as Spitz (1942) and Robertson and Bowlby (Robertson and Bowlby, 1952; Bowlby, 1960) is an "object loss" model. The mechanism here was separation and disruption of an attachment bond. Akiskal and McKinney reviewed the evidence for two specific issues regarding object loss and separation. The first issue was whether or not separation in adult life was an immediate precipitating stress leading to depression, and the second, whether bereavement or other types of early object loss in childhood could predispose an individual to the development of depression in adult life. Their review of the literature regarding the first issue led them to suggest that separation events did seem to act as precipitating events for the development of depression in adult life, but were *not* necessarily *specific* for depressive illness as opposed to other types of psychiatric disorders and as opposed to physical disorders. They also felt that the evidence suggested that a separation by itself was *not a sufficient* cause of depression because there was not a one-to-one relationship between separation and depression. In addition to not being a sufficient cause for depression, it was not felt to be a necessary cause because many depressed individuals did not have any evidence of separation.

With regard to the second issue, whether or not object loss in childhood can predispose an individual to the development of depression in adult life, they felt that the existing evidence was inconclusive.

The last psychoanalytic model discussed was Beck's model (1967) in which hopelessness was the central mechanism. A "cognitive triad" of negative conception of the self, negative interpretation of one's experience, and a negative view of the future led to the hopelessness, helplessness, and depression. Since the time of Akiskal and McKinney's review, Beck's model has been amplified, and cognitive therapy (discussed elsewhere in this volume) has been developed from this model.

Moving from the psychoanalytic to the behavioral school of thought, Akiskal and McKinney discussed two specific behavioral models: a "learned helplessness" model, put forth by Seligman (in press), and a model emphasizing "loss of reinforcement" emphasized by such authors as Lazarus (1968) and Lewinsohn (in press). The learned helplessness model was initially based on animal studies using uncontrollable aversive stimulation with dogs. They conceptualized learned helplessness as a behavioral state developing because the individual does not recognize a relationship between one's response and any relief from adverse events. Elsewhere in this volume, Petti discusses the value of the learned helplessness model in childhood depression, particularly in the area of developing behavioral models and methods of treatment.

The fourth and fifth schools of thought were sociological and existential. The sociological school, represented by such authors as Bart (1974), held that "loss of role status" played an important etiologic role. The existential school of thought was represented by authors such as Becker (1964) and asserted that "loss of meaning of existence" was an important etiologic factor. It can be seen that the sociological and existential schools overlap to some degree with the behavioral schools, which in turn overlap to some degree with Beck's idea of negative cognitive set.

The fifth school of thought discussed by Akiskal and McKinney in great detail was a biological one, emphasizing the biogenic amine and neurophysiological theories.

In their integration of all of these models, Akiskal and McKinney saw melancholic depression as a final common pathway of various processes involving at least four major areas: genetic factors, physiological stressors, psychosocial stressors, and developmental factors predisposing to the development of depression. Thus, certain genetic factors (such as a decrease in post-synaptic receptor sensitivity) may predispose individuals to develop depression. Likewise, early object loss or learned helplessness in childhood may act as developmental precursors and predisposers to depression. In the face of psychosocial stressors (such as object loss in adult life or chronic frustration) or in the course of physiological stressors (such as viral illness, illnesses such as hypothyroidism, or the use of certain drugs such as methyldopa and reserpine) these interacting factors produce changes in biochemistry leading to the final common pathway of melancholic depression. In this author's view Akiskal and McKinney's synthesis of the available evidence still stands as one of the best efforts to integrate the variety of schools of thought that exist in psychiatry into an overall conceptual framework to explain a common psychiatric disorder.

More recently, as discussed elsewhere in this volume, Kashani and his colleagues (1981) have picked up where Akiskal and McKinney left off and attempted to discuss the relevance of these various models for the etiology of depression in childhood.

The biochemical model has not had as much research behind it in children, but more data is becoming available in children. These are reviewed by Lowe and Cohen, and by Puig-Antich, in their chapters in this volume. Likewise, family-genetic studies have not been as common with children as they have been with adults. However, this is likewise becoming an active research area. The correct data are reviewed in Cantwell's chapter. The cognitive distortion model put forward by Beck is just being explored with children and is discussed in Emery's chapter on cognitive therapy. The learned helplessness model and other behavioral models are discussed by Petti in his chapter on behavioral methods of treatment. While life stresses have been studied by a variety of authors and related to the onset of certain types of childhood psychiatric medical problems, the life stress model has not been explored as much in childhood depression as it has been in adult depression by Paykel (1969), Brown et al (1973a, 1973b), and others.

Kashani points out that the sociological model is not as emphasized in the early childhood literature as it has been in the adolescent literature, although not necessarily specifically with regard to depression.

A complete discussion of the possible etiologic factors in childhood depression and the evidence for each is beyond the scope of this chapter and indeed of this book. The next four chapters present an overview of four areas that could be considered possibly etiologic in childhood depression, none of which are mutually exclusive. Puig-Antich discusses neuroendocrine factors, Lowe and Cohen discuss biochemical factors, and Cantwell discusses family and genetic factors. In his chapter, Eisenbruch looks at affective disorders in parents and discusses possible impact on children, not from a genetic standpoint but from an interactive standpoint. Eisenbruch's is an example of the type of work in family interaction at all levels that need to be done in the study of childhood depression.

These chapters are by no means meant to exhaust all that is known about etiologic factors in childhood depression. The whole area of the social origins of depression in adult life is itself a large literature and somewhat controversial. As mentioned, Paykel, Brown, and others have looked at the issue of life events as precipitating factors in the development of adult depression. Similar kinds of studies have not as yet been done in the study of childhood depression. It is expected that the next ten years will see a burgeoning of research in this area that rivals that which has been done in the area of depression with adults.

REFERENCES

Abraham K. Notes on the psychoanalytic investigation and treatment of manic-depressive insanity and allied conditions (1911). In: *Selected papers on psychoanalysis.* New York: Basic Books, 1960:137–156. Bryan D, Strachey A (trans.).

Akiskal HS, McKinney WT, Jr. Overview of recent research in depression: integration of ten conceptual models into a comprehensive clinical frame. *Arch Gen Psychiatry* 1975;32:285–305.

Bart P. Depression: a sociological theory. In: Roman P, Trice H, eds. *Explorations in psychiatric sociology.* Philadelphia: F.A. Davis, 1974:139–157.

Beck A. *Depression: clinical, experimental, and theoretical aspects.* New York: Harper & Row, 1967.

Becker E. *The revolution in psychiatry.* London: Free Press of Glencoe, Collier-MacMillian, 1964:108–135.

Bibring E. The mechanism of depression. In: Greenacre P, ed. *Affective disorders.* New York: International Universities Press, 1965:13–48.

Bowlby J. Grief and mourning in infancy and early childhood. *Psychoanal Study Child* 1960;15:9–52.

Brown GW, Harris TO, Peto J. Life events and psychiatric disorders. part 2: nature of causal link. *Psychol Med* 1973a;3:159–176.

Brown GW, Sklair F, Harris TO, Birley JLT. Life events and psychiatric disorders. part 1: some methodological issues. *Psychol Med* 1973b; 3:74–87.

Freud S. Mourning and melancholia, 1917. In: *Collected papers, vol. 4.* London: Hogarth Press, 1950:152–172.

Kashani JH, Husain A, Shekim WO, et al. Current perspectives on childhood depression: an overview. *Am J Psychiatry* 1981; 138; 2:143–153.

Lazarus A. Learning theory and the treatment of depression. *Behav Res Ther* 1968;6:83–89.

Lewinsohn P. A behavioral approach to depression. In: Friedman R, Katz M, eds. *The psychology of depression: contemporary theory and research.* Washington, D.C.: U.S. Government Printing House, (in press).

Paykel E, Myers J, Dienelt MN, et al. Life events and depression: a controlled study. *Arch Gen Psychiatry* 1969; 21:753–760.

Robertson J, Bowlby J. Response of young children to separation from their mothers. *Courrier Centre Inter Enfance* 1952; 2:131–142.
Seligman M. Learned helplessness and depression. In: Friedman R, Katz M, eds. *The psychology of depression: contemporary theory and research*. Washington, D.C.: U.S. Government Printing House, (in press).
Spitz R. Anaclitic depression: an inquiry into the genesis of psychiatric conditions in early childhood. *Psychoanal Study Child* 1942; 2:313–342.

Copyright © 1983 by Spectrum Publications, Inc.
*Affective Disorders in Childhood and Adolescence--
An Update.* Edited by D.P. Cantwell and G.A. Carlson.

11

Neuroendocrine and Sleep Correlates of Prepubertal Major Depressive Disorder: Current Status of the Evidence

Joaquim Puig-Antich

As reviewed in Chapter 9, the existence of major depression in prepuberty had been a subject of controversy for several years. Weinberg et al (1973) and Puig-Antich et al (1978b) found that by using diagnostic criteria for adult major depression it is possible to identify a population of severely depressed prepubertal children. Such findings have been confirmed later by other investigators (Carlson and Cantwell, 1980; Cytryn et al, 1980). These studies do not establish the final limits of the diagnosis of this age group, but they do identify a group which, if it turns out to be too restricted, is likely to be the most severely affected. From the point of view of research strategy, this fact opened the door to validation studies.

The investigator in the field of childhood affective disorders is in a historically privileged situation, because of the availability of techniques to measure psychobiological parameters which have been shown to be characteristically altered in adult major depression, at least during the period of illness. Therefore, validation of the syndrome can be undertaken using a much wider set of measures than those usually available to investigators of other psychiatric diagnoses at all ages.

For the last two years, the author and his team have been carrying out a controlled study, the objective of which is to test the validity of prepubertal major depressive disorder by comparing children fitting unmodified Research Diagnostic Criteria (RDC) (Spitzer et al, 1978) for this diagnosis with two groups of controls (normal and nondepressed children with emotional disorders) along seven psychobiological parameters shown to be associated with adult major depressive disorder. They are: (1) psychosocial factors: life events and interpersonal relationships; (2) polysomnography; (3) neuroendocrine circadian rhythms of plasma cortisol concentrations, and growth hormone response in insulin-induced hypoglycemia; (4) urinary MHPG excretion; (5) family psychiatric history; (6) response to imipramine; and (7) long-term outcome.

Given the well-known heterogeneity of disorders included under the diagnosis of major depression in adults, we also used the RDC criteria for endogenous subtype. About three-fifths of prepubertal children fitting criteria for major depression also fit criteria for endogenous subtype. Thus we split the depressive group into endogenous and nonendogenous subgroups in the hope of further increasing the homogeneity of at least one of the groupings.

In this chapter the author reviews only the sleep and neuroendocrine data already analyzed in this ongoing study, contrasting them with the results of similar studies in adult samples with major depressive disorders.

CORTISOL HYPERSECRETION

Adult Endogenous Depressive Cases

Since the initial observation by Gibbons (1964), a substantial amount of knowledge on cortisol secretion in adult major depression has been acquired. Thus, it is now known that about 50 percent of adult endogenous major depressive persons hypersecrete cortisol during illness and that this characteristic returns to normal upon recovery from the depressive syndrome (Sachar et al, 1973; Sachar, 1975). Cortisol hypersecretion, as measured by serial plasma concentrations every 20 minutes for 24 hours, expresses itself in a higher number of secretory episodes, higher peak values, higher minimal values (usually over 2 μg/100 ml), higher amount of secretion time, higher amount of cortisol secreted, higher 24-hour cortisol mean values, and no significant change in the half life of cortisol, indicating that the higher plasma concentrations are fully secondary to higher secretion and not due to decreased hormone catabolism (Sachar, 1975). Another source of evidence regarding hypersecretion of cortisol in adult endogenous major depressives is the work of Carroll (Carroll and Mendels, 1976; Carroll et al, 1976a, 1976b) and others (Brown and Shuey, 1980) measuring cortisol plasma concentrations nine, 17, and 24 hours after dexamethasone administration. Using 2 mg, about 30 to 40 percent of endogenous cases show lack of suppression of cortisol plasma levels. Using 1 mg this proportion increases to 59 percent (Carroll et al, 1981). Annis et al (1980) have conducted 24-hour studies on cortisol secretion and 2 mg dexamethasone suppression tests (DST) in the same sample of endogenous depressives. About 50 percent of cortisol hypersecretors are resistant to suppression of cortisol after 2 mg of dexamethasone. It is likely that most adult hypersecretors are resistant to the administration of 1 mg of dexamethasone. Schlesser et al (1979, 1980) have recently published strong evidence of an association between lack of suppression of cortisol secretion nine hours after bedtime administration of 1 mg of dexamethasone and certain subtypes of major depression: bipolar, unipolar sporadic depressive illness, and unipolar pure familial depressive illness. In contrast, patients with depressive spectrum disease (DSD) (Van Valkenburg and Winokur, 1979; Winokur, 1979) showed normal suppression of 8 AM cortisol after dexamethasone. Schlesser et al used an abbreviated dexamethasone test (without 4 PM and 11 PM sampling). It is open to question if the inclusion of these samples would have altered the overall results. Carroll et al (1980) have postulated a threshold model, which hypothesizes that patients with depression spectrum disease (Van Valkenburg and Winokur, 1979; Winokur, 1979), would hypersecrete cortisol only when very severely ill. In a small sample of delusional depressive patients they found that 60 percent of delusional DSD patients were nonsuppressors to dexamethasone when only the 8 AM sample was considered. This rate increased to 83 percent when all three standard samples were considered.

Cortisol hypersecretion is therefore one of the strongest psychobiological correlates of endogenous major depression in adults. The dexamethasone test has been proposed as a diagnostic test for endogenous depression, given its high specificity (Carroll, in press; Carroll et al, in press b), and also as a predictor of relapse (Greden et al, 1980).

Prepubertal Major Depressive Cases

Puig-Antich et al, in a preliminary paper (180), reported the presence of cortisol hypersecretion in two out of four prepubertal, medically healthy children, who fit unmodified RDC (Spitzer et al, 1978) for major depressive disorder, endogenous subtype. Analysis of the cortisol curves before treatment and drug-free after full recovery in the patient with a full 24-hour study with sampling every 20 minutes, revealed that during illness a nine-year-old boy had an almost threefold increase in mean 24 hour cortisol (8.45 μg/100 ml). During illness there was almost a doubling of number of secretory episodes, higher peak values, higher minimal values, and higher amount of time spent secreting. There was no change in the "decay" curve slopes during and after illness, indicating no differences in half-life of plasma cortisol. Thus, all the differences had to be attributed to changes in cortisol secretion. This hypersecretory pattern was therefore quite similar to the pattern described in adult endogenous depressive persons who hypersecrete cortisol (Sachar et al, 1973). This patient was restudied 15 days after the onset of a depressive recurrence six months later. His mean 24 hour cortisol was already almost double (5.7 μg/100 ml) from the one found when he was fully recovered (3.0 μg/100 ml).

Since that preliminary report, 24-hour studies have been carried out and analyzed in 20 prepubertal children fitting RDC criteria (Spitzer et al, 1978) for major depressive disorder. Fifteen fit criteria for possible or definite endogenous subtype and five did not. None of the nonendogenous cases hypersecreted cortisol while 20 percent of the endogenous group did. All hypersecretors have before and after treatment studies. This rate, if confirmed at the end of the study, represents about half the reported rate in adult endogenous cases. Such differences may be due to age effects or to the possible preponderance of cases who will ultimately fit criteria for depressive spectrum disease (Van Valkenburg and Winokur, 1979; Winokur, 1979) or to other unknown factors.

Age effects are hard to evaluate becasue of contradictory evidence. In Sachar's series of endogenous depressive adults (n = 26) there is a positive correlation between age and cortisol hypersecretion measured by 24-hour studies (Asnis et al, 1981). The majority of hypersecretors are older than 50 years of age, while depressive persons below 50 years are unlikely to show a hypersecretory pattern.

Using the 1 mg dexamethasone test (Carroll et al, 1980) in a sample of outpatient endogenous depressive persons, Carroll found no relationship between lack of suppression of cortisol secretion and age. Nonsuppressors were as likely to be over 50 as under 50 years.

The reasons for this discrepancy are difficult to pinpoint at present. Differences in sample size and outpatient versus inpatient status may be partially explanatory. The use of lower dexamethasone doses appears to increase sensitivity (59 percent) but not to decrease specificity (Carroll et al, 1981). This suggests that low-dose DST may be more sensitive than spontaneous hypersecretion. If this is supported by future work, it may indicate that there is an inversely age-related factor which increases the threshold for the appearance of spontaneous cortisol hypersecretion in younger depressed subjects. Finally, it is possible that the DST involves slightly different physiological mechanisms than spontaneous hypersecretion, and that one is age-related and the other is not.

To summarize, there are substantial indications that spontaneous cortisol hypersecretion measured by 24-hour multiple sampling may be an age-related phenomenon in adult endogenous depressive persons, and more frequent the older the group, while lack of suppression to dexamethasone may not be.

Another factor which may bear on the rate of cortisol hypersecretion in prepubertal endogenous depression is family history. It is difficult to judge how many prepubertal children will later be classified as depressive spectrum disease. In our pilot study (Puig-Antich et al, 1978) we were impressed by the high prevalence of alcoholism and antisocial personality among biological relatives of prepubertal major depressive persons. In an outgoing, blind, and controlled family history study the morbidity risks for alcoholism and antisocial personality among first degree biological relatives of prepubertal major depressive disorder probands are 0.29 and 0.18, respectively (n = 28). Although these rates are not very different from similar samples of major depressive adults, about one half of first degree relatives of the prepubertal depressive probands have not been born yet, and a substantial proportion of the other half have not reached age of risk for antisocial personality of alcoholism. Only follow-up family studies will be able to determine what proportion of prepubertal probands will end up classified as depressive spectrum disease (DSD). If this proportion turns out to be high, and if the data from Schlesser et al (1980) is confirmed, indicating that cortisol hypersecretion is quite rare among DSD patients, this may explain lower rates of cortisol hypersecretion among prepubertal depressive probands.

Studies of the use of the dexamethasone suppression test in prepubertal children with diagnosed affective disorder are limited. However, Poznanski and her colleagues (Poznanski et al, 1982) have recently reported on 18 children (ages six to 12), and their findings are quite intriguing. Of these 18 patients, eight (six boys and two girls) qualified for the RDC diagnosis of major depressive disorder, endogenous subtype. This is equivalent to the Diagnostic and Statistical Manual-III (DSM-III) diagnosis of major depressive disorder, melancholic subtype. One other boy met the criteria for major depressive disorder but did not have the endogenous subtype. There were nine other children who had dysphoric mood (four boys and five girls). However, they did not meet RDC criteria for an affective disorder diagnosis. Two of them had conduct disorders, two had attention deficit disorder, one was normal, one had a labile personality, one had a histrionic personality, one had separation anxiety disorder, and one had an academic under-achievement disorder.

The children were given 0.5 mg of dexamethasone, one tablet by mouth at 11 PM. The next day, one blood sample was drawn at 4 PM. Plasma cortisol concentrations were determined by the competitive protein binding method. The results were as follows. Five of the nine children with an RDC diagnosis of major depressive disorder had abnormal DST results. One other had a borderline abnormal test. This is a sensitivity of 56 percent. Eight of the nine children with diagnoses other than depressive disorder had normal DST results. Thus, the specificity was 89 percent in the nondepressed patients. Poznanski and her colleagues point out that these results on sensitivity and specificity are similar to that which are reported for the DST in adult depressed patients.

Considering only those depressed children with the endogenous subtype, the sensitivity was 63 percent, and the specificity was 90 percent. This suggests that the DST may in fact be as useful in prepubertal children with major depressive disorder as it is with adults. However, much more work needs to be done in this area.

In summary, the bulk of the evidence indicates that the phenomenon of cortisol hypersecretion occurs among prepubertal endogenous major depressives. The question of its prevalence is still open. Preliminary evidence indicates that about one-fifth of these children hypersecrete cortisol. Such data provides strong backing for the hypothesis that child and adult major depressive disorders are basically the same illness (or group of illnesses) occurring at different maturational stages.

GROWTH HORMONE RESPONSES

Adult Endogenous Depressive Cases

It has also been shown that about 40 to 50 percent of adult endogenous depressives hyposecrete growth hormone (GH) in response to insulin-induced hypoglycemia (ITT) (Gruen et al, 1975; Gregoire et al, 1977). This is a standard test of growth hormone secretion. Because of the confounding effects of estrogen on GH response, this finding was established in postmenopausal depressed and control subjects (Sachar, 1975).

Other provocative tests of GH secretion also have been reported showing a decrease in GH release by the pituitary in endogenous depressives. Specifically d-amphetamine (Langer et al, 1976), desmethylimipramine (DMI) (Laakman, 1979), and clonidine (Matussek, 1979) have been reported to induce significantly lower GH responses in adult endogenous depressive patients than in control subjects. The interpretation of the GH hyporresponsivity to some of the agents has been difficult because of age differences among the patients and control groups. The DMI-GH test has shown so far extremely high discriminating power between cases of endogenous depression, other depression, and normal control subjects (Laakman, 1979), with 100 percent specificity and 100 percent sensitivity using a cut-off of 10 ng/ml for GH peak value in the first four hours post-DMI administration (Laakman, 1979).

Prepubertal Endogenous Depressive Cases

To our knowledge only the author's team has studied GH response to ITT in this age group. This study is ongoing and its preliminary findings will be briefly reported on here (Tabrizi et al, 1979). GH-ITTs have been carried out and analyzed in ten endogenous depressive, ten nonendogenous depressive, and seven nondepressed emotionally disordered children, all prepubertal. GH samples were obtained every 15 minutes. Highly significant differences between the groups occurred for GH plasma concentrations at 30, 45, and 60 minutes after insulin injection. All differences were accounted for by hyposecretion of GH in the endogenous group. Ninety percent of the endogenous group had a peak GH in the first hour below 4 ng/ml, while 50 percent of the nonendogenous group and zero percent of the neurotic group had peak GH values below 4 ng/ml. Although all subjects included in the analysis had blood glucose drops of at least 50 percent of baseline values, there were significant differences in both speed and magnitude of glucose drop among the groups. These differences were fully accounted for by the endogenous group. Endogenous depressive children had glucose curves (sampled every five minutes) which fell less and more slowly than the other two groups. This finding suggests that prepubertal endogenous depressive children, like their adult counterparts (Mueller et al, 1972), may exhibit mild insulin resistance, at least during their illness.

Correlational analyses within each experimental group showed no evidence of a relationship between the speed and magitude of glucose drop on the one hand, and GH response on the other.

To the author's knowledge no studies have been carried out regarding GH responsibility to DMI or d-amphetamine in children with major depression. The GH-ITT data briefly reviewed here, if confirmed at the end of the study, provide further support for our hypothesis that child and adult major depressive disorders are basically the same illness (or group of illnesses) occurring at different maturational stages.

Two main points should be addressed regarding the sensitivity and specificity of GH-ITT in psychiatric populations and across age groups:

1. Sensitivity of GH-ITT in endogenous depressive patients across age groups: Our preliminary data indicate a much higher sensitivity of the GH-ITT test for prepubertal endogenous depressive children (90 percent) than for adult patients with the same diagnosis (40 to 50 percent). The most parsimonious explanation for such differences is the role of sexual hormones in particular estrogen. Estrogens potentiate GH response to a variety of stimuli (Frantz and Rubkin, 1965; Merimee and Feinberg, 1971) and they may therefore considerably affect response to ITT. In adult studies, this factor has been controlled for by restricting the sample to be studied to postmenopausal subjects. Prepubertal children, on the other hand, have minimal circulating estrogens, and therefore their GH responses to ITT are not subject to the possible influence of these hormones that may mask GH hyposecretion and which would otherwise appear if estrogen levels were lower.

The high sensitivity of the DMI-GH test in adult endogenous depressive patients (Laakman, 1979), casts doubt on estrogen being the only factor to explain the adult/prepubertal differences in sensitivity of the GH-ITT test in endogenous depression.

Among the four main GH stimulating agents which have been properly investigated in adult depressive patients (DMI, ITT, clonidine, d-amphetamine), functional increase of norepinephrine (NE) synaptic activity is the only common mechasims known. DMI is a purely NE reuptake inhibitor blocker (Javaid et al, 1979). D-amphetamine increases the release of NE, dopamine (DA), and serotonin (5HT) (Snyder, 1972). GH response to ITT is blocked by regitine (an alpha-adrenergic blocker) (Martin, 1976), and is not affected by dopamine blockers (Nathan et al, 1981). The role of serotonin and other putative neurotransmitters is still unclear.

It may be that the hypoglycemic stimulus is not as specific as DMI, in the sense that it may stimulate other neurotransmitter systems besides NE, which in turn may influence GH response in adult depressive patients and decrease the sensitivity of the test. If this hypothesis were to be true, our data would further suggest that in prepubertal endogenous depressive patients the hypoglycemic stimulus is more specific to NE systems. In summary, the evidence at hand suggests that maturational changes, like high levels of sexual hormones, may decrease the specificity of the hypoglycemic stimulus by permitting or potentiating the stimulation of neurotransmitter systems other than and in addition to NE.

Other alternative explanations are also available. Thus, the fact that in our sample 50 percent of cases classified as nonendogenous hyposecreted GH in response to ITT, the beginning evidence that prepubertal major depressive children may be a highly "genetically loaded" group, and the extremely early age of onset tend to support a hypothesis that major depressions of prepubertal onset may constitute a more severe form of disorder. This may in itself account for higher rates of GH hyporresponsivity to ITT.

2. Specificity of GH hyporresponse to ITT in prepubertal major depressives: Although inadequate psychoendocrine research has been carried out in prepubertal psychiatric disorders, GH hyporresponse to hypoglycemia has been reported in another condition: psychosocial dwarfism (PSD) (Money et al, 1976; Brown, 1976). Actually it was this work on psychosocial dwarfism which prompted Sachar to hypothesize that adult depressive persons may also hyposecrete GH in response to the same stimulus. Sachar based his hypothesis on the fact that some of the clinical features of psychosocial dwarfs appeared similar to what was described by Spitz (1945) as anaclitic depression in maternally deprived infants.

Nevertheless, several clinical characteristics of PSD and prepubertal major depression, as well as their respective GH hyporresponses to hypoglycemia, indicate that these are different and easily differentiated disorders, although it is conceivable that they may coexist. Thus, PSD children by definition present with abnormally short stature and severe sleeplessness (Wolf and Money, 1973); their sleep and growth disorders, as well as GH hyporresponse to ITT, quickly reverse when they are placed outside the home, be it in the hospital or in a residential center. In contrast, in our sample, prepubertal major depressive children are not shorter than control subjects, polysomnographic studies do not show any major differences from control subjects (Puig-Antich et al, 1979), and our preliminary data indicate that the endogenous group may continue to hyposecrete GH to hypoglycemia months after clinical recovery while still in a nondepressed state.

SUMMARY OF NEUROENDOCRINE STUDIES

Although other neuroendocrine abnormalities have been reported in adult endogenous depressive patients during illness, notably a blunting of thyroid stimulating hormone (TSH) response to intravenous injection of thyrotropin releasing hormone (TRH) (Prange, 1977; Takahasi et al, 1974; Kirkegaard et al, 1975), no such work has been carried out in prepubertal major depressive patients. Similarly, nothing is known at present regarding neuroendocrine correlates of adolescent major depression. This is surprising given the fact that the existence of major depressions among adolescents has been generally accepted, that it is likely to be more frequent than in prepuberty, and that it has been identified in well-conducted epidemiological studies of adolescent psychiatric disorders (Rutter et al, 1976).

Overall, the neuroendocrine results to date tend to validate the existence of prepubertal major depression and its similarity to adult major depression. Future work in this area appears to be promising regarding validating the disorder further, developing diagnostic tests for this condition, and providing guidelines to clinicians in the future on the solidity of apparent clinical recoveries and the appropriate timing for treatment discontinuation (Greden et al, 1980; Kirkegaard et al, 1975).

Finally, differences in rates of various neuroendocrine correlates of major depresson across different age groups may elucidate research leads into maturational changes in the brain regulation of mood and/or pleasure, and may help to define what correlates are specific to depressive disorders (or their subgroups) and which constitute epiphenomena where depression interacts with other age-dependent variables.

POLYSOMNOGRAPHY

Adult Major Depression

Electrophysiological recordings of brain, eye, and muscle activity which allow the characterization of different stages during sleep, have been extremely informative in studies of adult major depression. Several studies of drug-free adult depressive patients (Snyder, 1968; Kupfer and Foster, 1972; Mendels and Chernik, 1972; Chernik and Mendels, 1974; Gillen et al, 1975; Foster and Kupfer, 1975) reviewed by Kupfer and Foster (1979) have repeatedly shown a series of polysomnographic characteristics associated with these disorders: decreased total sleep time, decreased delta sleep, shortened REM latency, decreased sleep efficiency, intermittent awakenings, increased sleep latency, and early morning awakenings.

Once these findings had been established, the possibility remained that at least some were secondary to the decrease in total sleep time. Therefore, more recent studies have used primary insomniacs and also normal persons as control subjects. Thus, Gillen et al (1979), comparing these three groups, were able to show that they were significantly different in nine univariate comparisons: sleep latency, awake time, total sleep time, asleep efficiency, early morning awake time, delta sleep time, REM latency, REM density, and REM index. In addition, each group differed from the others in several univariate comparisons. Thus, insomniacs significantly differed from normal subjects in total sleep time, sleep latency, delta sleep, and sleep efficiency. Depressed subjects differed from normal subjects in total sleep time, sleep latency, early morning awake time, awake time, delta sleep, sleep efficiency, and REM latency. Finally, depressed and insomniacs differed significantly in early morning awake time, REM latency, REM index, and REM density.

Gillen et al (1979) also pioneered the use of multivariate comparisons between the groups, using not only variables which on their own yielded significant differences, but also all the other variables in standard sleep architecture. Using discriminant function analysis they were able to classify correctly 82.6 percent of subjects: all normal subjects, 73.2 percent of major depressive patients, and 77.8 percent of insomniacs. It is clear at the present time that sleep variables are likely to be useful in the clinical diagnosis of major depression in adults and they may also aid in subtyping more homogenous groups within the major depressive disorders.

Vogel et al (1980) have focused on REM sleep changes during endogenous depression. They have reported that depressive patients, compared to age matched and total sleep-time–matched insomniacs, present increased REM density and also an abnormal temporal distribution of REM sleep, so that the first rapid eye movement period (REMP) contains a higher percentage of REM time than control subjects. Vogel hypothesized that the neural oscillator which controls REM sleep is weakened in depression.

In summary, the use of polysomnographic techniques has been very productive in identifying correlates of endogenous major depression in adults. There is still very little data regarding possible uses of sleep correlates in predicting relapse after discontinuation of successful treatment of the depressive episode, the polysomnographic characteristics of drug-free recovered depressive patients, and the possible sleep correlates of nonendogenous, atypical depressive subjects.

Prepubertal Major Depressive Disorder

Kane et al (1977) reported on one case of prepubertal depression, an 11-year-old girl who presented with a shortened first REMP latency as compared with published age norms (Williams et al, 1974), disturbed sleep continuity, and low sleep efficiency.

The same group of investigators published a report (Kupfer et al, 1979) on the effect of antidepressant medication on polysomnographic patterns in a group of early adolescent and prepubertal depressive patients (n = 12). Before treatment, no significant differences were found in sleep architecture, sleep continuity, or REM latency between the depressive and normal patients in the literature (Williams et al, 1974). Findings from these open studies are difficult to interpret because clinical diagnosis was made using Weinberg et al (1973) criteria which have been shown to be less specific than DSM-III criteria for major depression (Carlson and Cantwell, 1980).

The author and his team are conducting a controlled study of polysomnographic patterns during illness of drug-free prepubertal subjects in the following four groups: RDC endogenous major depressive, nonendogenous major depressive, nondepressed emotionally disordered, and normal patients (Puig-Antich et al, 1979). Preliminary analyses were conducted when the sample size for each group were 24, 15, 12, and 11, respectively. At that point the results failed to reveal any significant differences between the groups, which may have helped to characterize the depressives. A few significant differences (total sleep period and total sleep time) during the first night were wholly accounted for by adaptation effects in the neurotic group, and had disappeared by the second night.

First REMP latencies were quite stable between 130 and 170 minutes in all four groups. The percentages of Stages I, II, III, IV, and REM showed no significant differences and no trends. Similarly, no differences appeared in sleep efficiency, number of minutes of awakenings and body movement, number of awakenings, sleep latency, and REM density.

These negative findings are surprising because in structured clinical interviews both the depressive children and their parents as a group report difficulty falling asleep and/or frequent middle-of-the-night awakenings. In addition, about one half of the endogenous group reported early morning awakenings, while a few described reappearance of naps and hypersomnia. Practically all prepubertal major depressive patients report a feeling of not sleeping well and that they did not feel well-rested upon awakening (nonrestorative sleep). These complaints usually subside during clinical recovery. Such discrepancy between clinical and polysomnographic findings is most intriguing and may be due to sleeping in the laboratory. We are specifically looking for possible polysomnographic correlates of nonrestorative sleep in the records of this sample at the present time.

The preliminary negative findings briefly summarized here if confirmed at the end of the study and replicated by other investigators, fail to support the validity of the diagnosis. Then the following question emerges: Does the virtual of cross-sectional sleep architecture differences in prepubertal major depressive children indicate that prepubertal and adult major depression are different disorders or does it only reflect maturational differences of the same disorder at different ages?

In our view, the evidence in our studies and in others points to the second possibility: The lack of sleep findings is likely to express a maturational difference, not a difference in the nature of prepubertal and adult major depression. The evidence for this tentative conclusion comes from two sources: studies of age differences in sleep correlates of young and older adult major depressive patients and studies of other psychobiological correlates of child and adolescent major depression.

Age Effects on Sleep Patterns in Normal Subjects and Depressive Patients

Normative data across age groups indicate a progressive decrease with age in percentage of delta sleep, REM latency, and sleep efficiency (Williams et al, 1974).

Coble et al (1980) have recently presented evidence that sleep correlates in adult depressive patients are also subject to an age effect. Thus they have compared polysomnographic data during illness in two groups of drug-free endogenous depressive patients: one group aged 18 to 30 years and the other 38 to 45 years. The older depressive patients differed significantly from the younger group in four variables. The older group presented higher REM density, lower REMP latency, lower sleep efficiency, and lower percentage of delta sleep. It should be noted that differences in clinical picture were reported to be minimal.

Ulrich et al (1982) have also reported a high negative correlation between age and first REMP latency in adult endogenous depressive patients during illness. The older the subject, the shorter the first REMP latency is.

Therefore, it would appear from these data that the lack of sleep findings characterizing prepubertal major depression may lie at one end of the curve in continuity with adult data, and that the polysomnographic findings reported as characteristic of adult endogenous depression may be the result of an interaction between this disorder and age. This would not detract from the future use of polysomnography in the diagnosis of adult endogenous depression, which is likely to become quite useful, sensitive, and specific (Carroll et al, in press; Gillin et al, 1979; Kupfer, 1976), but it would indicate that inferences regarding pathophysiology of endogenous depression from sleep data should consider the effects of aging on normal sleep. Future studies in adolescent major depressive patients will be crucial to test the hypothesis of continuity between lack of sleep findings in prepubertal depression and the well-esbablished sleep findings in adult depression.

The second source of evidence for the hypothesis that the lack of sleep findings in prepubertal major depression may represent a maturational difference and not a difference in the nature of the disorder at different ages comes from the assessment of current data on psychobiological correlates of prepubertal and adolescent major depressive disorder, which will be considered in the next and last section of this Chapter.

SUMMARY AND CONCLUSIONS

The hypothesis that the negative sleep findings may be due to maturational factors will be strengthened if the majority of other psychobiological correlates of major depressive disorder are similar in prepuberty and adulthood, thus indicating that the fundamental nature of major depressive disorder does not change with age.

In fact, the bulk of the evidence points in this direction. The data supporting the similarity of child and adult major depression at present, is enumerated below:

1. There is an almost identical clinical picture (same diagnostic criteria) (Weinberg et al, 1973; Puig-Antich et al, 1978; Carlson and Cantwell, 1980; Cytryn et al, 1980).
2. Growth hormone hyporresponsivity to insulin-induced hypoglycemia (Tabrizi et al, 1979) is present.
3. The phenomenon of cortisol hypersecretion definitely occurs in some prepubertal depressives (Puig-Antich et al, 1978).
4. An ongoing blind family history study of prepubertal major depressive disorders (n = 26) by the author and his team, recently analyzed at midpoint, indicates that the lifetime morbidity risk for major depressive disorder in first degree biological relatives over 16 years of age is 0.42. Morbidity risk for alcoholism is 0.29, for antisocial personality 0.18, for mania 0.04, and for schizophrenia is the same rate as in the general population. These figures are not yet age-corrected. Age correction will actually increase the rates for depression and alcoholism, given the youth of these relatives (late 20s to early 30s). In contrast, the lifetime morbidity risk for major depression in first degree biological relatives over 16 years of adult major depressives is 0.30 (Reich, personal communication, 1980). The data suggest that prepubertal major depressive patients are likely to be a highly genetically loaded group, and this may at least partially account for such an early onset.

In summary, preliminary data from family history studies of childhood major depressive disorders tend to validate the hypothesis of similarity of these disorders from prepuberty to adulthood.

Therefore, among the psychobiological parameters where data exist and have been analyzed, only sleep architecture shows major differences between adult and prepubertal studies. Very little work has been done in adolescent depressive patients. There is a strong possibility that the negative sleep findings are due to maturational factors. Sleep findings in adult major depressive patients may actually result from an interaction between age and major depressive disorder, although this does not detract from possible usefulness in diagnostic subtyping of depressive disorders in adults.

Future research in the psychobiology of major depressive disorders in children and adolescents offers exciting opportunities, not only for the development of refined diagnostic and treatment guidelines for these disorders in youngsters, but also for significantly furthering the understanding of which psychobiological markers are intrinsic to depressive disorders at all ages, for the possible development of age-universal markers of predisposition (or trait), for the subsequent elucidation of specific modes of genetic and/or cultural transmission of these disorders, and for the advancement of our knowledge on the pathophysiology of depression.

REFERENCES

Asnis G, Nathan S, Halbreich U, Sachar EJ. Cortisol and dexamethasone response in depression: neuroendocrine correlates. Presented at the Annual Meeting of the American Psychiatric Association, San Francisco, 1980.

Asnis G, Sachar EJ, Halbreich U, et al. Cortisol secretion in relation to age in major depression. *Psychosom Med* 1981;43:235–242.

Brown GM. Endocrine aspects of psychosocial dwarfism. In: Sachar EJ, ed. *Hormones, behavior and psychopathology*. New York: Raven Press, 1976: 253–261.

Brown WA, Shuey I. Response to dexamethasone and subtype of depression. *Arch Gen Psychiatry* 1980;37:747–752.

Carlson G, Cantwell D. Diagnosis of childhood depression: a comparison of Weinberg and DSM-III criteria. Presented at the American Psychiatric Association Annual Meeting, San Francisco, 1980.

Carlson G, Cantwell D. Unmasking masked depression. *Am J Psychiatry* 1980; 137:445–449.

Carroll BJ. Implications of biological research for the diagnosis of depression. In: Mendlewicz J, ed. *New advances in the diagnosis and treatment of depressive illness*. Amsterdam: Elsevier (in press).

Carroll BJ, Curtis GC, Mendels J. Neuroendocrine regulation in depression-I. Limbic system-adrenocortisol dysfunctions. *Arch Gen Psychiatry* 1976a; 33:1039–1044.

Carroll BJ, Curtis GC, Mendels J. Neuroendocrine regulation in depression-II. Discrimination of depressed from nondepressed patients. *Arch Gen Psychiatry* 1976b;33:1051–1058.

Carroll BJ, Feinberg M, Greden JF, et al. Diagnosis of endogenous depression: comparison of clinical, research and neuroendocrine criteria. *Arch Gen Psychiatry* 1981(2).

Carroll BJ, Feinberg M, Greden JF, et al. Neurodenocrine diagnostic criteria for depression. *Psychopharmacol Bull* 1980 (in press b).

Carroll BJ, Greden JF, Feinberg M. Neuroendocrine diagnosis of endogenous depression. *Psychoneuroendocrinology Lett* 1980; 2:151.

Carroll BJ, Greden JF, Feinberg M, et al. Neuroendocrine dysfunction in genetic subtypes of primary unipolar depression. *Psychiatry Res* 1980; 2:251–258.

Carroll BJ, Mendels J. Neuroendocrine regulations in affective disorders. In: Sachar EJ, ed. *Hormones, behavior and psychopathology*. New York: Raven Press, 1976:193–224.

Chernik DA, Mendels J. Sleep in bipolar and unipolar depressed patients. *Sleep Res* 1974; 3:123.

Coble P, Kupfer DJ, Spiker DG, et al. EEG sleep and clinical characteristics in young primary depressives. Presented at the Annual Meeting of the Association for the Psychophysiological Study of Sleep. Mexico City, 1980.

Cytryn L, McKnew D, Bunney W. Diagnosis of depression in children: reassessment. *Am J Psychiatry* 1980; 137:445–449.

Foster FG, Kupfer DJ. Psychomotor activity as a correlate of depression and sleep in acutely disturbed psychiatric inpatients. *Am J Psychiatry* 1975; 132:928.

Frantz AG, Rabkin MT. Effects of estrogen and sex differences on secretion of human growth hormone. *J Clin Endocrinol Metab* 1975; 25:1470–1480.

Gibbons JL. Cortisol secretion rate in depressive illness. *Arch Gen Psychiatry* 1964; 33:1051–1058.

Gillin JC, Bunney WE, Buchbinder R. Sleep changes in unipolar and bipolar depressed patients as compared with normals. Presented at the Second International Sleep Research Congress, Edinburgh, Scotland, and 15th Annual Meeting of the Association for the Psychophysiological Study of Sleep, 1975.

Gillin JC, Duncan W, Pettigrew KD, et al. Successful separation of depressed, normal and insomniac subjects by EEG sleep data. *Arch Gen Psychiatry* 1979; 36:85–90.

Greden JF, Albala AA, Haskett RF, et al. Normalization of the dexamethasone suppression test: a laboratory index of recovery from endogenous depression. *Biol Psychiatry* 1980; 15:449–458.

Gregoire F, Branman G, DeBuck R, Corvilain J. Hormone release in depressed patients before and after recovery. *Psychoneuroendocrinology* 1977; 2:303–312.

Gruen PH, Sachar EJ, Altman N, Sassin J. Growth hormone response to hypoglycemia in postmenopausal depressed women. *Arch Gen Psychiatry* 1975; 32:31–33.

Javaid JI, Perel JM, Davis JM. Inhibition of biogenic amines uptake by imipramine, desipramine, 2-OH-imipramine and 2-OH-desipramine in rat brain. *Life Sci* 1979; 24:21–28.

Kane J, Coble P, Conners CK, Kupfer DJ. EEG sleep in a child with severe depression. *Am J Psychiatry* 1977; 134:813–814.

Kirkegaard C, Norlem N, Lauridsen UB, et al. Protirelin stimulation test and thyroid function during treatment of depression. *Arch Gen Psychiatry* 1975;32:1115–1118.

Kupfer D. REM latency: a psychobiological marker for primary depressive disease. *Biol Psychiatry* 1976;11:159–174.

Kupfer DJ, Coble P, Kane J, et al. Imipramine and EEG sleep in children with depressive symptoms. *Psychopharmacology (Berlin)* 1979; 60:117–123.

Kupfer D, Foster FG. EEG sleep and depression. In: Williams RL, Karacan I, eds. *Disorders diagnosis and treatment*. New York: J Wiley, 1979:163–203.

Kupfer DJ, Foster FG. Interval between onset of sleep and rapid-eye-movement sleep as an indicator of depression. *Lancet* 1972; 2:684.

Laakman G. Neuroendocrine differences between endogenous and neurotic depression as seen in stimulation of growth hormone secretion. In: Miller EE, Agnoli A, eds. *Neuroendocrine correlates in neurology and psychiatry*. Amsterdam: Elsevier, 1979; 263–271.

Langer G, Heinze G, Reim B, Matussek N. Reduced growth hormone responses to amphetamine in endogenous depressive patients. *Arch Gen Psychiatry* 1976; 33:1471–1475.

Martin JB. Brain regulation of growth hormone secretion. In: *Frontiers in neuroendocrinology*, 1976; 4:129–168.

Matussek N. Neuroendocrinological studies in affective disorders. In: Shou M, Stromgren E, eds. *Origin prevention and treatment of affective disorders*. London: Academic Press, 1979:171–178.

Mendels J, Chernik DA. Sleep of manic-depressives and recurrent depressives. *Sleep Res* 1972; 1:142.

Merimee TJ, Fineberg SE. Studies of the sex based variation of human growth hormone secretion. *J Clin Endocrinol Metab* 1971; 33:896–902.

Money J, Annecillo C, Werlwas J. Hormonal and behavioral reversals in hyposomatotropic dwarfism. In: Sachar EJ, ed. *Hormones, behavior and psychopathology*. New York: Raven Press, 1976:243–252.

Mueller PS, Heninger GR, McDonald PK. Studies on glucose utilization and insulin sensitivity in affective disorders: In: Williams TA, Katz MM, Shield JA, eds. *Recent advances in the psychobiology of depressive illnesses*. Department of Health, Education, and Welfare Publication 70-9053, 1972: 235–245.

Nathan S, Sachar EJ, Ostrow L, et al. Failure of dopaminergic blockade to affect prolactin, GH, and cortisol responses to insulin-induced hypoglycemia in schizophrenia. *J Clin Endocrinol Metab* 1981; 52:802–809.

Poznanski EO, Carroll BJ, Banegas MC, et al. Dexamethasone suppression test in prepubertal depressed children. *Am J Psychiatry* 1972; 139; 3:321–324.

Prange AJ. Patterns of pituitary responses to TRH in depressed patients. In: Fann W, Karacan I, Pokorny AD, Williams RL, eds. *Phenomenology and treatment of depression*. New York: Spectrum, 1977:1–16.

Puig-Antich J, Blau S, Marx N, et al. Prepubertal major depressive disorders: pilot study. *J Am Acad Child Psychiatry* 1978; 17:695–707.

Puig-Antich J, Blau S, Marx N, et al. Prepubertal major depressive disorder. *J Am Acad Child Psychiatry* 1978b; 17:695–707.

Puig-Antich J, Hanlon C, Weitzman E, et al. Sleep correlates of prepubertal major depressive disorder. Presented at the Annual Meeting of the American Academy of Child Psychiatry, Atlanta, Georgia, 1979.

Rutter M, Graham P, Chadwick O, Yule W. Adolescent turmoil: fact or fiction. *J Child Psychol Psychiatry* 1976; 17:35–56.

Sachar EJ. Neuroendocrine abnormalities in depressive illness. In: Sachar EJ, ed. *Topics in psychoneuroendocrinology*. New York: Grune and Stratton, 1975:135–156.

Sachar EJ, Hellman L, Roffwarg HP, et al. Disrupted 24 hour pattern of cortisol secretion in psychotic depression. *Arch Gen Psychiatry* 1973; 28:19–25.

Schlesser M, Winokur G, Sherman BM. Genetic subtypes of unipolar primary depressive illness distinguished by hypothalamic-pituitary-adrenal axis activity. *Lancet* 1979; 1:739–741.

Schlesser M, Winokur G, Sherman BM. Hypothalamic-pituitary-adrenal axis activity in depressive illness. *Arch Gen Psychiatry* 1980; 37:737–743.

Snyder F. Electroencephalographic studies of sleep in depression. In: Kline NS, Laska E, eds. *Computers and electronic devices in psychiatry*. New York: Grune and Stratton, 1968:272.

Snyder SH. Catecholamines in the brain as mediators of amphetamine psychoses. *Arch Gen Psychiatry* 1972; 27:169–179.

Spitz RA. Hospitalism. *Psychoanal Stud Child* 1945; 1:53–74.

Spitzer RL, Endicott J, Robbins E. Research diagnostic criteria: rationale and reliability. *Arch Gen Psychiatry* 1978; 35:773–782.

Tabrizi MA, Puig-Antich J, Chambers WJ, et al. Growth hormone hyposecretion to insulin induced hypoglycemia in prepubertal major depressive disorder. Presented at the Annual Meeting of the American Academy of Child Psychiatry, Atlanta, Georgia, 1979.

Takahasi S, Kondo H, Yoshimura M, Ochi Y. Thyrotropin responses to TRH in depressive illness. *Folia Psychiat Neurol Jpn* 1974; 28:355–365.

Ulrich R, Shaw DH, Kupfer DJ. The effects of aging on sleep. *Sleep* 1982.

Van Valkenburg C, Winokur G. Depression spectrum disease. *Psychiat Clin North Am* 1979; 2:469–482.

Vogel GW, Vogel F, McAbee RS, Thurmond AJ. Improvement of depression by REM sleep deprivation. *Arch Gen Psychiatry* 1980; 37:247–253.

Weinberg WA, Rutman J, Sullivan L, et al. Depression in children referred to an educational diagnostic center. *J Pediat* 1973; 83:1065–1072.

Williams RL, Karacan I, Hursch C. *EEG of human sleep: clinical applications*. New York: J Wiley, 1974:37–47.

Winokur G. Unipolar depression. *Arch Gen Psychiatry* 1979; 36:47–53.

Wolf G, Money J. Relationship between sleep and growth in patients with reversible somatotropin deficiency (psychosocial dwarfism). *Psychol Med* 1973; 3:18–27.

Affective Disorders in Childhood and Adolescence--
An Update. Edited by D.P. Cantwell and G.A. Carlson.

12

Biological Research on Depression in Childhood

Thomas L. Lowe and Donald J. Cohen

Biological studies of neurochemical and neuroendocrine systems in depressed children represent an area of increasing investigation in child psychiatry and one of the potentially most valuable areas for the basic understanding and development of treatment modalities for affectively disordered children and adolescents. Although still in the initial phases of development, this research field is becoming increasingly active with several groups of biologically oriented child psychiatrists now actively pursuing biochemical studies of children exhibiting severe depressive symptomatology.

The movement toward increasing investigations of these children has been based on three main changes in psychiatric thought over the past decade. The first has been the reconceptualization of the existence in childhood of a depressive syndrome and not merely depressive symptoms. The work of Poznansky, Cytryn, Weinberg and others has provided increasing evidence that children are capable of exhibiting a constellation of symptoms similar to those fulfilling the criteria for adult unipolar depressive illness. This change in recognition has been described in other chapters of this volume.

The second important issue is the developing understanding of biologic distinguishing characteristics in depressed adults. Work over the past 15 years, since the development of Schildkraut and Kety's cathecholamine hypothesis of affective illness, has substantiated the fact that there are biochemical and endocrine abnormalities in a group of depressed adults that can be shown to differentiated them from their nondepressed counterparts. This increasing evidence for biological markers of depression has encouraged attempts at discovering similar abnormalities in children suffering from depression.

Third, there has developed during the recent past an increasing belief that childhood depression may well represent an early onset form of adult depression, sharing common underlying biological factors, as well as genetic predisposition. This belief, that depressed children represent the same basic pathological process occurring at an earlier stage of development, has led investigators toward attempts at replicating adult findings in depressed children and following similar avenues of research design in the elucidation of biochemical functioning in this group of children.

In order to better understand the biochemical and neuroendocrine work that has been accomplished and is in progress in childhood depression, we will summarize the major neuroendocrine and neurochemical findings in the field of affective disorders in adults. After that, we will discuss the work that has been completed or is in progress in the study of childhood depression, and conclude with thoughts about future directions for biological research in this area.

BIOLOGICAL STUDIES OF ADULT DEPRESSION

The history of biological studies in adult depression is closely linked to the pharmacological development of compounds which were discovered to have an effect on the mood of patients for whom they were prescribed. Particularly, drugs such as monoamine oxidase inhibitors (MAOIs), tricyclic antidepressants (TCAs), and lithium salts revealed major mood-altering capabilities and led to extensive neurochemical investigation of the spectrum from depressive illness to mania. With increased neuropharmacological understanding of the chemical effects of these medications, there developed a biogenic amine theory of affective disorder, described by Schildkraut and Kety, postulating a disturbance in central monoamine neurotransmitter regulations as the basis for major disorders in mood (Schildkraut, 1965). Work over the past 15 years has centered around studies of catecholamines, (dopamine and norepinephrine) and indoleamines (serotonin), which serve as neurotransmitters in the central nervous system. Study of these compounds has been carried out in two major ways: first, direct measurement of the compounds and their metabolites in the cerebrospinal fluid requiring lumbar puncture and analysis of cerebrospinal fluid, and second, analysis of catecholamine metabolites in the peripheral circulation and in the urine, where they are excreted. This latter method, obviously preferable to the former because of the discomfort associated with lumbar puncture and the difficulty of repeated sampling, has been made possible by the fact that one of the catecholamines, norepinephrine, is metabolized in the brain to 3-methoxy-4-hydroxyphenethylene glycol (MHPG) which is then excreted and can be measured in the urine. Because central metabolism primarily leads to MHPG production, while peripheral metabolism of norepinephrine primarily follows a different pathway leading to a separate final metabolite, measurement of urinary MHPG has been shown to reflect central nervous system norepinephrine metabolism in the main (Wilk and Watson, 1974). About 40 to 60 percent of urinary MHPG probably originates in the central nervous system (Maas et al, 1970; Swann et al, 1980). This fact has allowed a peripheral biochemical measure to be used in studying central norepinephrine systems without the necessity of invasive procedures in children and adults (Young et al, 1981b). The study of dopamine and serotonin systems in the brain has not as yet provided a peripheral compound reflecting primarily central activity and thus requires lumbar puncture for the measurement of their metabolites–homovanillic acid (HVA) for the dopamine system and 5-hydroxyindoleacetic acid (5-HIAA) for the serotonin system.

The findings of neurochemical studies of depression in adults have led to the recognition that all depressions are not clinically or biologically homogeneous. There appear to be at least two distinct subgroups that can be separated neurochemically (Maas, 1975; Schildkraut et al, 1981). One of these subgroups appears to have an abnormality in noradrenergic central nervous system functioning as reflected by decreased levels of urinary MHPG, the major metabolite of central norepinephrine. In comparison, other groups of clinically depressed adults have normal or slightly increased levels of MHPG production, and there is evidence that these distinctions may provide a biochemical criterion for predicting differential responses to treatment with different tricyclic antidepressant drugs (Schildkraut, 1973; Beckman and Goodwin, 1975). In addition, a subgroup of bipolar manic depressive adults has been described in which MHPG excretion appears to vary in relation to clinical state. Several groups of investigators have shown that MHPG levels are decreased during the depressed phase and increased during the manic phase of bipolar illness (Bond et al, 1972; Jones et al, 1973).

The second group of clinically depressed adults, who have been studied by the analysis of cerebrospinal fluid collected from lumbar puncture, has revealed a subgroup reflecting reduced levels of 5-HIAA, the metabolite of serotonin in the central nervous system (Coppen et al, 1972; Asberg, 1973). The evidence has been interpreted as suggesting that depressed adults may suffer from a defect in serotonin production leading to decreased levels of its metabolite, but the story is more complicated. Active work continues in the area of neurochemical findings in depressed adults, and the specific relationships between the groups exhibiting abnormalities in norepinephrine and serotonin metabolism await further elucidation. There is significant data, however, to support the hypothesis that an abnormality in monoamine neurotransmitter systems in the brain is related, in some patients, to clinical depression during adult life.

NEUROENDOCRINE FINDINGS IN ADULT DEPRESSION

Because of the recognized relationship between neurotransmitter compounds and the functioning of central endocrine systems mediated through the hypothalamus, active investigation has proceeded in an attempt to distinguish certain abnormalities in neuroendocrine functioning that can be related to the population of patients suffering from depressive illness. With the recognition of hypothalamic control of pituitary hormones, based on the effect of hypothalamic releasing factors, researchers have recognized the value of sensitive neuroendocrine determinations as a method of analyzing central nervous system activity and function. Rigorous investigation into the neuroendocrine functioning of depressed adults has taken place over the past decade. These studies have led to the recognition of impaired neuroendocrine functioning in several endocrine systems in depressed adults. These include the hypothalamic-pituitary-adrenal system, the growth hormone system, the leutinizing hormone system, and the thyroid-stimulating hormone system.

With regard to the hypothalamic-pituitary-adrenal axis, depressed adults have been shown to exhibit increased levels of plasma cortisol, a hormone secreted by the adrenal cortex in response to adrenocorticotrophic hormone (ACTH) from the pituitary, which is in turn thought to be induced by a releasing factor produced in the hypothalamus. In addition to increased plasma cortisol, investigators have found increased cerebrospinal fluid cortisol and increased 24-hour urinary-free cortisol in depressed adults (Carroll, 1972).

Additionally, depressed patients have been found to exhibit a different profile of cortisol secretion. While normal adults exhibit a definite circadian variation with relatively higher levels of cortisol during the early morning hours and lower levels in the evening, patients with depression have been shown to have increased secretion of cortisol, increased time per day during which that secretion occurs, increased plasma concentration, and active nighttime secretion of cortisol whether asleep or awake. These studies support an abnormality in neuroendocrine function in depression which consists of disinhibition of the hypothalamic-pituitary-adrenal axis and may well be related to levels of hypothalamic norepinephrine (Sachar et al, 1973; Carroll and Mendels, 1976).

Furthermore, study of the effect of the oral administration of dexamethasone, a steroid which normally suppresses plasma cortisol for at least 24 hours after a midnight dose, has revealed abnormalities in the response of depressed patients. Although the exact response pattern may differ with severity of depression, up to 70 percent of depressed patients exhibit "early escape" from dexamethasone suppression; plasma cortisol levels do not remain suppressed for the normal period after administration of dexamethasone (Carroll, 1972; Carroll and Mendels, 1976). Thus, alteration in at least two areas of adrenal functioning, baseline function, and response to dexamethasone suppression appear to be present in the population of depressed adults.

Evidence for impairment in the growth hormone (GH) system in depressed adults has come primarily from stimulation tests of GH secretion. Although basal GH levels are reported to be normal in depressed patients, GH response to provocative agents which normally produce elevation of plasma levels has shown abnormal responses in the depressed adult population. The most frequently used clinical procedure for stimulation of the GH system is insulin-induced hypoglycemia. Numerous investigators have now shown that subgroups of depressed patients tend to have blunted or absent GH responses to insulin-induced hypoglycemia (Garver et al, 1975; Carroll and Mendels, 1976). Because the GH system has been shown to be sensitive to both dopaminergic and noradrenergic effects, the role of these catecholamine neurotransmitters in this neuroendocrine system in depressed patients is an area for important further investigation.

The findings of impairment in the leutinizing hormone (LH) levels of depressed patients have mainly involved a specific subgroup of postmenopausal depressed women who have been found to have significantly reduced LH levels compared with age-matched postmenopausal nondepressed women (Altman et al, 1975). The understanding of this abnormality is again felt to be related to the fact that leutinizing hormone secretion is regulated by a hypothalamic releasing factor, and that regulation of this factor by the hypothalamus may be related to central nervous system catecholamines, particularly norepinephrine (Ojeda and McCann, 1973). It has been speculated that depletion of central norepinephrine, as described in the biogenic amine theory, may be implicated in the reduced level of LH found in this group of postmenopausal depressed women. It should be noted, however, that the relationships between gonadal hormones and disturbance in mood are both complex and, as yet, not well-understood.

Although levels of thyroid hormone, itself, appear to be normal in depressed patients, there is increasing evidence to show that a subgroup of depressed patients exhibit abnormally low levels of thyroid-stimulating hormone (TSH), produced by the pituitary in response to hypothalamic thyrotropin-releasing hormone (TRH). Furthermore, numerous investigators have found a blunted TSH response to exogenous TRH administrered to depressed patients (Ehrensing et al, 1974), a finding felt to be analogous to the reduced response of growth hormone to stimulation by hypoglycemia. The relationship between blunted TSH and growth hormone responses and hypersecretion of cortisol by the adrenal gland of depressed patients represents an area of possible neuroendocrine interaction that awaits further study since increased cortisol may blunt the TSH response to TRH (Otsuki et al, 1973).

The final neuroendocrine system which has been shown to function abnormally in depressed patients is the prolactin system (Halbreich et al, 1979). Prolactin, a pituitary hormone primarily under dopaminergic inhibitory control, was basally elevated in unipolar patients, due to increased secretion during wakefulness, and decreased secretion in bipolars, because of reduced nocturnal elevation (Mendlewicz et al, 1980). In studies of 24-hour profiles of prolactin concentration, the variability of prolactin levels appeared to be reduced around the 24-hour mean in both unipolar and bipolar patients. Alterations in daily prolactin profiles may reflect central monoaminergic disturbances; as with 24-hour profiles of dopamine-beta-hydroxylase, prolactin profiles were more atypical in bipolar than unipolar patients (Van Cauter and Mendlewicz, 1978).

In summary, studies of neurochemical and neuroendocrine mechanisms in adult depressive disorders have led to the recognition of several subgroups of patients exhibiting specific abnormalities in monoamine metabolism, as well as defects in neuroendocrine responsiveness in baseline levels and in dynamic stimulation testing.

BIOLOGICAL STUDIES OF DEPRESSION IN CHILDREN

The neurochemical and neuroendocrine studies of depressed children have represented a limited field of work and reporting in the literature up until this time. In part, this is because studies in children have awaited guidance and direction based on studies in adult depressed patients, and in part, because biological studies in child psychiatry and active research groups in this area have only developed over the past several years. Another major area that has limited the amount of biological studies in depressed children has been the disagreement as to diagnosis and classification of children exhibiting symptoms of disturbed affect. The recognition of childhood depression as a clinically definable syndrome only emerged in the 1970s and still remains a source of discussion among clinicians as to specific operational criteria for diagnosis. A more detailed discussion of these issues of diagnosis can be found in the chapters by Puig-Antich, Lang, and Weinberg which appear in this volume.

A major issue involved in biological studies of depressed children has been an ethical one. In comparison with biological studies of adult depressed patients where direct and informed consent for invasive procedures can be obtained, these same procedures in children, when authorized by parents, raise concerns in the minds of investigators. In particular, the technique of lumbar puncture which has been required for the understanding of certain neurochemical systems in adults, has not been attempted at this time with depressed children.

Since the development of the biogenic amine theory of affective disturbance and the subsequent work on norepinephrine metabolism in depressed adults, investigations into the noradrenergic functioning of children with depressive symptoms has been attempted. Because the norepinephrine system can be viewed indirectly by studying its principal metabolite, MHPG, in the urine of affected subjects, most neurochemical studies of depressed children have involved determination of urinary metabolites of catecholamines. Particularly prominent in the studies of urinary metabolites has been the work of Cytryn and McKnew. Over the past eight years, this group of investigators has attempted to replicate the adult findings of decreased MHPG excretion in depressed patients (Cytryn et al, 1974; McKnew and Cytryn, 1979). Inconsistent findings and possible group heterogeneity based on differences in diagnostic criteria have led to the conclusion that further investigation is necessary before definitive statements about noradrenergic functioning in depressed children can be made. Work presently in progress by several groups of investigators, including Puig-Antich and Chambers, using more highly refined diagnostic instruments may well provide data leading to the definition of a subgroup of depressed children exhibiting similar neurochemical findings to their adult depressive counterparts. At this time, it is too early to conclude that depressed children will exhibit these neurochemical manifestations, however.

Neuroendocrine techniques involved in defining central nervous system endocrine functioning and in attempting to replicate studies in the adult depressed population are presently underway in several groups in the United States. Perhaps most prominent is the Columbia research group, which is engaged in growth hormone and cortisol studies in a carefully defined group of latency-aged depressed children. Preliminary findings indicate that subgroups of these children may show defects in growth hormone response to hypoglycemic stimulation, as well as abnormal cortisol production consistent with the findings in adult depression (Puig-Antich et al, 1979; Poznanski et al, 1981).

In an attempt to define another homogeneous group of children exhibiting depressive symptomatology and possible disturbance in neurochemical and neuroendocrine functioning, our group focused on the children suffering from psychoendocrine growth disturbance or psychosocial dwarfism. These children exhibit a combination of findings, including retardation of height and weight to below the third percentile for age, abnormal and often bizarre eating patterns, seriously impaired maternal/child interactions, and clinical symptoms of depressed mood, social withdrawal, and developmental delay. Particularly interesting and related to the findings in adult depressive illness is the recognition of impaired growth hormone response to hypoglycemia and a defect in adrenocorticotrophic function (Brown, 1976; Genel et al, 1976). These children thus represent a potentially homogeneous group of young patients exhibiting both behavioral and neuroendocrine findings consistent with areas of dysfunction in adult depressed patients, and are felt to represent an important group for evaluation of further neuroendocrine and neruochemical system functioning. Studies now underway are designed to look at the noradrenergic system functioning in these children through measurement of urinary metabolites, particularly MHPG. Additionally, we have included both baseline studies and stimulation tests of hypothalamic and pituitary function in the areas of thyroid, ACTH, and growth hormone systems. Particularly valuable in the investigation of these systems is the differential response of patients to pharmacologic stimuli and probe compounds. It has become increasingly clear from the biological research in adult depression that abnormalities often represent alterations in function, as indicated by hyper- or hyposecretory states, rather than lack of functioning. The ability to measure responses of depressed children to graded stimuli and to compare those responses to normal control populations has the potential of providing valuable and significant biological findings in this group of affectively disordered children.

MECHANISMS OF DRUG ACTION

The "classical" biogenic amine theory of Schildkraut and Kety fit well with what was understood during the 1970s about the mechanism of action of TCA and MAOI antidepressants (Schildkraut, 1965). A relative deficiency of norepinephrine or serotonin was thought to be functionally reversed by the gradual accumulation of these neurotransmitters over the course of several weeks of pharmacological intervention. The two major groups of drugs eventuated in the same final metabolic re-adjustment: TCAs increased central monoaminergic activity by decreased reuptake of amines and MAOIs achieved this end by reducing the metabolic, enzymatic degradation of amines. Several powerful lines of evidence have now challenged this simple theory. There are newer, clinically effective antidepressants with minimal functional effect on the uptake of NE or 5-HT in the brain (Shopsin, 1980). For example, mianserin, a tetracyclic antidepressant, has proven clinical effectiveness but only weakly inhibits catecholamine uptake in the standard test systems. Second, the clinical effectiveness of TCAs requires up to three to four weeks to emerge; in contrast, these compounds block presynaptic uptake within a few minutes of administration (Glowinski and Axelrod, 1964) and the "classical" theory could not account for this differential. Finally, TCAs may act on more than one neurotransmitter or on their interaction; for example, there are changes in dopamine receptors which depend on the passage of time rather than on daily drug administration (Chiodo and Antelman, 1980). Along with the emergence of these doubts about the older theory has been a rapid increase in knowledge about neuronal regulatory mechanisms. This expanding, and still uncertain, field of knowledge has had profound impact on the understanding of drug mechanisms and hypothesis about pathogenesis of neuropsychiatric disorders. Three observations are particularly relevant: first, that there are different types of receptors for the same neurotransmitter; second, that a particular neuron may have receptors for multiple transmitters; and, third, that more than one transmitter may be stored in the same neuron, and that two transmitters may be released simultaneously. To further complicate the unravelling of drug action, it is now clear that a particular transmitter may have distinct effects in different parts of the nervous system. For example, there are inhibitory and facilitatory serotonergic neurons, and a drug acting on serotonin could affect either or both types of neurons (Davis, 1980).

The concept of multiple receptor types has had broad application to pharmacological theory. For example, there are presynaptic, postsynaptic, and soma-dendritic receptors at various sites in the dopamine pathways in the brain. Presynaptic receptors inhibit the synthesis and release of dopamine; postsynaptic receptors mediate the physiological effects of dopamine which are specific for a particular point in the pathway; and soma-dendritic receptors regulate dopaminergic neuronal activity (Aghajanian and Bunney, 1977). Compounds which are active at both pre- and postsynaptic receptors may have mixed effects physiologically (Sokoloff, 1980). Other agonists may be relatively more specific for one type of receptor (Goodale et al, 1980), although there are few such drugs available clinically. Finally, different classes of receptors may be differentially more sensitive to a specific agonist (Skirboll et al, 1979). For example, clonidine, an alpha-adrenergic agonist, is ten times more effective in stimulating presynaptic, alpha-2 autoreceptors than postsynaptic receptors. This differential effectiveness accounts for clonidine's ability to decrease central noradrenergic activity and reduce MHPG production. However, clonidine is also active at postsynaptic alpha-one receptors (leading to release of growth hormone).

In addition to feedback mechanisms utilizing the same neurotransmitter system, there are control mechanisms using more than one neurotransmitter system (Aghajanian and Cederbaum, 1979). For example, Bunney and collaborators have shown that low doses of d-amphetamine decrease the activity of midbrain dopaminergic neurons through a striato-nigral feedback system utilizing gamma-aminobutyric acid (GABA) as a transmitter (Bunney and Aghajanian, 1976, 1977). In addition, effects of pharmacological intervention may be expressed far "downstream" on postsynaptic cells distant from the initial site of drug action. For example, chronic treatment with desipramine and iprindole increases basal firing rate in hippocampal cells that are normally suppressed by locus ceruleus stimulation; this effect may be relevant both to the slowly developing therapeutic improvement with TCAs and to the more acute mood elevation with amphetamines experienced by some depressed patients (Huang, 1979a, 1979b).

An important method for studying central nervous system response to acute and prolonged drug treatment involves measurement of the firing rates and characteristics of individual neurons through single cell recordings (Aghajanian, 1978). After prolonged treatment with TCAs (imipramine and desipramine) and newer medications, neurons in several brain areas (hippocampus, cingulate, cerebellum) show a decrease in noradrenergic activity (Aghajanian, 1981). This observation is consistent with other findings indicating that TCAs decrease the sensitivity of beta-adrenergic receptors and produce a down-regulation of noradrenergic activity. Aghajanian and co-workers have shown that motor neurons facilitated by alpha-adrenergic receptors respond differently to prolonged treatment than beta receptors. Prolonged treatment with TCAs and iprindole appears to enhance alpha-adrenergic functioning. In contrast, it appears that TCAs may lead to gradual decrease in the sensitivity of presynaptic (alpha-2) auto-receptors in the noradrenergic system (Banerjee et al, 1977; Crews and Smith, 1978). On the basis of this observation, it has been hypothesized that increased sensitivity of presynaptic inhibitory receptors might account for decreased neuronal functioning (and thus lowered MHPG) in depression. Long-term administration of antidepressants may lead to clinical improvement through reduction of presynaptic, autoreceptor sensitivity and an upward regulation of noradrenergic activity. Other lines of evidence have highlighted the importance of serotonergic mechanisms in depression and response to medication. As noted earlier, there is a subgroup of depressed patients with reduced cerebrospinal fluid concentrations of the major serotonin metabolite, 5-HIAA. Prolonged treatment with TCAs facilitates the response of neurons to serotonin, suggesting that antidepressants increase the sensitivity of serotonergic receptors, perhaps postsynaptically (deMontigny and Aghajanian, 1978; Ögren, 1979).

Another area of active investigation focuses on the way in which TCAs are bound in the brain. Inhibition of imipramine binding by various compounds (such as norepinephrine or other drugs) can provide an index of the functional systems with which various compounds interact. High-affinity imipramine binding appears to be associated with the mechanism of serotonin, but not norepinephrine, uptake in the brain (Langer et al, 1980). The peripheral blood platelet exhibits the capacity for binding various endogenous and exogenous compounds and may serve as a partial model for central nervous system neurons (Stahl, 1977). Platelets from depressed patients have been reported to bind less imipramine than normal, suggesting that the corresponding receptor system in the central nervous system may likewise be altered (Briley et al, 1980). That platelets are particularly rich in serotonin receptors is consistent with the findings on imipramine binding in the brain.

Based on recent pharmacological and physiological advances, the 1970 version of the biogenic amine hypothesis requires renovation (Maas, 1979). Depression and mania appear to reflect disturbances in central nervous system regulation of catecholamines and indoleamines which may be associated with increased presynaptic sensitivity, decreased postsynaptic sensitivity, dysfunctional feedback mechanisms, disordered regulation in systems downstream from aminergic neurons, or a combination of factors. Mood disorders emerge from imbalance between mechanisms concerned with up and down regulation of biogenic amine metabolism and the responses of aminergic systems to environmental and internal processes. Antidepressants assert their therapeutic effectiveness by stabilizing noradrenergic and serotonergic functioning, in part through changes in receptor sensitivity and associated alterations in synthetic and degradative processes. Finally, depressed patients are biologically and psychologically heterogeneous; subgroups can be defined on the basis of neurotransmitter concentrations, neuroendocrine measures, response to medication, and natural history. This view is far more complex, and less gratifying, than the initial hypothesis in which depression was linked with deficient catecholamine synthesis and mania with excessive. Even this expanded biogenic amine set of hypotheses, however, does not seem sufficient to explain clinical disorders.

BIOPSYCHOLOGY AND METAPHARMACOLOGY

Fascinating achievements of biological research may obscure the obvious fact that depressions occur in psychologically meaningful contexts–following the loss of a human relationship, a painful assault on self-esteem, or the disruption of bodily integrity. In these situations, a period of increased arousal (with autonomic overactivity and heightened affect) is generally followed by the mobilization of defenses against psychological pain. The bereaved individual utilizes adaptive behavior to regain a sense of psychological integrity and personal value (through new relations, new achievements, reappraisal of old values) and the pain subsides. In pathological grief, the natural history of mourning is distorted. The patient does not move through the normal process of re-equilibration with acute pain and profound emptiness; acute episodes of remembering punctuated by lengthening periods of relief; and final achievement of resignation and re-engagement with life. Instead, he is unable to regain his sense of personal value and appreciation of pleasure, and he remains fixed in a state of painful longing, hopelessness, and despair; at times these painful affects may superficially be concealed. The phenomenology of mourning has been intensively studied for many decades in adults, and more recently in children (Parkes, 1972; Furman, 1974).

The clinical understanding of depression is based on a developmental model of psychological capacities and vulnerabilities, for example the individual's methods of self-esteem regulation, how he expresses aggression, and his capacity for object relations (Zetzel, 1970). This clinical approach is intrinsically historical and multivariate, looking back at the patient's early life and looking broadly at the current social and personal resources available to him. In contrast to this deep and rich viewpoint, biological research has tended to be narrow in scope (focusing on several measures) and cross-sectional rather than longitudinal. By necessity, biological researchers have studied depressed patients weeks or months after the onset of their disorder and many years after the life experiences and biological predispositions which shape vulnerability. Metabolic findings in depressed patients may, therefore, reflect long-term processes of adaptation to pain and sadness rather than the early biological alterations in depression or the basic pathobiology of the disorder. For example, studies of the noradrenergic system in depression reveal low concentrations of urinary MHPG and possibly increased presynaptic noradrenergic receptor sensitivity; similar studies done immediately after a major loss might lead to opposite findings. To guide future research, it appears useful to develop longitudinal hypotheses. For convenience, we will focus on the most straightforward model, a depressive syndrome following the loss of a child's parent (Bowlby, 1980). At least some child and adult depressive syndromes may be understood, phenomenologically, as not too distant from this situation.

As is well-known, children and other mammals develop specific, enduring attachments to their caregivers who provide comfort, food, and security. They seek proximity with their parents, especially in novel or frightening situations, and use internal representations of the parents to cope with anxiety. Disruption of a child's bond with his parents produces distress and rage which may be followed, sooner or later, by apathy and then, if all goes well, by regained liveliness as the child establishes new attachments (Robertson and Robertson, 1971; Bowlby, 1980). It seems reasonable to hypothesize that these processes—attachment and grief—are mediated neurochemically by central neurotransmitter systems.

Those transmitter systems which utilize opioid-like receptors seem especially suitable for this role in bonding and mourning. Active at brain sites rich in receptors for exogenous drugs such as morphine, enkepahalin and similar peptides are initially involved in the regulation of pain, pleasure, and arousal (Snyder, 1977). Addiction to narcotics, it is now postulated, is related to drug-induced alterations in this endogenous system. There is more than a surface analogy between drug addiction and drug withdrawal and the addiction to a beloved person and the pain at separation and loss, at whatever age these are experienced (Panksepp et al, 1978). In animals, separation distress can be exacerbated by the use of narcotic antagonists (which aggravate withdrawal symptoms) and can be muted by morphine (Panksepp et al, 1980; Herman and Panksepp, 1978).

During withdrawal from morphine, methadone, and similar compounds, addicts suffer marked increase in noradrenergic activity, manifested by anxiety, irritability, piloerection, tachycardia, insomnia, diarrhea, tremulousness, shivering, and other physical and psychological findings. This noradrenergic overactivity appears to result from the rich opioid receptor network located on the locus ceruleus, the dense brainstem cluster of neurons which controls central noradrenergic activity (Redmond and Huang, 1979). The physical and psychological manifestations of methadone withdrawal can be largely blocked by clonidine, an alpha-adrenergic agonist which inhibits the firing of locus ceruleus neurons by stimulating presynaptic, alpha-2 auto receptors (Gold et al, 1978; Cederbaum and Aghajanian, 1977; Aghajanian, 1978). It appears that during "cold turkey" withdrawal from methadone and with repeated electrical stimulation of the locus ceruleus, there is heightening of noradrenergic activity and, eventually, depletion; a similar process may be suggested for some depressive syndromes.

In children and adults with certain types of depressions, the process of grief and mourning may be initiated by opioid neuronal systems and may be mediated through the arousal mechanisms involving noradrenergic pathways. Noradrenergically mediated distress and heightened responsivity at separation would have adaptive value. The child's misery at separation is conveyed to others and to himself by motor agitation, crying, and marked unhappiness; these signs motivate the child to remain near his caregiver and are powerful stimuli for the return of the parents. However, what happens if the parents do not return? When a child's distress is not followed, after a long enough time, by the reappearance of the longed-for parent, normal metabolic processes might be expected to attenuate the distress and prepare the child to cope in other ways, either by finding substitutes or surviving on his own. With repeated loss, the establishment of new relations may become more difficult as the child learns that attachments are too often followed by painful withdrawal.

In depressive syndromes, the normal psychological and biological process of "detoxification" of painful affects does not proceed on course. Instead, the initial heightened arousal is followed by persistent pain and emptiness; the individual can neither fully detach from the past object nor find replacements. Psychodynamically, the inability to mourn can be traced to difficulties in self-esteem, repeated trauma, distortions in the channeling of aggression, and other such factors which influence the capacity for experiencing and dealing with loss and anguish, as well as the substitutes and supports which are realistically available. Biologically, we know relatively little about the predisposition to depression, nor about the influences of psychological and social history on the biological systems involved. There is no satisfactory genetic model that explains major depressive disorders—although a genetic disposition has been noted in some studies—and no biological marker of vulnerability. The postulated role of enkephalins in the origins of depression suggests new types of research; aimed at elucidating vulnerability, following the course of grieving, and intervening pharmacologically. For example, the discovery of agents that inhibit enkephalinases, the enzymes involved in metabolic degradation of enkephalins, may lead to pharmacological intervention closer to the roots of affective disorders (Roques et al, 1980).

FUTURE RESEARCH

Childhood depression appears to be a biologically and psychologically heterogenous disorder, as is adult depression. Research strategies borrowed from studies of adult disorders have suggested the involvement of catecholaminergic systems in childhood depression. There is no information about the role of indoleamines, such as measurements of cerebrospinal fluid metabolites, in childhood depression; whether there is a subgroup of children with reduced cerebrospinal fluid 5-HIAA, a major finding in adult depression, is not known. New strategies are suggested by available evidence and hypothesis. The role of central noradrenergic receptors can be evaluated through the use of provocative tests. For example, clonidine stimulates alpha-2-adrenergic auto-receptors (and thus reduces plasma and urinary MHPG) and stimulates alpha-1 receptors (leading to increased plasma growth hormone concentration). By measuring blood pressure, MHPG, and GH following clonidine, clinical investigators can gain access to central noradrenergic receptors at several sites in the central nervous system before and after the use of medications such as antidepressants (Leckman et al, 1980; Cohen et al, 1980). Other neuroendocrine strategies include the measurement of TSH following TRH and the dexamethasone supression test described earlier. Alterations in catecholamine and indoleamine metabolism may underlie neuroendocrine changes, and the complex relations between these systems needs further study. These various measures may lie downstream, temporally, from centrally active peptide neurotransmitters such as the enkephalins. Further study of the opioid-like transmitters is clearly indicated. It is obvious that the various types of neurochemical strategies should be used longitudinally, through the course of illness and into recovery, and with consideration for genetic and other subgroups.

Studies of depression in childhood should not be restricted to the models of investigation employed in research with adult patients.

First, there may be disorders which are unique to childhood and which may cast especially interesting light on psychosomatic correlations in general, and depression in particular. Among the areas which child psychiatric researchers are more likely to investigate than adult oriented researchers, and which require different methods, are the following: anaclitic-type depressions, failure to thrive, psychosocial dwarfism, offspring of depressed and other psychiatrically disturbed adults, children vulnerable to depression because of environmental factors (brief or prolonged separation from parents, multiple foster homes), and new animal models for depressive disorders during development (such as Harlow's monkeys and smaller mammals) (Kuhn et al, 1979).

Second, there may be biological approaches which are specifically more useful in relation to childhood disorders than adult disorders. For example, the standard methods for screening drugs for possible value in the treatment of depression (such as the potentiation of *L*-dopa or the antogonism of reserpine-induced sedation) may eliminate agents which are of value in children. Combinations of psychological and biological treatment at various stages of child development need assessment by researchers with interests and competence different from those in general psychiatry.

Third, child psychiatric investigators need to be mindful of the dramatic changes in central nervous system functioning during maturation. For example, we have found highly significant reduction in central dopaminergic activity (indexed by decreasing levels of cerebrospinal fluid HVA) during childhood and into adolescence (Leckman et al, 1980; Young et al, 1981).

Fourth, research on childhood depression must be integrated with studies on the normal development of affect. It is not enough to observe that certain children manifest the major criteria that would allow for the diagnosis of depression in adulthood, important as this fact may be. It is essential to understand the meaning of such findings in the context of cognitive and affective development and to understand the variety of ways in which children may experience and display painful affects and suffer from various types of disorders. The profound developmental shifts in neurochemical, cognitive, and affective functioning during the first years of life provide clinical investigators with special challenges. If child researchers follow only the methodological leads provided by research with adult depression, they are likely to miss unique opportunities for fundamental advancement of knowledge concerning affective disorders. It has been useful, as a motivating force, for there to be description and study of "adult-type" depressive disorders in childhood; this research, however, may be theoretically and practically far less exciting than the more clearly developmentally oriented research that remains to be done.

OVERVIEW

Depression is an integrated psychobiological response pattern; it may represent an attempt at adaptive withdrawal into a hypometabolic state following a period of increased autonomic and behavioral responsivity after major loss, physical insult, social disruption, or metabolic upset. Pharmacological and metabolic evidence suggests that in the midst of a major depression, there are alterations in indoleamine (serotonin) and catecholamine (norepinephrine) metabolism, perhaps as a result of increased presynaptic receptor sensivity, decreased postsynaptic sensitivity, changed receptor affinity, or various other factors. Biological research has focused on individuals with longstanding clinical syndromes; metabolic findings in such patients may be quite disparate from the metabolic state at the point of loss or early in the course of illness. The changes in MHPG and 5-HIAA, for example, may reflect complex attempts at psychobiological adaptation. We have suggested a role for the opioid system (eg, enkephalins) in the initial stages of depression. This system is involved in pain, pleasure, and arousal; opioid receptors are activated during withdrawal from addicting drugs and have been implicated in separation distress in animals. The resemblances between love and addiction and between loss and withdrawal seem worthy of further study, especially in relation to the "imprinting" of early childhood and its reawakening in intense love later in life. If opioid-type peptides play a role in depression, the symptoms of withdrawl initially may be mediated by noradrenergic mechanisms and later may involve the mobilization of compensatory serotonergic mechanisms. Over the course of illness, there may be a cascade of neurochemical and neuroendocrine alterations and adaptations, with subpatterns related to individual genetic and experiential differences, as well as developmental level. In the future, research on childhood depression is likely to focus on the ways in which affective disorders are different at various stages of life, as a reflection of biological, cognitive, and affective developmental transitions and the changes in a child's social world. Research on childhood depression will be advanced, without doubt, by future discoveries in the neurosciences. We are likely to see the rejection of current theories, some of which are quite vague, and the creation of more specific hypotheses. In the process of learning more about childhood depressions, clinical investigators will continue to play critical roles. Clinical sophistication will be called upon to delineate developmental and syndromic differences among depressed children, to highlight the complexities of affective development and the major force of environmental factors, and to provide necessary caution and skepticism about any fashionable biological theory.

ACKNOWLEDGMENT

We appreciate the clinical collaboration and suggestions of Dr. J. Gerald Young. This research was supported in part by Mental Health Clinical Research Center Grant MH30929, Children's Clinical Research Center Grant RR00125, National Institute of Child Health and Human Development Grant HD-03008, Mr. Leonard Berger, and the William T. Grant Foundation.

REFERENCES

Aghajanian GK. Feedback regulation of central monoaminergic neurons: evidence from single cell recording studies. In: Youdim M, Sharman D, Lovenberg W, Lagnado J, eds. *Essays in neurochemistry and neuropharmacology*. New York: John Wiley and Sons, 1978:1–32.

Aghajanian GK. Tolerance of locus coeruleus neurons to morphine: suppression of withdrawal response by clonidine. *Nature* 1978; 276:186–188.

Aghajanian GK. Tricyclic antidepressants and single-cell responses to serotonin and norepinephrine. A review of chronic studies. In: Usdin E, ed. *Neuroreceptors: basic and clinical aspects*. New York: Pergamon Press (in press).

Aghajanian GK, Bunney BS. Dopamine "autoreceptors": pharmacological characterization by microiontophoretic single cell recording studies. Nauyn-Schmied. *Arch Pharmacol* 1977; 297:1–7.

Aghajanian GK, Cederbaum JM, Central noradrenergic neurons: interaction of autoregulatory mechanisms with extrinsic influences. In: Usdin E, Kopin IJ, Barchas J, eds. *Catecholamines: basic and clinical frontiers*. New York: Pergamon Press, 1979:619–621.

Altman N, Sachar EJ, Gruen PH, Halpern FS, Eto S. Reduced plasma LH concentration in postmenopausal depressed women. *Psychosom Med* 1975; 37:274–276.

Asberg M, Bertilsson L, Tuck D, et al. Indolamine metabolites in the CSF of depressed patients before and during treatment with nortriptyline. *Clin Pharmacol Ther* 1973; 14:277–286.

Banerjee SP, Kung LS, Riggi SJ, Chanda SK. Development of beta-adrenergic receptor subsensitivity by antidepressants. *Nature* 1977; 268:455–456.

Beckman H, Goodwin FK. Antidepressant response to tricyclics and urinary MHPG in unipolar patients. *Arch Gen Psychiatry* 1975; 32:17–21.

Bond PA, Jenner FA, Sampson GA. Daily variations of the urine content of MHPG in two manic-depressive patients. *Psychol Med* 1972; 2:81–85.

Bowlby J. *Attachment and loss, volume 3, Loss.* New York: Basic Books, 1980.

Briley MS, Langer SZ, Raisman R, et al. Tritiated imipramine binding sites are decreased in platelets of untreated depressed patients. *Science* 1980; 209: 303–305.

Brown GM. Endocrine aspects of psychosocial dwarfism. In: Sachar EJ, ed. *Hormones, behavior and psychopathology.* New York: Raven Press, 1976: 253–262.

Bunney BS, Aghajanian GK. d-amphetamine-induced inhibition of central dopaminergic neurons: mediation by a striatonigral feedback pathway. *Science* 1976; 192:391–393.

Bunney BS, Aghajanian GK. d-amphetamine-induced inhibition of central dopaminergic neurons: direct effect or mediated by a striato-nigral feedback pathway? In: Costa E, Gessa GL, eds. *Non-striatal dopaminergic neurons.* New York: Raven Press, 1977:577–583.

Carroll BJ. The hypothalamic-pituitary-adrenal axis in depression. In: Davies B, Carroll BJ, Mowbray RM, eds. *Depressive illness: some research studies.* Springfield, Illinois: Charles C. Thomas, 1972:23–201.

Carroll BJ, Mendels J. Neuroendocrine regulation in affective disorders. In: Sachar EJ, ed. *Hormones, behavior and psychopathology.* New York: Raven Press, 1976:193–224.

Cedarbaum JM, Aghajanian GK. Catecholamine receptors on local coeruleus neurons: pharmacological characterization. *Eur J Pharmacol* 1977; 44: 375–385.

Chiodo LA, Antelman SM. Repeated tricyclics induce a progressive dopamine autoreceptor subsensitivity independent of daily drug treatment. *Nature* 1980; 287:451–454.

Cohen DJ, Detlor J, Young JG, Shaywitz B. Clonidine ameliorates gilles de la tourette syndrome. *Arch Gen Psychiatry* 1980; 37:1350–1357.

Cohen DJ, Young JG. Neurochemistry and child psychiatry. *J Am Acad Child Psychiatry* 1977; 16:353–411.

Cohen DJ, Shaywitz BA, Young JG, Bowers MB. Cerebrospinal fluid monoamine metabolites in neuropsychiatric disorders in childhood. In: Wood JH, ed. *Neurobiology of cerebrospinal fluid.* New York: Plenum, 1980:665–683.

Coppen A, Prange AJ, Jr, Whybraw PC. Abnormalities of indolamines in affective disorders. *Arch Gen Psychiatry* 1972; 26:474–478.

Crews FT, Smith CB. Presynaptic alpha-receptor subsensitivity after long-term antidepressant treatment. *Science* 1978; 202:322–324.

Cytryn L, McKnew DH, Logue M, Desai RB. Biochemical correlates of affective disorders in children. *Arch Gen Psychiatry* 1974;31:659–661.

Davis M. Neurochemical modulation of sensory-motor reactivity: acoustic and tactile startle reflex. *Neurosci Biobehav Rev* 1980;4:214–263.

deMontigny C, Aghajanian GK. Tricyclic antidepressants: long term treatment increases responsivity of rat forebrain neurons to serotonin. *Science* 1978; 202:1303–1306.

Ehrensing RH, Kastin AJ, Schalch DS, et al. Affective state and thyrotropin and prolactin responses after repeated injections of TRH in depressed patients. *Am J Psychiatry* 1974;131:714–718.

Furman E. *A child's parent dies: studies in childhood bereavement*. New Haven: Yale University Press, 1974.

Garver DL, Pandey GN, Dekirmenjian H, Deleon-Jones F. Growth hormone and catecholamines in affective disease. *Am J Psychiatry* 1975;132:1149–1154.

Genel M, Cohen DJ, Shaywitz BA, et al. Hypothalamic-pituitary studies in deprivation dwarfism: correlation with CSF monoamine metabolites. *Endoc (Suppl)* 1976;98:289.

Glowinski J, Axelrod J. Inhibition of uptake of tritiated noradrenaline in the intact rat brain by imipramine and structurally related compounds. *Nature* 1964;204:1318–1319.

Gold MS, Redmond DE, Kleber HD. Clonidine blocks acute opiate withdrawal symptoms. *Lancet* 1978;8090:599–602.

Goodale DB, Rusterholz DB, Long JP, et al. Neurochemical and behavioral evidence for a selective presynaptic dopamine receptor agonist. *Science* 1980;210:1141–1143.

Halbreich U, Grunhasu L, Ben-David M. Twenty-four hour rhythm of prolactin in depressive patients. *Arch Gen Psychiatry* 1979;36:1183–1186.

Herman BH, Panksepp J. Effects of morphine and naloxone on separation distress and approach attachment: evidence for opiate mediation of social affect. *Pharmacol Biochem Behav* 1978;9:213–220.

Huang YH. Net effect of acute administration of desipramine on the locus coeruleus-hippocampal system. *Life Sci* 1979a;25(9):739–746.

Huang YH. Chronic desipramine treatment increases activity of noradrenergic postsynaptic cells. *Life Sci* 1979b;25(8):709–716.

Jones F, Maas JW, Dekirmenjian H, et al. Urinary catecholamine metabolites during behavioral changes in a patient with manic-depressive cycles. *Science* 1973;179:300–302.

Kuhn CM, Evoniuk G, Schanberg SM. Loss of tissue sensitivity to growth hormone during maternal deprivation in rats. *Life Sci* 1979; 25:2089–2097.

Langer SZ, Moret C, Raisman R, Dubocovich ML, Briley M. High-affinity (H) imipramine binding in rat hypothalamus: association with uptake of serotonin but not of norepinephrine. *Science* 1980;210:1133–1135.

Leckman JF, Cohen DJ, Shaywitz BA, et al. CSF monoamine metabolites in child and adult psychiatric patients. *Arch Gen Psychiatry* 1980; 37; 6: 677–684.

Leckman JF, Maas JW, Redmond DE, Heninger GR. Effects of oral clonidine on plasma 3-methoxy-4-hydroxyphenethyleneglycol (MHPG) in man: preliminary report. *Life Sci* 1980;26;25:2179–2185.

Maas JW. Biogenic amines and depression. *Arch Gen Psychiatry* 1975; 32: 1357–1361.

Maas JW. Neurotransmitters in depression: too much, too little, or too unstable? *Trends Neuroscience* 1979; 2:306–308.

Maas JW, Hattox SE, Landis DH. Variance in the production of homovanillic acid and 3-methoxy-4-hydroxyphenethyleneglycol by the awake primate brain. *Life Sci* 1980; 26:929–934.

McKnew DH, Cytryn L. Urinary metabolites in chronically depressed children. *J Am Acad Child Psychiatry* 1979; 18; 4:608–615.

Mendlewicz J, Van Cauter E, Linkowski P, et al. The 24-hour profile of prolactin in depression. *Life Sci* 1980; 27:2015–2024.

Ögren SO, Fluxe K, Agnati LF, et al. Reevaluation of the indoleamine hypothesis of depression: evidence for a reduction of functional activity of central 5-HT systems of antidepressant drugs. *J Neural Trans* 1979; 46: 85–103.

Ojeda SR, McCann SM. Evidence for participation of a catecholaminergic mechanism in the post-castration rise in plasma gonadotropins. *Neuroendocrinology* 1973; 12:295–315.

Otsuki M, Dakoda M, Boba S. Influence of glucocorticoids on TRF induced TSH response in man. *J Clin Endocrinol Metab* 1973; 36:95–102.

Panksepp J, Herman B, Conner R, et al. The biology of social attachments: opiates alleviate separation distress. *Biol Psychiatry* 1978; 13:607–618.

Panksepp J, Meeker R, Bean NJ. The neurochemical control of crying. *Pharmacol Biochem Behav* 1980; 12:437–443.

Parkes CM. *Bereavement: studies of grief in adult life.* New York: International Universities Press, 1972.

Poznanski EO, Carroll BJ, Banegas M, et al. The dexamethasone suppression test in depressed children. Presented at the Annual Meeting of the American Psychiatric Association, New Orleans, Louisiana, 1981.

Puig-Antich J, Chambers W, Halpern F, et al. Cortisol hypersecretion in prepubertal depressive illness. preliminary report. *Psychoneuroendocrinology* 1979; 4:191–197.

Redmond DE, Huang YH. New evidence for a locus coeruleus–norepinephrine connection with anxiety. *Life Sci* 1979; 25:2149–2162.

Robertson J, Robertson J. Young children in brief separation: a fresh look. *Psychoanal Stud Child* 1971; 26:264–315.

Roques BP, Fournie-Zaluski MC, Soroca E, et al. The enkepalinase inhibitor thoiorphan shows antinociceptive activity in mice. *Nature* 1980; 5788: 288; 286–288.

Sachar EJ, Hellman L, Roffwarg HP, et al. Disrupted 24-hour patterns of cortisol secretion in psychotic depression. *Arch Gen Psychiatry* 1973; 28:19–24.

Schildkraut J. The catecholamine hypothesis of affective disorders: a review of supporting evidence. *Am J Psychiatry* 1965; 122:508–522.

Schildkraut J. Norepinephrine metabolites as biochemical criteria for classifying depressive disorders and predicting responses to treatment: preliminary findings. *Am J Psychiatry* 1973; 130:695–698.

Schildkraut J, Orsulak PR, Schatzberg AF, et al. Biochemical discrimination of subgroups of depressive disorders based on differences in catecholamine metabolism. Presented at Biological Markers in Psychiatry and Neurology Meeting, New Orleans, Louisiana, 1981.

Shopsin B. Second generation antidepressants. *J Clin Psychiatry* 1980; 41; 12; 2:45–56.

Skirboll LR, Grace AA, Bunney BS. Depaminergic auto and postsynaptic receptors: electrophysiological evidence for their differential sensitivity to dopamine agonists. *Science* 1979; 206:80–83.

Snyder SH. Opiate receptors in the brain. *N Engl J Med* 1977; 296:266–271.

Sokoloff P, Matres MP, Schwartz JC. H-apomorphine labels both dopamine postsynaptic receptors and autoreceptors. *Nature* 1980; 5788; 288:283-286.

Stahl SM. The human platelet: a diagnostic and research tool for the study of biogenic amines in psychiatric and neurological disorders. *Arch Gen Psychiatry* 1977; 34:509–516.

Swann AC, Maas JW, Hattox SE, Landis H. Catecholamine metabolites in human plasma as indices of brain function: effects of debrisoquin. *Life Sci* 1980; 27; 20:1857–1862.

Van Cauter E, Mendlewicz J. 24-hour dopamine-beta-hydroxylase pattern: a possible biological index of manic-depression. *Life Sci* 1978; 22; 2:147-155.

Wilk S, Watson E. Evaluation of pathways of cerebral catecholamine metabolism in men. In: Usdin E, Snyder S, eds. *Frontiers in catecholamine research*. New York: Pergamon Press, 1974.

Young JG, Cohen DJ, Anderson GA, Shaywitz BA. Neurotransmitter ontogeny as a perspective for studies of child development and pathology. In Shopsin B, Greenhill L, eds. *The psychobiology of childhood: a profile of current issues*. New York: Spectrum Press, 1983 (in press).

Young JG, Cohen DJ, Kavanagh ME, et al. Cerebrospinal fluid, plasma, and urinary MHPG in children. *Life Sci* 1981; 28(29):2837–2845.

Zetsel ER. *The capacity for emotional growth*. New York: International Universities Press, 1970.

Affective Disorders in Childhood and Adolescence--An Update. Edited by D.P. Cantwell and G.A. Carlson.

13

Family Genetic Factors

Dennis P. Cantwell

This chapter will review current evidence for genetic factors operating in the affective disorders of childhood. First, the usual genetic methods of investigation in clinical psychiatry will be reviewed. Then genetic studies will be reviewed in affective disorder. The rather relatively large number of studies in adults will be reviewed first. The relatively under-researched area of genetic factors in affective disorders in children will be reviewed and contrasted with what is known in adults. Finally, some generalizations for future research will be made.

GENETIC METHODS OF INVESTIGATION IN CLINICAL PSYCHIATRY

Rainer (1980) has reviewed the various methods that have been used for investigation of genetic factors in clinical psychiatry. These include: family studies, adoption studies, twin and twin family studies, high risk longitudinal studies, and linkage and marker studies.

Family studies can be subdivided into the following types: family history studies, direct family studies, segregation model studies, and threshold model studies. Family history studies are generally the starting point for the investigation of genetic factors in clinical psychiatric disorders. In general, a group of probands identified as having a specific psychiatric disorder are collected. Then family history data is collected on close family relatives (fathers, mothers, brothers, sisters, aunts, uncles, grandparents, and cousins). The prevalence rate for various types of psychiatric disorders is then calculated in the various family members. If genetic factors are thought to operate, there should be a greater prevalence rate of the same psychiatric disorder the proband has in close family members than in the general population. This rate should be greater than the prevalence rate for other psychiatric disorders in these family members. Family history studies have been helped by standardized methods of collecting family history data such as the Family History Research Diagnostic Criteria (FHRDC) devised by Andreasen and Winokur (1979). However, family history studies do suffer from the fact that there probably will be an under-reporting of certain psychiatric disorders simply because the informants are not aware of the psychiatric disorder occurring in certain family members. Also, family history studies often do not allow one to make a specific psychiatric diagnosis on a family member because of lack of available symptomatic information, even though it is clear that the family member in question has had a psychiatric disorder.

Direct family studies are an improvement over family history studies. In direct family studies, after the probands have been identified, the close family members (brothers, fathers, mothers, sisters, aunts, uncles, grandparents, cousins) are actually interviewed and the prevalence rate of various psychiatric disorders calculated The availability of standardized methods of evaluation such as the Diagnostic Interview Schedule (DIS) and the Schedule for Affective Disorders and Schizophrenia (SADS) have improved the family study method. The use of operational diagnostic criteria to identify probands and also to make psychiatric diagnosis in family members has also improved the family history method and the family study method.

In general, what family history studies and direct family studies can provide is prevalence rates for different psychiatric disorders in close family members of probands with a specified type of psychiatric disorder. Certain methods must be used to obtain a corrected expectancy rate in family members. One means of calculating this rate is Weinberg's abridged method (Rainer, 1980). This method yields the average expectancy of developing a given condition in the family members who remain alive through the period of its manifestation. The calculated expectancy rates can be compared for various groups of relatives and also for expectancy rates from the general population. Family history studies and family studies cannot provide any direct evidence on the mode of inheritance of a disorder without further information provided by two other types of studies, the segregation model study and the threshold model study.

By combining different pedigrees and comparing the observed proportion of relatives who have a particular disorder with that expected according to a given hypothesis, segregation model studies are able to test various specific genetic hypotheses (Emery, 1976; Rainer, 1980).

In the threshold model study, the liability to developing a certain psychiatric disorder is hypothesized to be distributed normally in the general population. It is also hypothesized to have a higher mean value in the relatives of probands with a specific psychiatric disorder. The liability to developing a particular disorder is considered to be the additive of both environmental factors and the genetic factors that together determine a person's likelihood of developing a given psychiatric disorder. The threshold is defined in such a way that the disorder is manifest above a particular level (Falconer, 1965;

Rainer, 1980). Using clinically collected data on prevalence of various psychiatric disorders in close family members of probands with a particular psychiatric disorder, a set of "best fit" parameters can be tested for the liability distribution so that "goodness of fit" can be tested between the observed prevalences of the psychiatric disorders to those expected by certain parameters. This method might enable one to rule out certain types of inheritance, and in the ideal case to specify uniquely the exact type of inheritance, whether it be sex-linked, single gene, autosomal, polygenic, etc.

All types of family studies in clinical psychiatry of course suffer from the fact that the biological probands have been raised by their parents along with their biological siblings. Thus, one could make a case for environmental transmission of a disorder rather than genetic transmission. It is in distinguishing between environmental and genetic factors that adoption studies find their greatest use. If adults with well-defined psychiatric disorders have children who were given up early in life to nonrelative adoptees, then the prevalence of psychiatric disorder can be studied in the biological parents, the adopted children, and the adopting parents. Thus, prevalence rates for psychiatric disorder can be compared in adopted children whose parents were ill with a particular psychiatric disorder, and this can be compared with the prevalence rate for psychiatric disorders in children who were adopted from parents who had no psychiatric disorder. A further refinement is the comparison of psychiatric disorder in the biological and adoptive parents of adopted probands who do not have a certain type of psychiatric disorder with biological and adoptive parents of control adoptees with either no psychopathology or with another type of psychiatric disorder.

In adoption studies mitigating factors such as social class, intelligence, religious factors, and others that lead to nonrandom assignment of adoptees should be taken into account. Also, a difficult child being raised by adoptive parents may in fact lead to the development of certain types of psychopathology in the adopting parents as the result of raising a difficult child (Bell, 1968, 1971).

Twin studies are also used to separate genetic and environmental factors. The classical methods have compared occurrence of psychiatric disorder in one or both twins who were either monozygotic or dizygotic. Monozygotic twins are the same sex, while two egg twins may either be of the same sex or of opposite sexes. Higher concordance of psychiatric disorder in monozygotic versus dizygotic twins generally is explained by operation of genetic factors in the discorder. In a further refinement called the twin family study, not only are the twins themselves studied, but also all of their siblings and their parents. Collecting of such pedigree data on large numbers of index twin cases with a certain psychiatric disorder allows one to compare prevalence rates for the disorder in monozygotic twins, dizygotic twins of the same sex, dizygotic twins of the opposite sex, full siblings, half siblings, and step siblings. If some twins have been brought up together and other twins in the population were raised apart, this allows for a further unique comparison of environmental and genetic factors.

Over the last ten years another type of investigation, high risk longitudinal studies, has broadened our understanding of genetic factors in certain types of psychiatric disorders, especially schizophrenia. In these studies, children of parents with a definable psychiatric disorder are observed over the years for the development of any type of psychopathology. This type of study best provides early signs, whether they are behavioral, cognitive, neurological, chemical, etc, of possible psychopathology. To date, this type of longitudinal high risk study has almost been exclusively confined to the study of children of schizophrenic parents.

The final types of genetics investigations in clinical psychiatry are linkage and marker studies. Basically, the hope is that a specific psychiatric disorder can be shown to be associated with a gene whose locus is linked to that of a known gene. A common such gene is a colorblindness gene known to be associated to a specific locus on the X-chromosome. There are about 110 known genes assigned to specific autosomes and 100 to the X-chromosome (Rainer, 1980). In a clinical study one can look at family pedigree to determine whether a given psychiatric syndrome appears together with a known trait such as colorblindness or the XGA blood group and if there are pedigrees in which they appear separately. There are mathematical models which now exist for describing the likelihood of the linkage and its closeness.

The basic aspects of psychiatric genetics have been covered in other comprehensive publications (Slater and Cowie, 1971). Specifically, genetic studies of mental retardation have often involved chromosomal or biochemical abnormalities. Such is not the case with the common psychiatric disorders in adults or in children, and specifically with affective disorders in adults and children.

GENETIC STUDIES IN AFFECTIVE DISORDERS

Genetic studies of affective disorders in adults have produced much useful information. Family history studies and direct family studies with adults have suggested the following. First, there is an increase in familial prevalence of affective disorder in bipolar-1 and bipolar-2 so that there is an increased prevalence of mania, depression, alcoholism, and suicide. There is more likely to be two generations with affective disorder in those individuals with bipolar illness. Studies suggest in some cases linkage with the genes for colorblindness and the XGA blood group, although others have not confirmed this. In twin studies there is an increased monozygotic to dizygotic ratio for bipolar individuals.

On the other hand, those who have primary unipolar depression have different family histories as manifested in the subtypes FPDD, SDD, and DSD. Andreasen and Winokur (1979), Schlesser et al (1980), and others have presented data on the validity of this classification of primary unipolar depression based on clinical and genetic studies and on response to the dexamethasone test. Studies suggest that SDD tends to be relatively severe and that it resembles FPDD more than it does DSD. Patients with DSD tended to respond better to major tranquillizers, while those with FPDD and SDD tended to respond better to antidepressants. There are some demographic differences as well. The PDD patients and SDD patients come from a higher SFS and have less parental divorce than the DSD patients. Some studies suggest that DSD may be linked to either alphahaptoglobin or to the third component of complement, C3. PDD's may be more likely to break away from dexamethasone suppression than the others, although this has not been found in all studies.

Findings of increased family psychopathology in probands with unipolar and bipolar disorder may suggest environmental or genetic etiologic factors or interaction of both. The overall monozygotic twin concordance rate is 76 percent as opposed to an overall dizygotic twin concordance rate of 19 percent. Monozygotic twins reared apart have a concordance rate for affective disorder of 67 percent. These findings strongly suggest genetic etiologic factors, although growing up in a family with a psychiatrically ill parent does have environmental consequences, even if they are not of primarily etiologic significance in the child's disorder. Two adoption studies (Mendlewicz and Rainer, 1977; Cadoret, 1978) have demonstrated increased prevalence rate for depression in adoptees whose biologic parents had a major affective disorder. The Mendlewicz and Rainer study was carried out in Belgium where adoptive registers are available. The subjects were the adoptive and biological parents of individuals with bipolar affective disorder. There were three sets of controls: (1) the parents of bipolar affective disorder individuals who were not adoptees; (2) the adoptive and biological parents of normal adoptees; and (3) the parents of individuals who had contracted polio during childhood or adolescence. This latter group was used to control for the affect on a parent of bringing up a child with a significant chronic handicap. The Feighner criteria were used to make the diagnoses. Only persons who had bipolar illness who had experienced both manic and depressive episodes were accepted as probands in the study. All of them had to have been adopted out before one year of age and have been raised by the adoptive parents until their adult life. Bipolar probands who were not adopted were selected from admission records of the same psychiatric facilities as the adoptees over a similar time period. Adoptees who were psychiatrically normal were obtained from adoption agencies, given clinical interviews, and only accepted if they were found to have no psychopathology. Pediatricians who had been treating patients with polio provided the control patients in that group.

All control groups were matched to the index group for age, sex, national origin, and socioeconomic status. All of the parents in the study were interviewed by clinicians who were blind to the clinical status of the probands and also to whether the probands were adopted or not.

The major finding of the study was that psychopathology in the biological parents was in excess of that found in the adoptive parents of the same bipolar probands. Bipolar affective disorder, unipolar affective disorder, schizoaffective disorder, and cyclothymic disorder were found to be significantly different at the level $p < 0.025$. The frequency of psychopathology of a nonaffective type was not higher in the biological parents of bipolar adoptees than in the normal adoptees. The degree of psychopathology in the biological parents of the bipolar adoptees was similar to that of the parents of the nonadopted bipolar probands. The rate of psychiatric disorder in the adoptive parents of the experimental group is similar to that of the adoptive parents of the normal offspring group. The degree of psychopathology in the parents of probands with polio is in the same range as in both groups of adoptive parents. All of these findings support the conclusion of the author that the experimental sets of parents were truly representative of the degree of psychiatric disorder which is present respectively in those parents who bring up and those who contribute genetically to bipolar illness individuals. No father to son transmission of bipolar illness was seen in the entire sample. This finding is consistent with a sex-linked model of bipolar affective disorder which has been suggested by other genetic studies. Another interesting finding was that bipolar illness had an early onset in all parents in whom it was present. However, in the adopting parents with unipolar illness, the unipolar illness occurred in every case after the onset in their children. This strengthens the genetic hypothesis by suggesting that the unipolar depression of the adoptive parents might be more reactive and less severe than that of their biological counterparts since early onset may be considered to be an index of severity.

Cadoret (1978) conducted a somewhat different type of adoption study. He looked for a sample of adoptees who ranged in age from 10 to 38 years at the time of follow-up. He interviewed those adoptees who were 18 years of age and older in the study of affective disorders since the thinking at that time was that this was the beginning of the period of risk for affective disorders. The experimental adoptee sample was selected to have the following four criteria: (1) evidence of any psychopathology in their biological parent; (2) being separated at birth from the biological mother; (3) having no further contact with biological parents or other biological relatives; and (4) the child had to be adopted. A control adoptee who met all of the above criteria except the first was selected for each experimental adoptee and matched on the basis of age, sex, and age of biological mother at the time of the adoptee's birth. The total sample was 126 (83 experimental adoptees and 43 control adoptees). Only 43 matched controls aged 18 and over were available. Feighner's diagnostic criteria were used. The diagnosis on the adoptee was made without knowledge of the biological background, and the diagnosis of the biologic parent was made blind to the findings of the adoptee. The major finding of the study was the significantly increased incidence of depression in the adoptees who had a biological parent with an affective disorder (three out of eight). No other parental diagnostic group showed as high an incidence of affective disorder in their adopted children.

Thus, the evidence is relatively strong in primary affective disorder in adults that there are genetic factors playing an etiological role. No exact mode of genetic transmission has been determined, but as mentioned previously, linkage studies have suggested an X-linked mode of transmission in some studies for bipolar affective disorder. Polygenic models and autosomal dominant models with incomplete penetrance have also been postulated as mechanisms of inheritance. A recent study by Baron and his colleagues (1981) of first degree relatives of 255 patients with both unipolar and bipolar illness found the following. The bipolar probands had more bipolar relatives and more relatives with all types of affective disorder than the unipolar probands. By applying a multiple threshold model of inheritance, the hypothesis of multifactorial inheritance was ruled out. Autosomal single major locus inheritance did provide an acceptable fit to the data. The conclusion of the authors was that bipolar and unipolar illness types seemed to occur at different thresholds on a single continuum of genetic-environment liability in which those with bipolar illness are more deviant genetically than those with unipolar illness.

Reich and his colleagues (in press) recently presented a preliminary analysis of the segregation distribution of primary major depressive disorder in adults. All patients were diagnosed as having primary depressive disorder with a young age of onset, peaking between the ages of 16 and 25. Compared to estimates of the population prevalence for primary depressive disorder, it was found that primary depressive disorder was much more common in the families of these probands (fathers, mothers, sisters, brothers, as well as spouses) than it was in the general population. The probands were then divided by sex, and the incidence of primary affective disorder in the siblings was measured, subdividing the data as to whether there was also a parent who had major affective disorder. These results showed a trend suggestive of segregation due to the fact that families who had at least one parent with a major affective disorder had a greater number of siblings who also had the same disorder. Female relatives were also more affected than male relatives. A relative deficiency of cross-sex transmission between parents and offspring was also found which had been reported by others. Thus, fathers tended to have sons who were affected and not daughters; mothers tended to have affected daughters and not sons. As observed in other previous studies, assortative mating had also occurred in that people with primary major depressive disorder tended to marry each other more than would be expected on the basis of population prevalence rates. With the increasing likelihood of finding biological markers and with newer mathematical models for genetic analysis, it is likely that genetic subtypes of primary affective disorder will be found.

FAMILY-GENETIC STUDIES WITH CHILDREN

Since the data are so strong with regard to the prevalence of major affective disorder in closer family members of probands with the illness, it is somewhat surprising that so little research has been done in this area regarding: (1) the children of depressed parents (a high risk group) and (2) family studies of children with primary affective disorder. Early studies such as those by Rutter (1966) did indeed find that children of psychiatrically ill parents were more likely to have psychiatric disorder than children whose parents had chronic medical illness. The latter children were more likely to have a psychiatric disorder than children of control parents. However, Rutter was unable to demonstrate a correlation between the type of psychiatric disorder in the parent and the type of psychiatric disorder in the child.

Orvaschel and her colleagues (1980) have recently reviewed some of the early studies on the children of depressed patients. Some of these early studies varied considerably in their methodology and in the nature of what they were trying to demonstrate. In some cases strict diagnostic criteria were used to make diagnoses in the children of depressed parents, in other cases only global sorts of information were sought. Weissman's study (1972) used interviews with the parent and clinic records. Rolf and Garmezy's study (1974) obtained information from the school only. Weintraub and colleagues (1975) used a parent interview, a child interview, school information, and psychological testing of the children, while Welner and her colleagues (1977) used both parent and child interviews. In general the early studies do suggest that children of depressed parents have a higher likelihood of having psychiatric disorder than children of normal parents. However, the findings are not necessarily specific with regard to the type of disorder. For example, Rolf and Garmezy found the children of depressed parents to be more socially isolated, withdrawn, and shy, while Weintraub and colleagues found a greater degree of acting out behavior in the classroom, inattention, and disrepectful and defiant behavior. Weissman, in investigating parental role performance of 35 depressed women, found that they were less involved with their children, had impaired communication, and also greater guilt, resentment, lack of affection, and increased friction when they were ill. Also, they demonstrated over-protection, irritability, preoccupation, and withdrawn and rejecting behavior with their children. Fifty-eight percent of the 109 children of the 35 depressed mothers did have some degree of disturbed functioning. However, the type of problem shown by the children varied widely. Besides depression, there were school problems, enuresis, and acting out behavior such as hyperactivity, truancy, and delinquency.

More recent studies have been more precise in their methodology. Welner and her colleagues examined 75 children and 29 parents hospitalized for depression. They compared these with 152 children in 41 families with well parents. Mothers and children were interviewed separately. According to the mothers, children of depressed mothers had more depressed mood, more death wishes, and frequent fights. The children agreed with this. According to the mothers, children of the depressed parents were more persistent in finishing projects and were more withdrawn. According to the children, the children of depressed parents showed more loss of interest in usual activities and more unexplained headaches. Both groups were also compared for a number of depressive symptoms and for a diagnosis of probable or definite depression, the criteria for which were set up by the examiners. The depressive symptoms investigated were: depressed and sad mood; moody; crying for no apparent reason; excessively worried over minor events; fearful; nervous or anxious most of the time with or without discrete phobias; significant death wishes; moderate to severe difficulties falling or staying asleep; being a loner; being apprehensive around other people; or being withdrawn. Eight of the 75 children (or 11 percent of the children of depressed parents) had five or more depressive symptoms. Seven of the eight were children of six mothers with depression (24 percent of all the hospitalized mothers). The eighth child had a father with depression (25 percent of all fathers). Thus, the results of this investigation would suggest that about a quarter of all parents who were hospitalized with a primary depressive disorder had at least one child with five or more depressive symptoms of the eight that were listed by the examiners. Seven of these children had at least one discrete episode lasting from one to 12 months in duration in which five or more depressive symptoms were present and had occurred within a year before the interview. Five of the eight children had received professional help because of their symptoms. None of the children of the well parents had five or more depressive symptoms. Five of the 75 children of depressed patients (or 70 percent) met the criteria for definite or probable depression (three definite and two probable). None of the controls met these diagnostic criteria.

There are a number of methodologic problems with this study. The interviews were not conducted blindly. Thus, knowledge of the parents having a psychiatric illness (and specifically depression) could have influenced the diagnosis in the children. Of probably more importance was the fact that information from others and from 86 percent of the children was obtained in the control group, whereas only half of the children of depressed parents were interviewed. This might in fact suggest an under-reporting of symptoms since many of the depressive symptoms are more easily obtainable and more reliably obtained from children than they are from parents. Likewise, the criteria for affective disorder are somewhat idiosyncratic.

In a similar study Kuyler and his colleagues (1980) examined 27 individuals with bipolar affective disorder at the New York State Psychiatric Institute. They interviewed each parent with a 63-item questionnaire developed by Stewart and Gath (1978). The eight symptoms noted by Stewart to be characteristic of childhood depression were used as criteria for depression. Children who had at least three of these symptoms were considered to have a depressive illness. The diagnoses of the adult patients were bipolar-1 in 24 individuals, bipolar-2 in nine individuals, and bipolar other in six. Of the 49 children interviewed, only three ever had treatment for a behavior disturbance. However, 22 (or 45 percent) were reported to have three or more symptoms and were considered to have some psychiatric disorder. Thirty-nine percent of the 18 children with one ill parent were ill as compared to 50 percent of the 28 children with two ill parents. Environmental factors seemed to play a role in the prevalence of psychiatric disorder in the children in that slightly less than a third of the 32 children whose parents were intact and living together were psychiatrically ill as compared to 71 percent if the parents were divorced. When a child had one parent with an affective illness, the rates of illness for children of divorced parents and for children living with both parents were comparable. Only four children had three or more of the eight symptoms characterizing depressive illness. All four of these children were at least 13 years of age. The other 18 ill children were given a diagnosis of undiagnosed psychiatric illness. Their symptoms suggested various personality disorders, adjustment reactions, and the attention deficit disorder with hyperactivity syndrome, as well as affective disorders. Thus, this study also suggests that the children of bipolar parents are likely to have psychiatric disorder. Only a minority could be definitely diagnosed as depressed by the authors' criteria, and an interview with the parent was the sole source of information, which again if anything may underestimate the presence of depressive symptoms in the child.

Conners and his colleagues (1979) examined symptoms ratings of 126 children of 59 families. One of the parents in each of 59 families was previously diagnosed as having a primary affective disorder of either bipolar or unipolar type. Both parents rated the children with the Conners' parent and teacher questionnaire, a 93-item checklist of common behavior disorders of childhood. Previous factor analysis of this rating scale had obtained eight factors: conduct problems, anxiety, impulsivity-hyperactivity, learning problems, psychosomatic, perfectionism, antisocial, and muscle tension. Twenty-seven percent of the parents had a bipolar illness; half of the children were male, half of the children were female. Children of bipolar parents were reported to have significantly fewer problems on four of the factors. Children from two-parent homes were reported to present significantly less symptomatology on both muscle tension and anxiety items than children from one parent or divorced homes. Children of unipolar parents were found to have significantly more symptoms on factors measuring conduct problems, anxiety, and impulsivity-hyperactivity. Divorced families had higher symptom sources on antisocial and muscle tension factors. Female children of unipolar parents were significantly more anxious than male unipolar children. While offering some valuable information on comparison of parent rated symptoms of unipolar and bipolar parents of children, this study tells little about prevalence of specific types of psychiatric disorder in children of depressed parents.

A more recent study by McKnew and his colleagues (1979) examined all children ages five to 15, of 14 consecutive patients, who had been admitted to the National Institute of Mental Health (NIMH) with either a diagnosis of bipolar affective disorder or a diagnosis of unipolar affective disorder. Each child was seen twice, four months apart, and was assessed by both interview and rating scales. The parents were also assessed. There were 30 children (16 girls and 14 boys). The parents completed the Conners' parent questionnaire and the children's personal data inventory from the children's ECDEU Battery. A structured interview was also conducted with the child at the two four-month intervals. Immediately after each interview, two observers of the interview and the interviewer himself rated the child independently on the following scales: the Children's Psychiatric Rating Scale from the ECDEU Battery, and the Children's Affective Rating Scale which had been developed by the authors with three major subscales: depressive mood and behavior, verbal expression, and fantasy. The diagnosis of a depressive disorder was made according to the Weinberg criteria. Of 14 boys, five were depressed at both interviews, three at one of the interviews, and six at neither interview. Of the 16 girls, four were depressed at both interviews, 11 were depressed at one interview only, and only one was depressed at either interview. Thus, combining the sexes, nine of the 30 children were depressed at both interviews, and 14 at one interview only. Seven children were not depressed at either interview. This study provides the most current evidence to date that indeed children of depressed adults may not only have higher rates of psychopathology in general, but higher rates of a diagnosable affective disorder using criteria similar to those which are used in adults. The data revealed no significant sex differences in the frequencies of depressive disorder in children. However, the presence of affective disorder was more consistent over the four-month period in boys compared to that in girls. Nevertheless, the study is open to question on the grounds of the use of the Weinberg criteria for the diagnosis of affective disorder in the children and the fact that other psychiatric diagnoses were not made, raising the possibility that the children may indeed have had another psychiatric disorder which predated the depressive episode and which may have been more persistent, such as attention deficit disorder, conduct disorder, etc. As noted above, this was true in the studies by Carlson and Cantwell, who also found that the Weinberg criteria were much broader compared to the Diagnostic and Statistical Manual-III (DSM-III) criteria.

Taken together, the findings from all of the studies do in fact suggest that investigations of the children of depressed parents is a fruitful area for an at-risk study analogous to that which has been done with children of schizophrenic parents. However, the definitive study of its type has not been done as of yet. What will need to be done is to take large groups of parents with affective disorder carefully defined by specified criteria such as the DSM-III criteria or the RDC criteria. These parents will then have to be subtyped according to bipolar-1, bipolar-2, unipolar, and various specific subtypes of unipolar. Their children will need to be studied blindly. Control groups of parents who have other psychiatric disorders such as antisocial personality, anxiety disorders, schizophrenia, etc, will also have to be studied; their children must be studied in the same way. The diagnosis of a psychiatric disorder in the child should be based on a comprehensive evaluation which includes not only interviews with the parent, but also direct interviews with the children, using a reliable interview such as DICA or the Kiddie SADS. These interviews should be supplemented by standardized parent and teacher rating scales such as the Achenbach. The diagnosis should be made using adult criteria unmodified, such as the DSM-III criteria rather than the Weinberg criteria which may include a broader group of children whose affective symptomatology may be part of another psychiatric disorder. Then these children and their parents will have to be followed over time longitudinally since the age of risk for the development of affective disorder extends to about 60 years. Thus, if children are not studied for a long period of time, it is impossible to say that a child who is not manifesting any disturbance when he is studied will not develop an affective disorder later on in life. Moreover, if the child is demonstrating a psychiatric disorder of any type at the time that he is seen, it is not possible to tell without an extensive follow-up well into adult life whether that disorder might be a prodrome of an affective disorder or simply a reaction to having an ill parent or some other psychiatric disorder altogether. A further elaboration on this type of family study could involve cousins of the children being studied as a control population. If genetic factors are strongly involved in the genesis of affective disorder in children, cousins who are related to the index parent who has an affective disorder would be expected to show more psychopathology than cousins related to the spouse of the affected parent. Their psychopathology would be expected to be only slightly higher than that of a random control population. Cousins might control for socioeconomic characteristics and provide a valuable source of information from a genetic viewpoint.

Clinical investigations of this nature could be combined with neuroendocrine, biochemical, physiological, sleep, and other biological studies to look for biological markers and correlates in children who manifest symptoms of an affective disorder in childhood.

The type of study which most needs to be done in the family-genetic area is significant family studies of children diagnosed by empirical criteria as having a depressive disorder in childhood. Very few of such studies have been done. This is not surprising in that without a clear-cut definition of childhood depression, the index population that would be studied is suspected from the beginning. With the debate over the existence of childhood depression, the data base necessary to do such a study has been lacking. However, there are some data again reviewed by Orvaschel and her colleagues (1980) from the studies of Poznanski and Zrull (1970), Poznanski et al (1976), Connell (1972), Cytryn and McKnew (1972), Brumback (1977), and Puig-Antich et al (1979). All of these looked at parental psychopathology one way or another. Some found parental rejection, others also found family discord. Brumback found that 89 percent of his depressed children had an affective disorder in their families. Sixty-four percent of the mothers of the depressed children were found to be depressed compared to 30 percent of the mothers of nondepressed control children. Poznanski and Zrull in an earlier study in 1970 found high rates of parents' depression in families of depressed children and also high rates of marital discord and rejecting, hostile behavior to the child on the part of the parents. In the 13 prepubertal depressed children originally described by Puig-Antich (1979), serious family discord or mistreatment of the children occurred in 11 of 13 cases, and a family history of either depression, mania, alcoholism, or schizophrenia occurred in 61 percent of the relatives of index children. Puig-Antich's study has been an ongoing one of carefully diagnosed prepubertal children using RDC criteria for major depressive disorder. First-degree relatives were interviewed blindly using the SADS-L, and RDC psychiatric diagnoses were made in first degree relatives over the age of 16 years. Morbidity rates were calculated and compared to base population rates for both sexes considered. Twenty-four children with major depression have now been studied. Morbidity risk for male and female first-degree relatives combined was found to be 0.40 for all the major depressives, 0.39 for endogenous depressives, and 0.41 for the nonendogenous depressives. This is compared to 0.07 for a neurotic control group, and 0.46 for a normal control group. The base rate epidemiological data for major depression would be 0.20. Base rates for mania for all the major depressed children was 0.04 compared to 0.0008 in the general population. Higher rates were also found for alcoholism, antisocial behavior, substance abuse disorder, and other RDC diagnoses. Puig-Antich's study is the first to date to use unmodified adult criteria for the diagnosis of prepubertal major depressive disorder, to break it down into subtypes of nonendogenous and endogenous, then to blindly interview first-degree relatives over the age of 16 using a standardized interview such as the SADS, and make diagnoses by standardized criteria such as the RDC.

Since these were all children who were raised by their biological parents, one could of course make the case that an environmental effect was operating as well as a genetic effect. Only adoption and linkage and segregation studies can add to the question of whether a genetic influence is operating as strongly in childhood depression as it is in depressive disorder in adults.

Nevertheless, the family studies of Puig-Antich very strongly suggest that when the studies are conducted in a way similar to that which has been done in adults, using standardized interviews and standardized criteria for diagnoses, the family pattern of psychiatric illness in prepubertal children with depressive disorder is very similar to that which is found in adults with major depressive disorder. The results of Puig-Antich's studies, when combined with other validating measures such as life events and family relationships, sleep studies, neuroendocrine, rhythms of plasma cortisol concentrations, and growth hormone response to insulin induced hypoglycemia, urinary MHPG excretion, response to imipramine, and long-term outcome, will go a long way to help subtyping major depressive disorder in childhood as it has been subtyped in adult life.

SUMMARY AND FUTURE DIRECTIONS FOR RESEARCH

This chapter has attempted to review relevant progress in the genetic study of affective disorders in children. While there is a substantial amount of information that has been forthcoming in the last ten years or so to indicate that there are children who do present with a clinical picture of depressive disorder analogous to that which is seen in adults, most of the studies of depressive disorder are still at the level of clinical descriptive research. In particular we know very little about the relative roles of genetic and environmental factors in the syndrome of affective disorder in childhood compared to what we know in adults. All types of studies (family history studies, direct family studies, adoption studies, twin studies, high risk studies, and linkage and segregation studies) have combined to produce strong evidence that a genetic factor is operating with affective disorder in adults. At the moment we have almost nothing except family and high risk studies to suggest genetic factors operating in the syndrome of affective disorder in childhood. As of yet there are no twin or twin family studies, no adoption studies, and no segregation or linkage studies.

Areas of future research should include the following. As a minimum, investigators need to agree on a core set of symptoms for the criteria for the diagnosis of the depressive and manic syndrome in childhood. Whether these should be unmodified adult criteria like the DSM-III criteria or the RDC criteria or whether they should be modified such as the Weinberg criteria is very much an open question at the moment. However, it is a question which is easily researchable. By studying children who meet modified criteria such as the Weinberg criteria but who do not meet DSM-III criteria and comparing them to children who meet both Weinberg and DSM-III criteria, one would be able to tell which criteria select the most homogeneous group with regard to natural history, response to treatment, and biological correlates. These criteria which provide the most homogeneous group should be used to select groups of children for genetic studies. As a starting point, once a significant number of probands with primary affective disorder in childhood have been identified, they should be subgrouped according to methods which have been proven to be successful in adults. These subgroups should then be studied by the direct family study method to look for prevalence rates of various types of affective disorder in their close family relatives. The next step would be to find adults with known affective disorder, as did Cardoret (1978), who adopted away their children at an early age. Children should then be studied in childhood before the age of 18 (unlike Cadoret who did not study those under the age of 18). These adoption studies, plus the type that select children with known affective disorder who have been adopted, and studies comparing psychopathology in their adopted and biologic parents, should go a long way towards clarifying gene-environment interaction in depressive disorder in childhood. Longitudinal high risk studying of adults with affective disorders for early manifestations of the syndrome in their children will also be helpful. Finally segregation and linkage studies which have been proven to be effective with adults can then be conducted.

REFERENCES

Andreasen NC, Winokur G. New experimental methods for classifying depression. *Arch Gen Psychiatry* 1979; 36:447–452.

Baron M, Klotz J, Mendlewicz J, Rainer J. Multiple-threshold transmission of affective disorders. *Arch Gen Psychiatry* 1981; 38:79–84.

Bell RQ. A reinterpretation of the direction of effects in studies of socialization. *Psychol Rev* 1968; 75:81–95.

Bell RQ. Stimulus control of parent or caretaker behavior by offspring. *Dev Psychology* 1971; 4; 1:63–72.

Brumback RA, Dietz-Schmidt S, Weinberg WA. Depression in children to an educational diagnostic center—diagnosis and treatment and analysis of criteria and literature review. *Dis Nerv Sys* 1977; 38:529–535.

Cadoret RJ. Evidence for genetic inheritance of primary affective disorder in adoptees. *Am J Psychiatry* 1978; 135:463–466.

Connell HM. Depression in childhood. *Child Psychiatr Hum Dev* 1972; 4:70-85.

Conners KC, Himmelhock J, Goyette CH, et al. Children of parents with affective illness. *J Am Acad Child Psychiatry* 1979; 18:600–607.

Cytryn L, McKnew DH, Jr. Proposed classification of childhood depression. *Am J Psychiatry* 1972; 129:149–155.

Emery AEH. *Methodology in medical genetics.* Edinburgh: Churchill Livingstone, 1976.

Falconer DS. The inheritance of liability to certain diseases, estimated from the incidence among relatives. *Ann Hum Genet* 1965; 29:51.

Kuyler PL, Rosenthal L, Igel G, et al. Psychopathology among children of manic-depressive patients. *Biol Psychiatry* 1980; 15; 4:589–597.

McKnew DH, Jr, Cytryn L, Efron AM, et al. Offspring of patients with affective disorders. *Br J Psychiatry* 1979; 134:148–152.

Mendlewicz J, Rainer JD. Adoption study supporting genetic transmission in manic-depressive illness. *Nature* 1977; 268:327–329.

Orvaschel H, Weissman MM, Kidd KK. Children and depression: the children of depressed parents; the childhood of depressed patients; depression in children. *J Affective Disord* 1980; 2:1–16.

Poznanski EO, Kraheneuhl V, Zrull JP. Childhood depression–a longitudinal perspective. *J Am Acad Child Psychiatry* 1976; 15:491–501.

Poznanski EO, Zrull JP. Childhood depression: clinical characteristics of overtly depressed children. *Arch Gen Psychiatry* 1970; 23:8–15.

Puig-Antich J, Perel JM, Lupatkin W, et al. Plasma levels of imipramine (IMI) and desmethylimipramine (DMI) and clinical response in prepubertal major depressive disorder: a preliminary report. *J Am Acad Child Psychiatry* 1979; 18; 4:616–627.

Rainer JD. Science of human behavior: contributions of the biological sciences. In: Kaplan HI, Freedman AM, Sadock BJ, eds. *Comprehensive textbook of psychiatry/III, vol. 1.* 3rd ed. Baltimore: Williams & Wilkins, 1980:135–154.

Reich T, Rice J, Andreasen N, Clayton P. A preliminary analysis of the segregation distribution of primary major depressive disorder. *Psychopharmacol Bull* (in press).

Rolf JE, Garmezy N. The school performance of children vulnerable to behavior pathology. In: Ricks DF, Alexander T, Roff M, eds. *Life history research in psychopathology, vol. III.* Minnesota: University of Minnesota Press, 1974:87–107.

Rutter M. *Children of sick parents.* Maudsley monograph no. 16. New York: Oxford University Press, 1966.

Schlesser MA, Winokur G, Sherman BM. Hypothalamic-pituitary-adrenal axis activity in depressive illness. *Arch Gen Psychiatry* 1980; 37:737–743.

Slater E, Cowie V. *The genetics of mental disorders.* London: Oxford University Press, 1971.

Stewart MA, Gath A. *Psychological disorders of children–a handbook for primary care physicians.* Baltimore: Williams & Wilkins, 1978.

Weintraub S, Neale JM, Liebert DE. Teacher ratings of children vulnerable to psychopathology. *Am J Orthopsychiatry* 1975; 45:839–845.

Weissman MM, Paykel ES, Klerman GL. The depressed woman as a mother. *Soc Psychiatry* 1972; 7:98–108.

Welner Z, Welner A, McCrary MD, Leonard MA. Psychopathology in children inpatients with depression–a controlled study. *J Nerv Ment Dis* 1977; 164:408–413.

SECTION V

Natural History

Childhood Depression: Issues Regarding Natural History

Dennis P. Cantwell

The essence of longitudinal natural history studies is that data are collected at least in two points in time, for example, in childhood and at least at one later date in time (adolescence or adult life). Follow-up studies in psychiatry have always played a large nosological role. As Robins (1979) has pointed out, psychiatry lacks laboratory tests for validation of psychiatric diagnoses. Thus, follow-up studies have been traditionally used as one means of validating a psychiatric diagnosis. So, if children who are diagnosed as having a particular psychiatric disorder (such as depression) always either continue to show that same psychiatric diagnosis at a later time or completely recover from it, this is suggestive evidence that they formed a homogeneous group initially and that the diagnosis is a valid one. On the other hand, if a group of children given a diagnosis of depression develop some other specific psychiatric diagnosis later on in life, this is suggestive evidence that the group was not homogeneous initially and that this diagnosis does not have predictive validity.

Robins (1979) has outlined the three types of designs that longitudinal natural history studies generally take. The first is the true prospective study, also called the real time prospective study. The second is the follow-back study, and the third is the catch-up prospective study. Each of these have their advantages and disadvantages in the study of psychiatric problems in general and particularly in the study of childhood depression. Each of these will be reviewed briefly here with regard to the role that they might play in the study of childhood depression.

In the real time prospective study, the investigator selects a population at time 1, collects the types of data specified, and then waits for an appropriate interval to take place before collecting data at time 2, time 3, time 4, etc. A second variation of the real time study allows the investigator to carry out a particular type of treatment in between time 1 and time 2 measurements. The real time prospective study has two distinct advantages. First, it is the only type which allows the investigator to collect the exact data he wants the way he wants it at time 1 (or indeed at multiple points in time) before the final evaluation is completed. Second, it is the only type of study which truly allows for the evaluation of the effect of any type of therapeutic intervention or for the study of comparative effects of different types of therapeutic intervention with the same disorder such as depression. The real time prospective study is the only one which allows the investigator to randomly assign individuals with the disorder to treatment or no treatment, or to one type of treatment versus another type of treatment. Other types of designs do allow for comparison of treatment effects, but since they do not allow for random assignment to various types of therapeutic intervention, it may be that entry into treatment is correlated with the outcome variables.

However, there are some distinct disadvantages to the real time prospective study, most of which are logistic. The obvious one in the study of children with depression is that if one wants to look at long-term outcome into late adolescence or even early adult life, the investigator has to be young when the study starts because he ages at the same age that the subjects do. For long-term studies, not only do children and the investigator grow, but also science grows. Thus, what may have looked like very sharp clinical or other measures 20 years ago look rather crude (Robins, 1979) now at the time of follow-up because of the way science has progressed. This is particularly likely to be true in the study of childhood depression. As mentioned in other chapters, standardized interviews such as the Kiddie-SADS and the DICA now make much more careful evaluation of depressive disorders and other psychiatirc disorders in children more reliable and presumably more valid than earlier attempts at standardized interviews and even earlier diagnoses made by unstandardized methods of investigation. The real time prospective study probably should be reserved for short-term studies involving stability of psychiatric diagnoses over a short period of time for which repeatable, reliable, and valid measures are necessary and for studies involving the short-term efficacy of treatment intervention.

However, in the field of childhood depression, it is important to recognize that there probably will not exist at the moment a body of data systematically collected in which a group of depressed children have been evaluated by modern methods that will allow for follow-up by designs other than the real time prospective study. In cases like this where there are no baseline data available for follow-back study, one has no choice but to collect data on a systematically selected sample and begin a true prospective study. One other problem with the true prospective study is the problem of maintaining the sample. The longer one follows a patient population, the more likely one is to lose a portion of the sample. Since follow-up studies have shown that those who fall into the group that are hardest to find often contain a disproportionately high number of those with significant social and psychopathology, loss of 20 percent or more of a sample can seriously distort the ability to generalize the findings. When one is talking about following children into adolescence and adult life, it also has to be recognized that the same measures may not be appropriate at different ages. For example, the use of something like the Children's Depression Inventory from the Adult Depression Inventory by Kovacs and Beck or the use of the Children's Depression Rating Scale (CDRS) developed by Poznanski may be appropriate for younger children. But what of these children when they reach late adolescence and early adult life? Does one then switch to the adult Beck Depression Inventory and the Hamilton Rating Scale? And, if so, how should that switch be taken into account in the data analysis?

The second design of a longitudinal natural history study is the follow-back study. In the follow-back study, one selects a sample at time 2 such as adolescence or adult life and then uses existing records that were available at the time of childhood to collect data at time 1. Thus, if one wanted to look at the connection between the presence of a depressive disorder in childhood and the likelihood of a depressive disorder in adult life, one might begin with a population of adults with definite depressive disorder and several control groups (adults with no psychiatric disorder and adults with other types of psychiatric disorder, such as anxiety disorders and schizophrenia). One would then have to find childhood records of all of the groups of adult patients with relatively complete and equal measures on each group. The finding of a consistent picture of childhood depressive disorder or indeed any type of childhood disorder that seems to be uniquely associated with depressive disorder in adult life would provide evidence of a link between that disorder in childhood and depressive disorder in adult life. The obvious advantage to the follow-back study is that it saves the lengthy period of waiting through a follow-up period for one to collect time 2 data. The disadvantage, of course, is that the investigator has to rely on whatever existing records he can find for time 1 data. Obviously, with the current and past state of research with childhood depression, it is unlikely that one is going to be able to find systematically collected information at time 1 for a group of adults with known depressive disorder.

Another possible disadvantage of the follow-back study design is that even if one can find a group of adults with the disorder who have a reasonably complete set of data available at time 1, the sample collected at time 2 in adult life must be an unbiased sample of the group with depressive disorder. Otherwise, this limits the ability to generalize the findings. For example, if one restricts the adult population to a group of private patients admitted to a specific private psychiatric hospital with a diagnosis of depressive disorder, it is unlikely that the findings will be generalizable to those who never appear in a psychiatric hospital or who appear in a county or city hospital for indigenous populations. Finally, the success of a follow-back study rests on collecting a complete set of data at time 1 on every patient on whom time 2 data is collected in adult life. The investigator generally does not know how much time 1 data he has missed on patients who should have had time 1 data collected.

The third type of design of the longitudinal natural history study outlined by Robins is what she labeled the catch-up prospective study. This type combines some elements of the first type and some elements of the second type. Thus, the sample is identified at time 1 rather than at time 2. However, unlike the first type of study, the data at time 1 has already been collected and exists in whatever existing records there are. This design allows the investigator to select an unbiased sample of the population that he wants to study, such as children with depression at time 1. It also allows him to eliminate the waiting period of a real time prospective study since he chooses his sample from records that have already "aged" before he begins his study. However, since the data at time 1 have already been collected, the investigator does not have the opportunity, as he does in the first type of study, to collect the type of data he wants in the way he wants to collect it. Robins' own classic study, "Deviant Children Grown Up" (Robins, 1966), is probably the best example of this type of study done with a child psychiatric population. If the investigator can be satisfied with the quality of records taken at time 1, and then finds the entire population or a very substantial number at time 2 (say in late adolescence or in adult life), this third type of study carries the same advantages as the second type of study in terms of economy and time. Thus, child psychiatric clinic sample populations, such as that studied by Dahl (1971), do allow for some generalization to be made about how frequent certain types of child psychiatric problems are associated with what types of depressive disorders in adult life. However, it must be stressed that the quality of records available in time 1 must be very good, that the sample be a relatively unbiased one of the population under study, and that the amount and quality of information collected at time 2 are also complete and accurate.

To date none of these three types of studies have been used extensively in the study of childhood depression. Each has advantages and disadvantages in what they can contribute to the elucidation of the natural history of childhood depression.

There are certain other issues that Robins (1979) has discussed in the general area of longitudinal studies that are relevant to our discussion of natural history studies of childhood depression. These include: selection of the index sample, selection of control or comparison cases, data to be collected initially in a prospective study, length of follow-up interval, measures of intervening variables, types of outcome measures, and proper statistical analysis. For those interested in a more detailed review of these issues, referral is made to Robins' excellent discussion (Robins, 1979). Some of these issues will be reviewed briefly here, specifically referring to the study of childhood depression.

First, in selecting the index sample in a real time prospective study, it is important to make sure that the patients are chosen by one set of diagnostic criteria that are applied operationally, that is, that are arrived at by methods that can be reproduced by other investigators. Thus, if one uses Diagnostic and Statistical Manual-III (DSM-III) criteria and uses the Diagnostic Interview

Schedule for Children (DISC) as an interviewing instrument for parents and children, such a study should easily be reproducible by other investigators using the same instruments. If one wishes to compare predictive validity of only one set of criteria, then the patient population should be as homogeneous as possible. Thus, if one wants to compare the predictive validity of a diagnosis of major depressive disorder in childhood, cases with secondary depression probably ought to be excluded since we do not know that children who develop a major depressive disorder out of the blue, as it were, compared to those who develop a major depressive disorder in the face of a long-standing conduct disorder or attention deficit disorder will have the same outcome. They should probably be separated out for an initial study of predictive validity of the DSM-III criteria. On the other hand, if one wants to look at the comparative predictive validities of the Weinberg criteria versus the DSM-III criteria, then the sample probably will not be as homogeneous as if one selects patients who only meet major depressive disorder criteria according to DSM-III. This planned heterogeneity will allow for a comparison of the Weinberg and DSM-III criteria. However, unplannned heterogeneity of a sample may leave the investigator with too few cases at time 2, time 3, time 4, etc of the outcomes he is interested in studying.

There are many available sources for selecting the initial sample to be studied. Thus, if one is looking for a group of children who meet DSM-III criteria for depression, one may select data from a private practitioner's practice, from hospital populations, from outpatient clinic populations, from residential treatment centers, from schools, etc. Whether or not the source of the depressed population is appropriate for the questions to be answered by the follow-up study depends on the degree to which that source provides a relatively unbiased sample of depressed children. It is probably likely that children selected from a psychiatric inpatient setting differ at least in severity if not in other factors from children with major depressive disorder treated solely as outpatients. Thus, the outcomes of the two may be different and may not be related to the diagnosis, but rather to severity or factors which led to hospitalization.

The selection of control and comparison cases is an important one. Issues to be considered are: what kind of control should be selected (normal or children with other types of deviant psychiatric disorders or both) and when should control populations be selected (initially, at follow-up) or should they differ from one type of investigator's study to another? Some types of studies, such as those that look at the effect of some type of treatment intervention, provide their own control group. Thus, one can compare a group of depressed children treated with tricyclic antidepressants to a group treated with placebo to a group given no treatment over a fixed period of time. If the tricyclic-treated group fares better than the no-treatment group and also better than the placebo-treated group, this strongly suggests that what we are witnessing is an actual effect of the medication, not simply the natural evolution of the disorder.

The inclusion of a placebo group versus a no-treatment group allows us to tell what effect "attention" has in depressed children. So if a placebo group improves more than a no-treatment group, it does suggest that some degree of the improvement obtained by the tricyclics was due to a placebo effect.

Comparisons with normal children are useful when studying depressed children over time, either treated or untreated. A comparison with a normal group will allow us to determine not only whether or not the depressed child has improved over time but how close to normal he has become in a variety of areas: academic performance, peer relationships, etc.

When any type of measurement instruments are used, comparison groups are a vital necessity. National norms are available for only a few measurement instruments; and even when instruments are used that do have national normative data, it is likely that the population under study may differ from the general population along a variety of parameters. Controlling for these parameters by the use of a comparison group will give more meaning to the findings on any particular measure. Instruments such as the Childhood Depression Inventory, the CDRS, and other specific depression measures do not yet have a large amount of normative data behind them. Thus, a normal comparison group and deviant comparison groups of children with other types of nondepressive psychiatric disorders are necessary in initial studies to determine which items on these measures are specifically endorsed more often by children with true depressive disorders. Same-sex siblings are one type of comparison group that are likely to be ideal from the standpoint of matching for such characteristics as sex; race; social status; family, genetic, and environmental factors; nonfamily environmental factors; etc. Thus, comparison of depressed children over time with their same-sex siblings for outcome is likely to lead to a firm conclusion that a particular type of outcome indeed is due to the presence of depressive disorder in the index child rather than family or demographic variables. However, since the same-sex siblings are matched for so many variables, these variables are then lost as predictor variables for outcome for children who do have a major depressive disorder. Moreover, the use of same-sex sibling controls requires that the indexed depressed child comes from a family in which there are at least two children of the same sex and may in fact bias toward the selection of depressed children from larger families.

Robins (1981) believes that a control group unselected for the index problem, such as childhood depression, is usually preferable to obtaining a "healthy" control sample. She recommends selecting all available index cases when the number of index cases is small. Thus, if the number of children who meet the criteria, for example, for a DSM-III diagnosis of bipolar affective disorder, is small, it would be important to collect all of these cases and then choose more control groups than index cases in order to increase the total sample size. When index cases are plentiful and when they are homogeneous, then index and control groups can be of equal size. She also recommends one-to-one matching rather than group matching for variables in the total sample. The reason for this is that one-to-one matching assures that the control subjects not only have the same distribution of the variables for which they are matched as the index cases do, but that the correlation between these characteristics is identical in the index group and the control group.

It is obvious that in a real time prospective study, as much data should be collected systematically as possible. These should include, as Robins points out, the descriptors of variables used as criteria for major depressive disorder; other subtypes of depression should be spelled out clearly. Secondly, enough identifiers should be collected to allow location at follow-up. This latter is particularly important when the index sample is young children. The index group of depressed children may be living in a single parent family in which over time remarriage is likely to occur. Thus, it is important to collect as much information as possible that would allow the child to be followed, regardless of whether the mother remains single, remarries (and thus carried a different name at follow-up), moves away, etc.

The third type of data to be collected are possible predictors. These predictors, with regard to the clinical picture, often include such things as: age of onset of the problem, the duration of the problem to the time the child is initially seen, degree of functional impairment, certain characteristics of the child (such as IQ, academic achievement), and characteristics of the family (including family history of psychiatric illness, family interaction factors, etc. Decisions about the length of follow-up need to be made with regard to the questions that are being asked. Obviously, if one wants to know whether the presence of a depressive disorder in childhood predisposes to the presence of a depressive disorder in adult life, then one has to follow the patients into adult life. On the other hand, if one is looking for information regarding the untreated natural history of one episode of major depression in a child, the follow-up period can be considerably shorter. Likewise, information regarding the effect of certain types of treatment on an episode of major depression can also be shorter than a study which is geared to answering whether or not the administration of certain medication prevents recurrent episodes of depression and/or mania in children.

The measurement of intervening variables during any follow-up study can prove to be difficult. Since life events have been postulated to affect both the timing and occurrence of major depressive disorder in adults (Brown et al, 1973), one would be interested in knowing something about life events occurring while children are being followed for major depressive disorder. Although there are instruments such as the Coddington Life Events Scale, they are not nearly as well-developed as instruments that have been used with adults.

The type of outcome measures to be collected also relate to the nature of the questions that are to be answered. If one is to postulate a relationship between certain types of clinical pictures in childhood and the presence of a major depressive disorder in adult life, then it is likely that structured interviewing of the individual himself or herself and probably a close relative is necessary to do the best kind of study. Relying only on hospital records or other types of records for the adult diagnosis is likely to miss a significant number of patients.

Finally, Robins makes a strong point for the type of data analysis that must be done in longitudinal studies. The reader is referred to work cited by Robins, including Joreskog and Sorbom (1976), Heise (1970), and Goodman (1970), for statistical handling of change in ways that simultaneously control for a variety of predictor variables and that assess the individual net contribution of each one of these predictor variables when all of the other variables are held constant.

In summary, we have reviewed various types of methodological aspects of natural history studies. Very few of these have been employed to any great extent yet in a study of childhood depression. What literature exists about the natural history of depression in childhood will be reviewed below.

The course of major affective disorder in adults is variable. There are individuals who have episodes separated by many years of normal functioning. On the other hand, other individuals have clusters of episodes that occur much more closely together. And a third group seem to have an increased number of episodes as they grow older. In the inter-illness period the level of function usually returns to the premorbid level. However, in as many as one third of the cases there may be a more chronic course which is associated with some residual symptomatic and social impairment. Fifty percent of individuals with an episode of major depression will eventually have another major depressive episode. Individuals who have recurrent episodes of major depression are at greater risk of developing a bipolar disorder than are those with a single episode (APA, 1980).

The course of bipolar and unipolar illness also seems to be different in a number of other ways. Aside from the obvious difference that bipolar depressed patients are at risk for the development of manic or hypomanic episodes, they also have more episodes in their lifetime (average three per lifetime), and the individual episodes are from three to six months in duration. Those with unipolar depression not only do not have episodes of mania or hypomania, but also have a lower total number of episodes (one to two per lifetime on the average). Individual episodes, however, are somewhat longer, lasting six to nine months. Among the unipolar depressed patients, those with depression spectrum disease (DSD) are more likely to have a variable illness with more interpersonal difficulties and are less likely to have long periods of chronicity. Those with familial pure depressive disease (FPDD) are more likely to have the latter. Patients with secondary affective disorder usually do not have episodes of depression as discrete as those patients with primary affective disorder. Their depressions tend to be more transient or chronic. It is likely that many of those with secondary depression using the Winokur subclassification would probably qualify for a diagnosis of dysthymic disorder in DSM-III.

In contrast to the relatively large amount of work that has been done with the natural history of adult psychiatric disorders, very little has been done with the untreated natural history of psychiatric disorders in childhood. With the rarer conditions that have a more severe outcome, such as infantile autism, natural history studies have proven to be fruitful. They do suggest that the majority of autistic children do not develop an adult schizophrenic-like picture. The studies also give guidelines as to which children are most likely to improve from among a total population of autistic children. A fair amount of information is beginning to accumulate about the untreated natural history of attention deficit disorder with hyperactivity and conduct disorder.

Much less is known about the course of prepubertal major depressive disorder. Such information could come from a variety of studies: (1) prospective follow-up studies of groups of depressive children diagnosed by operational diagnostic criteria; (2) follow-up studies of large groups of psychiatric patients in childhood well into adult life (this would supply information not only on those who present with a depressive disorder in childhood, but also on the other disorders with a nondepressive picture that may be associated with development of depression in adult life); (3) prospective and retrospective studies of the childhood of depressed adult patients. Such studies are few in number.

Orvaschel and her colleagues (1980) reviewed four such studies: those by Munro (1966), Perris (1966), Raskin (1977), and Jacobson et al (1975). All studies were retrospective; some were obtained by patient interview only, some by patient self-report only, and some involved interviewing relatives and the use of hospital records. The findings of all of the studies agree generally that adult depressive patients, when they were children, were likely to suffer from family discord, parental inattention, parental rejection, abuse; they also had parents who had high rates of mental illness. No unique clinical picture in childhood was described.

Solid prospective follow-up studies of large groups of depressed children are extremely rare. Poznanski and her colleagues (1976) did describe ten children at follow-up whom they had diagnosed as depressed some 6½ years previously. During adolescence at the time of follow-up, about half of the group were clinically depressed, and their clinical picture resembled the depressive syndrome of adults more than it had when they were seen in early childhood.

Herjanic (1976) conducted a similar study from the St. Louis Children's Hospital. Twenty children who received a discharge diagnosis of depression from the hospital made by their clinicians were followed up and interviewed systematically. At the time of follow-up, only one had a true affective disorder, one had schizoaffective disorder, and one patient had an undiagnosed illness which was likely to develop into affective disorder later in life. All three of these children had originally met the Weinberg criteria for depression. The 17 children who had been given a discharge diagnosis of depression by the clinicians taking care of them, but who did not meet the Weinberg criteria, had much more widely varying diagnoses at follow-up. Ten were found to have no psychiatric illness, two were found to have antisocial personality, and five were undiagnosed. Given that the Weinberg criteria identify a diagnostically more heterogeneous group than the DSM-III criteria, these data suggest that the DSM-III criteria might identify a much more homogeneous group of patients with a more characteristic course.

Several European studies come up with inconsistent results (Penot, 1971; Spiel, 1971; Nissen, 1971). For example, Penot, in a study of 17 children with depression (ages five to 11), suggested that the depression did not constitute a particular clinical entity and that there was a favorable course in about half the number of cases. Spiel (1971) reported on all manic depressive cases in children under the age of 15 who were admitted to the psychiatric department of the University of Vienna for clinical treatment during a 20-year period. Thirty cases were followed up for more than 18 years. Psychotic manifestations occurred on one occasion only. The transition from psychotic behavior in childhood to cyclic fluctuation was the rule. The cycles were mostly unipolar depressive states with relapses. There was a high rate of erroneous diagnosis in manic children.

Nissen from Berlin (1971) looked at 105 children and adolescents with severe depressive states. Six diagnostic syndromes were found which were believed to be variants of the agitated and inhibited syndromes. Four nosological groups were characterized: psychogenic, constitutional, somatogenic, and manic depressive states. Nissen felt that the prognosis of severe depressive states were unfavorable rather than favorable. The number of subsequent psychiatric illnesses and the frequency of admissions to a hospital ward indicated that. He also felt that neither diagnostic nor nosological syndrome diagnosis implied a definitive prognosis. Differing criteria for the diagnosis of depression and different etiological concepts and terminology make comparison to American studies somewhat difficult.

Long-term follow-up studies of groups of child psychiatric patients have not suggested that bipolar illness in adulthood is a common outcome. Dahl (1971) followed 146 male and 172 female patients 20 years after their initial admittance to two child psychiatric departments in Denmark. At the time of follow-up, they were between 20 and 35 years of age. At this point in their lives, a third of the female population and 27 percent of the males had been hospitalized in adult psychiatric patient departments. In no case was manic depressive disease a diagnosis at the time of adult hospitalization. Eight cases carried a diagnosis of depressive neurosis at the time of follow-up. Robins' follow-up (1966) of the St. Louis Child Guidance Clinic population also supports this view. In general, there does not seem to be evidence of a specific "predepressive" disorder occurring in childhood, that does not manifest itself as adult-like depression, which can identify a group of children who are likely to develop depression later in life any more than there seems to be a preschizophrenic picture. The classic review by Offord and Cross (1969) of the childhood antecedents of adult schizophrenia has shown that there does not seem to be a unique childhood picture associated with the development of schizophrenia in adult life. Rather what is shown is that depending on where the populations are selected from, the childhood picture of those who develop schizophrenia in adult life may differ. It is likely that the same thing will be found with children and the clinical picture of depression.

A rather unique study in the annals of child psychiatry is the New York longitudinal study. Chess (1980) followed 133 children from infancy through childhood; many were followed into young adult life. All but one have been interviewed and evaluated between the ages of 18 to 22 years of age. Chess reported on six of the 133 who had developed a clinical depression in childhood and adolescence. This study was unique in that the children were not selected for psychopathology, but rather were selected at the time of infancy to be followed longitudinally looking for temperamental characteristics in individuality and its functional significance for the course of psychological development.

Of the six cases that were found to have developed a clinical depression by the follow-up period of age 18 to 22, two were diagnosed as having a primary depression, and four as having a secondary depression. Chess concluded that the depressive syndrome, when it developed in childhood and adolescence, appeared to be continuous in its quality with depressive symptoms of early adult life. Stated another way, she did not feel that the data gave evidence for a separate clinical entity of childhood depression.

The primary depression cases were quite distinct from the secondary depression cases in a number of features. The primary depression cases had strong family histories of major affective disorder and did not have episodes that appeared to be precipitated by psychosocial stress. Psychosocial stress was prominent in the life of the four cases with secondary depression who also had negative family histories for depression. It was also noteworthy that the two cases of primary depression became clinically depressed quite early. One boy developed symptomatology at age eight with both anxiety and mood symptoms. By age 12 he was quite clearly depressed. By the age of 22 he had had recurrent depression six times in his life. The second case of primary depression was a girl who had been depressed off and on since the age of 12 but did not come to clinical attention until the age of 21.

In contrast, the secondary depression cases generally tended to develop symptomatology early that was of a different nature than the later developing depressive symptomatology. One boy first developed nondepressive clinical symptomatology at age five and depressive symptomatology at age ten. A second child, also a boy, had a long history of distractability and short attention span beginning at the age of 30 months with depressive symptomatology beginning for the first time at age 17, and a hypomanic episode at age 20, which responded to lithium. A girl was temperamentally difficult throughout most of her life but was accepted by her parents until a change in family constellation led to a poor "goodness of fit" and an episode of explosive anger, insomnia, and overeating at age 13, which qualified for a diagnosis of conduct disorder. It was not until age 16 that the depressive symptomatology became predominant. Finally, a boy developed a secondary depression at the age of 13 after a divorce in his family.

It is likely that follow-up studies of children diagnosed as depressed by operational criteria such as the DSM-III criteria will indeed show that they have a high likelihood of developing recurrent episodes of affective disorder, both unipolar and bipolar. Given that they have such an early age of onset, it may be that they will turn out to have a more severe form of the disorder in adult life. What will be needed are comparative studies using different criteria to select children with major depressive disorder. For example, comparative studies of children who meet the DSM-III criteria and the Weinberg criteria versus those who do not meet the DSM-III criteria but meet the Weinberg criteria need to be done. If the children who do not meet DSM-III criteria in childhood but who do meet the Weinberg criteria for depression have the same type of natural history, it may suggest that the broader Weinberg criteria are just as appropriate at least with regard to predictive validity.

One aspect of the natural history of depression in prepubertal children that has been relatively unexplored is its relationship to suicidal behavior. In adults there is a large literature on the demographic characteristics and the psychiatric diagnoses associated with both completed and attempted suicide. Over 90 percent of completed suicides are psychiatrically ill, and two thirds of completed suicides are accounted for by two psychiatric illnesses, major affective disorder making up about one half and alcoholism making up about 25 percent. Patients with terminal medical illness, schizophrenia, organic brain syndromes, and drug abuse also make minor contributions to successful suicides. It is important to note that in adults, antisocial personality, uncomplicated hysteria (somatization disorder), and emotional problems such as the anxiety disorders make little or no contribution to the pool of those who successfully commit suicide. The relationship of depression to suicidal behavior in children is reviewed in Chapter 19 in this volume.

REFERENCES

Brown GW, Harris TO, Peto J. Life events in psychiatric disorder: II. Nature of causal link. *Psychol Med* 1973;3:159–176.

Chess S. Depression in childhood and adolescence: a prospective study of six cases. Presented at the Arthur B. Richter Conference on Childhood Depression, University of Indiana, Indianapolis, Indiana, April 1980.

Dahl V. A follow-up study of child psychiatric clientele, with special regard to manic-depressive psychosis. In: Annell AL, ed. *Depressive states in child and adolescence*. Stockholm: Almquist and Wiksell, 1971:534–541.

Goodman LA. The multivariant analysis of qualitative data: interactions among multiple classifications. *J Am Stat Assoc* 1970; 65:225–256.

Heise DR. Causal inference from panel data. In: Borgheta EF, Bohrnstedt TW, eds. *Sociological methodology*. San Francisco: Jossey-Bass, 1970.

Herjanic B. Follow-up study of 20 children given a discharge diagnosis of depression—St. Louis Children's Hospital. Presented at the American Psychiatric Association Meeting, Miami, Florida, 1976.

Jacobson S, Fasman J, DiMascio A. Deprivation in the childhood of depressed women. *J Nerv Ment Dis* 1975; 166:5–14.

Joreskog KG, Sorbom D. Statistical models and methods for analysis of longitudinal data. In: Aigner DJ, Goldberger AS, Eds. *Latent variables in socioeconomic models*. New York: North Hall Publishing, 1976.

Munro A. Some familial and social factors in depressive illness. *Br J Psychiatry* 1966; 112:429–441.

Nissen G. Symptomatik und prognose depressiver Verstimmungszustande in Kindes–und Jungendalter. In: Annel A, ed. *Depressive states in childhood and adolescence*. Stockholm: Almquist and Wiksell, 1971:517–524.

Offord D, Cross L. Behavioral antecedents of adult schizophrenia. *Arch Gen Psychiatry* 1969; 21:267–283.

Orvaschel H, Weissman MM, Kidd KK. Children and depression: the children of depressed parents; the childhood of depressed parents; depression in children. *J Affective Disord* 1980; 2:1–16.

Penot D. Caracteristiques et devenir des depressions de la deuxieme enfance. In: Annel A, ed. *Depressive states in childhood and adolescence*. Stockholm: Almquist and Wiksell, 1971:525–533.

Perris C. A study of bipolar (manic-depressive) and unipolar recurrent depressive psychoses, part 2. Childhood environment and precipitating factors. *ACTA Psychiatr Scand* 1966; 42(suppl 194):45–57.

Poznanski EO, Kraheneuhl V, Zrull JP. Childhood depression—a longitudinal perspective. *J Am Acad Child Psychiatry* 1976; 15:491–501.

Raskin A. Depression in children: fact or fallacy. In: Schulterbrandt JG, Raskin A, eds. *Depression in childhood: diagnosis, treatment, and conceptual models*. New York: Raven Press, 1977: 141–146.

Robins LN. *Deviant children grown up*. Baltimore: Williams & Wilkins, 1966.

ROBINS LN. Longitudinal methods in the study of normal and pathological development. In: Kisker KP, Meyer JE, Muller C, Stromgren E, eds. *Psychiatrie der Gegenwart*, Band I., Forschung und Praxis, Gurndlagen und methoden der Psychiatrie Teil I. Heidelburg: Springer-Verlag, 1979:627–684.

Spiel W. Studien uber den verlauf und die Erscheinungs formen der kindlichen und juvenilen manisch-depressiven Psychofen. In: Annel A, ed. *Depressive states in childhood and adolescence*. Stockholm: Almquist and Wiksell, 1971:517–524.

Affective Disorders in Childhood and Adolescence--
An Update. Edited by D.P. Cantwell and G.A. Carlson.

14

Affective Disorders in Parents: Impact upon Children

Maurice Eisenbruch

Despite the long existence of depression or melancholia in the literature, application to the relationship between maternal depression and the child came much later. In Gregory Zilboorg's treatise "A History of Medical Psychology," "melancholia" merits twenty citations spanning the time from Hippocrates, while "childhood" or "mothering" receive none. The first retrospective reconstructions of a melancholy childhood was provided by Guibert of Nogent.

> She knew that I should be utterly an orphan with no one at all on whom to depend, for great as was my wealth of kinsfolk and connections, yet there was no one to give me the loving care a little child needs at such an age; though I did not lack for the necessities of food and clothing, I often suffered from the loss of that careful provision for the helplessness of tender years that only a woman can provide. . . . Although she knew that I would be condemned to such neglect, yet Thy love and fear, O God, hardened her heart . . . the tenderest in all the world, that it might not be tender to her own soul's harm.
>
> Guibert, abbot of Nogent-sous-Coucy: *Memoirs*, 1115.

In this passage, Guibert expresses his feelings toward his mother, both the intense ambivalence and the yearning for her love.

The awareness of the transmission of affects from mother to child was documented by Burton

> If she be over-dull, heavy, angry, peevish, discontented, and melancholy, not only at the time of conception, but even all the while she carries the child in her womb, her son will be so likewise affected and worse. If she grieve overmuch, be disquieted, or by any casualty be affrighted and terrified by some fearful object heard or seen, she endangers her child, and spoils the temperature of it; for the strange imagination of a woman works effectually upon her infant, that, as Baptista Porta proves, she leaves a mark upon it, which is most especially seen

> in such as prodigiously longing for such and such meats; the child will love those meats, saith Fernelius, and be addicted to like humours . . . our generation is corrupt, we have many weak persons, both in body and mind, crazed families, parentes peremptores (our parents are our ruin), our fathers bad, and we are like to be worse.
>
> Robert Burton; *The Anatomy of Melancholy*, 1621.

Herein are stated some parameters of mother-child interactional psychiatry. There are the matching of affects from mother to child, the power of influence of mother upon developing child, the notion that "the child will love those meats" that even the unpalatable food that is melancholia will be ingested. As expressed by Milton 17 years later in his poem "Il Penseroso"

> These pleasures, Melancholy, give,
> And I with thee will choose to live,
>
> Robert Milton: *Il Penseroso*, 1638.

THE PROBLEM

Child psychiatrists are agents for primary prevention through understanding the processes whereby children continue as "carriers" to transmit the seeds of mental disorder and suffering. In the past decade, attention has focused upon the relationship between psychotic parents and their children. Of particular relevance is the depressed mother and her child.

From the epidemiologic side, Fabian and Donahue (1956) noted that one third of the mothers of the children referred to their child guidance clinic were depressed. They felt that maternal depression was a family catastrophe and that the effects on infants and children would be disasterous. Walzer (1961) noted the frequency of depression in the parents of children referred to a child guidance clinic. Clarification of the nature of the depressed mother-child dyad, thus has considerable clinic relevance.

One's field of view of both the child's immediate reactions and his longer-range responses to depressive illness in his parent may take place at one or more of three levels. Closest to the surface are the social roles assumed by the child in his family. Then there is the range of phenomenology and symptomatology observable on examination. Finally, there are intrapsychic changes within the very core of the child's personality structure. These levels are interconnected, but what is seen depends upon which level is the focus of attention.

THE CHILD AND HIS SOCIAL ROLE IN THE FAMILY

Reactions of family members to disequilibrium "caused" by a change in one family member was first described by Koos (1946). Since then the growth of family systems and role theories has cast new light on this level in terms of general family reactions (Kreisman and Joy, 1974; Raymond et al, 1975). When a parent becomes psychiatrically "ill," he or she assumes a sick role; as a result other family members may suffer a disruption in complementarity of adult and child roles in the family. The child may take on "idiosyncratic" roles in attempts to maintain psychological equilibrium within the family system (Chagoya and Gutterman, 1971; Epstein et al, 1968; Lecker, 1976). Sturges (1978) describes eight idiosyncratic role performances played by children in their reactions to mental illness in the family. He classifies these roles under the descriptive labels of caretaker, baby, patient, mourner, recluse, escapee, good child, and bad child.

It is often the oldest daughter or the only child who assumes the caretaker role. At the other extreme is the child assuming the role of baby, most often taken on by a younger child who may regress to a clinging, whining, demanding state. The child in the role of mourner demonstrates excessive and prolonged grief over separation from the ill parent; this occurs commonly in younger children who may be expressing grief for the entire family, and some of whose members are suppressing their feelings of abandonment and loss. In the role of patient, the child may develop symptoms, become depressed, act like the sick family member, or actually become psychotic. It is often the adolescent who adopts the role of escapee, refusing involvement with the family altogether. This role can be adaptive, in that it may help differentiation from the illness and family problems, but while there may be physical distance between the child and the sick parent, the child may remain emotionally entrapped. On the other hand, the adolescent is prone to withdraw from peers, school, and family, taking on the role of recluse. Some children become extremely well-behaved, taking on the role of good child, perhaps through a feeling of guilt and responsibility for having caused the parental illness. On the other hand, the child may become openly aggressive or assume the role of bad child in some more subtle way.

Sturges makes the point that role flexibility within a family during a period of acute psychiatric illness in a parent can be a sign of strength, just as temporary changes in the child's role may be adaptive in meeting the needs of child and family. However, temporary changes can become fixed, particularly in cases of severe chronic depressive illness in the mother, and may lead to enduring changes in the child's personality. The determinants of these roles, together with the implications for permanent change in the child's developing personality, need to be clarified. Again, the impact of developmental crises and phase-specific childhood tasks upon these reaction patterns requires further resolution.

PHENOMENOLOGY AND PSYCHOPATHOLOGY

Children of psychiatrically ill parents seemingly present with more psychopathology and behavior problems than children of parents who are considered well (Preston and Antin, 1933; Baker et al, 1961; Cowie, 1961; Sussex et al, 1963; Ekdahl et al, 1962; Anthony, 1969; Welner et al, 1977; Cooper et al, 1977; Grunebaum et al, 1978; Orvaschel et al, 1979; McKnew et al, 1979; Kestenbaum, 1979, 1980; Kauffman et al, 1979). However, only some studies address the specific question of children whose parents suffer affective illness.

The study of children of psychotic mothers permits investigation of genetic and environmental factors which predisposed to psychopathology before the onset of illness and without the complicating effects of treatment (Mednick and Schulsinger, 1968; Garmezy, 1974; Hanson et al, 1976). The range of techniques for assessing clinical disturbance in children of depressed parents is broad and includes psychiatric interviews and diagnoses, hospital diagnoses, ratings by informants, ratings from index children, teachers, parents, and peers. Psychophysiological measures have been used and behavioral observation and other methods include questionnaires, birth records, and neurological examinations. Clinical evaluations using psychological tests including cognitive, visual-motor, attention, word association, and projective tests have also been used. As mentioned, children of schizophrenic mothers have been the more thoroughly studied (Beisser, 1967; Rolf, 1972; Raigins et al, 1975), usually in reports comparing high risk children and normal control subjects. Cohler et al (1977) found that five and six-year-old children of depressed mothers showed both greater impairment on a measure of intellectual ability and greater disturbance in the ability to deploy attention than was found among either the children of schizophrenic or well mothers. No differences in ratings of social or emotional behavior were found.

These results suggest that maternal depressive psychosis may have an even greater impact than schizophrenia on the child's cognitive development. In addition, the impact of depression upon overall ability of the mother to parent the child may be even more pervasive. These findings are supported by the work of Weintraub et al (1975), who found that teachers rated the classroom behavior of children of depressed and schizophrenic women as similarly deviant. It is suggested that children of depressed mothers are more vulnerable before adolescence while it is only at adolescence that the children of schizophrenic mothers become most vulnerable (Mednick et al, 1968). In addition, perhaps longstanding psychotic depression has a more pervasive impact on parenting and thus on a child than schizophrenia. The child may feel more responsible for his mother being depressed and rather less responsible for her states of schizophrenic irrationality.

Worland et al (1979) summarized part of a longitudinal perspective study of children at risk (Anthony, 1968, 1977), in which children of schizophrenic and manic depressive parents are evaluated to determine factors associated with parental psychosis irrespective of the type. Use of a control group of children with a physically ill parent allowed for evaluation of the influence of parental illness as such. Inclusion of children with parents who had no history of prolonged psychiatric or physical illness provided a normal control group. Worland et al tried to determine whether a psychodynamic evaluation of children at risk could isolate variables that characterized such children before the emergence of psychosis. The investigation employed a battery using the Wechsler Intelligence Scale for Children (WISC), figure drawings, Thematic Apperception Test (TAT), Rorschach Inkblot Test, and Beery-Buktenica Developmental Form Sequence, together with clinical disturbance ratings. Tests were administered individually to children (aged six to 20 years) from intact families with one schizophrenic, manic depressive, or physically ill parent, or two normal parents.

Children of schizophrenic and manic depressive parents differed from one another and from controls on two measures. In the aggressive content of their TAT stories, children with a schizophrenic parent showed less aggression than normal children, and children with a manic depressive parent showed more aggression than normal children. On the Rorschach, children of schizophrenic parents gave more primitive responses than children of manic depressive parents, and children of normal parents gave an intermediate number of such responses. Worland et al make the point that there are many possible reasons for this finding, and the high risk research methodology is not sufficient to answer the question of why pathology is greater among children of psychotic parents. Other than genetic influence, one possible reason is that the assessed pathology is the result of the disruption caused by the parents' psychotic behavior and hospitalization, a disruption that is greater in children of psychotic parents than for children of physically ill parents (Ekdahl et al, 1962). Another possible reason is that the pathology is due to parental psychopathology in the psychotic and/or the "well" parent. The third possible reason is that the pathology in the children may be a palpable or measurable precursor of the child's own potential to eventual psychosis.

These three explanations require comment. In the first place, it is too often assumed that the experience of acute parental psychosis with attendant admission to hospital is the "cause" of distress to the child. There is no evidence that this is the case. To the contrary, it could even be postulated that the more pernicious and insidious source of the "depressogenic environment" for the child is his ongoing "residence" in a habitat colored by his acutely depressed mother's character structure and organization. Again, the assumption that from the child's point of view a "psychiatric" parental admission is somehow different from a "nonpsychiatric" parental admission merit closer scrutiny. A growing body of work touching on focal suicide, accident-proneness, and psychosomatic research (Engel, 1970) suggests that so-called nonpsychiatric admissions of parents to hospital may represent the manifestation of long-term psychological disturbance. Though these manifestations may be occult and subclinical, there may lurk in this population a group of parents who from their child's point of view are equally as disturbed as those who are admitted with frank depressive illness.

Since it is possible that these findings of Cohler, Worland, and others may be relevant only at certain stages in the child's development, follow-up of original samples would be important. Grunebaum et al (1978) describe such a five-year follow-up study of the Cohler cohort. They found that while the previous study did not show differences in concentration, on follow-up it is indeed the children of depressed mothers, irrespective of sex of the child, who make the greatest errors. The earlier findings of lower scores on the Wechsler Preschool and Primary Scale of Intelligence (WPPSI) was not duplicated in the follow-up study using an abbreviated form of the WISC. Thus, early findings suggest a persistence rather than an evanescence of the cognitive characteristics found in children of depressed mothers.

Apart from the question of formal psychiatric diagnosis in the parent, there is the issues: is there a fundamental parental clinical state irrespective of formal diagnosis which in itself has an impact upon the child? Anthony (1969) in his study of children of schizophrenic parents drew attention to a nonspecific group of clinical disturbances. He referred to,

> the reactive environment . . . characterized by its inconsistency, chaotic management, contradictory communications, highly ambivalent but powerful affects, incoherent attentions and motions, and its disturbing degrees of intrusiveness into the lives of the children. This environment of irrationality envelops the family and makes for unpredictable storms and crises that hover over the lives of the children.

This description of reactive environment may apply equally to any family in which there is gross emotional turmoil. What is unclear is the specificity of the depressive environment as contrasted with, say, the schizophrenic environment or any other. The notion that formal diagnosis of depression is less important than the presence of emotional turmoil is supported by a study of children of psychiatric patients, in which Cooper et al (1977) found that families with disturbed children were characterized by the presence of frank marital discord, diagnosis of personality difficulties in the parents, inability of the father to tolerate angry situations, and the presence of siblings of under nine years of age. After a six month follow-up, nine of the nineteen children had improved considerably, and in almost every family this was associated with improvement in the condition of the parents. It is suggested that the psychiatric disorder of these children is reactive to the presence of emotional turmoil in the families.

What happens to these children later? Robins (1966) showed that childhood neurosis was not the best predictor of neurosis in adult life. Preliminary studies on the follow-up of children of "problem families" (Tonge, 1976) have shown interesting differences between anxious children who do well and "normal" children who grow up to repeat their parents pattern of maladjustment. The "normal" children who seemingly adjust to parental depression may be more damaged through internalization than others who react more vigorously and who are judged on the basis of presence of overt symptoms at the time to have psychiatric disorder.

THE IMPACT OF THE DEVELOPMENTAL LEVEL OF THE CHILD

An important variable in these comparative studies is the developmental level of the child. Symptoms in childhood are evanescent, changing with developmental progress. In addition, theoretical questions arise such as the prerequisite conditions of character development before which a depression may be present, and as well there is the impact of normal developmental vulnerability upon the child's proclivity to be affected by the depressed parent.

Grouping available comparative studies according to the ages of offspring examined, in the perinatal and infancy age bracket, Sameroff and Zax (1973) compared infants of schizophrenic, neurotic, depressive, and personality disordered mothers and found the prevalence of perinatal and infancy problems to be related to severity of the mother's psychopathology rather than to her diagnosis. De Horn and Strauss (1977) in comparing the birth weights of the offspring of schizophrenic, depressed, and other parents found no statistically significant difference among the three groups. In the preschool group, the study by Romano (1977) which compares preschool children of schizophrenic and neurotic depressed mothers is ongoing. In the school age group, the study by Grunebaum (1978) has already been referred to. Studies which include teacher's blind ratings (Beisser et al, 1967; Weintraub et al, 1975) demonstrate more disturbing school behavior for the offspring of diagnositc groups compared to normal control subjects, but there are no intergroup differences. Further evidence on this question is provided by Rutter et al (1975) in epidemiological studies.

In the adolescent age bracket, Remschmidt (1973) compared children of endogenously depressed, psychotic, and normal parents, and concluded that the problems of the offspring of depressives was intermediate between the other two groups. In the all-age samples, Post (1962), comparing the children of neurotic and psychotic mothers, reported the offspring of psychotics to be less affected than those of neurotics, while Cowie (1961) and Rutter (1966) reported more disturbance regardless of diagnosis if the mothers were ill. Garmezy (1974) found more withdrawn, shy, and socially isolated behavior for their "target" children, especially for children of depressive mothers than for control children. Weintraub et al (1975) noted higher levels of classroom disturbance, impatience, disrespect, or more defiant behavior, inattentiveness, and withdrawal, and lower levels of comprehension, creativity, and relating to teacher for both the children of schizophrenic mothers and the children of depressed mothers than for their control counterparts. Gamer et al (1977) found the children of psychiatrically ill parents to have disturbances in attention, particularly when dealing with complex tasks. Welner et al (1977) found that problems such as depressed mood, death wishes, fighting, psychosomatic concerns, and anhedonia were significantly more common in children with a depressed parent than in the control subjects. They also noted that 11 percent of the children of depressive parents had five or more depressive symptoms, with seven percent meeting the criteria for probable or definite depression, as compared with none of the control group.

However, the results of most studies should be interpreted in the light of their experimental design which largely homes in on the children of schizophrenic rather than depressed parents. Again, the range of diagnostic criteria, methodologies, and stages of development of children in each study makes it difficult to come to a general conclusion about a "specific" pattern of phenomenology of psychopathology of children whose mothers are depressed.

REACTION OF THE CHILD – TO WHAT?

Many of these studies report on mothers admitted to psychiatric facilities. Since children with a depressed parent may be especially vulnerable to separation and loss, an important consideration is whether the depressed parent had a long history of hospitalization or was indeed hospitalized at the time of the study. Clearly it is essential to differentiate childhood reactions to the state of depression in the parent from reactions primarily due to physical separation from the parent and changes in family and social adjustment, all modulated by the child's conscious and unconscious fantasies about the meaning of his mother's absence from home while hospitalized.

In a study of depressed parents admitted to an adult psychiatric service, Welner et al (1977) found that one quarter of parents hospitalized for depression had children with episodes of depression, while none of the children in "well" control groups had episodes of depression. Again, studies of this type suffer the limitation that while they are correlative, the causal links are most unclear. It is not known whether the childrens' depressive symptoms were associated with physical separation from the ill parent, recurrent illness in the ill parent, or some other factor rather than specifically with the parent's depression. As Rutter (1966) and Ekdahl (1962) have shown, children of parents with chronic physical illness are more likely to have neurotic and behavior disorders than children of normal parents. Clarification of this area is indicated.

Thus, it is important to disentangle the effects of physical separation of child from parent because of the parent's hospitalization from the effects of continued and continuing impaction upon the child by depressed parent who is not hospitalized and remains primarily within the family ambience. There is a tendency for depressed parents to be treated on an ambulatory basis, particularly with the advent of antidepressant medication available to general practitioners; thus children of depressed mothers may be experiencing greater exposure to the "depressogenic" effects of life with the depressed mother at home than if she were removed to hospital. For a given family, it is impossible to generalize as to which way the balance of the pendulum swings. Sometimes hospitalization may be in the interests of the developing child; in other instances the relationship between child and parent may mean it is not in the child's best interests.

Traditionally, psychiatric facilities have required that mothers admitted be separated from their children, thus necessitating a substitute caretaker. The last decade has witnessed innovative projects in which children of depressed mothers are admitted with their mothers to psychiatric facilities. It is not suggested that joint admission is the treatment of choice for all depressed mothers and their children. Although a careful assessment of the patient's interpersonal relationships is required before initiation of joint admission, it is difficult to establish which dynamic characteristics of family life and which dimensions of individual personality provide outcome predictors of joint admission, However, when a woman's problems center around an issue of mothering or where they are indeed precipitated by a particular child, joint admission may be specifically indicated. Again, the long-term impact on children admitted to such programs remains to be evaluated.

MATERNAL DEPRESSION AND MOTHERING

Turning to depressed women as mothers, McKnew et al (1979) studied the children aged five to 15 years of 14 consecutive patients admitted to hospital at the National Institute of Mental Health with a diagnosis of bipolar of unipolar primary affective disorder. The parents' diagnosis had been confirmed using the Research Diagnostic Criteria (RDC) modified by Gershon (Spitzer et al, 1977;

Lechman et al, 1977). On entry into the study, the parents were asked to complete a Conners' Parent Questionnaire and Children's Personal Data Inventory from the Children's Early Clinical Drug Evaluation Unit (ECDEU) Battery, 1973. A structured interview was conducted with the children who were seen twice over an interval of four months. Elicted were a history of depressive symptoms, evaluation of self-esteem, fantasy material, and other psychopathology such as anxiety or aggression. McKnew comments that all the children including the youngest, were capable of answering the questions, including those relating to self-esteem.

Of 14 boys, five were depressed at both interviews and three were depressed at one interview. Four of the 16 girls were depressed at both interviews and 11 were depressed at one interview. The clinical picture on the ratings showed the boys, not the girls, to have a significant correlation for depression on both interviews. Children diagnosed as suffering from depression were said to show symptoms of primary unipolar affective disorder without other significant pathology.

The investigators comment that other workers found a lower prevalence of depression of the offspring (Gershon et al, 1971; Zerbin-Rudin, 1971): in other studies the children often were not studied directly and their psychiatric status evaluated on the basis of the history given by the adult proband. The need for direct psychiatric examination of the children is obvious. But even where children are directly examined (Remschmidt et al, 1973), there are problems—a lack of uniformity of diagnostic criteria of childhood depression, a plethora of techiques which are employed (not all of which are validated), and a lack of precision in employing a phase-specific test which is attuned to the developmental tasks and crises of the age group of children being studied. In addition, there is a paucity of clinical studies that directly and specifically examine the dyadic relationship between the depressed mother and her child.

To dismantle the stereotype, not all of these women are "deficient" as mothers, nor are all "deficient" mothers depressed. Thus, an examination of social interpersonal and intrapsychic aspects of the depressed woman as a mother is relevant. While some investigators have commented on the difficulties depressed women have as mothers (Lesse, 1968; Rutter, 1966; Walzer, 1961), only a few have explored the interconnections between depressed women and their children (Deykin et al, 1966; Weissman et al, 1972, 1974; Anthony, 1975).

Weissman et al (1972, 1974), investigating the parental role performance of a group of 35 depressed women and a matched group of 27 normal women, observed that depressed women experience higher degrees of discord with their children than with members of their extended family, friends, neighbors, and work associates. These observations derived from two studies. The first study was a comparison with a matched normal group of a depressed group of women, in which maternal impairments in emotional involvement, guilt, hostility, resentment, and communicating affect were documented. The second study involved clinical investigation of the maternal impairment during the maternal stages in the family life cycle, from postpartum to empty nest. In the first study, highly significant differences in parental role functioning were found between the depressed and the normal women. The average rating of maternal role performance for the normal women was at the unimpaired end of the scales. In contrast, the depressed women felt only moderately involved in their children's daily lives, reported difficult communications, lessened affection, and were having considerable friction with their children.

The depressed women reported moderate degrees of guilt and considerable resentment and ambivalence toward family members. While they worried occasionally about their family, the worry was not significantly different than that reported by the normal women. Normal women did not report guilt or resentment. These trends led to more intensive clinical study of the depressed mothers and their children at different stages of the family life cycle.

In parallel with the concept of normative stages in individual development, stages in the life cycle of the nuclear family have been explored (Fleck, 1968; Lidz, 1968; Nye and Berado, 1966; Parsons and Bales, 1955). Such stages include care of the newborn, nurturance of the infant, enculturation of the young child, emancipation of the adolescent from the family, and termination of childrearing—the empty nest. A similar sequence may be characterized in terms of the tasks of parenthood (Anthony, 1975), involving a sequence of paramutuality. This latter sequence embraces not only the reactions of children but also that of parents to the toddler's drive for individuation, the oedipal child, the transition of the child into and out of latency, and the adolescence. Weissman compared and contrasted the adaptive performance of both the maternal role and the child's role in the normal as against the depressed mother at each successive stage in the family life cycle.

During the infancy stage, the maternal impairment of helplessness, overindulgence or hostility, excessive concern, and inability to separate self from the child were coupled with tyrannical behavior, inability to separate from the mother, vulnerability to subsequent separations, and potential damage to later development in the child.

During enculturation (younger children), the maternal impairment of emotional and physical overinvolvement or underinvolvement, friction, irritability, self-preoccupation, withdrawal, and emotional distance coupled with rivalry with peers and siblings for attention, feelings of isolation and depression, hyperactivity, school problems, enuresis or similar symptoms, and the potential for learning idiosyncratic behavior in the child.

During emancipation (adolescence), the maternal impairment of impaired communication, friction or withdrawal, worry, guilt, envy, and competition were coupled with deviant behavior, rebellion rather than exploration, and withdrawal in the child.

Finally, during termination or the empty nest (child leaves home), the maternal impairment of persisting in maintaining the maternal role, overt or latent friction, and resentment were coupled with rebellion, guilt, and interference with new roles by continued parental conflict in the child.

Weissman (1979) spells out the four areas of parental dysfunctioning in depression as follows. Acute depression impairs parents' ability to be involved in their children's lives. Younger children are deprived of parental involvement in play and physical care. Older children experience parental lack of interest and involvement in school progress, social activities, and friends. Adolescents may exploit the mother's helplessness rather than give her smypathy. Irritability and self-preoccupation prevent mothers from meeting their children's normal demands for attention. Children become less inclined to discuss deeper feelings and problems with the depressed parent, either taking their problems elsewhere or allowing them to build up. Depressed mothers report a lack of affection for their children and resultant feelings of guilt and inadequacy. This is particularly true for mothers of small children and infants who worry about not being able to love their children, or their anxiety about doing psychological or physical harm toward one or more children. This relates to upsurges of hostility which may erupt into episodes of violence toward particular children. But whether the hostility is consummated in a violent act, both mother and child may be painfully aware of what is simmering beneath the surface, expressed here:

> Looking on the lines
> Of my boy's face, methoughts I did recoil
> Twenty-three years, and saw myself unbreech'd.
> In my green velvet coat, my dagger muzzled,
> Lest it should bite its master, and so prove,
> As ornaments oft do, too dangerous.
>
> Shakespeare, W. *Winter's Tale.*
> act I, scene 2, line 153.

In some respects this constellation is similar to that in maltreatment, raising the possibility that the parent who maltreats her infant or toddler may then go on to "abuse" her child through his preschool and school age life through "attacks" of depression. However, no comparative studies in these areas have been reported.

How does the depressed mother arrive developmentally at this point? Albert Solnit so aptly summed up the notion of the "three-generational family" of Anthony and Benedek (1970) with the maxim: "Do unto your children as you would wish them to do unto your grandchildren." To clarify the relationships between childhood and adult depression, reconstructive studies of the childhood of adult depressive patients are illuminating. Often the focus is on the effect of childhood bereavement in the development of adult depression and other psychopathology. A significantly higher incidence of early parental death in the histories of depressed patients is reported (Beck et al, 1963; Birtchnell, 1970; Brown, 1977; Forrest et al, 1965; Gay and Tonge, 1967; Hill and Prince, 1967). Much of this work stemmed from the World Health Organization report of Bowlby (1951), "Maternal Care and Mental Health." The evolution and refinement in thinking about the nature of the separation and loss experience for the child is traced in Bowlby's three major volumes: Attachment; Separation: Anxiety and Anger; and Loss–Sadness and Depression. It is now evident that equally important as actual physical separation are the imaginary or threatened psychic losses which are the everyday experience for the child whose mother is emotionally moribund in a depressive state.

Frommer and Pratt (1971), examined through questionnaire and interview 89 women attending antenatal clinics, and contrasted those who had experienced early parental separation with normal control subjects. Depressive symptoms, marital difficulties, and problems around feeding and mothering were found in mothers who had experienced ealry separation, with symptoms only developing only at the end of the infant's first year. Frommer and Pratt postulate the delay to be due to cumulating exhaustion of the mother.

The influence of a bipolar affective environment on the child, at a psychodynamic level, is reviewed by Anthony (1975). One must correlate what is unfolding within the child and what is simultaneously taking place in his immediate ambience. The child perceives external reality in a way that is not only idiosyncratic to him but also idiomatic in his stage of development. Infantile elements persisting abnormally in the parent are taken up empathetically by the child as he passes through periods of development in which such elements would normally be phase-specific. This could lead to a reinforcement of the elements in the children. Clearly, developmental vulnerability at the time of exposure to a psychotic parent is crucial. In the case of younger children in whom the internal inhibitions against aggression have not been fully developed, there may be a greater acceptance of psychotic violence. The early latency child who is still struggling with defenses against destructiveness may have these reactivated by the external aggressions. On the other hand, the preschool child's animistic fears may be intensified by the objective anxieties to which he is exposed (Anthony, 1971).

The ingredients of affective disorder as manifested in the environment and the child's experience with it form an interplay which may at times involve the affective disorder psychopathology (when the patient is in a state of remission) and at times the affective disorder as a psychosis (when the patient is in a state of relapse).

The main ingredients in the bipolar affective environment are described by Anthony as cycles of omnipotence and impotence, of high and low self-esteem, or surplus and depleted energy, of adequate and defective reality testing, and of optimism and pessimism, and the variations in mood. During the manic phase the mother recreates the urgent environment of a narcissistically hungry infant. In the depressive stage, the family struggles to avoid becoming filled with depression themselves. He describes the child as a captive participant. The parent may need to be pacified, protected, sometimes fed and taken care of, and the children are susceptible to becoming "magic helpers" who wait vainly upon the omnipotent or impotent one as the case may be. The child learns his parent's vulnerability to minimal narcissistic injuries, and he may avoid inflicting any of these. Children may be left with the feeling that all of these objects, including themselves, are being manipulated for the gratification of the parent.

THE UNITY OF THE DEPRESSED MOTHER AND HER CHILD

O Mode and focus of the world;
I hold you deep within that well
you shall escape and not escape –
that mirrors still your sleeping shape;
that nurtures still your crescent all.

I wither and you break from me;
Yet though you dance in living light
I am the earth, I am the root,
I am the stem that fed the fruit,
the link that joins you to the night.

Judith Wright: *Woman to Child*, 1949

How may the permeability of the "skin" between mother and child protect against the child's vulnerability to his mother's depression? Developmentally, the mother together with her small infant involved in a mutual symbiotic union undergo a prolonged process of separation and individuation when the infant begins to "hatch" from the symbiotic tie in the first year of life (Mahler, 1952, 1975). This process can be difficult, particularly for dependent mothers with strong needs to be nurtured, who may have these needs met by involvement in care of a helpless dependent infant, and who are then faced with a motile toddler striving for autonomy. It is well-known clinically that such mothers may cast aside the previously-beloved toddler only to have a new "love affair" with the next pregnancy and infant-to-be. Uncertain developmental perils await the castoff toddler, especially since the mother's strategy in coping with her incipient feeling of depression may be brittle, temporary, and dependent upon the other "halves" of her symbiotic union with her children "cooperating" with her emotional needs.

Benedek (1973), Mahler (1966), and Anthony (1975) describe how with "bad" management, child's regression involves a return to symbiosis. The mother in her turn regresses stirring up the oral-dependent phase of her own development:

> depending on the outcome of the relationship, she will have sufficient or inadequate confidence in her own motherliness to take care of her child's disappointment. Through the process of introjection, a good mother-bad mother; good self-bad self representation is established within the child and becomes the "core of ambivalence." Through identifications with her mother and her child, the mother becomes both the delivering and receiving parts of the symbiosis. In failing to give successfully, she becomes the bad mother of her child and the bad child of her mother; as the frustrated receiver, the infant becomes her bad self as well as her own bad mother. Thus, in this two-way process, the ambivalent core is created in the infant and recreated in the mother. This leads to the establishment of Benedek's (1973) "depressive constellation."

The degree of individuation of child from mother might determine the child's emotional resilience against enmeshment in such a dyad. Perhaps one might discover intergenerational chains of incomplete separation and individuation running through family members who are vulnerable to clinical depression.

VULNERABILITY AND DEFENSE: COPING AND ADAPTATION

In describing the coping situation to the stress of a psychotic parent, Anthony (1976) reiterates that

> a rating on a process-reactive scale and an assessment of the mental health of the non-psychotic spouse proved better indications of the family's predicament; however, in the final appraisal it was the child's-eye-view, of being involved or not involved, supported by a rating of the helpfulness or harmfulness of the so-called well spouse which gave best impressions on the coping situation. An involving psychosis, therefore, came to mean one that incorporated the child into the psychotic system of the parent making him an integral part of the disorganized thinking and feeling of the parent as expressed in delusions, hallucinations, bizarre moods and behavior. . . . In the non-involving psychosis the parent undergoes a kind of psychic death and is largely unavailable to meet any of the child's needs. As far as emotional interchange is concerned, he is a non-person for the child, although a premorbid internal image that may reveal . . . suggesting that the child is keeping alive this otherwise lost parent within himself.

Anthony found the disturbances in the children to be heterogeneous, ranging from apparent normality to gross disorder. He cites Murphy (1970) in her discussion of the difficulty of separting defense and coping mechanisms. Coping has come to include the overcoming of objective anxiety, the mastering of subjective anxiety, and the tolerating of increasing doses of frustration and suffering. As Anthony puts it, "there was an implicit suggestion that whereas defenses must be analyzed, coping had to be taught and learned. The former tended towards stereotypy, whereas the latter could be creative and innovative. The main difference lay between habitual and spontaneous behavior, between the fixed and the flexible, the internally determined and the externally responsive."

The relationship between defense and coping mechansims underwent changes over a period of time, initially resembling one another with external avoidance reflected in internal denial, external intellectual preoccupations in internal isolation, external cancelling behavior in internal undoing. As time went on, coping mechanisms tended to become repetitive and stereotyped and were gradually incorporated into the character defense structure. Anthony notes that it is more difficult for the child than the adult to isolate and insulate an involving psychosis that disorganizes his life. These comments are especially relevant to the depressed mother and her child, since the mix of defenses and coping strategies will be phase-specific to not only the developmental levels and developmental crises of the child but also to the stage in evolution of his mother's depressive experience and the interaction between these two aspects as modulated by the family habitat.

In terms of vulnerability, each child in any sibling relationship will be especially placed. First, no two children will possess the same genetic and constitutional endowment. Thus, each child will be rendered more or less sensitive to a given pathogenic environment. Second, a unique environment will have existed for each child depending upon the concurrent psychosocial factors in his life. Finally, each member of a given sibling relationship will at any given point in time be negotiating a particular age-related developmental task, with its attendant difficulties. Thus a range of vulnerabilities is created for each child.

The evidence seems clear that during the symptomatic episode, the depressed mother is severely impaired in her affective relations with her children. Controlled therapeutic trials indicate that drug treatment and psychotherapy are effective in reducing the symptoms and improving social relationships in instrumental roles. However, they are more subtle impairments of emotional relationships and childrearing long before the clinical declaration of depression which persists after acute symptoms have subsided and after the patient and family may report that everything has returned to normal. It is this "normal" family habitat, which one might term "depressive culture" that merits scrutiny.

Furthermore, it is unclear whether all depressed women are equally impaired at every stage of not only their own life cycle but also that of the family.

But there is the other face of vulnerability. Garmezy (1974, 1978) and Kauffman et al (1979) describe groups of children with mentally ill parents who appeared to be "invulnerable." Anthony (1974) reported that ten percent of children of psychiatrically ill parents showed similar reactions, while Rutter (1978) reported that one in seven had some clear area of "outstanding ability." Kauffman (1979) suggests that these children seem to be a parallel population to the "superphrenic" successful adults found by Karlsson (1968). The difficulty lies in determining the extent of vulnerability in childhood, since in these children, psychopathology is still a *formes fruste*, to declare itself clinically later. Three issues regarding the development of super competent children of depressed parents arise: (1) How do these children manage to become so extremely competent given their depressogenic environment? (2) What are the unique development features of these children? (3) How can this subgroup be identified?

In a follow-up study of children of psychotic mothers, Kauffman et al (1979) examined a subgroup of outstandingly talented competent high risk children and their mothers, compared with a control group. The findings supported Anthony's hypothesis (1974) that invulnerable children of psychiatrically ill mothers had relationships with their mothers that are supportive and empathic but not intrusive. Such warm relationships would be consistent with Rutter's discussion (1978) of factors that reduce the impact of maternal psychiatric illness on the child's development. In the same way as it is observed clinically that mothers may function well in many respects and yet have a specific difficulty around parenting, so mothers who globally may be emotionally constricted may retain the ability to become involved in a warm and supportive relationship with the child. It might be expected that the impact of maternal depression on the developing child would tend toward blanketing of creativity in any case, and it is not surprising that Grunebaum (1977, 1978) and Cohler et al (1978) found a much more profound impact of severe maternal depression than of schizophrenia, with almost all mothers of the highly competent children having histories of schizophrenia rather than depression.

HIGH-RISK PERIODS

The role of stressful life events as precipitants of somatic illness and psychiatric disturbances is the focus of a number of studies (Rahe et al, 1972; Holmes and Rahe, 1967; Masuda and Holmes, 1967; Wyler et al, 1971; Dohrenwend, 1973; Paykel et al, 1969, 1975; Brown, 1977; Bart, 1971; Rabkin and Struening, 1976). On the one hand, life change events have been found not to precede the onset of clinical depression (Smith, 1971; Schless et al, 1974; Hudgens et al, 1967; Morrison et al, 1968). Against this point of view, Paykel et al (1969, 1975) have found a strong relationship between the onset of depression in mothers and life events in their families.

While Holmes and Rahe (1967) focused on the magnitude of the life change, Paykel (1975) examined the interpretation of events. The distinction is made between exit and entrance events, and an evaluative dimension is introduced—the desirability or vulnerability of an event. Events perceived as undesirable, and those involving exits or losses, distinguished the depressive from the control subjects (Paykel et al, 1969; Leff et al, 1970; Paykel and Uhlenhuth, 1972). Certainly, perception of desirability will be influenced by the depressed mother's weltenschaung.

There is little reported on the relationship between life events and psychiatric morbidity in childhood (Coddington, 1972), and there are no reports of the relationships between the life spaces of mothers and children. In his study of life events in childhood, Coddington (1972) surveyed 3,500 healthy children and devised a series of age-approrpiate life change scales. His investigation resulted in the construction of an age-related curve analogous to a growth curve. This curve is of interest. As a child expands his sphere of contact with the outer world, he risks the occurrence of more positive and negative life events, and the extent of adaptation increases. The first such increase is seen at age six to seven years ofentry into school, but the major jump occurs at age 12 to 14 years, coinciding with the onset of adolescence and the tasks of the second individuation (Blos, 1962). It is at precisely these times that upsurges in childhood depression have been reported. Perhaps there may be a fundamental link, but these correlations have not been explored.

A caveat is necessary here. The etiological relevance of comparison of high risk data is complex and theoretically difficult. Comparison of groups at high risk for pathology before the development of disturbances in the children cannot provide evidence that a given factor or characteristic of the groups contributes to the etiology of depression which may develop in children. For the data to become etiologically relevant, they must be studied as possible antecedents to disturbances identified by following the subjects. On the other hand, comparisons of high risk versus low risk groups are most appropriately interpreted as reflecting the characteristics, correlates, consequences (or some combination of these), and significance of the risk criterion.

THE DEPRESSED MOTHER AND HER CHILD: AN APPROACH TO MEASURING THE DYAD

A pilot study was carried out to draw together the methodologic, conceptual, and clinical strands described in this chapter. It was intended that the specific focus to be the mother-child dyad, with attention also to family functioning in general. Mothers admitted to a general hospital psychiatric unit with a clinical diagnosis of depression were considered, with the inclusion criteria that the depression was of such severity as to preclude management in an outpatient setting, that the admission Hamilton Rating Scale (Hamilton, 1960) score was 17, and that there was at least one child aged between three and 15 years, in a structurally intact family. Over six months, 12 mothers and 20 children were obtained. Although only a proportion of mothers was given a formal diagnosis of depressive illness, these were but a subset of a larger group with difficulties in mothering, associated with what Hill (1968) termed the depressive experience. Since the focus of study is the developmental transaction between mother and child, it seemed relevant to consider the broader group of mothers, who by virtue of their depressive core may have experienced similar difficulties, instead of mothers with formal depressive illness.

Despite attempts to differentiate the research interviews from parallel clinical management (of which the investigator was not a part), in most cases the mothers were highly relieved to be invited to discuss their mothering difficulties. They perceived difficulties in the prodrome, the admission in some instances being blamed on one particular child and then dealt with by self-recriminatory guilt at being responsible for the child's state.

Fathers when approached were willing to help with their wives "illness," but in several instances wished to keep the children out of any discussion, as if to isolate any possible connection between state of mother and child, and protect, at least in their own minds, the child from the depressed mother. Over an average two- or three-week admission, children of depressed mothers were brought to visit about twice weekly. Apart from weekend leave toward the latter stages of their admissions, no other direct contact existed between mother and child. When they were brought to visit their mothers, children seemed confused, anxious and overactive, or perhaps withdrawn. There was an air of discomfort and unease which seemed greater for the children of depressed mothers on the ward than for others. In some cases the mothers were withdrawn and uninterested, or otherwise had inappropriate responses to meeting their children.

An observer-rated scale which could be used in observation of mother or child was to be constructed. Clearly, symptoms mean different things at different developmental stages, and the meaning of symptoms and constructs to the external observer depends upon whether it is the mother or child being observed. Despite these difficulties, the potential advantages of a single scale which could be used to assess each member of the dyad were considered so significant that the enterprise was followed.

Attention was paid to the reactions of children to their mother's depression, perception of the mother's illness by both mother and children, caretaking and surrogation available for the children, a global measure of mothering, aspects of the mother-child interaction, and phenomenology, which would include depressive equivalents and disorders in regulatory balancee. These idiosyncratic roles and reactions of children to maternal depression were rated. Each role was operationally defined as follows: "patient" as acting like or developing symptoms like mother, "caretaker" as looking after others in family, "baby" as clinging, demanding, or regressed, "mourner" as grieving over the mother and her experience, "good child" as well-behaved and avoiding controversy, "bad child" as angry and uncooperative, and "escapee" as opting out of family involvement.

Perceptions of mother's illness was rated along five dimensions: (1) the extent to which mother and child saw the maternal depression as "a medical illness"; (2) the tendency to internalize or externalize blame for maternal illness; (3) the tendency to see depression in magical terms (this was included as a separate item from the first because severely depressed mothers and children, while apparently rationally comprehending the experience as "a medical illness," actually viewed it on quite magical and primitive levels); (4) the expectation of outcome assessed along the dimensions "self-limited, with eventual recovery" to "might go on forever–might die or go away or never get better; and (5) the feeling that the mother was losing control.

Also considered were the potentially mitigating or destructive effect of family interaction upon the child's capacity to deal with his mother's depression. The role of the father with the child was rated along the dimensions helpful-harmful, avoiding-engaging/approaching, and supportive-unsupportive. Contact between mother and father and between mother and children were each rated in terms of physical adequacy, emotional adequacy, and helpfulness-harmfulness. These dimensions were modified from the approach taken by Anthony (1975) in the St. Louis study of psychotic parents and their children.

It was difficult to operationally define the construct "mothering." Definition embracing the mother's perception of her child, her understanding of her child, and her response to her child was used. The quality of mothering was rated as appropriate-inappropriate.

Mother-child interaction was measured along nine dimensions. The degree of empathy together with the extent to which communication with the other member of the dyad was initiated or shut off were truncated into a single dimension. Again following Anthony (1975), an "actively engaging-actively avoiding" dimension was included in the dyadic scale to assess the extent of mirroring of mutual engagement and avoidance by mother and child. Following Weissman et al (1974), the extent of warmth-coldness, friction, ambivalence, anxiety, and resentment and hostility between mother and child were assessed. From the pilot work it was evident that mothers who experience difficulties with or concern about a particular child were often inclined to powerful identification with those children. Thus, a measure of identification was included, operationally defined as "seeing self as resembling other in dyad." Finally, a related dimension of "wishing to be like other in dyad" was included.

Phenomenologic parameters included four behavioral measures: speech (increased-mute), thought (pressure-poverty), memory and attention (intact-grossly impaired), and insight and judgment (intact-grossly impaired). These were included for two reasons. First, these parameters are part of the phenomenology of the depressed mother and her child. Second, if independent raters are using the scale reliably and validly, there should be evidence by consensus on relatively "molecular" parameters such as these, and where consensus is not achieved on these parameters then doubts would be cast upon the reliability and validity of the entire instrument. Thus, inclusion of thee four items serves as a built-in checking system.

While attention has been paid to the presence of "depressive equivalents" (Malmquist, 1971) in children, attempts to "match" equivalents between child and parent have not been described. Since it is possible that depressive-equivalents may be another facet of the symbiotic interlocking and parallel tracking between the depressed mother and child, they were included in the scale. With truncation, the parameters were: (1) loss of capacity to feel pleasure, sadness at the verbal behavioral or fantasy level, listlessness; (2) low frustration tolerance and irritability; (3) a conveyed sense of loss; (4) reversal of affect together with clowning, foolishness, buffoonery; (5) a tendency to passivity and expecting others to anticipate needs; (6) sensitivity; (7) high standards with readiness for self-condemnation for failures, guilt, self-punitive behavior; (8) shame; (9) obsessive behavior; (1) acting out behavior; (11) motor activity; (12) self-esteem.

From the postulate that in depression there is a fundamental disorder of regulatory balance of ego functions, these dimensions are also included. Following a similar line of reasoning to that mentioned earlier, it seemed relevant to determine whether these regulatory imbalances in the mother could be reflected or indeed measured in her child. Four functions were included in the final scale: hedonic capacity (can feel pleasure—cannot feel pleasure), self-confidence (feeling of power—feeling of helplessness), hopefulness (feeling of optimism—feeling of pessimism), and psychic input and output (feeling of fullness—feeling of emptiness).

Items were presented and rated on a 10 cm Visual Analog Scale, as described by Aitken (1970).

EXTERNAL VALIDATION OF THE DEPRESSED MOTHER-CHILD SCALE

The procedure for external validation was as follows. Mothers were interviewed as soon as practical after admission. Children and then the family were interviewed thereafter. Each of these interview segments was of 60 minutes duration. It was evident that the scope of material elicited in each of the three settings was complementary; each context on its own provided but an incomplete fragment of the picture. The sequence was repeated for each family approximately two months later, after discharge from hospital.

The interview room was arranged in a standardized form, subjects facing a remote-controlled motorized video camera unit. The children were invited to sit at a small table, on which there was a box containing a standardized set of play equipment appropriate to a range of developmental levels.

Invariably, themes relating to the illness and hospitalization of the mother spontaneously developed.

Various approaches to structuring the interview were attempted. Use of the Lynn Structured Doll Play Test was ruled out as too age-specific in its application. A series of miniature projective test items were found to be of some use, for example, "this child is hungry—what has happened?" "This child had a dream—what did he dream?" An attempt was made to mirror these inquiries for each mother and her child. A useful projective test was the Bellak Children's Apperception Test Supplement (CAT-S) (Bellak, 1976), the purpose of which is to elicit specific themes. One or more of the cards is presented as a storytelling game. This was particularly useful in a group situation with two members of a sibling relationship each responding to a card.

Many of these points are illustrated in the following excerpts from two interviews: Mr. and Mrs. S. and their children, 11-year-old Mike, and 9-year-old Sue. Mrs. S. had presented with suicidal ideation, and it was her first hospital admission.

Interview I: Mother's Admission

Mother Alone

Mrs. S.: . . . I have been worried about how this would affect the children—they are not stupid, and have worked out that something has not been right for some time, particularly Mike. He and I seem to be on the same wavelength. . . . It's unfair to them, as he is starting his nightmares again and sleepwalking, fingernail biting, and habits he gets when something is bothering him. Its easy to pick up when he is worried, that prompted me to do something about it (that is, seek admission to hospital). Sue is harder to work out . . . The first day of the holidays. They had done something—typical kids's stuff like mucking about and spilled milk on the lunch table. . . . I went off the deep end and layed into them, which is something I never do. That scared me . . . If I am going to do that I could end up going further in the long-term. When I was hitting them I lost control and I knew I was hurting them but I was so wound up that it was hard to stop.

The interviewer commented that Mrs. S. seemed to paint Mike and Sue very differently.

Mrs. S.: Yes completely different. Sue thinks life is just a big giggle. Mike would sit there and worry it would drive him crazy. He resembles me in a lot of ways . . . I can see a lot in him that I know is in me. He is very reticent about entering a room full of people he doesn't know, as I am. He is conscientious about things he has to do, like making his bed, it is always made properly whereas Sue just pulls the top covers up–it doesn't matter what is underneath. He is more serious than Sue is . . . as I am. He feels for people, not only me, but other people, he can pick when they are sad or cranky or cross and say things like "don't be cross about such and such, it will be alright." I know Sue is smaller but she always goes in feet first when people are cranky and you know it's not very pleasant really. Mike can feel these situations and if people are cross, he steers away from them. I find it hard to put my arms around the kids or even Jim sometimes to show them that I care and that upsets me 'cause I know I should. I don't do it as often as I should and that is a bit cruel (slumps and avoids eye contact). They all need a bit of love, even Jim does; I don't think he gets much from me–not as much as he should.

Children Alone

Mike: Mum's been here a week and a day.

Sue: We can't quite stand it without her.

Dr.: Why did Mum come to hospital?

Mike: Depression . . . she was a bit sad about things.

Sue: A bit tired.

Mike: She can't got to sleep at night and she is tired, and tired.

Dr.: What does it mean to be sad all the time?

Mike: There is something upsetting you and nothing can be done about it . . .

Dr.: I wonder what that something is?

Sue: When we have arguments . . . (pause) probably not.

Mike: She doesn't mind those really. (pause) We don't know.

Dr.: Do you know when she is worried. Can you tell when she is worried?

Sue: She has this necklace that I gave her for Mother's Day and . . .

Mike: (Interrupting) it changes colors. It is grayish and dullish when she is sad and gay colors when she is happy.

Dr.: You can tell by that . . .

Mike: In the middle it is purple, always purple in the middle for both feelings.

Sue: You feel worried when she hasn't got the stone on, we think she is happy and also think she is sad.

Mike: We don't know–she has a mask on her face and her mouth is a straight line. We can't do anything then.

Sue: We just keep out of her way.

Mike: I would like to talk with her and take her home . . . and keep her home.

Dr.: What would happen?

Sue: She wouldn't get better.

Mike: We want her to stay in hospital until she gets better . . .

The children each selected a card from the CAT Supplement. Sue selected Card 1 (4 mice children on a slide), Mike selected Card 5 (a kangaroo on crutches with a bandaged tail and foot).

Sue: We went on to the park . . . have a ride on the slides and swings. There's the mother, father, girl, and boy. She sat on the swing, fell and hurt her leg. They took her home and fixed up her leg. Then they went over to their Nan's house . . . They needed two bandages. They set them on her leg the way they usually do. Then they had a drink and went to their Nan's.

Mike then gave his story.

Mike: It has a name–how the kangaroo got such a hard tail. Once there was a kangaroo who went around boasting about his lovely soft tail. One day he fell asleep and a buffalo ran over it. "Good grief, look at my tail!" And he quickly bandaged it up, but unfortunately a few of the hairs came off, and they were coarse and hard and they rubbed against it. When he took it off he had nothing but a hard tail. It ended up not so well. The kangaroo felt awful.

The interviewer returned to their difficulties in "helping" mother.

Sue: I hope she gets better in a week . . . or less.

Mike: Find out what is wrong with her and how long she has to stay in the hospital. It could be a year at the least . . . if the circumstances get worse. They might have to put more research into her.

Family

The family interview followed. Neither child had seen their mother since her admission.

Mrs. S.: Hello! (Sue runs to her arms outstretched, gets a hug) How are you? How are you big boy! It has been a long time since I've seen you hasn't it? Been busy have you? Well how have you been doing? Well aren't you going to tell me anything?

Mike: I saw the "Cat from Outer Space."

Mrs. S.: Was it any good? He was a special cat wasn't he?

Mike: He has this collar on, and he used magic power, it was like five minds in one, this collar. It glowed and glowed and he could do anything.

Mrs. S.: Did you make a space ship?

Mike: Yeah. About this big.

Mrs. S.: Did it do anything? Did it have a motor in it . . .

Mike: It worked on friction and when you pushed it along the ground it whirred and it had a propeller and it went off the ground a little bit–about that much.

The family chatted about the past week's events.

Mrs. S.: It has been a long time. I have never been separated from them not even overnight . . . I think it has done everybody a bit of good.

Jim: That's right.

Mike: How long are you staying?

Mrs. S.: Oh, a bit longer.

Mike: (Insisting) How long?

Mrs. S.: (To herself) Well what have I been doing in the hospital.

Mike: Been playing sport . . . getting fit?

Mrs. S.: In a fashion yes.

Mike: I've been worried about you.

Sue: Me too!

Mrs. S.: Why have you been worried? What have you been thinking about?

Sue: I have the feeling that you won't come back.

Mrs. S.: Oh, I'll come back. You can't get rid of me.

Jim: Mike has had a lot of questions. When is mum coming home? How is Mum? Give her my love! Give her my regards! Its not the same is it?

Mike: That isn't enough. I have to see her.

Mrs. S.: The voice isn't the same. You have to touch me, don't you?

Sue: I'd forgotten how you look.

Mrs. S.: Had you? There's a photo somewhere.

Mike: You should have a picture of yourself. I have this picture frame and I could put it up and then I would know what you looked like.

Mrs. S.: Its not so much what you can do but what I can do, I suppose. Its more what I can do for you.

Interview II: Two-Month Follow-Up (One Month After Discharge)

Mother Alone

Mrs. S.: (Instantly obvious was an enormous weight gain) It's good to be home. I am disappointed that I haven't learned to handle myself better or come up with a solution to the whole thing. Particularly the eating caper. I can't concentrate.

If the children catch me when I am busy and ask for something or tell me they have to have something for school tomorrow, I don't seem to be able to handle more than one thing at a time. I can't organize myself to be able to cope. But I feel the kids understand a bit better. They are sensitive to moods and have been a big help, more considerate to Jim and to each other than they were before. I thought at one time it was his fault but I was looking for something to blame. Looking back I don't think there was a problem other than [of] my own making. I find people are understanding. I thought they mightn't be. I have always thought of this type of thing as a personality defect that you should be able to overcome. You know it's there so you should be able to handle it. People have really been terrific, except my mother! . . .

The kids . . . are happy to have me home. They have also realized what a lot Mum did that they didn't know about. We are thankful for each other a lot more. I realize now what a good backup your family can *be* if you let them. Looking back, I got too terribly engrossed with myself which is a selfish thing. I did very little for everyone else. For the kids I produced meals but that's as far as it went, there was no emotional backup. I can't say that it would never happen again.

Sue is a lot better, she sort of realizes, I mean life for her is a big giggle but she really has grown up a bit. She has realized that life is not all froth and bubble . . . that some things are sad and some things are serious . . . And, it sounds silly to say this, but adults are people as well as parents! She surprised me because I thought it wouldn't matter to Sue as long as she was fed and watered, put to bed, and had her pocket money. But it did, whether she is a deep person I don't know, I haven't a clue. I have to remember too that she is only eight years old after all.

Mike. He is throwing around a lot more hugs and touches and things than he did before, which is something I fully expected from Mike. We have had a few nightmares but not as badly as I thought he would.

Two kids is harder in a lot of respects than three, four, or five. He does need a lot more touching and closeness that way, a lot more than Sue does. Really he wants it–you can see by the way he comes and hedges around, puts a hand on the chair rather than you and looks at you then looks away and you can really tell that he wants an arm around him but he wouldn't admit it. Well, sometimes he does but not much.

The interviewer asked whether the family had talked together very much.

Mrs. S.: I don't suppose . . . I mean we have talked about me coming home, what I did here but not actually what happened. I have always been one for answering questions when they are there. I hope that if the kids want to talk about it they will say so. I suppose I could have knocked their questions back before I came into hospital. If it is bothering them it is probably why they are not talking about it now.

Children Alone

Mike: Once Mum got home we've been making things easier for her and helping her. We don't let her do the jobs she used to do and things like that.

Sue: Unless she wants to.

Mike: Unless she insists on it. We felt as if we were one big person, and felt something was missing.

The interviewer wondered why their mother had gone to hospital.

Sue: Because she was doing too much work probably.

Mike: And she was too tired and she wouldn't go to bed early. Like now she will go to bed before I do or Sue does sometimes.

Sue: She had a lot of worries at that time.

Mike: We don't know what they were.

Sue: She wouldn't spread them around the family.

Mike: She wouldn't let us take on part of the problems.

Mike: We knew because she moped around. And I asked her a few times "what's wrong?" and she said "nothing" . . .

Sue: When mum was in hospital, Nan was looking after us.

Mike: She still needs to be there. She is part of the family. We sent a note to her once asking her to be part of our family.

Sue: She still hasn't answered the note.

Mike: And mum's a great believer in God 'cause she said "if Skylab's going to hit me let it hit me. It's the way I am going to die."

Sue: We didn't believe that, though.

Mike: At night, we were waiting for it to land.

Mike: We knew it had landed. We felt safe 'cause no one was hurt. It had been worrying. They didn't have any control over it. It could go anywhere.

The interviewer reflected mother's earlier comment.

Mike: Let it. She won't run . . . we would probably do the same.

Sue: Mmm. If we were all in a group and it fell on us we wouldn't worry because we would be together up in heaven anyway. In a year . . . or a month there is going to be another spacecraft that will be falling.

Mike: That's Russian, and they have a lot of control. They'll make it fall in Russia.

Sue: I hope it's when relatives are having a party, and that would be better than just one person out of a family dying.

The interviewer referred to the earlier session in which the expectation of their mother's recovery was uncertain.

Mike: We felt as if we had lost something in the family.

Sue: Like we had lost something and we kept going back to find it and it wasn't there. Like you lost the families . . . There are special jewels of a family if you lost that you would keep going back to find it.

Dr.: Something precious.

Sue: Mom is precious.

The children were invited to each select a CAT-S card. Sue chose Card 2 (classroom situation with three little monkeys sitting at typical school desks). Mike did not choose a card.

Sue: One day, three monkeys were having their daily lesson, and one of them stood up and read a paragraph about how the bear lost his tail. The bear asked fox how he broke the rope and then he went out into the bush, and wished that he had some rope in the bush. And so the bear did that. And instead, from behind the bush there was a rustling of leaves, and fox jumped out and caught the bear and hung him by his tail. There was a fire underneath. The bear was very cheeky, and the bear's tail fell off and he fell into the fire. You should have seen what the funeral was like because hardly any one was there! Because the bear was so cheeky and nobody would like to go to his funeral.

Then Mike narrated a story without a card stimulus.

Mike: One day my friend and I were camping in a deserted ghost town. The next minute we were hopping into our sleeping bags and there was a sudden bright flash and a smell of burning smoke. And we ran out to look what was there, and before we got there we grabbed our rifles and ran to the door. A flash set alight the shack we were sleeping in, and we went out and ran for all we were worth until we bumped into something. It was a huge thing from outer-space. It picked us up and threw us into the back of his oval-shaped space ship. He rammed us in and locked the door. Then he grabbed our rifles and snapped them as if they were twigs. He took off with us held captive and when we got too high, the air was too thin, and we thought we were going to die of suffocation. Until the creature slapped oxygen masks on us. And then the oxygen was running out, and we found out that the creature was going to drop an atom bomb that would blow up the world. We fell down, holding each other, and our feet got caught in the main wire. We pulled it out and we sent the space ship crashing back to earth. We had just saved the earth.

Sue: Did you get a reward?

Mike: No we didn't.

Sue: Then really it wasn't worth doing . . . If it had gone somewhere like in the ocean it would have stopped it from blowing the whole world up.

Mike: You only want rewards for things like that Sue.

Sue: No. That's not what I mean.

(long pause)

Mike: What did you mean Sue?

Sue: I really can't explain. It's too hard . . . You know how most bombs if they land in water don't blow up—if it had landed in the ocean it wouldn't have blown up the world. That's what I mean.

Mike: It would make it more dangerous 'cause when it was opened it would go off. The creature died when he hit the earth because of the shock, though we survived because we had fallen on a mattress. When the ship hit the earth there was an earthquake and it only shook up the earth a bit. And now the creature is in a museum.

Sue: I think it went all right. The bear was always annoying the fox and I think he deserved to lose his tail. He looked more sensible anyway because bears don't usually have tails. If you went to his funeral it wouldn't be a nice funeral because all the musicians had been ordered . . . and they didn't want to play music at the annoying bear's funeral. And besides if they did come they wouldn't have played the music like they do at everyone else's funeral. They would have played but not nicely—they would have been making quite a few mistakes because they would have been thinking about how the bear and how the fox felt.

Family

Mike: How do you feel now you are home? A lot more settled? I'm glad you go to bed earlier!

Mrs. S.: It's good to be home.

Mike: I think your main problem was you didn't go to bed early enough.

Sue: I don't like it when you are too tired.

Mrs. S.: You reckon I am better for more sleep do you?

Mike: A lot better.

Sue: So do I.

Mrs. S.: Good.

Mike: We were just telling Dr. E. that when you were out of the family, when you were in hospital, we felt as if we were one person and we felt something was missing.

Mrs. S.: Did you? I felt as though a lot of me was missing too.

Sue: Yes, you would too.

Mike: (Suddenly) Why is Nan selling her house?

Mrs. S.: You would like Nan to live with us would you?

Mike: Yes.

Mrs. S.: Nan wants to live by herself for as long as she can! She has her own life! She would visit us every second minute I should imagine! But she doesn't want us to get too fed up with her!

Sue: We wouldn't!

Mrs. S.: Even though we know we wouldn't, she would like to be a little independent while she is healthy and while she can do things for herself.

Mike: I want her to be with us.

Sue: All the time.

Mrs. S.: After all this time in hospital Nan (my mum) came around and said we had been spending too much time together, because I had come to treat her as a friend, which is good, but we were seeing a lot of each other. She said "I was beginning to rely on you too much." I do think we were a bit too close.

Mike: Mom and Dad use this awful language . . . they keep secrets by saying "sasay non tata" or something like that.

Jim: (Laughs)

Mrs. S.: Since they have been to school, we have this language my father used, called Tottenham. They try to figure it out.

Sue: We worked out one word once . . .

Mike: It always means something that we can't have, I know that much!

Mrs. S.: Something that we don't want to mention now because you'll give us no peace until you get it.

Mike: . . . we have asked and asked, we have insisted and mum just says, "I'll tell you when you have your own children."

Mrs. S.: We are entitled to a few little secrets. Like you have things you won't tell us.

Mike: But you insist on hearing them!

Sue: Why don't we make up our own secret alphabet? . . .

Mrs. S.: Is that all you wanted to ask about?

Sue: No. We wanted to know what was worrying you before you went into hospital.

Mrs. S.: It wan't one particular thing. There were a few things . . . One was that I didn't think I was being good enough to you kids or dad.

Sue: You were!

Mrs. S.: Yes, but I thought I could do better. Just like your schoolwork, sometimes you think you could do better; and it made me tired and cranky and cross.

Mike: You were too good! We were worried when you were in hospital.

Mrs. S.: That shows you care. You're not worried now are you?

Mike: No, because you are out.

Mrs. S.: Would you worry if I went back in again?

Mike and Sue: Yes.

Mrs. S.: Mom's a funny person–she worried about things that other people don't worry about, and she gets all tied up . . .

Mike: But we understand.

Mrs. S.: Do we?

Sue: Mmmmm.

Mrs. S.: Good.

Jim: (to the children) Is that all you wanted to ask about?

Mike: Mom's taking pills that make her put on weight.

Mrs. S.: It's not exactly like that . . . Mom's eating and putting on weight!

Mike: She can't stop herself.

Sue: . . . and every time she loses a certain amount of weight . . . we get a chocolate bar . . . we get three chocolate bars and then an ice cream cake and then there is a party.

Jim: Mom's weight is one of the main things that has been worrying her.

Mike: Why do you eat Mum?

Mrs. S.: (angrily) Why do you eat?

Sue: Mom eats for the same reason I do. Mom eats because she is hungry.

Mike: (insisting) But why do you eat mum?

Mrs. S.: You can eat out of habit, or out of hunger, or because you like sweet things even though you know they are the wrong things, or you can eat because you are so fed up of having to think about not eating!

Mike: Which you do.

Here is a vivid account of each child's reactions to maternal prodromal depression, the ensuing hospitalization, and the phase of re-integration into the family. The power of mutual identification between Mrs. S. and Mike is evident as are the children's vigorous attempts to make sense of their mother's depression. Themes of death and the importance of the mother-child union and its maintenance were very evident.

With a total of 12 hours of video segments per family, the problem was to selectively reduce the material for rating by independent observers. An initial approach was by random time reduction. However, the continuity of the interview was disjointed. Instead, the original tapes were edited by the investigator selecting highlights of the relevant themes.

One of the limitations of the interviews was a tendency to focus on content. Unless care is taken, this could consolidate symptoms of depression. Another difficulty is that an "imaginary" picture of the child or mother is conjured up on the videotape recording. The task is then to match this image to the real child or mother. Of concern was the impact of video recording and studio environment upon a depressed and often ashamed mother. Interviews were held at an adult facility. The response-set of children being interviewed in an adult setting is different than what it would have been in a pediatric facility, and the impact of this bias has not been clarified. Also, it has been assumed that the second series of interviews demonstrates changes of mother and her family with presumed improvement in the clinical state of the mother. However, such a fleeting comparison is bound to be insensitive to significant areas of change in the mother-child dyad. An edited segment of a complete "before-and-after" series of interviews was prepared for external validation. Six fifth-year medical students were selected as presumptively "naive" raters. The first version of the interview rating scale was explained to them, but no elaboration was given of the operational definitions printed on the proforma. They viewed the first half of the video segment without comment or interruption. On the next day the process was repeated with the second half of the video segment.

The raters found it easy to complete all "quantitative" visual analog sections of the proforma, with greater difficulty in completing the "qualitative" comments and considerable range in some inter-rater consensus. There was a slight and statistically insignificant increase in inter-rater reliability from the first to the second day, consistent with some practicing effect.

A revised form was prepared. Modifications were as follows: ambiguous operational definitions were given qualifying phrases, and qualitative items were covered to visual analog form, by providing possible response sets in a forced-choice rather than free-choice situation. All items including those with low inter-rater reliability were retained. The intention was to see whether the low inter-rater reliability score obtained for certain items was due to: (1) ambiguity in the operational definitions, (2) inadequate preparation and training of raters, (3) excessive naiveté of the rater group, (4) inherent difficulty in gaining consensus on certain concepts regardless of format or preparation.

Edited video vignettes of the test family were then shown to three "expert" consultant child psychiatrist raters. On the basis of their scores and free comments, a further pilot scale was devised through further revision of operational definitions, separation of some previously bipolar items into unipolar items, and further randomization to reduce halo effects. A different edited video vignette of the test family was shown to a total of nine "expert" consultant child psychiatrist and child psychologist raters of diverse training and clinical and theoretical background. The original panel comprised ten experts, but one was deleted (Number 8) at her instigation. On a basis of these test scores and free comments, a statistical procedure for external validation was employed. The procedure for external validation was employed. The procedure is summarized in Fig. 1.

Before individual item analysis the extent of overall consensus by the ten "expert" raters was established. There were 82 parameters in the pilot scale completed by the "expert" raters, each parameter measured to a maximum of four occasions (for example, mother-child 1, mother-child 2, child 1-mother,

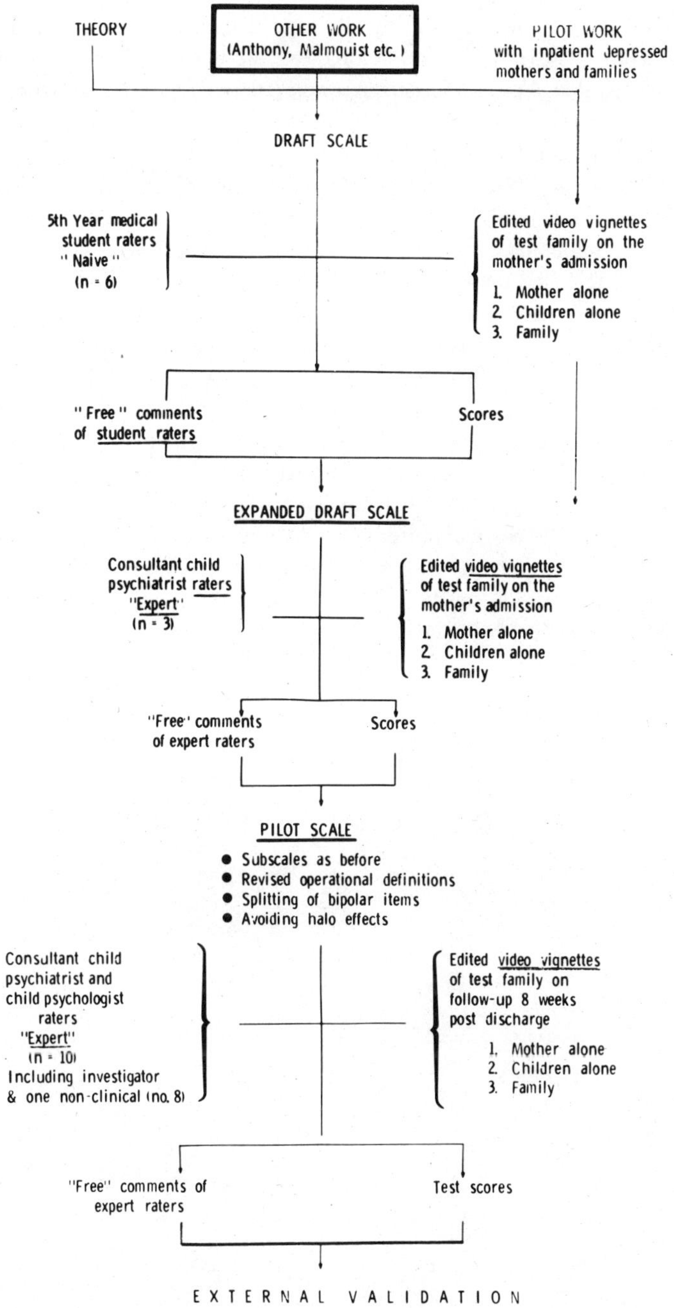

Fig. 1. Procedure for External Validation of Depressed Mother-Child Scale

child 2-mother). Thus the total of 189 sets of items had been scored by the ten expert raters. These items were collapsed, and an overall correlation matrix calculated (Table 1). A conservative nonparametric statistic, Kendall's Tau is 0.40 for approximately half the correlations, $p < 0.01$ for all correlations. Thus overall consensus was established.

It is apparent from the correlation matrix that the highest correlations were obtained between raters 10 and 7 and the other raters. Rater 10 is the investigator with the benefit of being the test constructor and also of continued clinical contact with the test family. Rater 7 was the most clinically experienced member of the expert group of raters. The greatest degree of consensus is expected to be between each expert rater and the investigator if overall face validity of the test has been achieved. This is the case, and an example is illustraded in Fig. 2.

The degree of consensus is represented by and inversely proportional to the magnitude of the coefficient of variation (standard deviation/mean). Ranking the 189 original items in this way does not differentiate apparent lack of consensus for a particular item due to low reliability or validity from, say, difficulty in measurement of that item in mother or in child due to developmental difference. Difficulties in consensus on items measuring regulatory balance (discussed below) clearly illustrates this point.

Table 1 Correlation Matrix of "Expert" Raters*

	Rater No.									
	1	2	3	4	5	6	7	8	9	10
1	1	.41	.32	.40	.34	.23	.47	.18	.41	.63
2		1	.37	.34	.49	.25	.40	.19	.34	.54
3			1	.31	.32	.34	.38	.29	.27	.46
4				1	.30	.26	.36	.21	.35	.50
5					1	.27	.33	.24	.39	.43
6						1	.25	.27	.23	.33
7							1	.26	.32	.61
8								1	.20	.30
9									1	.41
10										1

*Kendall's tau corrections, n = 189; for all corrections, $p < 0.01$.

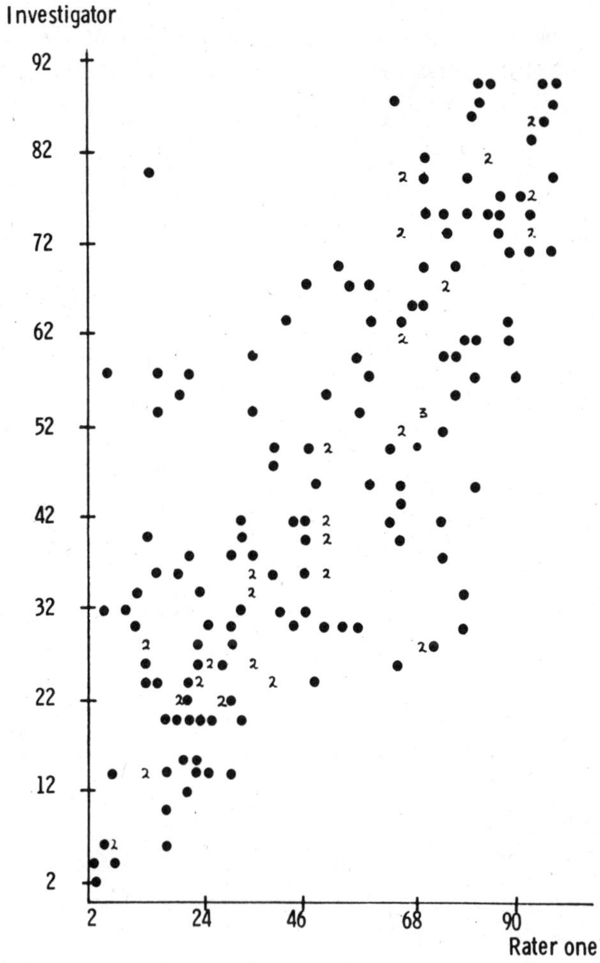

Fig. 2. Face Validity of Scale Overall
Scattergram of Scale Ratings: Investigator Against "Expert" Observer 1

To establish consensus for each parameter independently of either differences between each family member per se or developmental differences, residual variance derived from two-way analysis of variance was chosen as representing the error in ranking each parameter. The assumption that consensus is not affected by heterogeneity of family members for each parameter was tested by confirming a lack of correlation between family heterogeneity for each parameter (represented by the between-column variance on the two-way analysis of variance) *with* consensus for each parameter (represented by residual variance).

It can be seen from examination of each set of raw data that there is no correlation, and thus heterogeneity is not a significant source of bias. This is illustrated in the scattergram (Fig. 3).

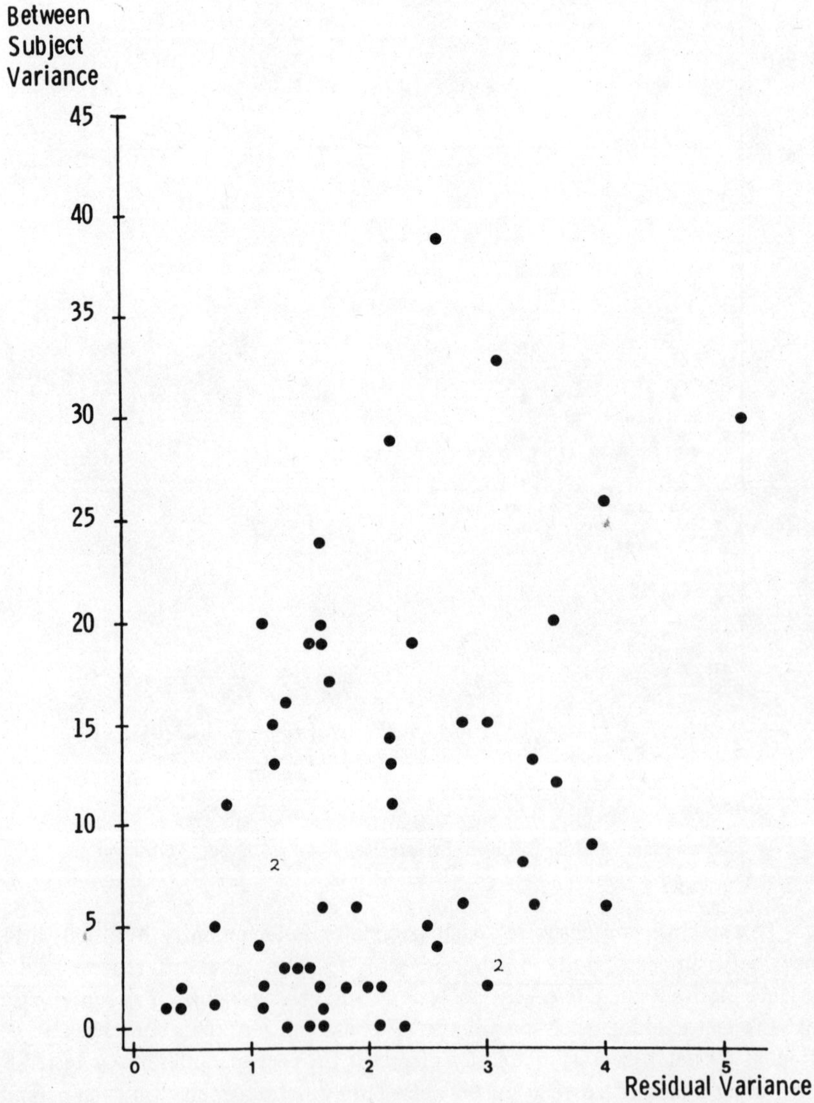

Fig. 3. Scattergram of Between-Subject Variances Against Residual Variances

Finally, for each subgroup (reactions, perceptions, and so forth), the correlation matrix was then weighted and a varimax-rotated factor matrix after rotation with Kaiser Normalization was derived. The procedure for item inclusion is represented by Fig. 4.

For each parameter, if the residual variance was found to be low (that is, consensus achieved across the parameter), the item was included. Where residual variance was high (that is, low consensus) the parameter was factor analyzed, and where found to form part of the factor, was included by trunction into that factor. Where on the other hand, the parameter with high residual variance did not form part of a factor, the coefficients of variation for that parameter were examined to establish whether there were major discrepancies between

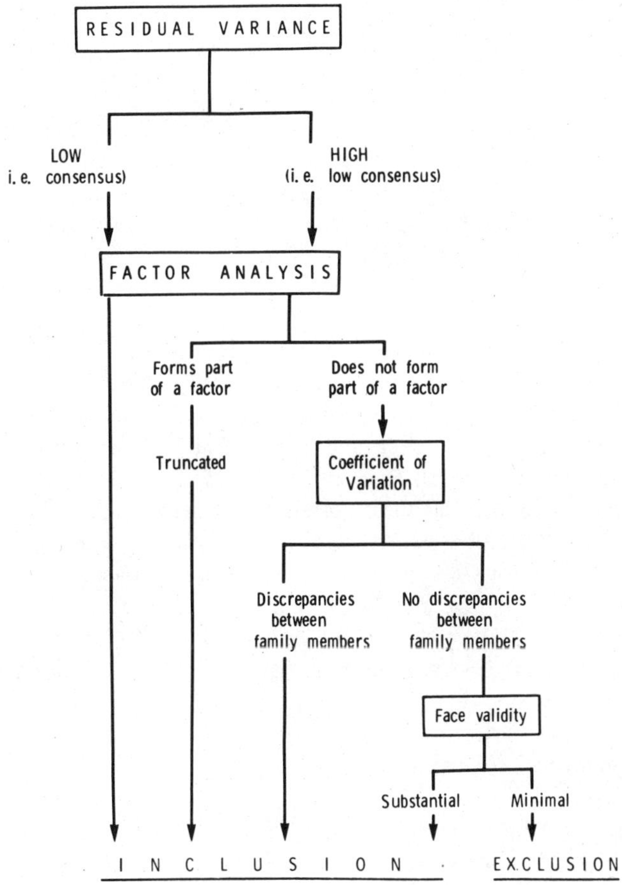

Fig. 4. Procedure for Item Inclusion

family members. Where it seemed that the discrepancies were responsible for low consensus or residual variance, the parameter was included. Where on the other hand, there were no discrepancies between family members, the final court of appeal was the face validity of the item. Where face validity was substantial, then the parameter was included regardless of score. Where on the other hand, face validity could not vindicate inclusion of the parameter, it was excluded from further use. This may seem a laborious process of justifying items which on strictly statistical grounds were ineligible to be retained. However, the aim of the procedure was to understand the statistical and methodologic limits of parameters which are used because of their clinical and substantive relevance, rather than to produce an instrument which though statistically watertight would be clinically and substantively void. Table 2 contains a summary of the results.

Reactions of Children

All eight parameters yielded residual variances within acceptable limits (0.50 to 2.56). Ranked from greatest to least consensus: bad child, mourner, good child, baby, patient, withdrawn, caretaker, and escapee. There was no correlation between residual variance ranking and between-family-member variance, confirming the earlier assumption about heterogeneity. (The same applies to all other sets.) The two parameters of least consensus, that is, caretaker and escapee, are seen (from the coefficients of variation for each child) to have significant discrepancies for each of the two children. It may be inferred that consensus was even greater than indicated by the individual variance values. The unrotated correlation matrix suggests high correlations between mourner and good child (0.64), good child and patient (0.63), bad child and escapee (0.62), and baby and patient (0.50).

The factor matrix clarifies these correlations. Factor 1 is a cluster: mourner (0.90) + good child (0.70) + patient (0.40) + baby (0.34), with an Eigen value of 2.87, accounting for 35.9 percent of the variance. Factor 2 represents a cluster: patient (0.81) + caretaker (0.61) + baby (0.55), with an Eigen value of 1.69, accounting for 21.1 percent of the variance. Factor 3 is a cluster: escapee (0.79) + bad child (0.78), with an Eigen value of 1.23, accounting for 15.4 percent of the variance.

Perception of Mother's Illness

The range of residual variance for this set of parameters was higher than for perception of mother's illness (1.04 to 3.36). The sequence from greatest to least consensus was: sees depression in magical terms, feeling that mother is losing control, tendency to blame, outcome, medical illness, cause in mother or life

Table 2 External Validation of Scale

	Residual variance (df = 8)	Between family variance (df = 1)	Consensus for each item measured		Factor matrix (Eigen value and p value in parentheses)					
			Child 1	Child 2	F1	F2	F3	F4	F5	F6
1. Reactions of children					(Eigen value:					
					2.87	1.69	1.23	0.91)		
					(Percentage:					
					35.9	21.1	15.4	11.4)		
Bad child	0.50	2.00	22	26	−0.07	−0.14	78			
Mourner	0.76	1.39	58	57	0.90	0.03	0.00			
Good child	1.38	8.00	64	53	0.70	0.36	−0.42			
Baby	1.47	0.22	26	11	0.34	0.55	0.27			
Patient	1.81	20.06	54	21	0.40	0.81	−0.14			
Withdrawn	2.31	0.06	28	22	0.21	0.26	−0.08			
Caretaker	2.47	14.22	76	28	−0.16	0.61	−0.11			
Escapee	2.56	0.06	27	18	−0.08	0.02	0.79			
2. Perception of mother's illness					(Eigen value:					
					2.10	1.53	0.98)			
					(Percentage:					
					30.0	21.8	14.0			
Magical terms	1.04	4.33	37	49	−0.47	−0.02				
Loss of control by mother	1.26	2.93	61	53	−0.30	0.62				
Blame: self/others	1.36	15.82	51	40	0.19	0.69				
Outcome	1.75	1.37	38	51	0.69	−0.14				
Medical illness	2.44	11.11	15	21	0.64	0.17				
Cause: mother-life situation	2.94	39.15	7	27	0.46	0.20				
Family complete	3.36	15.82	212	132	−0.15	−0.22				

(continued)

Table 2 (continued)

	Residual variance (df = 8)	Between family variance (df = 1)	Consensus for each item measured		Factor matrix (Eigen value and p value in parentheses)					
			Child 1	Child 2	F1	F2	F3	F4	F5	F6
3. Surrogation and family consensus for each item measured										
Surrogation	82									
Role of father with children										
helpful-harmful	33									
avoiding-engaging	43									
supportive-unsupportive	49									
Contact between mother and father										
physical and spatial	24									
emotional	37									
harmful-helpful	34									
Contact between mother and children										
physical and spatial	33									
emotional	42									
helpful-harmful	67									
4. Mothering–global					(Eigen value:					
					2.14	1.57	1.01	0.71)		
					(Percentage:					
					35.6	26.2	16.9	11.8)		

Currently on examination	0.38	0.50	25	26	−0.64	0.14		
At first presentation	1.13	0.50	47	60	0.99	0.08		
Before presentation	1.47	2.72	50	64	−0.14	0.08		
Currently on examination	1.56	0.06	48	41	0.16	0.33		
Before first presentation	1.63	2.00	38	34	−0.29	0.80		
At first presentation	1.97	6.72	47	55	−0.01	−0.64		
5. Interaction (mother-child)					(Eigen value:			
					3.69	1.67	1.16	0.93)
					(Percentage:			
					36.9	16.7	11.6	9.3)
Engaging-avoiding	1.22	20.47			−0.77	−0.28	−0.06	
Coldness-warmth	1.42	16.48			−0.73	−0.18	−0.17	
Resentment and hostility	1.60	3.81			0.23	0.79	−0.13	
Empathy	1.76	24.44			0.84	0.22	−0.06	
Communication: initiating-shutting off	2.47	29.26			0.74	0.13	−0.04	
Anxiety	2.93	4.56			0.34	0.06	0.42	
Friction	3.29	2.77			−0.23	−0.51	−0.25	
Ambivalence	3.39	3.89			0.25	0.32	−0.31	
Wish to be like other (in dyad)	3.70	8.62			0.07	0.50	−0.11	
Self perception as other in dyad	3.73	13.88			−0.02	−0.12	0.78	
6. Phenomenology–general					(Eigenvalue:			
					2.05	1.56	0.76)	
					(Percentage:			
					41.0	31.3	15.2)	
Orientation	0.32	1.15	6	4	−0.76	0.00		
Insight and judgment	0.83	5.33	70	84	0.56	−0.09		
Speech	1.32	8.48	24	19	−0.02	0.58		

(continued)

Table 2 (continued)

	Residual variance (df = 8)	Between family variance (df = 1)	Consensus for each item measured		Factor matrix (Eigen value and p value in parentheses)					
			Child 1	Child 2	F1	F2	F3	F4	F5	F6
Thought										
pressure-poverty	1.37	13.37	30	20	−0.06	1.00				
Memory and attention	1.45	3.37	95	75	0.82	0.01				
7. Phenomenology–depressive equivalents					(Eigen value:					
					4.00	2.53	1.96	1.70	1.36	1.07 0.93)
					(Percentage:					
					21.1	13.3	10.3	9.0	7.1	5.6 4.9)
Passivity, expecting others to anticipate	0.86	22.22	20	35	−0.19	−0.15	0.23	0.58	0.02	0.17
Self-punitive	1.62	19.70	32	47	0.52	−0.06	0.21	0.33	0.08	0.44
High standards, self-condemnation	1.76	19.59	72	46	0.66	0.05	0.07	0.06	0.06	0.03
Sadness (verbal, behavioral, fantasy)	1.78	0.44	50	68	0.25	0.02	0.49	−0.03	0.08	−0.01
Sensitivity	1.83	6.70	44	67	0.55	−0.15	−0.03	−0.21	0.20	0.02
Acting out	1.87	17.37	19	21	−0.23	0.58	−0.06	0.32	−0.28	0.02
Sense of need (conveyed)	1.97	2.93	44	67	0.39	0.32	0.10	−0.14	0.17	−0.14
Reversal of affect, clowning	2.25	2.33	23	22	−0.00	0.21	−0.03	0.10	−0.66	−0.01
Sense of feeling rejected	2.29	2.33	45	48	0.20	0.63	0.10	−0.06	−0.05	0.02
Motor activity	2.33	0.33	45	41	0.18	0.16	0.02	0.00	0.78	0.00
Low frustration, tolerance	2.44	13.82	25	26	0.02	−0.13	−0.04	0.65	−0.25	−0.11
Guilt	2.70	19.70	69	43	0.76	0.07	0.21	0.27	−0.12	0.18
Negative self-concept	2.82	5.82	35	35	0.18	−0.03	0.47	0.41	−0.03	0.15
Frozen, inhibited behavior	3.41	3.37	38	48	0.04	0.00	0.17	0.06	0.01	0.81

Shame	3.50	33.33	41	41	0.31	0.34	0.28	0.23	−0.27	0.33
Obsessive	3.75	6.04	40	31	−0.25	0.50	−0.01	−0.32	0.16	−0.01
Quality of discontent and anhedonia	4.03	12.44	42	45	0.24	0.18	0.61	0.19	0.90	0.33
Listlessness	4.43	6.26	43	53	−0.14	0.01	0.69	−0.07	−0.05	0.09
Somatizing	4.45	26.70	13	29	0.20	0.25	−0.10	0.63	0.07	0.18
8. Phenomenology–regulatory balance					(Eigen value: 3.09	0.65)				
					(Percentage: 61.8	13.0)				
Pleasure–cannot feel pleasure	3.09	15.59	61	50	0.65					
Superiority-inferiority	3.11	6.78	31	25	0.66					
Power-helplessness	3.97	20.26	39	43	0.74					
Optimism-pessimism	4.29	9.33	47	47	0.79					
Fullness-emptiness	5.28	29.04	28	47	0.76					

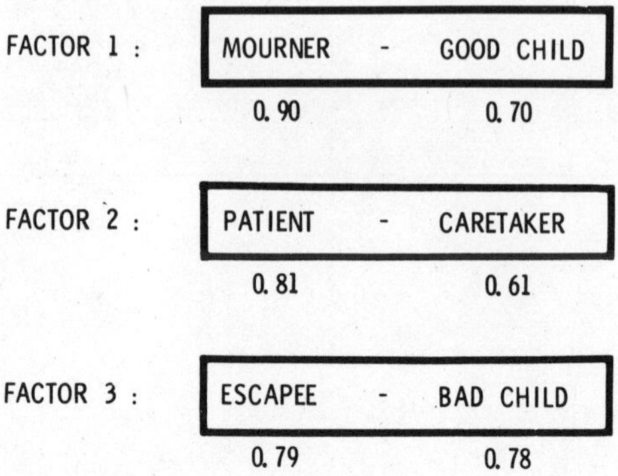

Fig. 5. Reactions of Children

situation, and family completeness. From coefficient of variation, inclusion of the item on family completeness could not be justified on statistical grounds, since not one of the sub-items of this parameter achieve consensus. However, the two other items could be justified for inclusion in that consensus was achieved for two out of the three items in each case. The unrotated correlation matrix did not reveal any outstanding correlations but after the next rotation, two factors were identified.

Factor 1 was a cluster: outcome (0.69) + medical illness (0.64) + cause in mother or life situation (0.46) with an Eigen value of 2.10, accounting for 30.0 percent of the variance. Factor 2 was a cluster: blaming self or others (0.69) + loss of control by mother (0.62) with an Eigen value of 1.53, representing 21.8 percent of the variance.

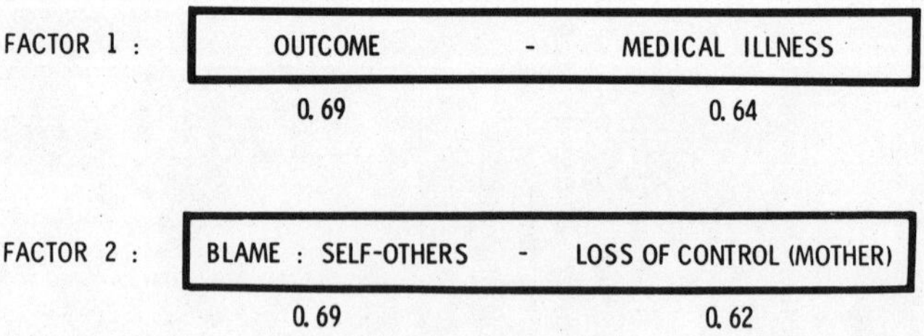

Fig. 6. Perceptions of Mother's Illness

Family Interaction and Surrogation

Since each parameter was only measured once per test family the results were interpreted directly on consensus for each item measured. It can be seen that for all parameters consensus was achieved.

Global Measure of Mothering

All residual variances fell within a range of acceptable consensus (0.38 to 1.97). Despite apparent statistical consensus, it was decided to delete all items referring to increase or decrease in mothering, these representing a quantification of "mothering" by the depressed subject, on examination. These are relative to: (1) the premorbid "baseline" level of mothering by the particular subject, and (2) a general baseline level of mothering against which the raters referenced all subjects.

In addition, retrospective reconstruction of the appropriateness of mothering at stages before that being observed on the video were deleted.

Mother-Child Interaction

Residual variance ranged from 1.22 to 3.73, all within consensus. From coefficients of variation, consensus was probably even greater than the residual variance values would suggest, since there seemed to be a systematic error in the

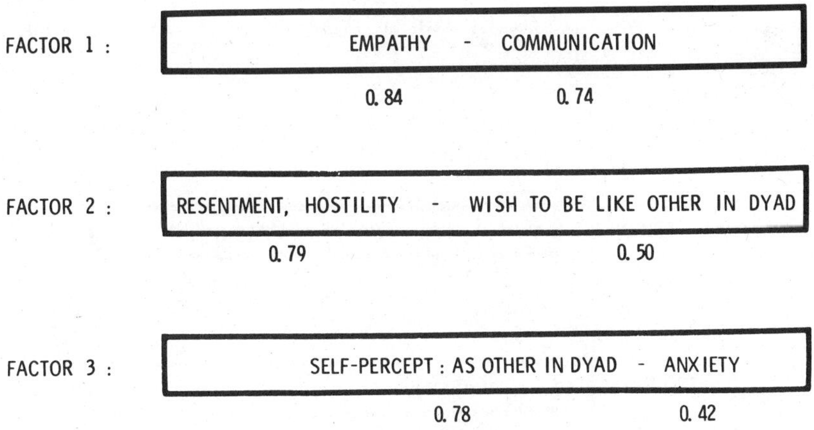

Fig. 7. Interaction (Mother-Child)

dyad between the mother and the elder child, with markedly higher values in this pair than in (mother-child 2, child 2-mother) dyad for resentment and hostility, 87 and 68 versus 37 and 43; empathy, 62 and 84 versus 36 and 37; communication, 66 and 107 versus 39 and 25; anxiety, 50 and 62 versus 42 and 34; frictions, 39 and 53 versus 22 and 32; and self-perception as other in dyad, 81 and 56 versus 35 and 35. The unrotated correlation matrix suggested a relationship between engaging-avoiding and warmth-coldness (0.70) and between empathy and initiating or shutting off communication (0.72), confirmed on factor matrix rotation.

Factor 1 represents the cluster: empathy (0.84) + communication (0.74), and to a lesser extent anxiety (0.304), with an Eigen value of 3.69, representing 36.9 percent of the variance. Factor 2 comprises a cluster: resentment and hostility (0.79) + wish to be like other in dyad (0.50) with an Eigen value of 1.67, representing 16.7 percent of the variance. Factor 3 comprises the cluster: self-perception as other in dyad (0.78) + anxiety (0.42), with an Eigen value of 1.16, representing 11.6 percent of the variance.

Phenomenology–General

As expected, the five items of general behavioral phenomenology yielded residual variances (0.32 to 1.45) of highest consensus, from orientation through insight and judgment, speech, pressure or poverty of thought, and memory and attention.

Factor analysis revealed two factors, the first comprising a cluster: memory and attention (0.82) + insight and judgment (0.56) with an Eigen value of 2.05, accounting for 41.0 percent of the variance; and factor 2 comprising a cluster: thought (1.00) + speech (0.58) with an Eigen value of 1.56, accounting for 31.3 percent of the variance.

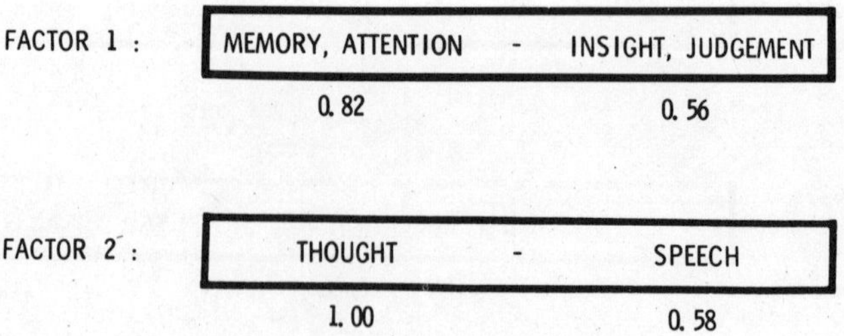

Fig. 8. Phenomenology–General

Phenomenology–Depressive Equivalents

Residual variances ranged from very low (0.86) to quite high (4.45), with a sequence passivity, self-punitive behaviors, high standards with readiness for self-condemnation, sadness, sensitivity, acting out, conveyed sense of need, reversal of affect, sense of feeling rejected, motor activity, low frustration tolerance, guilt, negative self-concept, frozen and inhibited behavior, shame, obsessive behavior, quality of discontent and anhedonia, listlessness, and somatizing. Apart from the last item (somatizing) with a coefficient of variation

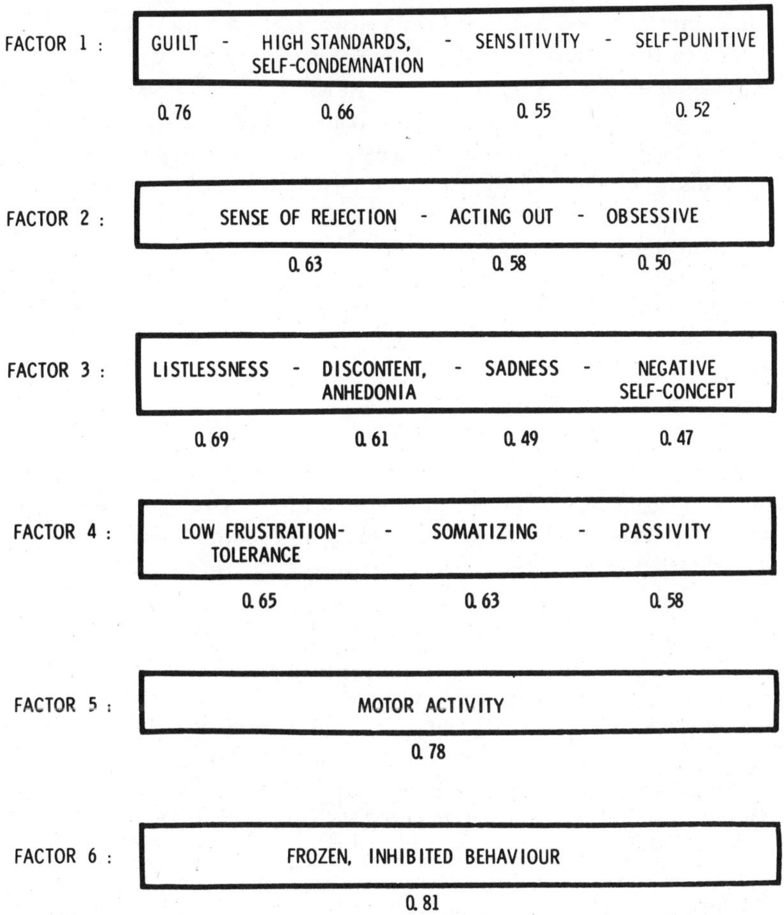

Fig. 9. Depressive Equivalents

of 58 for the mother versus 13 and 29 for child 1 and child 2 respectively, the low consensus for the other items could not be accounted for on the basis of within-family variation. Factor analysis produced six significant factors.

The first factor represented a cluster: guilt (0.76) + high standards with readiness for self-condemnation (0.66) + sensitivity (0.55) + self punitive behavior (0.52), with an Eigen value of 4.00, accounting for 21.1 percent of the variance. Factor 2 was a cluster: sense of rejection (0.63) + acting out behavior (0.58) + obsessive behavior (0.50), with an Eigen value of 2.53, representing 13.3 percent of the variance. Factor 3 was formed by a cluster: listlessness (0.69) + quality of discontent and anhedonia (0.61) + sadness (0.49) + negative self-concept (0.47), with an Eigen value of 1.96, representing 10.3 percent of the variance. Factor 4 was formed by a cluster: low frustration tolerance (0.65) + somatizing (0.63) + passivity (0.58), with an Eigen value of 1.70, representing 9.0 percent of the variance. Factor 5 was a single parameter, motor activity (0.78) with an Eigen value of 1.36, representing 7.1 percent of the variance. Factor 6 was a single parameter: frozen inhibited behavior (0.81) with an Eigen value of 1.07, representing 5.6 percent of the variance.

Phenomenology–Regulatory Balance

The residual variances (3.09 to 5.28) were of considerable lower consensus than on all other sections. Inspection of coefficients of variation reveals a possible explanation, for there is a systematic difference in scores between the mother (37, 18, 14, 25, and 16) and child 1 and child 2 (61 and 50, 31 and 25, 39 and 43, 47 and 47, and 28 and 47, respectively). Thus, it can be seen that scores for the mother alone are well within the limits of consensus but that apparent difficulty in consensus of scores for each child dragged the overall figure (on error variance) into a zone of no consensus. Factor analysis reveals a single factor encompassing all five variables.

CONCLUSIONS

It is commonly held that since "objective" phenomena (for example, motor activity) are more readily quantifiable than highly "subjective" phenomena (for example, empathy), then only the former are scientifically admissible. The findings reported in the external validation contradict this stereotype, in that a range of both "subjective" and "objective" items are perceived by nine raters with equal consensus.

The implications of approaches to the depressed mother-child dyad could be significant at theoretical and practical levels. With early identification of risk and vulnerability to adult depression, it might be possible to deploy primary and secondary preventive measures in such a way as to minimize the later development of clinical depression in adult life.

Secondary prevention for the depressed parent is actually primary prevention for the child. In time and space, the depressed mother and her family may come to attention as "at risk" from two complementary facets. First there is the child who through his difficulties may act as emissary for the family. Second, there is the mother who may be rendered vulnerable to "depressogenic mothering." In each case, there is a proclivity to dyadic dysfunction at points of developmental or traumatic discontinuity.

Application to effective primary prevention remains a challenge for the future, not only to protect the family before and during crisis, but also to harness the potential for adaptive growth in all family members confronting the face of change arising out of maternal depression.

ACKNOWLEDGMENT

The work reported in this chapter was carried out while the author was a Medical Postgraduate Research Scholar, National Health and Medical Research Council (Australia), at the Department of Psychiatry and Behavioural Science, Royal Children's Hospital, Melbourne, Victoria 3052, Australia.

REFERENCES

Aitken L. The visual analogue scale. Measurement of moods. *Br J Hosp Med* 1970;3:215–224.

Anthony EJ. A clinical evaluation of children with psychotic parents. *Am J Psychiatry* 1969;1262:177–184.

Anthony EJ. Folie a deaux: a developmental failure in the process of separation individuation. In: McDeuitt J, Settlage C, eds. *Separation-individuation: essays in honor of Margaret S. Mahler.* New York: International Universities Press, 1971.

Anthony EJ. How children cope in families with a psychotic parent: In: Rexford EN, Sander LW, Shapiro T, eds. *Infant psychiatry: a new synthesis.* Monographs of the J Am Acad Child Psychiatry. No. 2. New Haven and London, Yale University Press, 1976.

Anthony EJ. The developmental precursors of adult schizophrenia. In: Rosenthal D, Kety S, eds. *The transmission of schizophrenia.* New York: Pergamon Press, 1968.

Anthony EJ. The influence of a manic-depressive environment on the developing child. In: Anthony EJ, Benedek T, eds. *Depression and human existence.* Boston: Little Brown and Co., 1975:279–315.

Anthony EJ. The syndrome of the psychologically invulnerable child. In: Anthony E, Koupernik C, eds. *The child in his family: children at psychiatric risk.* New York: John Wiley and Sons, 1974.

Anthony EJ. In: Burrows GD, ed. *Handbook of studies in depression.* Amsterdam: Excerpta Medica, 1977.

Anthony EJ, Benedek T. *Parenthood: its psychology and psychopathology.* Boston: Little Brown and Co., 1970.

Anthony EJ, Scott P. Manic depressive psychosis in childhood. *J Child Psychol Psychiatry* 1976; 1:53–72.

Baker AA, Morrison M, Yame JA, Thorpe JY. Admitting schizophrenic mothers with their babies. *Lancet* 1961; 2:237–239.

Bart PB. Depression in middle-aged women. In: Gornick V, Morak BK, eds. *Women in sexist society.* New York: Basic Books, 1971.

Beck AT, Sethi BB, Tuthilly RW. Childhood bereavement and adult depression. *Arch Gen Psychiatry* 1963; 9:295–302.

Beisser AR, Glasser N, Grant M. Psychosocial adjustment in children of schizophrenic mothers. *J Nerv Ment Dis* 1967; 145:429–440.

Bellak L, Bellak S. *Manual for supplement to the children's apperception test (C.A.T.-S).* Larchmont, New York: C.P.S. Inc., 1976.

Benedek T. Toward the biology of the depressive constellation. In: *Psychoanalytic investigations: selected papers.* Chicago: Quadrangle Books, 1973.

Birtchnell J. Early parent death and mental illness. *Br J Psychiatry* 1970; 116:281–297.

Blos P. *The psychology of adolescence—a psychoanalytic interpretation.* Toronto: Free Press of Glencoe, 1962.

Bowlby J. *Attachment and loss, vol. 1. Attachment.* London: The Hogarth Press and the Institute of Psychoanalysis, 1969a.

Bowlby J. *Attachment and loss, vol. 3. Loss: sadness and depression.* London: The Hogarth Press and the Institute of Psychoanalysis, 1980.

Bowlby J. *Attachment and loss, vol. 2. Separation, anxiety and anger.* London: The Hogarth Press and the Institute of Psychoanalysis, 1969b.

Bowlby J. *Maternal care and mental health.* Geneva: World Health Organization, 1951.

Brown GW, Harris TO, Copeland TR. Depression and loss. *Br J Psychiatry* 1977; 130:1–18.

Chagoya L, Gutterman HA. *A guide to assess family functioning.* Montreal: Jewish General Hospital, July 1971.

Children's E.C.D.E.U. Battery. *Psychopharmacol Bull* Special Issue, 1973; 196–239.

Coddington D. The significance of life events as etiologic factors in the diseases of children—II. A study of the normal population. *J Psychosom Res* 1972; 16:205–213.

Cohler BJ, Gruenebaum H, Weis JL, et al. Disturbance of attention among schizophrenic, depressed and well mothers and their young children. *J Child Psychol Psychiatry* 1977; 18:115–136.

Cohler BJ, Gruenebaum H, Kauffman C, et al. Social adjustment among schizophrenic, depressed and well mothers and their children. Presented at the 131st Annual Meeting of the American Psychiatric Association, Atlanta, Ga. May 8–12, 1978.

Cooper SF, Leach C, Storer D, Tonge SL. The children of psychiatric patients: clinical findings. *Br J Psychiatry* 1977; 131:514–522.

Cowie V. The incidence of neurosis in the children of psychotics. *ACTA Psychiatr Scand* 1961; 37:37–71.

Cytryn L, McKnew DH, Jr. Proposed classification of childhood depression. *Am J Psychiatry* 1972; 129:149–155.

De Horn AB, Strauss ME. Brithweights of male and female schizophrenics' offspring. *ACTA Psychiatr Scand* 1977; 55:321–329.

Dennehy C. Childhood bereavement and psychiatric illness. *Br J Psychiatry* 1966; 112:1049–1069.

Deykin E, et al. The empty nest: psychosocial aspects of the conflict between depressed women and their grown children. *Am J Psychiatry* 1966; 22: 1422–1426.

Dohrenwend BS. Life events as stressors: a methodological enquiry. *J Health Soc Behav* 1973; 14; 2:167–175.

Ekdahl MC, Rice EP, Schmidt WM. Children of parents hospitalized for mental illness. *Am J Pub Health* 1962; 52:428–435.

El-Guebaly N, Offord DR, Sullivan KT, Lynch GW. Psycho-social adjustment of the offspring of psychiatric inpatients—the effect of alcoholic, depressive and schizophrenic parentage. *Can Psychiatry* 1978; 23:281–290.

Engel GL. Pain. In: MacBryde CM, Blacklow RS, eds. *Signs and symptoms.* Philadelphia: Lippincott, 1970:44.

Epstein NB, Segal JJ, Rakoff VM. *Family categories schemer.* Montreal: Family Research Group of Department of Psychiatry, Children's General Hospital, 1968.

Fleck TJ. Depression in hospital and general practice: a direct clinical comparison. *Br J Psychiatry* 1968; 124:240–242.

Forrest AD, Fraser RH, Priest RG. Environmenal factors in depressive illness. *Br J Psychiatry* 1965; 111:243–253.

Frommer EA, Pratt G. Childhood deprivation and mothering problems in a group of mothers with first babies. *Proceedings of Psychosomatic Medicine in Obstetrics and Gynaecology, 3rd International Congress,* London: 1971: 308–310.

Gamer E, Gallant D, Grunebaum H. Children of psychotic mothers: an evaluation of one year olds on a test of object permanence. *Arch Gen Psychiatry* 1976; 33:311–317.

Gamer E, Gallant D, Grunebaum H, Cohler BJ. Children of psychotic mothers. *Arch Gen Psychiatry* 1977; 34.

Garmezy N. The study of competence in children at risk for severe psychopathology. In: Anthony E, Koupernik D, eds. *The child in his family: children at psychiatric risk.* New York: John Wiley and Sons, 1974.

Garmezy N. Observtion on research with children at risk for child and adult psychopathology. In McMillan M, Henao S, eds. *Child psychiatry: treatment and research.* New York: Brunner/Mazel, 1978.

Gay MJ, Tonge WL. The late effects of loss of parents in childhood. *Br J Psychiatry* 1967; 113:753–759.

Gershon ES, Dunner DL, Goodwin FK. Toward a biology of affective disorders. *Arch Gen Psychiatry* 1971; 25:1–15.

Grunebaum H. Children at risk for psychosis and their families. In Henao S, McMillan M, eds. *Child psychiatry: treatment and research.* New York: Brunner/Mazel, 1977.

Gruenebaum H, Cohler B, Kauffman C, et al. Children of depressed and schizophrenic mothers. *Child Psychiatr Hum Dev* 1978; 8:219–228.

Hamilton M. A rating scale for depression. *J Neurol Neuros Psychiatry* 1960; 23:56–61.

Hanson DR, Gottesman II, Heston LL. Some possible childhood indicators of adult schizophrenia inferred from children of schizophrenics. *Br J Psychiatry* 1976; 129:142–154.

Hill DW, Prince JS. Childhood bereavement and adult depression. *Br J Psychiatry* 1967; 113:713–751.

Holmes TH, Rahe RH. The social adjustment rating scale. *J Psychosom Res* 1967; 11:213.

Hudgens RW, Morrison J, Barcha R. Life events and onset of primary affective disorders. *Arch Gen Psychiatry* 1967; 16:134–145.

Jacobson E. *Depression: comparative studies of normal, neurotic and psychotic conditions.* New York: International Universities Press, 1976.

Karlsson JL. Genealogic studies of schizophrenia. In: Rosenthal D, Kety S, eds. *Transmission of schizophrenia.* New York: Pergamon Press, 1968.

Kauffman K, Grunebaum H, Cohler B, Gamer E. Super kids: competent children of psychotic mothers. *Am J Psychiatry* 1979; 136; 9:1398–1406.

Kestenbaum CJ. Children at risk for manic-depressive illness: possible predictors. *Am J Psychiatry* 1979; 136; 11:1399–1402.

Koos EL. *Families in trouble.* New York: King's Crown Press, 1946.

Kovacs M, Beck AT. An empirical clinical approach towards a definition of childhood depression. In: Schulterbrandt JG, Rathkin A, eds. *Depression in childhood: diagnosis, treatment and conceptual models.* New York: Raven Press, 1977.

Kreisman DE, Joy VD. Family response to the mental illness of a relative: a review of the literature. *Schizophr Bull* 1974; 10:34–57.

Lechman JF. Reduced MAO activity in first degree relatives of individuals with bipolar affective disorders. *Arch Gen Psychiatry* 1977; 34:601–606.

Lecker S. Family therapies. In: Wojman BB, ed. *The therapists handbook.* New York: VanNostrand Reinhold, 1976.

Leff MJ, Roatch JF, Bunney WE. Environmental factors preceding the onset of severe depression. *Psychiatry* 1970; 33:292–311.

Lefkowitz L, Monroe M, Tesiny EP. Assessment of childhood depression. *J Consult Clin Psychol* 1980; 48; I:43–50.

Lesse S. The multivariate masks of depression. *Am J Psychiatry* 1968; 124: 35–40.

Lidz T. *Schizophrenia in the family.* New York: International University Press, 1968.

McKnew DH, Jr, Cytryn L, Efron AM, et al. Offspring of patients with affective disorders. *Br J Psychiatry* 1979; 134:148–152.

Mahler M. Notes on the development of basic moods: the depressive effect. In: Loewenstein RM, Newman LM, Schur M, Solnit AJ, eds. *Psychoanalysis: a general psychology. essays in honor of Heinz Harmann.* New York: International Universities Press, 1966.

Mahler M. On child psychosis and schizophrenia: autistic and symbiotic infantile psychoses. *Psychoanal Stud Child* 1952; 7:286–305.

Mahler MS, Pine F, Bergman A. *The psychological birth of the human infant: symbiosis and individuation.* London: Hutchinson of London, 1975.

Malmquist C. Depression in childhood and adolescence. Part I and II. *N Eng J Med* 1971; 284:887–955.

Masuda M, Holmes TH. Magnitude estimations of social readjustment. *J Psychosom Res* 1967; 11:219–225.

Mednick S, Schulsinger F. Some premorbid characteristics related to breakdown in children with schizophrenic mothers. In: Rosenthal D, Kety S, eds. *The transmission of schizophrenia*. New York: Pergamon Press, 1968.

Mednick BR. Breakdown in high risk subjects: familial and early environmental factors. *J Abnorm Soc Psychology* 1973; 82:469–476.

Mendelson M. *Psychoanalytic concepts of depression*. 2nd ed. New York: Spectrum Publications, 1974.

Morrison JR, Hudgens RW, Barchha RG. Live events and psychiatric illness. *Br J Psychiatry* 1968; 114:423–432.

Murphy LB. The problem of defense and the problem of coping. In: Anthony EJ, Konpernik C, eds. *The yearbook of the international association for child psychiatry and allied professions*. New York: Wiley-Interscience, 1970:65–86.

Nowicki S, Jr, Strickland BR. A locus of control scale for children. *J Consult Clin Psychol* 1973; 40:148–154.

Nye F, Berado F. *Emerging conceptual frameworks in family analysis*. New York: MacMillan, 1966.

Orvaschel H, Mednick S, Schulsinger F, Rock D. The children of psychiatrically disturbed parents: differences as a function of the sex of the sick parent. *Arch Gen Psychiatry* 1979; 36:691–695.

Parsons T, Bales RF. *Family, socialization and interactions process*. New York: The Free Press of Glencoe, 1955.

Paykel ES, Mayers JK, Dienelt MN, et al. Life events and depression: a controlled study. *Arch Gen Psychiatry* 19 ; 21:753–760.

Paykel ES, Prusoff BA, Myers JK. Suicide attempts and recent life events. *Arch Gen Psychiatry* 1975; 32; 3:327–333.

Paykel ES, Uhlenhuth EH. Rating the magnitude of life stress. *Can Psychiatry* 1972; 17:93–100.

Pearce J. Depressive disorders in childhood. *J Child Psychol Psychiatry* 1977; 18:79–83.

Phillips BS. *Social research*. 2nd ed. New York: The Macmillan Co; London: Collier-Macmillan, 1971.

Post F. The social orbit of psychiatric patients. *J Ment Sci* 1962; 108:147–156.

Poznanski E, Zrull JP. Childhood depression; clinical characteristics of overtly depressed children. *Arch Gen Psychiatry* 1970; 23:8–15.

Preston G, Antin R. A study of the children of psychotic parents. *Am J Orthopsychiatry* 1933; 2:231–241.

Rabkin JG, Struening EL. Life events, stress and illness. *Science* 1976; 194 (3.12.76), 1013–1020.

Rahe RH, Gunderson EKE, Pughe WM. Illness prediction studies. *Arch Environ Health* 1972; 25:192–197.

Raigins N, et al. Infants and children at risk for schizophrenia. *J Am Acad Child Psychiatry* 1975.

Raymond MA, Slaby AE, Lieb JA. Familial responses to mental illness. *Soc Case Work* 1975; 56:492–498.

Remschmidt H, Strunk P, Methner C, Tegeler E. Kinder endogen-depressiver eltern. *Fortschr Neurol Psychiatr* 1973; 41:326–340.

Rie HE. Depression in childhood. *J Am Acad Child Psychiatry* 1966; 5:653-685.

Robins LN. *Deviant children grown up*. Baltimore: Williams & Wilkins, 1966.

Rolf J. The academic and soical competence of children vulnerable to schizophrenia and other behaviour pathologies. *J Abnorm Psychol* 1972; 80: 225–243.

Romano J. Parent assessment in vulnerability research (Abstr No. 116). *Scientific Proceedings of the 130th Annual Meeting of American Psychiatric Association*, 1977.

Rutter M. Children of sick parents. An environmenal and psychiatric study. Institute of Psychiatry, Maudsley Monographs, No. 16. London: Oxford University Press, 1966.

Rutter M. The children of sick parents. Maudsley Monograph No. 16. London: Oxford University Press, 1969.

Rutter M, Cox A, Tupling C, et al. Attainment and adjustment in two geographical areas. 1. The relevance of psychiatric disorder. *Br J Psychiatry* 1975; 126:493–509.

Rutter M. Early sources of security and competence. In: Brunner J, Garton A, eds. *Human growth and development*. New York: Oxford University Press, 1978.

Rutter M. Six differences in response to family stress. In: Anthony EJ, Koupernik C, eds. *The child in his family*. New York: Wiley, 1970.

Sameroff AJ, Zax M. Perinatal characteristics of the offspring of of schizophrenic women. *J Nerv Ment Dis* 1973; 157:191–199.

Schulterbrandt JG, Rathkin A. *Depression in childhood: diagnosis, treatment and conceptual models*. New York: Raven Press, 1977.

Scless AP, Schwartz L, Goetz C, Mendels J. How depressives view the significance of life events. *Br J Psychiatry* 1974; 125:406–410.

Smith WG. Critical life events and prevention strategies in mental health. *Arch Gen Psychiatry* 1971; 25:103–109.

Spitzer RL, Endicott J, Robbins E. *Research diagnostic criteria*, 3rd ed. New York: Bionetics Research, N.W. York State Psychiatric Institute, 1977.

Stabenau JR. Genetic and other factors in schizophrenic, manic-depressive and schizo-affective psychoses. *J Nerv Ment Dis* 1977; 164:149–167.

Sussex JN, Cassman F, Raffel C. Adjustment of children with psychotic mothers in the home. *Am J Orthopsychiatry* 1963; 33:849–854.

Tonge WL. Problem family children grown up. Presented to the 10th International Congress of Psychotherapy. Paris, July 1976.

Tonge WL, James DS, Hillam SM. Familes without hope: a study of 33 problem families. *Br J Psychiatry* 1975; special publication no. 11; Ashford, Kent: Headley Bros.

Walzer H. Casework treatment of the depressed parent. *Soc Case Work* 1961; 42:505–512.

Weber M. *Basic concepts in sociology*. Secher HP, translator. New Jersey: Citadel Press, 1972.

Weinberg WA, et al. Depression in children referred to an educational diagnostic centre: diagnosis and treatment. *J Pediatr* 1973; 83:1065–1072.

Weintraub S, Neale JM, Liebert DE. Teacher ratings of children vulnerable to psychopathology. *Am J Orthopsychiatry* 1975; 45:838–845.

Weissman MM. Depressed parents and their children: implications for prevention. In: Berlin IN, Stone LA, eds. *Basic handbook of child psychiatry. IV. prevention and current issues.*

Weissman MM, Paykel ES, Klerman GL. The depressed woman as a mother. *Soc Psychiatry* 1972;7:98-108.

Weissman M, Paykel E. *The depressed women.* Chicago: University of Chicago Press, 1974.

Welner Z, Welner A, McCrary D, Leonard MA. Psychopathology in children of inpatients with depression: a controlled study. *J Nerv Ment Dis* 1977; 164;6:408-413.

Winnicott DW. The effect of psychotic parents of the emotional development of the child. In: *The family and individual development.* London: Tavistock, 1965.

Worland J. Rorschach developmental level in the offspring of patients with schizophrenia and manic-depressive illness. *J Personality Assess* 1979; 43: 591-594.

Wyler AR, Masuda M, Holmes TH. Magnitude of life events and seriousness of illness. *Psychosom Med* 1971; 33; 2:115-122.

Zerbin-Rubin E. Genetische aspeckte der endogenen Psychusen. *Fortschr Neurol Psychiatr* 1971; 39:459-494.

Affective Disorders in Childhood and Adolescence--
An Update. Edited by D.P. Cantwell and G.A. Carlson.

15

Depression and Suicidal Behavior in Children and Adolescents

Gabrielle A. Carlson

The complex nature of completed suicide and suicide attempts have made our understanding of its causes and thus its remedies elusive. There is no shortage of discourse on the topic; on the subject of youth suicide alone, the escalation of literature has paralleled the growth of the problem. From 1900 to 1967 there were approximately 200 papers written on youth suicide. In the past ten years alone there have been at least 300.

Rather than summarize the vast literature on youth suicide, this chapter will direct itself to two areas. Since the subject of the book is childhood affective disorder, the author will address what we know of the relationship of depression and suicidal behavior in young people. Secondly, some of the known similarities and differences between child and adult suicidal behavior will be examined. For those interested in further information, Seiden's review of youth suicide until 1968 (Seiden, 1969) is the most complete treatise on the subject. Recently, Pfeffer et al (1981) have reviewed the subject of suicidal behavior in children under age 15. Shaffer and Fisher (1981), Seiden and Freitas (1980), and Petzel and Cline (1978) have thoroughly reviewed the epidemiology of childhood and adolescent suicide.

Although the suicide rate in young people has fluctuated over time (Fig. 1), it has captured the attention of mental health professionals and the public in the last two decades because of its recent alarming increase. Accidents remain the leading cause of death in 15 to 24-year-olds; however, death rates from malignant neoplasms and cardiovascular renal disease have been displaced in frequency by death from violent causes. In 1975, young people were killed in homicidal incidents at a rate of 13.7/100,000; suicide deaths were ranked at 12.2/100,000. These two phenomena are now the second and third cause of death in the 15 to 24-year age group (Holinger, 1978).

Suicide in children under age 15, however, is a low frequency phenomenon. One hundred and seventy-five deaths were recorded between ages 5 to 14 in 1975 and although the rate has gone from about 0.2/100,000 in 1955 to 0.8/100,000

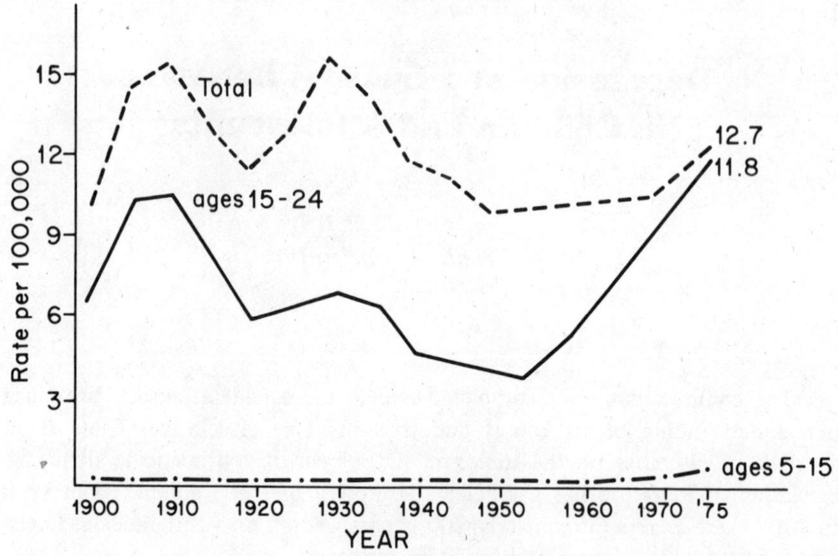

Fig. 1. Trends in suicide rate among youth (5-24) from 1900-1975. Extrapolated from *Suicide Among Youth*. National Clearinghouse for Mental Information, 1967.

in 1975 (Vital Statistics of the US), Shaffer (1981) has reported that in this young age group the rates have been relatively stable worldwide since 1955. The epidemiologic significance of suicide in this age group is twofold: since young people now die less frequently from medical causes (the suicide rate is equal in frequency to deaths from influenza and pneumonia combined) death from suicide is relatively more outstanding. Second, suicides in children under age 15 comprise a much lower percentage of total suicides than their proportion in the population (Table 1). Even in the 15 to 19-year-old age group where the suicide rate has almost doubled in the past ten years, and is higher than it has ever been, the phenomenon is under-represented in the age specific data.

The infrequency of completed suicide in children and younger adolescents is reflected by the paucity of studies on the subject. Bakwin (1972) has reviewed some of the earliest works and some of the world literature on children who committed suicide between the ages of three and ten. In those few case reports it would appear that the children were very unhappy. They either came from homes in which they were badly mistreated or had conduct problems which perhaps led them into difficulties to which they subsequently reacted. Shaffer (1974) reviewed the phenomenon of suicide in children between the ages of 10

Table 1

Age group	Suicides (*n*)	Total no. of suicides	Age group in general population
0-9	2	0.01	14.79
10-14	151	0.55	8.52
15-19	1606	5.88	9.63
19+	25,535	93.56	67.06

and 14 examining coroners' reports in Great Britain, and doing something of a psychological autopsy by reviewing all public records (but not interviewing parents) in the cases of completed suicide he found. He observed there were no cases under age 12 and that there were 31 verdicts of suicide returned for children between ages 12 to 14 in the seven-year period covered by his study.

Four additional studies (Jan-Tausch, 1964; Amir, 1973; Sanborn et al, 1973; Sathyavathi, 1975) address themselves to suicide rather than suicide attempts. Two of these reports cover populations in Bangalore, India, and Israel. The findings vary from those of the United States Census Bureau and Shaffer's study in Great Britain suggesting that in young people, as in adults, suicide statistics and the theories they generate cannot be generalized from country to country. Even in the United States, an examination of the extremely high suicide rate in some Native Americans, age 15 to 24 (47.5/100,000 versus 12.2/100,000 for all other races combined) indicates that from culture to culture within our country different factors exist among groups of young people (Frederick, 1978). Finally, there are some epidemiological data to suggest that rates of completed suicide in adolescents vary directly with the proportion of adolescents in the population (Holinger and Offer, 1982).

One question of particular interest to those concerned with suicide in young people, however, is whether what we know about suicide in adults can be generalized to suicide in children and adolescents.

Demographically, it appears that in the United States, the suicide rate in children under age 19 is considerably higher in males than in females. The sex ratio changes with age, however, dropping from 5.21:1 (males to females) in the 10 to 14-year-olds to 3.42:1 in 25 to 29-year-olds. Interestingly, in Amir's (1974) survey in Israel between 1963 and 1966, males and females up to age 17 have the same sex ratio; only after age 18 do males exceed females, 1.3:1. Finally, in Sathyavathi's survey (1975) of 45 suicides of children aged 14 or less over seven years in Bangalore, females outnumber males 3:1. Unfortunately adult data are not reported, but it appears that male youth domination among suicides isn't universal. The one finding all studies share, however, is the rarity of suicide in younger children and the increase with age after puberty.

The methods by which young persons kill themselves show a preponderance of active/violent means, as do adult suicides. In the United States, for 10 to 14-year olds, the means of suicide were about equally divided between firearms/explosives and hanging, strangulation, and suffocation. Drug or poison ingestion was uncommon. In Britain, Shaffer (1974) found that carbon monoxide and hanging were the most often used. In 15 to 19-year olds, firearms predominate as lethal means by almost 3:1 over hanging and, as with adults, death by drug or poison accounted for only ten percent of completed suicides (Shaffer and Fisher, 1981; Dorpat and Ripley, 1960). Again, as in adults, drug overdose is the means used most by women, though women are increasingly turning to firearms as a method for suicide (Browning, 1974). Finally, the method used for committing suicide in Bangalore differed from the United States and Britain (burning and drowning accounted for 38 percent of child suicides each, poisoning 13 percent, hanging nine percent; almost half the children chose an "active" means of killing themselves rather than a passive one (Sathyavathi, 1975).

Shaffer has found other similarities between suicides in the young adolescent population and the suicides of young adults and adults. For instance, almost half of the youngsters left suicide notes which seem to show more "outwardly directed hostility," a phenomenon also observed by Farberow and Schneidman (1957). As with adults, many of the children had discussed, threatened, or attempted suicide before their final attempt. The more premeditated the suicide, the higher the likelihood that a previous attempt had been made. Shaffer (1974) did not have access to the families of the suicide victims, but in having researched the ancillary records of a variety of psychiatric services he found that half of the children had been seen for psychiatric disturbances before their suicide, a finding noted in adult suicides (Robins et al, 1959a). While the relationship between suicide and specific psychopathology will be discussed later, Shaffer found two associations with suicide fairly specific to his young population. First, a disciplinary crisis accounted for over one third of the precipitating circumstances of the suicide, that is, the child was reprimanded or got into difficulty either with his parents or at school. Second, many children who killed themselves seemed to be larger, more physically mature, and, in general, brighter than the average population.

Sanborn et al (1973) found six of ten 11 to 17-year-old suicides in New Hampshire had made prior suicide threats or left suicide notes. These authors do not present data on means or motivation for suicide. Of the nine youngsters still in school, however, five were having adjustment problems and four had poor grades. Sathyavathi's data (1975) are not directly comparable to Shaffer's regarding the variables above. However, the report states that none of the relatives of the 45 young victims had any idea of their suicidal intentions. The suicides were considered impulsive, though 55 percent made sure they were entirely alone before making the attempt and 47 percent were dead at the time of discovery, suggesting a seriousness of intent on their part. Two children, though conscious at discovery, refused to say anything about their suicidal act.

The children from Bangalore came from a totally different school context; only 22 percent were students and 67 percent were either menial laborers or were doing household work in their respective homes. Of the 35 cases for whom data regarding motivation for suicide were available from police records, 43 percent seemed to be precipitated by disciplinary crises. Sathyavathi notes that these included "such things as being scolded and/or punishment by parent/relatives for various reasons (coming late to the house; disobedience in not carrying out instructions of the parents; not fulfilling parents' expectations; not going to school; mixing with bad company; going to movies without informing parents; indulging in play or roaming about with friends without paying attention to studies; ill-treatment by family members or employers; fear associated with examinations and the like)" (Sathyavathi, 1975).

In summary, the meager data that exist on the demographic variables of young suicide victims show both similarities and differences when compared to suicides in adults. Certainly, the incidence of suicide is considerably lower, the sex ratios are slightly different, and, where the precipitants have been described, they are often age-specific. However, those few children who succeed in killing themselves have obviously selected very lethal means and circumstantial evidence suggests that while the motivation may be impulsive, the actual act is quite deliberate. Shaffer's (1974) findings that successful young suicide victims are often both larger and brighter suggest some relationship of suicide to cognitive and biologic maturity.

CHILDREN'S CONCEPT OF DEATH AND COGNITIVE MATURITY

There are, in fact, no satisfying explanations for the very low suicide rate in children and young adolescents. Though some have hypothesized that the lack of real understanding children have about death is in some way "protective," one could also theorize that believing in death's reversibility would increase a child's risk. There is a growing literature on the subject of children's concept of death (Serafica and Walco, in press) beginning with Schilder and Wechsler's (1937) classic study of children aged 5 to 15. They used a questionnaire and pictures of death-related scenes to enable children to share their understanding and found that young children rarely thought about their own death. Later studies (Nagy, 1959) focused on changing concepts of death relating to increasing chronologic age. More recently, studies have shown that cognitive maturity rather than chronologic age was more responsible for increased sophistication regarding death. Koocher's study (1973) was the first to use a Piagetian model to explain changing responses. Koocher used the Similarities subtest of the WISC, Piagetian tasks of mass, volume, and number conservation, and a task of hypothesis testing and theory formulation. By asking children: (a) what makes things die? (b) how do you make dead things come back to life? (c) when will you die? (d) what will happen then? he found the following relationships: preoperational stage children provided unrealistic and egocentric explanations of what happens when you die and really could not grasp the concept of their own death. Older, operational stage children with the notion of reversibility could understand the finality of death, but only the more cognitively mature children in this group could truly conceive of their own death as final and irreversible. Weininger (1979) used a similar protocol but also examined children's ideas of death through play. He found that children under age nine expressed more understanding of death through play than they could verbally.

It has also been hypothesized that children's concept of death may be influenced by a number of noncognitive factors, the immediate experience of death being an obvious one and one that has been studied. Children facing death or having a sibling facing death have a much greater understanding of the event than cognitive levels would have predicted (Bluebond-Langner, 1977).

How an immature concept of death should keep someone from committing suicide is unclear. Recently, however, Orbach and Glaubman (1979) have begun to examine the concept of death in suicidal children. Using Koocher's (1973) questions, an assessment of the concept of life, and the similarities subtest of the WISC, they examined 27 children aged 10 to 12: nine suicidal, nine aggressive, and nine normal. There were no differences in the three groups on their similarities or concept of life scores. The suicidal children, however, felt that life processes continued after death significantly more often than the normal ($p < 0.01$) or the aggressive children ($p < 0.07$). In another similar study, moreover, they found that suicidal children conceived of another's death as final and irreversible but not their own (Orbach and Glaubman, 1979). These preliminary findings suggest that a child's concept of death may be independent of cognitive development and that it will not provide a satisfactory explanation of why very few children kill themselves.

Given the consistent findings that at least preoperational children have a fluid and egocentric concept of death, it is unclear whether a "suicide attempt" in a five-year-old (Fritz, 1980) or even the successful suicide in a five-year-old (Sathyavathi, 1975) was understood by the child in the same way it is by adults.

SUICIDE ATTEMPTS

It has been recognized for some time that there is overlap between the population of completed suicides and suicide attemptors (about ten to 15 percent of suicide attemptors ultimately kill themselves; 25 percent of completed suicide victims have made previous attempts [Robins et al, 1959; Dorpat and Ripley, 1960]. The highly lethal means used in some suicide attempts suggest they should be considered failed suicides and conversely there are probably some completed suicides that were unlucky and successful attempts). In general, however, suicide attempts, or "parasuicides" are made by a different population of people, using a different means, than completed suicides (Farberow and Schneidman, 1965).

Suicide attemptors are, in general, young (under age 30) and female (general sex ratio of 2:1). Consistent findings related to social class and marital status or a single personality type have not been demonstrated. However, the epidemiology of suicide attempts is fraught with even more methodologic difficulty than the epidemiology of suicides per se (Weissman, 1974). Still, as the suicide rate in young people has increased, so has the suicide attempt rate. This has occurred in many countries and the annual crude incidence rate of suicide attempts has been measured at anywhere from 160 to 300/100,000 with data coming from treatment facilities alone. Extrapolation of a survey done of persons in Los Angeles, aged 14 and older who admitted to making a suicide attempt, revealed a rate of 3900/100,000 (Mintz, 1970). Although these rates have not been broken down into different age groups, Weissman (1974) has specifically noted that the suicide attempt rate has shown a marked increase in persons aged 15 to 24. The ratio of suicide attempts to completed suicides in children and adolescents is felt to be as high as 100:1 (Jacobziner, 1965) in contrast to the 10:1 incidence in adults, though a recent study of this ratio has not been reported.

There is considerably more literature on the subject of parasuicide in children and adolescents than on suicide per se. It is a more frequent phenomenon accounting for anywhere between five and 15 percent of reasons for referral to psychiatric clinics (Lucianowitz, 1968; Pfeffer et al, 1979) and for 44 percent of emergency room intakes (Mattsson et al, 1969). Moreover, as with suicide, the frequency of suicidal behavior increased with age. In this population, as well as in young adults, girls outnumber boys in the frequency with which they are seen for suicidal rumination and attempt (Bergstrand and Otto, 1962; Mattsson et al, 1969). In the large Swedish study of 1,727 young parasuicides, three to four attempts per completed suicide were noted for boys; for girls, 25 to 30 attempts per completed suicide were found (Bergstrand and Otto, 1962). Finally, in contrast to completed suicide and as noted with suicide attemptors, drug overdose of all ages accounts for the majority of attempts followed by such self-inflicted injuries as wrist cutting (Weissman, 1974).

The prevalence of suicidal ideation in the general population is unknown, though there is reason to believe that many children in times of stress harbor thoughts of at least wishing they could die or disappear. In a psychiatrically ill population the incidence of suicidal ideation increases considerably. Over one third of psychiatrically referred children under the age of 13 admitted that they had at least thought of killing themselves at some time (Carlson, unpublished data). Hudgens (1974) found that 45 percent of 60 hospitalized adolescent psychiatric patients expressed the desire to die and, in fact, the intent to commit suicide. Besozzi (1972), studying suicidal ideation in normal high school students in Switzerland, found that 36 percent of the subjects could conceive of circumstances that might lead to a suicidal reaction and 22 percent had thought about killing themselves. However, of the 424 students surveyed in this study only six were seriously suicidal or felt that suicide was the only way out of their present difficulties.

A similar hierarchy of severity of suicidal intent exists for actual suicide attempts. The Barter et al (1968) study of adolescent suicide attempts found that 40 percent of the suicide attempts qualified as an insignificant suicidal gesture, 47 percent fit the category of a suicidal act requiring medical attention but without significant risk to life or health, nine percent were moderate to severe self-injury, and 5 percent were an unequivocal attempt to end the child's life.

FOLLOW-UP OF SUICIDE ATTEMPTORS

The follow-up of suicidal attemptors into young adulthood reveals that continued suicidal behavior is not uncommon. In Barter's study (1968) 42 percent of subjects admitted to repeat attempts when he had restudied them approximately two years later; 31 percent of McIntyre's 26 subjects had made repeated attempts in her six to 24-month follow-up of her population of adolescents (McIntyre et al, 1977). There is also a higher incidence of completed suicides in the suicide attemptor group—best documented by Otto and his follow-up of 1,700 parasuicides (Otto, 1971). In following up these children a total of 15 years later, 67 of them had committed suicide, a figure much higher than would have been expected for the normal population. Most of these suicides took place within one to two years of the initial suicide attempt. Finally, children and adolescents who have made suicide attempts have a considerably higher risk for having an unstable relationship with another person; more were on welfare, more were likely to have committed criminal acts, more were alcoholic, and more were physically ill. In attempting to look at factors that might lead one to predict which population would be more likely to have a worse outcome, McIntyre et al (1977) compared the lethality of the initial suicide attempt with the outcome of her 26 adolescents and found that there was no relationship between lethality and ultimate outcome.

Dahlgren's (1977) long-term follow-up study of suicide attemptors between age 15 and 45 completed some 59 to 75 years after the initial attempt continues to suggest both the initial year or two after the suicidal attempt carries the greatest risk for completed suicide but that long-term these patients also are significantly more at risk for suicide than the nonattemptor population. Diagnoses of alcoholism and hysteria made at the time of initial attempt were considerably more common in the late suicide group (16.7 and 19.4 percent, respectively) than psychosis (9.9 percent).

In a study of death patterns in suicide attemptors, a psychiatric population, and a general population, Tefft et al (1977) found that suicide is by far the leading cause of death for suicide attemptors through age 44. While there were no recorded suicidal attempts or suicides in the Monroe County, New York case register (from which data were taken) in the zero to 14-year age group, in the 15 to 24-year group the following average annual mortality rates per 100,000 were noted: for suicidal attemptors, the suicide rate was 37.0, for psychiatric (but nonattemptor) registry patients 9.6, and for the general population 3.2. Even through age 55, suicide attemptors have the highest age-specific mortality accounted for mostly by suicide, but by other nondisease conditions as well.

In summary, the high morbidity noted in follow-up of suicide attemptors as well as the high mortality lends credence to the seriousness of this problem both to the individual and society.

PSYCHOPATHOLOGY

In adults, studies of suicide victims (Robins et al, 1959a, 1959b; Barraclough et al, 1974) reveal that major psychiatric illness is almost always present and that major depression (or primary affective disorder) and alcoholism account for over three fourths of the diagnoses. In addition, depression is the most common diagnosis cited in suicide attemptors, although these diagnoses have often been gleaned from depression inventories (the assumption being that anyone making a suicide attempt must be depressed) and from cross-sectional assessments of dysphoric individuals who do not meet diagnostic criteria for depression (Goldney, 1980). The consistent observations of suicide attemptors as individuals with chronic histories of chaotic, hostile, and impulsive behavior whose attempts are usually in the context of interpersonal conflict fit more in the diagnostic context of personality disorders. Some feel that these individuals have a secondary rather than primary affective disorder and that hysteria (Briquet's syndrome), alcoholism, and antisocial personality disorder are the primary diagnoses (Bibb and Guze, 1972; Morgan et al, 1975). High levels of hostility have been found consistently in suicide attemptors in contrast to depressed but non-suicide-attempting patients, suggesting that more than depression is involved in this self-destructive behavior. We must postulate that this is true for completed suicide as well, since, although 15 percent of patients with primary affective disorder die by suicide (Robins and Guze, 1971),

85 percent do not. An interesting biological correlation between hostility and suicide has recently been found in 26 young men (without psychiatric history) in the United States Navy who had significant past histories of tantrums, discipline problems, antisocial behavior, and current difficulties with the military judicial system. Not only were they significantly more "aggressive" than 26 control subjects, there were significant negative correlations with the cerebrospinal fluid serotonim metabolite (HIAA) and positive correlation with the norepinephrine metabolite (MHPG); the most extreme correlations were achieved in the aggressive men, 11 of whom had made suicide attempts (Brown et al, 1979). Traskman and Asberg (1981) also have studied this association and found low cerebrospinal fluid HIAA levels to correlate better with ultimate suicide in suicide attemptors than depression levels. These findings need further study and replication but lend credence to the theory that something in addition to depression is necessary to explain suicidal behavior.

What do we know about the diagnostic psychopathology in child and adolescent suicide victims? There are currently few systematic diagnostic studies on completed suicide in young people to shed light on this issue. The methodology of Shaffer's study (1974) precludes the making of a definitive diagnosis in the completed suicides of 10 to 15-year olds, as he was unable to interview the victim's parents. He did find that 17 percent of these youngsters had come to the attention of school authorities for fighting, stealing, truancy, and running away from home. Such emotional symptoms as depressed mood, somatic concerns, excessive fears, morbid preoccupation, and school phobia were present in 13 percent of subjects. Mixed antisocial and affective symptoms were noted in 57 percent of cases. There was adequate information in a few cases to clarify that the behavior change had been recent. Whether these young suicides had primary affective disorder with so-called acting out (that is, antisocial) behaviors or a conduct disorder with secondary depression is unclear. This young population is similar to adult suicide victims in its preponderance of males, the lethality of method, histories of previous suicidal behavior in 46 percent of cases, and previous known psychiatric disorders in themselves and family members. They are like suicide attemptors in the mixture of personality disorder/affective psychopathology and degree of hostility as recorded in suicide notes which 14 of 30 children left behind.

In spite of the increase in suicides in 15 to 19-year olds, there are no systematic psychological autopsy data that would clarify diagnosis in youngsters of this age group. Welner's follow-up of 77 of 110 hospitalized adolescents reported that six patients had ultimately died by suicide (though in their 20s at the time), two males had schizophrenia, three females were diagnosed as bipolar manic depressive, and one woman had unipolar depression and alcoholism (Welner et al, 1980).

The extensive literature on parasuicide in children and adolescents reflects that the young person attempting self harm almost invariably comes from a disturbed psychosocial system (Seiden, 1969). There is usually a history of repeated separations and losses and parents with inadequate coping skills who have difficulty managing their own lives let alone noticing their children's distress. The youngster often has a fairly long history of behavioral and academic problems and interpersonal difficulties as well. Suicidal behavior in children may be a cry for help and a manifestation of frustration with their present reality and aggression towards themselves and their depriving "love objects" even more often than is the case in young adults. Although a few children attempt suicide as a response to a hallucinatory command, or to join a dead relative (Toolan, 1975), they are in the minority. As noted above, long-term follow-up of attemptors continues to demonstrate the interpersonal difficulties and poor coping skills of this population. Short-term follow-up underlines the environmental chaos which bred the attempt. Parents are often notoriously unreliable about initiating or continuing treatment. The many hospitalizations and placements that may result from the attempts only continue the process of separation and loss (McIntyre et al, 1977).

While one might hypothesize that depression or depressive symptoms might be rampant in such depressing circumstances, are there any data to this effect? Otto's study (1966) of 581 suicidal children and adolescents reports that only 38 percent of subjects had had depressive changes noted up to three months before the suicide attempt. Pfeffer et al (1979) and Mattsson et al (1969) also found depressive symptoms significantly more often in suicidal than in nonsuicidal children. Hudgens (1974), using systematic interviews to make diagnoses on 110 hospitalized adolescents, found that only one third of the 45 adolescent attemptors met criteria for a depressive syndrome. The remainder were undiagnosed and, on follow-up (Welner et al, 1980), many fit criteria for antisocial personality disorder. Thus, while depressive symptomatology is present in some young attemptors, the frequency seems somewhat less than has been reported in the adult literature.

In an attempt to study the relationship between depressive symptoms, major depressive disorder, suicidal ideation, and suicide attempt, Carlson and Cantwell (1982) examined systematic interview and depression inventory data gathered on 102 psychiatrically referred children and adolescents. They found that:

1. Suicidal ideation increased with chronologic age.
2. The 45 of 102 youngsters who denied suicidal ideation rarely met criteria for depression; the 12 youngsters who felt seriously suicidal and had high depression inventory scores frequently (83 percent) met criteria for major depressive disorder. However, 45 youngsters who admitted only to thinking

about suicide were only slightly depressed; one third met criteria for depressive disorders, one third for behavior disorders, and one third for other psychiatric disorders.

3. Family history of depression and alcoholism was mirrored in this hierarchy, being least common in nonsuicidal youngsters and most common in seriously suicidal youngsters.

We concluded that the intensity of suicidal ideation was usually a reflection of the severity of depression but that many youngsters who thought about suicide were not depressed at all.

In this study, 22 young people had a history of suicide attempt; for 11 of these youngsters the index psychiatric admission resulted. These two groups differed in that those hospitalized felt depressed, were observed at interview to be depressed, and 8 of 11 cases were diagnosed as having either primary, secondary or probable depressive disorder. The fact of the attempt, not the lethality per se, in the context of depression prompted both referral and hospitalization regardless of the age of the child. By contrast, the 11 youngsters who had given a history of at least one suicide attempt in the past more often met criteria for behavior disorder diagnoses, had been referred for "behavioral" problems, and though more depressed than nonsuicidal youngsters, were significantly less depressed than hospitalized attemptors. The most troubling finding of the study was the enunciation of what has been observed before. A sizable number of youngsters can feel suicidal without being or feeling depressed. Their suicide attempts may be as serious as their depressed counterparts but are less likely to be noticed and taken seriously. While in suicide attemptors the risk of suicide increases in patients with major affective disorder (McHugh and Goodell, 1971), the suicide potential in young people with other psychiatric disorders should not be underestimated.

It would appear that depression has a contributory but not constant relationship to a suicide attempt, but is neither necessary nor sufficient for it. The major advantage of depression may be that people take depression more seriously these days and there are treatments for it. While the author has seen a number of suicidal youngsters who are not depressed, she has never seen a suicidal youngster, even when clear-cut diagnostic criteria for unipolar or bipolar depression are met, who did not come from a severely disturbed living situation which usually antedated the suicidal behavior.

EXAMINATION

Any discussion of suicide and parasuicide must acknowledge the broad spectrum nonserious expression of a death wish—"I wish I were dead" to a very lethal and, for all practical purposes, fatal act. The former may not come to psychiatric attention and, as mentioned above, the incidence of suicidal thought is not uncommon in the general population of young people. The suicide attempt, on the other hand by its very nature is a barometer both of the young person's inability to cope productively with stress and the immediate environment's inability to recognize the person's distress. A suicide attempt needs prompt evaluation. Ultimately, assessment of the completed suicide while no longer of benefit to the victim, might be useful to friends and family and to society which needs a greater understanding of this phenomenon in young people.

Assessment of a young person who makes a suicide attempt should focus itself on two items: the imminent risk to the person's life, and, given the long-term morbidity and mortality, what can be understood and remedied to improve the ultimate prognosis.

Imminent Risk

While a psychiatric diagnosis is not sufficient to explain a suicide attempt, we do know that people meeting criteria for a major affective disorder carry a higher risk of suicide. Hence, it is important to systematically assess depressive disorder, gathering data from subject, family, and/or friends and using all of the DSM III inclusionary and exclusionary criteria. Since suicide attempts almost invariably take place in the context of some major psychiatric disorder (the others most often being conduct disorders, attention deficit disorder, schizophrenia), a thorough diagnostic evaluation is warranted.

The details of the suicide attempt must be examined for degree of seriousness of intent. What circumstances preceded the attempt? Was the attempt impulsive or well-planned? Were there previous communications of intent or previous attempts? Was anyone around when the child made the attempt? If the child has not made an attempt, it is useful to know what has kept him from it. If he did make an attempt, did he tell anyone about it subsequently? Was he found serendipitously? What was his understanding about the lethality of the means? It is possible that the interaction of the child's developmental level on the nature of a suicide or attempt has more to do with his ability to plan and conceive of consequences than it does his concept of death.

Finally, it is important to discuss the implications of the suicide attempt with the youngster. The person will often verbalize she wanted to hurt parents or boyfriend, or wished to join a recently deceased relative, or felt too miserable to live. A scenario may be portrayed where the child, though he has imagined himself dead, also has the satisfaction of seeing the grief and regret of friends and family. This unrealistic view of death is understandable in young children who do not comprehend the irreversibility of death; however, such fantasies also occur in adolescents and adults who should know better. This lends additional credence to the fact that more than the person's intellectual knowledge is involved in contemplation of suicide.

Morbidity Assessment

The young person's interpersonal, family, social, and school functioning needs to be evaluated. Specific items such as family history of psychiatric illness (especially depression and alcoholism), and histories of other suicidal behavior in the family help in ascertaining diagnosis, genetic vulnerabilities, and in getting a sense of the family's coping skills. Clarifying the nature of the whole system's distress as well as the assets it has in dealing with the difficulties is important. Moreover, the interaction between a major depression and environmental chaos is reciprocal. Those circumstances in which a previously well-functioning adolescent becomes acutely depressed and suicidal should disrupt the functioning of most families.

Assessment of the circumstances surrounding completed suicide is best elaborated by Schneidman (1976):

1. Identifying information for victim (name, age, address, marital status, religious practices, occupation, and other details).
2. Details of the death (including the cause or method and other pertinent details).
3. Brief outline of victim's history (siblings, marriage, medical illnesses, medical treatment, psychotherapy, previous suicide attempts).
4. Death history of victim's family (suicides, cancer, other fatal illnesses, ages at death, and other details).
5. Description of the personality and life style of the victim.
6. Victim's typical patterns of reaction to stress, emotional upsets, and periods of dysequilibrium.
7. Any recent–from last few days to last 12 months–upsets, pressures, tensions, or anticipations of trouble.
8. Role of alcohol and drugs in (a) overall life style of victim and (b) his death.
9. Nature of victim's interpersonal relationships (including physicians).
10. Fantasies, dreams, thoughts, premonitions, or fears of victim relating to death, accident, or suicide.
11. Changes in the victim before death (of habits, hobbies, eating, sexual patterns, and other life routines).
12. Information relating to the "life side" of victim (upswings, successes, plans).
13. Assessment of intention, that is, role of the victim in his own demise.
14. Rating of lethality.
15. Reactions of informants to victim's death.
16. Comments, special features, etc.

Specific additions to this examination for children might include:

1. What was the child's basic personality? Had there been any recent changes?

2. What was the child's school functioning academically? Had there been any changes (for example, school refusal, change in grades, increased friction with school authorities)?

3. What kinds of relationships did the child have with family members? With peers?

4. Was there a past history of psychiatric referral? Psychiatric problems?

5. Was any suicidal behavior known to the child?

6. What was the child's understanding of death?

7. How available were lethal means (such as, guns, pills, poisons) and how knowledgeable was the child?

TREATMENT

Minimizing the risk of suicide is the first step in treatment. This may require hospitalization or, in less serious cases, close monitoring by family and therapist. Subsequent steps depend on what the evaluation reveals. In adults, the more closely a suicide attempt is tied to the diagnosis of serious depression, the greater the likelihood that at least that episode can be treated. Electroconvulsive therapy has been considered the treatment of choice for seriously suicidal patients for many years. Certainly, hospitalization and medication are indicated in such depressions. The foregoing is equally applicable to adolescents. In prepubertal children, where the identification of discrete depressive syndromes is only now being formulated and the continuity with adult depressive disorders has not yet been ascertained, the issue of treatment becomes more complicated. In adults, the more chaotic and influential the psychosocial situation the more discouraging the response. This observation seems more relevant to parasuicides in children and adolescents whose families are often disturbed, deprived and unwilling or unable to continue treatment. Although the youngster may achieve the immediate gratification demanded by his attempt, there is rarely any constructive or lasting change that occurs as a result so that future attempts and continued marginal existence, as noted in the follow-up studies, is likely.

It is clear that both the child and his psychosocial system need to be taught improved coping skills. Insofar at the mental health team can acccomplish this, either by hospitalization, or family and individual therapy, the prognosis is probably improved. A recent small study of adult suicide attempts (Liberman and Eckman, 1981) suggests an improved outcome (at two years) when the group was followed closely and aggressively and when subjects were taught social skills training, anxiety management, and family contingency contracting. There is also some suggestion that cognitive therapy may be helpful for long-term as well as short-term prognosis in that it teaches the subject better ways of dealing with frustration. The limited resources of the families involved, as well as the limited resources of the entire mental health interdisciplinary, require that innovative measures be developed to respond to this growing problem.

REFERENCES

Ackerly WC. Latency-age children who threaten or attempt to kill themselves. *J Am Acad Child Psychiatry* 1971;6:242-261.

Amir A. Suicide among minors in Israel. *Israel Am Psychiat Related Disciplines* 1973;11:219-269.

Bakwin H, and Bakwin R. "Suicide." In: *Behavior disorders in children*. New York: W. B. Saunders, 1972:613-629.

Barraclough B, Bunch J, Nelson B, Sainbury P. A hundred cases of suicide: clinical aspects. *Br J Psychiatry* 1974; 125:355-373.

Barter JO, Swabck DO, Todd P. Adolescent suicide attempts: a follow up study of hospitalized patients. *Arch Gen Psychiatry* 1968; 19:523-527.

Bergstrand CG, Otto U. Suicidal attempts in adolescence and childhood. *ACTA Paediatr* 1962;51:17-26.

Besozzi C. On the epidemiology of suicidal thoughts of students. In: Litman RE, ed. *Proceedings of the 6th International Conference for Suicide Prevention*. Mexico City, December 5-8, 1972. Los Angeles: Suicide Prevention Center, 216-221.

Bibb RC, Guze SB. Hysteria (Briquet's syndrome) in a psychiatric hospital: the significance of secondary depression. *Am J Psychiatry* 1972; 129:224-228.

Bluebond-Langner M. Meanings of death to children. In: Feifel H, ed. *New meanings of death*, New York: McGraw-Hill, 1977.

Brown GL, Goodwin FK, Ballenger JC, Goyu PF, Major LF. Aggression in humans correlates with cerebrospinal fluid amine metabolites. *Psychiat Res* 1979; 1:131-139.

Browning CH. Epidemiology of suicide firearms. *Compr Psychiatry* 1974; 15: 549-553.

Carlson GA, Cantwell DP. Suicidal behavior and depression in children and adolescents. *J Am Acad Child Psychiatry* (in press).

Cazzullo CL, Balestri L, Generali L. Some remarks on the attempted suicide in the period of adolescence. *ACTA Paedopsychiatr* 1968; 35:373-375.

Dahlgren KG. Attempted suicides–35 years afterwards. *Suicide Life Threat Behav* 1977; 7:75-79.

DeLong WB, Robins E. The communication of suicidal intent prior to psychiatric hospitalization–a study of 87 patients. *Am J Psychiatry* 1961; 117: 695-705.

Dorpat TL, Ripley HS. A study of suicide in the Seattle area. *Compr Psychiatry* 1960; 1:334-359.

Farberow NLM, Schneidman ES. Suicide and age. In: Schneidman ES, Farberow NL, eds. *Clues to suicide*, New York: McGraw-Hill, 1957.

Farberow NL, Schneidman ES. *The cry for help*. New York: McGraw-Hill, 1965.

Frederick Calvin. Current trends in suicidal behavior in the United States. *Am J Psychother* 1978;32:169-200.

Fritz GK. Attempted suicide in a 5-year-old boy. *Clin Pediatr* 1980; 19:447-450.

Goldney RD, Pilowski I. Depression in young women who have attempted suicide. *Aus NZ J Psychiatry* 1980; 14:203-211.

Guze S, Robins E. Suicide and primary affective disorders. *Br J Psychiatry* 1970; 117:437-438.

Holinger PC. Adolescent suicide: an epidemiologic study of recent trends. *Am J Psychiatry* 1978; 135:754–756.

Holinger PC, Offer D. Prediction of adolescent suicide: a population model. *Am J Psychiatry* 1982; 139:302–307.

Hudgens RW. *Psychiatric disorders in adolescents.* Baltimore: Williams & Wilkins, 1974.

Jacobziner H. Attempted suicide in adolescents. *JAMA* 1965; 191:7-12.

Jan-Tausch J. *Suicide of children, 1960-63.* Trenton, New Jersey: New Jersey Public Schools, Department of Education, 1964.

Koocher GP. Childhood, death, and cognitive development. *Dev Psych* 1973; 9:369-375.

Liberman RP, Eckman T. Behavior therapy vs. insight-oriented therapy for repeated suicide attemptors. *Arch Gen Psychiatry* 1981; 38:1126–1139.

Lukianowicz N. Attempted suicide in children. *ACTA Psychiatr Scand* 1968; 44:415–435.

Mattsson A, Seese L, Hawkins JW. Suicidal behavior as a child psychiatric emergency. *Arch Gen Psychiatry* 1969; 20:100-109.

McHugh PR, Goodell H. Suicidal behavior: a distinction in patients with sedative poisoning seen in a general hospital. *Arch Gen Psychiatry* 1971; 25: 456-464.

McIntyre MS, Angle CR, Wilcoff RL, Schlict ML. Recurrent adolescent suicidal behavior. *Pediatrics* 1977; 60:605-608.

Mintz RS. Prevalence of persons in the city of Los Angeles who have attempted suicide: a pilot study. *Bull Suicidol* 1970; 7:9-16.

Morgan HG, Barton J, Pottle S, et al. Deliberate self-harm: a follow-up study of 279 patients. *Br J Psychiatry* 1976; 128:361-368.

Morgan HG, Burns-Cox CJ, Pocock H, Pottle S. Deliberate self-harm: clinical and socioeconomic characteristics of 368 patients. *Br J Psychiatry* 1975; 127:564-574.

Murphy GE, Robins E. Social factors in suicide. *JAMA* 1967; 199:303-308.

Nagy M. The child's view of death. In: Feifel H, ed. *The meaning of death*, New York: McGraw-Hill, 1959.

Orbach I, Glaubman H. Children's perception of death as a defensive process. *J Abnorm Psychol* 1979; 88:671-674.

Orbach I, Glaubman H. Suicidal, aggressive, and normal children's perception of personal and impersonal death. *J Clin Psychol* 1978; 34:850-857.

Orbach I, Glaubman H. The concept of death and suicidal behavior in young children: three case studies. *J Am Acad Child Psychiatry* 1979; 18:668-678.

Orbach I, Gross Y, Glaubman H. Some common characteristics of suicidal latency age children: a tentative model based on case study analyses. *Suicide Life Threat Behav* 1981; 4:180-190.

Otto Ulf. Changes in the behavior of children and adolescents preceding suicidal attempts. *ACTA Psychiatr Scand* 1961; 40:366-403.

Otto Ulf. Suicidal attempts in childhood and adolescence—today and after 10 years. A follow-up study. In: *Depressive states in childhood and adolescence* 1971:357-366.

Otto Ulf. Suicide attempts made by children. *ACTA Psychiatr Scand* 1966; 55:64-72.

Petzel SV, Cline D. Adolescent suicide: epidemiological and biological aspects. *Adolesc Psychiatry* 1978; 6:239-266.

Pfeffer CR, Conte HR, Plutchik R, Jerrett I. Suicidal behavior in latency age children. *J Am Acad Child Psychiatry* 1979; 18:679–692.

Pfeffer CR. Suicidal behavior of children: a review with implications for research and practice. *Am J Psychiatry* 1981; 138:154–159.

Robins E, Gassner A, Kayes J, et al. The communication of suicidal intent: a study of 134 consecutive cases of successful (completed) suicides. *Am J Psychiatry* 1959a; 115:724-733.

Robins E, Murphy GE, Wilkinson RJ, Jr, et al. Some clinical considerations in the prevention of suicide based on a study of 134 successful suicides. *Am J Pub Health* 1959b; 49:888-899.

Sanborn DE, Sanborn CJ, Cimbolie P. Two years of suicide: a study of adolescent suicide. In: New Hampshire *Child psychiatry and human development* 1973; 3:234-242.

Sathyavathi K. Suicide among children in Bangalore. *Indian Pediatr* 1975; 42:149-157.

Schneidman ES. Suicide among the gifted. In: Schneidman ES, ed. *Suicidology: contemporary developments.* New York: Grune and Stratton, 1976.

Seiden RH. Suicide among youth–a review of the literature, 1900-1967. U.S. Govt. Printing Office: *Bull Suicidol (Suppl),* 1969.

Seiden RH, Freitas RP. Shifting patterns of deadly violence. *Suicide Life Threat Behav* 1980; 10:195-209.

Serafica FC, Walco GA. Children's concepts of illness and death: a review, personal communication.

Shaffer D. Suicide in childhood and early adolescence. *J Child Psychol Psychiatry* 1974; 15:275-291.

Shaffer D, Fisher P. The epidemiology of suicide in children and young adolescents. *J Am Acad Child Psychiatry* 1981; 20:545-565.

Tefft BM, Pederson AM, Babigian H. Patterns of death among suicide attemptors, a psychiatric population and a general population. *Arch Gen Psychiatry* 1979; 34:1155-1161.

Toolan JM. Suicide in children and adolescents. *Am J Psychother* 1974; 339-344.

Toolan JM. Suicide in children and adolescents. *Am J Psychother* 1975; 29: 339–344.

Traskman L, Asberg M, Bertilsson L, Sjostrand L. Monoamine metabolites in CSF and suicidal behavior. *Arch Gen Psychiatry* 1981; 38:631-641.

Weininger O. Young children's concept of dying and dead. *Psychol Rep* 1979; 44:395-407.

Weissman MM. The epidemiology of suicide attempts, 1960-1971. *Arch Gen Psychiatry* 1974; 30:737-746.

Welner A, Welner Z, Fishman R. Psychiatric adolescent inpatients 8 to 10 year followup. *Arch Gen Psychiatry* 1980; 36:698-700.

Vital statistics of the United States, 1961-1975: mortality. Washington, DC: U.S. Government Printing Office.

SECTION VI

Management

Issues in the Management of Childhood Depression

Dennis P. Cantwell

TREATMENT

It is an unfortunate truth in child psychiatry that treatment is more often based on the theoretical orientation of the clinician than it is on evidence for the efficacy of the treatment modality used. In a seminal article Akiskal and McKinney (1975) reviewed ten models of depression. These ten models reflected five dominant schools of thought about the etiology of depression: psychoanalytic, behavioral, sociological, existential, and biological. The four psychoanalytic models included: aggression turned inward, object loss, loss of self-esteem, and negative cognitive set. The two behavioral models included learned helplessness and loss of reinforcement. The biological models included the biogenic amine theories, and neurophysiological theories. Very recently Kashani and his colleagues (1981) reviewed the similar models for their relevance for depression in childhood.

With so many etiological theories it is not surprising that a variety of different therapeutic modalities are postulated for childhood psychiatric disorders in general and depressive disorders in particular. However, whatever one's theoretical orientation, it would be hard to argue with the viewpoint that childhood psychiatric disorders and depression in particular are most likely multifactorial in etiology. Thus, it is a crucial part of the diagnostic formulation of an individual child to ascertain not only what diagnostic category the child's disorder may be (such as major depressive disorder), but also a variety of other factors that are related to treatment planning. These factors have been described in a previous chapter and include: in a particular child with depressive disorder, what are the likely intrapsychic, biological, intrafamilial, psychosocial, and other roots of this disorder, and what are the relative strengths of these roots? In this individual child what are the factors that seem to be maintaining the problem? (These may be different from factors that were originally causal.) In this individual child what factors are helping to maintain normal development? In this child and in this family what are the strengths and competencies that one has to work with in the variety of therapeutic modalities that may be prescribed? Based on this type of evaluation a multimodality treatment approach will probably be prescribed for most childhood psychiatric disorders, including depression. The Satterfields and Cantwell have demonstrated the utility of this multimodality approach in the treatment of attention deficit disorder with hyperactivity in children (Satterfield et al, 1979). Petti and his colleagues (1980) have recently outlined a multimodality treatment approach of a depressed girl in an attempt to provide a framework for assessing and treating chronically depressed multiproblem children.

The exact components of this multimodality treatment program will vary from child to child depending on the results of a comprehensive diagnostic evaluation of each child and family. The modalities to be considered would include: biological therapies such as antidepressant drugs, lithium, and electroconvulsive therapy; various types of psychotherapy including individual therapy for the child, group and family therapy; various behavior modification programs; and various types of psychoeducational intervention. Klein and his colleagues (Klein et al, 1980) have outlined a stepwise approach to the clinical management of affective disorders in adults. Various chapters in this book have addressed the use of tricyclic antidepressants and other types of psychopharmacologic intervention, behavior modification procedures, and cognitive therapy with depressed children. Unfortunately, as with other psychiatric disorders of childhood, there is very little controlled evidence for the efficacy of most of the psychological interventions.

In contrast to the situation with depressive disorder in adults, there is also very little in the way of controlled studies of psychopharmacologic intervention. It is an established fact now that tricyclic antidepressant medications such as imipramine and amitriptyline have a substantial positive effect on major depressive disorders in adult life. There are over 200 double-blind placebo-controlled studies of tricyclic antidepressants with depessive disorders in adult life. In addition, newer antidepressant agents such as mianserin, veloxazine, and maprotiline are being introduced at a very rapid rate. Some of these are proposed to be at least as efficacious as the tricyclics, but since they have a different mode of action, they may have fewer adverse effects. Quadricyclics, for example, are felt to have less in the way of cardiotoxicity than the tricyclics, and they are touted as being as affective in the treatment of the major depressive disorders. Other types of antidepressant medication such as the MAO inhibitors probably also play a role in the treatment of depressive disorders in adult life. There is some suggestion that the MAO inhibitors are helpful in depressive patients who have phobic anxiety features as well. Lithium was introduced primarily to treat the manic phase of bipolar affective disorder, but there is increasing evidence that it not only has antimanic effects, but it may have a prophylactic effect in preventing manic and depressive episodes in individuals who have bipolar disorder and a prophylactic effect against depression for those individuals who have recurrent unipolar depression. Electroconvulsive therapy continues to play a significant role in depressive disorders in adult life. It is primarily used in the cases of treatment-resistent depressions, those who have serious suicidal behavior, those with psychotic delusional depressions, and persistent manics and catatonics. The most up-to-date review of the use of these biological agents in the treatment of major depressive disorder in adult life can be found by Klein et al in their recent edition of their book on psychopharmacologic treatment of psychiatric disorders (Klein et al, 1980). The book also gives a nice outline of the major side effects of these drugs and their management, and also outlines a rational plan for the clinical management of affective disorders.

The situation with regard to the psychopharmacologic management of depressive disorders in childhood is not as clear-cut as it is with adults. Tricyclic antidepressants, MAO inhibitors, and lithium have been occasionally used in children diagnosed as having affective disorder. But from the standpoint of significant amount of evidence from double-blind placebo controlled studies, the literature is very scarce. Imipramine is known to be effective in the treatment of other types of psychiatric disorders in childhood. Attention deficit disorder with hyperactivity, separation anxiety disorder, and enuresis are three conditions in which imipramine has been used effectively. In some cases a response to an antidepressant in a child has been used as evidence that the child is therefore depressed, regardless of what the clinical picture was originally. This type of thinking is circular and is characteristic of the type of thinking that has led to the use of such terms as "masked depression" and "depressive equivalent." However, imipramine like all drugs, affects many biological functions and it is much more likely that the effects in enuresis, separation anxiety disorder, and attention deficit disorder can be quite distinct from one another and also from the effect that occurs when it is used as an antidepressant.

The use of tricyclics in children has been reviewed by Puig-Antich (in press), Rapoport (1976), Petti (in this volume), and Elkins and Rapoport (in this volume). In general, what this literature reveals is that there are suggestions from a variety of open studies that about three quarters of children diagnosed as having depression respond to tricyclic antidepressants. However, most studies are uncontrolled, lack specific diagnostic criteria for the diagnosis of depression and duration of treatment, and had greatly varying dosage. Frommer (1967) conducted a controlled study of antidepressant medication in 32 children comparing a combination of MAO inhibitor and chlordiazepoxide to phenobarbitol, each given two weeks in a double-blind crossover design. More than three quarters improved with the antidepressant-antianxiety combination compared to about one half with phenobarbitol. Unfortunately, the design of the study does not allow one to make definite conclusions on the effect of the antidepressant alone, and diagnostic criteria for the diagnosis were lacking. Although Frommer does propose that her three different types of depression (pure, phobic, and enuretic) respond differently to different drugs, the evidence for this has not been forthcoming from double-blind controlled studies. A major advance in the field resulted from Weinberg's open trial (1973). Using his own criteria for depression which were modified from the Feighner criteria for adult depression, 42 children from the St. Louis Children's Hospital Pediatric Outpatient Clinic were diagnosed as depressed. Nineteen were treated in an open trial by their pediatricians with either amitriptyline or imipramine. On follow-up, 18 of the 19 children who were treated were found to have improved compared with only six of those who were not treated. The length of the trials obviously varied, the dosages varied, and follow-up measures were not systematically reported. However, this study did use operational diagnostic criteria very similar to that found with adult disorders and did find a striking difference between treated and nontreated children.

Puig-Antich et al (1978), in a preliminary report of eight prepubertal children who met Research and Diagnostic Criteria (RDC) for major depressive disorder, found that giving imipramine up to 4.5 mg/kg per day for a period of six to eight weeks resulted in a substantial improvement in six of eight cases. The criteria for considering a child improved were quite strict, and a seventh child was found to respond after the dose was raised to 5 mg/kg per day. Since that time, Puig-Antich and his colleagues have been conducting one of the first double-blind placebo controlled studies of imipramine treatment of prepubertal major depressive disorder. All of the children met RDC criteria for major depressive disorder and were unresponsive to two weeks of psychosocial intervention on an inpatient unit. This study involved a five-week double-blind placebo controlled study of imipramine to doses ranging up to a maximum of 5 mg/kg per day. The imipramine is raised to 5 mg/kg per day over a 12-day period using three roughly equally divided daily dosages. Every third day the dose is raised, beginning with 1.5 mg/kg, then 3 mg, then 4 mg, and then 5 mg. Appropriate electrocardiographic, blood pressure, and clinical side effects are monitored. In a preliminary report of 26 cases the placebo group response rate is 60 percent, and the imipramine response rate is 60 percent. This would suggest that a dosage of 5 mg/kg does no better than placebo over a five-week period of time. However, Puig-Antich and his colleagues have also been looking at the relationship between steady state plasma level of imipramine plus its immediate metabolic product, desmethylimipramine, and relating that to clinical response. When their population is divided into a steady state plasma level above and below the median figure (which was 152 ng/ml), all of those above this level are positive responders while only one third of those below that level are positive responders. They hypothesize that if plasma levels could be systematically measured and dose adjustments made to produce a steady state over 200 ng/ml, the response rate would be 100 percent. In a personal communication, Puig-Antich noted that some of those who were nonresponders at 5 mg/kg responded at higher dosages when the steady state plasma level was raised. Their safety measures were a 5 mg/kg per day dose ceiling and three specific electrocardiographic safety limits (resting heart rate not over 130, P-R interval length not over 0.18 seconds, and a QRS width not over 130 percent of baseline). Subsequent review of their data with cardiology consultation suggested that the electrocardiographic limits were too conservative and that a P-R interval of 0.21 seconds as the upper limit of safety would be more reasonable. If Puig-Antich's data are replicated, they do suggest that children with prepubertal major depressive disorder diagnosed by adult criteria such as RDC or Diagnostic and Statistical Manual-III (DSM-III) would indeed have a substantial improvement rate with tricyclic antidepressants given adequate steady state plasma levels of drug. Moreover, with careful clinical and laboratory monitoring, dosage needed to obtain the steady state plasma level would be tolerated by the majority of children.

Given that antidepressants will have some role to play in the treatment of major depressive disorder in children, the question is what role do they play with regard to other types of intervention. Part of Puig-Antich's study has revealed that mother-child relationships and peer relationships are markedly impaired in depressed children during the acute phase of their illness. Moreover, after the children have recovered from their illness, peer relationships remain almost as bad as they were during the acute phase while mother-child relationships had improved to some degree. Thus, psychosocial intervention directed towards improving social skills and parent-child interaction would seem to be mandatory in the treatment of depressed children. Unfortunately, scientific evidence supporting the efficacies of various types of psychosocial intervention with depressed children are lacking. Pelham and his associates have found a similar situation for children with attention deficit disorder with hyperactivity. That is, even though they have been rated as improved on a variety of parameters after treatment with stimulant medication, peer relationships were still found to be seriously impaired. The addition of a social skills training program plus the use of stimulant medication has been found to improve the peer relationships, an improvement that was not obtained by the use of stimulant medication alone, which was in fact effective for other aspects of the child's problem.

In the field of depressive disorders with adults, however, a substantial amount of evidence regarding efficacies of various types of psychotherapy have been forthcoming in the past several years. The various types of psychotherapy that have been tested include the following: traditional behavior therapy, cognitive-behavior therapy, cognitive therapy, interpersonal psychotherapy, group therapy, and marital therapy. These data have been recently reviewed by Kovacs (1980) and by Weissman (1979). Traditional behavior therapy accounts for the development of depression in stimulus-response terms. Traditional behavior therapists postulate that certain symptoms of the depressive syndrome are elicited from an individual by a low rate of positive reinforcement. When there is a lack of available positive reinforcement and there are negative reinforcing instruments in the environment, a depressive syndrome develops. The emphasis generally in traditional behavior therapy is on measurement of specific overt behaviors and on their modification through the use of external reinforcers.

Cognitive behavior therapy is a term used to describe therapy used by a number of behaviorists who have elaborated on the traditional stimulus response paradigm. They have defined cognitions to be internal or covert behaviors that act as moderating or mediating processes between stimulus and response. They see these cognitions also as appropriate goals for modification. On the other hand, cognitive therapy as developed by Beck states that the depressed person's affective experiences are determined by their interpretation of internal and external events. Thus, Beck's cognitive therapy focuses on the depressed patient's characteristic negative thoughts and attitudes and seeks to modify these and the maladaptive ways in which the patient processes information.

Interpersonal psychotherapy defines depression as having three component processes: (a) symptom formation, (b) social adjustment, and (c) personality. Those who practice interpersonal therapy postulate that depression develops in a social and interpersonal context and is determined by the interpersonal relationships between the depressed patient and his environment. Interpersonal therapy attempts to intervene in symptom formation and social adjustment and does not attempt to intervene in the underlying enduring aspects of the personality. Marital therapy likewise can be conceptualized as a form of interpersonal therapy. Marital therapy focuses on the interaction between the marital partners and attempts to modify these interactions. Marital therapy is based on the postulate that the marital relationship affects all types of thoughts, feelings, and behavior. Thus, by changing the marital system interaction, depressive symptoms can improve. In group therapy, a trained psychotherapist and a group of patients attempt to change the symptomatology and behavior of the patient. Interpersonal therapy, the behavior therapies, and cognitive therapies have more in the way of specified techniques than do group therapy and marital therapy.

With regard to their use with depressed patients, social skills therapy as described by Lewinsohn and his colleagues (1969a, 1969b, 1972, 1974) bears a close relationship to traditional behavior therapy, as does McLean's (McLean et al, 1976, 1979) social skills therapy. Self-control behavior therapy is a form of cognitive behavior therapy that has been applied to depression, and Beck's cognitive therapy has been tested and compared with other forms of therapy with depressed adults. Weissman's review presents six controlled studies of cognitive therapy, eight of behavior therapy, three of interpersonal psychotherapy, and two of group therapy and conjoint marital therapy. Weissman's review revealed nine studies comparing various types of psychotherapy with a no-treatment control group or a very low contact control group. All of the studies supported the fact that psychotherapy alone was effective for the treatment of depression compared with a control group. There were five studies comparing various types of psychotherapy with drugs. One of these found cognitive therapy superior to imipramine in symptom reduction and in dropout rate. One found drugs and psychotherapy about equal for symptom reduction, and three of these studies found drugs better than psychotherapy in the prevention of relapse and in the reduction of symptoms. However, psychotherapy was slightly superior to drugs in improving social functioning. Five studies tested the combined effect of psychotherapy plus a tricyclic antidepressant and all showed superiority of a combination of psychotherapy and pharmacotherapy and a no-treatment group or of people treated with either psychotherapy or drugs by themselves. There are limitations in all of these studies involving the type of depression that was treated, the diagnostic criteria for the diagnostic depression, indices of improvement, intensity and duration of therapy, duration of improvement, dosage of drugs in the psychopharmacologic studies, duration of drug treatment, and other factors. However, taken together, these studies with adult depression do suggest that various types of psychotherapy are effective in the treatment of depression. Moreover, these seem to be additive effects of antidepressant drugs and psychotherapy with no negative interactions of drugs and psychotherapy reported. There are also some suggestions that psychotherapy and drugs have differential effects, with drugs helping the more vegetative aspects of the depressive syndrome such as appetite, depression, somatic complaints, and sleep disturbance, whereas psychotherapy may be more effective for social functioning over time.

Since children are very intimately involved both in families and in school and are developing organisms, it is likely that psychosocial intervention will play at least as important a role in depressive disorders in childhood as it does with adults. The description of the multimodality treatment program designed by Petti and his colleagues (Petti et al, 1980) in the treatment of a 10½-year-old girl who had depression, educational problems, and family and foster family problems is a good example of a stepwise progression of therapeutic intervention in a child with a depressive disorder. This child was hospitalized and was given individual psychotherapy targeted at developing understanding of her conflicts, especially her relationship with her natural and her foster parents. Psychotherapy was also geared to improving her self-image. At the same time psychoeducational intervention was conducted in the school by an individualized teaching prescription. The goals were to provide positive achievement and develop more appropriate school behavior which would ultimately increase self-esteem. Social skills training was used to help with both peer relationships and to facilitate placement in a foster home setting. Family therapy was geared to helping both foster and biological parents provide a more favorable home environment by teaching the parents to focus on the girl's positive behaviors while at the same time developing better ways of managing her problem behaviors. Imipramine was given at a dose of 5 mg/kg after five weeks of hospitalization. Response to imipramine over time enhanced her ability to respond to other forms of the therapeutic program.

One issue in the management of the depressed child has to do with when the patient should be hospitalized and how suicidal behavior should be managed. The indications for hospitalization of a child with depression are probably similar to the indications for hospitalization of an adult with depression. A definite indication is serious suicidal intent which can only be managed by hospitalization. A second indication is severe dysfunction as a result of the depression. A child who is unable to go to school, is apathetic, spends much of the time in bed, and refuses to take proper personal care of himself or herself probably needs to be hospitalized. Management of suicidal behavior as it occurs in the course of depression has been discussed by Carlson in her chapter on depression.

The following chapters in this section on treatment outline in more detail various forms of intervention to be used with depressed children. Evidence for the efficacy of these intervention modalities either alone or in combination is largely anecdotal at the moment. It is hoped that in the future, systematic studies will be conducted of various forms of psychological intervention with depressed children, both with and without the use of antidepressant medication, in a similar way to what has been done with depressive disorder in adults.

REFERENCES

Akiskal HW, McKinney WT Jr. Overview of recent research in depression: Integration of ten conceptual models into a comprehensive clinical frame. *Arch Gen Psychiatry* 1975;32:285-305.

Elkins R, Rapoport JL. Psychopharmacology of adult and childhood depression: an overview. In: Cantwell DP, Carlson GA, eds. *Affective disorders in childhood and adolescence*. New York: Spectrum, 1983.

Frommer EA. Depressive illness in childhood. *Br J Psychiatry* 1967;2:117-136.

Kashani JH, Husain A, Shekim WO, et al. Current perspectives on childhood depression: an overview. *Am J Psychiatry* 1981;138;2:143-153.

Klein DF, Gittelman R, Quitkin R, Rifkin R. *Diagnosis and drug treatment of psychiatric disorder in adults and children*. Baltimore: Williams & Wilkins, 1980.

Kovacs M. The efficacy of cognitive and behavior therapies for depression. *Am J Psychiatry* 1980;137:12.

Lewinsohn PM. A behavioral approach to depression. In: Friedman RJ, Katz MM, eds. *The psychology of depression: contemporary theory and research*. New York: John Wiley & Sons, 1974.

Lewinsohn PM, Atwood GE. Depression: a clinical research approach. *Psychother: Theory Res Pract* 1969a;6:166–171.

Lewinsohn PM, Libet J. Pleasant events, activity schedules, and despression. *J Abnorm Psychol* 1972;79:291-295.

Lewinsohn PM, Shaw DA. Feedback about interpersonal behavior as an agent of behavior change: a case study in the treatment of depression. *Psychother Psychosom* 1969b; 17:82-88.

McLean PD. Therapeutic decision-making in the behavioral treatment of depression. In: Davidson PO, ed. *Behavioral management of anxiety, depression, and pain.* New York: Brunner/Mazel, 1976.

McLean PD, Hakstian AR. Clinical depression: comparative efficacy of outpatient treatments. *J Consult Clin Psychol* 1979; 47:818-836.

Petti TA. Imipramine in the treatment of depressed children. In: Cantwell DP, Carlson, GA, eds. *Affective disorders in childhood and adolescence.* New York: Spectrum, 1983.

Petti TA, Bornstein M, Delamator A, Conners CK. Evaluation and multimodality treatment of a depressed prepubertal girl. *J Am Acad Child Psychiatry* 1980; 19, 690-702.

Puig-Antich J. Antidepressant treatment in children: current state of the evidence. In: Friedman E, Gershon S, Mann J, eds. *Depression and antidepressants: implications for cause and treatment* (in press).

Puig-Antich J, Blau S, Marx N, et al. Prepubertal major depressive disorders: pilot study. *J Am Acad Child Psychiatry* 1978; 17:695-707.

Rapoport JL. Psychopharmacology of childhood depression. In: Klein DF, Gittelman-Klein R, eds. *Progress in psychiatric drug treatment.* New York: Brunner/Mazel, 1976:493-505.

Satterfield JH, Cantwell DP, Satterfield BT. Multimodality treatment: a one-year follow-up of 84 hyperactive boys. *Arch Gen Psychiatry* 1979; 36: 965-974.

Weinberg WA, Rutman J, Sullivan L, et al. Depression in children referred to an education diagnostic center. *J Pediatr* 1973; 83:1065-1072.

Weissman MM. The psychological treatment of depression. *Arch Gen Psychiatry* 1979; 36:1261-1269.

Copyright © 1983 by Spectrum Publications, Inc.
*Affective Disorders in Childhood and Adolescence--
An Update.* Edited by D.P. Cantwell and G.A. Carlson.

16

Psychopharmacology of Adult and Childhood Depression: An Overview

Robert Elkins and Judith L. Rapoport

This chapter will discuss the treatment of childhood affective disorders from the perspective of pharmacological treatment of adult disorders. Adult treatment and response will be reviewed and compared to child treatment. Differences in findings can be explained by different methodological approaches, and possibly by differences in neurochemical response. The comparison of adult and child studies suggests several hypothetical approaches to child treatment.

TREATMENT OF ADULT AFFECTIVE DISORDERS

Table 1 (Mindham, 1979; Green and Costain, 1979), Table 2 (Cantwell and Carlson, 1979; Akiskal and McKinney, 1975; Andreasen and Winokur, 1978; Gershon, 1975; Goodwin, 1977a, 1977b; Winokur, 1979; Murphy et al, 1978), and Table 3 (DiMascio et al, 1979; Weissman, 1979) represent a selected overview of adult studies of affective disorder. The following general points from these studies stand as contrasts with child studies.

There are many methodologically rigorous adult studies, while there are only a few controlled child studies, most flawed methodologically.

There is an array of antidepressants used in adults with a broad spectrum of pharmacological mechanisms of action (Table 1). These include differences in postulated location of action, for example, pre and postsynaptic, and differences in biochemical effect, for example, varying effects on functional levels of serotonin, norepinephrine, and dopamine. An array of treatments increases the chance of biochemically dissecting depression. The methodology of child studies limits the evaluation of drug efficiency of any single drug, and thus drugs with different effects can not be compared as effectively in children as adults.

Table 1 Psychopharmacological Treatment of Adult Affective Disorders

Agent	Comment
Tricyclic antidepressants, eg, imipramine	Over 200 adult blind placebo-controlled trials. About 1/4 of trials do not show significant effect
Newer antidepressant agents, eg, maprotiline, mianserin, veloxazine	Different modes of action from tricyclics. No firm evidence for improved efficacy, or fewer side effects
Amine precursors, eg, L-dopa, L-tryptophan, 5-OH-triptamine	No advantage to tricyclics alone
MAO inhibitors, eg, phenelzine	More helpful in nonpsychotic outpatients with phobic-anxiety features
Lithium	Antimanic and prophylactic for bipolar and unipolar depressions, many other controversial uses
Electroconvulsive treatment	Most useful for psychotic delusional depressions, treatment-resistant mania and catatonia
Other treatments: alteration of circadian rhythms, sleep deprivation, diet change	Experimental, but beneficial reports in bipolar patients

Table 2 Example of Selective Drug Effects in Treatment of Adult Affective Disorders

Primary Depression		
Bipolar	Unipolar	Secondary Depression
Dextroamphetamine elevates mood	Dextroamphetamine shows no mood elevation	No double-blind studies
More marked antidepressant response to lithium	Equivocal antidepressant response to lithium	Less likely to respond to antidepressants
More likely to respond to imipramine and desipramine	More likely to respond to amiptriptyline	
L-dopa can induce mania	L-dopa generally does not induce mania	

Table 3 Treatment of Adult Affective Disorders: Psychotherapy Alone or Combined with Medication

1. There are additive effects of drugs and psychotherapy with no negative interactions.
2. This additive effect may be due to a different effect. Drugs seem to help vegetative signs, sleep disturbance, somatic complaints and appetite. Psychotherapy effects mood, suicidal ideation, interests, and guilt.
3. The efficacy of drugs alone and psychotherapy alone are about equal and both are better than control.

Selective pharmacological effects in adults reveal a difference between primary and secondary affective disorder and within primary affective disorder between bipolar and unipolar depressed patients. Some of these effects are reviewed in Table 2. There are selective pharmacological effects in children also, but these have not as yet aided in confirming diagnostic groups.

There may be syndrome selective drugs in adults, for example, MAO inhibitors for phobic/anxious, atypical depressions (Quitkin et al, 1979). There are some syndrome-specific drug effects in children (for example, time of onset of imipramine in hyperactivity or enuresis), but selective drug treatment of specific childhood syndromes remains to be investigated.

There is a growing literature of adult depressed subjects comparing psychotherapy alone or combined with medication (Table 3). The findings, although preliminary, are perhaps most relevant for child psychiatry. Children have fewer vegetative signs and therefore may be relatively poorer candidates for drugs and better for psychotherapy.

Finally, new research in affective disorders involving diet and manipulation of circadian rhythms may hold promise for child treatment.

TREATMENT OF CHILDHOOD AFFECTIVE DISORDERS

Selected trials of drug treatment of childhood depression are listed in Table 4.

The gap between our knowledge of child and adult treatment makes direct comparison difficult. Methodological, neurobiological, and other treatment response variables will be examined.

Methodological Variables

Cantwell (1979) contends that one major drawback to defining depression in childhood is the lack of methodology similar to that found in adults. This includes rating scales such as the Schedule for Affective Disorders and

Table 4 Selected Trials of Antidepressant Drugs in Child Affective Disorder

	Drug	Dose	N	Length	Diagnoses	Comment
Puig-Antich et al, 1978, 1979	Imipramine	5 mg/kg/day	38	5 wks	Major depressive disorder (RDC)	5 wks, parallel pbo, see text
Weinberg et al, 1973	Amitriptyline Imipramine	min. dose 25 mg	34	3-7 mos	Based on Feighner criteria	Not double-blind, no placebo, 40% response of non-treatment gp
Frommer, 1967, 1968	Phenobarbitone Chlordiazepoxide	30 mg 20 mg 30 mg	32	2 wks	Phobic gp Mood disorder gp	No pbo, no objective ratings, low dose
Lucas et al, 1965	Amiptriptyline	30-75 mg	14	12 wks	Secondary depression with schizophrenia and personality disorder	

Schizophrenia (SADS) (Spitzer et al, 1978), and those of severity such as the Hamilton (1967) and Beck (1967). Child diagnostic interviews, a rapidly growing area, are discussed in this volume; it is fair to say that at this time there is no accepted child interview with demonstrated reliability and validity.

Rapoport et al (1974) report that responses to a self-concept scale (Piers and Harris, 1963) containing 30 items about self-worth such as "I do bad things," or "I have a pleasant face," showed no difference at six weeks on stimulant or tricyclic drugs compared to placebo. It was observed almost universally that grade school children (and not older children) object to considering and/or sharing introspections of this sort. Does this negative finding indicate an insensitivity of the rating instrument? Is there an age attributional effect to labeling feelings (Schaechter and Singer, 1962), or is there a true qualitative difference in response to stimulants? Children on stimulants often give others an impression of seriousness or sadness even when there is marked clinical benefit from drugs in other areas of functioning. This supports the latter explanation.

The varying length of child clinical trials (Table 4) contributes to the heterogenous child treatment data. Improvements observed over inconsistent periods are interpreted as being due to drug effects. This tends to inflate treatment efficacy, since depression is usually a remitting disease (Puig-Antich et al, 1982).

Minimal operational criteria for the concept of childhood depression as a syndrome is still another poorly controlled variable, although some progress is being made. Weinberg et al (1973) (Table 4) first modified the Feighner (Feighner et al, 1972) criteria for adult depression, delineating ten symptoms as characteristic of childhood depression with an array of behaviors for each symptom. Puig-Antich et al (1978, 1979) have also found this approach useful, and have gone on to carry out the best of the few double-blind controlled drug studies. Puig-Antich used the unmodified Research Diagnostic Criteria (RDC) (Spitzer et al, 1978) to identify prepubertal children with a major depressive disorder. In a pilot open clinical study of 13 children, the depressed children all had other difficulties, such as separation anxiety, antisocial behavior, or severe familial stress. He treated eight of these children with imipramine after a lack of response to milieu, group, family, and individual therapy for at least one month. All were inpatients and continued their nondrug therapy. Six showed a beneficial response after a four-week period. All three endogenous subtypes were responders. These pilot data stimulated a double-blind, five-week placebo-controlled study of imipramine in carefully diagnosed depressed children. Preliminary data in 13 nonpsychotic depressed children, of which two were inpatients and ten outpatients (Puig-Antich et al, 1979), suggested that the degree of improvement in mood is significantly associated with plasma levels of imipramine and metabolites. By the end of 1979, 38 cases had completed the double-blind protocol with 22 assigned to placebo and 16 to imipramine (Puig-Antich, personal communication). To date there is no difference in clinical response between drug and placebo groups, regardless of method of measurement of the depressive syndrome. However, when the drug group was split into two subgroups by high or low plasma drug levels (above or below the group mean of 165 ng/ml) and when each subgroup was compared to placebo, it was found that high level cases consistently do better than placebo. Low level imipramine may actually be harmful, as these children do substantially and consistently worse than with placebo. This is the first study in adults or children that measures plasma levels of drug and placebo-controlled treatment response at the same time. The placebo group of this study was divided into responders and nonresponders. Sixty percent of the placebo group were responders, a figure quoted in other child studies (Eisenberg et al, 1961).

Puig-Antich's work is the only child study that stands with the best of adult research. Certain problems, however, have to be addressed. Compliance in outpatients is related to the supportive nature of the home. Although there was no significant correlation between maintenance dose and plasma levels, compliance can't be monitored exactly in outpatients. Thus, home environment may have mediated good outcome in this study and needs to be controlled.

The high placebo response and the specific response of anhedonia, depressed mood, and some vegetative signs to drug therapy bring the cited adult work on psychotherapy and medication to mind. In adults, there was a differential effect of the two therapies. Would this be true also in children? Perhaps one explanation of the high placebo response rate is that children, who usually don't have vegetative depressive symptoms, simply may not respond to drugs and may be more like the subgroup of adult depressive patients who respond to psychotherapy. A comparative study of psychotherapy and drug response in children should be conducted using the Weissman model.

Neurobiological Variables

Central regulatory mechanisms of normal mood seem to differ in early versus later life. Thus pathological dysregulation would not be expected to follow a similar pattern across ages (Klein et al, 1980). When one compares responses to stimulant drugs and steroids in preadolescent children and adults, they seem to differ, although this had not been rigorously documented. Response to stimulants shows a lack of euphoric effect in hyperactive (Rapoport, 1977) and normal children (Rapoport et al, 1978). Many other stimulant effects, however, are the same in the child and adult group (Rapoport et al, 1980a).

The response of preadolescent children to endogenous and exogenous corticosteroids had not been shown to be associated with depression, as has adult Cushing's disease and steroid therapy (Rapoport, 1977). Differences in affective response to stimulants and steroids are of particular interest when the rates of naturally occurring affective disturbance in adults and children are compared. The most agreed upon difference is the extreme rarity of mania in the preadolescent age group (Campbell, 1952; Conners, 1976).

Underlying mood regulatory processes may be different in children and adults. Children seem to display more spontaneous social behavior than adults and their usual mood seems more elevated and labile than adults (Klein et al, 1980). Different biological mechanisms may help to explain the difference in drug response between these groups. These findings suggest that directly comparing adult and child responses to drugs in the same experimental paradigm may be a useful research approach.

Other Response Variables

MAO inhibitors are superior to placebo in 76 percent of studies of atypical neurotic adult depressions (Quitkin et al, 1979). This is similar to the percentage of studies of tricyclic antidepressants showing efficacy in a more typical group of adult depressive patients (Quitkin et al, 1979). Other work has suggested that MAO inhibitors are syndromally specific for the above cited subgroup (Tyrer, 1979); however, comparative trials of MAO inhibitors versus tricyclics are not definitive (Quitkin et al, 1979). There is only one comparative study of a MAO inhibitor (phenelzine) in children (Frommer, 1967). It is not placebo-controlled. A comparison of MAO inhibitors and tricyclics in specific child subgroups may be useful, particularly if also compared to psychotherapy. School phobic children, for example, if resistant to more traditional therapy could be treated with MAO inhibitors (Gittelman-Klein and Klein, 1971). Other anxiety disorders of childhood, also resistant to traditional therapy, could be investigated as possible drug responsive states, using a MAO inhibitor/tricyclic/placebo comparison. For example, excessive concern about external judgment, an anxiety state seen in middle childhood, might be a fruitful clinical variable to explore. Obsessive compulsive disease of childhood is a rare treatment-resistant ailment (Elkins et al, 1980). Our group's preliminary findings indicate that hospitalization and therapy may be as or more effective than tricyclic antidepressants (Rapoport et al, 1980b), MAO inhibitors may be useful in this condition, especially if there were a "mixed" phobic element, which is more common.

Time course of antidepressant effect in children may help validate broader child nosological categories, in a fashion similar to MAO inhibitors validating adult affective subgroups. Tricyclic antidepressants have an immediate onset of action in children with hyperactivity or enuresis, conditions often regarded as "developmental delays." This is in contrast to the probable delayed clinical effect seen after two to four weeks in school phobic children, for example, a neurotic disorder (Rapoport et al, 1979). (In the studies showing delayed onset of action, dose was increased gradually over one to two weeks so there is some confounding of dose with time.)

A pilot study by McKnew et al (1980) is an interesting attempt to pharmacologically dissect a distinct syndrome of childhood affective illness. It questions whether the response to lithium is inherited regardless of the psychopathology of the child. Six patients aged six to 12 years with mixed "incapacitating" symptomatology, for example, some hyperactive/behavior-disordered, others depressed or highly anxious, have entered a 16-week double-blind crossover trial which includes two lithium and two placebo periods. Five of the children had a lithium responding parent with primary affective illness, while one child had an affectively ill responding grandmother. Two of the children, diagnosed as having a bipolar affective disorder, responded to lithium. Other responses were open to question because of rater disagreement about behavior change. The sample is small at present. When completed, the research may provide evidence for a lithium responsive subgroup. However, unless the response rate of these children can be compared with that of children with similar disorders *without* family history of lithium responsive illness, the genetic component will remain unknown.

NEWER TREATMENTS

Recent adult studies of bipolar affective disorder hypothesize a circadian rhythm desynchronization as an important etiological factor (Wehr et al, 1978, 1979a, 1979b, 1979c). Mechanisms which synchronize circadian rhythms with one another (internal synchronization) or with the environment (external synchronization) are impaired in affective illness. For example, body temperature and motor activity become desynchronized in isolated normal subjects and some cycling bipolar patients. Progressive changes in time of going to sleep (phase advance) is an effort to realign activity with other rhythms. Sleep deprivation may work by this mechanism. Although the circadian clock "wobbles" in early infancy, that is, there is increasing or decreasing motor activity in relation to other cyclic variables such as temperature, it is thought to stabilize at an early age. Changing bedtime could be a painless simple treatment of child depression. Circadian rhythm disturbances in childhood may prove to be an extremely useful field of investigation, even though vegetative signs are not prominent.

Diet has been associated with behavior change in adults and children (Wurtman and Wurtman, 1979). Caffeine use, for example, can cause symptoms of anxiety and depression in adults (Gilbert, 1980; Ritchie, 1975; Greden, 1974).

Trytophan and choline have been used equivocably to treat adult affective disorder (Green and Costain, 1979; Wurtman and Wurtman, 1977, 1979). The developing central nervous system may be uniquely sensitive to dietary manipulation. Although the efficacy of the Feingold diet is unsettled for hyperactive children (Lipton et al, 1979), other more simple dietary changes could be investigated in children's mood disorders and anxiety. Caffeine is found in cola beverages and tea, and is heavily used by some children (Elkins et al, 1980). What is its effect on mood? Dietary manipulation is an ethical and perhaps efficacious treatment in children, and could be easily investigated.

SUMMARY

Adult psychopharmacology provides some methodologic examples which may benefit studies of drug treatment of childhood depression. At this time, the gap between the two areas is so wide that one can only speculate on the possibilities for research in the pediatric area.

On the other hand, it may be that psychopharmacologic studies will prove less fruitful with depressed children. Children may have more immediate response to non-drug therapies, and may tend to have fewer of those symptoms which are primarily drug responsive. In addition, other chemical manipulations, such as diet, may be more acceptable for pediatric research. These are researchable issues which can and should be addressed. Recent advances in methodology in child psychiatry will facilitate these investigations.

REFERENCES

Akiskal HS, McKinney WT, Jr. Overview of recent research in depression: integration of ten conceptual models into a comprehensive clinical frame. *Arch Gen Psychiatry* 1975; 32:285-305.

Andreasen NC, Winokur G. Secondary depression, familial, clinical and research perspectives. *Am J Psychiatry* 1978; 136:62-66.

Beck AT. *Depression: clinical, experimental, and theoretical aspects.* New York: Harper and Row, 1967.

Campbell JD. Manic-depressive psychosis in children: report of 18 cases. *J Nerv Ment Dis* 1952; 116:424-439.

Cantwell DP, Carlson G. Problems and prospects in the study of childhood depression. *J Nerv Ment Dis* 1979; 167:522-529.

Conners CK. Classification and treatment of childhood depression and depressive equivalents. In: Gallant, Simpson, eds. *Depression: behavioral, biochemical, diagnostic and treatment concepts.* New York: Spectrum, 1976.

DiMascio A, Weissman MM, Prusoff BA, et al. Differential symptom reduction by drugs and psychotherapy in acute depression. *Arch Gen Psychiatry* 1979; 36:1450-1456.

Eisenberg L, Gilbert A, Cytryn L, Molling PA. The effectiveness of psychotherapy alone and in conjunction with perphenazine or placebo in the treatment of neurotic and hyperkinetic children. *Am J Psychiatry* 1961; 117:1088-1093.

Elkins R, Rapoport JL, Zahn RP, et al. Acute effects of caffeine in normal prepubertal boys. Presented at American Psychiatric Association Annual Meeting, San Francisco, May 5-13, 1980.

Elkins R, Rapoport JL, Lipsky A. Obsessive-compulsive disorder of childhood and adolescence: a neurobiologic viewpoint. *J Am Acad Child Psychiatry* 1980; 19:213-224.

Feighner JP, Robins E, Guze SB, et al. Diagnostic criteria for use in psychiatric research. *Arch Gen Psychiatry* 1972; 26:57-63.

Frommer EA. Treatment of childhood depression with antidepressant drugs. *Br Med J* 1967; 1:729-732.

Frommer EA. Depressive illness in childhood. *Br J Psychiatry* 1968; 2:117-136.

Gershon S. The treatment of manic-depressive states. In: Shader RI, ed. *Manual of psychiatric therapeutics*. Boston: Little Brown and Co., 1975.

Gilbert R. Adverse consequences of excessive caffeine use. Paper presented at the conference entitled "Nutrition and Behavior" Conference sponsored by the Franklin Institute. Williamsburg, Virginia, March 10-12, 1980.

Gittelman-Klein R, Klein DF. Controlled imipramine treatment of school phobia. *Arch Gen Psychiatry* 1971; 25:204-207.

Goodwin FK. Biological basis of drug action in the affective disorders. In: Jarvik, ed. *Psychopharmacology in the practice of medicine*. New York: Appleton-Century-Crofts, 1977a.

Goodwin FK. Diagnosis of affective disorder. In: Jarvik, ed. *Psychopharmacology in the practice of medicine*. New York: Appleton-Century-Crofts, 1977b.

Greden J. Anxiety of caffeinism: a diagnostic dilemma. *Am J Psychiatry* 1974; 131:1089-1092.

Green AR, Costain DW. The biochemistry of depression. In: Paykel E, Coppen A, eds. *Psychopharmacology of affective disorders*. New York: Oxford University Press, 1979.

Hamilton M. Development of a rating scale for primary depressive illness. *Br J Soc Clin Psychol* 1967; 6:278-289.

Klein DF, Zitrin CM, Woerner M. Antidepressants, anxiety, panic and phobia. In: Lipton M, DiMascio A, Killam K, eds. *Psychopharmacology: a generation of progress*. New York: Raven Press, 1978.

Klein DF, Gittelman R, Quitkin F, Rifkin R. *Diagnosis and drug treatment of psychiatric disorder, adults and children*. Baltimore: Williams & Wilkins, 1980.

Lipton MA, Nemeroff CB, Mailman RB. Hyperkinesis and food additives. In: Wurtman, Wurtman, eds. *Nutrition and the brain. Vol. 4*. New York: Raven Press, 1979.

Lucas AR, Lockett HJ, Grimm F. Amitriptyline in childhood depressions. *Dis Nerv Sys* 1965; 26:105-110.

McKnew DH, Cytryn L, Rapoport JL, et al. Paper presented at the annual meeting of the American Psychiatric Association, San Francisco, May 5-13, 1980.

Mindham RHS. Tricyclic antidepressants and amine precursors. In: Paykel E, Coppen A, eds. *Psychopharmacology of affective disorders*. New York: Oxford University Press, 1979.

Murphy DL, Shiling DJ, Murray RM. Psychoactive drug responder subgroups: possible contributions to psychiatric classification. In: Lipton M, DiMascio A, Killam K, eds. *Psychopharmacology, a generation of progress*. New York: Raven Press, 1978:807-820.

Piers EV, Harris DB. Age and other correlates of self concept in children. *J Educ Psychol* 1963; 55:91-95.

Puig-Antich J. Personal communication, 1980.

Puig-Antich J, Blau S, Marx N, et al. Prepubertal major depressive disorder, a pilot study. *J Am Acad Child Psychiatry* 1978; 17:695-707.

Puig-Antich J, Gittelman R. Depression in childhood and adolescence. In: Paykel E, ed. *Handbook of affective disorders*. New York: Basic Books, 1982:379-392.

Puig-Antich J, Perel JM, Lupatkin W, et al. Plasma levels of imipramine (IMI) and desmethylimipramine (DMI) and clinical response to prepubertal major depressive disorder. *J Am Acad Child Psychiatry* 1979; 18:616-627.

Quitkin F, Rifkin A, Klein DF. Monoamine oxidase inhibitors. *Arch Gen Psychiatry* 1979; 36:749-760.

Rapoport JL, Quinn PO, Bradbard G, Riddle K, Brooks E. Imipramine and methylphenidate treatments of hyperactive boys. *Arch Gen Psychiatry* 1974; 30:789-793.

Rapoport JL. Pediatric psychopharmacology and childhood depression. In: Schulterbrandt J, Raskin A, eds. *Depression in childhood: diagnoses, treatment, and conceptual models*. New York: Raven Press, 1977.

Rapoport J, Buchsbaum MS, Zahn TP, et al. Dextroamphetamine: cognitive and behavioral effects in normal prepubertal boys. *Science* 1978; 199:560-563.

Rapoport JL, Buchsbaum MS, Weingartner H, et al. Dextroamphetamine: cognitive and behavioral effects in normal and hyperactive children and normal adults. *Arch Gen Psychiatry* 1980a; 37:933–946.

Rapoport J, Elkins R, Mikkelsen E, Lipsky A. Clinical controlled trial of chlorimipramine in adolescents with obsessive-compulsive disorder. *Psychopharmacol Bull* 1980b; 16:61–63.

Rapoport JL, Potter WZ. Tricyclic antidepressants and children. In: Raskin A, Robinson D, eds. *The influence of age on the pharmacology of psychoactive drugs*. New York: Basic Books, 1981.

Ritchie JM. Central nervous system stimulants. In: Goodman, Gilman, eds. *The pharmacological basis of therapeutics*. New York: Macmillan, 1975: 367-368.

Schachter S, Singer JE. Cognitive social and physiological determinants of emotional state. *Psycholog Rev* 1962; 69:379-399.

Spitzer R, Endicott J, Rollins E. Research diagnostic criteria: rationale and reliability. *Arch Gen Psychiatry* 1978; 35:773-782.

Tyrer P. Clinical use of monoamine oxidase inhibitors. In: Paykel E, Coppen A, eds. *Psychopharmacology of affective disorders*. Oxford: Oxford University Press, 1979.

Wehr TA, Goodwin FK. Biological rhythms and affective illness. *Weekly Psychiatry Update Series* 2:1-7, 1978.

Wehr TA, Goodwin FK. Desynchronization of circadian rhythms as a possible source of manic-depressive cycles. (unpublished material) 1979.

Wehr TA, Muscettola G, Goodwin FK. Urinary 3-methoxy-4-hydroxyphenylglycol circadian rhythm. *Arch Gen Psychiatry* 1979a; 37:257-262.

Wehr TA, Wirz-Justice A, Goodwin FK, et al. Phase advance of the circadian sleep wake cycle as an antidepressant. *Science* 1979b; 206:710-713.

Weinberg WA, Rutman J, Sullivan L, et al. Depression in children referred to an educational diagnostic center: diagnosis and treatment. *Behav Pediatr* 1973; 83:1065-1072.

Weissman MM. The psychological treatment of depression. *Arch Gen Psychiatry* 1979; 36:1261-1269.

Winokur G. Unipolar depression. *Arch Gen Psychiatry* 1979; 36:47-56.

Wurtman RJ, Wurtman J. Precursor control of transmitter synthesis. In: *Nutrition and the brain. Vol. 1.* New York: Raven Press, 1977:1–324.

Wurtman RJ, Wurtman J. Sources of choline and lecithin in the diet. In: *Nutrition and the brain. Vol. 5.* New York: Raven Press, 1979:73–82.

Affective Disorders in Childhood and Adolescence--An Update. Edited by D.P. Cantwell and G.A. Carlson.

17

Imipramine in the Treatment of Depressed Children

Theodore A. Petti

There is general consensus among clinicians who evaluate and treat disturbed and disturbing children that depression is a frequently occurring problem. A variety of classification schemes have been developed or proposed to assist in the task of clarifying the plethora of issues surrounding the phenomenon of childhood depression (Malmquist, 1972; Petti, 1978).

The position that seems most rational regarding this elusive (in terms of nosology) phenomenon is that adopted by Akiskal and McKinney (1975) with respect to depression seen in adults. They conclude from their extensive review of the literature that depression is the final common pathway of several factors which play varying roles, depending on the individual's constitutional make-up, genetic structure, environment, past experiences, psychosocial adaptive mechanisms, and cognitive organization.

A similar scheme can be developed to explain the clinically depressed affect and mood experienced by children. Two leading proponents of behavioral/cognitive etiologies for depression (Lewinsohn, 1979; Seligman, 1979) have noted the role that physiologic components play once depression is established. An animal model based on separation-induced socal disorders in rhesus monkeys provides an analog for separation/abandonment or anaclitic-type depression in infants and has contributed data on neuropharmacologic changes (Young et al, 1973) and psychopharmacologic response to imipramine treatment, which parallels changes observed in depressed adults (Suomi et al, 1978).

Although there seem to be many types of depression in children with a variety of contradictory symptoms (hyperactivity versus hypoactivity, aggression versus withdrawal, hypersomnia versus insomnia, hyperphasia versus anorexia), data has begun to accumulate to indicate physiologic changes do occur in children meeting objective criteria for depression which are similar to those found in depressed adults. For instance, changes in all-night electroencephalogram-monitored sleep, similar to those reported for depressed adults who meet Research and Diagnostic Criteria (RDC) criteria for a major depressive disorder, have been found in children (Kane et al, 1977; Coble et al, 1977; Kupfer et al, 1979). A shortened rapid eye movement latency (REML) is the parameter that seems the most consistent. This is the time that elapses between the onset of sleep and the beginning of the first REM period. There seems to be a developmental component to this potential biological index since the REML of depressed children is not as short as that of adults. However, depressed adolescents have shortened REML that is very similar to that of depressed adults. This may be especially important in the future for evaluating depression and monitoring its treatment.

Recent work suggests that the dexamethasone suppression test (DST) may be a neurophysiologic marker for major depression in dysphoric children (Poznanski et al, 1982). The response of growth hormone to a test of insulin-induced hypoglycemia may be an even more promising marker (Puig-Antich, 1982).

This chapter will briefly describe the use of tricyclic antidepressants (TCA) in treating adults, spend more time reviewing the literature of TCA treatment of symptoms commonly associated with depression in children, and finally move to studies directly related to therapy of depressed children. It is important to note that the depression may refer to a symptom, a symptom complex, a syndrome, or a specific disease entity, depending on the biases of the individual investigators.

TRICYCLIC ANTIDEPRESSANT THERAPY WITH ADULTS

A recent review succinctly describes the field of neuropharmacology as "still in its infancy" (Kupfer and Detre, 1978). About 10,000 papers have been published concerning the experience with imipramine between 1957 and 1978 (Bickel, 1977). A number of comprehensive reviews summarize this rich literature (Klein and Davis, 1969; Morris and Beck, 1974; Angst and Theobald, 1970). Morris and Beck (1974), in their comprehensive review, found that tricyclics are generally superior to placebo; placebo has never been shown in a controlled study to be superior to TCA.

Klein and Davis (1969) note that with so many controlled studies employing (TCA) versus placebo, demonstrating the superiority of TCA over placebo, the efficacy of this class of drugs has been satisfactorily demonstrated. Davis (1976) goes one step further when he notes that TCA maintenance treatment of drug responders is significantly superior to placebo for its antidepressant prophylactic effect. More recent supporting studies, including one for patients who meet criteria for major depressive disorder, have been reported (Stein et al, 1980). Progress in the field remains obscured by our inability to predict whether a given TCA will be effective or not. We also can only guess as to which portion of the molecule exerts its antidepressant effect. The recent agreement on diagnostic criteria (Diagnostic and Statistical Manual-III [DSM-III]) has provided some stability in diagnosing and selecting treatment modalities.

Much of the DSM-III schema for depression relates to the pioneering work of the Washington University-St. Louis group of researchers. These workers made a distinction between primary and secondary depressions. The primary depressions consisted of individuals with "normal" premorbid personalities, except for episodes of depression and or mania. The secondary depressions included individuals with prior antecedent psychopathology, such as the neuroses, personality disorders, alcoholism substance abuse, or other toxic organic or medical conditions (Andreasen and Winokur, 1979).

The primary affective disorder has been further divided into bipolar and unipolar groups. Winokur has suggested, based on a number of studies he and his collaborators have conducted, that the unipolar group can be further divided into nonfamilial, and pure and depression spectrum disease. These workers have demonstrated that such a classification is supported by family history for psychiatric disorder and sociodemographic variables, symptomatology beyond the core symptoms of major depressive disorder (that is, differing in degree of restless sleep, suspiciousness, bizzareness, and self-blame, but not in appetite disturbance, poor concentration, and decreased energy), and response to treatment (Andreasen and Winokur, 1979).

Winokur (Schlesser et al, 1979) has reported that the dexamethasone suppression test (DST) correlates highly with familial pure depression and, hence, provides a clearer indicator of individuals most likely to respond to TCA or electroconvulsive treatment and least likely to respond to major tranquilizers. This test involves the association between the hypothalmic-pituitary-adrenal (HPA) axis and depression (Carroll et al, 1976).

A dose of 1 to 2 mg of dexamethasone is given orally around midnight and plasma cortisol levels are collected over the next 24 to 48 hours. Carroll and his Michigan group have reported that depressed patients fail to show the normal suppression of cortisol secretion that one would expect. However, as the depression clears, the patient shows the expected suppression. Brown et al (1979) found that 40 percent of male RDC-diagnosed psychiatric patients with a major depressive disorder showed escape from suppression with the DST, while all the patients with diagnosed schizophrenia, neuroses, alcoholism, and drug abuse showed normal pituitary-adrenal suppression. Patients who showed the escape phenomenon tended to respond better to therapy and were rated as being initially more severely depressed. Also, all the patients who escaped from the DST had elevated midnight cortisol levels.

Dysken et al (1979) have described the correlation between depression ratings and the ability to suppress cortisol secretion in a 56-year-old depressed man treated with electroconvulsive therapy and who was followed with serial

DST before and during the treatment. Albala and Greden (1980) report similar results and note that failure to normalize the DST cortisol production during treatment with electroconvulsive treatment or TCA has dire prognostic significance.

Kupfer and associates (Kupfer and Detre, 1978) have taken a different classification approach using a different set of psychobiological indices. In their schema, depression is divided into anxious-hyperactive and anergic-hypoactive major subtypes. The former type is the most common recurring unipolar depression and is distinguished by intermittent wakefulness, early morning awakening, increased psychomotor activity, and anorexia. The secondary form of this subtype generally follows the abuse of alcohol, other general central nervous system depressants, and narcotic analgesics. The anergic-hypoactive subtype is composed of two groups of primary and three groups of secondary depressions. The primary type of depression is composed predominantly of bipolar (manic depressive) disorders where the anergia is profound and sleep is either unchanged or increased, except in the younger age group where falling asleep might be problematic. Postpsychotic depression, depressions following amphetamine, related cogeners, and cocaine, and those associated with toxic-infectious exhaustive states make up the secondary forms of anergic-hypoactive depression.

Kupfer et al (1976) reviews the work of the Pittsburgh group with polysomnography and describes REM latency as a psychobiologic marker for differentiating primary from secondary depressive disease. The shortened REM latency is also observed in patients suffering from schizoaffective illness and in certain schizophrenic patients who require TCA in their management. Kupfer notes that this marker is present in virtually all primary depressive illnesses and absent in secondary depression. This marker is state dependent. Like the DST, shortened REM latency returns to normal levels as the depression clears. During the depression it is consistently found and has been noted to be independent of age, drug effect, or changes in other sleep parameters.

A number of other clinical and biological parameters which may be helpful in differentiating primary and secondary depression have been described (Akiskal et al, 1979). The relation of thyroid and thyrotropic hormones to depression, particularly in women (Prange et al, 1976), has engendered ongoing discussion. This is illustrated by the work of Gold et al (1979), who have been able to distinguish unipolar and bipolar depression by the thyrotropin release test. They found that patients with similar symptomatology and severity of illness reliably fell into unipolar and bipolar specific responses; they suggest that procedures such as a challenge with thyrotropin releasing hormone (TSH) may be useful in predicting whether a patient would respond to lithium (bipolar) or a tricyclic (unipolar).

Thus, a number of approaches to clarify diagnosis and provide a guide to treatment have been advanced. However, a statement the author can readily endorse signifies the state of the art at present: "Actually, there is little known as to what type of depression is most likely to respond to tricyclics and even less regarding the choice of tricyclic drugs" (Kupfer and Detre, 1978). The reader is invited to make his own judgment. Some recent papers which might be helpful include those by Wold and Dwight (1979), Freyhan (1979), Helmchen (1979), and Kupfer and Foster (1978).

Similar problems beset us in child psychiatry as a smaller number of researchers and clinicians attempt to grapple with similar issues in a population that routinely is experiencing developmental, cognitive, and physiologic changes (Petti, 1978).

Attempts have been made to delineate some of the biopsychosocial issues. The Washington group (Cytryn et al, 1974; McKnew and Cytryn, 1979) has attempted, with confusing results, to correlate urinary metabolites such as norepinephrine, vanillylmandelic acid, and 3-methoxy-4-hydroxyphenlethylene glycol in depressed patients. Puig-Antich et al (1979a) have studied cortisol secretion and the Pittsburgh group is studying the physiology of all night sleep electroencelphalogram analysis in normal and depressed children (Kupfer et al, 1979; Coble, in press). As mentioned previously, a positive DST may be helpful in delineating certain types of major depressions in children (Poznanski et al, 1982) and the response to growth hormone to insulin-induced hypoglycemia may be a specific marker for the depressive trait (Puig-Antich, 1982), rather than a state-bound characteristic. The advantage of using the latter may be the preliminary finding that it is not influenced by age as are the DST and all-night sleep electroencephalogram results.

TRICYCLIC ANTIDEPRESSANT TREATMENT OF SYMPTOMS RELATED TO DEPRESSION

The whole concept of depression in children and its treatment has been enigmatic. Many symptom complexes, such as school phobia, hyperactivity, psychosomatic illness, delinquency, and aggressive behavior, have been directly associated with childhood depressive disorders. These symptoms have been treated in a number of ways with a variety of therapeutic modalities, including different classes of drugs. The following discussion will detail how some of these major symptom complexes have been treated with the TCA. Imipramine has been the drug most frequently used in these studies.

School refusal or phobia is a symptom complex which frequently has accompanying depression, anxiety, stomach aches, and general discomfort. Gittelman-Klein and Klein (1971, 1973) in a double-blind, placebo-controlled study of the effects of imipramine reported significant changes on a number of measures for school phobic children. The 35 children, ages six to 14 years, had been absent or refused to attend school for at least two weeks. They were randomly assigned, on the basis of age or sex, to matching placebo or imipramine pills. Regular contact with a case worker who offered supportive therapy, regular contact with the school, and persuasive and desensitization techniques for the child and family were also provided.

Results demonstrate imipramine to be significantly superior to placebo in helping the child return to school. The psychiatrists, the mothers, and the children themselves all rated the imipramine group as showing significantly greater improvement. This included physical complaints and reported fear when going to school. A lessening of depression was the only one of the ten items rated by the mothers which differed significantly between the two groups. The fact that all of the children who received imipramine treatment rated themselves as much improved compared to 21 percent of the placebo group ($p < 0.005$) is very significant to the clinician. Moreover, almost 75 percent of the children receiving placebo, including five of nine of the children who returned to school, reported not feeling better; while three imipramine group children did not return to school, they all reported feeling better. This raises further questions of whether school refusal can truly be said to have its roots in the area of agoraphobia rather than depression.

Conners (1976), in his scholarly review, notes that early separation may predispose an individual to subsequent depression, in childhood or later. We must, of course, wait for more scientific data in this area. Suffice it to say that children who refuse to attend school respond to TCA therapy by returning to school, that some of those who return are still fearful, and that all of those who had been treated with TCA felt better, including those who did not attend school. This study (Gittelman-Klein and Klein, 1971, 1973) follows earlier work (Rabiner and Klein, 1969) which treated school phobic children aged seven to 14 years with imipramine in an open study. They targeted school refusal and anxious, angry, or depressed mood and reported similar results to the later controlled study: return to school was effected for 24 of the 28 children who completed the trial; 75 percent of the 24 who returned to school showed positive change in mood and sociability.

Agitated, aggressive, or hyperkinetic behaviors frequently accompany depression in children. Though there is some disagreement in the field (Poznanski et al, 1979; White, 1977) most workers feel that psychomotor retardation is low on the symptom checklist of depressed children. The exception, of course, may be children hospitalized for medical conditions. A number of reports, though uncontrolled, note that imipramine is highly effective in the treatment of the hyperkinetic syndrome. Huessy and Wright (1970), for example, in a noncontrolled study, used imipramine up to 125 mg per day in children three to 14 years of age (mean seven years). Monitoring progress with parent and school reports of behavior and performance and targeting such items as hyperkinesis, mood swings, aggressiveness, and sleep and school difficulties, they found that 67 percent responded with marked improvement. Ryback et al (1973) were more positive, noting "uniformly excellent results" in several hundred hyperkinetic children treated with imipramine. In this uncontrolled study, depression, hyperactivity, distractability, and short attention span were the monitored symptoms. Brown et al (1973) report on three hyperactive/aggressive children who responded to imipramine.

Watter and Dreifus (1973) diagnosed and treated 118 hyperactive behavior children (aged two to 15 years) with nortriptyline, 20 to 75 mg per day. The children were subjectively rated by teachers, parents, and attending physicians for their extreme activity, attentional deficits, emotional lability, impulsivity, and temper outbursts. Improvement was found in 55 percent, no improvement in 36 percent, and adverse reactions in six percent. The authors concluded that the results were significantly better than those with methylphenidate. Controlled studies using TCA with hyperactive children have tempered this enthusiasm. Greenberg et al (1975) conducted a double-blind, crossover study with 58 children, six to 13 years of age, who had shown a positive response to methylphenidate in comparing the stimulant to imipramine. They found methylphenidate to have greater efficacy with fewer adverse effects and with improved social relatedness; imipramine was better for irritability, whining, clinging behaviors commonly associated with depression, and sleeping difficulties.

Another double-blind, placebo-imipramine, non-crossover comparison with methylphenidate for hyperactive boys was conducted by Rapoport et al (1974). Utilizing a number of reliable and valid instruments, they found imipramine as significantly superior to placebo but not as good as methylphenidate. On follow-up two years later (Riddle and Rapoport, 1976), they found that the children continued to have academic and behavioral problems, with a significantly greater incidence of depression ratings as compared to control subjects, matched for age. But no significant correlation was obtained between the baseline and two-year follow-up data for depression.

Winsberg et al (1972) in a study of hospitalized "neuropsychiatrically impaired" school age children, most of whom were hyperkinetic, aggressive, and inattentive, compared dextroamphetamine to imipramine in a double-blind counterbalanced order. Their data support the use of imirpamine as an effective agent with this type of child. Further use of imipramine to treat hyperactive defiant, inattentive children has been described by Waizer et al (1974). They treated 19 children with a diagnosis of hyperkinetic reaction of childhood and gave a trial of placebo after treatment with imipramine. Results indicated significant improvement in overall ranking of items often considered manifestations of depression—hyperactivity, somatic complaints, affect disturbance, depression, temper tantrums, poor concentration, and anxiety. Even with significant deterioration in target symptoms during the post-imipramine treatment period, positive changes were significantly present compared with the baseline nondrug period. Yepes et al (1977) in a double-blind crossover comparison of amitriptyline and methylphenidate to placebo in a study similar to Winsberg et al (1972) found both active agents to be equally efficacious in attenuating hyperactivity and aggression.

Nocturnal enuresis has been another symptom which has been associated with depression in children. Frommer (1968) has actually designated a category of childhood depression as enuretic-depressive and notes that 54 of the 190 children she reports on fit into this subtype. In her uncontrolled study, she treated these children, three to 16 years of age, with therapeutic groups, amitriptyline, monamine oxidase (MAO) inhibitors, and special help in school and reported good results. Some of the earliest and best controlled studies of imipramine related compounds were in the treatment of enuresis (Blackwell and Currah, 1973). About half of the studies have utilized a double-blind control design and the report by Pouissant and Ditman (1965) is frequently cited as demonstrating the highly significant superiority of imipramine over placebo. Werry et al (1976) report an increase in pleasant feelings in children with enuresis who have not been diagnosed as suffering from emotional problems.

A similar finding was reported by Fromm et al (1972). Six children who had myoclonic or akinetic seizures that were unresponsive to conventional anticonvulsant medications, experienced a decrease in such seizures with imipramine treatment. They also became brighter (by parent report) and more alert during physician visits. Schoolwork was markedly improved and one youngster was able for the first time to use school instruction.

Autistic or young psychotic children comprise another group which have been reported to show improvement with TCA. Kurtis (1966) treated children with schizophrenia or postencephalitic syndrome between the ages of four and 15 years with nortriptyline. In this uncontrolled study which employed rating scales, he found that 76 percent improved in the targeted behaviors of depression, aggressiveness, destructiveness, and self-destructiveness. Petti and Campbell (1975) elaborate on a young depressed psychotic child who showed a dramatic response to imipramine. The use of imipramine with borderline psychotic depressed children has also been found to be effective (Petti and Unis, 1981; Petti and Law, 1982).

Amitriptyline was used in outpatient treatment of emotionally disturbed children who manifested multiple neurotic and behavioral symptoms. Results based on interviews with the parents and child indicated excellent to good response in 68 percent. Those diagnosed as having neurosis with depression (six of seven) had a positive response. McLaughlin (1964), in a double-blind crossover study with Ensidon (opipramol) and placebo, treated nonpsychotic severely disturbed children with targeted behaviors closely approximating the diagnosis of childhood depression: apprehension, tearfulness, loss of interest, hopelessness, insomnia, psychosomatic symptoms, etc. The TCA was found helpful in conjunction with supportive psychotherapy and other services in sufficiently improving behavior to allow for a satisfacotry adjustment. In a similar uncontrolled study of children and young adults, aged five to 21 years with most in early adolescence (Rapoport, 1965), behavior and learning problems were treated with low dose (5 to 40 mg per day) imipramine. Complete or marked remission of all symptoms (enuresis, compulsive behaviors, depression, anxiety, poor learning patterns) occurred after six to 24 months.

ROLE OF TRICYCLIC ANTIDEPRESSANTS IN CHILDHOOD DEPRESSION

Beside the reported studies of depression in children for related or associated behaviors, there is an expanding literature on children treated with TCA who have been diagnosed as depressed. This section will be divided into controlled and noncontrolled studies to facilitate assessment of the data. A preliminary caution: all that glitters is not gold, and the diagnosis of childhood depression may have a unique meaning to the individual investigators.

Uncontrolled Studies

The majority of studies and case reports utilizing TCA for treating children diagnosed as depressed fall into this category. One of the earliest studies is by Crot (1961) who treated a number of children and adolescents aged nine to 18 years for dysphoric states, reactive depression, neurotic origin depression, and psychasthenic depression of adolescence with imipramine. He concluded that imipramine acts for depressed children as it does with depressed adults and allows a child to become more active, develop a better attitude, be more attentive, and be less fearful. He also noted that the very withdrawn, depressed child who has feelings of being persecuted and rejected often is able to lose such symptoms. He in general recommended low dose imipramine therapy for such children but cautioned that consideration of the environment, particularly of the parents, needs to be addressed in therapeutic planning.

Kuhn (1963) provides a very nice overview from the European model of the occurrence in treatment of endogenous depression in children. He cites some of the earlier literature and presentations and concludes that many behavioral problems in children respond well to therapy with antidepressant thymoleptic drugs. His comments certainly highlight some of the author's experiences when he states, "In any case, anyone who is familiar with the special characteristics of depression in children, briefly detailed here, in anyone who experiences just a few times how a child receiving such therapy is strikingly transformed into another hardly recognizable individual, develops a much keener diagnostic sense of recognition for such disturbances. . . . Many children thus live on quite unaffected, following the drug-induced remission as it would follow in the spontaneous course of the depression, while for others the experience poses a great problem which must be resolved by psychotherapy." Dr. Kuhn relates his experience in treating children with imipramine going back to 1958. He has hypothesized from his experience that many pediatric behavioral problems, both functional and psychosomatic, as well as those seemingly related to environmental influences, have depressive states as their basis. Again, from the European model, he recommends low dose therapy.

In a retrospective review of 20 children who had made suicidal attempts, Lawler et al (1963) found that imipramine was the drug of choice in the few cases where there were vegetative signs of depression such as changes in weight or insomnia and or associated with slowing of thought processes. None of the children made suicidal attempts in the follow-up. Westman (1965) describes the result of treating a number of children, aged 11 to 19 years, with imipramine. They had manifested a variety of behaviors subsumed under a number of subclassifications of depression, including endogenous, manic depressive, neurotic, asthenic, and psychogenic. In the endogenous, they found 14 remissions with four positive responders; in the manic depressives there were two remissions and two with no effect; in the neurotic depressions there were 13 positive responses and three with no effect; in the asthenic, two remissions, four positive responders, and four with no effect; in the psychogenic depressions there were six positives; in children presenting initially with depression but later diagnosed as schizophrenia, there were two with positive responses and three with no effect; in the other categories there were two positives and three with no effect. Westman concluded that imipramine is a valuable agent in treating depressions that occur during the age of puberty.

A fascinating paper which describes very low dose imipramine (10 mg per day) is that of Christe (1966) who describes four types of depression in children (anaclitic, neurotic, abandonment, and reactive) which responded to imipramine treatment. Response was determined by the Koch Draw-a-Tree test, the Rorschach, and clinical examination. Target behaviors included scholastic difficulties, enuresis, and encopresis. Christe noted that secondary symptoms disappeared in 70 percent of the cases and that the patients frequently appeared more open and straightforward and that their sadness, dejection, and bitterness usually gave way to feelings of serenity and contentment. The children seemed to become detached from the previous traumas that they had undergone. Christe reports that the changes in the Draw-a-Tree test were remarkable for positive change at a statistically significant level.

Frommer (1967) compared phobic and mood disorder depressive children aged nine to 15 years, mostly prepubertal, in a double-blind, crossover study comparing phenobarbitone and phenelzine/chlordiazepoxide. Measurement consisted of the parent's report and patient interview and compared behavior to previous state as worse, unchanged, slight improvement, or improvement.

The behaviors were related to the inference of depression. There was a suggestion of improvement on the phenelzine/chlordiazepoxide regimen, but the research design was unsatisfactory for a number of reasons (Graham, 1974). In a later work, Frommer studied enuretic depressive, depressive, phobic depressive, manic depressive patients in an uncontrolled study. The therapeutic regimen was geared to the specific subtype of depression. In the enuretic depressive patients, Frommer advocated therapeutic groups, amitriptyline, MAO inhibitors, and special help in school. These were children between three and 16 years with half being between nine and 12 years. There is no indication of measurement for establishing criteria for change in the target behaviors, but the results are reported as good.

Murray (1970) describes several cases in which children exhibiting depressive symptomatology were treated with a variety of medications including MAO inhibitors, TCA, and minor tranquilizers. In the cases described, target behaviors such as depression, sleep disturbance, social withdrawal, fears about death, nonattendance in school, aggression, somatic symptoms, and general anxiety were improved by the treatment.

Children who presented with migraine and nonmigraine headaches and met research criteria for depression were treated by Ling et al (1970) with amitriptyline, imipramine, analgesics, and no medication. The children were four to 16 years of age with 80 percent 12 and under. This was not a controlled study and improvement was measured by changes in complaints of headache and depressive symptoms as either marked, mild, or no improvement. The results indicated that of the children with both depression and migraine, four of six showed marked improvement and one of six mild improvement.

Connell (1972) divides childhood depression into two subcategories: high and low neuroticism categories on the basis of the Junior Eysenck Personality Inventory. The six children in the low neuroticism group showed a persistent fluctuating course in a long (four-year) history of dysphoric mood; two of the six children responded to group psychotherapy and manipulation of the environment to diminish stress but the other four required and responded with dramatically positive results to tricyclic antidepressants. The 12 high neuroticism children had a shorter duration of symptomatology which spanned a few months to two years and a depression seen as a response to specific events. They responded to environmental manipulation and group therapy. Four of the 12 needed tricyclic treatment and "responded well, but not so dramatically." Measurement included assessment of self-concept. The symptoms were scored from interviews of the child and parents and by the Junior Eysenck Personality Inventory. Target behaviors included social withdrawal, feeling rejected, irritability, negative self-concept, and morbid ideas. Connell's hope was that treatments such as his might prevent a great deal of unhappiness in such children.

In a very provocative paper, Ossofsky (1974) analyzes the response of 220 children between the ages of one and 12 years who were treated with imipramine for a variety of disorders and in whom depression was felt to dominate the clinical picture. These were all children that Dr. Ossofsky classified as endogenous depressive. She followed the course of treatment with parent response data, teacher and school report, examination of the child, and, in a small portion of the children, the Wechsler Intelligence Scale for Children–Revised (WISC-R). Imipramine was started at 10 mg per day with a maximum dosage of 300 mg per day. Target behaviors included irritability, easy frustration, short attention span, temper tantrums, and hyperactivity. She reports very good results—particularly when the verbal IQ was greater than the performance IQ. When the verbal IQ was equal to or less than the performance IQ, the addition of phenothiazine medication was often needed.

A number of uncontrolled studies are described in one volume (Annell, 1972). These include work done by Kuhn and Kuhn, Lelord, Stock, Frommer, and other English and European investigators. The results are generally reported as positive.

Weinberg et al (1973) report a comparison study of depressed children who were treated with a TCA versus those who were not so treated. Of the 72 children who comprised their study group referred for school performance or behavior problems in the school setting, 42 were found to be depressed. On follow-up three to seven months after the initial evaluation, 41 depressed and 26 nondepressed children were available. Antidepressant treatment had been recommended for the 35 "actively depressed" children, of whom 19 received this treatment and 15 did not. There was no difference between these two groups regarding age, sex, IQ, grades in school, family history, or number of depressive symptoms. Treatment consisted of a dosage of 25 mg per day or more of imipramine or amitriptyline for at least one month. They found that 12 of the 19 treated showed marked improvement as compared to three of the 15 nontreated. Mild to moderate improvement was found in six treated compared to three nontreated. Only one treated child showed no changes compared to six of the nontreated, and three of the latter group became worse. These differences were significant at the 0.001 level.

Moreover, none of these children received psychotherapy or other counseling assistance. The data is further delineated in a later study (Brumback et al, 1977) and demonstrates the differences between the treated and untreated groups at follow-up at the $p < 0.001$ level for the following categories: dysphoric mood, self-deprecatory ideation, and sleep disturbance. These workers comment on their 95 percent rate of improvement in children treated with the TCAs utilizing modified RDC criteria (Weinberg et al, 1973). This work has been criticized for the lack of a double-blind placebo control but it certainly presents dramatic results!

McConville and Boag (1976), in a fascinating paper which attempts to delineate a typology of childhood depression and discusses therapeutic approaches, noted that TCAs can be very helpful as part of a total treatment program. Imipramine, the one most commonly used, was employed in 17 percent (one of six) in the affectual self-esteem group (D1) and in all six of the children with guilt type depression (D3 mixed) in which the symptoms were very similar to those found with depressed adults. It was also used for the "high feeling intensities" of the mixed D1 and D2 group in 58 percent (11 of 19 cases). In the D2 group it was used in "an attempt to externalize anger." They observed clear clinical benefit after seven to ten days of imipramine treatment in the guilt depressions (D3 mixed) using their 15-item total depression rating scale. They felt that the externalizing of anger was helpful but could not conclude what degree of benefit could be ascribed to the medication, since it was used in conjunction with multiple therapeutic interventions.

Utilizing unmodified adult RDC–DSM-III criteria of depression, Puig-Antich et al (1978) reported on an open uncontrolled study which treated prepubertal children with "major depressive disorders" with imipramine to 5 mg/kg per day. Six cases were found to be responders and two were nonresponders after four continuous weeks of maximum dosage (pre-post imipramine levels were at the $p < 0.004$ level).

A similar open study utilizing modified RDC criteria, the Bellevue Index of Depression (Petti, 1978), found significant overall improvement in the 20 children studied (Petti and Conners, 1981). The children were given imipramine to 5 mg/kg per day (mean 4.5 mg/kg per day) and were followed by twice daily scoring of the total Children's Behavior Inventory of Burdock and Hardesty (1964). They showed significant improvement in many of the nine factor scale scores and the total score. Thus, there is a preponderance of clinical experience to demonstrate that TCAs are an effective form of treatment for clinically depressed children.

Controlled Studies

A major problem has been the lack of double-blind controlled studies. One of the few is that of Lucas et al (1965) who treated a diagnostically heterogenous group of 14 children aged ten to 17 years whose clinical symptoms were marked by a major depressive component. In a 12-week placebo-controlled double-blind crossover between amitriptyline and placebo, monitored by daily ratings of nine behavioral characteristics in the midst of a total milieu program, they found some statistically significant differences ($p < 0.001$) in individual patients for each of these factors: somatic complaints–3, participation in activities–2, spontaneous relationships–2, need for controls–3, response to controls–5, eating difficulties–2, settling at bedtime–3, and depressed appearance–1. None of the children showed differences between placebo and drug periods for sleeping difficulties. The dosage levels were comparatively low (30 to 75 mg per day). Some of the children showed a worsening in some of these factors as well.

A double-blind, between-patient design comparing placebo, perphenazine, amitriptyline, and a perphenazine-amitriptyline combination was conducted by Weise et al (1972). The subjects were 111 underachieving elementary students, grades four to six. A primary depressive reaction diagnosis was made for 46 percent of the children, while the remainder presented symptoms of mixed anxiety and depression; all had Otis IQ scores of 80 or more. Exclusionary conditions included psychosis, organic disorders, epilepsy, and cardiovascular disorders. The children were randomly assigned to each of the four groups. All pills were identical. Maximal dosage level of the TCA was 30 mg per day. A number of assessment measures were used, many modified from adult forms.

The results are interesting because of the manner in which the data was handled. Taking the group as a whole, there were no significant drug differences at the end of eight weeks. However, when the study population was divided into high depressed and low depressed groups, utilizing measures of depression and depressed mood, they found that severity of depression was a major variable. The more depressed patients received greater symptomatic relief, while the less depressed patients showed improvement in classroom performance. But there were no significant differences between drug groups. Of highest interest was the comparison of a "no pill" group (eight) to the placebo group (15); 28 percent of the former showed improved as compared to 60 percent of the latter. Thus, a very significant placebo response seems to operate in some samples of depressed children. Results of a double-blind controlled pilot study reported by Petti and Law (1982) suggest the superiority of imipramine over placebo for children who meet research criteria for depression. Major indicators of depression (dysphroic mood, suicidal ideation, hopelessness, withdrawal, and helplessness) in the three children treated with imipramine decreased appreciably as compared with a lack of such change in the three children treated with placebo. A number of issues peculiar to depressed children and the use of imipramine in their treatment (Petti and Conners, 1981) make double-blind studies on a large group basis difficult to conduct. This strengthens the need for more extensive double-blind studies, both group and individual case studies. Many of the former have or are in the process of being funded. We have conducted several of the latter at the University of Pittsburgh (Petti and Unis, 1981; Petti and Wells, 1980; Taska et al, 1980). It is obvious that much more work needs to be done in this area.

THE EFFECT OF TRICYCLIC ANTIDEPRESSANTS ON CHILDREN

We know, as demonstrated in the material thus far discussed, that TCAs are effective in treating a number of childhood disorders. The primary questions, of course, are how and why. Looking at specific effects of the TCA might shed some light in this area.

Gualtieri (1977) notes that imipramine may be effective in nocturnal enuresis for a number of reasons including an anticholinergic effect on detrusor muscles, an adrenergic effect on the internal sphincter, an influence on both autonomic systems in effecting a balance between them regarding micturition, an action as an antidepressant or anxiolytic agent to decrease the emotional component, and a possible ability to change sleep patterns in children. Rapoport and Mikkelsen (1978) elaborate on these issues and note the conflicting data.

The similar multiplicity of potential actions of imipramine and the TCAs make the specific mechanisms of action in the successful treatment of hyperactive children unclear. The problem of course is that hyperactivity, like depression, is a final common pathway for predisposed or troubled children. Both are symptoms with multiple roots and it is likely that the TCAs act by redistributing the equilibrium of a number of neurotransmitter systems.

Gualtieri (1977) notes the parallel between adult depressives development of tolerance to the anticholinergic side effects but not to the antidepressant action and the seeming tolerance of hyperactive children to the effective action of TCA and suggests an anticholinergic influence as important in its action with children.

There are definite physiologic changes which occur with imipramine treatment of children. A number of workers have described all-night sleep electroencephalogram changes with imipramine and tricyclic medication (Rivto et al, 1969; Kupfer et al, 1979; Taska et al, 1980). Work conducted by Kupfer and associates (Coble et al, 1976; Kupfer, 1976; Kupfer and Foster, 1978) has shown that all-night electroencephalographic sleep parameters can be used as objective measurements in the diagnosis and classification of adult disorders. They have also shown (Kupfer et al, 1976) that electroencephalographic sleep may be useful in predicting the efficacy of antidepressant therapy and as an objective measurement of the effect of the drugs.

Kupfer et al (1979) described the electroencephalographic sleep of 12 children with significant depressive symptomatology who after a two-week drug-free period, were given imipramine up to 5 mg/kg per day and received that dose for at least seven to ten days. Each of the children met the Bellevue Index of Depression criteria (Petti, 1978) for moderate to severe depressive symptomatology. Significant differences between pre- and post-drug conditions included more time spent awake ($p < 0.01$). Wakefulness, which is the percentage of time awake over the total time asleep, was also significantly increased at the 0.01 level. The time spent asleep in minutes was markedly shortened (0.05 level of significance) and sleep efficiency, which is the percentage of total time spent asleep over the total recording period, was also decreased at the 0.002 level of significance. In terms of the REM sleep architecture, latency was markedly increased at the 0.01 level. This is the time elapsed from the moment the child falls asleep to the moment that REM begins. REM time was markedly decreased as were the number of REM periods, going from 4.3 ± 0.3 in the pre-drug to 2.3 ± 0.3 in the drug condition. REM density, which is REM activity over total REM time, increased during the drug period.

An attempt to compare improvers to nonimprovers in the various sleep parameters was not possible because of the high rate of improvement in this group of 12 children; however, certain changes appeared constant, whether the child improved or not. These included: decreased sleep efficiency, increase in stage two sleep, and decrease in stage four sleep. However, all of the children who improved with the medication had a lengthening of REM latency while two of the nonimprovers showed little change, and a third had a REM latency that was even shorter than in the drug-free period. We know that the shift toward an increased arousal state differs from reports in adults whose total time spent sleeping, delta state, and efficiency of sleep are increased by tricyclic administration. All-night sleep electroencephalographic analysis may be an effective means of monitoring depression in children and perhaps in predicting those who may or may not respond to antidepressant medication. It may also help to provide a physiologic measure or monitor of the effectiveness of treatment.

Kraft et al (1966) aptly characterized their perception of the effect of amitriptyline in childhood disturbance when they state that it is as if the drug reduces the physiological effect of tension enough to allow the child to function in circumstances in which, before the medication, he or she was ineffective. They see this as leading to an increase in maturation and development in ego strength, which, in turn, allows for growth within the child and within his environment. This is seen as creating an environment in which the child is apt to benefit from the available ambient positive reinforcers.

Rapoport and Elkins (this volume, Chapter 16) fully describe the psychopharmacology of this group of drugs. Cognitive functioning, which when delayed or disordered may lead to or enhance depression in children, may be affected by TCA. A stimulant-like effect demonstrated by increasing vigilance on the Continuous Performance Task and decreasing impulsivity on the Porteus Maze Test and similar other works is elaborated upon by Rapoport and Mikkelsen (1978).

Aman (1978) reviews the effects of drugs on learning and notes that antidepressants have been found to cause both a significant improvement and a slight nonsignificant improvement in attention using the Continuous Performance

Task and reaction time as measures of change. He also notes that no studies have been done regarding verbal learning as measured by Paired Associate Learning and that antidepressants have not been shown to change reflection-impulsivity as assessed by the Matching Familiar Figures test. None of the antidepressants have been shown to have an effect on short-term memory or on intelligence as measured by the WISC. Conners et al (unpublished data) have noted that imipramine has little effect on a continuous performance test, specifically the Zero Input Tracking with Alternate Distraction (ZITA). When children receiving stimulants were compared to children taking imipramine, the before and after data were significant for increased accuracy for children with the stimulants as compared with no change for children taking imipramine.

Our experience in treating over 60 inpatient hospital children with high dose imipramine has been that children become more in contact with their feelings, have a decreased feeling of anxiety, and have an increased feeling of well-being. This feeling of well-being is often accompanied by a transient experience of depressed mood and affect; the child for the first time comes to grip with these feelings. The child then becomes more in contact with these emotions and develops the ability to describe such feelings and his sense of helplessness and hopelessness. Most of the children also responded by becoming less defiant and oppositional and more compliant and cooperative.

However, some of the children (Pallmeyer and Petti, 1979) became more angry, hostile, and aggressive. We have postulated that this may be related to similar findings reported in adults. Kaplan et al (1961) noted that the response of depressed adults to imipramine was manifested by increased physical and verbal activity and greater interaction with the environment while their former depression, helplessness, and hopelessness decreased. Thus, as in adults and some children, the lethargy, dejection, suicidal ideation, and other depressive symptomatology has been seen to decrease with TCA after which the child is able to deal with some of his feelings in the hospital setting. The two cases presented by Pallmeyer and Petti (1979) were both very depressed children who showed lethargy and dejection. Table 1 contains the data obtained by our unit staff monitoring the Children's Behavior Inventory (CBI) of Burdock and Hardesty (1964) twice daily throughout each child's hospitalization. Two scales on the CBI, the Anger and Hostility and the Lethargy and Dejection scale, are the ones that make the point.

In Case 1, a boy who accidentally killed his twin brother three weeks before admission to our unit, one can note a very high level of lethargy and dejection initially and with imipramine treatment see how that dropped as the anger and hostility increased significantly. As the imipramine was discontinued, his anger and hostility also decreased and the lethargy and dejection continued on the decline.

Table 1 Measurements of Aggression and Dejection of Two Children During Imipramine Treatment

	Pre-imipramine	Imipramine initiated	Optimal imipramine dosage	Imipramine decreased and discontinued
Case 1				
Length of period over which data was collected	2 weeks	2 weeks	13 weeks	2 weeks
Mean number of lethargy/dejection items checked per day	5.2	2.4	2.8	0.4
Mean number of anger/hostility items checked per day	0.6	1.2	4.0	2.6
Case 2				
Length of period over which data was collected	2 weeks	2 weeks	5 weeks	2 weeks
Mean number of lethargy/dejection items checked per day	9.0	7.8	7.8	4.6
Mean number of anger/hostility items checked per day	4.4	9.0	8.6	6.6
Mean number of suicidal statements per week	4.0	3.5	1.2	0.0
Mean number of aggressive acts necessitating locked seclusion per week	0	0	6.4	2.0

Case 2, a 6½-year-old boy who had had numerous unsuccessful foster home placements, including a rejection by adopted parents, presented with social withdrawal, irritability, frequent tearfulness, and extreme feelings of sadness, loneliness, and low self-esteem. He also often thought of suicidal and homicidal activities and felt worthless and rejected. His CBI data closely paralleled that of the older boy. The anger and hostility increased as imipramine therapy was instituted and decreased once it was stopped. The lethargy and dejection showed the opposite effect. In the second case we recorded the number of suicidal statements, which parallel the lethargy and dejection scores; these were completely absent after the medicine was increased and discontinued. The number of aggressive acts dramatically increased following the institution of medication and decreased precipitously once medication was discontinued. These results are quite dramatic and reflect the ability of the child to get in better contact with feeling states; however, degree and direction is not typical for children treated with imipramine.

We have noted and it will be demonstrated in the next chapter that many of the children lack the ability to derive pleasure and positive reinforcement from their environment. We have treated many children with social skills/assertion/conflict resolution skills and have found that children are better able to use such training, as well as their own individual dynamically oriented therapy, during or after treatment with imipramine.

SIDE EFFECTS

A number of side effects have been reported when children are treated with a TCA. Gualtieri (1977) provides a partial review of this issue. One of the few studies that compares placebo and imipramine (Gittelman-Klein and Klein, 1973) lists the side effects of the two conditions in children treated for school refusal. The only symptom that significantly differentiated the two groups was dryness of mouth, which was more frequent in imipramine-treated children. Fortunately, all the side effects are of a minor nature and are those generally found with drug therapy of any type.

Kuhn and Kuhn (1972) report side effects in one fifth of their cases, but only rarely did they necessitate changing the therapy. The chief side effects included gastric upsets, nausea and vomiting, dizziness, and headache. They note that the children suffered from similar side effects as those in adults but less frequently. Kurtis (1966) lists such symptoms as dryness of mouth, restlessness, epigastric distress, tremulousness, weakness, fatigue, confusional state, excess weight gain, and temper tantrums as present in one or two of the 16 children treated with amitriptyline. However, six showed no side effects.

Gittelman-Klein (1974) lists a number of side effects with imipramine four weeks after a mean dosage of 167 mg per day. After 12 weeks of treatment, the mean dose was 161 mg per day and the percentage of children with no side effects increased from 17 to 44 percent. There were no children with one side effect, 22 percent with two, 11 percent with three, and 22 percent with four or five side effects. Difficulty in falling asleep and dry mouth were the ones reported by greatest number of children. Her clinical impression was that imipramine did not seem as problematic as had methylphenidate in the past and seemed potentially easier to manage than stimulant medication. She noted that her sample of 12 was small.

Frommer (1968) using low dose amitriptyline found that children given a morning dose often complained of sleepiness and could not go to school. Once the dose was given in the evening, the problems stopped. Nausea was a complaint that caused change of treatment to imipramine. A few children developed constipation and required laxatives and one or two developed "hysterical behavior." She reports constipation in one or two children as a side effect of imipramine.

Lucas et al (1965) found that only one child out of the 14 patients treated with amitriptyline had a side effect. This was a girl who became drowsy an hour after each administration of 25 mg of the medication. One adolescent girl who was not in the study seemed to develop an acute schizophrenic episode with suicidal preoccupations, delusions, and depersonalization. Ossofsky (1974) on the other hand noted the absence of toxic reactions or side effects except for dilation of pupils in the 220 children she had treated in that study and in other children she has treated with imipramine. She also assessed routine complete blood counts, including platelet counts, slit lamp examinations, and liver and kidney function tests, and reports them as unimpaired in children who had received maintenance therapy for as long as seven years.

Lucas et al (1965) note that the poorest response with amitriptyline occurred in individuals who had chronically poor adjustment histories and inadequate control of hostility and negativism. These patients showed an aggravation of symptomatology. Crot (1961) states that children might become antagonistic or rebellious as part of the response to imipramine. Tec (1963) has noted a similar phenomenon in an eight-year-old boy who became increasingly aggressive. Pouissant and Ditman (1965) report increased irritability as one of the side effects in a number of children who they treated with relatively low doses of imipramine for nocturnal enuresis. In a double-blind controlled study by Weise et al (1972), medication with a TCA produced significantly more side effects at two weeks than the placebo or the phenothiazine medication ($p < 0.001$). This difference held at the eighth week of treatment, in which the primary side effect was sedation.

The two areas in which side effects are of most concern are those dealing with the cardiovascular and central nervous systems. Cardiovascular changes have been reported for adults on TCA therapy and a number of investigators have reported similar changes in children (Winsberg et al, 1975; Saraf et al, 1974, 1978; Greenberg et al, 1975; Lake et al, 1979).

Winsberg et al (1975) report seven cases where electrocardiographic abnormalities occurred in children ages seven to ten years who were receiving high dose imipramine therapy. A first degree atrioventricular block was present in three of these children. In all the cases, the repolarization process was altered, as shown by an increase in T-wave width and a decrease in T-wave magnitude. One patient showed a minor shift of the P and T axes and another had a shift of the P axis to the left. Koehl and Wenzel (1971) report on hypotension and a subsequent electrocardiogram revealing first degree atrioventricular block in a nine-year-old girl treated with 25 mg of imipramine twice a day for enuresis. Saraf et al (1978) analyzed the effects of imipramine on the electrocardiogram of 25 hyperactive and eight school phobic children who were receiving 3.5 mg/kg per day or more. They found an increase in P-R interval of 0.02 second or more, particularly in those with a small pretreatment P-R interval; in seven children a prolongation of the P-R interval above the rate-corrected norm period. Greenberg et al (1975) report increases in systolic and diastolic blood pressure with high dose imipramine therapy and Lake et al (1979) report similar changes. On the other hand, Martin and Zaug (1975) monitored electrocardiographic tracings monthly on 27 children with normal cardiovascular function receiving therapy for enuresis and found no substantial electrocardiogram changes in any of these children. The doses range from 25 to 75 mg per day. Rapoport et al (1974), using dosages averaging 80 mg per day in two divided doses, found no electrocardiogram changes.

The central nervous system effects have an equally important role regarding potential contraindications or complications for therapy. A number of case reports are available describing seizures accompanying imipramine therapy. A review (Petti and Campbell, 1975) describes a number of these studies. Brown et al (1973) describe the seizures of three brain-damaged children who were receiving imipramine therapy. Another case (Petti and Law, unpublished) describes a depressed, borderline child who responded well to imipramine treatment, developed a viral infection with a high fever, and had one grand mal episode. A pre-drug electroencelphalogram showed a number of slow wave patterns in the left temporal region but no paroxysmal features were present in either of two tracings, one of which was a sleep record. The child was placed on 5 mg/kg per day imipramine and received this regimen for one week when the seizure occurred. An electroencephalogram conducted shortly after the seizure indicated scattered slow waves without paroxysmal features. The child was not cooperative for the electroencephalogram. This child was maintained on half the maximal dosage for a period of time and was not able to maintain the previous degree of clinical progress. On follow-up of three months he has not developed any subsequent seizures and has been said to have maintained good clinical progress.

Fromm et al (1972) reported an exacerbation of grand mal psychomotor seizures in five of 20 patients who were given imipramine to control their minor motor and petit mal seizures because they had failed to respond to conventional anticonvulsant medication. This was handled by increasing their diphenylhydantoin or primidone which they had already been taking. These workers note that imipramine never provoked an increase in major uncontrollable seizures. However, the case described by Petti and Campbell (1975) reported that a two year, ten-month-old child continued to have intractable seizures over time. They also note that seizures often accompany child psychotic disorders. A recent report further confirms this impression (Deykin and MacMahon, 1979).

In our experience, an abnormal electroencephalogram per se should not be viewed as a contraindication to TCA treatment, even at the relatively high dose levels described in this review. We have treated several children who have had electroencephalograms reported as diffusely abnormal with or without paroxysmal features. Generally, we try to find alternatives to TCA treatment. When these fail, we then turn to imipramine.

One child for instance, a 6¾ year old white girl who met BID criteria for depression, was referred for longstanding behavioral and emotional problems including impulsivity, suicidal ideation, and hyperactivity. She scored 17 on the CDI (Kovacs, revised). Her electroencephalogram was described as "mildly and diffusely abnormal and paroxysmal." During sleep "there is one poorly organized bilateral and diffuse spike wave discharge with a duration of one to two seconds and maximum amplitude of 400 V. There are no focal features. Photic simulation produced bilateral diffuse spike wave discharges with maximum amplitude of 400 mV." The child failed to respond to an intensive therapeutic program and her depression persisted. Imipramine was begun at 25 mg at bedtime and slowly increased to 100 mg per day (5 mg/kg per day) over 15 days. Electroencephalograms were obtained at 50 mg per day and shortly after she reached the 75 mg per day and 100 mg per day doses. There were no changes in the electroencephalograms then or after she received the 100 mg per day dose for one week. There was no clinical evidence of seizure activity.

The ad hoc committee on TCA cardiac cardiotoxicity (Robinson and Barker, 1975) suggested the following labeling changes for imipramine-type medication:

1. That imipramine, in the treatment of enuresis, should not exceed 2.5 mg/kg per day.

2. That the mean lethal dose of imipramine in an acute overdose is 30 mg/kg and the lowest reported lethal dose is 8 mg/kg.

3. That in the warning section, preexisting cardiovascular disease should be listed and extra precautions required; and in the precautions section, that

careful monitoring should be undertaken in any patient with preexisting cardiac disease or cardiographic abnormalities, and during initial TCA therapy until steady state levels are achieved.

It was also recommended that the Bureau of Drugs should permit doses up to 5 mg/kg per day for imipramine in research protocols involving children, provided that adequate cardiac monitoring is carried out. Goldstein et al (1977) describe their findings of left ventricular performance in electrocardiographic changes during imipramine therapy in seven hyperactive aggressive children treated with 5 mg/kg per day of imipramine. They again observed nonspecific T-wave changes and prolonged P-R intervals with the drug. Only the pre-injection peak of the first derivative of the apex cardiogram (R-dA/dt) changed significantly with imipramine therapy. They note that the impact of this finding is diminished somewhat because of the small sample size and the skew in the degree of R-dA/dt increase. But note also that the one child who showed a large change in this parameter was also one whose pre-injection period over left ventricular ejection time increased. They conclued that when doses not exceeding 5 mg/kg per day are used, in three divided doses, imipramine does not adversely affect left ventricular performance in children. They caution that this does not mean that the drug is unequivocally safe for all children and that electrocardiographic changes do occur and may be significant. They also question whether desmethylimipramine which is less cardiosensitive can be used as a substitute of equal clinical efficacy but with less cardiotoxicity than imipramine.

Saraf et al (1974) note minor side effects which occurred in 83 percent of the 65 children and young adolescents receiving imipramine treatment as compared to 70 percent in 37 similar children receiving placebo. Over four percent of the imipramine group had what they considered to be significant side effects with the majority occurring during the first three weeks of treatment. One child in this study died, possibly due to high dosage (300 mg per day given at bedtime for a six-year-old). This may have been a drug cardiotoxic idiosyncratic effect. None of the other side effects were significant enough to necessitate withdrawal of the drug.

Another side effect that has been encountered in the use of TCAs is the phenomenon of withdrawal symptoms after abrupt cessation of high dose TCA. Gualtieri and Staye (1979) report on a child who developed severe gastrointestinal symptoms when his amitriptyline was stopped abruptly. There was no other evidence to suggest a toxic or infectious origin for the nausea and vomiting. Petti and Law (1981) report on two children who in the course of treatment had high dose imipramine (3.5 to 5 mg/kg per day) abruptly stopped. Similar gastrointestinal signs and symptoms occurred with such children. The symptoms were of short duration. Another study (Law et al, 1981) describes withdrawal-like symptoms in a number of children who were gradually tapered from imipramine medication. Three of these children had what appeared to be acute decompensation with bizarre, psychotic-like behavior. This is certainly something that clinicians need to take into account when they use high dose medication. It is important to note that nausea and vomiting were symptoms that occurred to a significant degree in many of these children. Increased moodiness and irritability were also frequently reported. These symptoms are often cited as side effects of the TCA and as reason to decrease or terminate the medication. We suggest the dosage be tapered over a ten to 14-day period as has been recommended for adults (Kupfer and Detre, 1978). Gittelman-Klein (1974) suggests that maintenance on the lower doses of imipramine for several days before total discontinuation generally reduces the withdrawal phenomenon. We have had a similar experience.

DOSAGE SCHEDULES

The dosage for TCA therapy, particularly the tertiary forms, imipramine and amitriptyline, varies greatly in the literature. Early workers, the English and Europeans in particular, advocated starting with 10 mg per day dosages and gradually working up to 30 to 60 mg per day. Many of the references cited above used maximal doses for 11 to 12-year-olds that were 100 mg per day or less. Gittelman-Klein and Klein (1971) reported 75 mg per day as the minimally effective dose for school-phobic children. Westman (1965) reports not needing dosages greater than 250 mg per day in depressed children 11 to 19 years of age.

Ossofsky (1974) administered imipramine to children one to 12 years of age on a dosage schedule that began at 10 mg per day and was increased by 10 mg per day every third day until the expected clinical improvement was noted. The maximal dose used (300 mg per day) was for a five-year-old. She divided the dose into one or two daily administrations and did not tailor the total daily dose to weight. She maintained children under the age of five years for indefinite periods of time, and otherwise would taper and discontinue the medication at the end of the school year for those children who had been treated for at least six months. The 300 mg per day for the five-year-old, and the relatively high doses given to some of the other children, were maintained for six to eight weeks or until no further improvement was apparent, and then tapered to the lower level where improvement was maintained. Ossofsky regulated the dose according to the needs of the child, as related to stress or physical illness.

Most investigators are adhering to the recommended Food and Drug Administration (FDA) guidelines of 5 mg/kg per day in divided doses (Hayes et al, 1975). We (Petti and Conners, 1981; Petti et al, 1980) have noticed that, in many instances, going the full distance to 5 mg/kg per day as the FDA recommends is necessary for optimal clinical results. Though Puig-Antich et al (1978,

1979b) report that dosage levels below this are entirely satisfactory, particularly if plasma imipramine levels can be monitored, we have found that the smaller children (40 kg or less), require the full 5 mg/kg per day. We had also set an arbitrary limit of 200 mg per day but have revised this based on the clinical experience of the Columbia group and will now got to 250 mg per day for the child weighing 50 kg or more (Perel, 1979). However, the monitoring of plasma tricyclic levels may obviate this problem. Weller et al (1981), in a preliminary study comparing clinical response to imipramine in children meeting research criteria for major depression, also found a strong correlation between positive changes in behavior and plasma level. These data also suggest a possible "therapeutic window" between 150 and 300 mg/ml. We report (Petti and Law, 1982) one similar case. Further findings confirming this data are forthcoming (Perel, 1982).

The schedule we employ is given in Table 2. You will note that we begin with 25 mg at bedtime and gradually increase to the optimal or maximal dose by day 7. Puig-Antich et al (1978, 1979a, 1979b), on the other hand, move in a stepwise progression as specified by the FDA for research purposes. Our original research protocol negotiated with the FDA is similar to this (Table 3). We have agreed to the FDA requirement of maintaining a dosage of less than 4 mg/kg per day for three days before advancing to the maximal dosage for the child and of monitoring the electrocardiogram by obtaining a daily rhythm strip for three days once the dosage exceeds 4 mg/kg per day in children on research protocol.

The schedule we employ in Pittsburgh is for hospitalized children where time restraints can be of critical importance. The Columbia group is generally treating outpatients. For our outpatient, clinically depressed children, we carry out the dosage schedule over a two to four-week period of time.

The duration of treatment varies from clinician to clinician as do the dosage level and schedules. The schedule we employ for our inpatient children, of seven days to reach maximal dosage, 21 days on maximal dosage, and ten to 14 days to taper off and discontinue the medication is brief compared to most other reports. We have had good clinical responses to this regimen and have needed to reinstitute or continue a high dosage of imipramine in less than 20 percent of the cases.

Several cases in which imipramine was reinstituted occurred early in our experience with the high dose schedules. In retrospect, some of these children were probably experiencing the symptoms of withdrawal. None of the last 15 children we have treated with high dose medication have required reinstitution of medication.

When we reinstitute imipramine treatment, we generally do this at one-half the maximal dosage, maintain this level for three to four weeks, and again taper and discontinue the drug. Very few children have required further

Table 2

Weight (kg)	Day 1	Day 2	Day 3	Day 4	Day 5	Day 6	Day 7
10 or more	25 mg hs	25 mg hs	25 mg hs	25 mg hs	25 mg hs	25 mg hs	25 mg AM 25 mg hs
15 or more	25 mg hs	25 mg hs	25 mg AM 25 mg hs	25 mg AM 25 mg hs	25 mg AM 25 mg hs	25 mg AM 25 mg hs	25 mg AM 25 mg 5 PM 25 mg hs
20 or more	25 mg hs	25 mg hs	25 mg AM 25 mg hs	25 mg AM 25 mg hs	25 mg AM 25 mg 5 PM 25 mg hs	25 mg AM 25 mg 5 PM 25 mg hs	25 mg AM 25 mg 5 PM 50 mg hs
25 or more	25 mg hs	25 mg hs	25 mg AM 25 mg hs	25 mg AM 25 mg 5 PM 25 mg hs	25 mg AM 25 mg 5 PM 50 mg hs	25 mg AM 25 mg 5 PM 50 mg hs	50 mg AM 25 mg 5 PM 50 mg hs
30 or more	25 mg hs	25 mg hs	25 mg AM 25 mg hs	25 mg AM 25 mg 5 PM 25 mg hs	25 mg AM 25 mg 5 PM 50 mg hs	50 mg AM 25 mg 5 PM 50 mg hs	50 mg AM 50 mg 5 PM 50 mg hs
35 or more	25 mg hs	25 mg AM 25 mg hs	25 mg AM 25 mg 5 PM 25 mg hs	25 mg AM 25 mg 5 PM 50 mg hs	50 mg AM 25 mg 5PM 50 mg hs	50 mg AM 50 mg 5PM 50 mg hs	50 mg AM 50 mg 5 PM 75 mg hs
40 or more	25 mg hs	25 mg AM 50 mg hs	25 mg AM 25 mg 5 PM 50 mg hs	50 mg AM 25 mg 5 PM 50 mg hs	50 mg AM 50 mg 5 PM 50 mg hs	50 mg AM 50 mg 5 PM 75 mg hs	75 mg AM 50 mg 5 PM 75 mg hs
45 or more	25 mg hs	25 mg AM 50 mg hs	50 mg AM 25 mg 5 PM 50 mg hs	50 mg AM 50 mg 5 PM 50 mg hs	50 mg AM 50 mg 5 PM 75 mg hs	75 mg AM 50 mg 5 PM 75 mg hs	75 mg AM 75 mg 5 PM 75 mg hs
50 or more	50 mg hs	50 mg AM 50 mg hs	50 mg AM 50 mg 5 PM 50 mg hs	50 mg AM 50 mg 5 PM 75 mg hs	75 mg AM 50 mg 5 PM 75 mg hs	75 mg AM 75 mg 5 PM 75 mg hs	75 mg AM 50 mg 5 PM 100 mg hs

Table 3 Protocol for Tofranil Study

Weight (kg)	Day 1	Day 2	Day 3	Day 4	Day 5	Day 6	Day 7	
10 or more	25 mg hs	25 mg hs	25 mg hs	25 mg hs	25 mg hs	25 mg hs	25 mg AM 25 mg hs	50
15 or more	25 mg hs	25 mg hs	25 mg hs	25 mg AM 25 mg hs	25 mg AM 25 mg hs	25 mg AM 25 mg hs	25 mg AM 25 mg 5 PM 25 mg hs	75
20 or more	25 mg hs	25 mg AM 25 mg hs	25 mg AM 25 mg hs	25 mg AM 25 mg 5 PM 25 mg hs	25 mg AM 25 mg 5 PM 25 mg hs	25 mg AM 25 mg 5 PM 25 mg hs	25 mg AM 25 mg 5 PM 50 mg hs	100
25 or more	25 mg hs	25 mg AM 25 mg hs	25 mg AM 25 mg hs	25 mg AM 25 mg 5 PM 25 mg hs	25 mg AM 25 mg 5 PM 25 mg hs	25 mg AM 25 mg 5 PM 25 mg hs	50 mg AM 25 mg 5 PM 50 mg hs	125
30 or more	25 mg hs	25 mg AM 25 mg hs	25 mg AM 25 mg 5 PM 25 mg hs	25 mg AM 25 mg 5 PM 50 mg hs	25 mg AM 25 mg 5 PM 50 mg hs	25 mg AM 25 mg 5 PM 50 mg hs	50 mg AM 50 mg 5 PM 50 ms hs	150
35 or more	25 mg hs	25 mg AM 25 mg 5 PM 25 mg hs	25 mg AM 25 mg 5 PM 50 mg hs	50 mg AM 25 mg 5 PM 50 mg hs	50 mg AM 25 mg 5 PM 50 mg hs	50 mg AM 25 mg 5 PM 50 mg hs	50 mg AM 50 mg 5 PM 75 mg hs	175
40 or more	50 mg hs	25 mg AM 50 mg hs	25 mg AM 25 mg 5 PM 50 mg hs	50 mg AM 50 mg 5 PM 50 mg hs	50 mg AM 50 mg 5 PM 50 mg hs	50 mg AM 50 mg 5 PM 50 mg hs	75 mg AM 50 mg 5 PM 75 mg hs	200
45 or more	50 mg hs	25 mg AM 50 mg hs	25 mg AM 25 mg 5 PM 50 mg hs	50 mg AM 50 mg 5 PM 50 mg hs	50 mg AM 50 mg 5 PM 50 mg hs	50 mg AM 50 mg 5 PM 50 mg hs	75 mg AM 75 mg 5 PM 75 mg hs	225
50 or more	50 mg hs	25 mg AM 25 mg 5 PM 50 mg hs	25 mg AM 25 mg 5 PM 50 mg hs	50 mg AM 50 mg 5 PM 75 mg hs	50 mg AM 50 mg 5 PM 75 mg hs	50 mg AM 50 mg 5 PM 75 mg hs	75 mg AM 75 mg 5 PM 100 mg hs	

imipramine treatment following this regimen. Relapse can occur from two weeks to seven months after decreasing from the maximal level.

One child who was treated on our unit is an example of our experience. Lynn is a 13-year-old girl who was referred for school refusal and depression. The child had a chronic history of reluctance to attend school but for the five months before hospitalization absolutely refused to go, would barricade herself in her room, and become aggressive if attempts were made to force her to school. She scored very high on the BID (Petti, 1978) in all areas, particularly dysphoric mood, self-depreciatory ideation, sleep problems, and somatic complaints. The family was extremely dysfunctional. With imipramine to 200 mg per day in divided doses (4.3 mg/kg per day) she became less depressed, and her lethargy dejection scale on the CBI (Burdock and Hardesty, 1964) dropped; however, it increased just before discharge after two months of hospitalization. She was able to be more open concerning her ambivalence about leaving the hospital, worries concerning her inability to talk with her parents, and fears that she would step back into her old habits. The staff considered her to be mildly improved and the author felt she was markedly improved over her admission levels.

Lynn was referred to a special school for emotionally disturbed children and she and her family were referred to our Family Therapy Clinic. A one-year follow-up revealed substantial gains in all areas. Our educational psychologist visited the school and reported that Lynn's overall academic functioning had greatly improved and that she had been on the honor roll during the last two marking periods. Her peer group relationships had steadily improved and she was viewed as the "most popular" person in the program by her peers. Lynn had been tapered from imipramine during the six weeks after discharge from the hospital. She was receiving weekly psychotherapy, she and her parents were being seen monthly in family therapy, and the family therapist related significant gains over the year's time. The mother reported similar improvement and noted that Lynn was happier, had more interests, was dating, had more girlfriends, was participating with them regularly, and was spending more time out of her room and with her family. Difficulty falling asleep and trouble awakening in the morning were less problematic than previously. She was less moody and irritable and better able to share feelings and handle frustration.

Lynn requested to see me about three years after discharge from the hospital. Her parents had made some changes, particularly her mother, but her brother and father wre continuing to drink heavily. She said that she was returning to the state she was in before her earlier hospitalization—being unable to fall asleep, feeling fatigued all the time, losing her interest in things, having multiple somatic complaints, avoiding school, and having suicidal ideation. Moreover, she feared that she too might start "hitting the bottle" in order to assuage her helpless feelings. Her BID was again very positive. She was begun on imipramine at 50 mg in the morning and 100 mg at bedtime and showed rapid improvement. She reported no longer having to drag herself to school, her sleeping improved dramatically, she was able to deal with a number of environmental conflicts, and she was no longer feeling depressed. In this case, as has been my experience previously, it was not necessary to go to the full dose of medication for a second course of treatment.

PATIENT SELECTION AND MONITORING TRICYCLIC ANTIDEPRESSANT TREATMENT

We have found the BID to be an effective screening instrument for determining which children should be given a trial of TCA. This is an instrument which combines both the child and the parenting figures' perceptions to provide the best clinically available data which can be reasonably obtained in a clinical setting. Obtaining data solely by child report or by interviewing parents provides too many false negatives for depression. Some children, for whatever reason, simply deny their depressive symptoms—in fact, some of the most depressed children we have treated score close to zero on their section of the BID or on the Children's Depression Inventory (CDI) (Kovacs et al, 1976). There are a number of parents who also deny even the most overtly severe depressive behavior in their children. (Occasionally, we experience both parents and children who deny the presence of depressive symptomatology.)

Children treated on an inpatient unit are generally given two weeks of intensive milieu, behavioral, psychoeducational, and individual therapy before medication is considered. In the past, we have often given an intensive course of social skills training as an alternative to medication (Petti, 1981).

A number of assessment instruments are used, some of which are standard, others individualized depending on the particular symptoms of the children. The CDI is a research assessment we routinely employ. We also utilize an instrument—the Pittsburgh Activities of Living Scale—Children (PALS-C)—which monitors daily functioning in four basic areas: (1) activities of daily living (ADL) such as basic hygiene, (2) compliance (Comp) to specified unit procedures, (3) mealtime social interaction (MSI), and (4) adaptive peer interactions (API) (Petti and Unis, 1981). Direct observations in the classroom of on-task, neutral, and disruptive (dis) behavior are routinely collected using time sampling procedures (Williamson et al, 1981). The Teacher Affect Rating Scale (TARS), a 26-item scale with three factors—depression, behavioral, and academic—has also proven to be very useful in monitoring depression in many children. Direct, time-sampled observations in a free play setting to measure adaptive (API), maladaptive (MPI), isolation or solitary play (SP), and interactive play with staff (SI) have also proven useful.

The School Age Depression Listed Inventory (SADLI), a psychiatric interview, helps determine whether a child continues to be depressed or whether the child has responded to individualized treatments such as TCA or social skills training. It is important to note that the author has not found any single instrument or source of data which provides a valid assessment of the need for or response to medication or other treatment. The BID, for the author, has proven to be the single most useful instrument.

We also monitor for side effects utilizing a format similar to that described by Gittelman-Klein and Klein (1973) with modification. Routine electrocardiograms are obtained to monitor for the variety of cardiac changes reported in the literature. We have, parenthetically, not experienced a single case of first degree heart block or any other cardiac change requiring decreasing or terminating imipramine. One child did develop orthostatic hypotension. The dose schedule of imipramine was reduced and increased slowly to the maximal dose and no futher problems were encountered.

We use TCAs other than imipramine when we have a history of previous positive response or a family history of positive response to another TCA, such as amitriptyline. We have not found that delusional-like or borderline psychotic behavior is a contraindication to TCA therapy and, in fact, have had reportable success with such children (Petti and Wells, 1980; Petti and Unis, 1981).

Our previous case reports (Pallmeyer and Petti, 1979; Petti and Wells, 1980; Petti et al, 1980; Michelson et al, in press; Petti and Unis, 1981; Sonis et al, 1981; Williamson et al, 1981) describe how we monitor response to treatment. The problem with monitoring depressed children treated with TCAs is that, if you use solely what the child is saying and experiencing, you might misjudge the utility of the drug. Since imipramine is expected to allow the child greater access to his/her feelings and to facilitate more appropriate and less deviant behavior, we do not get overly concerned when a child who formerly denied ever feeling depressed, worthless, negative, or oppositional begins to cry, relates his feelings of depression, helplessness, and hopelessness, or begins to become more assertive, sometimes even in a negative way.

Lonny is a good example of such a case. He presented as a nine-year-old bi-racial child who was removed from his natural mother at age 5 years because of physical abuse and from a foster family a few months before admission because of emotional abuse. He spent time in a children's shelter and then was placed in a truly ideal foster placement. Because his volatile, impulsive, violent behavior alternated with loving and caring, he was referred to us for evaluation and short-term treatment. He met BID criteria for depression and had markedly elevated scores on the TARS and SADLI. The following is excerpted from his treatment plan:

Short-term Goals of Hospitalization for Lonny

1. *Aggression*
   Goal: To significantly decrease aggression
   Target measurement:
   a. Decrease locked quiet room—either eliminate or decrease by 50 percent or more
   b. Adaptive peer interaction (API) at 60 percent or increase by 20 percent over baseline
   c. API to 75 percent or increase by 20 percent on PALS
   Intervention:
   a. Milieu time-out procedure
   b. Individual psychotherapy
   c. Consideration of medication
   d. Possible social skills training; behavior program
   e. Self monitoring and self-control program

2. *Depression*
   Goal: Measurement: decrease or eliminate
   Target measurement:
   a. TARS, SADLI, CDI—if problem, decrease by 50 percent
   b. Increase API as in Number 1
   Intervention:
   a. Milieu
   b. Individual psychotherapy
   c. Consider medication
   d. Social skills training, if possible
   e. Resolution of family situation, if possible

3. *Learning or school problem*: behavior and/or academic
   Goal: Assess for learning disability and devise individualized educational prescription
   Target measures:
   a. Psychoeducational evaluation
   b. TARS and direct observations of disruptive and on-task behavior intervention
   Intervention:
   a. Individualized and educational prescription

4. *Assess for presence of stealing behavior*: eliminate if present
   Target measurement:
   a. Daily inventory of room contents

Intervention:

a. If stealing behavior is present, stealing protocol

5. *Well child care–multiple somatic complaints*: rule out physical disease
Intervention:
a. Physical examination
b. Admission tests
c. Ophthalmology consultation if indicated
d. Visual acuity testing

6. *Oppositionalism*
Goal: To significantly decrease oppositionalism
Target measurements:
a. Compliance to 80 percent or 20 percent over baseline on PALS
b. Absence of oppositional behavior on SADLI
Intervention:
a. Milieu
b. Time-out procedure
c. Individual psychotherapy
d. Consider medication
e. Self control program

7. *Sexual acting out*
Goal: To assess for inappropriate behavior and eliminate or significantly decrease behavior, if present
Target measurements:
a. Direct observation to assess occurrence and/or frequency of behavior
Intervention:
a. If behavior persists, formulate treatment plan

8. *Fire-setting by history*
Goal: To assess degrees of problem and eliminate, if present
Target measurements:
a. Direct observations
Intervention: If behavior occurs, direct intervention and formulation of treatment program

Long-Term Goals:

1. Significantly decrease aggression and oppositionalism
2. Eliminate depression
3. Eliminate stealing, fire-setting, and sexually provocative behavior if found to be problems

4. Increase adaptive peer interaction
5. Increase Lonny's insight as to reasons for his oppositional behavior
6. Placement in appropriate educational setting
7. Resolution of foster home placement—legal difficulties

After the diagnostic conference at the end of his first two weeks of hospitalization, Lonny was placed on a self-control program where he monitored his behavior and was rewarded for accurate monitoring as well as maintaining control during stressful situations. He made substantial gains, developed a brighter affect, and a better self-concept over the next month. He was using his social skills (on occasion to redirect his peers) was decreasing the destruction of his own property, and increasing his positive interactions with his new step family. The short term goals 1 and 6 were achieved and goals 4 and 8 required no intervention since no associated problems were seen. His explosive behavior had decreased significantly. In individual psychotherapy, he continued to seek magical solutions and voiced wishes of leaving the hospital and seeing his former foster parents. His frustration level was viewed as markedly improved.

In the next two weeks, his behavior again became erratic, with a dramatic increase in noncompliant behavior outside those measured on the PALS-C, pouting, sexual acting out, testing limits, and deviant behavior. This is demonstrated on Table 4 in the Direct Observations from the class and free play settings and in locked and open quiet room statistics. There were multiple episodes of careless, dangerous behavior. He also complained of increasing difficulty in falling asleep. His foster parents had instituted a time out procedure for all the children in the family and on weekend pass Lonny was the only one who did not require this form of punishment. In individual psychotherapy, he was still discussing magical solutions to his problems. Because of the failure to meet the goals regarding his depression, the evident regression in areas not highly structured, his failure to develop insight into his difficulties, and his excessively controlled behavior which would degenerate into destructive acts, a trial of imipramine was instituted.

After one week of full dose (125 mg per day, 5 mg/kg per day in three divided doses) significant gains were made in all areas (Table 4). He reported sleeping and feeling better. In individual therapy, he appeared more cheerful, was able to discuss issues more clearly and realistically but was unable to role-play anger inducing situations. All the short-term goals, except for depression, had been met. By discharge, his depression had decreased significantly, he was hopeful about the future, and he was able to verbalize realistic concerns and potential conflicts he would need to handle. There was a regression noted in areas where consequences for noncompliance were minimal. All the short and long-term goals of hospitalization had been met. A CDI (Kovacs, revised) was completely negative.

Table 4

	Weeks					
	1-2	3-4	5-6	7-8	9-10*	11-12*
PALS-C	%	%	%	%	%	%
ADL	75	81	78	79	81	89
MSI	80	84	83	83	83	87
Comp	82	85	87	89	86	90
API	69	76	75	78	78	81
Direct observation	%	%	%	%	%	%
API	53	77	72	61	94	27
MPI	2	2	3	11	0	4
SP	38	19	11	19	3	69
SI	7	2	14	9	3	0
Gross Motor Behavior	42	35	41	64	19	56
TARS	27	27				9
Classroom	%	%	%	%	%	%
On-task	–	88	83	62	89	47
Dis	–	0	7	25	4	43
Neutral	–	12	10	13	7	10
LOR per day	1.8	0.9	0	0.25	0	0
OQR per day	3.5	down	0.4	1.9	down	<1

Compilation of data by two-week periods. Pittsburgh Activities of Living Scale (PALS-C): activities of daily living (ADL), mealtime social interactions (MSI), compliance (Comp), and adaptive peer interactions (API). Direct observations in a free-play setting: adaptive peer interactions (API), maladaptive peer interactions (MPI), solitary play (SP), interactions with staff (SI), and gross motor behavior (GMB). Teacher Affect Rating Scale (TARS). Direct Observations in the Classroom: on task, disruptive (Dis), and neutral. Behaviors requiring seclusion: locked quiet room (LQR), or time out in room or open quiet room (OQR).

*Imipramine treatment.

The child continued his outpatient individual therapy, was referred to a special school program, and was tapered from the imipramine. A follow-up at one month indicated maintenance and actual improvement in his behavioral gains. His BID, parents as informants, was negative.

NEW DIRECTIONS

It has been demonstrated that imipramine and the group of TCAs are effective agents in the armamentarium of clinicians treating disturbed children, particularly those manifesting behaviors related to childhood depression. We are embarking on a very exciting era, with the possibility of all-night electroencephalographic monitoring of sleep for both diagnosing and following depressed children and their responses to medication and other therapeutic modalities. We are also entering the era where we may be able to routinely monitor plasma imipramine, amitriptyline, and related TCA compounds and their metabolites in a way which will open up the field so that correlations can be made between treatment, blood levels, and clinical effect. Puig-Antich et al (1979b) report on plasma levels of imipramine and desipramine and the clinical response to children with nondelusional prepubertal major depressive disorder to tricyclic treatment. From their data, they suggest that the clinician should aim for a plasma level of imipramine and desipramine above 146 mg/ml to obtain maximal clinical effect over a five-week treatment time. They also note that the dose in itself may not be a good guideline for predicting clinical changes. The data with adult work is also subject to much debate and attempted clarification to determine the potential for utilizing TCA plasma levels. Weller et al (1981) report similar findings.

Using techniques of learning theory and behavioral approaches to psychotherapy in drawing the expertise for clinically monitoring the behaviors and symptoms of children treated with TCA will also be a great help in the future. We are very much involved in the art of psychopharmacologic treatment of depressed children and the next decade should open up some new, fruitful approaches.

CONCLUSION

Depressed children require a variety of interventions. Changing the internal physiology or altering biochemical systems seems to be one very critical component of a total therapeutic regimen. Children demonstrating depressive symptomatology or behaviors often related to childhood depression do respond to psychopharmacologic treatment. The tricyclic group of antidepressants are presented as highly efficacious agents. An unequivocal statement regarding their use awaits the documentation of double-blind controlled studies. We must not, however, allow the semantic confusion concerning nosology and absence of reliable assessment instruments deter us from studying and treating depressed youngsters. We must exercise sound clinical judgment and be willing to monitor clinical changes and potential side effects when using substances such as the tricyclics. This chapter should have provided sufficient breadth for awareness of the rationale, potential uses, method of utilization, and potential hazards associated with this group of compounds. The next five years should provide us with the tools and experience to permit us to treat depressed children from a more scientifically based approach.

REFERENCES

Akiskal HS, McKinney WT, Jr. Overview of recent research in depression. *Arch Gen Psychiatry* 1975;32:285-305.

Akiskal HS, Rosenthal RH, Rosenthal TL, et al. Differentiation of primary affective illness from situational, symptomatic, and secondary depressions. *Arch Gen Psychiatry* 1979;36:535-543.

Albala AA, Greden JF. Serial dexamethasone suppression tests in affective disorders. *Am J Psychiatry* 1980;137:383.

Aman MG. Drug, learning and the psychotherapies. In: Werry J, ed. *Pediatric psychopharmacology*. New York: Brunner/Mazel, 1978.

Andreasen NC, Winokur G. Newer experimental methods for classifying depression. *Arch Gen Psychiatry* 1979;36:447-452.

Angst J, Theobald W. *Tofranil*. Berne: Verland Stamfli & Cie, 1970.

Annell AL. *Depressive states in childhood and adolescence*. New York: Halsten Press, 1972.

Bickel MH. Imipramine series. In: Usdin E, Forrest I, eds. *Psychotherapeutic drugs*. Rockville: National Institute of Mental Health, 1977.

Blackwell B, Currah J. The psychopharmacology of nocturnal enuresis. In: Kolvin I, MacKeith R, Meadow S, eds. *Bladder control and enuresis*. Philadelphia: J. B. Lippincott Co, 1973.

Brown D, Winsberg B, Bialer R, Press M. Imipramine therapy and seizures: three children treated for hyperactive behavior disorders. *Am J Psychiatry* 1973;130:210-212.

Brown WA, Johnston R, Mayfield D. Twenty-four hour dexamethasone suppression test in a clinical setting: relationship to diagnosis, symptoms and response to treatment. *Am J Psychiatry* 1979;136:543-547.

Brumback RA, Dietz-Schmidt SG, Weinberg WA. Depression in children referred to an educational center: diagnosis and treatment and analysis of criteria and literature review. *Dis Nerv Sys* 1977;38:529-535.

Burdock EL, Hardest AS. A children's behavior diagnostic inventory. *Ann NY Acad Sci* 1964;105:890-896.

Carroll BJ, Curtis GC, Mendels J. Neuroendocrine regulation in depression II. Discrimination of depressed from nondepressed patients. *Arch Gen Psychiatry* 1976;33:1051-1058.

Christe P. Contribution to the study of depressions in children and their treatment with imipramine. *Ann Paediatr* 1966;206:47-83.

Coble P, Foster FG, Kupfer DJ. Electroencephalographic sleep diagnosis of primary depression. *Arch Gen Psychiatry* 1976;33:1124-1127.

Coble P, Kupfer D, Petti T, et al. EEG of hospitalized boys with depressed symptomatology. In: Chase M, Millter M, Walter P, eds. *Sleep research*. Los Angeles: B.I.S./B.R.I., 1977.

Connell HM. Depression in childhood. *Child Psychiatr Hum Dev* 1972;4:71–85.

Conners CK. Classification and treatment of childhood depression and depressive equivalents. In: Gallant D, Simpson G, eds. *Depression: behavioral, biochemical, diagnostic and treatment concepts*. New York: Halsted Press, 1976.

Crot PM. Preliminary investigation of Tofranil in the treatment of children at the Swiss Medical-Pedagogical office. *Praxis* 1961;50:202-206.

Cytryn L, Logue M, Desai RB. Biochemical correlates of affective disorders in children. *Arch Gen Psychiatry* 1974;31:659-661.

Davis JM. Overview: maintenance therapy in psychiatry: II. affective disorders. *Am J Psychiatry* 1976; 133:1-13.

Deykin EY, MacMahon B. The incidence of seizures among children with autistic symptoms. *Am J Psychiatry* 1979; 136:1310-1312.

Dysken MW, Pandey GN, Chang SS, et al. Serial postdexamethasone cortisol levels in a patient undergoing ECT. *Am J Psychiatry* 1979; 136: 1328-1329.

Freyhan FA. The target symptoms for treatment of depressive illness revisited. *Compr Psychiatry* 1979; 20:495-501.

Fromm GH, Amores CY, Thies W. Imipramine in epilepsy. *Arch Neurol* 1972; 27:198-204.

Frommer E. Treatment of childhood depression with antidepressant drugs. *Br Med J* 1967; 1:729-732.

Frommer EA. Depressive illness in childhood. *Br J Psychiatry* (Special publications) 1968; 2:117-136.

Gittelman-Klein R. Pilot clinical trial of imipramine in hyperkinetic children. In Conners C, ed. *Clinical use of stimulant drugs in children.* The Hague: Excerpta Medica, 1974.

Gittelman-Klein R, Klein DF. Controlled imipramine treatment of school phobia. *Arch Gen Psychiatry* 1971; 25:204-207.

Gittelman-Klein R, Klein DF. School phobia: diagnostic considerations in the light of imipramine effects. *J Nerv Ment Dis* 1973; 156-199-215.

Gold MS, Pottash LC, Davies RK, et al. Distinguishing unipolar and bipolar depression by thyrotropin release test. *Lancet* 1979; 2:411–412.

Goldstein S, Camp JA, Winsberg BG, et al. Left ventricular performance and electrocardiographic changes during imipramine pharmacotherapy in hyperactive children. In: Obilis J, Ballus C, Monclus EG, Piyul J, eds. *Biological psychiatry today*. North Amsterdam: Elsevier, 1977.

Graham P. Depression in pre-pubertal children. *Developm Med Child Neurol* 1974; 16:340-349.

Greenberg LM, Yellin AM. Blood pressure and pulse changes in hyperactive children treated with imipramine and methylphenidate. *Am J Psychiatry* 1975; 132:1325-1326.

Greenberg LM, Yellin AM, Spring C, Metcalf M. Clinical effects of imipramine and methylphenidate in hyperactive children. *Recent advances in child psychopharmacology. Int J Ment Health* 1975; 4:144–156.

Gualtieri CT, Imipramine and children: a review and some speculations about the mechanism of drug action. *Dis Nerv Sys* 1977; 33:368–375.

Gualtieri CT, Staye J. Withdrawal symptoms after abrupt cessation of amitriptyline in an eight year old boy. *Am J Psychiatry* 1979; 135:457–458.

Hayes TA, Panitch ML, Barker E. Imiparmine dosage in children. *Am J Psychiatry* 1975; 132:546–547.

Helmchen H. Current trends of research on anti-depressive treatment and prophylaxis. *Compr Psychiatry* 1979; 20:201-214.

Huessy HR, Wright AL. The use of imipramine in children's behavior disorders. *ACTA Paedopsychiatr* 1970; 37:194-199.

Kane J, Coble P, Conners CK, Kupfer DJ. EEG sleep in a child with severe depression. *Am J Psychiatry* 1977: 134:813-814.

Kaplan DM, Kravetz RS, Rose WD. The effects of imipramine on the depressive components of mental disorders. In: *Proceedings of the third world congress of psychiatry, Montreal 1961. Vol. 2.* Toronto: McGill University Press, 1961:1362-1367.

Klein DF, Davis JM. *Diagnosis and drug treatment of psychiatric disorders.* Baltimore: Williams & Wilkins, 1969:187–322.

Koehl GW, Wenzel JE. Severe postural hypotension due to imipramine therapy. *Pediatrics* 1971;47:132-133.

Kovacs M, Betof NG, Celebre JE, et al. Childhood depression: myth or clinical syndrome? (unpublished manuscript) 1976.

Kraft IA, Ardali C, Duffy J, et al. Use of amitriptyline in childhood behavioral disturbances. *Int J Neuropsychiatry* 1966; 2:611-614.

Kuhn R. The occurrence and treatment of endogenous depression in children. *Schw. Med. Wsch* 1963; 93:89-90.

Kuhn V, Kuhn R. Drug therapy for depression in children. indications and methods. In: Annell A, ed. *Depressive states in childhood and adolescence.* New York: Halsted Press, 1972.

Kupfer DJ. REM latency: a psychobiologic marker for primary depressive disease. *Biol Psychiatry* 1976; 11:159-174.

Kupfer DJ, Coble P, Kane J, et al. Imipramine and EEG sleep in children with depressive symptoms. *Psychopharmacol* 1979; 60:117-123.

Kupfer DJ, Detre TP. Tricyclic and monamine oxidase-inhibitor antidepressants: clinical use. In: Iverson L, Iverson D, Snyder S, eds. *Handbook of psychopharmacology.* New York: Plenum, 1978:14:199–232.

Kupfer D, Foster FG, Reich L, et al. EEG sleep changes as predictors in depression. *Am J Psychiatry* 1976; 133:622-626.

Kupfer DJ, Foster FG. EEG sleep and depression. In: Williams R, Karacan I, eds. *Sleep disorders: diagnosis and treatment.* New York: John Wiley and Sons, 1978.

Kurtis LB. Clinical study of the response to nortriptyline in autistic children. *Int J Neuropsychiatry* 1966; 26:298-301.

Lake CR, Mikkelsen EJ, Rapoport JL, et al. Effect of imipramine on norepinephrine and blood pressure in enuretic boys. *Clin Pharmacol Therapeut* 1979; 26:647-653.

Law W, Petti TA, Kazdin AE. Withdrawal symptoms after graduated cessation of imipramine in children. *Am J Psychiatry* 1981; 138:647-650.

Lawler RH, Nakielny W, Wright NA. Suicidal attempts in children. *Can Med* 1963; 89:751-754.

Lewinsohn PM. Depression—a social learning perspective. Presentation at Western Psychiatric Clinic and Institute, Pittsburgh, 1979.

Ling W, Oftedal G, Weinberg W. Depressive illness in childhood presenting as severe headache. *Am J Dis Child* 1970; 120:122-124.

Lucas AR, Lockett HJ, Grimm F. Amitriptyline in childhood depressions. *Dis Nerv Sys* 1965; 26:105-111.

Malmquist CP. Depression in childhood and adolescence. *N Eng J Med* 1971; 284:887-893, 955-961.

Martin GI, Zaug PJ. Electrocardiographic monitoring of enuretic children receiving therapeutic doses of imipramine. *Am J Psychiatry* 1975; 132: 540-542.

Matson JL, Esveldt-Dawson K, Andrasik F, et al. Observation and generalization effects of social skills training with emotionally disturbed children. *Behav Ther* 1980; 11:522–531.

McConville BJ, Boag LC. Therapeutic approaches in childhood depression. Presented at the Annual Meeting of the American Academy of Child Psychiatry, Toronto, 1976.

McKnew DH, Cytryn L. Urinary metabolites in chronically depressed children. *J Am Acad Child Psychiatry* 1979; 18:608-615.

McLaughlin BE. A double blind study involving thirty emotionally disturbed children (outpatients). *Psychosom* 1964; 5:40-43.

Michelson L, DiLorenzo T, Petti TA. Behavioral assessment of imipramine effects in a depressed child. *J Behav Assess* 1981; 3:253–262.

Morris JB, Beck AT. The efficacy of antidepressant drugs. *Arch Gen Psychiatry* 1974; 30:667-674.

Murray PA. The clinical picture of depression in schoolchildren. *Irish Med J* 1970; 63:53-56.

Ossofsky HJ. Endogenous depression in infancy and childhood. *Compr Psychiatry* 1974; 15:19-25.

Pallmeyer T, Petti TA. Effects of imipramine on aggression and dejection in depressed children. *Am J Psychiatry* 1979; 136:1472-1473.

Perel, J. Personal communication, 1979.

Perel, J. Personal communication, 1982.

Petti TA. Depression in hospitalized child psychiatry patients: approaches to measuring depression. *J Am Acad Child Psychiatry* 1978; 17:49-59.

Petti TA. Depression of children—behavioral and other treatment strategies. In: Clarkin J, Glazer H, eds. *Depression: behavior and directive treatment strategies*. New York: Garland Press, 1981.

Petti TA, Bornstein M, Delamater A, Conners CK. Evaluation and multi-modality treatment of a depressed pre-pubertal girl. *J Am Acad Child Psychiatry* 1980; 19:690-702.

Petti TA, Campbell M. Imipramine and seizures. *Am J Psychiatry* 1975; 132: 538-540.

Petti TA, Conners CK. Depression in childhood, literature review. 1977; (unpublished material).

Petti TA, Conners CK. Changes in behavioral ratings of depressed children treated with imipramine. *J Am Acad Child Psychiatry* (in press).

Petti TA, Law W. Abrupt cessation of high dose imipramine treatment in children. *JAMA* 1981; 246:768–769.

Petti TA, Law W. Imipramine treatment of depressed children: a double-blind pilot study. *J Clin Psychopharmacol* 1982; 2:107–110.

Petti TA, Unis AS. Treating the borderline psychotic child with imipramine: a controlled study. *Am J Psychiatry* 1981; 138:515-518.

Petti TA, Wells K. Crisis treatment of a preadolescent who accidentally killed his twin. *Am J Psychother* 1980; 34:434-443.

Pfeffer CR, Conte HR, Plutchik R, Jerrett I. Suicidal behavior in latency-age children: an empirical study. *J Am Acad Child Psychiatry* 1979; 18:679-692.

Poussaint AF, Ditman KS. A controlled study of imipramine (Tofranil) in the treatment of childhood enuresis. *J Pediatr* 1965; 67:283-290.

Poznanski E, Carroll BJ, Banegas MC, et al. The dexamethason suppression test in prepubertal depressed children. *Am J Psychiatry* 1982; 139:321-324.

Poznanski EO, Cook SC, Carroll BJ. A depression rating scale for children. *Pediatrics* 1979; 64:442-450.

Prange AJ, Wilson I, Breese G, Lipton MA. Hormonal alteration of imipramine response: a review. In: Sachar E, ed. *Hormones, behavior and psychopathology*. New York: Raven Press, 1976.

Puig-Antich J. Discussion at the Annual Meeting, American Academy of Child Psychiatry, Atlanta, Georgia, 1979.

Puig-Antich J. Biological correlates of depression in prepubertal children. Presented at Recent Developments in the Study of Childhood and Adolescent Depression, New York, February 5, 1982.

Puig-Antich J, Blau S, Marx N, et al. Prepubertal major depressive disorder, a pilot study. *J Am Acad Child Psychiatry* 1978; 17:695-707.

Puig-Antich J, Chambers W, Halpern F, et al. Cortisol hypersecretion in prepubertal depressive illness: a preliminary report. *Psychoneuroendocrinology* 1979a; 4:191-197.

Puig-Antich J, Perel JM, Lupatkin W, et al. Plasma levels of imipramine (IMI) and desmethylimipramine (DMI) and clinical response in prepubertal major depressive disorder. a preliminary report. *J Am Acad Child Psychiatry* 1979b; 18:616-627.

Rabiner CJ, Klein DF. Imipramine treatment of school phobia. *Compr Psychiatry* 1969; 10:387-390.

Rapoport J. Childhood behavior and learning problems treated with imipramine. *Int J Neuropsychiatry* 1965; 1:635-642.

Rapoport JL, Mikkelsen EJ. Antidepressants. In: Werry J, ed. *Pediatric psychopharmacology: the use of behavior modifying drugs in children.* New York: Brunner/Mazel, 1978.

Rapoport JL, Potter W. Tricyclic antidepressants and children. In: Raskin, ed. *The influence of age on the pharmacology of psychoactive drugs conference.* New York: Raven Press, 1979.

Rapoport JL, Quinn PO, Bradbard G, et al. A double-blind comparison of imipramine and methylphenidate treatments of hyperactive boys. *Arch Gen Psychiatry* 1974; 30:789-793.

Riddle KD, Rapoport JL. A 2-year follow-up of 72 hyperactive boys: classroom behavior and peer acceptance. *J Nerv Ment Dis* 1976; 162:126-134.

Ritvo ER, Ornitz EM, Gottlieb F, et al. Arousal and non-arousal enuretic events. *Am J Psychiatry* 1969; 126:77-84.

Robinson DS, Barker E. Official minutes and chairman's report: ad hoc committee on tricyclic antidepressant activity. Bureau of drugs, food and drug administration, Rockville, Maryland, September 10, 1975.

Ryback WS, Jorgensen PA, Jorgensen S. Sensitivity reaction to imipramine. *Am J Psychiatry* 1973; 130:940.

Saraf K, Klein DF, Gittelman-Klein R, Groff S. Imipramine side effects in children. *Psychopharmacology* 1974; 37:265-274.

Saraf KR, Klein DF, Gittelman-Klein R, et al. EKG effects of imipramine treatment in children. *J Am Acad Child Psychiatry* 1978; 17:61-69.

Seligman M. Learned helplessness. Pittsburgh: Western Psychiatric Institute and Clinic, 1979.

Schlesser MA, Winokur G, Sherman BM. Genetic subtypes of unipolar primary depressive illness distinguished by hypothalamic-pituitary-adrenal axis activity. *Lancet* 1979; April:739-741.

Sonis WA, Petti TA, Richey ET. Epilepsy and psychopathology in childhood: a controlled case study with Tegretol. *J Am Acad Child Psychiatry* 1981; 20:398-407.

Stein MK, Rickels K, Weise CC. Maintenance therapy with amitriptyline: a controlled trial. *Am J Psychiatry* 1980; 137:370-371.

Suomi SJ, Seaman SF, Lewis JK, et al. Effects of imipramine treatment of separation-induced social disorders in rhesus monkeys. *Arch Gen Psychiatry* 1978;35:321–325.

Taska BA, Kupfer DJ, Coble PA, et al. EEG sleep in depressed children: changes during inpatient treatment. Presented at the Annual Meeting of the American Psychophysiological Study of Sleep, Mexico City, 1980.

Tec L. Unexpected effects in children treated with imipramine. *Am J Psychiatry* 1963; 12:603.

Waizer J, Hoffman SP, Polizos P, Engelhardt DM. Outpatient treatment of hyperactive school children with imipramine. *Am J Psychiatry* 1974; 131:587-591.

Watter N, Dreifuss FE. Modification of hyperkinetic behavior by nortriptyline. *VA Med Mon* 1973; 100:123-126.

Weinberg WA, Rutman J, Sullivan L, et al. Depression in children referred to an educational diagnostic center: diagnosis and treatment. *Pediatrics* 1973; 83:1065-1072.

Weise CC, O'Reilly PP, Hesbacher P. Perphenazine-amitriptyline in neurotic underachieving students: a controlled study. *Dis Nerv Sys* 1972; 5:318-325.

Weller EB, Weller RA, Preskorn SH, Glotzbach R. Steady-state plasma imipramine levels in prepubertal depressed children. Delivered at the American Academy of Child Psychiatry Annual Meeting, Dallas, October, 1981.

Werry J, Dowrick P, Lampen E, Vamos M. Imipramine in enuresis-psychological and physiological effects. *J Child Psychol Psychiatry* 1975; 16:289-300.

Westman M. Tofranil treatment of depressions in adolescence. *Lakartidningen (suppl II)* 1965; 62:87-92.

White JH. *Pediatric psychopharmacology. Practical guide to clinical application.* Baltimore: Waverly Press, 1977:125–133.

Williamson D, Calpin J, DiLorenzo T, et al. Combining dexedrine and feedback for the treatment of hyperactivity. *Behav Modif* 1981; 5:399-416.

Winsberg BG, Bialer I, Kupietz S, Tobias J. Effects of imipramine and dextroamphetamine on behavior of neuropsychiatrically impaired children. *Am J Psychiatry* 1972; 128:1425-1431.

Winsberg BG, Goldstein S, Yepes LE, Perel JM. Imipramine and electrocardiographic abnormalities in hyperactive children. *Am J Psychiatry* 1975; 132: 542-545.

Wold PM, Dwight K. Subtypes of depression identified by the KDS-3A: a pilot study. *Am J Psychiatry* 1979; 136:1415-1419.

Yepes LE, Balka EB, Winsberg BG, Bailer I. Amitriptyline and methylphenidate treatment of behaviorally disordered children. *J Child Psychol Psychiatry* 1977; 18:39-52.

Young L, McKinney WT, Lewis JK, et al. Induction of adrenal catecholamine synthesizing enzymes following mother-infant separation. *Nature* 1973; 246:94-96.

Affective Disorders in Childhood and Adolescence--
An Update. Edited by D.P. Cantwell and G.A. Carlson.

18

Behavioral Approaches in the Treatment of Depressed Children

Theodore A. Petti

In the treatment of depressed children, it is critical that the clinician be aware of the multiple etiologies which play a role in the development and maintenance of the symptomatology. Akiskal and McKinney (1975) review the nonbiological schools of psychiatry which have provided models for explaining and conceptualizing the basis of depression. Many relate to therapies based on learning theory which utilize behavioral approaches. Lazare (1973) describes four conceptual models that psychiatrists interweave in their approaches to patients—the medical, psychological, behavioral, and social, and notes that one or a combination of these models are utilized in formulating diagnosis and treatment. Child psychiatrists traditionally have employed these models in combination, though most concentrate on the psychological and social, including school; more recently, increasing numbers have been employing the biological or medical model. Learning principles as related to behavioral approaches are sometimes formally used but more often are incorporated in the individual, insight, or supportive psychotherapy.

This chapter will present behavioral models of depression, describe how they relate to depression in children, briefly review the literature of behavioral approaches to the psychopathology of children, and, finally, elaborate on how such approaches relate to treating the symptoms related to the depressed child. The behavioral model of depression consists of the following major constructs: (1) learned helplessness; (2) loss of reinforcement, chronic frustration, and lack of control over interpersonal relationships; and (3) negative cognitive set, hopelessness, and helplessness.

Learned helplessness is a concept derived from animal experimentation that involved subjecting animals to inescapable electric shock (Seligman and Maier, 1967). A normal animal, when shocked, would actively attempt to escape the aversive stimulus. The animal who had been subjected previously to an inescapable stimulus would not attempt to escape before the repeated shock, but would instead simply move around and around in a confused state or just lie down in a passive, accepting pose. Several subsequent studies (Seligman, 1979) have correlated learned helplessness and depression and arrived at the following conclusions:

1. Motivation is impaired in both. Both animals and humans (usually college students) who were faced with an inescapable unpleasant situation or repeated failure did not try new solutions to subsequent situations they faced.

2. Cognition is impaired in both. Even when the animal or person who experienced an inescapable situation did initiate action, and even when that action was effective, they did not expect it to be effective and would not accept that it was effective.

3. Lowered self-esteem occurs when individuals feel responsible for their ineffectiveness.

4. Aggression or assertive deficits occur.

5. Apetitive deficits occur.

6. Physiological deficits occur.

Approaches to both treatment (Seligman, 1979) and immunization against learned helplessness have been proposed (Klee and Meyer, 1979). Akiskal and McKinney (1975) note that Seligman's model includes aspects of the cognitive, existential, and sociological under the fabric of a behavioral framework. Recently, Seligman (1979) has introduced the biological into this construct as well when he discusses breaking up learned helplessness in the rat with electroconvulsive therapy, tricyclic antidepressants, monamine oxidose inhibitors and sleep deprivation. The strategies he proposes for treating depression derived from or related to learned helplessness include:

1. Assisting the individual in changing expectations for unpleasant events by making the environment more pleasantly rewarding and assisting the depressed person in relinquishing nonattainable goals.

2. Providing the individual with the skills necessary to achieve attainable goals by social skills or decision making training, and

3. Changing their cognitive style of attribution.

In this author's experience, learned helplessness plays a major role in the genesis and/or maintenance of depression in children hospitalized for psychiatric disorders. Many come from the lower socioeconomic strata of society and are constantly faced with a no-win situation—due to the all encompassing poverty which may involve abuse, neglect, or rejection from meaningful adults, and high expectancy bombardment (through television, eg, "you too, can have a super specto spaceship with accompanying thousand people, an electronic game, and a teaching computer"). Part of the repetitive inescapable aversive situation relates to the educational system as well. The author's experience has led to a hypothesis that a combination of specific learning difficulties, internal conflict, and a nonsupportive home environment causes these children to do poorly in school, which in turn leads to school avoidance, increased deviant behavior in school, repeatedly negative consequences, and increased frustration; this culminates in depression withdrawal, hyperactivity, aggression, or other deviant behaviors. Rutter (1972) and Wolkind and Renton (1979) note that moderately disturbed children remain so over long periods of time. The former relates this to the prolonged exposure to adverse environmental influences, usually from within the family, that operate throughout the child's life, the latter workers suggest that disordered children, requiring long-term residential care, get into a viscious cycle of adult rejection and unacceptable behavior.

Dweck (1977) notes that even if childhood depression as an entity does not exist, helplessness as described by Seligman is still applicable to the various mood disorders which play major roles in childhood psychopathology. She redefines helplessness to mean that the involved individual perceives the aversive event to mean that the situation cannot be put under control by him and that such events are likely to continue, even if he tries to change them. Her earlier work (Dweck and Reppucci, 1973; Dweck, 1975) demonstrates the relation of negative cognition and helplessness to the responses children make after experiencing failure. Though both helpless and nonhelpless children shared equal competence at problem solving, the helpless children tended to attribute failure to their lack of competence or to external, noncontrollable sources, while the nonhelpless viewed failure as something that could be modified by changes in their behavior, such as increasing their effort. When faced with failure, the helpless children became incapable of solving problems they had just completed successfully; they became demoralized and passive. The nonhelpless children, on the other hand, attacked the failed problem with creative vigor, using the failure to systematically review their approach and to improve their achievement. Dweck notes that the learned helpless children can alter their strategies in an active manner when they are taught to perceive failure as controllable by the use of alternative approaches.

Two other studies support such a position relating faulty attribution to childhood depression. Moyal (1977) investigated the relationship between depressive symptoms, self-esteem, locus of control, and stimulus appraisal in a group of nonreferred fifth and sixth grade Toronto school children. Three self-completion questionnaires were administered—the Piers-Harris Children's Self-Concept Scale to which seven items related to depression were added, the Nowicki-Strickland Children's Locus of Control Scale, and the Moyal-Miezitis Stimulus Appraisal Scale. The Piers-Harris scale is scored toward increasing self-esteem, the depression cluster toward increasing depression, the Nowicki-Strickland in the direction of external perception of control, and the stimulus appraisal scale as the tendency to choose an adaptive, helpless, blaming, or self-blaming choice.

The 213 complete sets of scales of the 225 administered were analyzed and revealed a strong negative correlation between self-esteem and depression.

Locus of control or perceived helplessness over one's situation was correlated negatively ($p < 0.01$) with self-esteem and with choice of adaptive responses, and was correlated positively ($p < 0.01$) with depression score, choice of helplessness, self-blaming, or externalized blaming responses. Other significant correlations as would be expected for adults were found: depression was correlated in a negative direction with choice of adaptive responses and positively with choices of helplessness, self-blaming, or externalized blaming; low self-esteem was similarly correlated. This support for learned helplessness, if one is willing to accept an external locus of control as related to this concept, has been well-documented in children. However, the two may not be synononomous. We have (Petti and Davidman, 1977) described how an external locus of control is related to homicidal or depressed, suicidal behavior because of the decreased behavioral options made available with an external locus of control.

In a large study (Lefkowitz and Tesiny, 1980), a Peer Nominating Inventory of Depression, the Children's Depression Inventory, a modified Zung Self-Rating Depression Scale–MMPI "yes" or "no" depression scale, the Coopersmith Self-Esteem Inventory, the Nowicki-Strickland Locus of Control Scale, a human figure drawing, a teacher rating scale, and academic records were obtained for 944 children with a mean age of 10.24 + 0.78 years. As expected, the results demonstrated highly significant correlations between high peer nominations for depression, depressed intellectual functioning, poor social behavior, apathy, and self-ratings of depression. They conclude that the clinical symptoms of childhood depression may consist of three predominant factors: loneliness, inadequacy, and dejection. The depressed children tended to view events in their lives as externally controlled.

Loss of positive reinforcement is another major behavioral model of depression. Lewinsohn et al (1969) were the first to systematically apply behavioral assessment to depression in a research manner and found that depressed individuals lacked access to an adequate schedule of positive reinforcement. They suggested that the historical antecedents of depressive behavior was a deficient rate of response-contingent positive rewards or reinforcers. This deficit could have its roots in a general absence of available reinforcers (as in a ghetto neighborhood with alcoholic parents) or in the inability of individuals to access themselves to the "goodies" due to their lack of appropriate skills (as in children who demand friends but lack basic friendship building skills).

Lewinsohn (1979) integrates this process as follows: (1) few potentially reinforcing events related to personal characteristics are available and (2) there is little availability of reinforcement in the environment, which may lead to (3) behavior by the individual to elicit some reinforcement. Out of this input comes a low rate of reinforcement which in turn leads to depression and a cycle is perpetuated with feedback to the individual for more behavior, a continued deficit of reinforcement in the environment, and a low rate of reinforcement.

McLean et al (1973) summarize this and the learned helplessness model by delineating the process of depression into these categories:

1. extinction of appropriate behavior through nonreinforcement;

2. production of a state of powerlessness as a response to the lack of reinforcement and the failure of "coercive techniques" applied in desperation to elicit appropriate behavior; and

3. the subsequent development, reinforcement, and maintenance of depressive behaviors. Observations of adults reveal an initial sympathetic response of the environment toward the depressed individual. However, this phase is short-lived as peers and colleagues get frustrated or discouraged and withdraw whatever attention they had provided with the resultant lack of any support for the depressed. Some depressed females have been reported as especially aggressive and histrionic in these endeavors.

McLean (1975) summarizes the systematically collected data by Lewinsohn and his associates:

1. compared to normal controls, the depressed elicit fewer behaviors;

2. the number and kind of pleasant activities engaged in are related to the mood of an individual;

3. less positive reinforcement is obtained by depressed than nondepressed persons;

4. a greater sensitivity to aversive stimuli is found in depressed as compared to nondepressed individuals.

5. fewer social skills are exhibited by depressed than nondepressed subjects. Lewinsohn (1979), however, noted that depressed individuals know what to do and may even say they use appropriate social skills but, when systematically observed, fail to demonstrate their use. McLean (1975) cautions that reinforcer effectiveness may operate as a function of mood state and be related both to endogenous biological changes or alterations in the chain of reinforcers, for example, being promised an opportunity for downhill skiing in Tuscon during August.

Lewinsohn (1974) lists three ways in which the reduced rate of response-contingent positive reinforcement might occur: the diminished capacity of reinforcer effectiveness, the lack of available reinforcing events, and the lack of the necessary social behaviors to attain the available reinforcers. This is especially applicable to children when one pictures their lives and activities. Their major time commitments are television, school, and sleeping. Television does a fine conditioning job on increasing expectations, but with few programs such as "Mr. Roger's Neighborhood," does little to provide positive support or modeling. School is fine for the child with an accepting and supportive family, but for the child with learning or emotional problems or demanding unrealistic parents, school can be as aversive as positive. For the inner-city child who must attend a school marked by lack of discipline, arbitrary decisions, lack of predictability, and constant fear of personal injury, school becomes more of a source of discomfort and negative expectations than the fountain of knowledge and support. Yet, school is the major interpersonal part of their day! Moreover, many of these children may come from lower income families, and have parents who may be depressed, have psychiatric or chronic medical problems, and who serve as poor role models for effective social interactions (McLean, 1976).

As noted in Chapter 17, depression in children may be accompanied by multiple symptom complexes ranging from apathy, lethargy, and withdrawal to hyperactivity, impulsivity, and aggressiveness. Studies of both of these extreme behaviors have shown lack of social skills to be a predominant factor (Campbell and Paulauskas, 1979; Camp, 1977; LaGreca and Mesibov, 1979; Bornstein et al, 1977) and that unpopular or isolated children—an indirect way of ascribing social skills utilization—have a more guarded prognosis than those not so labeled (Gottman et al, 1975). Assessing social interaction, social competence, and friendship in children, Gottman et al (1975) found that popular children were more skillful in social interactions than their unpopular counterparts, were more likely to praise and be accepted by their peers, and were more knowledgeable about how to make friends.

The importance of a "chum" relationship for preadolescent children has been emphasized by Sullivan (1953) and recently expanded upon by Mannarino (1978) who studied 30 sixth grade boys with a chum and 30 without. Using the Piers-Harris Children's Self-Concept Scale, he found that boys with a chum scored significantly higher on self-concept than those without a chum. This relates to being reinforced and validated consentually by the environment. A child without rudimentary social skills or the motivation to use them would be precluded from such a positive interaction.

Teacher and parent-pleasing behaviors may fit in here. The cognitive model of depression espoused by Beck (1970) assumes that depression is a collection of symptoms and that the diagnosis is based on perceived changes in the subject's psychobiological system. This model is an integration of ego-psychology and behavioral psychology and is based on the importance of the negative cognitive triad of expectations—a negative view of the self, of the world, and of the future. Hopelessness and helpless thinking are postulated as changing mood states.

In many ways, this model pulls together the concept of learned helplessness and loss of reinforcement and adds a twist of cognition. For example, the negative view of self is based on a self-perception of inadequacy and lack of worth; attribution for unpleasant experiences is assigned to a defect within the self. The negative view of the world hinges on a constantly frustrating and withholding environment which sets unreasonable expectations and results in demeaning of the self. The negative view of the future is comprised of never-ending failure, suffering, and hopelessness. This negative set is at once distorted, unrealistic, exaggerated, extreme, and based on negative cognitions extracted solely from the negative aspects of the individual's experiences. A failure in such an individual would be expected to lead to even more negative expectations as the mechanisms of exaggeration and overgeneralization are utilized (Kovacs and Beck, 1977). Themes of loss and deprivation which are frequent in depressed children are considered pivotal to the development of the negative triad. These in turn can lead to an externally perceived locus of control, an enhancement of helplessness and hopelessness, and firm entrenchment in depression. Moyal (1977) in her survey of nonreferred Grade 5 and Grade 6 children noted that depressed children tended to reach faulty, nonadaptive conclusions and to distort situations much as one would expect from depressed adults caught in a negative cognitive triad.

HISTORY OF BEHAVIORAL THERAPIES WITH CHILDREN

A number of reviews and overviews describe the application of learning theory and behavioral approaches to childhood psychopathology (Gelfand and Hartman, 1968; Werry and Wollersheim, 1967; Yates, 1970; Graziano, 1971; Phillips and Ray, 1980; Petti, this volume). Behavior therapy has developed accepted and effective treatment strategies for most childhood disorders. The symptoms or syndromes successfully treated range from infantile autism and early childhood psychosis, delusions in retarded children, phobias, rituals, anorexia, enuresis, encopresis, hyperactivity, asthma, aggressiveness, withdrawal, and other symptoms related to deviant behavior. A major issue has been the failure to demonstrate generalization or carry-over of gains from the treatment to other settings or situations (Wahler, 1969).

Early studies by Jones, in 1924, demonstrated how the classical work by Watson and Rayner with "Peter and the rabbit" could be applied clinically to ameliorating the fears of young children. She also was able to show how role modeling and systematic deconditioning could both relieve the fearful reactions of a 34-month-old boy and generalized to decreasing the child's fears to objects beside the rabbit to which he was deconditioned. Systematic desensitization was later shown to be highly effective in treating phobic children (Lazarus et al, 1965). This area of behavioral treatment of children's fears is well-reviewed (Graziano et al, 1979).

Other areas of interest to those treating children include reprogramming the social environment (Patterson et al, 1967), punishment essays (MacPherson et al, 1974), behaviorally oriented milieus (Monkman, 1972; Pizzat, 1973), social skills training (Combs et al, 1977; Van Hasselt et al, 1979; Ollendick and Hersen, 1979; Elder et al, 1979), cognitive behavioral therapy (Kendall and Finch, 1978), verbal self-instruction (Kendall, 1977; Camp et al, 1977), and multimodality therapies (Keat, 1976; Petti et al, 1980).

The number of papers reporting single case and group studies utilizing behavioral approaches in treating children with a psychiatric disturbance has increased at a phenomenal rate; the number of reported studies utilizing behavioral strategies in the treatment of depressed adults has also been increasing (Rehm and Kornblith, 1979). However, there has been a glaring absence in the formal use of behavioral approaches with depressed children. The following section will describe how behavioral approaches have been utilized in symptoms and syndromes commonly associated with depression.

BEHAVIOR THERAPY OF SYMPTOMS ASSOCIATED WITH DEPRESSION

Depression, as noted earlier (Petti, 1978), is a symptom complex which cuts across a number of diagnostic categories. The descriptions unhappy, depressed, and sad often occur in children who are hyperactive, impulsive, inattentive, isolative, school phobic, and withdrawn.

The hyperactive, so called minimally brain-damaged child, as part of his total symptom complex often has a low sense of self-esteem, has difficulty interacting in social situations, and is tearful and sensitive. Such a child is likely to develop significant dysphoria when his hyperactivity/inattentiveness are controlled by stimulant medication (Conners, 1976). The author has suggested that this dysphoria is based more on the child's newfound ability to perceive the awful negative situation he finds himself in, now that he is no longer in a state of "Brownian movement" and is able finally to analyze all the negative systems that he is a participant in, than a secondary psychopharmacologic response. What would the goals be in treating hyperactive/inattentive children manifesting symptoms related to depression? Using the conceptual models described above, it is an easy task to hypothesize how such children might get depressed or, using a psychodynamic perspective, how they might use a number of defenses to ward off depression. Such children are frequently of at least average intelligence, yet often are failing or are manifesting academic difficulties and always are performing below their expected potential. Such children are placed daily in what seems to many of them to be an inhumane shock box called "classroom" that closely models the unavoidable aversive consequence paradigm of Seligman. Moreover, because a negative cycle has been established between their efforts and the lack of success, and because they begin to manifest some deviant behaviors as a response to the frustration, they continue to deplete the number of positive reinforcers available in their school environment, though they may elicit a number of negative responses, and the issue of low self-esteem and demeaned self-worth comes to the forefront. It is not an incidental finding that a greater percentage of such children have been found to be depressed (Weinberg et al, 1973) as compared to emotionally disturbed clinic patients. This whole process leads to the negative cognitive triad, where school is seen as a hopeless situation. For those children whose hyperactive, inattentive, immature behavior is not confined to the school, but spills over into home and community, the problem is multiply intensified. This is particularly true for children from homes which are unstable or non-supportive. The ghetto children the author has encountered in New York, Brooklyn, and Pittsburgh, who are quick, bright, and "street-wise," and the middle class children whose parents set realistic expectations do not develop depressive symptoms.

The children whose immaturity and impulsivity spill over into the home setting often report being friendless or overprotected or rejected by the mothering figure, have no escape from lowered self-worth, and frequently develop depressive, aggressive, or isolative behaviors.

The behavioral interventions for hyperactive/inattentive behavior range from teachers attending to and praising appropriate behaviors and ignoring or verbally and nonverbally expressing disapproval of deviant actions (Ayllon and Rosenbaum, 1977), to token economy systems, home-based reinforcement, and biofeedback. The earliest studies were conducted in specially designed research settings and lack the property of comparability to regular or typical classrooms for the learning disabled or emotionally disturbed. Gittelman et al (1979) describe a number of studies conducted in regular classrooms which demonstrate the efficacy of behavioral approaches in treating hyperactive children. Ayllon and Rosenbaum (1977) present further examples and a bibliography of behavior therapy for the "hyperkinetic behavior syndrome" is available (Reatig, 1980).

Recent reviews comparing behavioral with psychopharmacologic (stimulant medication) approaches suggest that behavioral approaches may be helpful but often inferior to psychomotor stimulants. Backman and Firestone (1979) note that academic performance has been reported to improve with behavioral treatments, but that the data they reviewed support the stimulant as superior, particularly regarding attentional processes and classroom behavior. Gittelman et al (1979) have demonstrated this in a very well-designed and thought out study. They conclude that methylphenidate is clearly superior to behavior modification in treating hyperactive children. However, they did find that the combination of behavior therapy and stimulant medication was helpful in certain children and should be used when medication alone is not enough. Williamson et al (1980) and Backman and Firestone (1979) come to similar conclusions.

This is especially true for hyperactive children who may be depressed or who, as described above, lack the skills or environment in which they can compensate for their deficits. Zrull et al (1970) postulated a relationship between the hyperkinetic syndrome and depression and provide poignant examples of hyperactive behaviorally disordered children who clearly demonstrated depression. Brumback and Weinberg (1977) present their findings, which demonstrate that hyperactivity and depression do occur independently but, more importantly, that there is a frequent association between hyperactivity and depression, particularly when the hyperactivity is episodic.

Satterfield et al (1980) describe their multimodality therapeutic approach in treating 84 hyperactive boys. They note that long-term studies have indicated that medication alone is insufficient for favorable outcome. For many of their children, low self-esteem was a major problem and this, they felt, was related to overall poor interpersonal relations with all meaningful persons and to both academic and social failures in school. Depression was viewed as a major therapeutic problem, sometimes warranting use of antidepressant medication. Though behavioral therapy per se was not employed, the goals were identical to those that a behaviorist would prescribe: to increase his self-esteem by being able to do something well; to encourage the development of rewarding and positive interactions free of distractibility in therapy so that "success at building and creating" could generalize beyond the therapeutic sessions; verbalizing responsibility for his own behavior; to place him in group therapy to decrease social isolation and increase meaningful relationships; to develop task oriented family therapy, for those so motivated; to provide consistent, predictable structure and nonpunitive discipline; and to establish educational therapy oriented toward academic and social skills in the school setting.

Some of these hyperactive children were so depressed that they required hospitalization, often for suicidal ideation. From their description, one is left with the impression that hyperactive children do develop significant depression which requires a truly comprehensive approach. Moreover, unless the therapeutic program for hyperactive children takes into account the variables above, the prognosis for such children is grim. Numerous follow-up studies attest to this fact. The child's perceived locus of control also plays a role in the response to particular therapeutic strategies. Whalen and Henker (1976) review the literature dealing with perceived causal attribution and use of medication. A pilot study (Bugental et al, 1977) demonstrated no short-term differences between hyperactive elementary aged boys treated with contingent social reinforcement from those provided with a form of cognitive manipulation which focused on self-control. However, when controlling for medication, it was noted that children who benefited most from the cognitive manipulation were those not receiving medication and who had a high internal locus of control. The social reinforcement group showed trends indicating that it was more effective for children on medication with a low internal locus of control. On six month follow-up (Bugental et al, 1978) several interesting results were noted. Children from the social reinforcement group showed greater improvement on teacher rating scales than their peers who had received self-control training. But those from the self-control group had a higher sense of personal control over themselves than the boys from the other group. The teacher's perceived greater control over the boys treated with contingent social reinforcement, which was probably related to the boy's ability to respond more positively and to elicit more positive responses from the adults. The authors suggest sequential treatment of hyperactive children to decrease impulsivity and to improve social behavior through contingent social reinforcement, followed by self-control procedures to develop long-term improvement of personal causality.

Williamson et al (1980) utilized a program which sequentially provided medication and graduated levels of self-control techniques for an incredibly hyperactive nine-year-old boy who was extremely distractible and lacked basic social skills. The interventions were provided in a highly therapeutic environment that consistently reinforced positive adaptive behavior in both academic and nonacademic environments. This child met modified Research and Diagnostic Criteria (RDC) criteria for depression on the Bellevue Index of Depression (BID) (Petti, 1978). He improved in all areas, including social interactions, on-task behavior, and academics. His depression cleared. His medication (dextroamphetamine, 20 mg orally, twice daily) was decreased by half. We had great difficulty in training the mother on appropriate responses to the deviant behavior of her three disturbed children. However, the boy that received our comprehensive treatment continued to make gains with special school placement, group therapy, and medication. The general impression was that greater gains could have been effected had we been able to engage the mother in treatment.

A variety of other approaches to training self-control in disruptive or hyperactive children have been utilized. Drabman et al (1973) employed social reinforcement through the use of a token system to initially decrease disruptive behavior and improve and increase academic output. Following this, the students were reinforced on a declining schedule for matching on self-evaluation the teacher's rating of their social and academic achievement. The exciting aspects of this work are that the students maintained their previous gains even while the reinforcement was being tapered and eliminated and, more importantly, that these improved behaviors were also demonstrated at times of the day when no program was used. A series of papers (Kendall and Finch, 1976, 1978) describes one form of verbal self-instructional procedures which use a cognitive-behavioral framework in treating impulsive children. Douglas et al (1976) describe an effective cognitive protocol which taught self-verbalization and self-reinforcement techniques to hyperactive boys. These involved employing effective strategies for social situations, cognitive tasks, and academic problems in a more deliberate manner. Biofeedback, as the most mechanically oriented of the behavioral self-control techniques, has also been demonstrated to be highly effective in decreasing deviant behaviors, particularly motor activity, in hyperactive children (Lubar and Shouse, 1977).

Poor school performance is often associated with hyperactive inattentive or impulsive behavior but may be quite independent of that complex as well. Most depressed children have academic or behavioral problems in school. There is usually an associated drop in grades, inability to concentrate, lack of energy for schoolwork, and occasional desire to avoid the school situation. Hollon (1970) describes four cases of children referred to a psychologist for testing because of their poor academic achievement despite good learning capacities. Hollon refers to masked depression as the underlying disorder, but each of these children gave clear evidence of dysphoria. They all verbalized feelings of low self-esteem, guilt, rejection, and futility once the issues underlying the depression were addressed. Therapeutically, the children made behavioral and academic improvement.

It should be of no surprise that children with learning disabilities and poor academic performance, on the other hand, are particularly susceptible to developing clinically significant depression. But this is not simply because they get poor grades. Serafica and Harway (1979) note that children with learning disabilities are less popular than comparison groups of children on peer sociometric ratings, adults also perceive learning disabled children as doing poorly in social interactions. These workers comment on the generally accepted relationship between low academic achievement and diminished self-esteem but note that children with learning problems will often rate themselves higher in sociometric status than they actually deserve. This they relate to "ego-defensiveness" on the child's part.

The whole issue of learned helplessness with regard to the learning disabled or academic underachiever is highlighted by Bryan and Pearl (1979). They note that studies concerned with the relationship between self-concept and locus of control of learning disabled children have found that such youngsters perceive themselves as more externally than internally controlled (more subject to luck and the vagaries of their environment than their own efforts) and more prone to have a negative view of themselves. More importantly, they comment on the observation that such attitudes and concepts of responsibility and causality are established by the age of nine years and become progressively more negative with advancing years. Of equal importance, the teachers and parents have the same negative view of the learning-disabled child—harboring more negative expectations of them than of other children without such a handicap and usually a more pessimistic view than the children have of themselves.

The interventions used for such children really depend upon the basic reasons for the lack of achievement and for the failure to socialize adequately. Many are described in other sections of this chapter. Other specific techniques include training in "teacher pleasing behaviors," dealing with the specific type of disability and assisting the child in developing alternate problem solving strategies, increasing the perception of internal attribution and mastery while decreasing learned helplessness (Zigmond, 1979; Schroeder et al, 1978; Petti, 1980).

Children with epilepsy are a similarly handicapped group who are subject to a variety of behavioral and more serious psychiatric disability (Rutter et al, 1970; Sonis et al, 1980). These children manifest psychiatric distrubance at a rate of three times that of the general population. Many of these children are extremely vulnerable to depression when the very real episodic lack of control over their behavior, the degree of academic and social deficits they experience, and the ever-present fear of "having a fit" are considered. Aside from those children who have toxic behavior reactions to diphenhydantoin or the barbiturate derivatives, most children whose seizures, particularly the psychomotor and major motor variety, come under control or remit spontaneously feel a greater sense of security and decreased anxiety and depression. Fromm et al (1974) beautifully illustrate this when describing children with atypical, treatment-resistant seizures who responded to imipramine with seizure control. My own clinical experience substantially bears this out, particularly with the use of carbamazepine for children with psychomotor seizures.

Behavioral therapies have been successfully applied to seizure disorders, both functional and organic. Gardner (1967) describes the elimination of hysterical seizures in a ten-year-old child who was involved in sibling rivalry and competition for her mother's attention. There has been an increase in somatic complaints and tantruming before the first "seizure" episode. A hospital inpatient evaluation was positive only for a functional diagnosis in a girl experiencing a high degree of sibling rivalry with a high potential for conversion reaction behavior given her "hysteric type personality." The parents assisted in developing a home treatment program which emphasized ignoring seizures, tantrums, or other highly deviant behaviors—being "deaf and dumb"—and giving attention to her when she was involved in appropriate behaviors. The seizures were eliminated and other deviant behaviors dropped well below the baseline level. A reversal, where the parents attended to the somatic complaints, lead to a marked increase in deviant behavior and a "seizure." A return to the "deaf and dumb" intervention precluded any further seizure activity and decreased inappropriate behavior to the acceptable level.

Balaschak (1976) used a similar strategy in the treatment of an 11-year-old child with organically based seizures who had not responded to medication. The child had been referred because an added hysterical component consisting of prolonged seizure-like activity had become a problem. This component had responded successfully to dynamic psychotherapy but the child's ability to express feelings or to increase her sense of self-esteem had not. General immaturity, marked inability of independent functioning, frequent denial of her seizures, and lack of friends were also viewed as significant emotional difficulties.

There was good evidence that she was aware of an impending seizure and that the seizure did have some correlation to external stimuli, such as perceived rejection by her peers and criticism by the teachers as well as anxiety provoking situations related to novelty, frustration, or anger. The teacher saw a causal relationship to lack of self-confidence as illustrated by her inability to make even basic decisions and inordinate dependency on peers, teacher, and adults alike.

The program consisted of the teacher praising the girl and giving her a reward for seizure-free periods during the school day and of a "good times chart" for monitoring. No specific directions to prevent the seizures were given but she was urged to talk to the teacher whenever she became tense or anxious. A second chart to monitor assertive or self-initiated behaviors, independent of rewards, was also kept. There was a dramatic decrease in seizure activity during this phase of treatment and her self-initiated assertive behaviors increased rapidly to the point that the teacher felt that the child's lack of self-confidence and dependency were no longer problems requiring intervention. The child evidenced enjoyment at the challenge of the seizure control program. Following a break for vacation, the girl's medication was increased and she began wearing a helmet for protection. The seizures remained at a low but slightly higher level than the previous phase at school. At home they occurred frequently until the mother instituted her own informal contingency program for seizure-free periods and the child's seizure activity at home also decreased. The child then developed mononucleosis and was out of school for about two months. On return to school, the teacher elected not to restart the program preferring instead to concentrate on academic goals. The seizure rate returned to its pretreatment level. A variety of hypotheses are offered by Balaschak to explain the results, including the increase of self-esteem, resulting from self-control over the seizures, and the development of assertiveness and independence to replace seizures as an acceptable response. The issue of attribution and locus of control would logically apply in cases of epilepsy. The case presented clearly demonstrates a number of features associated with learned helplessness, except that the child was not feeling completely hopeless, as is often the case with depressed children (Symonds, 1968b), and hence was open to a hopeful solution. Children with secondary depression often will evidence marked improvement when entering therapy or an inpatient setting for the first time.

A number of other studies have demonstrated varying degrees of efficacy in the application of behavioral techniques to seizure disorders in children. These include biofeedback control of seizures in children who had not responded to anticonvulsant therapy (Finley et al, 1974), interrupting the chain of events leading to the seizures with a loud shout of "no" and shaking of the shoulders during the prodromal state (Zlutnik et al, 1975), time out, self-control with relaxation, contingent electrical shock (Siegel and Richards, 1978) and other types of biofeedback that have been reviewed (Lubar and Shouse, 1977; Conners, 1979). The issue once again evolves around the concepts of competence versus inadequacy and a sense of inner control and responsibility versus helplessness. Providing a convulsive disordered child with a sense of inner control over his seizures is one way of immunizing him against present and future feelings of learned helplessness.

A large number of depressed children present to psychiatrists with a history of hostile, oppositional, and aggressive behavior. Poznanski and Zrull (1970) after screening very carefully for depressed children from those seen at the psychiatric clinics of the University of Michigan, found that aggression and hostility were the predominant chief complaints occurring in 12 of 14 children. Petti (1978) found that symptoms related to agitation and aggression were the highest ranking behaviors, aside from dysphoric mood, for hospitalized children diagnosed as depressed by both research criteria (BID) and clinician's judgment.

An earlier study (Burks and Harrison, 1962) poignantly describes the manner in which aggressive children ward off a basic state of helplessness or powerlessness associated with a depressed affect. Such children were noted by the staff as being unable to experience any real fun and only able occasionally to experience transient periods of infantile enjoyment with a trusted staff person. It is of particular interest to note that the natural course of the depressed but aggressive children described by Poznanski and Zrull (1970) was not into delinquent, violent behavior but rather to the passivity and withdrawal more often associated with depression in adults (Poznanski et al, 1976).

Symonds (1970) eloquently illustrates the dynamics behind the behavior of depressed adolescents. He notes that though such individuals present with problems surrounding school and academic performance, the psychiatrist quickly discerns the patient to be angry and overly involved with his own suffering. They are seen as anxious and clinging to adults while at the same time as being unhappy and angry and despising themselves for those weaknesses. Symonds (1968b) describes depressed children and adolescents as chronically pessimistic and suffering from a modified "Charlie Brown Syndrome" marked by thinly suppressed anger, passive resistance and oppositional behavior (a modified negative cognitive triad).

Symonds (1968b) notes that children lack the verbal and cognitive ability to express their depression and need to act out their feelings. Such children "feel sad but act bad" and adults who might respond positively to their sadness and depression are alienated by their badness. Children who feel inferior (Symonds, 1968a) may use defensive aggressiveness, occasional disruptive assaultiveness, and denial in their effort to compensate. Petti and Davidman (1981) comment that school age children who contemplate or attempt homicide are frequently faced with a "nothing left but . . . murder" situation due to their perceived inability to respond in a more adaptive manner to an overwhelmingly aversive and noxious environment.

A number of behavioral approaches have been employed in helping such troubled youngsters. Patterson (1976) and his colleagues at the Oregon Research Institute were among the first to develop behavioral approaches to the treatment of aggressive children. In the systematic analysis of the families of such children compared to their nonaggressive counterparts, they found that aggressive children were both the victims and the architects of coercive family systems. Coercion was defined as a "general process of control-by-pain." The families were characterized by high rates of such behaviors but the parents were inconsistent in their responses to most behaviors and often used weak punishments. The children, particularly the middle or problem child, learned this mode of interaction from their parents and began using it with increasing frequency. Finally, the family system becomes disrupted and all members use coercion more frequently and more intensely. The problem child receives more punishment, is labelled deviant, and ends up not responding to positive social interactions. He increases the coercive behaviors when punished, develops a negative sense of himself and others, experiences rejection from his family as a result of his maladaptive behavior, and has general stunting of his developing basic social skills which are necessary for customary interactions, for example, initiating and sustaining a conversation. Such children were often punished, even when they were behaving appropriately, and were doing poorly in school. Utilizing the hypothesized etiologies of depression described above, such children were prime candidates for significant depression.

Given such an assessment for understanding the aggressive child, the Patterson (1976) group aimed at changing the family system equilibrium through "parenting skills" training in such concepts as: behavior observation and record keeping, implementation of effective punishment for coercive behavior, and reinforcing prosocial behaviors through effective social and material reinforcers. Children who were highly disruptive in school were provided with a special program oriented to rewarding nondisruptive behaviors or "survival skills" which were shared with the peer group. The parents were trained to provide remedial tutoring for the children who lacked academic skills.

Results of this intensive intervention indicated statistically significant change in the levels of coercive and deviant behaviors manifested by the boys. The parents felt that all the children had improved. Moreover, a majority rated their child as "happier" and their whole family as functionally improved. Similarly, disturbed boys whose parents participated in placebo groups showed nonsignificant increases in deviant symptom scores. The carry-over of effective parenting to the siblings of disturbed children has been verified in other populations (Klein et al, 1977; Humphreys et al, 1978). This rise of stability and appropriate parental authority for the family produces a warmer, less tense, healthier home environment for all family members.

Social skills or conflict resolution skills training is another area of behavior therapy which has been demonstrated to be effective in treating aggressive children. Patterson et al (1967) note that in analyzing the behavior of deviant children and assessing their levels of skills, one must differentiate between children in whom the skills already exist to some extent and those in whom such skills must be trained almost from a zero baseline. Bornstein et al (1980) describe social skills training for highly aggressive children who were treated on our inpatient unit. The training was completed in a multiple baseline across behaviors design; behaviors which received attention included the ability to maintain eye contact (as a rate of duration of speech), hostile tone, requests for new behavior, and overall assertiveness. Smiles was a behavior target for one girl. The two boys and two girls ranged in age from eight to 12 years. An initial assessment was conducted to obtain a baseline and to determine the type of intervention required. This was done by describing situations to the children and recording their responses. Feedback was then provided concerning performance with regard to the targeted behavior; this feedback was discussed and appropriate responses were modelled. The child was allowed to respond again following specific instructions by the therapist. The child kept rehearsing the behaviors until the therapist was satisfied that the appropriate type of response was achieved. New interpersonal situations were presented and the process continued. Behaviors were also monitored in a separate therapy group conducted with other children on the unit. Results of the treatment were very positive regarding the targeted behaviors. However, at follow-up, which ranged from four to 26 weeks, the children showed inconsistent maintenance of their behavioral gains. All continued to show improvement in decreasing their hostile tone and one subject maintained her gains at six months. The others showed variability and poor generalization of their new skills over the time span. The authors raise numerous hypotheses to explain their results. Three of these children met accepted criteria for depression (BID) (Petti, 1978) and one is described more fully elsewhere (Petti et al, 1980).

A similar study was conducted in four males, aged nine to 11 years, hospitalized for their aggressive behavior and poor peer relations. All had done poorly on a scale which assessed social skills (Calpin and Kornblith, 1978). All of the boys were depressed. The format was essentially that of the Bornstein et al (1980) study except that the targeted behaviors were affect statements, requests for new behavior, and overall social skills. The behaviors were trained sequentially. All the boys showed marked improvement as a response to the specific interventions. All showed generalization to scenes that they had not been trained for, though this occurred only after the concomitant use of dextroamphetamine in one child. This child failed to maintain his gains on a three month follow-up assessment while the other three boys retained most of their therapeutic gains. Depression improved in the two boys treated with imipramine but not in the two boys who received other psychopharmacologic treatment.

Successful modification of the aggressive behavior of adolescent hospital patients through the use of social skills training has been described (Elder et al, 1979). By training socially appropriate alternative responses for the former aggressive reactions that would characterize the manner in which the youngsters would respond to troublesome situations, the number of required seclusions and other deviant behaviors dropped significantly and positive behaviors increased. Also, the adaptive responses generalized to other ward settings such as the lunchroom and classroom. This approach has also been applied to other groups of deviant children (Ollendick and Hersen, 1979).

Although, in the author's experience, most depressed children present with aggressive and impulsive behavior, a picture of a withdrawn, social isolate with low energy and a "sad sack" face is the picture most people have of the depressed child. This seems to be the case for children diagnosed as depressed who are hospitalized on pediatric wards (Poznanski et al, 1979; Kashani and Simonds, 1980). If one employs the anaclitic model of depression, these children would be fully in the latter two stages—despair and detachment. These would be children for whom learned helplessness is in full bloom, for whom reaping the benefits from the positive reinforcers in the environment is highly improbable, and for whom the negative cognitive triad is well established. Such depressed children, in my experience, are the most difficult to treat and effect a positive outcome in unless one "shoots the works" and provides truly comprehensive treatment (Petti and Wells, 1980; Petti et al, 1980).

The majority of reports and case studies describing behavioral approaches to treating isolated or withdrawn children deal with preschoolers (O'Connor, 1969, 1972). Very few describe the affective state of the children or provide data that would permit the inference of depression. A major difficulty is that such children infrequently cause a disruption in the class or neighborhood, may be viewed as model children, and go undetected until they become depressed, aggressive, psychotic, or school refusing in adolescence.

Walker and Hops (1973) describe the successful use of group and individual reinforcement in the treatment of withdrawn children in first and second grade who were scored highest on teacher ratings of withdrawal and low social interactions and had these observations substantiated by direct systematic observation. Three children met these criteria out of 1,067 children screened. The first child, a second-grade girl, was taught specific social interaction skills and rewarded only when she used those skills and her peers initiated interactions with her. She was not rewarded simply for initiating interactions with them. In a design in which a baseline period was followed by the intervention, then a no-treatment baseline followed by a repetition of the treatment period (ABAB), the child showed marked increases in interaction rates with her peers during the treatment phases (B) which were well above both her baseline rates and the mean rates of her peers. The duration of her interactions did not increase.

For the second withdrawn child, the complementary situation was employed. This first-grade girl's classmates were trained in social interaction skills and then they were rewarded a point for each initiation the withdrawn girl made to any of her peers. The peers as a group earned a preselected reward for a given number of points. An ABAB design was again employed. The results were as positive as those obtained for the first child.

The third child, a severely withdrawn second-grade girl, was provided both treatment procedures used in the previous two subjects. However, the child could not receive her individual reward and the class could not receive the group reward unless both the girl and the class met their quota of interactions. An ABAB design was again employed and the results were again dramatically positive. For all children, the second baseline level (B) never dropped as low as the initial baseline level. A primary aim was to access the withdrawn children to the natural reinforcement system in the environment and this was accomplished (Walker and Hops, 1973). However, generalization of the changes to other situations was not studied.

Gelfand (1978) discusses shyness and social withdrawal, notes that informal efforts and "socialization experiences" such as individual nondirective play therapy, collaborative activity with peers, and advising parents have been found to be ineffective and states that programs which do not deal with "the child's social skills deficit are doomed to failure." She then reviews modeling, reinforcement procedures and indirect methods (such as passing out candy) and provides guidelines to effective and noneffective use of such modalities.

An innovative approach to training social skills in unassertive children is described in the work of Bornstein et al (1977). Twelve youngsters, aged eight to 11 years, were referred by their teachers because they were shy, passive, unassertive, and conforming. The four children chosen for treatment were found on assessment to be deficient in at least three of the following verbal and nonverbal behaviors: poor eye contact, short duration of speech, inability to make requests, and inaudible responses. Following the baseline assessment, each of these children trained squentially and cumulatively to the deficit behaviors over a three-week period. The following training protocol was employed: (1) a scene was presented, a model gave a prompt, and the child responded; (2) feedback was provided to the child concerning the appropriateness of the response to the targeted behavior; (3) the feedback was discussed to insure understanding; (4) role models modeled appropriate responses; (5) specific instructions were provided concerning the desired behavior and the child was asked to respond a second time; (6) rehearsal continued for that scene until criterion for the behavior was achieved; (7) training then advanced to new interpersonal scenes following the above sequence. The results indicated marked improvement in all the targeted components in overall assertiveness and in generalization to untreated scenes in all four children; these gains were maintained at two and four-week follow-up evaluations. These workers (Bornstein et al, 1977) note that the generalization to the natural environment with other children was not studied. However, this study does suggest that specific deficits in verbal and nonverbal social skills can be identified in children who are functioning inadequately in social situations and that these deficits can be corrected in unassertive, shy, passive children. Rhodes et al (1979) carried these procedures out with an unassertive adolescent with similar results. Moreover, the effects generalized to actual children whose names had been used in the training scenes and to other peers as well.

Whitehill et al (1980) in a similarly constituted study employing instructions, modeling, behavior rehearsal, performance feedback, and programmed generalization treated four socially isolated children, aged eight to ten years, with training in conversational behaviors. All four improved in the component skills of making informative statements, asking open-ended questions, and making requests to share in an activity. Their overall conversational ability increased, the mean length of pauses between scenes decreased, and mean duration of speech increased. They also decreased their percentage of time spent alone during free play from about 57 to 20 percent. These gains were not maintained consistently at follow-up and generalization was inconsistently made to the school setting. Minimal post-treatment gains as measured by positive and negative peer nominations were disappointing. A comprehensive review (Van Hasselt et al, 1979) is available which critiques the various techniques, classification issues and determination of skill components, generalization, and maintenance of treatment effects of social skill assessment and training for children with the major focus of withdrawal, lack of assertiveness, and isolation.

A different focus on the behavioral treatment of social withdrawal in early grade school children is provided by Weinrott et al (1979). An experimental group of teachers was trained in the use of symbolic modeling, social reinforcement, contingency management, and individual and group reinforcement. Twenty-five children were identifed by objective criteria as withdrawn. The 20 children in the experimental group showed a significant increase in peer interactions compared to baseline on multiple measures of withdrawal; the gains persisted through a follow-up period. At follow-up, the experimental group no longer differed from normal peers and were more sociable than the untreated control subjects who were still functioning at a social level well below that of their classmates. Anecdotal reports by teachers indicated that the treated children were "happier, more alert, and eager to assume tasks of greater responsibility." This increased interaction with peers generalized to the cafeteria, playground, and home where they began inviting and being invited by friends to visit. These workers also found that the teachers demand for social interaction, without any of the other behavioral interventions, itself had a positive but unsustained effect during a second baseline.

Thus withdrawal and social isolation, symptoms which to some extent often accompany depression in children, have been shown to respond to specific behavioral approaches. Providing children with access to rewarding experiences and success allows them a greater feeling of mastery and confidence. This, in turn, should make them less susceptible to a perpetuation of their helplessness and social ineptitude.

Few studies have been specifically directed to the behavioral treatment of children who meet research criteria for depression. Two single case, multiple baseline studies of such children have been described (Petti and Wells, 1980; Petti et al, 1980) in which behavioral interventions were combined with anti-depressant medication within a highly intensive, comprehensive therapeutic milieu.

Matson et al (1980) treated four children, boys aged nine and 11 years and girls aged 11 years, who met BID criteria for depression. These children had failed to respond to an intensive behaviorally oriented milieu and insight-oriented psychotherapy. The children were given social skills training in a group format. Individualized assessments were conducted and the children were taught how to make appropriate eye contact, to demonstrate affect appropriate for the given situation, to use adaptive psychomotor behavior, and to be selective in their verbal responses in particular settings. The social skills format was similar to those described above. The training effects were immediate and the study clearly demonstrates that social skills can be trained effectively in a group and that peer modeling alone is not an effective strategy in teaching social skills to such children, particularly those with few skills.

A noncontrolled study comparing intensive social skills training to imipramine and matched placebo within the same intensive milieu showed that children trained in social skills did about as well as children treated with placebo but not as well as children treted with imipramine. But in the area of social skills assessment and use of social skills in the environment they excelled by far the other two groups. However, these children still remained clinically depressed and, unlike the imipramine treated children, failed to show changes in all-night sleep electroencephalographic analysis which would indicate a positive response to antidepressant treatment (Taska et al, 1980). A detailed description of one of these cases is described elsewhere (Petti, 1980).

The case description in Chapter 17 should help illustrate some of these points and give the reader an appreciation for the role of social skills, self-control, and behavioral approaches, highlight the complex therapeutic and assessment issues, and demonstrate the need for a comprehensive treatment strategy.

SUMMARY

The whole area of depression, with its roots in learning theory and abberant cognition, has come a long way from the statement that "the new developments in behavior modification techniques . . . have not been applied to depressive illness. Even the newer theoretical developments along these lines tend to ignore depression" (Costello and Belton, 1969). In the past five years there has been a steady increase in attention directed toward these issues in general psychiatry and we are just beginning to look at behavioral, cognitive, and related therapies for depressed children. A major stumbling block continues to be the lack of general agreement as to what makes up depression in children. The strength of the behavioral approaches is in delineating target symptoms and behavior. A focus on these issues along with physiological concomitants of childhood depression may provide the tools to better define the disorder and to objectively determine appropriate therapeutic approaches.

It is the unusual case in which a depressed child has his/her symptoms clear up as readily as described elsewhere (Cytryn and McKnew, 1979). Most of the depressed hospitalized children we have treated required intensive behavioral programming, focus on self-control and adaptive social interactions, and re-programming of their perceptions of school, family, and community environment which would enhance and help maintain their therapeutic gains. When everything falls into place, as it did for instance in the child Lonny presented in Chapter 17, the prognosis can be excellent. As the available number of factors necessary for adequate treatment decrease (for example, parents' refusal to be involved, recalcitrant schools, failure to respond to medication, or impenetrable defenses), the prognosis correspondingly decreases. The next ten years should show an exponential growth in the amount of published behavioral and cognitive work reporting the results of treating symptoms of childhood depression. Piaget (1962) noted that both affect and cognition are necessary for normal characterologic development. All the components of these two factors as they are detailed above should consume our interest for some time.

REFERENCES

Akiskal HS, McKinney WT, Jr. Overview of recent research in depression. *Arch Gen Psychiatry* 1975; 32:285-305.

Ayllon T, Rosenbaum MS. The behavioral treatment of disruption and hyperactivity in school settings. In Lahey B, Kazdin A, eds. *Advances in clinical child psychology*. New York: Plenum Press, 1977:85-115.

Backman J, Firestone P. A review of psychopharmacological and behavioral approaches to the treatment of hyperactive children. *Am J Orthopsychiatry* 1979; 49; 3:500-504.

Balaschak BA. Teacher implemented behavior modification in a case of organically based epilepsy. *J Consult Clin Psychol* 1976; 44:218-223.

Beck AT. The core problem in depression: The cognitive triad. In: Masserman J, ed. *Depression: theories and therapies*. New York: Grune & Stratton, 1970.

Bornstein M, Bellack AD. Social skills training for highly aggressive children in an inpatient psychiatric setting. *Behav Mod* 1980;4:173-186.

Bornstein MR, Bellack AS, Hersen M. Social-skills training for unassertive children: a multiple-baseline analysis. *J Applied Behav Analy* 1977; 10: 183-195.

Brumback RA, Weinberg WA. Relationship of hyperactivity and depression in children. *Percept Mot Skills* 1977;45:247-251.

Bryan T, Pearl R. Self concepts and locus of control of learning disabled children. *J Clin Child Psychol* 1979;8:223-226.

Bugental DB, Whalen CK, Henker B. Casual attributions of hyperactive children and motivational assumptions of two behavior change approaches: evidence for an interactionist position. *Child Dev* 1977;48:874-884.

Bugenthal DB, Collins S, Collins L, Chaney LA. Attributional and behavior management interventions with hyperactive boys: a follow-up study. *Child Dev* 1978;49:247-250.

Burks HL, Harrison SI. Aggressive behavior as a means of avoiding depression. *Am J Orthopsychiatry* 1962;32:416-422.

Calpin JP, Kornblith SJ. Training aggressive children in conflict resolution skills. Presented at the American Association of Behavior Therapy, Toronto, 1978.

Camp BW. Verbal mediation in young aggressive boys. *J Abnorm Psychol* 1977;86(2):145-153.

Camp BW, Bloom GE, Frederick H, van Doorninck WJ. Think aloud: a program for developing self-control in young aggressive boys. *J Abnorm Child Psychol* 1977;5:157-169.

Campbell S, Paulauskas S. Peer relations in hyperactive children. *J Child Psychol Psychiatry* 1979; 20:233-246.

Combs ML. Arezzo-Slaby D. Social skills training with children. In: Lahey B, Kazdin A, eds. *Adv Clin Child Psychol* New York: Plenum Press, 1977: 161-197.

Conners CK. Classification and treatment of childhood depression and depressive equivalents. In: Gallant D, Simpson G, eds. *Depression: behavioral, biochemical, diagnostic, and treatment concepts.* New York: Halsted Press, 1976:181-204.

Conners CK. Application of biofeedback to treatment of children. *J Am Acad Child Psychiatry* 1979;18;1:143, 151.

Costello CG, Belton GP. Depression: treatment. In Costello C, ed. *Sympt Psychopathol* New York: John Wiley and Sons, 1970:201-215.

Cytryn L, McKnew DH, Jr. *Disturbances in development of the basic handbook of child psychiatry. Volume Two.* New York: Basic Books, 1979. 321-340.

Douglas VI, Parry P, Marton P, Garson C. Assessment of a cognitive training program for hyperactive children. *J Abnorm Child Psychol* 1976; 4:389–410.

Drabman RS, Spitalnik R, O'Leary KD. Teaching self-control to disruptive children. *J Abnorm Psychol* 1973;82:10–15.

Dweck CS. The role of expectations and attributions in the alleviation of learned helplessness. *J Personal Soc Psychol* 1975;31:674–685.

Dweck CS. Learned helplessness: a developmental approach. In Schulterbrandt J, Raskin A, eds. *Depression in childhood diagnosis, treatment and conceptual models.* New York: Raven Press, 1977:135–138.

Dweck CS, Reppucci ND. Learned helplessness and reinforcement responsibility in children. *J Personal Soc Psychol* 1973; 25:109–116.

Elder JP, Eldestein BA, Narick MM. Adolescent psychiatric patients: modifying aggressive behavior with social skills training. *Behav Mod* 1979; 3:161-178.

Finley WW, Smith HA, Etherton MD. Reduction of seizures and normalization of the EEG in a severe epileptic following sensori-motor biofeedback training: a preliminary study. *Biolog Psychol* 1974; 2:189-203.

Fromm GH, Amores CY, Thies W. Imipramine in epilepsy. *Arch Neurol* 1972; 27:198-204.

Gardner JE. Behavior therapy treatment approach to a psychogenic seizure case. *J Consult Psychol* 1967; 31:209-212.

Gelfand DM. Social withdrawal and negative emotional states: behavior therapy. In: Wolman B, Egan J, Ross A, eds. *Handbook of treatment of mental disorders in childhood and adolescence*. Englewood Cliffs: Prentice-Hall, 1978: 330-353.

Gelfand DM, Hartman DP. Behavior therapy with children: a review and evaluation of research methodology. *Psychol Bull* 1968; 79:204-215.

Gittelman R, Abikoff H, Klein DF, Mattes J. A controlled trial of behavior modification and methylphenidate in hyperactive children. Paper presented at the American Academy of Child Psychiatry, Atlanta, Georgia, 1979.

Gottman J, Gonso J, Rasmussen B. Social interaction, social competence and friendship in children. *Child Dev* 1975; 46:709-718.

Graziano AM. *Behavior therapy with children*. Chicago: Aldine Atherton, 1971.

Graziano AM. Behavior therapy. In: Wolman B, Egan J, Ross A, eds. *Handbook of treatment of mental disorders in childhood and adolescence*. Englewood Cliffs: Prentice-Hall, 1978:28.

Hollon TH. Poor school performance as a symptom of masked depression in children and adolescents. *Am J Psychotherapy* 1970; 25:258–263.

Humphreys L, Forehand R, McMahon R, Roberts M. Parent behavioral training to modify child noncompliance: effects on untreated siblings. *J Behav Ther Exp Psychiatry* 1978; 9:235-238.

Kashani J, Simonds JF. The incidence of depression in children. *Am J Psychiatry* 1979; 136:1203-1205.

Keat DB, II. Multimodal therapy with children: two case histories. In: Lazarus, ed. *Multimodal behavior therapy*. New York: Springer, 1976:116-132.

Kendall PC. On the efficacious use of verbal self-instructional procedures with children. *Cogn Ther Res* 1977; 1:331-341.

Kendall PC, Finch AJ, Jr. A cognitive-behavioral treatment for impulse control: a case study. *J Consult Clin Psychol* 1976; 44:852-857.

Kendall PC, Finch AJ, Jr. A cognitive-behavioral treatment for impulsivity: a group comparison study. *J Consult Clin Psychol* 1978; 46:110-118.

Klee S, Meyer RG. Prevention of learned helplessness in humans. *J Consult Clin Psychol* 1979; 47; 2:411-412.

Klein NC, Alexander JF. Impact of family systems intervention on recidivism and sibling delinquency: a model of primary prevention and program evaluation. *J Consult Clin Psychol* 1977; 45:469-474.

Kovacs M, Beck AT. An empirical-clinical approach toward a definition of childhood depression. In: Schulterbrandt J, Allen A, eds. *Depression in childhood: diagnosis, treatment and conceptual models*. New York: Raven Press, 1977:1–25.

LaGrega AM, Mesibov GB. Social skills intervention with learning disabled children: selecting skills and implementing training. *J Clin Child Psychol* 1979;8:234–241.

Lazare A. Hidden conceptual models in clinical psychiatry. *N Eng J Med* 1973; 288:345-351.

Lazarus AA, Davison GC, Polefka DA. Classical and operant factors in the treatment of a school phobia. *J Abnorm Psychol* 1965;70:225-229.

Lefkowitz MM, Tesiny EP. Assessment of childhood depression. *J Consult Clin Psychol* 1980; 87:43-50.

Lewinsohn PM. Behavioral study and treatment in depression. In: Hersen M, Eisler R, Miller P, eds. *Progress in behavior modification.* New York: Academic Press, 1974:19–64.

Lewinsohn PM. Depression: a social learning perspective. Paper presented at Western Psychiatric Institute and Clinic, Pittsburgh, 1979.

Lewinsohn PM, Weinstein M, Shaw D. Depression: a clinical-research approach. In: Rubin R, Frank C, eds. *Advances in behavior therapy 1968.* New York: Academic Press, 1969:231–240.

Lubar JF, Shouse MN. Use of biofeedback in the treatment of seizure disorders and hyperactivity. In: Lahey B, Kazdin A, eds. *Advances in clinical child psychology.* New York: Plenum Press, 1977:204-261.

MacPherson EM, Candee BL, Hohman RJ. A comparison of three methods for eliminating disruptive lunchroom behavior. *J Appl Behav Anal* 1974; 7:287-297.

Mannarino AP. Friendship patterns and self-concept development in preadolescent males. *J Genet Psychol* 1978;133:105-110.

Matson JL, Esveldt-Dawson K, Andrasik F, et al. Observation and generalization effects of social skills training with emotionally disturbed children. *Behav Ther* (in press).

McLean PD. Therapeutic decision-making in the behavioral treatment of depression. In: Davidson P, ed. *The behavioral management of anxiety, depression and pain.* New York: Brunner/Mazel, 1975:54–90.

McLean PD. Parental depression: incompatible with effective parenting. In: Mash E, Handy L, Hamerlynck L, eds. *Behavior modification approaches to parenting.* New York: Brunner/Mazel, 1976:209-220.

McLean PD, Ogston K, Grauer L. A behavioral approach to the treatment of depression. *J Behav Ther Exp Psychiatry* 1973;4:323-330.

Monkman MM. *A milieu therapy program for behaviorally disturbed children.* Springfield: Charles C. Thomas, 1972:113-135.

Moyal BR. Locus of control, self-esteem, stimulus appraisal, and depressive symptoms in children. *J Consult Clin Psychol* 1977;45:951-952.

O'Connor RD. Modification of social withdrawal through symbolic modeling. *J Appl Behav Anal* 1969;2:15-22.

O'Connor RD. Relative efficacy of modeling, shaping and the combined procedures for modification of social withdrawal. *J Abnorm Psychol* 1972; 73:327-334.

Ollendick TH, Hersen M. Social skill training for juvenile delinquents. *Behav Res Ther* 1979;17:547-554.

Patterson GR. The aggressive child: victim and architect of a coercive system. In: Mash E, Hamerlynck L, Handy L, eds. *Behavior modification and families.* New York: Brunner/Mazel, 1976:267–316.

Patterson BR, McNeal S, Hawkins N, Phelps R. Reprogramming the social environment. *J Child Psychol Psychiatry* 1967;8:181–195.

Petti TA. Depression in hospitalized child psychiatry patients: approaches to measuring depression. *J Am Acad Child Psychiatry* 1978;17:49–59.

Petti TA. Active treatment of childhood depression. In: Clarkin J, Glazer H, eds. *Depression: behavioral and directive treatment strategies.* New York: Garland Press, 1981.

Petti TA. Imipramine in the treatment of depressed children. In: Cantwell D, Carlson G, eds. *Affective disorders in childhood and adolescence.* New York: Spectrum, 1983.

Petti TA, Bornstein M, Delamater A, Conners CK. Evaluation and multimodality treatment of a depressed pre-pubertal girl. *J Am Acad Child Psychiatry* 1980.

Petti TA, Davidman L. Homicidal school-age children: cognitive style and demographic features. *Child Psych Hum Dev* 1981;12:82–89.

Petti TA, Wells, K. Crisis treatment of a preadolescent who accidentally killed his twin. *Am J Psychother* 1980.

Phillips JS, Ray RS. Behavioral approaches to childhood disorders. *Behav Mod* 1980;4:3-34.

Piaget J. The relation of affectivity to intelligence in the mental development of the child. *Bull Menninger Clin* 1962;26:129-137.

Pizzat FJ. *Behavior modification in residental treatment for children: model of a program.* New York: Behavior publications, 1973.

Poznanski E, Krahenbuhl V, Zrull JP. Childhood depression: a longitudinal perspective. *J Child Psychiatry* 1976;15:491-501.

Poznanski EO, Cook SC, Carroll BJ. A depression rating scale for children. *Pediatrics* 1979;64:442-450.

Poznanski E, Zrull JP. Childhood depression. *Arch Gen Psychiatry* 1970;23:8-15.

Reatig NA, ed. *Proceedings of the National Institute of Mental Health Workshop on the Hyperkinetic Behavior Syndrome.* Washington, DC, 1978.

Rehm LP, Kornblith SJ. Behavior therapy for depression: a review of recent developments. *Progr Behav Mod* 1979;7:277-317.

Rhodes WA, Redd WH, Berggren L. Social skills training for an unassertive adolescent. *J Clin Child Psychol* 1979;8:81-121.

Rutter M. *Maternal deprivation–reassessed.* London: Penguin, 1972.

Rutter M, Graham P, Yule W. *A neuropsychiatric study of childhood.* Philadelphia: J. B. Lippincott, 1970.

Satterfield JH, Satterfield MS, Cantwell DP. Multimodality treatment of hyperactive children. In: Reatig NA, ed. *Proceedings of the NIMH Workshop on the Hyperkinetic Behavior Syndrome.* Washington, DC, 1980.

Schroeder CS, Schroeder SR, Davine MA. Learning disabilities: assessment and management of reading problems: In: Wolman B, ed. *Handbook of treatment of mental disorders in childhood and adolescence.* Englewood Cliffs: Prentice-Hall, 1978:212–237.

Seligman M. Learned helplessness. Paper presented at Western Psychiatric Institute and Clinic, Pittsburgh, 1979.

Seligman M, Maier S. Failure to escape traumatic shock. *J Exp Psychol* 1967;74:1–9.

Serafica FC, Harway NI. Social realtions and self-esteem of children with learning disabilities. *J Clin Child Psychol* 1979; 8:227–233.

Siegel LJ, Richard CS. Behavioral intervention with somatic disorders in children. In: Marholin D, ed. *Child behavior therapy*. New York: Gardner Press, 1978:339–394.

Sonis WA, Petti TA, Richet ET. Epilepsy and psychopathology in childhood: a controlled case study with Tegretol. *J Am Acad Child Psychiatry* 1981; 20:398–407.

Sullivan HS. *The interpersonal theory of psychiatry*. New York: Norton, 1953.

Symonds M. Our youth: apathy, rebellion and growth. A symposium. Disadvantaged children growing in a climate of hopelessness and despair. *Am J Psychoanal* 1968a; 28:15-22.

Symonds M. The depressions in childhood and adolescence. *Am J Psychoanal* 1968b; 28:189-195.

Symonds M. Depression in adolescence. *Sci Psychoanal* 1970; 17:66-74.

Taska BA, Kupfer DJ, Coble PA, et al. EEG sleep in depressed children: changes during inpatient treatment. Presented at the Annual Meeting of the American Psychophysiological Study of Sleep, Mexico City, 1980.

Van Hasselt VB, Hersen M, Whitehill MB, Bellack AS. Social skill assessment and training for children: an evaluative review. *Behav Res Ther* 1978; 17: 413-437.

Wahler RG. Setting generality: some specific and general effects of child behavior therapy. *J Appl Behav Anal* 1969; 2:239-246.

Walker HM, Hops H. The use of group and individual reinforcement contingencies in the modification of social withdrawal. In: Hamerlynck L, Handy L, Mash E, eds. *Behavior change: methodology, concepts and practice*. Champaign: Research Press, 1973:193.

Weinberg WA, Rutman J, Sullivan L, et al. Depression in children referred to an educational diagnostic center. *J Pediatr* 1973; 83:1065-1072.

Weinrott MR, Corson JA, Wilchesky M. Teacher mediated treatment of social withdrawal. *Behav Ther* 1979; 10:281-294.

Werry JS, Wollersheim JP. Behavior therapy with children: a broad overview. *J Am Acad Child Psychiatry* 1967; 6:346-370.

Whalen CK, Henker B. Psychostimulants and children: a review and analysis. *Psychol Bull* 1976; 83:1113-1130.

Whitehill MB, Hersen M, Bellack AS. Conversation skills training for socially isolated children. *Behav Res Ther* 1980; 18:217–225.

Williamson D, Calpin J, DiLorenzo T, et al. Combining dexedrine and feedback for the treatment of hyperactivity. *Behav Mod* 1981; 5:399–416.

Wolkind S, Renton G. Psychiatric disorders in children in long term residential care: a follow-up study. *Br J Psychiatry* 1979; 135:129-135.

Yates AJ. *Behavior therapy*. New York: John Wiley and Sons, 1970.

Zigmond N. Assessment of adolescents in preparation for intervention. Paper presented at Learning Disabilities: Untying the Gordian Knot of Assessment and Intervention, Pittsburgh, 1979.

Zlutnick S, Mayville W, Moffat S. Modification of seizure disorders: the interruption of behavioral chains. *J Appl Behav Anal* 1975; 8:1-12.

Zrull JP, McDermott JF, Poznanski E. Hyperkinetic syndrome: the role of depression. *Child Psychiatry Hum Dev* 1970; 1:33-40.

Affective Disorders in Childhood and Adolescence--
An Update. Edited by D.P. Cantwell and G.A. Carlson.

19

Cognitive Therapy with Depressed Children and Adolescents

Gary Emery, Richard Bedrosian, and Judy Garber

Cognitive therapy is based on the cognitive model of emotional disorders (Beck, 1976). The model holds that a person's cognitions (verbal and pictorial events in a stream of consciousness) determine how the person feels and acts. In depression, the person reacts to stress or a series of stresses by activating a set of dysfunctional beliefs. This has been referred to as the negative triad: a negative view of the self, the world, and the future.

Depressed persons systematically distort experiences to agree with their negative conclusions. The person maintains the depression through a series of cognitive errors, such as overgeneralization, all-or-nothing thinking, minimization of the positives, and selective abstraction. They mishear, misperceive, and misconstrue events to fit this prevailing negative line.

Often the therapist has to inquire about the patient's internal world to gather this information.

Below are excerpts from diaries and letters written by several depressed adolescents who initially had offered the therapist little information upon direct questioning. Notice the typical depressive themes, such as negative self-image, expectation of rejection from the therapist, hopelessness, and victimization at the hands of family and peers.

> . . . I'm not too good at letter writing, so I hope you'll excuse this letter if it sounds dumb. . . . You said I could write to you if I needed to. I can't talk to my parents. My mom and dad refuse to believe that I'm not "sick" and it's starting to hurt. Then they always have to discuss it with you before they let me do things. It just makes me feel so unnormal. I must sound very bratty, but I have been going to bed crying every night. . . . I'm real sorry about this letter. I guess these things really don't deserve me sending a letter of complaint. I wish I could get my act together and not need a doctor. Sorry if the writing's a little messy. I know this letter is dumb, but I had to talk to someone.

> . . . I wanted to mail you a nice letter but now I can't. When I felt this bad I used to cry but now I can't and won't. I won't give them the satisfaction. My stomach feels kind of sick. I'm not sure about anything. I don't want to give up on life. Sometimes I would just like to not care about anything. I'm not going to do that though. It might be easier. . . . For a while I was trying to think positive. Maybe school is nice, but it's not. I tried to think of good things, but I can't keep lying to myself. I wish I was the type of person that runs away, but I'm not. P.S. This is not my idea of how life should be!

> . . . I feel my biggest problem has been the way I look. I'm so goddamn ugly it's pathetic. I've been ugly all my life. I wish I was dead! I have no boyfriend. They all think I'm shitty looking. I wish I was better looking, smarter, different, I don't know. FUCKIN UGLY!!! That's what I am. I'll never go to college or make people proud of me. I mean people cringe when they see me. I just can't take it anymore!!!

In cognitive therapy, therapists and patients work together to identify and correct distortions such as those found above. The therapy is active and time limited. Patients learn to master problems they consider insurmountable by reevaluating their thinking. Patients first obtain symptom relief. Later, therapy focuses on uncovering beliefs that lead to depression and subjecting these beliefs to reality testing.

This chapter is divided into two main sections. The first covers the application of cognitive therapy to childhood depression. The standard methods of cognitive therapy (Beck et al, 1979) are outlined in this section. Theoretical questions that pertain to the use of cognitive therapy with children are also discussed in this section.

The second section deals with cognitive therapy with depressed adolescents. While the first section is concerned more with theoretical and empirical questions, the second section focuses on clinical concerns. Common themes found among depressed adolescents are outlined and clinical strategies for dealing with these problems are discussed.

CHILDHOOD DEPRESSION

Is cognitive therapy an appropriate and useful treatment for childhood depression? This question needs to be considered from both a theoretical and developmental perspective. First, is childhood depression theoretically consistent with a cognitive model? Second, do developmental limitations make the experience of depression different in children or interfere with its treatment by a cognitive therapy?

While there is considerable empirical support for Beck's cognitive model of depression in adults (Blaney, 1977; Hollon and Beck, 1979), few studies have focused on the cognitive aspects of childhood depression. The few studies that have been conducted with depressed children have been concerned with such cognitive variables as attributions (Leon et al, 1980), self-esteem (Garber, 1982b; Kaslow, 1981), standards of performance (Schultz, 1981), and locus of control (Lefkowitz et al, 1980). The evidence suggesting thinking errors among depressed children is limited.

Kendall (1981) believes that the nature of the cognitive problems differs between adults and children and the treatment should differ as a result. He suggests that whereas the targets of adult cognitive therapies can be classified as *cognitive errors*, the focus of treatment in children should be on *cognitive deficits.*

> Unlike therapy with adult clients, where the cognitive-behavioral therapist has to identify maladaptive cognitive processes, remove dysfunctional cognitions, and teach the client more adaptive thinking, the child cognitive-behavioral therapist can proceed more directly from identifying the cognitive absences to teaching the cognitive skills that help to remedy problems and foster adjustments (page 54).

Researchers have used cognitive interventions with cognitive deficits found among children. This has included deficits in role-taking ability, empathy, interpersonal problem-solving, and interpersonal understanding (Kendall et al, 1981).

While it is possible that cognitive deficits occur in depressed children, it is also plausible that the cognitive errors found in depressed adults can be found in children as well. Cognitive therapy of depression emphasizes changing the depressive's negative beliefs and illogical patterns of thinking. To build a case for using cognitive therapy with depressed children, it is necessary first to demonstrate that depressed children do have such thinking errors.

A second consideration regarding the appropriateness and, even more importantly, the feasibility of cognitive therapy concerns the child's cognitive level of development. Do children have the cognitive capacity: (1) to experience depression, and (2) to alter their ways of thinking in the manner described by cognitive therapy?

According to cognitive developmentalists such as Piaget (1970) and Flavell (1977), prepubertal children between the ages of seven and 12 are in the midst of the concrete-operational period. This stage is characterized by inferences, decentering, and reversibility. The child is closely tied to the concrete reality of the here and now; however, the child is capable of making inferences about reality that go beyond mere appearances.

Do children have the cognitive capacity to misinterpret and distort reality? Children can perceive reality and make inferences about it. While the inference may be consistent with the perceived reality, it's not necessary accurate. For example, the belief that the world is flat is consistent with what people see when they look out over the horizon, even though this belief isn't accurate. One child, for example, observed that her father was never around and inferred from this that he didn't care about her, when in fact the father was simply away on business.

In addition, children develop perspective-taking ability during middle childhood; this allows them to infer motives and attribute beliefs to others, even if they aren't always accurate. Thus, the concrete-operational child is capable of perceiving and inferring from reality as well as misinterpreting and distorting this reality.

Children also have the ability to perceive intentionality in their own or others' actions. At the same time, they have the parallel capacity to overapply or overattribute personal motives and intentions (Flavell, 1977). Therefore, children can experience self-blame and guilt, as well as anger and projection of blame onto others.

Finally, latency age children begin to develop a sense of their own and others' personalities. Livesly and Bromley (1973) found that during middle childhood, children tend to focus on traits and dispositions in their descriptions of themselves and others. During this stage, children's concept of self develops and children get a sense of their own competence.

Thus, children in the concrete-operational stage of development can make inferences from the concrete reality. They have the cognitive capacity to experience such symptoms of depression as guilt, low self-esteem, misattributions of blame, and feelings of rejection. One symptom that children may not yet have the cognitive capacity to experience fully is hopelessness. The concrete-operational children are closely tied to the realities of the here and now; as a result, they have more difficulty in anticipating the future and inferring consequences that may occur later. This cognitive limitation will be discussed further in a subsequent section concerned with the notion of "catastrophizing" (Ellis, 1971).

While it seems plausible that children in the concrete-operational stage of cognitive development have the capacity to experience many of the symptoms of depression, do they also have the capacity to remove these symptoms through cognitive means? Unfortunately, the process of undoing the depression is a bit more complex.

Cognitive therapy consists in a large part of the systematic application of empirical procedures to the cognitive, behavioral, and emotional symptoms of the depressed patient. One of the key techniques used in cognitive therapy is hypothesis testing. This procedure involves treating beliefs, assumptions, and expectations as hypotheses to be tested in a scientific inquiry. Together, the patient and therapist identify problem areas and design experiments that the client carries out to test the various thoughts and beliefs. The data generated by these tests provide the evidence and thus the new reality to be understood and interpreted. Are children able to use this method of hypothesis testing as a means of changing their beliefs?

The formal-operational adolescent is capable of hypothetico-deductive reasoning, the concrete-operational preadolescent, on the other hand, uses empirico-inductive reasoning (Flavell, 1977). That is, the formal operational thinker is capable of generating hypotheses and deducing logically about what ought to occur, whereas the concrete-operational thinker is more nonspeculative and more tied to the detected empirical reality. "Reality is subordinated to possibility in the former case, whereas possibility is subordinated to reality in the latter case" (Flavell, 1977).

Although concrete-operational children can produce, comprehend, and verify propositions, they tend to consider them singly and in isolation from one another. In contrast, the formal-operational thinker can reason about the logical relations that hold among two or more propositions. Latency age children have the capacity to generate and test propositions and can comprehend the technique of hypothesis testing. They may need assistance both with altering their reality and identifying alternative inferences from the new and existing realities. This is one aspect of cognitive therapy that may require the active participation of the parents.

Parents can become involved in the child's treatment by providing the opportunities that will allow the child to acquire new information. For example, Leah felt she couldn't "do anything." Her mother helped her to become involved in a music activity in which she experienced some success. She also encouraged friendships for Leah, who thought no one wanted to play with her, by driving the child to friends' homes and by making her home available to other children to come over to play.

Once the child and therapist have generated the hypothesis and designed the prospective test, the parent can facilitate the process. They can do this by providing the child with opportunities to test these hypotheses. For example, Leah believed she couldn't do anything right; she had a chance to disprove this in the music lessons.

Simply engaging in the behaviors, however, is not sufficient, or at least is not maximally efficient in producing change. Bandura (1977) argued that enactive procedures are most likely to produce the desired cognitive changes. Hollon and associates (Hollon and Beck, 1979; Hollon and Garber, 1980), however, have argued that the behavioral procedures should be accompanied by cognitive-symbolic techniques. Without this, children (as well as adults) may continue to assimilate external stimuli into their existing internal mental structures. Rather, they need to adapt their mental structures to the structures of the external stimuli. That is, concrete-operational children may have difficulty generating alternative explanations for events and may simply interpret them to be consistent with their existing beliefs. The therapist and parent can help the child to explore other explanations and to review the evidence supporting them. Giving Leah piano lessons wasn't enough. She needed to see that this meant she could develop some competencies.

In sum, children are capable of developing the negative thinking associated with depression, as well as the ability to change this thinking through cognitive strategies. Although they may have difficulty coming up with new explanations and testing them by themselves, with the assistance of parents or other significant adults they can do this; thus, cognitive strategies for altering their beliefs have a chance to work.

Specific Techniques

Self-Monitoring

The self-monitoring of mood, ongoing activities, pleasant events, and mastery experiences can provide both therapists and children with a fairly accurate description of how children spend their time and how they evaluate this. This can be done in the format of a diary or weekly self-monitoring record. Children are asked to use a notebook to record their activities. Researchers have found that children as young as four or five years old can be taught to self-monitor their behavior and can do so fairly accurately (Fixsen et al, 1972; Risley and Hart, 1968).

The accuracy of the child's report can be checked by asking parents as well as the child to complete the weekly activity record about the child. The parents' records about the child might serve as interesting data to share with the child. For example, one boy had a tendency to under-report or forget how he spent his time, particularly the more pleasant activities. Comparisons between the child's and the parents' recordings helped to highlight this tendency. This was then used as evidence to counter his idea that he "never" had any fun. This is one of the advantages of working with children; since parents can provide an important source of information not typically available with adult patients, this resource should be used when possible.

One aspect of self-monitoring that may be more difficult for children is their ability to report their mood. Young children's limited cognitive development often leads to all-or-nothing thinking and extreme responding. Children's thinking develops gradually, progressing from the global, undifferentiated, and concrete to the more differentiated and abstract.

As part of the self-monitoring procedure, clients are instructed to rate their mood on a 100-point scale. Zero (0) represents the "worst you ever felt in your whole life," and 100 represents the "best you ever felt in your whole life." While this is completely beyond the capacity of most younger children, many children can use a ten-point scale.

DiGuiseppe (1981) noted that although children's ideas about emotions are limited and tend to be dichotomous, they can be taught to identify a continuum of feelings and an accompanying vocabulary to describe them. Although young children may not be able to use the ten-point scale with much validity, the therapist can teach them a range of feelings through other means. For example, by role playing various feelings, children can experience different intensity of feelings and can perceive gradations in reactions to the same event.

Children who find it too difficult to use the ten-point scale for reporting mood can use alternative procedures. These children may be better able to respond to pictures of faces as in the Children's Event Schedule (Garber, 1982a), or simple word descriptors such as "happy," "sad," "just okay," "mad," and "scared." Using word descriptors such as these, Barden et al (1980) found that children as young as kindergartners could describe, with some consensus, the expected emotional reaction to hypothetical events described to them. This study suggests that children are capable of accurately describing and differentiating among various emotions. The degree of differentiation tends to increase with age, and thus, the degree to which children will be able to describe their mood will increase with age.

Behavioral Techniques

Behavioral techniques in cognitive therapy involve the systematic alteration of the patients' ongoing behavior. As mentioned earlier, behavior procedures designed to test hypotheses about beliefs should be used in conjunction with cognitive techniques that help them reinterpret events, and ultimately to alter their cognitions. The process of making predictions and then evaluating them on the basis of new information generated by their own behavior is the core of cognitive therapy for depression. The important behavioral techniques which may be used with depressed children include activity scheduling, contingent reinforcement, pleasurable events scheduling, and graded task assignment.

Activity Scheduling

Activity scheduling involves systematically and specifically planning the patient's day. The process of planning hourly and daily activities for children to engage in helps them to reduce passivity and the time spent ruminating. Parents can become activitly involved in this procedure. Parents known their own and their children's daily routines better than anybody, and therefore they can help schedule hourly and daily activities with the children. Even more importantly, parents can increase the probability that the children will actually carry out the activities by involving themselves as part of the plan.

One important note about the process of activity scheduling is that the child should be an active participant in the planning. Depressed children should be given choices and a sense of control over their lives; for some children a sense of lack of control may serve to exacerbate their depression (Seligman, 1975). Depressed children need to be gently, consistently, and persistently coaxed to participate in the scheduled activities. They should, however, ultimately realize that how they feel and what they want makes a difference.

Contingent Reinforcement

One of the most common and useful ways of modifying behavior, particularly children's behavior, is the careful application of reinforcement procedures (Graziano, 1971; Marholm, 1978). Such techniques as manipulation of social contingencies, punishment, positive reinforcement, systematic desensitizations, and modeling procedures have been used to modify children's behavior with considerable success (Petti, 1981).

Behavioral theories of depression (Ferster, 1973, 1974; Lewinsohn, 1973, 1974) have speculated that depression may be produced and maintained by low rates of response-contingent positive reinforcement. This may be particularly true for latency-age children whose moods seem to be more closely tied to the concrete reality of the here and now. Thus, increasing the amount of positive reinforcement may alter the depressed child's mood.

A problem with using contingent reinforcement to alter depressed children's mood and behavior is that children often have difficulty identifying what is rewarding them. One of the classic symptoms of depression is loss of interest or pleasure in usual activities and an apparent lack of responsiveness to rewards. What used to be pleasurable to depressed children or what is typically rewarding to most children of their age, such as candy, toys, or game, may no longer be appealing to depressed children.

Potential rewards can be identified in several ways. Asking children what used to be fun, or what would be fun if they didn't feel so sad, may be useful. Carefully observing how depressed children spend their time, or reviewing the weekly self-monitoring record, may help to identify activities that still seem enjoyable to them, or that at least are engaged in with some frequency. Premack (1965) suggests that high frequency behavior may be used successfully to reinforce lower frequency behavior. Thus, the therapist can use the child's own behaviors to reinforce other behavior.

Once the desirable reinforcers have been identified, the therapist and parents can reward the child for engaging in the prescribed behaviors such as self-monitoring or recording thoughts. Moreover, the reinforcement itself may produce at least temporary elevations in the child's mood; during this period the child can be encouraged to meet with friends or complete neglected school assignments.

Scheduling Pleasurable Activities

Depressed children may refuse to engage in activities because they don't expect to have fun. The therapist can encourage them to do the activity anyway as an experiment to see what will happen. The therapist can say that the children don't have to enjoy it; they only have to try it. Children should record their expectations before engaging in the activity, as well as their subsequent reactions to it. Often depressed children will end up enjoying an activity once they become involved in it, despite initial expectations to the contrary. Through this process, they may learn that despite their original negative expectations they can still have fun. Even if they say they don't enjoy it, they can be reinforced for trying and use the event as a means to see what they were thinking while doing the activity.

An instrument known as the Pleasant Events Schedule was constructed by Lewinsohn and his colleagues (Lewinsohn and Graf, 1973) in order to define a set of potentially pleasurable events. Garber (1982a) has developed a similar measure for children called the Children's Event Schedule which contains 75 pleasant and 75 unpleasant events to be rated for frequency and pleasure. This instrument may be helpful in identifying pleasurable activities as well as high frequency behaviors, and can be used when scheduling pleasurable activities.

Graded Task Assignments

Graded task assignments, breaking tasks into smaller steps, reduce the difficulty of a task for patients; they also provide more frequent success experiences throughout the process of completing the task. Children's beliefs about their own competence should be monitored throughout the process of task completion. Here again, children's initial negative expectations, in this case about their inability to complete the task, can be dismantled by their own behaviors. Each step can be set up as an experiment to try.

The use of graded task assignments is a particularly good strategy for dealing with school work. Depressed children often show decreased school performance (Weinberg et al, 1973) that may be a result of feeling overwhelmed or of their perceived lack of competence in completing large assignments. With the collaboration of the teacher, the therapist can assign smaller, more manageable tasks to the depressed children until they are capable of taking on larger amounts of work. Reducing the workload allows depressed children to complete some of their work, while at the same time acquiring a sense of accomplishment. Ultimately, this procedure often will produce a snowballing effect: the more the children believe that they are accomplishing, the more they will actually get done, and so on.

Cognitive Techniques

To conduct cognitive therapy with depressed children, the therapist has to teach them how to identify and modify their cognitions. The first step in identifying their thoughts involves a cognitive analysis. What are the children thinking when they perform a target behavior or when there is a significant shift in mood? What ideas or pictures run through their minds when they run into difficulty?

Central to this process is children's ability to recognize and report their thoughts. The typical technique for collecting an individual's thoughts and inferences has been self-report. However, the use of self-report methodologies with children has been under-used and under-rated as a viable assessment technique, and thus, few good strategies for assessing children's thoughts exist.

Historically, projective techniques, behavioral observation, and parent report have been used as the primary methods of assessing and understanding children. Children's subjective reports generally have been considered to be unreliable, inaccurate, and wishful thinking. However, according to Quay and Werry (1979), in areas such as "child abuse, childhood depression, and pediatric psychopharmacology, self-rating would appear to be not only desirable but necessary."

Recently, other researchers in childhood depression have emphasized the importance of obtaining children's thoughts and feelings directly through interviews and self-report inventories (Cytryn et al, 1980; Garber, 1981). Several strategies for assessing cognitions and self-statements relevant to cognitive interventions with children have been reviewed recently (Kendall and Hollon, 1981; Kendall et al, 1981). Methods relevant to the cognitive treatment of depressed children will be discussed below.

Assessment of Children's Cognitions

Several strategies can be used to obtain children's thoughts and ideas both in the clinic and at home between sessions. Children can be instructed to think aloud either directly to the therapist or into a tape recorder while working on a task or playing a game. This method of assessing self-statements requires that children verbalize their thoughts continuously while engaged in some behavior.

A similar think-aloud procedure can be used while the child imagines certain situations. Children may describe something that happened during the week that bothered them, but for some reason they neglected to record their thoughts at the time. Children can try to imagine themselves back in the disturbing situation and describe aloud their thoughts while imagining it.

An interesting variation of the think-aloud procedure is to videotape children while they are talking to others or playing a game. The videotape is then replayed to children and they say what they were thinking or feeling during the behavior. The advantage is that children aren't artificially forced to verbalize continuously while performing a task. Children usually enjoy seeing themselves on videotape, so they are often more willing to cooperate. One disadvantage of this procedure, as well as the imagining procedure, is that the children are reporting their thoughts after the fact, so they are apt to forget or to distort how they were actually thinking at the time.

Children should be encouraged to record their thoughts between sessions. Specific times can be set aside each day to record thoughts, or records can be kept in a more or less continuous fashion. When the child experiences a significant shift in mood, the accompanying cognitions should be recorded immediately. Children can write their thoughts into a daily diary or on structured response columns known as the Dysfunctional Thought Record (Beck et al, 1979), or they can record their thoughts into a tape recorder.

Parents can be actively involved in this component of therapy. Parents can remind children to record their thoughts at certain times and help them to elicit their thoughts. Parents can pay attention to the child's mood shifts and ask what the child is thinking; such on-the-spot prompting by parents can be extremely valuable to therapy.

Finally, children's cognitions can be discovered through the use of more structured self-report inventories. Although there aren't an abundance of children's self-report inventories, a few do exist that can be used to assess cognitions relevant to depression. Measures of self-concept (Coopersmith, 1967; Piers, 1969), attributions (Kaslow et al, 1979), anxiety (Casteneda et al, 1956; Reynolds and Richmond, 1978), and depression (Kovacs and Beck, 1977) can be used to identify specific cognitions or more generalized underlying assumptions. Once the beliefs and thoughts are identified, the therapist and children can examine and develop strategies for changing them.

Cognitive Change Strategies

Social psychologists (Fishbein and Ajzen, 1975; Oskamp, 1977) have suggested that beliefs and attitudes can be changed by persuasive communication, instruction, direct experience, and logical inference. Cognitive therapy with children uses all of these techniques; the child's level of cognitive functioning dictates which is the most appropriate and effective.

Children below age seven who are still in Piaget's preoperational stage of cognitive development may respond best to the simple instruction to replace certain thoughts with other thoughts. In a method known as self-affirmation, the child is instructed to repeat certain prescribed statements several times daily. Such affirmations as "I like myself," "I can do it if I try," or "I know mommy loves me" if stated repeatedly can enhance the child's positive feelings; they can be even more helpful if a parallel set of statements are reaffirmed by a parent or other significant adult.

Similarly, coping self-statements can be used to help children respond more adaptively in certain situations. Cognitive-behavioral therapy with impulsive children, in particular (Kendall and Finch, 1978; Meichenbaum and Genest, 1980), emphasizes the use of directive self-statements. The applicability of the self-talk method to the treatment of depressed children remains to be investigated. The self-reward component of this procedure, where children tell themselves, "Good job, I did that well," or "I tried my best," may be especially relevant to depression.

A difficulty with both the self-affirmation method and the coping self-statements is that their effectiveness may be short-lived and situation-specific. For this reason, these procedures, if possible, need to be accompanied by more generalized cognitive change strategies.

The core of cognitive therapy involves examining the validity of the patient's beliefs. In order to challenge their beliefs, patients need to distance themselves from them and to learn that believing something doesn't necessarily make it so. This can be difficult for younger children; they often maintain a form of magical thinking: they assume their beliefs represent reality and can actually influence what happens. For example, a young girl may secretly wish that her teacher would go away and never come back. If the next day the teacher is killed in a car accident, the child may actually believe that her thoughts or wishes caused this to happen.

Young children also have difficulty disentangling other people's remarks from fact. Children who are repeatedly told that they are "a loser" by other children or by family members tend to believe the others' opinions as if they were a fact. Children can be taught that regardless of the strength of the other persons' convictions, their saying it or believing it does not serve as evidence of the accuracy of the statement (DiGiuseppe, 1981).

The therapist's job is to teach children strategies for subjecting their beliefs to critical scrutiny. Once children have learned to identify their thoughts and record them, they should learn the three methods of challenging these beliefs: (1) looking at the evidence, (2) exploring alternative explanations, and (3) examining the consequences, if what they believe turns out to be true.

The first question the child should be taught to ask is "What is the evidence that this belief is true?" The primary strategy for answering this question involves "empirical analysis" (Ellis, 1977) or "hypothesis testing." Despite Ellis' labeling this approach the inelegant solution, as compared to the more elegant philosophical disrupting, it may be a more appropriate strategy for dealing with children's beliefs. Children learn more from action than from words, more from concrete experience than from sophisticated arguments (Bemporad, 1978). Therefore, designing an experiment with children that they can actually complete may be the best strategy for changing their beliefs.

The technique of hypothesis testing was discussed briefly in an early section. To reiterate, (1) latency age children's level of cognitive development usually allows them to understand the process of hypothesis-testing and gives them the ability to help in the design and implementation of the appropriate experiments, and (2) the assistance of parents or other significant adults in carrying out the experiments is recommended.

The second question the child should be taught to ask is, "What is another way of looking at this or explaining this?" Of all the cognitive strategies, the process of generating alternative attributions is probably the most feasible and potentially the most effective for changing children's beliefs. Researchers have found that depressed children have a greater tendency to attribute negative events to external factors and positive events to external factors than do nondepressed children (Kaslow et al, 1979; Leon et al, 1980).

Moreover, researchers have discovered that children can successfully participate in an attribution retraining procedure; this retraining results in more positive attributions and improved performance. Dweck (1975) trained children, identified to be "helpless," to take responsibility for failure and to attribute this to lack of effort, rather than lack of ability. As a result of such reattribution training, the children demonstrated unimpaired performance after failure, as compared to "helpless" children who had received success experiences only. A similar kind of reattribution training procedure can be used with depressed children; this the therapist can use to encourage children to explore alternative explanations for events.

A second set of procedures that can be used to teach children to examine others' ways of looking at things involves Interpersonal Cognitive Problem Solving skills (ICPS) (Spivack and Shure, 1975). Spivack and Shure (1975) emphasize that such interpersonal problem solving skills as alternative-solution thinking, means-ends thinking, consequential thinking, and causal thinking are important mediators of children's social, emotional, and behavioral adjustment. Spivack and his colleagues developed several instruments to assess these interpersonal problem-solving skills and to evaluate the success of the many recently developed problem-solving skill training programs for children.

The Children's Means-Ends Problem-Solving test (MEPS) (Shure and Spivack, 1972) can be used with depressed children; the therapist can use this to see if the children have any deficits in interpersonal problem-solving skills and to identify the nature of these deficits. If such deficits exist among depressed children, then the Children's MEPS can be useful as a teaching instrument in social skills training programs. This training should be included as one of the procedures to be used in the overall cognitive therapy with depressed children.

Finally, the third question depressed children should be taught to consider is, "Even if what I think turns out to be true, how bad is it?" Ellis (1977) emphasized the idea of decatastrophizing, whereby no outcome is ever really awful; it is only uncomfortable or inconvenient. There are times when children have to deal with aversive events over which they have no actual control, such as parents' divorce, or moving to a new city. In such cases, there is a realistic disruption in their lives with which they must learn to cope. The problem-solving or hypothesis testing strategies can't alter the event. These strategies can only influence their reactions to it. Since not all children who experience realistic negative events become depressed, there may be some form of cognitive distortion occurring in those who do.

Grief Reaction

When children experience an uncontrollable aversive event, therapists should tell parents it is important that children be provided with accurate information about it. Children who lose a parent through death or divorce should be told the truth about the finality and often the irreversibility of the event. If they aren't given this information, they will be unable to develop a viable coping strategy. Some parents feel it's better to alter or omit information from the children in order to protect them from any pain. However, the absence of information or the deliberate misrepresentation of the facts may ultimately produce more emotional harm than if the truth had been dealt with directly at the time.

Once children are provided with the truth, their feelings and thoughts about what they believe will be the consequence of the event should be carefully explored. The children may dwell on the worst possible outcome of the negative event and thus may not consider less severe consequences.

The parents' reactions to the shared family crisis also may have an important influence on the child. If parents themselves become depressed about the divorce or other significant life change, then the children may be affected; this may be by directly modeling the parents' maladaptive coping attempts, or by experiencing the ramifications of the parents' distress. In this situation, teaching the parent cognitive coping strategies for dealing with an uncontrollable event not only helps the child to cope, but also may help the parent to deal with the reality as well.

One interesting aspect of children's more limited cognitive ability is that this may actually protect them from engaging in extensive catastrophizing. Since young children are tied so closely to the here and now, they are often unable to anticipate all of the bad things that could occur as a result of the negative event. The death of a loved one is an example of a circumstance in which children's limited cognitive capacity to anticipate future consequences may play a role in their reaction. For some reason, children often do not show an adult-like grief reaction. Their mourning is often short-lived or delayed (Miller, 1971; Robertson, 1956).

Early psychoanalytic writers (Deutsch, 1937; Freud, 1960; Wolfenstein, 1966) believed that young children didn't show a true grief reaction and they didn't believe mourning is possible until the resolution of adolescence. They observed that children responded to death with an overt or covert denial of the irreversibility of the loss. Piaget (Inhelder and Piaget, 1955) also has suggested that children don't really comprehend the finality of death until adolescence.

Furman (1973), however, argues that the absence of an externally visible grief reaction isn't necessarily evidence of children's lack of an intrapsychic ability to mourn. Rather, as Schowalter (1975) suggests, the phenomenon of mourning is an evolving psychic function for which the developing child has a varying capacity; what one observes are the defenses against the pain of mourning.

What may be developing is children's capacity to anticipate future consequences of a here and now event. In the case of a death, children may not fully understand the finality and irreversibility of the loss. However, once they begin to experience the negative effects of the loss, they then may manifest what looks like a delayed grief reaction. Thus, the negative view of the future associated with depression may be one component of the negative cognitive triad that children are spared until adolescence. Despite that children's limited cognitive capacity to anticipate negative consequences may initially protect them, once they experience the actual impact of the event, they may then develop an equally maladaptive reaction.

Children are often forced to deal on a more immediate basis with realistic negative events and they may react to these circumstances by "catastrophizing." For example, children with physical or intellectual handicaps must learn to sort out their realistic limitations from their distortions. Mark, an 11-year-old boy with a perceptual-motor learning disability, found that he was unable to keep up with the other children in his class. He developed a generalized low self-concept; he believed that he was incapable of doing anything right so he should not bother trying. He began to get into more and more trouble at school and was visibly unhappy about his perceived generalized incompetence.

The therapist explored with Mark his thoughts about his learning disability and discovered that he thought that this meant he would never be able to do anything worthwhile. The therapist helped Mark to accept the realistic limitation of his problem and also helped him to examine more carefully whether this meant that there was nothing he could do well. After giving it some thought, Mark was able to list skills that he was capable of doing, and doing fairly well, such as art and running. By carefully examining and challenging his beliefs about the consequences of his problem, Mark was eventually able to conclude that his situation wasn't as bad as he had originally thought.

The final line of cognitive questioning that asks "so what?" is especially important for children with low self-esteem. Children that perceive themselves to have a problem with respect to one aspect of their life (for example, they are too tall, short, fat, or learning-disabled) often generalize the ramifications of their deficit. The strategy of challenging their assumptions about the meaning of the problem helps them to keep them within realistic proportions.

In sum, cognitive strategies for treating depression in children first involve the careful acquisition and description of the child's thoughts. Once the children's beliefs and attitudes have been identified, they can be challenged by searching for evidence, looking for alternative explanations, and considering the consequences. Although these techniques basically are the same as those used with adult depressives, their implementation and efficacy vary depending upon the child's age and level of cognitive functioning.

DEPRESSED ADOLESCENTS

Role of Family

Clinical impressions indicate that few adolescents are referred for treatment *specifically* for complaints of depression, for example, low self-esteem, poor morale, sleeplessness, and so on (an exception to this observation would involve the teenager who enters treatment following a suicide attempt or a report of suicidal ideation). Most adolescents find their way to treatment as a result of poor school performance, substance abuse, precocious sexual behavior, or defiance towards authority figures. Adolescents and their families often simply fail to recognize depression and the real problem underlying the presenting complaints.

Parents may describe the troubled adolescent as rebellious, lazy, hostile, manipulative, or immoral, and thereby attribute the presenting complaints to their child's inherent character defects. On the other hand, adolescents will often externalize blame for their difficulties onto parents, school, or siblings. Parents and their teenage children may then become locked into a series of mutually destructive power struggles, while the real issues such as the young person's self-esteem, remain unaffected.

The therapist often needs to work at the outset to change the family's attributions regarding the presenting complaints; this can be done by relabeling the adolescent's problem as a depressive episode. For example, a divorced mother sought treatment for her 12-year-old son, Larry. He was doing poorly in school and had joined in recent neighborhood episodes of truancy, vandalism, and drinking. His mother responded to the unacceptable behaviors with powerful bursts of rage, and prolonged arguments resulted. When she became angry with her son she would think, "He's just like his father," and become even more enraged as she remembered her sociopathic, abusive ex-husband.

Larry meanwhile alternated between angry defiance towards his mother and highly immature, dependent behaviors (such as jumping onto his mother's lap and embracing her during a family session). Both the therapist and the school personnel agreed that the boy concealed his essential fearfulness and inadequacy with a veneer of rebelliousness. He seemed desperate for attention and affection, particularly from adult males.

The therapist worked to sensitize the mother to the numerous manifestations of her son's poor self-image. He emphasized the connection between her son's low self-esteem and his vulnerability to negative peer influences. She began to recognize that the boy's acting out behavior reflected his desire for recognition and peer status, not his inherently antisocial nature. The therapist also encouraged the mother to enumerate the differences between her ex-husband and her son, so that she could begin to resist the tendency to scapegoat the boy. Gradually, she began to react to his provocative behavior in a calmer, less hysterical fashion, and therapy avoided a number of destructive confrontations. From a more detached position, she was able to see more clearly the effects of his strong sense of inadequacy (as opposed to his "bad genes") upon his behavior. As she changed, she was surprised to see his behavior change also.

Concurrently, the therapist also worked on an individual basis with the son. For the most part, he ignored the boy's expressions of distrust and hostility early in their relationship. The therapist played games and lifted weights with the boy all the while discussing his relationships with his peers and his parents. For over a year, Larry had nurtured the belief, at times encouraged by remarks from both parents, that he would be able to move in with his father, who lived several states away, if his mother would only allow him to make the transition. He would say, "I'm miserable because my mother won't let me go to live with my father."

The therapist enabled the boy to reconsider more carefully who was truly responsible for his living arrangements. He began to acknowledge that the reason he had not moved in with his father was that both parents had agreed it was preferable for him to remain with his mother. Moreover, he recognized that he often raised the issue of custody in order to make his mother angry. As he became more comfortable with the therapist, Larry was able to discuss issues in his life which did not directly involve his mother, such as his poor school performance and his unsatisfying friendships.

As the preceding vignette illustrates, a therapist can work to modify cognitions even when the presenting complaint seems "unworkable" in cognitive terms. A note of caution: families with conflictual relationships of great duration and intensity may not be able to tolerate the kinds of interventions described in the preceding case example.

Guidelines

Regardless of the therapeutic techniques they employ, all therapists who work with adolescents must learn to tolerate dramatic departures from adult treatment norms. Cognitive therapy works best as a problem-focused treatment;

however adolescents will sometimes subvert the process by remaining silent for long periods, by refusing to discuss significant topics, or by skipping from one seemingly unrelated issue to another.

Consequently, the pace of therapy is slower and the scope of the therapist's knowledge is narrower than with the adult patient. Moreover, the therapist more easily alienates the teenager with too many probing questions, too many homework assignments, and so on. Adult norms for self-disclosure and prolonged self-exploration aren't appropriate for adolescents. Developing one or two major treatment themes per session is a suitable goal for the therapist who works with teenage patients.

It may be useful to reiterate a few earlier recommendations (Bedrosian, 1980; 1981a) for the application of cognitive therapy techniques for adolescents: (1) utilize briefer sessions than the traditional 50-minute hour; (2) spend as much time as possible reducing threat and building rapport with the teenager; (3) tolerate a modicum of noncompliance with treatment norms, for example, lateness for sessions, refusal to talk, and so on; (4) maintain ongoing family contact, so that systematic interventions can occur whenever needed; (5) respect the adolescent's sense of privacy and remember that not all sensitive topics require attention during one course of treatment; (6) maintain a collaborative atmosphere by attempting to reach an agreement with the teenager regarding the goals of therapy; (7) avoid assigning complex homework assignments to adolescents who are already experiencing school and/or learning difficulties: stick to more concrete, behavioral tasks between sessions.

Many teenagers find it difficult to tolerate face-to-face encounters with a therapist. As discussed elsewhere (Bedrosian, 1981b), the therapist may include activities such as backgammon and checkers as a part of the interview, in order to help the adolescent warm up to a discussion of sensitive topics. Games also provide other types of useful data regarding the young person's attitudes toward competition, his or her ability to sustain concentration, and so on.

Even when the therapist has established good rapport and a benign therapeutic atmosphere, the adolescent patient may still offer little therapeutic material. In such situations, the therapist may wish to offer the adolescent alternatives ways of expressing his or her concerns. Instead of speaking directly to a therapist, adolescents can keep diaries, write letters, or make phone calls to the therapist, talk to tape recorders, pick out poems or popular songs which reflect their experiences, and so on. Some teenagers who initially appear ill-suited to individual therapy will flourish in treatment, if they are allowed to choose the method by which they communicate to the therapist.

Family Therapy

The patient's negative view of the self is a major focus in the cognitive model of depression. Depressed adolescents often see themselves as stupid, ugly, defective, and so on. Unfortunately, many teenagers find ample confirmation of their negative self-images in the critical reactions of family members and peers. Consequently, the therapist may often need to reduce the tangible pressures on the adolescent by blocking scapegoating in the family or by restructuring parental expectations. Without such interventions, the significant others may inadvertently reinforce the adolescent's dysfunctional cognitions. The following case example illustrates how cognitive and family interventions can be interwoven. Readers interested in further description of such interventions may wish to consult recent work by Shaw (1981) and Bedrosian (1981a).

Following a suicide attempt (a low lethality overdose of a minor tranquilizer) which resulted in a brief psychiatric hospitalization, the parents of a 16-year-old female sought outpatient treatment for their daughter. The couple had been childless for a number of years before adopting the girl, Patty, at age nine. Abandoned by her mother as a toddler, Patty had shuttled between a series of cheerless, sometimes physically and sexually abusive foster homes, before she came into contact with her adoptive parents. The parents, particularly the mother who held a psychology degree, clearly had made a "project" out of Patty. Interestingly, a year or so after they adopted the girl, they finally conceived a child of their own.

In an intrusive, frequently critical manner, her mother tried to help Patty resolve her numerous social, scholastic, and personal difficulties. If Patty wanted to lose weight, her mother would purchase and prepare all the low calorie foods; she would then become angry when Patty abandoned her diet. Patty's reaction would be to think, "There I go again, screwing up and letting everyone down," or "Mom doesn't understand me, nobody understands me."

The mother's overinvolvement reinforced Patty's sense of helplessness and worthlessness and also inhibited her psychosocial maturation. The therapist alternated between individual sessions with Patty and meetings with various family configurations. In the sessions with the parents, he worked to disengage mother and daughter, while promoting a stronger working alliance between mother and father. The mother was able to recognize that her overconcern for Patty generally made her tense and irritable, produced more friction in the family and seldom led to improvements in her daughter's functioning. The father, who had encouraged his wife to take less responsibility for Patty for some time, was asked to alert her when her demands on their daughter seemed too harsh.

Since the suicide attempt, the parents had reluctantly curtailed their own social activities outside the home. Unfortunately their decision left mother with more opportunities to become irritated with her daughter. With the therapist's encouragement, the couple began to resume a normal social life and even spent a long weekend together at a nearby resort. In the meantime, friction between mother and daughter decreased substantially.

With the overt conflict in the home at a more manageable level, the therapist was able to focus more intensively upon Patty's psychological problems. She consistently verbalized dysfunctional cognitions such as, "I'm fat and ugly," "No one will ever find me attractive," and "I'll always be different from other people." As a result of her long history of abuse and deprivation, Patty suffered from minimal self-esteem, a low frustration tolerance, and a desperate need for approval.

The therapist knew that the girl would require long-term treatment, regardless of the modality employed. He began the complex task of chipping away at her dysfunctional beliefs about herself. In her case, even as the depressive affect disappeared, substantial psychological and social deficits persisted.

Boredom and Apathy

Parents often fail to recognize depression in the teenager who withdraws into an apathetic, possibly sullen state. Depressed adolescents may complain of boredom with school, friends, family, and extracurricular activities in a whining, "entitled" manner which antagonizes adults. Nonetheless, their complaints may reflect anhedonia, hopelessness, isolation from mastery and pleasure activities, poor concentration, low frustration tolerance, and a profound sense of alienation.

A major component in the cognitive therapy of depression involves stimulating the patient's participation in mastery and pleasure activities (Beck et al, 1979). The therapist should take care to tailor any behavioral assignments as closely as possible to the adolescent's interests and areas of competency. Otherwise, the therapist may recede into the background as one more adult who makes unreasonable demands upon the depressed teenager.

Identity and Self-Esteem

A key feature of adolescent depression is a negative view of the self. Adolescents tend to lack the personal and environmental resources to cope adequately with severe reductions in self-esteem. Preserving a positive self-image in the face of dramatic physical changes and rapid shifting role expectations represents a formidable task even for the well-adjusted teenager. Depressed adolescents find themselves acutely sensitive to their perceived deficiencies, and tend to magnify the significance of any teasing or criticism they receive from their peers or significant others. Moreover, the adolescent subculture can be nonsupportive at its best, frankly hostile at its worst.

The cognitions of depressed teenagers often reveal rigid, all-or-nothing beliefs, for example, "People only respect the jocks," or "Guys will never be attracted to overweight girls." Such rigid beliefs are reinforced by adolescent peer groups which overemphasize conformity and punish deviations from group norms. One teenager stated, "At our school there are the 'stats' (high status), the 'jocks,' and the 'druggies.' If you're not in one of those groups, you can just forget about a social life." She then went on to discuss in some detail the typical dress and behavior associated with each group.

To some degree, her assessment of the oppressive regimentation of her school peers was correct. The therapist's task involved helping the young woman identify the "shades of grey" in her social environment. What about the young people who didn't associate with one of the three groups? Were they all bored and lonely? What other activities were available to her which did not involve the same old kids and the same old rules?

Depressed adolescents often assume that other individuals, especially peers, don't have to struggle with similar troublesome thoughts and feelings. Consequently, they persist in viewing themselves as different from (and therefore inferior to) others, and isolate themselves further as a result. Group therapy, which offers a number of additional advantages, allows teenagers to discover that other young people are also trying to cope with similar difficulties. Other methods for normalizing the adolescent's view of his or her experiences involve the use of bibliotherapy and self-disclosure by parents or other significant adults. Teenagers are often surprised to hear that their parents, whom they may view as hyper-adequate, also struggled with sensations of despair and inferiority at one time or another.

Helplessness

Helplessness is often a major theme in the cognitions of depressed adolescents. Although adolescents may exert a tremendous influence upon their families, particularly through the use of various acting out behaviors, they may also view themselves as totally powerless at any other time. Some depressed teenagers do find themselves in the midst of disturbed family situations which are nearly impervious to external influence. In such situations, unless modifications can occur in the family system, the therapist can only aid the young patient in learning to tolerate a bad situation until he or she can leave home.

A 16-year-old female with no previous psychiatric history experienced a psychotic depressive episode which required a two-month hospitalization. The young woman was an excellent student, attractive, popular, and a skilled athlete. The father was in his late sixties, while the mother was over 20 years his junior. The parents had long since settled into an angry isolation from one another. The house was disorganized and in poor repair. Father showered unreasonable demands upon the children; the mother quietly sabotaged his every move. Meanwhile, she would drink herself into a stupor each evening on the living room couch, in full view of everyone.

Within a month after her discharge from the hospital, the teenager once again had immersed herself in her normal activites. More importantly, the chronic parental friction was now in the open, available for comment by everyone in the family, and by the therapist. Mother had stopped her drinking entirely, and now openly threatened her husband with separation. He meanwhile began to modulate his harsh uncompromising stance as a parent, since it was clear from the family sessions that unless he offered more support to his children, he would continue to be alienated from the rest of the household.

The marital tension didn't disappear, but the daughter now knew that she could bring any family issues into the conjoint treatment sessions, instead of quietly slipping into another depressive episode. Moreover, two of her siblings now also verbalized concerns about the parents' relationship. Clearly, ongoing family treatment provided the identified patient with a means of avoiding being overwhelmed by the chronic conflicts between her parents.

Since depressed teenagers are prone to fail in school, engage in acting out behavior, or break family rules, they may end up being labeled as stubborn, lazy, or defiant by their parents. Parents often submit the identified patient to excessively harsh restrictions as a consequence. Instead of providing motivation for improved performance, the restrictions may drive the teenager deeper into a sense of hopelessness and helplessness. Runaway episodes and suicidal behaviors are potential risks in such situations. The therapist can help by insuring that parents don't cut off the teenager totally from sources of reinforcement outside the home, and that the adolescent has a mechanism for earning back privileges on an incremental basis.

Rejection and Loss

A pattern of multiple losses and rejections tends to "prime" an adolescent for a depression episode. The deaths of significant others or friends, loss of dating partners, and parental separation or divorce all may leave the teenager progressively more vulnerable to depressogenic thinking. Teenagers not only lack the psychological tools used by adults to cope with losses, they also find it hard to ask for and receive support from others.

Lilly, a 13-year-old, attempted suicide by ingesting 30 to 40 aspirin tablets shortly after her closest friend moved to a neighboring state. An interview with the family revealed that when Lilly was eight years old, a teenage brother had died during an apparent episode of "Russian Roulette." Two years later, her father left the family and moved several hundred miles away. She rarely spoke with her father and had seen him but a few times over a period of several years. Both Lilly and her mother became tearful at the merest mention of either the father or the deceased brother. The situation in the home was chaotic, as illustrated by the fact that Lilly's 19-year-old brother lived there with his

15-year-old girlfriend. The brother and his girlfriend openly flaunted their drinking and marijuana smoking in front of the mother.

Since she had grown nearly a head taller than most of her peers, Lilly was frequently an object of ridicule in school, despite her sweet disposition and her pretty, expressive face. Although she had above average abilities in many areas, she showed little interest in most activities except for the approval of others. The friend who had moved away had served as Lilly's confidant and primary source of support. Understandably, Lilly viewed the loss as a catastrophe.

The therapist allowed Lilly and her mother to mourn and resolve their various losses. He consistently implied that Lilly's recovery was tied to the mother's resolution of similar grief issues. He also included an older sister who lived in a nearby town in the sessions. She related warmly to Lilly and demanded a more assertive stance on the part of the mother.

The therapist stressed to all parties the apparent irreversibility of the parents' separation, as he explored with mother why she had not yet filed for divorce, dated other men, or made a number of family financial decisions. Slowly she began to assume a less passive posture. The mother eventually found a male friend, kicked her troublesome son out of the house, and filed for divorce. Lilly's sister coaxed the girl into a more active social life. She began to participate in the school orchestra, while boys suddenly seemed to find her interesting. After five months of intermittent contact, the family was discharged from treatment.

A year after termination, Lilly's guidance counselor called the therapist to request an immediate appointment for the girl, whom she described as suicidal. When the therapist saw her later that day, Lilly readily discussed the precipitant of her suicidal wishes—rejection at the hands of a boyfriend. She explained, "He was the only guy who liked me. I'll never find anyone else. Nobody could ever love me," and so on.

The therapist asked her to pretend that he was a friend of hers who needed her help because he had just lost his girlfriend. One by one, he verbalized the dysfunctional cognitions she had revealed to him. Lilly performed her role quite well, as she offered rational responses such as, "Just because she left you, that doesn't mean there's something wrong with you," and "You'll find someone else. You found her, didn't you?" The therapist was not easily convinced however, so he maintained his lament for several minutes. Midway through the exercise, Lilly burst into a smile.

By the end of the session, Lilly achieved a dramatic affective shift, probably because she had acquired a more realistic perspective on the current loss. The therapist saw Lilly and her mother for three sessions thereafter to focus on some current issues regarding the impact of mother's boyfriend upon the household. Although he discharged the family from treatment within two months, he was confident that Lilly would request his services if she again became depressed in the future.

In summary, many of the typical cognitive therapy techniques developed for adults can be applied effectively with depressed adolescents. Because adolescents have a variety of special problems, there are unique difficulties associated with their treatment. The methods of cognitive therapy have to be modified to deal with these problems.

REFERENCES

Bandura A. Self-efficacy: toward a unifying theory of behavioral change. *Psychol Rev* 1977;84:191-215.

Barden RC, Zelko FA, Duncan SW, Masters JC. Children's consensual knowledge about the experiential determinants of emotion. *J Pers Social Psychol* 1980;39:968-976.

Beck AT. *Cognitive therapy and the emotional disorders*. New York: International Universities Press, 1976.

Beck AT, Rush AJ, Shaw B, Emery G. *Cognitive therapy of depression*. New York: Guilford Press, 1979.

Bedrosian RC. The adolescent in cognitive therapy. Presented at the Annual Convention of the American Psychological Association. Montreal, Canada, 1980.

Bedrosian RC. Ecological factions in cognitive therapy: the use of significant others. In: Emery G, Hollon S, Bedrosian R, eds. *New directions in cognitive therapy*. New York: Guilford Press, 1981a.

Bedrosian RC. The application of cognitive therapy techniques to adolescents. In Emery G, Hollon S, Bedrosian R, eds. *New directions in cognitive therapy*. New York: Guilford Press, 1981b.

Bemporad J. Psychotherapy of depression in children and adolescents. In: Arieti S, Bemporad J, eds. *Severe and mild depression*. New York: Basic Books, 1978.

Blaney TH. Contemporary theories of depression: critique and comparison. *J Abnorm Psychol* 1977;86:203-223.

Casteneda A, McCandless B, Palermo D. The children's form of the manifest anxiety scale. *Child Dev* 1956;27:317-326.

Coopersmith S. *The antecedents of self-esteem*. San Francisco: W.H. Freeman & Co, 1967.

Cytryn L, McKnew DH, Bunney WE. Diagnosis of depression in children: a reassessment. *Am J Psychiatry* 1980;137:22-25.

Deutsch H. Absence of grief. *Psychoanal Q* 1937;6:12-22.

DiGiuseppe RA. Cognitive therapy with children. In: Emery G, Hollon S, Bedrosian R, eds. *New directions in cognitive therapy*. New York: The Guilford Press, 1981.

Dweck CS. The role of expectations and attributions in the alleviation of learned helplessness. *J Personal Soc Psychol* 1975;31:674-685.

Ellis A. Rejoiner: elegant and inelegant RET. *Counsel Psychol* 1977;7:73-82.

Ellis A. *Growth through reason: verbatim cases in rational-emotive psychotherapy*. Palo Alto: Science & Behavior Books, 1971.
Ferster CB. A functional analysis of depression. *Am Psychol* 1973; 28:857-870.
Ferster CB. Behavioral approaches to depression. In: Friedman, Katz, eds. *The psychology of depression: contemporary theory and research*. Washington, DC: Winston/Wiley, 1974.
Fishbein M, Ajzen I. *Belief, attitude, intention, and behavior*. Massachusetts: Addison-Wesley, 1975.
Fixsen DL, Phillips EL, Wolf MM. Achievement place: the reliability of self-reporting and peer-reporting and their effects on behavior. *J Appl Behav Anal* 1972; 5:19-30.
Flavell JH. *Cognitive development*. New Jersey: Prentice-Hall, 1977.
Freud A. Discussion of Dr. John Bowlby's paper. *The psychoanalytic study of the child*. New York: International Universities Press, 1960; 15:53.
Furman R. A child's capacity for mourning. In: Anthony EJ, Koupernik C, eds. *The child in his family*. New York: John Wiley and Sons, 1973.
Garber J. The children's events schedule, unpublished manuscript, University of Minnesota, 1982a.
Garber J. Conceptual issues in the diagnosis of childhood depression. Paper presented at the Annual Meeting of the American Psychological Association, Los Angeles, 1981.
Garber J. Self-concept and depression in children, unpublished manuscript, University of Minnesota, 1982b.
Graziano AM, ed. *Behavior therapy with children*. Chicago: Aldine, 1971.
Hollon SD, Beck AT. Cognitive-behavioral intervention for depression. In: Kendall PC, Hollon SD, eds. *Cognitive-behavioral interventions: theory, research and procedures*. New York: Academic Press, 1979.
Hollon S, Garber J. A cognitive-expectancy theory of therapy for helplessness and depression. In: Garber, Seligman, eds. *Human helplessness: theory and applications*. New York Academic Press, 1980.
Inhelder P, Piaget J. *The growth of logical thinking*. New York: Basic Books, 1958.
Kaslow N. Social and cognitive correlates of depression in children from a developmental perspective. Paper presented at the Annual Meeting of the American Psychological Association, Los Angeles, 1981.
Kaslow N, Tanenbaum R, Seligman MEP, et al. Depression in children: problem-solving, attributional style, and parents' attributional style. University of Pennsylvania, 1979; (unpublished material).
Kendall PC. Cognitive-behavioral interventions with children. In: Lahey BB, Kazdin AE, eds. *Advances in clinical child psychology. Volume 4*. New York: Plenum Press, 1981.
Kendall PC, Finch AJ. A cognitive-behavioral treatment for impulsivity: a group comparison study. *J Consult Clin Psychol* 1978; 46:110-118.
Kendall PC, Hollon SD. *Assessment strategies for cognitive-behavioral interventions*. New York: Academic Press, 1981.
Kendall PC, Pelligrini D, Urbain ES. Approaches to assessment for cognitive-behavioral interventions with children. In: Kendall PC, Hollon SD, eds. *Assessment strategies for cognitive-behavioral interventions*. New York: Academic Press, 1981.

Kovacs M, Beck AT. An empirical-clinical approach toward a definition of childhood depression. In: Schulterbrandt JG, Raskins A, eds. *Depression in childhood: diagnosis, treatment and conceptual models.* New York: Raven Press, 1977.

Lefkowitz MM, Tesiny EP, Gordon NH. Childhood depression, family income, and locus of control. *J Nerv Ment Dis* 980; 168:732–735.

Leon GR, Kendall PC, Garber J. Depression in children: parent, child and teacher perspectives. *J Abnorm Child Psychol* 1980; 8:221–235.

Lewinsohn PM. A behavioral approach to depression. In: Friedman MM, Katz RJ, eds. *The psychology of depression: contemporary theory and research.* Washington, DC: Winston/Wiley, 1974.

Lewinsohn PM. Clinical and theoretical aspects of depression. In Calhoun KS, Adams HE, Mitchell KM, eds. *Innovative treatment methods in psychotherapy.* New York: Wiley and Sons, 1973.

Lewinsohn PM, Graf M. Pleasant activities and depression. *J Counsel Clin Psychol* 1973; 41:261-268.

Livesley WJ, Bromley DB. *Person perception in childhood and adolescence.* London: Wiley and Sons, 1973.

Marholm D, II, ed. *Child behavior therapy.* New York: Gardner, 1978.

Meichenbaum D, Genest M. Cognitive behavioral modification: an integration of cognitive and behavioral methods. In: Kanfer, Goldstein, eds. *Helping people change* 2nd ed. New York: Pergamon, 1980.

Miller JBM. Children's reactions to the death of a parent: a review of the psychoanalytic literature. *J Am Psychoanal Assoc* 1971; 19:697.

Oskamp S. *Attitudes and opinions.* New Jersey: Prentice-Hall, 1977.

Petti TA. Active treatment of childhood depression. In: Clarkin, Glazer, eds. *Depression: behavioral and directive intervention strategies.* New York: Garland Press, 1981.

Piaget J. Piaget's theory. In: Mussen PH, ed. *Carmichael's manual of child psychology. Vol. I.* New York: Wiley and Sons, 1970.

Piers EV. *Manual for the Piers-Harris children's self-concept scale.* Nashville, Tennessee: Counselor Recordings and Tests, 1969.

Premack D. Reinforcement theory. In: Levine, ed. *Nebraska symposium on motivation.* Lincoln: University of Nebraska Press, 1965.

Quay HC, Werry JS, eds. *Psychopathological disorders of childhood.* New York: Wiley and Sons, 1979.

Reynolds CR, Richmond BO. What I think and feel: a revised measure of children's manifest anxiety. *J Abnorm Child Psychol* 1978; 6:271-280.

Risley TR, Hart B. Developing correspondence between the non-verbal and verbal behavior of school children. *J Appl Behav Anal* 1968; 1:267-281.

Robertson J. Some responses of young children to loss to maternal care. *Child-Fam Dig* 1956; 15:7-22.

Schowalter JE. Parent deaths and child bereavement. In: Schoenberg B, Gerber I, Wiener A, et al. eds. *Bereavement: its psychosocial aspects.* New York: Columbia University Press, 1975.

Schultz HT. Correlates of depression in a clinical sample of children and their mothers. Presented at the Annual Meeting of the American Psychological Association, Los Angeles, 1981.

Seligman MEP. *Helplessness: on depression, development and death.* San Francisco: W. H. Freeman, 1975.

Shaw BF. Cognitive therapy with an inpatient population. In: Emery G, Hollon S, Bedrosian R, eds. *New directions in cognitive therapy.* New York: Guilford Press, 1981.

Shure MB, Spivack G. Means-ends thinking, adjustment and social class among elementary school-aged children. *J Consult Clin Psychol* 1972; 38:348-353.

Spivack G, Shure M. *The social adjustment of young children.* San Francisco: Jossey-Bass, 1975.

Weinberg WA, Rutman J, Sullivan L, et al. Depression in children referred to an educational diagnostic center. *J Pediatr* 1973; 83:1068-1072.

Wolfenstein M. How is mourning possible? *The psychoanalytic study of the child.* New York: International Universities Press, 1966; 21:93.

Index